*The Dividing Line Histories of
William Byrd* II *of Westover*

The Dividing Line Histories of William Byrd II of Westover

Edited by

KEVIN JOEL BERLAND

Published for the
Omohundro Institute
of Early American
History and Culture,
Williamsburg, Virginia,
by the University of
North Carolina Press,
Chapel Hill

The Omohundro Institute of Early American History and Culture is sponsored jointly by the College of William and Mary and the Colonial Williamsburg Foundation. On November 15, 1996, the Institute adopted the present name in honor of a bequest from Malvern H. Omohundro, Jr.

This volume received support from a publication grant by the William P. McDowell Endowment, Penn State Shenango.

Designed by Richard Hendel
Set by Tseng Information Systems, Inc.
in Arnhem type
Manufactured in the United States of America.

The paper in this book meets the guidelines for permanence and durability of the Committee on Production Guidelines for Book Longevity of the Council on Library Resources.

The University of North Carolina Press has been a member of the Green Press Initiative since 2003.

In discussing indigenous people, the author has followed the "Guide to Writing about Virginia Indians and Virginia Indian History" issued by the Virginia Council of Indians in 2008.

Complete cataloging information for this title is available from the Library of Congress.
ISBN 978-1-4696-0693-4

17 16 15 14 13   5 4 3 2 1

Pages 64, 342: *The Virginia–North Carolina Dividing Line.* Engraving, modern print from the original copperplate. Rawlinson Collection, Bodleian Library, accession #R1986-9. The Colonial Williamsburg Foundation. Gift of the Bodleian Library.

FRONTISPIECE
Portrait of William Byrd II. *Studio of Sir Godfrey Kneller. England, ca. 1700–1704 or 1715–1717. Oil on canvas, accession #1956-561. The Colonial Williamsburg Foundation. Museum purchase*

Acknowledgments

Scholarly projects would be difficult or impossible without the support of networks of generous and accommodating people. It is a pleasure to acknowledge my debt to libraries and librarians, including Fran Freed, Gail Mancuso, Becky Albitz, Matthew Ciszek, the Lartz Memorial Library staff, and interlibrary loan staff working valiantly behind the scenes. Thanks to Jim Green, Connie King, and John Van Horn at the Library Company of Philadelphia, where I started my work on Byrd, and to Sandy Stelts and Charles Mann at Penn State's F. L. Pattee Library Special Collections, and to the staff at the American Philosophical Society Library, the British Library, the Folger Shakespeare Library, the Houghton Library, the Huntington Library, the National Archives at Kew, the New-York Historical Society, the New York Public Library, the Rockefeller Library at Colonial Williamsburg, and the Virginia Historical Society Library. My work has been nourished by discussions and consultations in the virtual common rooms of online discussion groups, especially C18-L, and also EARAM-L, Ex Libris, Ficino, H-HISTSEX, H-OIEAHC, SHARP-L, and VA-HIST.

One of the chief satisfactions of completing a long-term research project is the opportunity of acknowledging the generous support of research foundations and libraries. This project was made possible by grants from the Library Company of Philadelphia, the National Endowment for the Humanities, the Gilder-Lehrman Institute of American History, the American Philosophical Society, the Rockefeller Library at Colonial Williamsburg, the Virginia Historical Society, and the McDowell Endowment at Penn State Shenango. Support for travel to research collections was also provided by Penn State's College of Liberal Arts, Penn State's University College, and the Academic Affairs office of Penn State Shenango.

Friends, colleagues, research assistants, support staff, and others have generously provided assistance, advice, suggestions, questions, answers, and encouragement. Thanks to Joel Berson, Sylvia Bowerbank, Donna Brodish, Louise Brydon, Brycchan Carey, Liz Denlinger, Diane Eiland, Kevin Hardwick, Kevin Hayes, James Horn, Dale Katherine Ireland, Gil Kelly, Jon Kukla, Elizabeth Latshaw-Foti, Fredric Leeds, Leo Lemay, Jack Lynch, Robert Maccubbin, Charles Mann, Jim May, Donald Mell, Linda Merians, Frank Parks, Ruth Perry, Patricia Popovich, Pat Rogers, Laura Rosenthal, David Shields, Frank Shuffleton, Laura Stevens, Brent Tarter, Fredrika Teute, Nadine Zimmerli, and the Omohundro Institute and its editorial readers. Thanks also to Jan Gilliam and Ken Lockridge, my coeditors of Byrd's *Commonplace Book*.

Thanks to my parents, Jayne and Alwyn Berland, for modeling a life of reading and thinking and writing. Thanks also to my writing group friends and colleagues, Natalie Hayes, Jack Smith, Jeanne Mahon, Don Feigert, John Woge, and Brad Isles, whose long-running wisecracks about my tendency to write half books must now come to an end. And very special thanks to Rebecca Shapiro: באַששערט.

Preface

In the spring and fall of 1728, an expedition of Virginia and North Carolina officials, surveyors, and woodsmen set out to resolve the disputed boundary between the two colonies, running nearly 242 miles west from the Atlantic shoreline to the foothills of the Blue Ridge Mountains. Over the decades following the expedition, William Byrd revised and expanded the official report he had submitted to Virginia's governor into two remarkable narratives, never published in his lifetime but now considered classics of early American literature: *The History of the Dividing Line betwixt Virginia and North Carolina* and *The Secret History of the Line*.

The History of the Dividing Line was a public history designed for British readers always eager to read about travels in distant lands. Byrd dressed up his narrative with an abundance of botanical, zoological, and historical information together with literary allusion, anecdotes, historical sketches, tidbits of ethnographic information, erudite jests, and unacknowledged appropriations from earlier authors, both ancient and modern. The range of Byrd's accumulation of materials will be of great interest for modern readers to observe, using this edition's annotations and commentary. In refashioning the official report, Byrd was faithful to the Horatian warrant for literature: its purpose is to instruct and delight. The resulting narrative functions at once as historical chronicle, literary entertainment, and encyclopedic survey of nearly everything that could be said about its subject, the Virginia–North Carolina backcountry in the early 1700s.

What led Byrd to write such a book? It must have been in part a desire to establish himself in England as the leading expert on Virginia. He had a taste of reputation as an expert when John Oldmixons's 1708 *History of the British Empire in America* borrowed—and praised—a sketch of Virginia history Byrd had written. And it might have been in part a desire to contribute to the collection and dissemination of useful information that characterized the writings of the Royal Society's correspondents. Byrd had been a proud member of the Royal Society from the age of twenty-two and participated in the correspondence network that supported the scientific project. It might have been in part a desire to display the breadth of his knowledge, insight, practical wisdom, political skill, social status, wit, and literary talent. Whatever the combination of motives, *The History of the Dividing Line* was exactly the kind of book his education, his scientific and cultural interests, and his sense of his position in society prepared him to write.

The other narrative, the *The Secret History of the Line,* took an entirely different approach. Specifically recasting the story for private circulation, Byrd added to the chronicle of the expedition episodes of political maneuvering, scandal, rakish anecdote, and libertine humor. The manuscript was designed for a select, private readership, the sort of readers who would be amused by accounts of political intrigue, bad characters, and risqué antics. In *The Secret History* Byrd submerges serious intent—the depiction of his understanding of the proper way to manage life in the colonies—beneath a surface of raillery against sloth, selfishness, and uncouth behavior.

William Byrd II of Westover, Virginia (1674–1744), was a prominent eighteenth-century Virginia planter, trader, lawyer, politician, amateur naturalist and Fellow of the Royal Society, colonial landowner and developer, diarist, booklover, and man of letters. A member of the Executive Council (the upper house of the colonial Virginia legislature), in 1728 Byrd was the senior Virginia member of the joint commission to survey and fix the previously uncertain Virginia–North Carolina boundary. After long, drawn-out negotiations and delays, the expedition set out to map the border, a line running due west from the beach at Coratuck (now known as New Currituck Inlet), across streams, swamps, plantations, rivers and up into the foothills of the Blue Ridge. Long-standing differences between the governments of Virginia and North Carolina affected the expedition from the start, the company was often divided and quarrelsome, and the North Carolina delegation decided to return home before the assigned task was completed—at least according to Virginia's point of view.

Byrd first submitted a report of the expedition to Virginia governor Sir William Gooch, and it passed next to the Lords Commissioners of Trade and Plantations (usually called the Board of Trade) in London. This body supervised colonial government and commerce on behalf of the crown, appointing colonial governors and council members, approving or striking down colonial legislation, and managing colonial offices and revenues. Byrd's official report (preserved in the British National Archives at Kew) provided a textual base on which Byrd elaborated to produce the Dividing Line narratives.

The History of the Dividing Line and *The Secret History* are hybrid texts. That is to say, neither can be understood properly as a straightforward eyewitness account of the events of 1728. Rather, they combine field observations (of surveying detail, natural history, topography, and personal character) with a copious supply of other material, the production of long sessions in the author's library adding more and more to the original chronological outline of events. Byrd's narratives are embedded in historical issues and contexts not always apparent to a modern reader, personal opinions color his representation of historical personages and events, and these representations are framed and manipulated by sophisticated literary techniques. It is well known that literary critics often overlook historical contexts and that historians often disregard the rhetorical effects of literary technique on the composition of historical texts. Therefore, this edition of Byrd's narratives is itself a hybrid production, drawing on material from the historical archive, networks of social and cultural knowledge, the legacy of critical views, and close textual readings. Annotations and commentary bring together materials to allow recovery or reconstruction of cultural assumptions and language instrumental to Byrd's narrative but possibly obscure to modern readers.

Historians approaching the Dividing Line texts have generally considered them as valuable repositories of historical fact. However, it is important to consider how Byrd selected and arranged these facts. Modern historians and theorists of historiography agree that there is really no such thing as a truly impartial or objective chronicling of events. In a manner approximating what psychologists call confirmation bias—the tendency to search for or favor evidence that fits an inquirer's preconceptions—writers of histories, such as Byrd, preselect evidence even in what might appear to be objective accounts. That is to say, their preconceptions tend to determine the choice of which events are significant even before the writer arranges and interprets them. Whatever Byrd's Dividing Line histories may be, they are not evenhanded accounts. Rather, they are works designed to appeal to a specific audience and to serve specific functions of persuasion and entertainment. A more or less factual chronicle of actual events underlies the structural elements of his narratives (intended audience and polemical design). Some of the events in Byrd's narratives are verifiable and reliable, and others less so. What is required at the outset is a frank acknowledgment that Byrd's stories of the events leading up to and during the 1728 expedition to settle the Virginia–North Carolina border are everywhere affected by his powerful bias for Virginia's superiority and his concern for Virginia's welfare and by the sophisticated use of literary techniques establishing two narrative personae, "Steddy" (in *The Secret History*) and "Byrd" (in *The History of the Dividing Line*). These are both narrative constructions, *invented* voices, not to be confused with the actual personal character, public and private, of William Byrd himself. The narratives are framed and mediated by literary presentation. Granted, some readers may discern in Byrd's created personae something of what he must have wished his readers to think of him. At the same time, readers may do well to be alert to the operations of Byrd's persuasive bias.

That Byrd's rhetorical strategies have succeeded may be seen in the reception history of the Dividing Line narratives. Over the years since they were first published, many historians and critics have accepted his version of the story, including the legitimacy of Virginia's concerns, the negligible value of North Carolina's concerns, and indeed the negligible value of the North Carolinians themselves. In documenting the composition, structure, and purpose of the narratives, this edition should invite a more careful consideration of such matters. In my treatment of the Dividing Line narratives, I have combined historical and literary approaches, paying close attention to the social, political, and economic contexts of eighteenth-century Virginia and Carolina, to make sense (as much as possible) of Byrd's opinions. I have also pointed out instances of what might be called the "writtenness" of the narratives, the literary processes that transmute simple records of events into adventure stories complete with characterized narrators, fashioning a linear story interrupted by diversions and digressions, and adding a swarm of detail designed to educate and entertain. Thus I have included copious references to documentary evidence providing contexts for some of Byrd's opinions. For instance, minutes of the Virginia Executive Council and papers in the records of the Board of Trade corroborate Byrd's impression of the fractious Richard Fitzwilliam, one of the Virginia Commissioners. Other evidence tends in the opposite direction, suggesting that some of Byrd's representations of other people and events are not entirely accurate.

In a manner perhaps unusual for editions of historical manuscripts, the text of this edition is accompanied by and supported with copious annotation, commentary, and extensive sources and analogues, designed to give the reader access to to the cultural, political, and scientific contexts in which Byrd lived and wrote. This additional material provides an entry to a wide range of topics important to Byrd, matters that affected his opinions and his practice in the field. Wherever possible, reference has been made to books in Byrd's own library, especially when evidence indicates he consulted them in adding detail to the narratives. Evidence, both internal and external, establishes that Byrd worked on his manuscripts for many years after the expedition was concluded. During this time he expanded on his field observations, revised and improved passages, and inserted new material. A good deal of this expansion involved bringing in material drawn from other writers, which suggests that he often worked in his library with one or more books open before him. In some passages, phrases, and ideas Byrd owes an unacknowledged debt to earlier colonial writers such as John Smith, Robert Beverley, and John Lawson. Other debts to classical authors, early modern travel writers, naturalists, and Royal Society publications appear from time to time.

The method of *The History of the Dividing Line,* Byrd's unfinished masterpiece, is accretional. An accretional narrative absorbs disparate materials bit by bit, without necessarily paraphrasing or transforming them and without explicitly acknowledging them as sources. This is not the same thing as allusion, though Byrd's narratives are frequently allusive, incorporating easily recognizable references to other texts (scripture, poetry, the classics). For instance, Byrd reports that the inhabitants of Norfolk regarded the crossing of the Dismal Swamp the plan of "Men devoted, like Codrus and the 2 Decii, to certain destruction." But the accretional narrative does more than enrich the story with such biblical, classical, and contemporary cultural allusions. It silently appropriates factual content from a myriad of sources, providing a cumulative effect on his intended reader of the author's ethos or expertise.

Of course, it was not uncommon for writers in Byrd's era to depend upon the words of earlier authors. Many travel writers and chroniclers thought it fitting to interweave their own experiences and observations with those of ancient authorities or earlier travelers. Nonetheless, it has seemed important to indicate here wherever Byrd has borrowed and where he might have been influenced by what he read. Very little scholarly work has been done so far on such accretional narratives and their relation to their sources. The blurred line between what Byrd wrote from firsthand experience and what he wrote (or assembled) in his library is not always easy to fix, and this uncertainty should produce in modern readers, historians, and critics increased careful attention (if not skepticism) when mining the Dividing Line narratives for ostensibly firsthand historical evidence.

The formal complexity of *The History of the Dividing Line* is the product both of the accretional method and of the author's diverse intentions. Byrd clearly meant to create a stimulating book for London readers, and to this end he combined a chronicle of the events of 1728 with a complex, digressive account of Virginia and North Carolina, a hybrid admixture of historical, topographic, economic, scientific, and personal presentation. As well, Byrd makes himself the hero of his story. Considering Byrd's strategies of self-presentation in historical contexts will afford the modern reader the opportunity to view the author at work behind (or through) the narration. Considering the way Byrd incorporated ancient and modern cultural and scientific matters will afford the modern reader insight into Byrd's participation in the common culture of his era. Considering the way the narratives evolved from official chronology to expansive narrative will afford the modern reader insight into the eighteenth-century understanding of authorship.

In preparing this edition I have endeavored to demonstrate the way Byrd's Dividing Line histories carry out a chorographical "deep mapping" of Virginia. Mike Pearson and Michael Shanks explain this approach:

Reflecting eighteenth century antiquarian approaches to place which in-cluded history, folklore, natural history, and hearsay, the deep map attempts to record and represent the grain and patina of place through juxtapositions and interpenetrations of the historical and the contemporary, the political and the poetic, the factual and the fictional, the discursive and and the sen-sual; the conflation of oral testimony, anthology, memoir, biography, natu-ral history and everything you might ever want to say about a place.
—*Theatre/Archeology* (London, 2001), 64–65. See also Vladimir Jankovic, "The Place of Nature and the Nature of Place: The Chorographic Challenge to the History of British Provincial Science," *History of Science,* XXXVIII (2000), 79–113

The History of the Dividing Line was never completed, perhaps because Byrd never quite ran out of things he wanted to say about Virginia. This edition, then, provides a trove of historical and cultural contexts allowing modern readers to take in and appreciate the encyclopedic range of Byrd's heroic endeavor.

Contents

Illustrations

Abbreviations and Short Titles

APS.d
  American Philosophical Society manuscript of *DL* (975.5 B99h)
APS.s
  American Philosophical Society manuscript of *SH* (975.5 B99h)
Aristotle
  The Complete Works of Aristotle. The Revised Oxford Translation. Ed.
  Jonathan Barnes. Princeton, N.J., 1984
ASD
  Maude H. Woodfin and Marion Tinling, eds. *Another Secret Diary of
  William Byrd II of Westover, 1739–1741, with Letters and Literary Exercises,
  1696–1726*. Richmond, Va., 1942
Banister
  Joseph Ewan and Nesta Ewan, eds. *John Banister and His Natural History of
  Virginia, 1678–1692*. Urbana, Ill., 1970
Beverley
  [Robert Beverley]. *The History and Present State of Virginia*. London, 1705
BL
  "A Journal of the Divideing line Drawn between the Colonies of Virginia
  & North Carolina begun March 5: 1728 — per Colo. Byrd & others." British
  Library Add. MS 28260
Boyd
  William K. Boyd, ed. *William Byrd's Histories of the Dividing Line betwixt
  Virginia and North Carolina*. Raleigh, N.C., 1929
C&P
  Nell Marion Nugent, ed. *Cavaliers and Pioneers: Abstracts of Virginia Land
  Patents and Grants, 1623–1800*. Richmond, Va., 1934-
Catesby
  Alan Feduccia, ed. *Catesby's Birds of Colonial America*. Chapel Hill, N.C.,
  1985. Includes the text of the 1731 edition of Mark Catesby, *The Natural
  History of Carolina, Florida, and the Bahama Islands*
Commonplace Book
  Kevin Berland, Jan Kirsten Gilliam, and Kenneth A. Lockridge, eds. *The
  Commonplace Book of William Byrd II of Westover*. Chapel Hill, N.C., 2001
Correspondence
  Marion Tinling, ed. *The Correspondence of the Three William Byrds of
  Westover, Virginia, 1684–1776*. Charlottesville, Va., 1977

Council

H. R. McIlwaine, Wilmer L. Hall, and Benjamin Hillman, eds. *Executive Journals of the Council of Colonial Virginia.* Richmond, Va., 1927

CRNC

Colonial Records of North Carolina

CSP

Great Britain, Public Record Office. *Calendar of State Papers,* Colonial Series, *America and West Indies.* London, 1860–1969

CWR.d

Fragment of *DL.* Rockefeller Library, Colonial Williamsburg, MS 40.2

CWR.s

Fragment of *SH.* Rockefeller Library, Colonial Williamsburg, MS 40.2

DL

William Byrd, *The History of the Dividing Line betwixt Virginia and North Carolina, Run in the Year of Our Lord 1728*

DNCB

William S. Powell, ed. *Dictionary of North Carolina Biography.* Chapel Hill, N.C., 1979–1996

DVB

John T. Kneebone et al., eds. *Dictionary of Virginia Biography.* Richmond, Va., 1998–

Fields

Darin Evan Fields. "William Byrd's 'History of the Dividing Line betwixt Virginia and North Carolina Run in the Year of Our Lord 1728': A Genetic Text." Ph.D. diss., Univ. of Delaware, 1992

H

Fragment of *Secret History.* Huntington Library, MS BR box 256.28

Hayes

Kevin J. Hayes. *The Library of William Byrd of Westover.* Madison, Wis., 1997

Hening

William Waller Hening, comp. *The Statutes at Large: Being a Collection of All the Laws of Virginia.* Richmond, Va., and Philadelphia, 1823

Herodotus

A. D. Godley, trans. *Herodotus.* London, 1928–1931

Jones

Hugh Jones. *The Present State of Virginia: From Whence Is Inferred a Short View of Maryland and Carolina* (1724). Ed. Richard L. Morton. Chapel Hill, N.C., 1956

Lahontan

[Louis Armand de Lom d'Arce], Baron [de] Lahontan. *New Voyages to North-America*. London, 1703

Lawson

John Lawson. *The History of Carolina: Containing the Exact Description and Natural History of That Country. . . .* London, 1714.

LD

William Byrd. *The London Diary (1717–1721) and Other Writings.* Ed. Louis B. Wright and Marion Tinling. New York, 1958

Lederer

John Lederer. *The Discoveries of John Lederer* (1672). Ed. William P. Cumming. Charlottesville, Va., 1958

NAE

Native American Ethnobotany. University of Michigan–Dearborn. http://herb.umd.umich.edu

NCHGR

North Carolina Historical and Genealogical Register

ODNB

The Oxford Dictionary of National Biography. http://www.oxforddnb.com

OED

The Oxford English Dictionary. http://oed.com

Oldmixon

[John] Oldmixon. *The British Empire in America: Containing the History of the Discovery, Settlement, Progress, and Present State of All the British Colonies on the Continent and Islands of America.* London, 1708

Plants

PLANTS Database. United States Department of Agriculture. http://plants.usda.gov/

Pliny

Pliny. *Natural History.* Trans. H. Rackham et al. Cambridge, Mass., 1967–

Prose Works

Louis B. Wright, ed. *The Prose Works of William Byrd of Westover: Narratives of a Colonial Virginian.* Cambridge, Mass., 1966

SD

William Byrd. *The Secret Diary of William Byrd of Westover, 1709–1712.* Ed. Louis B. Wright and Marion Tinling. Richmond, Va., 1941

SH

The Secret History of the Line

"Surveyors' Journal or Field Book"
> "A Journal or Field Book of the Proceedings of the Surveyors appointed for determining the Bounds between the Colonies of Virginia and North Carolina." CO 5, 1321, 120–135

Smith
> *The Complete Works of Captain John Smith (1580–1631).* Ed. Philip L. Barbour. Chapel Hill, N.C., 1986

SPG
> Society for the Propagation of the Gospel in Foreign Parts

V
> The Westover Manuscripts. Virginia Historical Society manuscript MSS1 B9966a

VMHB
> *Virginia Magazine of History and Biography*

WMQ
> *William and Mary Quarterly* (including early variant titles)

The Dividing Line Histories of
William Byrd II *of Westover*

PLATE 2. Bookplate of William Byrd II. *England, ca. 1690, engraving. Image #79-DS-131. Special Collections, John D. Rockefeller, Jr. Library, The Colonial Williamsburg Foundation*

Introduction

The most succinct biographical sketch of William Byrd is his epitaph. At the junction of two paths in the gardens of Westover, the fine Georgian house he built on the banks of the James River, his monument still stands, bearing this summation of what was especially memorable about his life:

> Being born to one of the amplest fortunes in this country,
> He was early sent to England for his education,
> Where under the care and direction of Sir Robert Southwell,
> And ever favored with his particular instructions,
> He made a happy proficiency in polite and varied learning.
> By means of the same noble friend,
> He was introduced to the acquaintance of many of the first persons of the
>   age
> For knowledge, wit, virtue, birth, of high station,
> And particularly contracted a most intimate and bosom friendship
> With the learned and illustrious Charles Boyle, Earl of Orrery.
> He was called to the bar in the Middle Temple,
> Studied for some time in the Low Countries,
> Visited the Court of France,
> And was chosen Fellow of the Royal Society.
> Thus eminently fitted for the service and ornament of his country,
> He was made Receiver-General of His Majesty's revenues here,
> Was thrice appointed public agent to the Court and Ministry of England,
> And being thirty-seven years a member,
> At last became President of the Council of that Colony.
> To all this were added a great elegance of taste and life,
> The well-bred gentleman and polite companion,
> The splendid economist and prudent father of a family,
> With the constant enemy of all exorbitant power,
> And hearty friend to the liberties of his country.[1]

1. For details of Byrd's life, see Pierre Marambaud, *William Byrd of Westover, 1674–1744* (Charlottesville, Va., 1971); "Byrd, William (1674–1744)," *ODNB*. For a psychological interpretation of Byrd's development, see Kenneth A. Lockridge, *The Diary, and Life, of William Byrd II of Virginia, 1674–1744* (Chapel Hill, N.C., 1987).

The epitaph is reprinted in *LD*, 11. An early Byrd editor, John Spencer Bassett, opined

William Byrd II was born on March 28, 1674, the first surviving child of William Byrd I (1652–1704) and Mary Horsmanden Filmer (1650–1699). His father had come to Virginia at the age of seventeen at the request of his uncle, Thomas Stegge, a substantial planter and Indian trader, one of the leading entrepreneurs who exchanged English trade goods (cloth, tools, weapons, and decorative items such as beads) for Indian goods (primarily furs and deer-skins). Stegge brought his nephew into his business and made him his heir. At Stegge's death in 1670, William Byrd I inherited his uncle's property and busi-ness, swiftly rising to a prominent position in Virginia's patrician elite. The Indian trade prospered, as did his trade in English commodities to colonists, tobacco production, the slave trade and indentured servant contracts, the pur-chase and sale of land, and investment in ships and cargoes.

Upon his death Byrd I left his son an ample fortune: vast properties, a flour-ishing Indian trade, and membership in the highest circle of elite Virginia so-ciety, a patrician network of gentlemen whose status sprang from the accu-mulation of land, wealth, and power, held and improved over two or more generations. A genteel pedigree was not required for this group—Byrd I's father had been a London goldsmith, and his maternal grandfather a sea captain—though descent from a "good" family was an added benefit.

At the age of seven William Byrd II was sent to Felsted Grammar School, Essex, where under the tutelage of Christopher Glasscock he gained the strong classical education that prepared him for a lifetime of reading Greek, Latin, and Hebrew. This education gave Byrd access to the common culture of an English gentleman, the personal importance of which is signaled by his lifelong daily ritual of reading classical authors and scriptures in Hebrew and Greek. Leaving Felsted at the age of sixteen, Byrd observed trade practices in the Rotterdam offices of Jacob Senserff. Returning to London, he continued his study of trade in the offices of his father's London agents, Perry and Lane. Soon after, in 1692, he took up the study of law in the Middle Temple. A young Templar like Byrd would be exposed to a great deal of good company and culture as well as oppor-tunities for rowdiness. Byrd frequented plays and coffeehouses and pursued sundry libertine pastimes, which he documented in his *London Diary*. And yet

---

that the epitaph was "written by some warm admirer" (Bassett, ed., *The Writings of "Colonel William Byrd of Westover in Virginia Esqr."* (New York, 1901), xl. Byrd's biogra-phers do not discuss the epitaph's authorship, but it is worth noting that it was not un-usual for early modern gentlefolk to compose their own epitaphs, as a pious exercise in the face of death, whether distant or imminent, or else to guarantee a good image for pos-terity. Either possibility would fit Byrd's situation, and so I conclude Byrd composed the epitaph; he was certainly capable of "warm admiration" for himself.

the course of study was very demanding. On April 12, 1694/5, Byrd was called to the bar and was admitted to Lincoln's Inn, October 22, 1697.[2]

As a resident and student in the Inns of Court, Byrd had access to a fascinating cultural circle. He probably knew the playwright William Congreve (1670–1729), admitted to the Middle Temple in 1691, and the poet Nicholas Rowe (1674–1718), admitted in the same year as Congreve. Byrd's London diaries are packed with the names of writers, politicians, ladies, gentlemen, and members of the nobility. Byrd had occasion to meet a number of people who would influence his life in important ways and whose friendship he would consider among his most substantial achievements throughout the rest of his life. Foremost in Byrd's estimation was Sir Robert Southwell (1634–1702), sometime clerk of the Privy Council, commissioner of Customs, secretary of state for Ireland, vice admiral, Oxford L.L.D, long a fellow of the Royal Society and its president from 1690. It is not clear what Byrd meant when he said Southwell had given him "particular instruction." Southwell took learning very seriously, supervising the education of his son Edward and other young relatives from the King and Perceval families. In 1701, Southwell arranged for Byrd to accompany his grandnephew, John Perceval (1683–1748), on a tour of England after he left Oxford. Byrd and Perceval traveled for four months through the northeast counties, visiting universities and churches and the homes of gentlemen, crossing the

2. On Byrd's education and the common culture, see *Commonplace Book,* chap. 2, "Making a Gentleman: William Byrd and Early Modern Education." Kevin Hayes explains that Rotterdam was considered "a good place for young English-speaking men to learn mercantile business," for the Dutch were experts in international trade (*Hayes,* 8). Years later Byrd wrote to Senserff, reporting on his many enterprises on his busy plantation. Though his letter was concerned with "all my little affairs," he asked Senserff's patience, since it was "the story of one who had the early example of your good example and advice. If there be any good in me, you had a hand in the forming of my mind to it, and it [may] be some pleasure to you, that I do well because I was under your ca[re]." Byrd to Senserff, ca. June 25, 1729, *Correspondence,* I, 410–411.

Kevin Hayes points out Byrd's library contained many books on the more philosophical branches of natural law and political thought, including "nearly all of the important books advocating enlightened political ideas." Among Byrd's books at Westover were interleaved and copiously annotated copies of major legal texts. *Hayes,* 10–12, 82–83.

Byrd's period of study was shorter than the customary seven years, so he must have invoked a "call of grace," a special arrangement allowing a candidate to be called to the bar early, with the support of a senior member and the payment of a fine of thirty shillings for each term short of the requisite sixteen. J. Bruce Williamson, *The History of the Temple, London: From the Institution of the Order of Knights of the Temple to the Close of the Stuart Period* (London, 1924), 557; see also E. Alfred Jones, *American Members of the Inns of Court* (London, 1924), 35.

border into Scotland, and then returning to London. Perceval kept a diary of the journey that featured comments on antiquities and touristical sights, social conditions, religious dissent, architecture, manufactures, the preparation of herring, the extraction of salt from seawater, agricultural improvements, and other samples of useful knowledge. The diary also contained numerous quotations from and allusions to books read before and during the journey. Whatever Southwell's contributions to Byrd's education might have been, the crowning achievement was Southwell's sponsorship when Byrd was elected a member of the Royal Society on April 29, 1696.[3]

Other friendships with metropolitan nobles and gentlemen continued. Byrd maintained a friendly correspondence with John Campbell (1680–1743), second duke of Argyll in the Scottish peerage and (after 1705) duke of Greenwich and, with his brother Archibald Campbell (1682–1761), earl of Ilay (Islay) and later the third duke. Another important friendship was with Charles Boyle (1674–1731), fourth earl of Orrery, best known for his Greek and Latin edition of the *Epistles of Phalaris,* which attracted the scornful attention of the great scholar Richard Bentley. The Byrd-Orrery correspondence lasted thirty years and continued with Lord Orrery's son John Boyle (1707–1762), later fifth earl of Cork and fifth earl of Orrery. Lord Ilay was an avid botanist and collector of trees; Lord Orrery was a fellow of the Royal Society and the patron of the artificer George Graham, who built the first clockwork model of the solar system, named the "Orrery" in his honor.

"Eminently fitted for the service . . . of his country," in 1692 Byrd entered Virginia politics, first as a London agent for the Virginia Assembly while he was

3. *ODNB:* "Congreve, William (1670–1729)"; "Rowe, Nicholas (1674–1718)"; "Southwell, Sir Robert (1635–1702)"; "Perceval, John, first earl of Egmont (1683–1748)." During his London years (1714–1722), Byrd recorded meeting Congreve socially on several occasions (*LD,* 64, 261, 273). Pierre Marambaud speculates Byrd knew Southwell through his father's business acquaintances. Alternately, the connection might have arisen from Byrd I's botanical correspondence with, and gifts of plants and seeds to, English botanists. Or possibly they met in or around the Inns of Court, for Southwell was himself a member of Lincoln's Inn. *William Byrd,* 18; Jones, *American Members of the Inns of Court,* 35.

On Byrd and Perceval's tour: Mark K. Wenger, ed., *The English Travels of Sir John Percival and William Byrd II: The Percival Diary of 1701* (Columbia, Mo., 1989). Byrd and Perceval (who became Baron Perceval in 1715, Viscount Perceval in 1722, and first earl of Egmont in 1733) remained friends for many years. The warm exchange of letters stopped only in 1737, when Byrd included in a letter to Perceval complaints about Georgia's laws requiring Virginia traders to the Cherokee to obtain a license, a comment also featured in *The History of the Dividing Line.* Perceval was a close associate of Georgia's founder, James Edward Oglethorpe, and was himself first president of the colony's trustees. After Byrd's complaint there were no further letters.

still a law student, and in 1696 as burgess for Henrico County. In 1698 and again in 1715, Byrd represented the Virginia legislature in London communicating the colony's dissatisfaction with the administration of governors to the Board of Trade. When his father died, Byrd succeeded to the positions of auditor and receiver general of Virginia, though shortly thereafter the positions were separated and Byrd retained only the latter. Away in England from 1714 to 1719 and confronted with mandatory forfeiture of colonial offices held during a long absence, he sold his interest in the receiver general's office in 1716. Byrd gained a seat on the Executive Council in 1709, a position he retained to his death. In his political life, Byrd exercised considerable power and influence, appropriate (in his view) to a prominent member of the patrician elite of Virginia. This attitude is everywhere apparent in the Dividing Line histories, where Byrd casts himself as a rightful and levelheaded leader. As well, Byrd, who was a reasonably devout member of the Church of England, clearly considered the established church the appropriate religious affiliation for one of his patrician position. Byrd's vision of a steadfast and loyal Anglican Virginia informs the commentary on religious practices that runs throughout the two narratives.[4]

Another important element of Byrd's life was his strong attraction to literature, both classical and contemporary, reflected in his commitment to expanding his library, references in his diaries to continual reading in Greek, Hebrew, and English, and the practice of excerpting and paraphrasing recorded in his commonplace book. Among early evidence of Byrd's authorship was his gentlemanly participation in the production of epigrammatic verse praising the ladies at the English spa, Tunbridge Wells. He translated the Ephesian Matron episode from the *Satyricon* of Petronius and wrote Theophrastian characters, including one describing himself at a critical juncture in life. His correspondence, too, is polished and literate. These literary exercises, as David S. Shields has observed, served as an instrument for confirming his status as a gentleman. Indeed, it could be argued that literary activities were an integral part of Byrd's self-definition, allowing him to accord himself in his epitaph the acclaim of being a "well-bred gentleman and polite companion."[5]

4. Byrd to John Custis, Oct. 2, 1716, *Correspondence,* I, 293; Marambaud, *William Byrd,* 25–26. On Byrd's religion, see Patricia U. Bonomi, *Under the Cope of Heaven: Religion, Society, and Politics in Colonial America* (New York, 1986), 98–99; Lauren F. Winner, *A Cheerful and Comfortable Faith: Anglican Practice in the Elite Households of Eighteenth-Century Virginia* (New Haven, Conn., 2010), 102–108; and *Commonplace Book,* 58–64.

5. Selections by "Mr. Burrard" from *Tunbrigalia; or, Tunbridge Miscellanies for the Year 1719* (London, 1719) and "A Poem upon Some Ladies at Tunbridge, 1700" are reproduced in *ASD,* 401–409, 248–249, respectively. On Byrd's poetry, see Carl Dolmetsch, "William Byrd of Westover as an Augustan Poet," *Studies in the Literary Imagination,* IX, no. 2 (Fall

It was equally important to Byrd to participate in the scientific project. The Royal Society's appetite for information was insatiable; it collected both morsels of information and full-blown theoretical discourses. Its journal, *Philosophical Transactions,* published accounts of experiments, reports of unusual phenomena, and detailed letters from wayfarers in distant lands. The exchange of letters between people interested in natural phenomena was a solid underpinning of more public scientific activity. Historian of science Andrea Rusnock has demonstrated the importance of letter writing to the New Science, noting that letters of interest were presented to the society by recipients and other interested parties. In this sense, Byrd worked within a model of correspondence networks of scientific inquirers, and as a volunteer correspondent Byrd collected field data—the minute particulars of natural history—and tested observation against popular tradition. This interest led him to support naturalists working in British America (John Banister, Mark Catesby, John Bartram, and others), to correspond with eminent scientists (Hans Sloane, Peter Collinson), and to provide samples of flora and fauna to metropolitan collectors. The abundance of natural history detail in the Dividing Line narratives indicates Byrd's commitment to the empirical mission of the Royal Society.[6]

1976), 69–77; Kevin Hayes's section "London Litterateur," *Hayes,* 25–31; *Commonplace Book,* 36–43; David S. Shields, *Civil Tongues and Polite Letters in British America* (Chapel Hill, N.C., 1997), 41–42.

Byrd's translation of Petronius appears in *ASD,* 224–227; see *Commonplace Book,* 37. On the literary quality of Byrd's letter writing, see Robert D. Arner, "Style, Substance, and Self in William Byrd's Familiar Letters," in J. A. Leo Lemay, ed., *Essays in Early Virginia Literature Honoring Richard Beale Davis* (New York, 1997), 101–119. For Addison's influence on Byrd's letter writing, see Susan Manning, "Industry and Idleness in Colonial Virginia: A New Approach to William Byrd II," *Journal of American Studies,* XXVIII (1994), 174–180. Patterning correspondence on accepted literary models may be seen as deliberate participation in the metropolitan cultural community; for the effect of improved transatlantic communications on feeding the sense of community, see Richard D. Brown, *Knowledge Is Power: The Diffusion of Information in Early America, 1700–1865* (New York, 1989), esp. chap. 2, "William Byrd and the Challenge of Rusticity among the Tidewater Gentry"; and Ian K. Steele, *The English Atlantic, 1675–1740: An Exploration of Communication and Community* (New York, 1986).

6. Andrea Rusnock, "Correspondence Networks and the Royal Society, 1700–1750," *British Journal for the History of Science,* XXXII (1999), 155–169. For an example of a transmitted letter, see "An Experiment concerning the Spirit of Coals, Being Part of a Letter to the Hon. Rob. Boyle, Esq; from the Late Rev. John Clayton, D.D. Communicated by the Right Rev. Father in God Robert Lord Bishop of Corke to the Right Hon. John Earl of Egmont, F.R.S.," *Philosophical Transactions,* LI (1739–1741), 59–61. On the participation of British American amateurs in the "specimen-centered empiricism" that placed special

In 1706, Byrd married Lucy Parke, youngest daughter of Colonel Daniel Parke II. Parke was a remarkable character, a wealthy Virginia planter, burgess, and member of the Executive Council—and a man of ill repute, a notorious rake whom the head of the Church of England in Virginia, Commissary James Blair, chided from the pulpit. But Parke's good reputation in England grew, especially with his service as aide-de-camp to John Churchill, first duke of Marlborough. His best-known accomplishment was bringing the news of Marlborough's victory at Blenheim to Queen Anne. Later he served in the British House of Commons but was ejected for bribery, though he retained enough influence with Marlborough to overcome this disgrace and to secure a potentially lucrative appointment as governor of the Leeward Islands. There his unpopularity reached epic proportions, until he was killed in 1710 during a riot in Antigua sparked by his brutal and arbitrary rule.

The terms of Parke's will would precipitate long-lasting economic difficulties. Byrd's claim in his epitaph to have been a "splendid economist" is undermined somewhat by his long struggle to emerge from debt, but at last, during the years when he was working on his Dividing Line narratives, he had finally attained a respectable degree of comfort. When he died in 1744, he left his heirs no burden of debt and a prodigious quantity of land. The marriage of William and Lucy Parke Byrd was frequently turbulent, but, as Byrd's biographer Pierre Marambaud concludes, their quarrels were never long-lasting, their reconciliations were swift, and evidence points to "the sincerity of their mutual affection." Of their four children, only Evelyn and Wilhelmina lived past infancy.[7]

In 1706 when Byrd was courting Lucy Parke, her father had promised—but neglected to deliver—a wedding present of one thousand pounds. When he died, his daughters and their families were surprised to learn all his Caribbean estate went in trust to a favorite illegitimate daughter, Lucy Chester. Should she die before she came into her estate, the will granted her mother a life interest,

---

value on "local expertise and local access," see Susan Scott Parrish, *American Curiosity: Cultures of Natural History in the Colonial British Atlantic World* (Chapel Hill, N.C., 2006), esp. 16.

7. "Parke, Daniel (1664/5–1710)," *ODNB.* For Parke's life and particular details on Parke's debts, see Helen Hill Miller, *Colonel Parke of Virginia: "The Greatest Hector in the Town": A Biography* (Chapel Hill, N.C., 1989); Jacob M. Price, *Perry of London: A Family and a Firm on the Seaborne Frontier, 1615–1753* (Cambridge, Mass., 1992), 68–70.

On quarrels: Marambaud, *William Byrd,* 27. See also Michael Zuckerman, "William Byrd's Family," *Perspectives in American History,* XII (1979), 253–311. Richard Godbeer sees evidence of "gentle affection" and love despite frequent arguments in "William Byrd's 'Flourish': The Sexual Cosmos of a Southern Planter," in Merril D. Smith, ed., *Sex and Sexuality in Early America* (New York, 1998), 140.

and upon her decease the remaining estate would go to yet another illegitimate child, Julius Caesar Parke. To his elder legitimate daughter in Virginia, Frances Parke Custis, Parke left "all estate in Virginia and England," out of which she was to pay a legacy of one thousand pounds to his younger daughter "Lucy Bird," and other legacies (including an additional fifty pounds per annum to the "godson" Julius Caesar Parke). Byrd's London agent, Micajah Perry, commented: "But what shall we say to such a man that would make his bastard children so easy to have all that he had mulk't together and was as ready money; and tye all his debts and legacys upon his estate in England and Virginia. We can't with patience reflect upon his unkindness." The will slighted Lucy Parke Byrd, on whose behalf Byrd was so deeply disappointed that he boldly proposed that he would take on Parke's English estates (Whitchurch, in Dorset) and all those Virginia properties scheduled to be sold to discharge debts, including Mount Folly, Taskenask, Skimino, and Skimino Mill, all on the York River. He would sell these estates and pay the debts out of the proceeds himself. It might have been a good arrangement, since Byrd knew very well how to profit from land acquisition, except for one minor detail: Parke's estate was far more gravely encumbered than Byrd could have anticipated. Parke owed £6,280 in England alone, and funds from the sale of his English property met less than half that liability.[8]

The Virginia debts, too, were outrageous, and storms had severely damaged most of the buildings at the Folly and Taskanask plantations. Byrd was long oppressed by efforts to clear the burden of his unfortunate investment, as revenue from public office did not clear the debts. Doubtless it was the pressure of his debts that lent urgency to Byrd's drive to acquire more and more land. Remarkably, though, he was sanguine about being able to resolve the problem. After Lucy's death, he was able to tell the father of a young woman he hoped to marry in 1718 that he owned forty-three thousand acres and 220 slaves in Virginia and that his average annual income was more than seventeen hundred pounds. In addition to his home plantation, Westover, Byrd left eleven Virginia plantations, with a population of 240.[9]

In 1715 Byrd was back in London, attempting to clear up the debts of his father-in-law, working for the interests of the Virginia Council, and—after his

8. Micajah Perry to Byrd, May 12, 1711, *Correspondence,* I, 280–282. Parke's will, along with a biographical sketch and some letters, is reproduced in "Virginia Gleanings in England," *VMHB,* XX (1912), 372–381.

9. Byrd to "Vigilante" [John Smith], [Feb. 18, 1718], *Correspondence,* I, 311; Huntington Library manuscript "Inventory of the Estate of William Byrd Esqr deceasd In the County of Henrico at the Falls of James River in the Yeare 1746" (HM 27224).

wife Lucy died of smallpox in the winter of 1716—searching for a woman of family and fortune to marry. At the same time, he immersed himself in the libertine pleasures London could offer a man of means with powerful appetites, diversions noted in his diary. After several false starts with eligible young women, Byrd proposed to Maria Taylor, a young English woman with a gratifying knowledge of Greek, though without a large fortune, and was accepted. They were married on May 9, 1724.

It was expensive to live in London, and so the Byrds went home to Virginia. To remain in Virginia permanently was definitely not in Byrd's plans, but that is how matters turned out. They settled in at Westover, Byrd still anticipating that some lucrative office or another would come his way. Four children, including son and heir William Byrd III (1728–1777), were born there. By April 1726, Byrd was back sitting on the Virginia Council. Financially, the appointment to the Dividing Line commission came at a good time, even though the stipend to be awarded to the commissioners was not determined in advance.[10]

During the years following the expedition, Byrd was busy planning and remodeling his house at Westover, paying especial attention to his library. Meanwhile, he turned his attention to other means of restoring his fortune. From the North Carolina Commissioners who had been granted land in lieu of cash payment, he purchased a large tract of land (twenty thousand acres) in the area he called the Land of Eden, near the confluence of the Dan and Smith Rivers. In 1733 he traveled to this region to survey his holdings with the surveyor William Mayo, in the company of James Mumford, John Banister (the son of the naturalist), Peter Jones, and several other woodsmen, some of whom had participated in the expedition of 1728. Byrd's journal of this excursion, "A Journey to the Land of Eden," is found in the Westover Manuscripts in the Virginia Historical Society. He continued to buy large tracts of land in the area—eventually his holdings amounted to seventy thousand acres—hoping to settle Swiss farmers there, and promoting immigration by engaging a Swiss agent, Samuel Jenner, supported by a tract, *Neu-gefundenes Eden* (Bern, 1737). Tragically, the ship carrying 250 Swiss emigrants sank as it approached Virginia, and very few survived.[11]

10. Douglas Anderson, "Plotting William Byrd," *WMQ*, 3d Ser., LVI (1999), 704; *Commonplace Book*, 186–192; *ASD*, 371–380. *Correspondence*, I, 348, reproduces Byrd's letter courting Maria Taylor (written in Greek).

11. "A Journey to the Land of Eden" may be found in *Prose Works*, 381–415. Jenner's *Neu-gefundenes Eden* was translated from the German and edited by Richmond Croom Beatty and William J. Mulloy and published as *William Byrd's Natural History of Virginia; or, The Newly Discovered Eden* (Richmond, Va., 1940). Beatty and Mulloy contended that Byrd was

Byrd was more successful with the two other Virginia settlements he founded, Petersburg (1733) and Richmond (1737). When after two years he hadn't managed to settle the requisite one hundred families on another 105,000 acres on the Roanoke River granted in 1735, Byrd was compelled to pay taxes of £525 per annum. Still, most of his land investments performed well.[12]

Alexander Spotswood's ironworks at Germanna prompted Byrd's own dreams of mining and smelting wealth. He visited Spotswood in 1732, hoping to find encouragement for such an enterprise. Overwhelmed by the risks and complexity, he elected not to pursue the dream of a metallurgical fortune, but he did write of his hopes in a manuscript known as the "Progress to the Mines" in the Westover Manuscripts, a text that resembles the Dividing Line histories in some stylistic qualities and details. In 1736, Byrd participated in yet another surveying expedition, this time to fix the limits of the Northern Neck, an expanse along the Chesapeake Bay between the Potomac and Rappahannock Rivers, granted to a loyal supporter in 1661 by Charles II. The proprietor's

---

the primary author of "the basic information which Jenner incorporated into his own account of the colony" (xxvi–xxviii). Percy G. Adams, in *Travelers and Travel Liars, 1660–1800* (Berkeley, Calif., 1972), 142–161, proposed that Jenner had "borrowed the name of William Byrd" for his tract, which Adams believed was essentially a reworking of John Lawson's *History of Carolina.* Marambaud concluded that Jenner "used notes provided by Byrd but had made far greater use of Lawson's *New Voyage [to Carolina]*" (*William Byrd,* 53). Adams and Marambaud were in the right when they discerned a strong resemblance between Lawson and Jenner's *Neu-gefundenes Eden.* However, in their conclusion that Jenner had borrowed from Lawson, they missed Byrd's own extensive borrowing from Lawson. The Jenner-Lawson parallels indicate that Jenner must have used a manuscript of *DL* (at some stage of revision and development), for every one of Jenner's passages appropriating Lawson was also subsumed by Byrd in *The History of the Dividing Line.*

On the development of the "Land of Eden," see Christopher Hendricks, *The Backcountry Towns of Colonial Virginia* (Knoxville, Tenn., 2006), 64–70. On the Swiss disaster, see Michael L. Nicholls, "Searching for Eden: William Byrd, the Switzers, and the Disaster of 1739," *Virginia Cavalcade,* XXXVI, no. 2 (Autumn 1986), 88–95.

12. The *Virginia Gazette*'s advertisement of Byrd's Richmond project reflects the enthusiasm of development: "This is to give Notice, That on the *North* Side of *James* River, near the Uppermost Landing, and a little below the Falls, is lately laid off by Major *Mayo,* a Town, called *Richmond,* with Streets 65 Feet wide, in a pleasant and healthy Situation, and well supply'd with Springs of good Water. It lies near the Publick Warehouse at Shoccoe's, and in the midst of great Quantities of Grain, and all kind of Provisions. The Lots will be granted in Fee Simple, on Condition only of building a House in Three Years Time, of 24 by 16 Feet, fronting within 5 Feet of the Street. The Lots to be rated according to the Convenience of their Situation, and to be sold after this *April* General Court, by *me, William Byrd." Virginia Gazette,* Apr. 15–22, 1737.

right to all the Northern Neck was asserted some ninety years later by his heir, Thomas, sixth Baron Fairfax.[13]

Thwarted in his attempts to secure the highest colonial office for himself— he was unsuccessful in getting himself appointed governor—Byrd supported the "liberties of his country" by defending the prerogatives of the Executive Council and resisting any tendency toward "exorbitant power" in the administration of Virginia's governors. Most notable among these was Colonel Alexander Spotswood (1676–1740), whose vigorous campaign to establish and maintain the supremacy of the governor brought him into conflict with both branches of the Virginia legislature. Spotswood was determined to strengthen the viceregal powers of his office, but the Burgesses and Council regarded efforts to curtail their sphere of authority with alarm. Though some biographers and historians have made much of Byrd's antipathy toward and rivalry with Spotswood, Byrd was by no means alone in clashing with the governor. In point of fact, power struggles between colonial governors and their councils were hardly unusual. The *Calendar of State Papers* notes dozens of such complaints occurring in nearly every colony. Members of the Virginia Council— singly, in small groups, or unanimously—attempted to persuade London to recall several governors on several occasions. Although Spotswood at last left office under suspicion of questionable dealings in the acquisition of very large properties through surrogates, Byrd and Spotswood reconciled and appear to have maintained good relations. Byrd visited him in 1732 to inquire about the details of mining, and a cordial letter of 1735 survives as well.[14]

Upon the outbreak of hostilities between Britain and Spain in 1741, Virginia's governor William Gooch set out with Virginian troops for Cartagena. Commissary Blair, already eighty-five years old, was named president of the Council— that is, acting governor—but he was old and infirm. Byrd, who was next in seniority, handled most of the presidential duties and stepped into the position as president of the Council himself at Blair's death on August 1, 1743. Just a year later, on August 26, 1744, William Byrd died and was buried in the Westover Parish churchyard. In the gardens of Westover his monument still stands, bearing the epitaph he composed for himself.

13. See "A Progress to the Mines in the Year 1732," *Prose Works,* 339–378. On Fairfax's claim, see Stuart E. Brown, Jr., *Virginia Baron: The Story of Thomas, Sixth Lord Fairfax* (Berryville, Va., 1965); Josiah Look Dickinson, *The Fairfax Proprietary: The Northern Neck, the Fairfax Manors, and Beginnings of Warren County in Virginia* (Front Royal, Va., 1959).

14. For an interpretation of the Spotswood-Byrd antipathy as a definitive element in Byrd's life, see Lockridge, *The Diary, and Life,* esp. 77, 117. See also Alexander Spotswood to Byrd, Dec. 23, 1735, *Correspondence,* II, 466–468.

TAKING UP LAND

In Virginia and North Carolina the pressing need for new land was compounded by what had rapidly become a tobacco monoculture economy. Clearing forests for tobacco fields rapidly used up the nutritive qualities of the soil while little or no effort was undertaken for refertilization, and so, as the Anglican divine and naturalist John Clayton reported to the Royal Society, "every three or four Years they must be for clearing a new piece of Ground out of Woods. . . . Thus their Plantations run over vast Tracts of Ground, each ambitioning to engross as much as they can, that they may be sure to have enough to Plant, and for their Stocks and Herds of Cattle to range and feed in, that Plantations of 1000, 2000, or 3000 Acres are common." Thus the need for new land created an agricultural westward expansion.[15]

Land patents provided a steady stream of income to the crown. The laws governing colonial landownership were founded on the theory of royal domain. All "new" and lapsed land belonged to the crown, which granted title through the appropriate authorities; patents were granted by the Executive Council and recorded by the colony's secretary. Title did not free the owner of obligation to the crown; lands granted by patent were subject to a modest quitrent of two shillings per hundred acres, to be collected by the receiver general, and held or dispersed by the auditor general at the crown's command. Through the correspondence of colonial governors with the Board of Trade runs a steady stream of assurances to metropolitan authorities about colonial efforts to maintain and improve quitrent income.

The history of the disputed border region between North Carolina and Virginia is bound up with government and individual profits from ownership of land. The archives documenting this history are rife with contravening impulses. At the same time that both colonies issued urgent calls for resolution of the boundary predicament, a prolonged series of delays allowed certain public officials, who proved to be anything but disinterested, to capitalize on the unsettled state of affairs. The uncertainty of the boundary was complicated by the fact that the terms of the two Carolina charters of 1663 and 1665 blurred the names of the boundary landmarks and their precise location. In 1663, the conjectural boundary line started at the Atlantic shore at a point on "the North end of the Island called Luck Island, which lies in the southern Virginia Seas and within six and Thirty degrees of the Northern latitude." In 1665 the starting point was "the north end of Carahtuke River or Gullet; upon a straight westerly

15. "Mr. John Clayton, Rector of Crofton at Wakefield, His Letter to the Royal Society, Giving a Farther Account of the Soil, and Other Observables of Virginia," *Philosophical Transactions*, XVII (1693), 979.

line to Wyonoake Creeke, which lies within or about the degrees of thirty-six and thirty Minutes, Northern latitude." The rewording of the second charter was not a clarification. It established the Carolina border at the latitude of 36° 30', some thirty miles farther north than the original formulation. From Virginia's point of view, these few careless words threatened to deprive it of a wide swath of land and to divert quitrent income from the crown to Carolina's Lords Proprietors.[16]

Without an established boundary line, there was no way to control who patented land in which jurisdiction. The disputed border zone or controverted region was a broad strip running as far west as the colonies extended, to the "Southern Sea"—the Pacific Ocean—as the charters and maps of the day proclaimed with a grand though hazy optimism. Lord Berkeley estimated the region comprised a strip of territory thirty-one miles in breadth, as Byrd mentions in *The History of the Dividing Line*. According to this estimation, within the region extending from the Atlantic coast to the westernmost reach of the 1728 line there were 7,471 square miles, or 4,781,440 acres, at stake. Virginia and Carolina officials continually accused each other of taking advantage of the uncertain boundary. Whenever the Virginia government learned that North Carolina's surveyors were surveying and patenting tracts of land in the disputed region, their protests brought assurances from North Carolina that this activity would be suspended until the boundary was established. And yet protests, assurances, and broken promises continued right up to the 1728 boundary survey.[17]

HOW THE SURVEY WAS EXECUTED

The task of a civil surveyor charged with measuring and recording the limits of property in irregularly shaped tracts required a multitude of complex geometric and mathematical calculations. The task of the boundary surveyors was somewhat simpler, consisting in just two processes. First, it was necessary to establish the easternmost starting point for the boundary line on the shore at Currituck Inlet, and then to extend the line straight west. Regular checks were also necessary to ensure that the due-westward line remained true to the agreed latitude; this was accomplished by means of solar observation and sidereal measurement. The second task was measuring and recording distances along

16. Mattie Erma Edwards Parker, ed., *North Carolina Charters and Constitutions, 1578–1698*, CRNC, I (Raleigh, N.C., 1963), 76–77, 91.

17. A more temperate estimation would measure the gap between the two charters' boundaries as closer to 15 miles. This would still result in a disputed region of 3,615 square miles, or 2,313,600 acres.

the line, noting major geographical features to be recorded in maps and leaving markers for future reference.[18]

To establish the latitude the surveyors employed the same techniques of celestial observation used by navigators on the high seas. One method was to observe the sun at noon, which the surveyors did at Currituck. Solar observation involves some complex mathematics, but it is reliable, as Arthur Pierce Middleton explains: "At the vernal and autumnal equinoxes (March 21 and September 23) each year, when the sun is on the equinoctial circle, the altitude of the sun subtracted from 90° yields the latitude of the observer." Tables of solar declination allowed navigators and surveyors to adjust for the angular distance north or south of the equinoctial line. The second method was sidereal observation, measuring the height of Polaris, the North Star, by night. Byrd reported that the surveyors "turn'd out about 2 in the Morning, to try the Variation by a Meridian taken from the North Star, and found it to be somewhat less than three degrees West." This observation confirmed that they had maintained the due west course of the line with an acceptable degree of accuracy. Again, Middleton explains: "As the elevation of the celestial pole is axiomatically equivalent to the observer's latitude and as Polaris nearly coincides with the north celestial pole, the navigator merely determined the altitude of Polaris. This yielded his latitude without calculation and without lapse of time."[19]

The principal navigational / surveying tool the surveyors used was the quadrant, an instrument consisting of a metal arc, one-quarter of a circle, with marks graduating from 0° to 90°. The surveyors calculated the angle by using a plumb line (to establish a line perpendicular to the earth) and a radial arm. The 1728 surveyors came much better prepared than those of the failed survey of 1710, when the North Carolina Commissioners had found fault with a loosely fixed instrument furnished by the Virginians that produced erratic readings. In *The History of the Dividing Line* Byrd acknowledged the justice of their com-

18. On the state and methodology of surveying at the time of the Dividing Line expedition, see Sarah S. Hughes, *Surveyors and Statesmen: Land Measuring in Colonial Virginia* (Richmond, Va., 1979); John Noble Wilford, *The Mapmakers,* rev. ed. (New York, 2000); Frank Emerson Clark, *Clark on Surveying and Boundaries,* 7th ed., ed. Walter G. Robillard and Lane J. Bouman (Charlottesville, Va., 1997); Pat Rogers, "Dividing Lines: Surveyors and the Crossing of the Colonies," *Lumen,* XXXI (2012), 41–64. On colonial surveying as the act of "bringing into bounds" territory still in "a state of nature" as it applied to the 1728 expedition, see David Smith, "William Byrd Surveys America," *Early American Literature,* XI (1976–1977), 296–310.

19. Arthur Pierce Middleton, *Tobacco Coast: A Maritime History of the Chesapeake Bay in the Colonial Era* (Baltimore, 1984), 21–23.

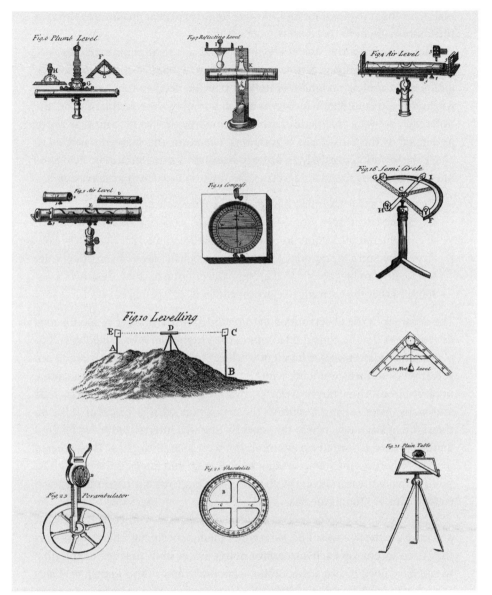

PLATE 3. Surveying Instruments. *Detail. Ephraim Chambers,* Cyclopaedia; or, An Universal Dictionary of Arts and Sciences *(London, 1728). This item is reproduced by permission of the Huntington Library, San Marino, California*

plaint, for the 1710 quadrant had allowed "an Error of near 30 Minutes either in the Instrument, or in those, who made use of it."

Another process that the surveyors needed to revisit continually was the variation of the compass. Since the earliest days of magnetic compasses, navigators and travelers on land had noticed that the needle often deviated from true north, a phenomenon known as magnetic variation or declination, or "the difference between magnetic north as defined by the needle and true north as defined by the earth's axis of rotation." Therefore, the surveyors needed to check the variation regularly, in order to maintain a true course. The field journal maintained by the 1728 surveyors opens with just such an observation:

> They found a true Meridian Line by means of the Pole Star and the first in the Tail of the Great Bear, from which the Needle varyed 3° towards the West, so that the due West Line to run was by the Needle N. 87° West. They observed the Sun's Meridional Altitude on the North Shore of Currituck Inlet and found it to be 52° 25′ 56″. The Suns Declination for that Time is 1° 2′ 21″ South so that the Latitude of Currituck Inlet is 36° [32]′ 13″.

The accuracy of the observations Byrd recorded in *The History of the Dividing Line* suggests that he consulted a copy of the Virginia surveyors' fieldbook.[20]

It was standard practice for eighteenth-century surveyors to mark their observations and measurements with physical indicators such as posts, cairns, or blazed trees. These physical marks corresponded with the surveying records and maps. After leaving Currituck the expedition set a large cedar stake on the shore of Back Bay, where the westerly line was interrupted by water, and another where it started up again on the west side of the bay. They erected markers wherever the line crossed a road or trail, and finally the westernmost point of the line was indicated with marks on a large red oak tree and blazes on a circle of trees around the oak.

Once the starting point was established, the surveyors proceeded to lay out and measure the due-west line. No record remains specifying what instruments they used to line up each successive point, but current practice at the time would have been to use a theodolite, a circumferentor (also known as a surveyor's compass), or a plane table. The most precise of these instruments was the theodolite, which consisted of a graduated brass circle with 360° mark-

---

20. Board of Trade archives, C.O. 5, 1321, 120r; Deborah Jean Warner, "True North—and Why It Mattered in Eighteenth-Century America," *American Philosophical Society, Proceedings,* CXLIX (2005), 373. Warner's account of the scientific background of surveying and its instruments in the colonial setting is very valuable, though she discusses no surveys earlier than the 1740s.

ings, on which a compass was centrally mounted. From each already-surveyed
point, the surveyor looked through sights fixed at each end of the diameter,
which allowed him to direct the assistant to place a surveying staff exactly at
the correct point. Theodolites sometimes had an attached quadrant for calculating the height of geographical features. The circumferentor was somewhat less complicated, a straight brass bar with vertical sights at either end and
a center-mounted compass. Simpler still was the plane table, little more than
a flat board fitted with sights, the table allowing paper to be affixed for drawing maps. All three instruments were fitted with spirit levels. It is interesting
to note that a cartouche on William Mayo's 1722 "accurate Mapp of Barbadoes"
shows details of surveying, including a plane table, though this does not necessarily mean that it was Mayo's instrument of choice.[21]

Distances were measured with a special chain of one hundred links, extending four poles, or sixty-six feet. The Gunter chain, named for its deviser the
English mathematician Edmund Gunter, ordinarily had an indicator every ten
links to make keeping count much easier. The chain measured "four Poles . . .
divided into 100 Links, one Links being four times the length of the other . . .
each perch to contain 16½ Feet, then each Link of this Chain will contain [7.91
inches], the whole Chain 792 Inches, or 66 Foot." On a good day, Byrd noted,
the surveyors advanced "6 Miles and 35 Chains, the Woods being pretty clear,
and interrupted with no Swamp, or other wet Ground." Struggling through the
Dismal Swamp, they could progress only three miles in five days. The surveyors'
crew often had a great deal of very hard work to do. Probably the most demanding work was the pioneers' task of clearing brush and timber along the boundary, since a clear sight line was necessary. The chainmen worked in pairs, one
at the last survey marker and the other extending the chain to the next, where
yet another man held the staff or pole used to establish the due-west direction
of the line. Still more men were required to transport supplies and bedding.[22]

When the line was interrupted by an obstacle such as a large body of
water—the waters of Currituck Sound and Back Bay, and one difficult pocosin
(swamp)—the surveyors established the point on the far side where the line
should resume with the same methods used to determine the starting point of

21. William Leybourn, *The Compleat Surveyor: Containing the Whole Art of Surveying of
Land, by the Plain Table, Theodolite, Circumferentor, Peractor, and Other Instruments,* 3d ed.
(London, 1674), 41, 44; William Mayo, *A New and Exact Map of the Island of Barbadoes in
America, according to an Actual and Accurate Survey Made in the Years 1717–1721, Approved
by the Royal Society and Authorized by His Majesty Royal Licence* (London, 1722). The map
is reproduced in Margaret Beck Pritchard and Henry G. Taliaferro, *Degrees of Latitude:
Mapping Colonial America* (Williamsburg, Va., 2002).

22. Leybourn, *Compleat Surveyor,* 51.

the survey. They considered making a circuit around the Dismal Swamp, which would have entailed leaving an end marker, perhaps a post, at the eastern margin, riding a long arc to the north, and resuming the line at the appropriate latitude on the west side of the swamp as their instruments directed. However, as it happened, the surveyors and a team of assistants opted to venture straight through the swamp. Though it might not have been quite as perilous as Byrd describes with relish in both narratives, the route must have been very difficult because of the thick growth of trees, the heavy, matted undergrowth, the slashes and deep pockets of water, and the waterlogged ground.

The final task of the surveyors was to produce a fair copy of their field book and to prepare a plat, a diagram or map of the area surveyed, indicating major geographical features and distances. At the end of the first part of the expedition the North Carolina and Virginia surveyors made a plat together, and they made another when the North Carolinians left in the midst of the second stage of the expedition. The Virginians produced a third plat when they finally turned back at the foot of the mountains. These plats were the source for Mayo's map of the expedition, submitted to the Board of Trade with Byrd's journal.

ACCRETION, EXPANSION, AND AMPLIFICATION

In turning his official documents concerning the 1728 expedition into two narratives, one meant for a small coterie of readers with specialized tastes and the other for the London literary marketplace, Byrd had no compunction about filling in the empty spaces and enriching his writing with material borrowed from any number of sources. His approach included allusion, discursive asides, tipped-in anecdotes, natural-historical digressions, and various passages borrowed from other writers.

Byrd was fond of allusion, which is not the same thing as borrowing. Rather, it is a figurative expression that draws the reader in through a process of recognition, creating a tacit relationship, a community of shared meaning. In the richly allusive *History of the Dividing Line,* Byrd frequently appeals to the cultural literacy common to his intended readers. For instance, he compliments the Widow Allen by saying she "had copied Solomon's Complete Houswife exactly." Byrd's readers would be likely to recognize the feminine ideal set forth in Proverbs 31, indicating that Mrs. Allen was industrious, trustworthy, attentive to family and household, charitable, and neither reproachful nor gossipmongering.

It is a short step, however, from allusion to appropriation. As Samuel Johnson once observed to James Boswell, "The greatest part of a writer's time is spent in reading, in order to write: a man will turn over half a library to make one book." We may see the truth of Johnson's observation in Byrd's lifelong pattern of reading and writing. Though his diary entries mentioning his morning reading often omit the names of the books and newspapers he read, sometimes evidence of his reading emerges in letters or in notes or extracts in his commonplace book. In his diary Byrd also noted occasions when he wrote in English; he did not specify what he was writing, but he might well have been taking notes, making entries in a commonplace book, or annotating a draft of one of the narratives. His diaries also record occasions when he read aloud to friends from (unnamed) manuscripts. The single extant Byrd commonplace book predates the editorial period, but once there might have been other volumes of extracts related to composing the Dividing Line histories. There is no doubt that he turned over his library to make his narratives; the annotations in this edition demonstrate how Byrd enriched his writing by inserting interesting tidbits, phrases, and entire passages from other authors. Sometimes these insertions are relevant, while at other times they are only tangentially appropriate.[23]

Byrd used extraneous material plentifully to bolster his authoritative declarations. In the first pages of *The History of the Dividing Line,* Byrd describes the origin of the British settlement of Virginia, drawing on earlier accounts by Captain John Smith and others. Byrd follows his sources by stressing the royal authority behind the colonial enterprise, just as Smith opened his account of the founding of Virginia with a royal command: "The most famous, renowned, and ever worthy of all memory, for her courage, learning, judgement, and vertue, Queene Elizabeth, granted her Letters Patents to Sir Walter Raleigh for the discovering and planting new Lands and Countries." The strong correspondence between Byrd's phrasing and the words of such earlier writers is too close for coincidence. No doubt Byrd worked on his narratives in his library, sometimes consulting books from his collection or notes taken during earlier sessions of reading. Here Byrd has enriched his own summary of the founding of Virginia

---

23. James Boswell, *Boswell's Life of Johnson,* ed. George Birkbeck Hill, rev. L. F. Powell (Oxford, 1934–1950), II, 344. Critics influenced by the theoretical work of Gérard Genette might designate elements added to narrative *paratexts.* However, Genette uses the term to indicate liminal devices and conventions not actually part of the main narrative itself, though affecting the reader. Titles, prefaces, and introductory materials are paratexts, but not elements embedded in (and not immediately distinguished from) the narrative, as with the accretional narrative. Genette also introduces the term *hypotext* for references to or imitations of antecedent or source texts. See Gérard Genette, "Introduction to the Paratext," trans. Marie Maclean, *New Literary History,* XXII (1991), 261–272. Byrd's combined imitation, allusion, and unacknowledged appropriation is infinitely more complex and jumbled than the neatly parallel hypotextual relation, say, of an eighteenth-century picaresque novel to *Don Quixote.*

by infusing it with historically legitimate observations—legitimate insofar as they were excerpted from the most authoritative texts.[24]

Byrd owes a hitherto-unrecognized debt to his predecessors, including Smith, Beverley, Lawson, and many others, in instances too numerous to list here but that this edition documents often for the first time. Byrd's hybrid writing combines the more or less straightforward chronicle of the events of 1728 with all sorts of antecedent material. This component of hybrid writing raises serious historiographic questions. What are we to make of material borrowed without acknowledgment, or even proffered as firsthand observation? After all, firsthand observations contribute to the reader's sense of a narrative's authority—that is, the "power to inspire belief, title to be believed." Historians have recently used the term "autoptic"—"belonging to . . . the nature of an eyewitness; based on or characterized by personal observation"—to indicate the persuasive quality of first-handedness. In a seminal chapter, "The Autoptic Imagination," Anthony Pagden discusses the way early New World writers achieved an effect of authority through the use of an autoptic voice; Karen Ordahl Kupperman has demonstrated the usefulness of providing ostensibly firsthand promotional accounts of the colonies to the metropolitan center of power. A large part of the authority of Byrd's narratives springs from the eyewitness mode in which they were written.[25]

However, as it happens, a writer of fiction such as Defoe may also consciously adopt the autoptic stance as a narrative strategy, producing the *effect* of firsthand observation in accounts that are in part or wholly borrowed or fabricated. Because modern historians have been accustomed to relying on firsthand accounts, they are often unprepared for writers who, like Byrd, embed material gathered from diverse sources into what only *appear* to be firsthand observations. This process may strike some readers as bordering on forgery or theft, and yet it may be better understood as a matter of enlisting materials from diverse sources to forge a new understanding of the time and place under discussion. Early modern writers had an understanding of the proprieties of historical reporting very different from our own. Most modern studies of plagiarism have focused on literary offenses, but the matter is somewhat different in historical writing. Joseph Levine has pointed out that the practice of the early

24. *Smith*, II, 63. See also Fayrer Hall, *A Short Account of the First Settlement of the Provinces of Virginia, Maryland, New-York, New-Jersey, and Pennsylvania* (London, 1735), [3].

25. Definitions from the *OED*. On importance of the autoptic mode in the writing of histories, see Anthony Pagden, *European Encounters with the New World, from Renaissance to Romanticism* (New Haven, Conn., 1993); Karen Ordahl Kupperman, *The Jamestown Project* (Cambridge, Mass., 2007).

modern historian was essentially cumulative and imitative of earlier models, so that "the writing of history meant essentially the rewriting of histories. His task was thus to choose the best narrative and to recast it with the help of other convenient works, adding his own gifts of style, organization, and political insight." Thus, Levine suggests, the notion of history writing as the production of an individual author is of relatively recent vintage. Early modern history writing established authority not simply by the presentation of verifiable factual data but through an affectively credible narration. Successful early modern historians recast history to induce in the reader a sense of trust and belief in the telling. Engagement with tradition and familiar texts and confident assertion of insight bolstered reader confidence as it constructed an authoritative narrative voice. Without such support, how could readers trust a book to be what it claimed to be, especially in an age when history writing was so often polemical or panegyrical and fiction masqueraded as travel narrative, personal letters, or secret histories?[26]

Thus, modern readers need not dismiss Byrd as a plagiarist or fraud, for reliance on other authors was a characteristic shared by many writers of his day. Even apparently respectable authors published works that were partly or completely lifted from other writers. Recognizing Byrd's extensive borrowing should not lead us to dismiss Byrd's version of history. Certainly, he often told the truth about some things he observed, and he helpfully passed on received opinion about other things, but, for the most part, his intent was not to deceive. Rather, he set out to construct a text containing those elements he believed—based on exemplary histories—would contribute to the authority of his narration. History and travel writing pursue a common goal, the construction of recognizable reality or verisimilitude. Detlev Fehling observes: "Verisimilitude and truth are not contrasts. Verisimilitude can often be thought to give an even better (because simpler and clearer) picture of deeper truths than is furnished by reality, where the fundamentals can be obscured by any amount of irrelevant detail." That is to say, verisimilitude supports the *impression* of authority; this is what drives Byrd's raiding of other authors for material.[27]

In the light of Byrd's appropriations of other texts, one further cautionary note seems appropriate. It should be clear to careful readers that it is not always safe to take Byrd's word at face value. What has passed for firsthand observation is not necessarily so. Byrd's accretional mode of composition often over-

---

26. Joseph M. Levine, *Humanism and History: Origins of Modern English Historiography* (Ithaca, N.Y., 1987), 167.

27. Detlev Fehling, "The Art of Herodotus and the Margins of the World," in Zweder von Martels, ed., *Travel Fact and Travel Fiction* . . . (Leiden, 1994), 9.

lays episodes with expansions and digressions until the original eyewitness moment is practically unrecognizable in the midst of material often appropriated from multiple sources. One example will illustrate Byrd's accretional expansion. In the Board of Trade report this laconic sentence appeared in the entry for September 23: "Our men kill'd four wild Turkeys." To the original report the British Library manuscript adds some concrete detail: "Our Hunters brought us four wild Turkeys, which at that Season began to be fat and very delicious, especially the Hens." Expanding the entry for *The History of the Dividing Line,* Byrd appended to the simple observation a discursus on turkeys that fused the field observation, material recycled from earlier books, and witty commentary. The scientific identification of species—they "seem to be of the Bustard kind"—comes from the ornithology of John Ray. Byrd attributes to a "bold Historian" comments about prodigiously heavy birds; this was Carolina natural historian John Lawson. Detail about Indian arrows tipped with turkey spurs came from Smith's *Generall Historie of Virginia* (or Beverley's borrowing from Smith in his *History and Present State of Virginia*). By adding new material to the early matter-of-fact chronicle, Byrd implicitly gained authority by providing his readers with an assortment of appealing detail—such as that colorful and learned discussion of the wild turkeys of Virginia—only loosely anchored to the day-to-day events of the expedition.[28]

Additionally, Byrd's revisions significantly alter the tone of the histories, developing and polishing the authorial persona's wit, penetration, and easy mastery of detail. In this Byrd exemplifies what David Shields has outlined as the sociable mode of belles lettres: "The tone of intimacy, the explicit cultivation of pleasure, the avoidance of didacticism, the easy use of pagan classicism, and the playfulness were stylistic marks available for emulation."[29]

BYRD AMONG THE LITERARY CRITICS AND HISTORIANS
Though Byrd's Dividing Line histories were not published in his lifetime, once they appeared in print they achieved status as classic artifacts of the colonial

28. John Ray, *The Ornithology of Francis Willughby . . .* (London, 1678), 178 (*Hayes* 790). Cf. John Wilkins, *An Essay towards a Real Character, and a Philosophical Language* (London, 1668), 148 (*Hayes* 93); Richard Bradley, who called the North American turkey "the *Virginian* Bustard," in *The Country Gentleman and Farmer's Monthly Director* (London, 1728), 62.

Lawson reported, "I never weigh'd any myself, but have been inform'd of one that weigh'd near sixty Pound Weight. I have seen half a Turkey feed eight hungry Men two Meals" (*Lawson,* 149). Smith, *Generall Historie,* in *Smith,* II, 117; and *A Map of Virginia,* in *Smith,* I, 163; *Beverley,* book 3, 60.

29. Shields, *Civil Tongues and Polite Letters,* 37.

era, sometimes considered as historical documents, and sometimes as literary expressions. They have been lauded and anthologized as small masterpieces of early American literature and humor, mined for historical data, praised for their embodiment of patriotic values, and castigated for their representation of repressive political and economic processes at work. It may be useful for readers of the Dividing Line histories to review some of the principal responses to and interpretations of Byrd's texts taken by literary critics and historians. Naturally, the scope of an introduction such as this precludes a thorough survey of secondary criticism; it must suffice to set forth some of the principal approaches. Perhaps because Byrd's writings fall into the category of belles lettres, a form David S. Shields demonstrates has traditionally been neglected by literary critics, the Dividing Line histories have been more frequently extracted in anthologies and reprinted than subjected to formal literary analysis. In practice, the most rewarding literary analyses have often partaken of historical methodologies. How then did Byrd's narratives contribute to the development of the American literary canon?[30]

From the outset, whenever Byrd's *History of the Dividing Line* was considered under the rubric of American literature, it was esteemed for wit rather than profundity. In their 1855/1875 *Cyclopaedia of American Literature,* Evert and George Duyckinck praised Byrd's narrative for its humor in the vein of Henry Fielding. According to the author of a 1909 critical survey of American literature, Byrd was colonial Virginia's "wittiest writer," *The History of the Dividing Line* "a picaresque and racy account of an interesting experience" written with spirit, vivacity, and humor. A few years later, another critical survey framed the same qualities as "Cavalier" style—urbanity, charm, (mostly) good-natured mockery, scandal, and superficial jocularity. Unfortunately, according to this commentator, "the gay Cavalier who must have his jest at any cost" was more interested in amusing his reader than in providing an accurate "picture of the pioneers." Byrd's penchant for ridicule displeases; ultimately "we are skeptical of Byrd's fitness as a historian; but we are delighted with him as a writer." The lingering notion of Byrd as a Cavalier writer recurs with dismissal of his literary aspirations as a superficial component of his gentility. Writing of the Dividing Line histories in 1947, Louis B. Wright insisted, "Although the author was clearly ambitious to be regarded as a man of letters, he preferred to pursue his avocation in the genteel manner, without rushing precipitately into print."[31]

30. Ibid., xxii.

31. Rose Marie Cutting, "America Discovers Its Literary Past: Early American Literature in Nineteenth-Century Anthologies," *Early American Literature,* IX (1975), 243; William Edward Simonds, *A Student's History of American Literature* (Boston, 1909), 47–48;

The casual offerings of genteel dilettantes—witty British Americans still emulating London genres—struck many nineteenth- and twentieth-century literary historians as an inauspicious starting point for American literature, especially when compared with the high seriousness of the literary production of New England. As William C. Spengemann has cogently observed, for many years specialists in American literature insisted that the true native tradition began in the nineteenth century; they regarded British American literature as "a tail wagged by a nineteenth-century dog." What did not fit the prescription for a national cultural identity was ignored or excluded: it was not really "literature." Thus, the literary reception of Byrd's writings until the last quarter of the twentieth century consists mostly of dismissive commentary or, at best, faint praise.[32]

Nonetheless, some critics took Byrd more seriously. In one area Byrd attained eminence for his contributions to the evolution of American regional humor. Leo Lemay placed Byrd's "satirical passages about low-life frontier types" among the ten key colonial works giving rise to the tradition of southern humor, emphasizing the trope Walter Blair described as the "tradition of comic barbarians on the frontier." Byrd's biographer, Pierre Marambaud, explains that his "essential aim . . . was literary." This led Byrd to add character sketches and humor to make the narrative more "readable." Marambaud likens "the mischievous twinkle in Byrd's eye" to Fielding and Tobias Smollett and proposes that Joseph Addison influenced his best humorous passages, "bathed in a light of indulgent irony," all managed with "an easy and elegant style."[33]

For many years, then, Byrd's style, and its resonances with great English wits, occupied the critics. Anthologies of early American literature reprinted extracts of the most readable bits. Critics searched in Byrd's writing for parallels with British models, as for instance when Robert D. Arner interpreted Byrd's

---

William J. Long, *American Literature: A Study of the Men and the Books That in the Earlier and Later Times Reflect the American Spirit* (Boston, 1913), 33–35. Louis B. Wright, "Literature in the Colonial South," *Huntington Library Quarterly,* X (1946–1947), 306. Wright made similar comments in his 1966 edition, *Prose Works,* 1.

32. William C. Spengemann, "Discovering the Literature of British America," *Early American Literature,* XVIII (1983–1984), 5.

33. J. A. Leo Lemay, "The Origins of the Humor of the Old South," *Southern Literary Journal,* XXIII, no. 2 (Spring 1991), 5; Walter Blair, "Traditions in Southern Humor," *American Quarterly,* V (1953), 132. See also Shields McIlwaine, *The Southern Poor-White, from Lubberland to Tobacco Road* (Norman, Okla., 1939); W. Howland Kenney, ed., *Laughter in the Wilderness: Early American Humor to 1783* (Kent, Ohio, 1976); Marambaud, *William Byrd,* 124, 126, 128.

life at Westover and his journeys into the wilderness as a New World accommodation of pastoral attitudes and language. The publication of Byrd's secret diaries introduced a new element to considerations of Byrd as a stylist. The distance between *The History of the Dividing Line* and the cruder, laconic diaries puzzled many and contributed to the rise of studies investigating the process of writing as the construction of Byrd's personal identity.[34]

In recent decades literary scholarship has focused on literature as a production or epiphenomenon of social circumstances and conflicts, psychological states, linguistic conditions, and cultural constructions. Focusing on factors affecting Byrd's authorship—writing as compensation for personal problems or to counter anxiety, writing as the construction or presentation of an idealized self—most literary critics turned away from formal considerations. Theoretically driven readings of Byrd as author supplanted examinations of the texts themselves, and, as the growth of cultural studies rendered disciplinary borders less distinct, the methodology of literary and historical interpretations tended to overlap. The discussion that follows, therefore, necessarily combines the literary and historical, often under the heading of cultural studies.

But, first, an important point about history writing. All historians who have studied and interpreted Byrd have framed his narratives according to their own worldviews, historiographical methods, and interpretive frameworks. That is to say, their interpretations have been constructed within a state of understanding or interpretive framework belonging to their own historical era and values. This framework of understanding produces what theorists of history writing call the *metanarrative,* the pattern, narrative structure, or set of abstract ideas underlying historical interpretation. The metanarrative allows an interpreter to collect and explain evidence in a particular way, as if organizing evidence in accordance with a dominant theme. History writing filtered through an individual historian's predispositions may produce special insights, but it may also produce partial views or polemical distortions in service of a historical, political, or theoretical position. Mary Fulbrook has cogently explained this process, contending that historians do not pluck significant elements out of thin air. Rather, they operate "within pre-existing, collectively developed frameworks of assumptions, knowledge (or lack of it) and questions." She adds, "In short, historians work within collective traditions of inquiry which set certain parameters and puzzles for which they seek solutions." I will briefly touch on

34. Robert D. Arner, "Westover and the Wilderness: William Byrd's Images of Virginia," *Southern Literary Journal,* VII, no. 2 (Spring 1975), 105–123. The critical issues of style and identity are well outlined by Ross Pudaloff, "'A Certain Amount of Excellent English': The Secret Diaries of William Byrd," *Southern Literary Journal,* XV, no. 1 (Fall 1982), 101–119.

the principal puzzle-solving approaches employed in the major historical interpretations of Byrd's Dividing Line histories.[35]

Byrd's first popularizer was Edmund Ruffin (1794–1865), an agricultural
writer, journalist, soldier, loyal Virginian, and self-styled southern patriot. Ruffin saw in Byrd an exemplar of the genteel Old South, employing Byrd in his
own campaign to generate a newly mythologized cultural identity based on a
romantic version of the past. The idealization of public figures from colonial
times generated the romantic myth of Cavalier Virginia, distinctively southern
and fundamentally aristocratic. Virginia was founded by loyal monarchists, so
the story goes, unlike the unruly Dissenting emigrants of New England. Virginia remained loyal to the royal martyr, Charles I, while, as Gordon Wood has
described the myth, "the northern colonies had been settled by Roundhead
Puritans, by narrow-minded plebeian people who had no aristocratic taste or
grace." According to Ruffin's Cavalier metanarrative, then, Byrd figured as the
archetypal Virginia aristocrat, and his *History of the Dividing Line* was the memoir of a witty but righteous patrician leader determined to preserve the Cavalier
ascendancy.[36]

From the late nineteenth to the mid-twentieth centuries historians extended
the notion of American exceptionalism—the doctrine that the United States
was founded on principles different from (and superior to) those of other countries and therefore has a superior destiny—to a kind of proleptic historiography. That is to say, exceptionalist historians anachronistically sought out early
signs of the Revolutionary spirit years, decades, and even centuries before 1776.
Nicholas Canny has observed that such historians treated the colonial period
"as nothing more than a prelude to the real thing, which . . . began only with the

35. Mary Fulbrook, *Historical Theory* (London, 2002), 67. Fulbrook goes on to note:
"Historians frequently work, whether explicitly or implicitly, within the context of collective 'controversies.'" She expands, "A great deal of history is, thus, not so much about
individual historians 'emplotting' the past out of the blue, as it were, but rather about
puzzle-solving within the context of particular controversies or wider frameworks of investigation."

36. William Byrd, *The Westover Manuscripts: Containing the History of the Dividing
Line betwixt Virginia and North Carolina; A Journey to the Land of Eden, A.D. 1733; and A
Progress to the Mines: Written from 1728 to 1736, and Now First Published* (Petersburg, Va.,
1841). Gordon S. Wood, "The Relevance and Irrelevance of American Colonial History," in
Anthony Molho and Gordon S. Wood, eds., *Imagined Histories: American Historians Inter-
pret the Past* (Princeton, N.J., 1998), 144. Wood explains: "Since Americans, unlike other
Western nations, lack a misty past where the historical record is remote and obscure,
they have tended to turn authentic historical figures and events of their colonial past into
mythical characters and legends" (147–148).

Declaration of Independence or even with the ratification of the Constitution." Proleptic historiography foregrounds any acts that might be construed as a tendency toward Independence, sometimes attributing to them a significance not supported by context. For instance, struggles between provincial executive councils and their governors demonstrated the taste for liberty and rejection of tyranny that led to the founding of the Republic. But colonial councillors, a reasonable counterargument might say, had no interest in popular liberty; rather, they were concerned with maintaining their own elite privileges in the face of arbitrary royal power, consistent with the English constitutional tradition. Specific events could be framed proleptically, as when in 1893 Philip A. Bruce constructed a version of Bacon's rebellion as a precursor of the American Revolution, arguing that the name "Patriot" would be more accurate than "Rebel," for Bacon "headed a powerful popular movement in which the sovereignty of the people was for the first time relied upon on American soil by a great leader as the justification of his acts." Few modern historians would agree with Bruce's assertion, which stands as an example of how historical events can be viewed backward, imposing the interpreter's polemical tunnel vision on events more complex and ambiguous than they are made to appear. According to this metanarrative, then, Byrd's representation of the interests of the Virginia legislature and his resistance to the increase of viceregal power, taken together with the language of Byrd's epitaph—"constant enemy of all exorbitant power . . . friend to the liberties of his country"—transform him into an antecedent for the democratic spirit of the late 1700s.[37]

Still more influential was the early-twentieth-century metanarrative of Frederick Jackson Turner, whose myth of the formative nature of westward expansion gave rise to the frontier school of historiography. Another true exceptionalist, Turner saw in the frontier a fusion of civilization and wildness, the spirit of settlement and the energy of wilderness. Out of this synthesis emerged the unique identity of America. The archetypal American gained sufficient strength from the wilderness to bring it under control, a key element of America's destiny. The influence of Turner's doctrine has persisted to this day, though many

---

37. Nicholas Canny, "Writing Atlantic History; or, Reconfiguring the History of Colonial British America," *Journal of American History,* LXXXVI (1999-2000), 1096; Philip A. Bruce, as quoted by Thomas J. Wertenbaker, *Virginia under the Stuarts, 1607-1688* (1914; New York, 1959), v. Wertenbaker calls Bacon "the torchbearer of the Revolution" (vi). Similarly, James Franklin Shinn reinvents North Carolina councillor and surveyor general Edward Moseley as an antecedent to American Revolutionary principles in "Edward Moseley: A North Carolina Colonial Patriot and Statesman," Southern History Association, *Publications,* III (1899), 15-34.

important counterarguments have appeared. Frontier-centered histories are ubiquitous, and they often adduce Byrd as an example of expansionist leadership. It should not be difficult to see how adherents of Turner's theory came to view Byrd as just such a frontier American, especially in his westward expeditions and his projections of settlements in the "Land of Eden" and Richmond.[38]

Since the heyday of frontier historiography, numerous other approaches have arisen. Sociocultural historicism emerged from the egalitarian boom of the 1960s, as Dorothy Ross explains:

> Moved by populist, socialist, and/or feminist political sympathies, social-cultural historians often valorized their subjects' resistance to oppression and sturdy survival, or conversely, their victimization by oppressors. Using a symbolic anthropology that depicted culture as the primary realm of integration and meaning in people's lives, these historians viewed culture as the site of indigenous strength.

Sociohistorical interpreters have adduced Byrd as an archetypical agent of oppression. His status as a slaveholder, his quasi-aristocratic power, and his condescending attitude toward women all provide sufficient cause for equity-minded historians to portray him negatively. Similarly, the New Historians who apply a microscope to the economics of plantation life, searching the archive for such details as land transfers, criminal court records, and changes in the regulation of transatlantic commerce, also discover evidence for the sort of charges leveled by sociohistorians.[39]

This approach has been renewed and newly theorized by postcolonial and gender theorists, who posit an integral link between social elitism, race, and sexual exploitation—and again Byrd has served as a negative exemplar. In his diaries and letters Byrd casually referred to the central role he played in an idealized agrarian economic community. Describing his life to his friend Lord Orrery, he asserted:

---

38. Frederick Jackson Turner, *The Frontier in American History* (New York, 1920). Turner says a little more about Byrd I than Byrd II, but he clearly sees both as key participants in the move westward. There are far too many Turner-influenced histories to list here, but for a fair sense of Turner's influence, see Wilbur R. Jacobs, *On Turner's Trail: One Hundred Years of Writing Western History* (Lawrence, Kans., 1994); John Mack Faragher, in *Rereading Frederick Jackson Turner: "The Significance of the Frontier in American History" and Other Essays* (New York, 1994), 1–10, 225–241.

39. Dorothy Ross, "The New and Newer Histories: Social Theory and Historiography in an American Key," in Molho and Wood, eds., *Imagined Histories*, 95.

Like one of the patriarchs, I have my flocks and my herds, my bond-men, and bond-women, and every soart of trade amongst my own servants, so that I live in a kind of independance on every one, but Providence. However tho' this soart of life is without expence yet it is attended with a great deal of trouble. I must take care to keep all my people to their duty, to set all the springs in motion, and to make every one draw his equal share to carry the machine forward. But then tis an amusement in this silent country, and a continual exercise of our patience and oeconomy.[40]

Feminist critics have made useful contributions to Byrd studies. Annette Kolodny, for instance, discovers in early frontier literature the beginnings of a gendered American pastoral, based upon "a yearning to know and to respond to the landscape as feminine." When Byrd observes the resemblance of a peak in the Blue Ridge mountains to a woman's breast, Kolodny observes, "topography and anatomy were at least analogous." The feminizing metaphor resists the impression of the wilderness as "threatening, alien, and potentially emasculating," by reinscribing the new land as a mother, taking in those who have cast off the bonds of Europe, and nurturing a new culture and improved human possibilities.[41]

A less optimistic view may be seen in the view of scholars who have explained Byrd's attachment to the patriarchal nature of the plantation in terms of personal self-realization within a conservative, misogynistic authoritarian notion of gentility. There is much to recommend in the historical deconstruction and analysis of what has come to be known as "patriarchy," with its grotesquely unjust, oppressive, cruel dimensions. Not the least significant contribution of this approach is the exploding of the misty-eyed romanticism of earlier views of the South. This change has been effected by emphasizing the opportunism, exploitation, and ruthless coercion that made the genteel lives of the planters possible. The planters' tacit assumption that their way was natural does not detract from the essential cruelty of the position, nor does the gentility that disguises it. As John Carey has observed, "One of history's most useful tasks is to bring home to us how keenly, honestly and painfully past generations pursued aims that now seem to us wrong or disgraceful."[42]

40. Byrd to Charles Boyle, earl of Orrery, July 5, 1726, *Correspondence*, I, 354–356.

41. Annette Kolodny, *The Lay of the Land: Metaphor as Experience and History in American Life and Letters* (Chapel Hill, N.C., 1975), 9. See also Virginia Scharff, ed., *Seeing Nature through Gender* (Lawrence, Kans., 2003).

42. See especially Kathleen M. Brown, *Good Wives, Nasty Wenches, and Anxious Patriarchs: Gender, Race, and Power in Colonial Virginia* (Chapel Hill, N.C., 1996); Kenneth A.

Critics and historians have engaged with the misogynistic attitudes and comments running through many of Byrd's writings. For Kenneth Lockridge, misognyny is a source of the anxiety and rage that threatened to consume Byrd; Lockridge adduces evidence for this interpretation in his diaries, the *Commonplace Book,* and the libertine episodes of the Dividing Line histories. The influence of misogyny in British America was pervasive; as Kathleen Brown explains, "Traditions saanctioning male sexual dominance had long provided Virginia's planters with both a language expressive of power and a means to practice it." According to Brown, Byrd described the sexual activities of the Dividing Line expedition with aggressive language only partly masked by a tone of libertine amusement. His language "reflected male fears of being dominated sexually by women as well as male desires for conquest." Byrd's sexual metaphors were drawn from the military lexicon, indicating that "dominance and aggression were thus encoded in the very terms with which elite men described their sexual activities." Moreover, Byrd has also served feminist historians as an archetype of the abusive southern patriarch. Kathleen Wilson explains how colonial forms of servitude and slavery entrenched male power in British America: the whip enforced the patriarch's will. Male authority was primarily concerned with "the regulation of sexual behaviour"—and hence it follows that Byrd's interest in sexual activity in the Dividing Line histories is a manifestation of the patriarchal urge for control. It is interesting to note the way in which this argument connects in a new way to the argument of colonial anxiety. Kathleen Brown, for instance, maintains, "For elite men such as Beverley and Byrd, however, public affirmations of masculine identity and the creation of an equally affirming domestic landscape were not sufficient compensation for the insecurity of their position within the colony and the British empire."[43]

At the same time, it is vitally important that scholars historicize—that is, come to terms with—what Virginia planters themselves thought of their role

---

Lockridge, *The Diary, and Life,* and *On the Sources of Patriarchal Rage: The Commonplace Books of William Byrd and Thomas Jefferson and the Gendering of Power in the Eighteenth Century* (New York, 1992); John Carey, as quoted by Margaret MacMillan, *Dangerous Games: The Uses and Abuses of History* (New York, 2008), 169.

43. Lockridge, *The Diary, and Life,* and *On the Sources of Patriarchal Rage;* Brown, *Good Wives;* Kathleen Wilson, "Empire, Gender, and Modernity in the Eighteenth Century," in Philippa Levine, ed., *Gender, and Empire* (Oxford, 2004), 26. See also Kirsten Fischer, *Suspect Relations: Sex, Race, and Resistance in Colonial Virginia* (Ithaca, N.Y., 2002). After describing the sexual importuning of the men on the expedition, Fischer comments, "The touted sexual aggression of European Men was analogous to the New World takeover that colonizers planned" (69). See also Terri L. Snyder, *Brabbling Women: Disorderly Speech and the Law in Early Virginia* (Ithaca, N.Y., 2003); Brown, *Good Wives,* 231.

in the colonial economy. As Michal Rozbicki has observed, eighteenth-century accounts of the plantation tended toward "the Renaissance landed ideal, pastoral and serene in comparison with the chaos of cities and providing everyone with a secure livelihood." It was therefore natural for Byrd and other members of the patrician elite to assume the legitimacy of their position, based on "the traditional landed ideal, with the authoritarian but benevolent master as the axis, responsible for setting the mechanisms of the plantation microcosm in motion, with the large 'family' of servants, slaves, and other dependents gravitating around him and with his own independence limited by no one." It was by no means unusual for a gentleman of Byrd's standing to believe in and practice this ideal sincerely and without hypocrisy, and to single him out as uniquely oppressive is perhaps unfair. The underlying premise of the patrician elite to which Byrd belonged was the firm belief that the entire community benefited from the benevolent rule of appropriate authorities. In his active life as a senior participant in governance and in the cultural context of his narratives, Byrd proclaimed the natural hierarchy of a traditional social structure. His commitment to the patrician order may be seen in his struggle, shared by his fellow councillors, to maintain the power and perquisites of the elite. To stand up for the rights of the colonial patrician order against infringements by arbitrary rule was truly a form of patriotic loyalty in the British constitutional tradition; hence, again, the language Byrd scripted for his own monument. Byrd understood political liberty to mean the free exercise of the rights and privileges of the different orders of society—especially his own.[44]

Yet another influential historical approach has been psychohistorical, emphasizing the impact on representative individuals of "social strains." Historians and biographers introduced personality theory to explain social conditions in certain historical periods. Especially compelling has been the New Historicist concept of self-fashioning pioneered by Stephen Greenblatt, focusing on the way individuals forge their own identity in relation to power configurations outside the self. As Dorothy Ross explains, "Status anxiety, deviance, relative deprivation, and a host of psychological disorders defined the tensions emerg-

44. Michal J. Rozbicki, *The Complete Colonial Gentleman: Cultural Legitimacy in Plantation America* (Charlottesville, Va., 1998), 74, 121. David Hackett Fischer and James Kelly have also pointed out that the Virginian understanding of "family" was extended and hierarchical: "*Patriarch* was a word that came often to Virginian lips, and *family* referred to everyone under his protection. Demographic conditions reinforced the importance of the extended family by the disruption of nuclear units," in *Bound Away: Virginia and the Westward Movement* (Charlottesville, Va., 2000), 50. See also Jack P. Greene, *Pursuits of Happiness: The Social Development of Early Modern British Colonies and the Formation of American Culture* (Chapel Hill, N.C., 1988), 95.

ing from society understood in a functionalist way." A common psychohistorical argument is that the most potent source of strain felt by colonial gentlemen
was anxiety generated by London-based metropolitan disregard or contempt
for their status, a position well expressed by Michal Rozbicki:

> Condescension directed by genteel society in the metropolis toward colo-
> nists in the New World was a persistent theme in British writing of the seven-
> teenth and eighteenth centuries. Derogatory stereotypes appeared in a wide
> cross section of English publications, from scientific treatises and travel ac-
> counts to journals, belles lettres, and graphic images. This barrage of hau-
> teur and ridicule struck those colonists who, by the eighteenth century, as-
> pired to legitimate status as gentlemen.

Rozbicki concludes, however, that metropolitan contempt did not in the end
deter "colonial elites from the quest for gentility."[45]

Nonetheless, other interpreters have insisted that the colonial quest for
acceptance was a deep, existential struggle. Combining the notions of self-
fashioning and social strain, modern students of Byrd's life have explored what
they consider to be the key element of Byrd's identity: anxiety. Donald Siebert,
for instance, contends that the Dividing Line histories provide insight into "a
more human William Byrd, with passions not always under control, with fears
and self-doubts, a man *struggling* to fashion himself in his own ideal image."
In the differences between *The Secret History* and *The History of the Dividing
Line* Siebert discovers "evidence of Byrd's own doubts concerning how best to
portray himself." Byrd's "struggle to be Steddy" drives *The Secret History*'s narrative, and the self-portrait in *The History of the Dividing Line* communicates
"an impression of ease, confidence, and control, all necessary qualities of his
idealized self-identity." According to Siebert, anxiety drove Byrd to live up to
the ideal self, imagined in *The Secret History* and created in a kind of literary or
imaginative wish-fulfillment in *The History of the Dividing Line*.[46]

45. Stephen Greenblatt, *Renaissance Self-Fashioning: From More to Shakespeare* (Chi-
cago, 1980); Ross, "The New and Newer Histories," in Molho and Wood, eds., *Imagined
Histories,* 95; Michal J. Rozbicki, "The Curse of Provincialism: Negative Perceptions of
Colonial American Plantation Gentry," *Journal of Southern History,* LXIII (1997), 727, 751.

46. Donald T. Siebert, Jr., "William Byrd's Histories of the Line: The Fashioning of a
Hero," *American Literature,* XLVII (1975–1976), 536, 538, 539. See also Wayne Franklin,
who explains Byrd's irony as a self-deprecating response to the possibility that his elabo-
rate schemes might collapse:

> Likewise, a witty attention to wayside annoyances may act within the text as a
> release for very real tensions developing in the traveler. In the case of a land-hungry

The most thorough account of the influence of anxiety may be found in the work of Kenneth Lockridge, who in several compelling studies presents a view of Byrd's life as a constant struggle with forces that threaten to undermine and diminish his sense of worth and his very identity. Lockridge's method has produced fruitful insights, but emphasis on psychobiography, not always firmly anchored in historical contexts, has sometimes led other interpreters to confuse or conflate historical and personal processes. This tendency has been aggravated by the social constructivist and postmodernist renegotiation of historical narrative. Beginning with the premise that individuals and social groups construct the ways they perceive reality, scholars of history writing have become increasingly aware of the ways that shared perceptions of the significance of phenomena affect the way writers attribute significance to what they relate in historical narratives.[47]

---

figure like William Byrd, for instance . . . irony serves to clarify rather than dismiss drives which are almost absurd in their pretension. Byrd's wit is less a means of acknowledging history than a symptom of his attempt to laugh off the confusions with which history threatens his schemes. Unable to deal directly with such threats, Byrd diminishes them by diminishing himself, by deflating intentions which he has no plan to abandon.

—*Discoverers, Explorers, Settlers: The Diligent Writers of Early America* (Chicago, 1979), 127

47. Lockridge, *The Diary, and Life, On the Sources of Patriarchal Rage,* and "The Commonplace Book of a Colonial Gentleman in Crisis: An Essay," in *Commonplace Book,* 90–115. The influence of Lockridge's argument may be seen in many studies of Byrd. For instance, Katherine Ledford explains Byrd's entire career in terms of frustrated ambition: "Byrd strove to reach a social position that was ultimately beyond him," courted socially unattainable women, and "lobbied unsuccessfully throughout his life for the governorship of Virginia." His personal anxieties had a marked impact upon not only his representations of women but also his representation of frontier people; see Katherine Ledford, "A Landscape and a People Set Apart: Narratives of Exploration and Travel in Early Appalachia," in Dwight B. Billings, Gurney Norman, and Katherine Ledford, eds., *Confronting Appalachian Stereotypes: Back Talk from an American Region* (Lexington, Ky., 1999), 47–66, esp. 56. Similarly, Geoffrey Kaeuper sees Byrd as unable to deal with the question of which world he belonged in—the metropolitan world from which he was exiled or the land of his exile:

For approximately the first fifty years of his life Byrd attempted to deal with that question by pursuing English nobility. In his later life, however, when forced to acknowledge his inability to achieve his desired status within that sphere, Byrd began to look more pointedly to Virginia as the forum for his ambitions; and in doing so he underwent a distinct alteration in self-conception.

—"New Dominance in the Old Dominion: Steadying William Byrd in *The Secret History of the Line,*" *Southern Literary Journal,* XXXVI, no. 1 (Fall 2003), 121

The focus of theorists such as Hayden White on the essential subjectivity of all history writing, Mary Fulbrook observes, has led to the assertion that "stories are imposed, not given or found in the past. In White's view, relationships among historical events exist 'only' in the mind of the historian." Postmodernist views of Byrd identify the events of the Dividing Line expedition as the production of Byrd's own mind; in this view the Dividing Line narratives document the projection of Byrd's psyche onto the landscape. Such explanations effectively detach the author of histories from historical contexts, conflating event and narration. Thus, postmodernists and postcolonialists sometimes assert claims for events that might be more reasonably applied to the *narration* of events. Attributing an extraordinary degree of agency to Byrd, they insist that the cultural demarcations of the project lay in Byrd's own conception and execution of the task, thus making him an agent of empire. One objection to this approach occurs: it is not consistent with the historical context of the survey. Seeking the origin of the Dividing Line itself in Byrd's own urge for control reverses the order of events, in effect placing the mapping ink before the surveyor's marks on the trees. Byrd did not invent the Line in order to alter the landscape. The Line did not so much subjugate the wild landscape as assist in the commodification of frontier land, making it potentially profitable to the patrician elite. As such it is imperialism writ small. Postmodern and postcolonial interpretations point to the fact that the 1728 expedition ignored natural geography, instead striking out in a straight, artificially imposed westerly direction. The significance of this route, apparently, is that Byrd imposed upon the natural terrain a man-made division, bringing it into accord with imperial measurement. But such arguments tend to overlook the fact that that was the way colonial boundary surveys were conducted—all of them, not just Byrd's. Without historical contextualization, then, theoretically oriented historians have sometimes run the risk of confusing or conflating interior and exterior causation and significance, treating events and their narration as indistinguishable.[48]

48. Fulbrook, *Historical Theory,* 66. L. Scott Philyaw, for instance, posits a special significance in the difference between the natural itinerary followed by earlier travelers and the straight line of the survey:

Instead of following the well-established paths of the Indian Trader, William Byrd II struck out across the landscape, translating an invisible line of latitude into a legal and, in Byrd's mind, cultural demarcation. As his crew transformed the draftsman's ink into the surveyor's blaze, Byrd engaged in the larger goal of subjugating the natural landscape under the purely abstract rationale of imperial decree. Unwilling

Literary criticism can provide historians with a corrective reminder about the nature of narration. Byrd's Dividing Line narratives *appear* to be autobiographical, but, as Norman S. Grabo warns, "Autobiography is always contrived, too, although its contrivance includes the appearance of artlessness." Byrd's contrivance produces what may be called a mediated autoptic effect, an artificially constructed sense of eyewitness narration. Everything that appears to the reader as the author's authentic personal experience is produced by deliberate rhetorical artifice. And so the principle that *narrated* events exist in the mind of the author has its uses, stressing the degree of control authors may exert over meaning. The question seems to be, Is history "about" the past—as Fulbrook puts it—or is it about our ways of creating meaning from the neutral debris of the past? Historical stories are not "out there" in the midst of historical reality, as postmodernists insist, waiting to be discovered—they are produced by the historical writer operating within cultural conventions. And yet the need to distinguish between event and narration leads us back to the vexing nature of historical contexts. We may see Byrd's cultural conventions at work in the way he creates a plot for his narratives, and we may see these conventions at work in the array of historical contexts and events he represents. The Dividing Line narratives may be approached on both levels, event and narration, and thus require recognition of the contexts in which the events unfolded. The political and economic pressures that made the survey necessary, the public concerns for preserving an orderly development of the colonial economy, the private benefits expected by all the commissioners, and finally Byrd's framing of these matters in emplotted, narrator-mediated accounts—all these are essential to understanding Byrd's histories.[49]

Practitioners of both the sociohistorical and psychohistorical approaches have sometimes identified Byrd's narratives as candid expressions of cultural values or personal struggles with these values, an approach that has furnished

---

to meet the New World on its own terms, Byrd instead molded it to fit his own notions.

—*Virginia's Western Visions: Political and Cultural Expansion on an Early American Frontier* (Knoxville, Tenn., 2004), 16

See also Ralph Bauer, who explains the survey as a quixotic attempt to impose "a geometric abstraction upon the American landscape": *The Cultural Geography of Colonial American Literatures: Empire, Travel, Modernity* (Cambridge, 2003), 193.

49. Norman S. Grabo, "Going Steddy: William Byrd's Literary Masquerade," *Yearbook of English Studies,* XIII (1983), 84. Grabo's initial point is essential, even if one does not agree with the analysis into which it leads him. And see Fulbrook, *Historical Theory,* 108.

some valuable insights. Still, the Dividing Line narratives are not unmediated expressions of the writer's inmost thoughts, and Byrd's conscious practice as a writer involves deliberate rhetorical artifices designed to affect his readers in certain ways. Undoubtedly Byrd's narration is compelling, but it is salutary to remember that the narratives recount Byrd's highly partial version of the events in which he participated and that they calculatingly project carefully structured positions for his reader's consumption and approbation. His narratives are not autobiographical in the modern sense; that is, they were not really an outpouring of character. Rather, they are deliberately constructed, artificial, rhetorically inflected accounts delivered by a narrative voice that is a fictional creation of the author. The narrative voice is *not* the author's personal voice. Examining the Dividing Line narratives may just as easily bring Byrd's modern readers to differ with those who attribute to Byrd the "unnatural" configuration of the boundary, or to agree substantively with many of their findings. But it must be conceded that the symbolism of a boundary separating genteel Virginia from slothful, disorderly North Carolina belongs to Byrd's narration, and not to the task of running the line itself.

To elide from the microscopic to the macroscopic, for several decades historians and critics have been widely concerned with the place of empire in colonial culture. This concern has taken several forms: first, under the influence of Edward Said and Homi Bhabha, historians and critics have investigated the radical differences in the construction of metropolitan and colonial identity; of especial interest are what Simon Gikandi identifies as the "unstable zones and contested boundaries that conjoin and divide metropolitan cultures and colonial spaces." Colonial culture neither mimics nor replicates metropolitan culture, instead adapting it to the special environment and circumstances of the colony. This adaptation is often explained as hybridizing or "creolizing," indicating a transatlantic admixture of resistance to and adaptation of metropolitan influences and authority. Some leading historians have introduced a new framework, considering the Atlantic colonial world as "a relatively homogenous unit, moving in common response to common requirements and pressures," and investigating how these movements formed "distinctive colonial identities." Michael Zuckerman maintains that "the colonists of British America always strove to be Britons": they were unable or unwilling "to see themselves as a people with a cultural identity of their own," despite the fact that their circumstances were so markedly different.[50]

---

50. Edward W. Said, *Culture and Imperialism* (New York, 1994); Homi Bhabha, "Of Mimicry and Man: The Ambivalence of Colonial Discourse," *October*, XXVIII, no. 1 (1984), 125–133, and *The Location of Culture* (Abingdon, 1994); Simon Gikandi, *Maps of English-*

Zuckerman's survey of the conflicting motives in creating colonial identity—whether reconstructing Old World culture or replacing the decadent Old World culture with something radically new—is especially useful. Others have combined theories of creolism with the notion of anxiety-based construction of anxiety, as when Ralph Bauer declares, "Creoles such as Byrd always had to prove that they were in fact what they could not assume to be: English gentlemen." Similarly, Susan Scott Parish explains: "Byrd, as a member of the creole elite, understood how the empire and its English-born agents curtailed his and other Virginia planters' authority in their home territory. His identification with the ground also comes out of that local sense of resentment at distant measures. And the notion of creolism has been applied to Byrd's authorial positions, as when Bauer reads Byrd's Dividing Line histories as "parody of the imperial production of knowledge," or when Parrish describes Byrd's shifts in authorial mode, from the "imperial virtuoso mode," in which he "attaches British verbal and material signs to New World nature in a 'ceremony of possession' (to use Patricia Seed's phrase)" to "transatlantic wit mode." Thus the Dividing Line histories "enact imperial land possession as a disinterested, improving, and chivalric rite, showing how science and empire work in tandem."[51]

One of the most perplexing characteristics of historiography, and one that is not often enough acknowledged, is that there is always evidence suitable for supporting nearly any argument. A plenitude of evidence supports every metanarrative. Thus, critics and historians whose understanding of Byrd begins, for instance, with the a priori premise that he was driven by anxiety can readily find evidence to support their explanations. At the same time, other explanations of the same evidence are always possible. There is ample evidence, for ex-

<hr>

ness: Writing Identity in the Culture of Colonialism (New York, 1996), 2. While Said and Bhabha focus primarily on nineteenth-century colonization of non-English peoples, their arguments have been adapted to the circumstances of British America: see John H. Elliott, "Introduction: Colonial Identity in the Atlantic World," in Nicholas Canny and Anthony Pagden, eds., *Colonial Identity in the Atlantic World, 1500–1800* (Princeton, N.J., 1987), 4, and Michael Zuckerman, "Identity in British America: Unease in Zion," 115.

51. Useful perspectives on this topic may be found in Ralph Bauer and José Antonio Mazzotti, eds., *Creole Subjects in the Colonial Americas: Empires, Texts, Identities* (Chapel Hill, N.C., 2009). In her essay in this collection, "William Byrd and the Crossed Languages of Science, Satire, and Empire in British America," Susan Scott Parrish discusses the differences between Bhabha's critique of empire and the colonial mimicry of British Americans (362). And see Ralph Bauer, *The Cultural Geography of Colonial American Literatures: Empire, Travel, Modernity* (Cambridge, 2003), 184. For a discussion of the place of travel literature in constructing colonial identity, see Mary Louise Pratt, *Imperial Eyes: Travel Writing and Transculturation* (New York, 1992).

ample, that Byrd derived much satisfaction from the elite power he possessed, rather than being always consumed by frustrations over his social limitations. His sense of superiority over the lesser ranks, frontier people, and women, explainable as his way of bolstering a shaky sense of self-worth, is also explicable as a manifestation of the sturdy sense of social superiority common to men of his economic rank, cultural background, and patrician social class. Plausible explanations of the importance of social strain in Byrd's life and writing may be modified in the light of a closer examination of his peers that reveals a similar array of attitudes and actions. Was Byrd afflicted with unrealistic pretensions? Perhaps. He might well have been frustrated by the difficulty of getting recognized by the class of English society to which he thought he belonged and into which he hoped to marry. The same London diaries that chronicle his frustration in the marriage market also indicate that he traveled comfortably in genteel circles, and he maintained contact with distinguished members of the metropolitan elite throughout his life. While he was rebuffed in his campaign for the governorship, he was not the only unsuccessful colonial aspirant to the office.

Furthermore, it may be useful to balance the view of Byrd's frustrations with a revaluation of his actual achievements. This inevitably leads to the question, Were his real successes so mediocre that he must necessarily have been haunted by a sense of inferiority? After all, Byrd was in fact a very powerful member of Virginia's small patrician elite, he wielded considerable economic and legal power as a key member of the Virginia Council, and he was recognized by his social peers and by a great many of his social inferiors as a great man. That Byrd himself agreed with this estimation may be concluded from evidence of his confidence in his social status and power. Moreover, despite his long-lasting struggles with debt, many of his large-scale enterprises met with marked success. Ultimately, therefore, the historiography of anxiety can neither be proven nor disproven. Strong evidence supports it, and equally strong evidence calls some of its conclusions into question.

The predominant feature of history writing, as Mary Fulbrook explains, is "its engagement with the past from the perspective of the present." There is no question that my account of Byrd scholarship as well as my own ordering of archival evidence and explanatory materials has been conducted within a framework of twenty-first-century understanding. I make no claim to freedom from historically determined views nor any claim to that remote ideal, objectivity. Like the predecessors I have mentioned, as editor, critic, and historian I have interpreted Byrd's texts and drawn facts from the archive in patterns that make sense to me, observing as much as possible the widely accepted rules of evidence—and yet I have been conscious of the truth of Thomas L. Haskell's wise caution: "Facts only take shape under the aegis of paradigms, presuppo-sitions, theories, and the like." Therefore, I freely acknowledge that I have pre-sented evidence and conclusions that may be subject to criticism. My read-ing in the field has prepared me to recognize the inevitable limitations of any selection and interpretation of facts, including my own. As Margaret MacMil-lan observes, "If the study of history does nothing more than teach us humility, skepticism and awareness of ourselves, then it has done something useful." It is my hope that this edition of Byrd's Dividing Line manuscripts, the archival evi-dence I have introduced, and the contextual explanations I have provided will be of use. Meanwhile, the field of interpretation is always open.[52]

---

52. Fulbrook, *Historical Theory*, 13; Thomas L. Haskell, *Objectivity Is Not Neutrality: Explanatory Schemes in History* (Baltimore, 1998), 157; MacMillan, *Dangerous Games*, 169.

Textual History

BYRD'S NARRATIVES

The Dividing Line histories have passed down to posterity in several manuscript forms: there remain only one nearly complete copy of the *Secret History of the Line* and two of *The History of the Dividing Line*. Several fragments also remain, useful for filling in missing parts and providing evidence of Byrd's revisions. In 1962 the Virginia Historical Society acquired the "Westover Manuscripts," a volume of Byrd's manuscripts passed down through his descendants, who over the years occasionally granted friends and visitors the opportunity to read it. The "Westover Manuscripts" narrowly escaped oblivion when in 1912 the Equitable Trust Co., in whose New York vault the volume was stored, burned to the ground in a five-alarm fire.[1]

The Westover version of *The History of the Dividing Line* is the copy-text used here, collated with another version now in the American Philosophical Society Library in Philadelphia. This copy, also owned by a branch of the Byrd family, came to the APS in 1815 missing some thirty-two pages. The APS considered publishing an abbreviated and expurgated version; pencil marks of the would-be editor are still visible on the pages. The APS committee for publications wrote to Thomas Jefferson, requesting the loan of a Byrd manuscript in his possession to compare, and hoped to supply the missing pages. Jefferson had acquired his copy from Benjamin Harrison; however, Jefferson's manuscript was, not another version of *The History of the Dividing Line,* but a copy of Byrd's *Secret History of the Line,* which Jefferson deposited in the APS Library in 1817.[2]

Several fragments of the two narratives are extant. The collection of Virginia antiquary Robert Alonzo Brock (now in the Huntington Library) includes pages of the *Secret History* on which the partially erased names of expedition members are still visible under Byrd's overwriting with aliases. Fragments of both histories are preserved in the Rockefeller Library at Colonial Williamsburg; these were among the papers of William Blathwayt (1649–1714), secretary to the Board of Trade, and his son, also William Blathwayt. Many of the senior Blath-

---

1. On the Virginia Historical Society's acquisition, see "The Westover Manuscripts," Virginia Historical Society, *Occasional Bulletin,* no. 5 (October 1962), 2–5, *Fields,* xvi.

2. On the history of the APS manuscripts, see Maude H. Woodfin, "Thomas Jefferson and William Byrd's Manuscript Histories of the Dividing Line," *WMQ,* 3d Ser., I (1944), 363–373; Kathleen L. Leonard, "Notes on the Text and Provenance of the Byrd Manuscripts," in Louis B. Wright, ed., *The Prose Works of William Byrd of Westover: Narratives of a Colonial Virginian* (Cambridge, Mass., 1966), 417–423; *Fields,* xiv–xxix.

wayt's papers passed to his son-in-law, Edward Southwell, and eventually this collection made its way to the Huntington Library. Other papers passed to the younger Blathwayt son and were eventually purchased by John D. Rockefeller, Jr., for the Colonial Williamsburg collection. Another manuscript of unknown provenance, "A Journal of the Divideing line Drawn between the Colonies of Virginia & North Carolina begun Mar 5: 1728—[per] Colo. Byrd & others," is in the British Library. Details of these manuscripts appear in Appendix 2.[3]

Both the *Secret History* and *The History of the Dividing Line* were works in progress. Both sprang from a common source, and, though the originating text is no longer extant, the evolution of the two narratives may be discerned in existing records. Several stages of composition came before Byrd wrote the two narratives presented in this edition. Some of these stages are observable in extant manuscript sources, but others are conjectural. *The History of the Dividing Line* and the *Secret History* are not field journals, though some have called them so. Byrd might well have taken notes in a diary or field book, but these notes do not remain, nor are there traces of intermediate drafts or revisions as he wrote his official report. Perhaps the British Library's manuscript was an early draft revision of a field journal, but its place in the manuscript history is unclear. Its early pages record laconic entries, but, as the chronicle advances, longer, more detailed entries gradually appear. The last section features detail and stylistic touches preserved in later versions.[4]

Whether or not Byrd kept his own journal, a copy of the surveyors' journal still exists in the Board of Trade archives. Byrd mentions in the *Secret History* that Virginia surveyor Alexander Irvin gave him "the Minutes which he had kept of our Proceedings by Order of the Commissioners." Byrd possibly consulted this log of dates and distances to supply his own narrative with a temporal and geographical framework or as an aid in building a coherent structure to which he could add from his own notes and memory. Soon after his return from the expedition, Byrd wrote summaries of the journey in letters to English friends, containing descriptive passages that were either derived from drafts or absorbed into later versions of the narrative. These epistolary descriptions may be considered another stage in the composition of the Dividing Line narratives.[5]

---

3. Maude H. Woodfin, "The Missing Pages of William Byrd's Secret History of the Line," *WMQ*, 3d Ser., II (1945), 63–70; Lester J. Cappon, "The Blathwayt Papers of Colonial Williamsburg, Inc.," *WMQ*, 3d Ser., IV (1947), 317–331.

4. "A Journal of the Divideing line Drawn between the Colonies of Virginia & North Carolina begun March 5: 1728—[per] Colo. Byrd & others," BL.

5. "A Journal or Field Book of the Proceedings of the Surveyors appointed for deter-

As the senior commissioner for Virginia, Byrd was responsible for reporting the work of the surveying expedition, a task which he undertook early in the expedition by dispatching a letter to Governor William Gooch from Norfolk (mentioned in the *Secret History*). No trace of this letter has been found, but two extant letters from Byrd to the governor exist, written during the interval between the spring and fall segments of the expedition, requesting that his position as commander be more firmly established. Byrd afterward furnished the governor with a full-length report, which Gooch conveyed to the Board of Trade in London together with a cover letter, the surveyors' journal, and copies of the king's charge to the Virginia Commissioners. All these documents, together with the report of North Carolina Commissioners, letters from the two governors, and other related items, are preserved in the Board of Trade papers now in the British National Archives.[6]

THE TWO HISTORIES

It has been common for editors and critics to assume that the composition of *Secret History* preceded and generated *The History of the Dividing Line.* The logic of this assumption seems to be that the *Secret History* is vigorous, crude, and private, whereas *The History of the Dividing Line* is polished, genteel, factual, learned, and public. Ostensibly the cruder version underwent a process of refinement and civilization to transform it from a spontaneous, artless expression of often vulgar private sentiments into something more generally palatable in the public sphere.[7]

---

mining the Bounds between the Colonies of Virginia and Carolina." This journal bears the signature of Alexander Irvin. *CSP,* V, 1321, ff. 120–135; Byrd to Charles Boyle, earl of Orrery, May 27, 1728, and May 26, 1729, *Correspondence,* I, 373–375, 395–397, Byrd to John Boyle, Baron Boyle of Broghill, May 20, 1729, I, 393–394, Byrd to John Perceval, Viscount Perceval, June 10, 1729, I, 402–405, Byrd to Peter Collinson, I, 408–409. On June 13, 1729, Byrd also wrote to Martin Bladen of the Board of Trade, alerting him to the effect of the new boundary on property he and his wife's family held in the Currituck region, I, 405–406.

6. Byrd to Gooch, Sept. 1, 5, 1728, *Correspondence,* I, 387–389; "A Journal of the Proceedings of the Commissioners for Settling the Bounds Betwixt Virginia and Carolina," CO 5, 1321. During the expedition's summer adjournment Gooch had sent a copy of the first part of the "Proceedings" with maps, received by the Board of Trade on July 30, 1728. Byrd's letter and the full text of the "Journal of the Commissioners for settling the boundary between Virginia and Carolina" were received June 27, 1729, and marked "read" on Oct. 4, 1729, *CSP,* XXXVI, 414, no. 795 (CO 5, 1322).

7. See Richard Beale Davis, who declares, "Almost surely 'The Secret History' is the earlier," because it is half as long as *The History of the Dividing Line,* omits the prefatory history, uses tag names, and is more satirical, "even sarcastic" (*Literature and Society in Early Virginia* [Baton Rouge, La., 1973], 122). Donald T. Siebert, Jr., traces "the pro-

However, a careful reading of the two manuscripts does not corroborate claims of direct genetic relation. Such claims rest, not on textual evidence, but on an untested theory of the civilizing process of composition, a theory that presumes writing involving scandal and libertine humor must be simpler and less mature than writing that eschews or transcends such matters. Unarguably *The History of the Dividing Line* is more complex, dignified, and cultured than the *Secret History,* but these factors do not establish which narrative came first. The essential difference between them concerns, not style, but purpose. Byrd's writing in the *Secret History* is neither undeveloped nor unsophisticated. Rather, its michievous, rakish tone is a highly sophisticated literary mode founded on well-established libertine precedents and satirical traditions, here developed specifically for the select audience among whom Byrd passed the manuscript. Differences in content between the two versions are best understood as deliberate rhetorical choices rather than personal or stylistic evolution. To contend that the *Secret History* was cleaned up and transformed into *The History of the Dividing Line* polarizes the actual content of the two narratives, glossing over the fact that the *Secret History* is not always jesting, and that *The History of the Dividing Line* is not always grave. Indeed, each features many passages of the sort supposedly characteristic of the other. The *Secret History* includes serious detail (such as transcriptions of official documents) not present in *The History of the Dividing Line,* and *The History of the Dividing Line* includes its fair share of scandal and bawdy humor. In place of the conventional view of a linear relationship between the two narratives, then, an alternative explanation is in order. Simply put, the two narratives were developed in parallel for wholly different audiences, drawing on a common text. Both concern themselves with the events of 1728, but internal evidence reveals that Byrd reworked both for many years after the events.

Because Byrd saw his narratives through a number of stages over an ex-

---

cess which transformed *Secret* into *History*," in "William Byrd's Histories of the Line: The Fashioning of a Hero," *American Literature,* XLVII (1975–1976), 545. Valerie Babb asserts, "Scholars generally agree that the *Secret History* represents Byrd's immediate recollections and responses and that the *History* is the version that was edited for public consumption, one that scaled down gossip and the divulging of the crew's sexual escapades and rendered in more detail the topography and the process of surveying," in *Whiteness Visible: The Meaning of Whiteness in American Literature and Culture* (New York, 1998), 34. A. James Wohlpart grounds his study on the assumption that the *Secret History* was "written first," in "The Creation of the Ordered State: William Byrd's (Re)Vision in the *History of the Dividing Line*," *Southern Literary Journal,* XXV, no. 1 (Fall 1992), 4. See also April D. Gentry, "William Byrd II (March 28, 1674–August 26, 1744)," in Daniel Patterson, ed., *Early American Nature Writers: A Biographical Encylopedia* (Westport, Conn., 2007), 78.

tended period, readers should be careful not to assume any passage was written on or near the given date of 1728. Writers have long been accustomed to praise Byrd as a discerning observer; sometimes their praise for what appears to be field observation in fact refers to material brought in during sessions of revision and expansion, added much later than Byrd's months in the field. By framing his narratives in the form of dated-entry chronicles, Byrd imparted a sense of in-the-field verisimilitude, implicitly suggesting he was relating what he observed at the time of the events themselves. Readers should beware of overlooking this authorial distance. If we tacitly accept the authorially contrived sense of narrative immediacy—what may be called the indirection of the travel narrative—our attention is guided away from the operation of Byrd's narrative artifice. The dated-journal format might well have been inherited directly from the original template (a bound journal), but in practice the ostensibly daily from-the-field reporting masks a great deal of in-the-study artifice. This comprehends a wide variety of activities, ranging from simple editorial polishing and replacement of words and phrases with more refined writing, to amplification with telling detail and literary allusion, to borrowing of detail and phrasing from earlier histories, to the careful construction of a narrative persona, a voice crafted for the telling of this story.[8]

One further characteristic commonly attributed to Byrd remains to be addressed: the frequently adduced notion that *The History of the Dividing Line* went unpublished during Byrd's lifetime because of his genteel reluctance to demean himself by courting popular approval in print. This was the opinion of his first editor, Edmund Ruffin, who in 1841 established the standard explanation of *The History of the Dividing Line* as the private writing of a colonial gentleman:

> The manuscripts offer abundant internal evidence that they were written merely for the amusement of the author, and for the perusal of his family and friends, and not with any view to their being printed. This adds much to their other and important value. For there prevails throughout, as in the

8. John Fiske in 1897 typically identified Byrd as "the historian," describing him as a trustworthy observer of admirable penetration and accuracy: "He wrote a narrative of his proceedings so full of keen observations on the people and times as to make it an extremely valuable contribution to history" (*Old Virginia and Her Neighbours* [Boston, 1897], II, 257). Dating everything Byrd wrote in the Dividing Line histories specifically as 1728 is common. In 1897 Fiske noted what Byrd said "in 1728" about timber poaching in Norfolk (II, 211); in 2002 Kirsten Fischer dated certain of Byrd's accounts of the border country "as late as 1728" (*Suspect Relations: Sex, Race, and Resistance in Colonial North Carolina* [Ithaca, N.Y., 2002], 25, 36).

private letters of an accomplished writer, a carelessness in the mode of expression, and a manifest freedom from all restraint, which together serve to render subjects pleasing and interesting, that, however worthy of consideration, would be dry and tedious if the writer had sought for the applause, or feared the censure, of the reading public. The author was a man "too proud to be vain," and who neither cared for, nor thought of seeking, public applause for his writings.

A century and a quarter later, Byrd editor Louis B. Wright observed that Byrd "never permitted his account to be printed in his lifetime," explaining Byrd's motives partly as genteel disdain for public applause and partly as a preference for polishing. The origin of the notion that eighteenth-century gentlemen held print in contempt remains a mystery, for scholarship in the history of authorship and publication clearly establishes the opposite. Numberless counterexamples could be presented, gentlemen of considerable status acting in a manner that displays no fear of being considered common scribblers. But Wright was not mistaken in stressing Byrd's proclivity for extensive polishing. Delays in completing *The History of the Dividing Line* probably had less to do with diffidence or distaste for vulgar display than with practical matters. He was continually busy with estate management, trade, politics, and land development, so the prime cause of delay might well been preoccupation.[9]

Byrd transformed his record of the expedition into two very different stories, using his early drafts as a template and refashioning the material in such a way that each narrative took on a unique style, fit for his intended audience. The *Secret History* is a private account of the feckless, scandalous conduct of certain Carolinians and Virginians during the expedition. *The History of the Dividing*

---

9. Edmund Ruffin, "Editor's Preface," *The Westover Manuscripts: Containing the History of the Dividing Line betwixt Virginia and North Carolina; A Journey to the Land of Eden, A.D. 1733; and A Progress to the Mines. Written from 1728 to 1736, and Now First Published* (Petersburg, Va., 1841), [iii]. This position is well expressed by Louis B. Wright's eloquent (and imaginative) explanation:

> Byrd was not one to hide his light under a bushel, but he was a perfectionist about his writing, and he was unwilling to turn over the manuscript to a publisher until he had given it an ultimate polishing. As a proud and dandified colonial gentleman, eager to retain the good opinion of aristocratic friends in England, he felt a certain diffidence about rushing into print like any common scribbler. As was the way of dilettantes of letters, he preferred to have his writings circulate genteelly in manuscript until such a time as he could bring them out in a manner befitting a gentleman.
> —"Introduction," *Prose Works,* 1

Line is a public account of the expedition as a manifestation of Virginian culture, conjoining civic and scientific observations with the linear chronology of the daily tasks undertaken by the commissioners, surveyors, and their support team of woodsmen. To effect these transformations, Byrd expanded and added to the material in various ways, and the two narratives took shape slowly. The Huntington fragments of the *Secret History* vividly show the process of Byrd's editorial work, right at the moment when he began to conceal the names of the surveying party with comic nicknames. Their real names still show as palimpsests on the manuscript pages, through hasty erasure and overwriting. Other manuscripts contain many revisions and additions in Byrd's hand, as the editorial apparatus indicates.

PREHISTORY OF *THE HISTORY OF THE DIVIDING LINE*

The History of the Dividing Line begins with a chronicle of the division of the territory once known as Virginia into separate colonies. It is likely that Byrd based this passage on a historical sketch he had devised decades earlier. In 1708 the English historian John Oldmixon acknowledged that he had help with the Virginia chapter of his *British Empire in America*—an unpublished history "written with a great deal of Spirit and Judgment by a Gentleman of the Province, to whom this *Historian* confesses he is very much indebted." In the second edition, Oldmixon identified the Virginian author as "Col. *Bird,* whom the Author knew when he was of the *Temple.*" Oldmixon was not himself a member of the Inns of Court, but he designated Byrd as "of the Temple" because that was Byrd's London identity at the time, for he had studied and resided in the Middle Temple from 1692. Byrd and Oldmixon probably met in literary circles.[10]

Byrd's correspondence records that in 1719 he furnished his friends the duke of Argyll and Lord Ilay in 1719 with copies of a manuscript to which he referred as a "description of Virginia." Neither the pre-1708 Oldmixon manuscript nor the 1719 Argyll-Ilay manuscripts are extant today, so it is impossible to tell whether they were the same version or different versions thereof or whether they might have furnished Byrd with material useful in composing the Dividing

---

10. Preface, *Oldmixon,* I, x, and 2d ed. (London, 1741), I, x. Oldmixon's first poems appeared in the *Gentleman's Journal* in 1692; his *Poems on Several Occasions* appeared in 1694. He wrote Whig panegyrics and pamphlets, verse epistles, prologues, an opera libretto, a tragedy, a newspaper (*The Muses' Mercury,* 1707-1708), and numerous historical volumes. For more on Oldmixon, see "Oldmixon, John (1672/3-1742)," *ODNB;* Pat Rogers, "An Early Colonial Historian: John Oldmixon and *The British Empire in America," Journal of American Studies,* VII (1973), 113-123, and *The Letters, Life, and Works of John Oldmixon: Politics and Professional Authorship in Early Hanoverian England* (Lewiston, N.Y., 2004).

Line histories. Additionally, in 1736 Byrd promised to send a manuscript to the naturalist Peter Collinson, modestly describing it as "the skeleton and ground-work of what I intend, which may some time or other come to be filld up with vessels, and flesh, and have a decent skin drawn over all to keep things tight in their places, and prevent their looking frightfull." There is no way of telling whether Byrd kept his promise, for no such manuscript has been found among the Collinson papers. Could it have been a draft of *The History of the Dividing Line?* Possibly, for Byrd's modest words about filling in and tightening truly fit the process of revision that everywhere affects the extant *History of the Dividing Line* manuscripts. Still later, one of Byrd's manuscripts was substantially re-cycled to produce the book *Neu-Gefundenes Eden,* translated by Samuel Jenner into German from the English of "Wilhelm Vogel." The book was published in Bern, Switzerland, in 1737, to support Byrd's efforts to develop his holdings in North Carolina.[11]

Oldmixon praised Byrd's early account of Virginia as "one of the most perfect of these Histories of our Plantations," especially for its "Ability and Exactness." Not every reader will agree with Oldmixon's claim for outstanding historical ex-actness in Byrd's writing, but we can easily agree with Oldmixon's declaration that the history of Virginia that reappeared in *The History of the Dividing Line* "is written with a great deal of Spirit and Judgment."[12]

BYRD'S REVISIONS

The early writings listed above served as preliminaries contributing to the more mature efforts Byrd produced between 1729 and the 1740s. Accounts of the ex-

11. Byrd's diary entry, Nov. 20, 1719, mentions leaving copies of his "description of Virginia" for Lord Ilay and his brother the duke of Argyll, *LD,* 343, Byrd to Peter Collinson, July 18, 1736, *Correspondence,* I, 494. However, Marion Tinling has plausibly suggested that the manuscript offered to Collinson could have been a draft of Byrd's *Journey to the Land of Eden, Anno. 1733,* in *Correspondence,* II, 494. Other historians have identified the manuscript Byrd promised to send Collinson as a copy of the *Secret History* (*Hayes,* 66). But the *Secret History* is not a draft for *The History of the Dividing Line,* nor a skeleton or outline, but a fully developed narrative in its own right. Tinged throughout by scandal and rakish anecdotes, the *Secret History* would not have been something Byrd would have shared with his serious, mild-mannered Quaker correspondent.

It is clear that *Neu-Gefundenes Eden* has its genesis in the *Dividing Line,* though which stage of Byrd's revised text Jenner consulted cannot be determined. See Richard Croom Beatty and William J. Molloy, eds. and trans., *William Byrd's Natural History of Virginia; or, The Newly Discovered Eden* (Richmond, Va., 1940), xxiv–xxviii; *LD,* 343n; *Prose Works,* 32; Richard Beale Davis, "William Byrd: Taste and Tolerance," in Everett Emerson, ed., *Major Writers of Early American Literature* (Madison, Wis., 1972), 156.

12. *Oldmixon* (1708), I, 10.

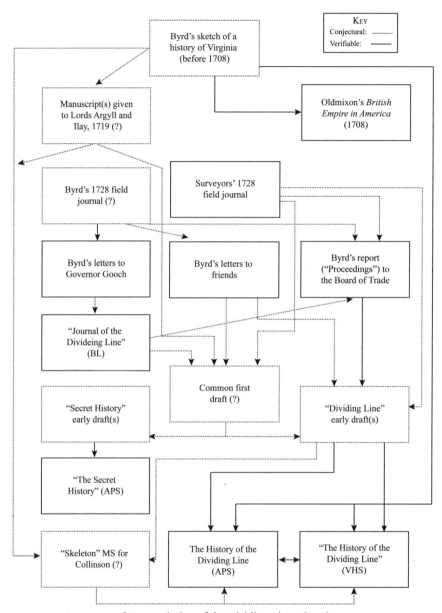

KEY
Conjectural: ....
Verifiable: ——————

Byrd's sketch of a history of Virginia (before 1708)

Manuscript(s) given to Lords Argyll and Ilay, 1719 (?)

Oldmixon's *British Empire in America* (1708)

Byrd's 1728 field journal (?)

Surveyors' 1728 field journal

Byrd's letters to Governor Gooch

Byrd's letters to friends

Byrd's report ("Proceedings") to the Board of Trade

"Journal of the Divideing Line" (BL)

Common first draft (?)

"Secret History" early draft(s)

"Dividing Line" early draft(s)

"The Secret History" (APS)

"Skeleton" MS for Collinson (?)

The History of the Dividing Line (APS)

"The History of the Dividing Line" (VHS)

FIGURE 1. Ancestry and Transmission of the Dividing Line Histories

pedition in his personal letters parallel his Board of Trade report and parts of *The History of the Dividing Line* and the *Secret History of the Line;* distinct touches of Byrd's style may be seen in these letters, just as they can be seen in the official "Proceedings" sent to London. As an aid to discerning the textual history of the narratives, I have constructed a conjectural diagram.

As a further aid in identifying Byrd's engagement in revision, this edition indicates where he took care to alter or expand specific passages in the extant manuscripts, a broken line designating erasure.

EDITIONS OF THE DIVIDING LINE HISTORIES

From the first publication of Byrd's histories, editors have treated the texts with a surprising lack of care, transcribing inaccurately, silently excising passages, modernizing spelling and punctuation, and altering grammatical constructions. The problem has been compounded by the fact that successive editors actually recycled the texts of their predecessors, thus transmitting old errors as well as introducing new mistakes, as Darin E. Fields has conclusively demonstrated.[13]

In 1822, the Petersburg newspaper the *Republican* printed a series of extracts from *The History of the Dividing Line,* containing about a quarter of the Westover manuscript text. Nineteen years later, Edmund Ruffin published *The Westover Manuscripts,* the heavily abridged edition of *The History of the Dividing Line* and two other narratives by Byrd, as a special supplement to the *Farmer's Register.* Ruffin's transcription was not scrupulous, he censored passages he considered provocative, and he modernized spelling, punctuation, and usage. But it is this highly unreliable 1841 version, as Fields has established, that became the copytext for most later editions.[14]

In 1866, Thomas Hicks Wynne published an edition of *The Dividing Line,* together with several other texts from the Westover Manuscripts. The title page declared it was "Printed from the Original Manuscript," and Wynne claimed he had scrupulously followed Byrd's "accidental and chaotic Arrangement, or

13. Darin E. Fields, "William Byrd's History of the Dividing Line betwixt Virginia and North Carolina Run in the Year of Our Lord 1728: A Genetic Text in Two Volumes" (Ph.D. diss., University of Delaware, 1992), xi–xv *(Fields).*

14. *Republican* (Petersburg), Aug. [9]–Oct. 18, 1822. Maude H. Woodfin states that variations in the *Republican* extracts suggest the newspaper worked with a different manuscript from that used by Ruffin and later editors. "Thomas Jefferson and William Byrd's Manuscript Histories of the Dividing Line," *WMQ,* 3d Ser., I (1944), 363–364, and *Fields,* xlvii; Byrd, *The Westover Manuscripts.* As editor of the Petersburg-based *Farmer's Register,* Ruffin had earlier published Byrd's "Proposal to Drain the Dismal Swamp," with commentary: *Farmer's Register,* IV, no. 9 (Jan. 1, 1837), 521–524.

rather Want of all Arrangement" in this new edition, or "Reprint." Wynne's design was "to give, as far as it was practicable with Types, *fac-simile* Copies of his Transcript," and he assured his readers "the Whole is here given with perfect Fidelity." Wynne's standard of textual fidelity, however, was not strict, for, as Fields has noted, Wynne's transcription of the first manuscript page contains some thirty-eight silent revisions (or errors) in punctuation, spelling, capitalization, and emphasis.[15]

The next version was John Spencer Bassett's elegant limited-edition folio volume of 1901, *The Writings of "Colonel William Byrd of Westover in Virginia, Esqr."* Bassett did not specify his textual source, nor did he mention any personal encounter with the Westover Manuscripts. Instead, he named Wynne's edition "an exact reprint of the manuscript," and so it is reasonable to conclude that Bassett simply recycled Wynne's transcription.[16]

Mark Van Doren's 1928 collection of writings by Byrd, *Journey to the Land of Eden and Other Papers,* again used the 1841 Ruffin volume as a copy-text. Van Doren did not identify the textual source on which he drew, nor did he alert his readers to the fact that parts of the original text were missing.[17]

Byrd's *Secret History* was first published in William K. Boyd's edition, *William Byrd's Histories of the Dividing Line betwixt Virginia and North Carolina.* Boyd arranged the two narratives on facing pages, an arrangement that facilitates comparisons of Byrd's treatment of characters, issues, and incidents, but at the same time the arrangement inhibits reading each history as an independent text. Furthermore, the texts themselves are problematic, for Boyd's transcription of the *Secret History* introduces errors and modernizations, and his Wynne-derived *History of the Dividing Line* transmits and multiplies earlier errors.[18]

15. Thomas H. Wynne, ed., *History of the Dividing Line and Other Tracts: From the Papers of William Byrd, of Westover, in Virginia, Esquire* (Richmond, Va., 1866), I, vii; *Fields,* xii.

16. John Spencer Bassett, ed., *The Writings of "Colonel William Byrd of Westover in Virginia, Esqr."* (New York, 1901). Louis B. Wright noted that Bassett and Boyd perpetuated many of Wynne's errors (*Prose Works,* 20); *Fields* demonstrates conclusively that Bassett simply copied Wynne, along the way introducing new errors of transcription (xii).

17. Mark Van Doren, ed., *Journey to the Land of Eden and Other Papers* (New York, 1928). The volume includes the *Dividing Line, A Journey to the Land of Eden,* and *A Progress to the Mines.*

18. William K. Boyd, ed., *William Byrd's Histories of the Dividing Line betwixt Virginia and North Carolina* (Raleigh, N.C., 1929). For Boyd's dependence on Wynne for the text of *The History of the Dividing Line,* see Wright, *Prose Works,* 20, and *Fields,* xii. Boyd's *Secret History* features several curious errors, sometimes supported by extravagantly obscure glosses. Transcribing Byrd's account of Capricorn's reluctance to leave his wife "to the

In 1958, Louis B. Wright and Marion Tinling included a version of *The History of the Dividing Line* in their edition of Byrd's *London Diary*. This version, they informed the reader, was abridged and modernized "to increase the ease of reading." They reached back to 1841 for Ruffin's already heavily abridged and modernized edition for their copy-text. For his comprehensive 1966 *Prose Works of William Byrd of Westover,* long established as the best scholarly edition, Wright returned to the Westover Manuscripts. But, instead of carrying out a fresh transcription from the manuscripts themselves, Wright's assistants began with the Ruffin text, collating it against a microfilm copy of the Westover Papers. As a result of what Fields has rightly called "careless editing," Wright retained many of Ruffin's errors and introduced new transcription errors as well as extensive emendations and modernizations.[19]

In 1967, Dover Press published *William Byrd's Histories of the Dividing Line betwixt Virginia and North Carolina,* reproducing the 1929 Boyd edition with a new introduction by Percy G. Adams. The version of the *Secret History* published in the 1994 Penguin collection *Colonial American Travel Narratives* comes directly from the Dover edition.[20]

It is appropriate here to acknowledge the significant debt that Byrd studies owe to Darin E. Fields's dissertation, a genetic text that endeavors to show in detail the order in which Byrd composed and revised his narrative. Fields made an important contribution to Byrd studies with his scrupulous comparison of editions of *The History of the Dividing Line* and his conclusions about the serial recycling of early and inaccurate transcriptions. Had Fields proceeded with his project, he would no doubt have produced a far better edition than any preceding him; however, several limitations would have had to be addressed. First, by focusing solely on *The History of the Dividing Line,* Fields passed up the opportunity to compare the two narratives' treatment of sources and analogues. Sec-

---

Mercy of a Physician," Boyd recorded the phrase as "the Merch of a Physician," glossing the word as Old English for "marrow." Again, he transcribes Byrd's phrase "Essay of the Variation" as "Essary of the Variation," which he explained is "a corruption of essart, the art of grubbing land to make it arable" (249). Some errors stand unjustified; he renders the phrase "Spirit of Divination" inexplicably as "Spirit of Dwinahun," with no explanation (184). On several occasions he mistranscribed names: "Wilson" for "Wilkins," "Captain Toot" for "Captain Foot."

19. Louis B. Wright and Marion Tinling, eds., *The London Diary (1717–1721) and Other Writings* (New York, 1958), v; Wright, ed., *The Prose Works of William Byrd,* 20–21. See *Fields,* xii–xiv.

20. *William Byrd's Histories of the Dividing Line betwixt Virginia and North Carolina* (New York, 1967); Wendy Martin, ed., *Colonial American Travel Narratives* (New York, 1994).

ond, while I concur with many of his observations, we frequently arrive at different conclusions, and our transcriptions from the Westover Manuscripts do not always agree. Finally, the pages of the genetic text Fields establishes faithfully record every minute particular of revision. The text is crowded with sigla identifying each contributing stage, producing what the editorial specialist Mary-Jo Kline has elsewhere called "a densely packed trail of symbols" to allow the reader to track multiple versions of the same passage. Foregrounding genetic detail makes sense for intensive textual study, but would make very heavy going for readers not concerned with technical detail. I acknowledge Fields's contributions where appropriate, but for this edition I have adopted a less intrusive form of markup, just enough to indicate where revisions occurred.[21]

21. *Fields;* Mary-Jo Kline, *A Guide to Documentary Editing,* 2d ed. (Baltimore, 1998), 178–179. Despite its many strengths, Fields's edition falls short of the accuracy he set out to achieve. His transcription includes errors such as omission and addition of words, misreading of the long *s,* anticipation of consistent or modern spelling, typographical errors, and unexplained emendations.

Editorial Matters

EDITORIAL METHOD
The editorial method employed in this edition largely conforms to accepted principles of scholarly editing, together with a few variations necessitated by certain peculiar characteristics of the manuscripts.

Basic Format: Transcription of the manuscripts has been carried out as faithfully to the originals as possible. This edition does not reproduce the exact appearance of the manuscripts line by line or page by page. Those parts recorded in journal format, but with dates moved in from the left margin, are given as provided. Authorial comments or revisions written in the margins of the manuscript have been moved into the text and annotated.

Running Dates: The extant manuscripts feature different arrangements of dates, often in the top left margin of the page. Since the pagination of this edition does not reproduce manuscript pagination, those dates are omitted.

Pagination: Copy-text manuscript pages were numbered, though not necessarily at the time of composition or transcription. These numbers appear in square brackets within the text [18] immediately before the first word of text on the next manuscript page.

Catchwords provided by the copyist at the bottom of the manuscript page to link it to the next page are omitted silently. When the copyist forgot to carry the catchword over to the beginning of the next page, the catchword supplies the omission.

Spelling: Spelling is reproduced as written in the copy-text. Many minor variations in spelling exist between manuscripts—such as "oil" and "oyl." Because spelling probably reflects, not the author's intention, but the copyist's habits of spelling, such small variants are generally not noted, except for variations in Byrd's own hand.

Hyphenation: When a word is divided between two manuscript pages, the hyphen is silently removed, and the full word appears as if it were entirely written on the page where it began. In the present text, no editorial end-of-line hyphens are introduced.

Capitalization: Capitalization is reproduced as written, but it is often a matter of subjective judgment whether upper- or lowercase forms are being used, especially in the case of *C, E,* and other letters. The copyists did not always capitalize the initial letter of new sentences, and abstract nouns appear in upper- or lowercase almost at random.

Punctuation is reproduced as written, with the caveat that distinguishing between commas and periods is also subjective. Similarly, in the manuscripts contracting apostrophes (shou'd) are often obscured by the left recurving loop of the cursive *d,* or omitted; here they are reproduced or supplied silently.

Paragraphs: Paragraphing and indentation are reproduced as written—again a matter of judgment.

Insertions: Text inserted interlineally—letters, numbers, words, and phrases— appears ^within raised carets^, indicating copyist correction or authorial revision.

Deletions: Deleted text—letters, numbers, words, and phrases—appears canceled <~~within angle brackets~~>, but only when canceled text is legible and provides evidence of substantive changes in wording or meaning. Indecipherable deleted text is ignored.

Erasure and Overwriting: When manuscript text is scraped or erased and then overwritten, the site is indicated by broken underscoring. This indication provides useful genetic evidence of composition and revision.

Lines: Dashes or lines added by Byrd or his copyist to fill space after erasure and overwriting are omitted, as are dashes or lines filling the space out to the right margin at the end of a line or paragraph.

Superscripts: Conventional usage in Byrd's era often featured abbreviations with superscripts (Govr, M^r). In the copy-texts this usage is inconsistent. Therefore, to avoid confusion superscripts have been brought down to the line and treated as standard abbreviations (Govr., Colo., Mr.). An exception is made for S^r, which is silently expanded (Sir). A period is supplied silently when appropriate if there is no colon or period indicating the abbreviation. In cases of longer words that are not standard abbreviations or only partially abbreviated [w^{ch}, Commission^{rs}], however, no period is added (wch, Commissionrs).

Thorn Abbreviation: The *y* often employed as the runic letter thorn [y^t, y^e] has been transcribed as *th,* and the abbreviated word is silently expanded (that, the).

Names: The names of persons, places, ships, and words in other languages are given as written.

Compass Points: Compass directions are preserved as written, as are bearings, with degrees (°), minutes (') and seconds (") also indicated as written; these marks are not supplied when not given in the manuscript.

Ampersand: The ampersand (&) is retained as written in manuscripts. Variant handwritten symbols (+) for "and" are silently given as ampersands.

Emphasis: Words written large in the manuscripts for emphasis are rendered in italics.

Emendations: Words or parts of words obliterated where the manuscript is damaged are supplied [within square brackets], whether the reading is conjectural or obvious. Questionable readings are followed by a (?).

Hiatus: A totally missing word or phrase in the copy-text is rendered as [————], unless it can be supplied from another manuscript, in which case the replaced text is enclosed in [square brackets] and its source noted.

Ellipsis: A blank space within a manuscript text is represented by a blank space (of 3 ems:) within [square brackets], to indicate a space left for an insertion that was not filled in.

Textual Notes: Occasional textual notes are provided at the bottom of the page, principally descriptions of the manuscript, and indicated by alphabetical footnote references, sequences renewed ad libitum.

Annotations: Historical and contextual annotations are given in endnotes, indicated by numeric superscript references, continuous through each text. Both narratives follow a common source and contain much material in common. Readers are advised that many annotations to *The History of the Dividing Line* are not duplicated in *The Secret History of the Line,* to avoid excessive repetition.

INTERNAL EVIDENCE

Both Dividing Line histories contain internal evidence establishing that Byrd worked on them for a lengthy period after the given date of 1728, when the events chronicled took place. Several of the most cogent instances are listed here, first in *The History of the Dividing Line.*

1. Byrd writes, "Of late the new colony of Georgia has made an Act. . . ." Georgia was chartered in 1732, and the new colony's bill establishing regulation of the Indian trade was passed March 21, 1733.

2. Byrd refers to the famous castrato Carlo Farinelli and to rival Italian sopranos Faustina Bordoni Hasse and Francesca Cuzzoni. The battle of the sopranos occurred in 1727 but continued to resurface in print for many years; the story even turned up in the *Virginia Gazette* in 1736. Farinelli sang in London between 1734 and 1737.

3. Byrd compares the South African herb kanna with ginseng and mentions an animal "call'd a stinker." Lord Perceval's letter of 1730 discusses Peter Kolb's mention of kanna in his account of the Cape of Good Hope. Kolb's book, published in 1731, also mentions the "stinker."

4. Byrd enriches his storytelling with a digression about a remarkable lightning strike in the summer of 1736 at York, Virginia, reported later that year in several American newspapers.

5. Byrd mentions a "recent" discovery of the efficacy of Seneca rattlesnake

root against the gout. Virginia practitioner Dr. John Tennent published a short treatise on the subject in 1736, defended his findings in the *Virginia Gazette* in 1736–1737, and traveled to London with letters of introduction from Byrd in 1738.

6. Byrd mentions the 1711 death of John Lawson as occurring twenty-five years previous, thus dating this comment to 1736.

7. Byrd draws on the expanded third edition of John Tennent's *Every Man His Own Doctor* (1736) for his comments on Saint Andrew's Cross.

8. Byrd compares the expedition chaplain's outdoor sermon to the open-air preaching of Methodist leader George Whitefield. Whitefield did not begin this famous practice until the summer of 1739.

9. Byrd echoes a phrase from Pierre Lambert de Saumery, *The Devil Turn'd Hermit; or, The Adventures of Astaroth Banish'd from Hell,* first published in 1741.

Next, several other pieces of internal evidence may be found in *The Secret History.*

1. Byrd describes a mountain "which we call'd Mount Pleasant, for the Beauty of the Prospect from thence." However beautiful the view, the expedition did not actually travel so far in 1728. Thus, while Byrd and his companions might have given the peak the name it still bears, the *explanation* of the name derives from a later date, when someone else had scaled the mountain and reported on the view.

2. Byrd identifies Alexander Irvin as "Professor of the Mathematics in the College of William & Mary," a post he was not granted until the year after the expedition.

3. In the entry for March 11 Byrd refers to the misadventure of the French marshal, the duc de Broglie, who escaped without his trousers from a surprise attack. The incident occurred in 1734 and reappeared in English satirical verse in the early 1740s.

4. One of Byrd's rakish passages describes the forestalling of a rape by the willing participation ("timely *consent*") of the kitchen helper who would otherwise have been ravished. This phrase almost perfectly matches or echoes a line from Henry Fielding's 1743 novel, *Jonathan Wild.*

5. Byrd jokingly praises William Dandridge's facility with a sewing needle, asserting that he'd learned "the *Use* of that little *Implement at Sea.*" Dandridge was not a sailor, but a wealthy merchant, planter, and Norfolk shipowner. However, after 1737 he was commissioned in the Royal Navy, commanding several ships and participating in important naval engagements between 1741 and his death in 1743.

A NOTE ON THE ILLUSTRATIONS

In a letter to Peter Collinson, Byrd wrote in 1736 of his wish to commission some illustrations for a manuscript he was preparing and wondered whether, perhaps, Mark Catesby might undertake the task. No evidence remains to indicate whether Byrd or Collinson approached Catesby, but it is safe to assume that Byrd envisioned his completed *History of the Dividing Line* as an illustrated volume.[1]

Other evidence has emerged suggesting that Byrd, or somebody acting on his behalf, did commission illustrations suitable for publication in such a volume. In 1993, Margaret Beck Pritchard and Virginia Lascara Sites proposed that Byrd might have commissioned a set of copperplate engravings discovered in Oxford's Bodleian Library, suggesting "the embryo of a larger project." Linking two of these plates with Byrd—one depicting the Williamsburg buildings and the other a map of the Dividing Line and assorted historical images—is quite plausible. Several images on these plates depict things not mentioned in the extant Dividing Line manuscripts, and the other plates deal with the Caribbean and South America. Pritchard and Sites, acknowledging that these images "reach beyond the scope of Byrd's *History of the Dividing Line*," extrapolate "a more complex account of the Americas," a history unfortunately never completed and now lost. While the argument for such a conjectural history is flawed, Pritchard and Sites are more convincing in their identification of images on the Williamsburg and Dividing Line plates.[2]

Specifically, these plates feature images directly corresponding to passages in *The History of the Dividing Line:* the tarantula and the musical cure, the emetic ipecacuanha, the mulberry tree that ought to support silkworm culture, the cash crops of tobacco and hemp, the rattlesnake charming a squirrel down from a tree, the female opossum and her young. One of the two birds depicted, the passenger pigeon, is featured in *The History of the Dividing Line* in

1. Byrd to Peter Collinson, July 18, 1736, *Correspondence*, II, 494.

2. Pearce S. Grove, "Eighteenth-Century Copperplates Discovered," *WMQ*, 3d Ser., XLIV (1987), 333–335; Luis Marden, "The Adventure of the Copper Plates," *Colonial Williamsburg*, IX, no. 4 (Summer 1987), 5–18; Margaret Beck Pritchard and Virginia Lascara Sites, *William Byrd II and His Lost History: Engravings of the Americas* (Williamsburg, Va., 1993), 19, 64. The Bodleian plate illustrating Williamsburg buildings was known earlier and proved invaluable in the reconstruction of the colonial capital. Pritchard and Sites, attempting to connect the subject matter of *all* the plates, stray into the more hazardous zones of conjecture. On problems with evidence and argument, see the review by Kevin J. Hayes, *American Literature*, LXVI (1994), 155–156, who contends that the authors overlook "crucial evidence," which "renders their thesis untenable." See also the review by Martin S. Quitt, *VMHB*, CIII (1995), 376–377.

a passage inspired by or borrowed from Lawson—and the rattlesnake image is clearly copied from Lawson's illustration of the same topic. The Indian man smoking a pipe and the Indian woman carrying an infant on her back might serve as illustrations for Byrd's description of the Nottoway. Pritchard and Sites identify the second bird as the frigate bird, referring to similar illustrations from Jean Baptiste Labat's 1724 *Nouveau voyage aux isles de l'Amérique,* though Byrd never mentions this species. Nor are there extant parallels in Byrd's text for the beetle, seahorse, or flying fish; however, he might have intended to add descriptions of these creatures to *The History of the Dividing Line* at some time.[3]

I have included several other images not specifically authorized by Byrd; most of them were found in books known to Byrd. Two illustrations corroborate my view of Byrd's borrowing from earlier texts: the image of a squirrel using his tail for a sail (from Olaus Magnus) and the image of the rattlesnake charming a squirrel down from a tree (from Lawson, also replicated in the Bodleian plate). The chart of surveying instruments should assist the reader in visualizing the technical aspects of the expedition. The rest of the illustrations show plants about which Byrd expressed a marked interest: these come from various herbals and botanical texts. Of particular interest is the frontispiece from Virginia physician John Tennent's 1738 *Epistle to Dr. Richard Mead, concerning the Epidemical Diseases of Virginia,* depicting the Seneca rattlesnake root, which Tennent proposed as an effective cure for several illnesses. Byrd, ever interested in botanical medicine, wrote effective letters of introduction for Tennent when he traveled to London to share his discoveries with the scientific and medical community.

Thanks to the Huntington Library for permission to publish the images from Olaus Magnus, Gerard, Pomet, Salmon, Lawson, and Chambers. Thanks to the Virginia Historical Society for permission to publish the Tennent frontispiece. And thanks to the Colonial Williamsburg Foundation for permission to publish Byrd's portrait and bookplate.

---

3. See Pritchard and Sites, *William Byrd II and His Lost History,* 116–138. They note the similarity of Byrd's account of the passenger pigeon to Catesby (127) but overlook the similarity of Byrd and Lawson, nor do they mention Lawson's account of the rattlesnake charm (132–137).

The History of the Dividing Line betwixt Virginia and North Carolina Run in the Year of Our Lord 1728.

Before I enter upon the Journal of the Line between Virginia and North Carolina, it will be necessary to clear the way to it, by shewing, how the other British Colonies on the main, have one after another, been carved out of Virginia, by Grants from his Majesty's Royal Predecessors. All that part of the northern American Continent, now under the Dominion of the King of Great Britain, and stretching quite as far as the Cape of Florida, went at first under the General Name of Virginia.

The only Distinction in those early Days, was, that all the Coast, to the southward of Chesapeak Bay, was called South Virginia, and all to the Northward[a] of it, North Virginia.[1]

The first Settlement of this fine Country was owing to that great Ornament of the British Nation, Sir Walter Raleigh, who obtain'd a Grant thereof from Queen Elizabeth of ever glorious Memory, by Letters Patents dated March the 25th 1584.

But whether that Gentleman ever made a Voyage thither himself, is uncertain, because those who have favour'd the Publick with an Account of his Life, mention nothing of it. However thus much may be depended on, that Sir Walter invited sundry persons of Distinction to share in his Charter, and join their purses in the laudable project of fitting out a Colony to Virginia.[2]

Accordingly 2 Ships were sent away that very Year, under the Command of his good Friends, Amidas and Barlow, to take the Possession of the Country in the Name of his Roial Mistress the Queen of England.[3]

These worthy Commanders for the advantage of the Trade-Winds, shap'd their Course, first to the Charibbe Islands, thence stretching away by the Gulph of Florida, drop't Anchor not far from Roanoak Inlet. They ventured ashoar near that Place, upon an Island, now called Colleton Island, where they set up the Arms of England, and claimed the Adjacent Country in Right of their Sovereign Lady the Queen, and this Ceremony being duely performed, they kindly invited the neighbouring Indians to traffick with them.

These poor People at first approacht the English with great Caution, having heard much of the Treachery of the Spaniards, and not knowing but

---

[a]A (APS.d): north

these Strangers might be as treacherous as they. But at length discovering a kind of good nature in their looks, they ventured to draw near, and barter their Skins and Furrs for the Bawbles and Trinkets of the English.

These first Adventurers made a very profitable Voyage, raising at least a Thousand Per Cent upon their Cargo. Amongst other Indian Commodities, they brought over some of that bewitching Vegetable, Tobacco, and this being the first that ever came to England, Sir Walter thought he could do no less, than make a Present of some of the brightest of it to His Roial Mistress for her own Smoaking.

The Queen graciously accepted of it, but finding her Stomach [sicken after two or three] Whiffs, ['twas presently whispered by the Earl][b] [2] of Leicester's Faction, that Sir Walter had certainly poison'd her. But Her Majesty soon recovering her disorder, obliged the Countess of Nottingham and all her Maids to Smoak a whole Pipe out amongst them.[4]

As it happen'd some Ages before to be the Fashion, to santer to the Holy Land, and go upon other Quixot[c] Adventures, so it was now grown the Humour to take a Trip to America. The Spaniards had lately discover'd Rich Mines in their Part of the West Indies, which made their Maritime Neighbours eager to do so too. This Modish Frenzy being still more inflam'd by the charming Account given of Virginia by the first Adventurers, made many fond of removeing to such a Paradise.[5]

Happy was he, and still happier she, that cou'd get themselves transported, fondly expecting their coarsest Utensils, in that happy place, would be of massy Silver.

This made it easy for the Company to procure as many Volunteers as they wanted for their new Colony; but like most other Undertakers, who have no Assistance ^from^ the Publick, they starved the design by too much Frugality; for unwilling to Launch out at first into too much Expence, They ship't off but few People at a time, and those but scantily provided. The Adventurers were besides idle and extravagant, and expected they might live without work in so plentiful a Country.

These Wretches were set ashoar not far from Roanoak-Inlet, but by some fatal disagreement, or Laziness, were either starv'd, or cut to pieces by the Indians.

Several repeated Misadventures of this kind did for some time allay the Itch of Sailing to this New World: but the Distemper broke out again about the Year 1606. Then it happened that the Earl of Southampton, and several

[b]V: *The bottom of the page is worn and illegible; text supplied from A.*   [c]A: Quixote

other persons, eminent for their Quality and Estates, were invited into the Company, who apply'd themselves ^once more^ to people the then almost abandon'd Colony: For this purpose they embark't about an Hundred Men, most of them Riprobates of good Familys, and related to some of the Company who were Men of Quality and Fortune.

The Ships that carried them, made a Shift to find a more direct way to Virginia, and ventured thro' the Capes into the Bay of Chesapeak. The same Night they came to an Anchor at the Mouth of Powatan, the same as James River, where they built a small Fort at a Place call'd Point Comfort.

This Settlement stood its ground from that time forward, in spite of all the Blunders and Disagreement of the first Adventurers, and the many Calamitys that befell the Colony afterwards.*d

[The six gentlemen who were first nam'd by the company were empower'd to chuse an annual President from among themselves, were always engaged in factions and quarrels, while the rest detested Work] more than Famine. At this rate the Colony must have come to nothing had it not been [for the vigila]nce and Bravery of Capt. Smith, who struck a Terrour into all the Indians round about. This Gentleman took some pains to perswade the Men to plant [Indian C]orn, but they lookt upon all Labour as a Curse. They chose rather to depend upon the musty Provisions that were sent from England, and when they fail'd were forc't to take more pains to seek for Wild Fruits in the Woods, than they wou'd have taken in tilling the Ground. Besides this expos'd them to be knockt [in the head] by the Indians, and gave them Fluxes into the Bargain, which thin'd the Plantation very much. To supply this Mortality they were reinforct [the year en]suing with a greater number of People, amongst which were fewer Gentlemen, and more Labourers, who however took care not to kill themselves with Work.

These found the First Adventurers in a very starving condition but reliev'd their Wants with the fresh supply they brought ^with^ them. From Kiquotan they extended themselves as far as James Town, where like true Englishmen they built a Church that cost no more than Fifty Pounds and a Tavern that cost Five^e hundred.

They had now made peace with the Indians, but there was one thing wanting to make that Peace lasting. The Natives cou'd by no means perswade themselves that the English were heartily their Friends, so long as they

<hr>

dV: *An asterisk here signals an addition in the left margin. The page is damaged, worn, and illegible; text in the following paragraph is supplied from A.*   eV: *Lowercase* f *with stroke added to make it uppercase.*

disdained to intermarry with them. And in earnest, had the English consulted their own Security, and the good of the Colony, Had they intended either to civilize or convert these Gentiles, they would have brought their Stomachs to embrace this prudent Alliance.[6]

The Indians are generally tall and well proportion'd, which may make [full Amends] for the Darkness of their Complexions. [Add] to [3] this that they are healthy & strong, with Constitutions untainted by Lewdness, and not enfeebled by Luxury. Besides, Morals and all considered, I can't think the Indians were much greater Heathens than the first Adventurers, who had they been good Christians, would have had the Charity to take this only method of converting the Natives to Christianity. For after all that can be said[f], a sprightly Lover is the most prevailing Missionary that can be sent amongst these, or any other Infidels.[7]

Besides, the poor Indians would have had less reason to complain, that the English took away their Land, if they had received it by way of Portion with their Daughters. Had such Affinities been contracted in the Beginning, how much Bloodshed had been prevented, and how populous would the Country have been, and consequently how considerable? Nor wou'd the Shade of the Skin have been any reproach at this day, for if a Moor may be wash't white in 3 Generations surely an Indian might have been blanch't in two.[8]

The French for their parts have not been so squeamish in Canada, who upon Trial find abundance of attraction in the Indians. Their late Grand Monarch thought it not below even the Dignity of a Frenchman to become one Flesh[g] with this people, and therefore ordered 100 Livres for any of his Subjects, Man or Woman, that wou'd inter-marry with a Native.[9]

By this piece of Policy we find the French Interest very much strengthen'd amongst the Savages, and their Religion, such as it is, propagated just as far as their Love. And I heartily wish this well concerted scheme don't hereafter give the French an Advantage over his Majesty's good Subjects on the northern Continent of America.

About the same time New England was pared off from Virginia by Letters Patents bearing Date April the 10th 1608. Several Gentlemen of the Town and Neighbourhood of Plymouth obtain'd this Grant, with ^the^ Ld: Chief Justice Popham at their Head.[10]

Their Bounds were specified to Extend from 38 to 45 Degrees of Northern Latitude, with a Breadth of some Hundred Miles from the Sea-Shore. The first 14 Years this Company encounter'd many Difficulties, and lost many men, tho' far from being discourag'd, they sent over numerous Recruits

[f]A: For after all, a   [g]V: *Another lowercase* f *with stroke added to make it uppercase.*

of Presbyterians every year, who for all that, had much to do to stand their Ground, with all their Fighting and Praying.

But about the year 1620 a Large Swarm of Dissenters fled thither from the Severities of their Stepmother the Church. These Saints conceiving the same Aversion to the Copper-Complexions of the Natives, with that of the first Adventurers to Virginia, would on no Terms contract Alliances with them, afraid perhaps, like the Jews of Old, lest they might be drawn into Idolatry by those strange Women.[11]

Whatever disgusted them I can't say, but this false delicacy creating in the Indians a Jealousy that the English were ill-affected towards them, was the Cause that many of them were cut off, and the rest exposed to various Distresses.

This Reinforcement was landed not far from Cape Codd, where for their greater Security they built a Fort, and near it, a small Town, which in Honour of the Proprietors was call'd New Plymouth. But they still had many discouragements to struggle with, tho' by being well supported from Home, they by Degrees triumph't over them all. [4]

Their Brethren after this flock't over so fast, that in a few Years they extended the Settlement one hundred Miles along the Coast, including Rhode-Island and Martha's Vineyard.

Thus the Colony throve apace, and was throng'd with large Detachments of Independants and Presbyterians, who thought themselves persecuted at home.

Tho' these People may be ridicul'd for some Pharasaical Particularity's in their Worship and Behaviour, yet they were very useful Subjects, as being Frugal and Industrious, giving no Scandal or bad Example, at least by any open and publick Vices. By which excellent Qualities they had much the advantage of the Southern Colony, who thought their being Members of the Establish't Church sufficient to sanctifie very loose and Profligate Morals: For this Reason New-England improved much Faster than Virginia, and in seven or eight Years New Plimouth, like Switzerland, seem'd too narrow a Territory for its Inhabitants.[12]

For this Reason several Gentlemen of Fortune purchas'd of the Company that Canton of New-England, now call'd Massachuset-Colony. And King James confirm'd the Purchase by his Royal Charter dated March the 4th 1628. In less than 2 years after, above 1000 of the Puritanical Sect removed thither with considerable Effects, and these were followed by such Crowds, that a Proclamation issued in England, forbidding any more of his Majesty's Subjects to be ship't off. But this had the usual Effect of things forbidden, and serv'd only to make the willful Independants flock over the faster: And about this time it was, that Messrs. Hampden and Pimm, and (some say) Oliver Cromwell, to shew how little they valued the King's Authority, took a Trip to New-England.[13]

In the Year 1630 the famous City of Boston was built in a commodious Situation for Trade and Navigation, the same being on a Peninsula at the Bottom of Massachuset-Bay.

This Town is now the most considerable of any on the British Continent, containing at least 8,000 Houses, and 40,000 Inhabitants. The Trade it drives is very great to Europe, and to every part of the West Indies, having near 1000 Ships and lesser Vessels belonging to it.[14]

Altho' the Extent of the Massachuset-Colony reach't near one Hundred and Ten Miles in Length, and half as much in Breadth, yet many of the Inhabitants, thinking they wanted Elbow-room, quitted their old Seats in the Year 1636, and formed 2 new Colonies, that of Connecticut, and New Haven: These King Charles the 2d. erected into one Government in 1664, and gave them many valuable Priviledges, and among the rest that of chusing their own Governors. The extent of these united Colonies may be about seventy Miles long, and fifty broad.[15]

Besides these several Settlements there sprang up still another a little more northerly called New Hampshire. But that consisting of no more than two Counties, and not being in condition to support the Charge of a distinct Government, was glad to be incorporated with that of Massachuset, But upon Condition however of being named in all Publick Acts, for fear of being quite lost and forgot in the Coalition.

In like manner New Plymouth joyn'd it self to Massachuset, except only R^h^ode Island, which tho' of small extent got [5] itself erected into a Seperate Government, by a Charter from King Charles the 2d. soon after the Restoration, and continues so to this day.

These Governments all continued in possession of their Respective Rights and Priviledges till the Year 1683, when that of Massachuset was made Void in England by a *Quo Warranto*.[16]

In consequence of which the King was pleased to name Sir Edmund Andros His first Governor of that Colony. This Gentleman it seems ruled them with a Rod of Iron, till the Revolution, when they laid unhallowed Hands upon Him, and sent him Prisoner to England.[17]

This undutiful proceeding met with an easy forgiveness at that happy Juncture. King William and his Royal Consort were not only pleas'd to overlook this Indignity offered to their Governor, ^but^ being made sensible how unfairly their Charter had been taken away, most graciously granted them a new one.

By this, some new Franchises were given them, as an Equivalent for those of coining Money, and electing a Governour, which was taken away. However the other Colonies of Connecticut and Rhode Island[h] had the luck to remain in Possession of their Original Charters, which to this Day have never been call'd in Question.

The next Country dismember'd from Virginia, was New Scotland, claim'd by the Crown of England in Virtue of the first Discovery by Sebastian Cabot. By Colour of this Title, King James the first granted it to Sir William Alexander by Patent, dated September the 10th 1631[i].[18]

But this Patentee never sending any Colony thither, and the French believing it very convenient for them, obtain'd a Surrender of it from their good Friend and Ally, King Charles the 2d. by the Treaty of Breda. And to show their gratitude, they stirred up the Indians soon after to annoy their Neighbours of New England. Murders happen'd continually to his Majesty's Subjects by their means, till Sir William Phipps took their Town of Port Royal in the Year 1690. But as the English are better at takeing, than keeping strong places, the French retook it soon, and remain'd Masters of it till 1710, when General Nicholson wrested it once more out of their Hands.[19]

Afterwards the Queen of Great Britain's Right to it was recogniz'd and confirmed by the treaty of Utrecht.[20]

Another Limb lopt off from Virginia, was New-York, which the Dutch seized very unfairly, on pretence of having purchas'd it from Captain Hudson, the first Discoverer. Nor was their way of taking possession of it a whit more justifiable, than their pretended Title.

Their West India Company tamper'd with some worthy English Skippers (who had contracted with a Swarm of English Dissenters to transport them to Hudson River) by no means to land them there, but to carry 'em some Leagues more Northerly.

The Dutch Finesse took exactly, and gave the Company the means to seize Hudson-River for themselves. But Sir Samuel Argall, then Governor of Virginia, understanding how the King's Subjects had been abused by these Republicans, march't thither with a good Force and oblig'd them to renounce all pretensions to that Country. The worst of it was, the Knight depended on their Parole to ship themselves for Brasile, but took no measures to make this slippery People as good as their Word.

No sooner was the good Governor retired, but the honest Dutch began to build Forts, and strengthen themselves in their ill-gotten Possessions; nor did any of the King's Liege People take the trouble to drive these Intruders

---

[h]A: Rhode Island and Connecticut   [i]A: 1621

thence. [The Civil war in]^j England [6] and the Confusions it brought forth, allowed no Leisure for such distant Considerations. Tho' tis strange that the Protector, who neglected no Occasion to mortify the Dutch, did not afterwards call them to Account for this breach of Faith. However after the Restoration the King sent a Squadron of his Ships of War under the Command of Sir Robert Carr, and reduced that^k Province to his Obedience.^{l,21}

Some time after His Majesty was pleas'd to grant that Country to his Roial Highness the Duke of York, by Letters Patents dated March the 12th 1664. But to shew the Modesty of the Dutch to the Life, tho' they had no Shadow of a Right to New-York, yet they demanded Surinam, a more valuable Country, as an Equivalent for it, and our able Ministers at the time had the Generosity to give it them.[22]

But what wounded Virginia deepest was the cutting off *Maryland* from it by Charter from King Charles the 1st to Sir George Calvert, afterwards Lord Baltimore, bearing Date the 20th of June 1632. The Truth of it is, it begat much Speculation in those days, how it came about, that a good Protestant King should bestow so bountiful a Grant upon a Zealous Roman Catholick. But 'tis probable it was one fatal Instance amongst many others of his Majesty's complaisance to the Queen.[23]

However that happen'd, 'tis certain this Province afterwards prov'd a commodious Retreat for Persons of that Communion. The Memory of the Gun-Powder-Treason-Plot was still fresh in every body's Mind, and made England too hot for Papists to live in, without danger of being burnt with the Pope every 5th of November, for which reason Legions of them transplanted themselves to Maryland, in order to be safe, as well as from the Insolence of the Populace, as the Rigour of the Government.[24]

Not only the Gun-Powder-Treason, but every other Plot, both pretended and real, that had been trump't up in England ever since, has help't to people his Lordship's Propriety.

But what has prov'd most serviceable to it, was the Grand Rebellion against King Charles the 1st, when every thing that bore the least tokens of Popery, was sure to be demolisht, and every man, that profest it, in Jeopardy of suffering the same kind of Martyrdom, the Romish Priests do in Sweden.[25]

Soon after the Reduction of New-York, the Duke was pleas'd to grant out of it all that Tract of Land included between Hudson & Delaware Rivers, to the Lord Berkeley and Sir George Carteret, by Deed dated June the 24th 1664: And

---

^{j}V: *The bottom of the page is worn and illegible; text supplied from A.* ^{k}A: the ^{l}*A does not break for a new paragraph.*

when these Grantees came to make Partition of this Territory, His Lordps. Moiety was call'd West-Jersey, and that to Sir George, East-Jersey.

But before the Date of this Grant the Swedes began to gain Footing in part of that Country, tho' after they saw the Fate of New-York, they were glad to submit to the King of England, on the easy Terms of remaining in their Possessions, and rendering a moderate Quitrent. Their Posterity continue there to this Day, and think their Lot cast in a much fairer Land than Dalicarlia.[26]

The Proprietors of New-Jersey finding more Trouble than Profit in their new Dominions, made over their Right to several other Persons, who obtain'd a fresh Grant from his Royal Highness, dated March the 14th 1682.[27]

Several of the Grantees being Quakers, and Anabaptists, fail'd [7] not to encourage many of their own Perswasion to remove to this peacefull Region. Amongst them were a swarm of Scots Quakers, who were not tolerated to exercise the Gifts of the Spirit in their own Country.

Besides the hopes of being safe from Persecution in this Retreat, the new Proprietors inveigled many over by this tempting Account of the Country: That it was a place free from those 3 great Scourges of Mankind, Priests, Lawyers, and Physicians. Nor did they tell them a Word of a Lye, for the People were yet too poor to maintain these Learned Gentlemen, who every where love to be well paid for what they do, and, like the Jews, can't breath in a Climate, where nothing is to be got.

The Jerseys continued under the Government of these[m] Proprietors, till the Year 1702, when they made a formal surrender of the Dominion to the Queen, reserving however the property of the Soil to themselves. So soon as the Bounds of New-Jersey came to be distinctly laid off, it appeared there was still a narrow Slipe of Land, lying betwixt[n] that Colony, and Maryland. Of this William Penn, a Man of much Wordly Wisdom, and some eminence amongst the Quakers, got early Notice, and by the Credit he had with the Duke of York, obtain'd a Patent for it Dated March the 4th 1680.[28]

It was a little surprizing to some People, how a Quaker shou'd be so much in the good Graces of a Popish Prince, tho' after all it may be pretty well accounted for. This ingenious Person had not been bred a Quaker, but in his earlier days had been a Man of Pleasure about the Town. He had a beautiful form, and very taking Address, which made him successful with the Ladies, and particularly with a Mistress of the Duke of Monmouth. By this Gentlewoman he had a Daughter who had Beauty enough to raise her to be a Duchess, and continued to be a Toast full 30 Years.

[m]A: the   [n]A: between

But this Amour had like to have brought our Fine Gentleman in Danger of a Duell, had he not discreetly shelter'd himself under this peaceable Perswasion. Besides his Father haveing been a Flag-Officer in the Navy, while the Duke of York was Lord High Admiral, might recommend the Son to his Favour. This piece of Secret History I thought proper to mention, to wipe off the suspicion of his having been Popishly inclin'd.[29]

This Gentleman's first Grant confin'd Him within pretty narrow Bounds, giving him only that Portion of Land, which contains Buckingham, Philadelphia, and Chester Counties.° But to get these Bounds a little extended, He push't His Interest still farther with His Royal Highness, and obtain'd a fresh Grant of the three Lower Counties, called New-Castle, Kent, and Sussex, which still remain'd within the New-York Patent, and had been luckily left out of the Grant of New-Jersey.

The Six Counties being thus incorporated, the Proprietor dignify'd the whole with the name of Pensilvania.

The Quakers flock't over to that Country in Shoals, being averse to go to Heaven the same way with the Bishops. Amongst them were not a few of good Substance, who went vigorously upon every kind of Improvement: and thus much I may truly say in their Praise, that by Diligence and Frugality, For which this Harmless Sect is remarkable, and by haveing no Vices, but such as are Private, they have in a few Years made Pensilvania a very fine Country.

The Truth is, they have observ'd exact Justice with all the Nations [8] that border upon them; they have purchas'd all their Lands from the Indians, and tho' they paid but a Triffle for them, it has procured them the Credit of being more righteous than their Neighbours. They have likewise had the Prudence to treat them kindly upon all Occasions, which has sav'd them from many Wars, and Massacres, wherein the other Colonies have been indiscreetly involved. The truth of it is, a People whose Principles forbid them to draw the carnal Sword, were in the Right to give no Provocation.[30]

Both the French and Spaniards had in the Name of their Respective Monarchs, long ago taken Possession of that Part of the Northern Continent, that now goes by the Name of Carolina: but finding it produced neither Gold nor Silver, as they greedily expected, and meeting such returns from the Indians, as their own Cruelty and Treachery deserved, they totally abandon'd it. In this deserted Condition that Country lay for the space of 90 Years, 'till King Charles the 2d. finding it a *Derilict,* granted it away to the Earl of Clarendon and others by His Royal Charter, dated March the 24th 1663. The Boundary of that Grant towards Virginia was a due West Line from Luck-

°A: contains Philadelphia, Buckingham, Philadelphia, and Chester counties

Island (the same as Colleton-Island) lying in 36 Degrees of N. Latitude, quite to the South Sea.

But afterwards Sir William Berkely, who was one of the Grantees and at that time Governour of Virginia, finding a Territory of 31 Miles in Breadth between the inhabited part of Virginia, and the above-mentioned Boundary of Carolina, advis'd the Lord Clarendon of it, and His Lordp. had Interest enough with the King, to obtain a Second Patent to include it, dated June the 30th 1665.

This last Grant describes the Bounds between Virginia and Carolina in these Words: "To run from the North-End of Corotuck-Inlet due West to Weyanoak Creek, lying within or about the Degree of Thirty Six, and thirty Minutes of Northern Latitude, and from thence West in a direct Line as far as the South-Sea." Without question this Boundary was well known at the time the Charter was Granted, but in a long course of years Weyanoak Creek lost its name, so that it became a Controversy, where it lay. Some ancient Persons in Virginia, affirm'd it was the same with Wicocon, and others again in Carolina were as positive it was Notoway River.

In the mean time the People on the Frontiers enter'd for Land, & took out Patents by Guess, either from the King or the Lords Proprietors. But the Crown was like to be the loser by this Incertainty, because the Terms both of taking up, and seating Land, were easier much in Carolina. The Yearly Taxes to the Publick were likewise there less burthensome, which laid Virginia under a plain disadvantage.

This consideration put that Government upon entering into Measures with North Carolina, to terminate the Dispute, and settle a certain Boundary between the two colonies. All the Difficulty was, to find out which was truly Weyanoak Creek. The Difference was too considerable to be given up by either side, there being a Territory of 15 Miles betwixt the two Streams in controversy.

However till that Matter could be adjusted, it was agreed on both sides, that no Lands at all should be granted within the disputed Bounds. Virginia observed this Agreement punctually, but I am sorry, I can't say the same of North-Carolina. The [9] great Officers of that Province were loath to lose the Fees accrueing from the Grants of Land, and so private Interest got the better of publick Spirit, and I wish that were the only place in the World, where such Politicks are fashionable.

All the Steps, that were taken afterwards in that Affair, will best appear by the Report of the Virginia-Commissioners, recited in the Order of Council given at St. James's March the 1st 1710 set down in the Appendix.

It must be owned, the Report of those Gentlemen was severe upon the then Commissioners of North-Carolina, and particularly upon Mr. M——[y][p] I won't take upon me to say with how much Justice they said so many hard things, tho' it had been fairer Play, to have given the Parties accus'd a copy of such Representation, that they might have answer'd what they could for themselves.[31]

But since that was not done, I must beg leave to say this much on behalf of Mr Moseley[q], that he was not much in the Wrong to find fault with the Quadrant produced by the Surveyors of Virginia, because that Instrument plac't the Mouth of Notoway River in the Latitude of 37 Degrees, whereas by an Accurate Observation made since, it appears to lie in 36°, 30′½ so that there was an Error of near 30 Minutes either in the Instrument, or in those, who made use of it.

Besides it is evident, the Mouth of Notoway River agrees much better with the Latitude, wherein the Carolina Charter supposed Wyanoak Creek, (namely in or about 36 Degrees and 30 Minutes) than it does with Wicocon Creek which is about 15 Miles more Southerly.

This being manifest, the Intention of the King's Grant will be pretty exactly answer'd, by a due West Line drawn from Corotuck Inlet to the Mouth of Notoway River, for which reason 'tis probable, that was formerly call'd Wyanoak-Creek, and might change its Name when the Notoway Indians came to live upon it, which was since the Date of the last Carolina Charter.

The Lieut. Governor of Virginia. at that time Colo. Spotswood, searching into the Bottom of this Affair, made very Equitable Proposals to Mr. Eden at that time Governour of North-Carolina, in order to put an End to this Controversy. These being form'd into Preliminaries were sign'd by both Governours, and transmitted to England, where they had the Honour to be ratifyed by his late Majesty, and assented to by the Lord Proprietors of Carolina.[32]

Accordingly an Order was sent by the late King, to Mr. Gooch afterwards Lieut. Governor of Virginia to pursue those Preliminarys exactly. In Obedience thereunto he was pleased to appoint Three of the Council of that Colony, to be Commissioners on the Part of Virginia, who in conjunction with others, to be named by the Governor of North-Carolina, were to settle the Boundary between the 2 Governments upon the Plan of the abovemention'd Articles.

Two experience't Surveyors were at the same time directed to wait upon the Commissioners Mr. Mayo[r], who made the accurate Mapp of Barbadoes,

[p]A: M. . . . . .] V: M. . . . .y *(the* y *has been mostly erased). In both MSS the number of dots in the ellipsis corresponds to the number of letters missing in the name Moseley.* [q]A: Moseley
[r]A: Mr. Mayo

and Mr Irvin[s] the Mathematick Professor of William and Mary Colledge. And because a good Number of Men were to go upon this Expedition, a Chaplain was appointed to attend them, and the rather because the People on the Frontiers of North-Carolina, who have no Minister near them, might have [10] an Opportunity to get themselves, and their Children baptiz'd.[33]

Of these proceedings on our Part immediate Notice was sent to Sir Richard Everard, Governor of North-Carolina, who was desired to name Commissioners for that Province, to meet those of Virginia at Corotuck-Inlet the Spring following. Accordingly he appointed Four Members of the Council of that Province to take care of the Interests of the Lds. Proprietors. Of these Mr. Moseley was to serve in a Double Capacity both as Commissioner, and Surveyor. For that reason there was but one other Surveyor from thence, Mr. Swan. All the Persons being thus agreed upon they settled the time of Meeting to be at Coratuck March the 5th 1728.[34]

In the mean time the requisite Preparations were made for so long and tiresome a Journey; and because there was much work to be done, and some Danger from the Indians in the uninhabited Part of the Country, it was necessary to provide a competent number of Men. Accordingly seventeen able Hands were listed on the Part of Virginia, who were most of them Indian Traders, and expert Woodsmen.

1728. FEBRUARY[t]

27   These good men were ordered to come armed – with a Musquet, and a Tomahack, or large Hatchet, and provided with a sufficient Quantity of Ammunition.

They likewise brought Provisions of their own for ten days, after which time they were to be furnisht by the Government. Their March was appointed to be on the 27th of February, on which day one of the Commissioners met them at their Rendezvous, and proceeded with them as far as Colo. Allens. This Gentleman is a great Oeconomist, and skill'd in all the Arts of living well at an easy expence.[35]

28.   They proceeded in good Order through Surry County, as far as the Widdow Allens, who had copied Solomon's Complete Houswife exactly. At this Gentlewoman's House the other two Commissioners had appointed to

<hr>

[s]A: Mr. Irwin] V: *Both proper names initially gave only the first and last letters; omitted letters were later overwritten in another hand.*   [t]V: *The first date given, on upper left-hand corner of the page. In A, the year is given in the left-hand margin at the beginning of the paragraph.*

join them, but were detain'd by some Accident at Williamsburg longer, than their Appointment.[36]

29.   They pursued their March thro' the Isle of Wight, and observ'd a most dreadfull Havock made by a late Hurricane, which happen'd in August 1726. The Violence of it had not reach't above a Quarter of a Mile in Breadth, but ^within^ that Compass had levell'd all before it. Both Trees and Houses were laid flat on the Ground, and several things hurl'd to an incredible distance. 'Tis happy such violent Gusts are confin'd to so narrow a Channel, because they carry desolation, wherever they go. In the Evening they reach't Mr. Godwins on the South Branch of Nansemond River, were[u] they were treated with abundance Primitive Hospitality.[37]

March.1.   This Gentleman was so kind as to shorten their Journey by setting them over the River. They coasted the N.E. side of the Dismal for several miles together, and found all the Grounds bordering upon it very full of Sloughs. The Trees, that grow near it look't very Reverend, with the long Moss that hung dangling from their Branches. Both Cattle and Horses eat this Moss greedily in Winter[v], when other Provender is scarce, tho it is apt to scour them at first. In that moist soil too grows abundance [11] of that kind of Myrtle, which bears the Candle-Berries. There was likewise here and there a Gall-bush, which is a beautiful Evergreen, and may be cut into any shape. It derives its name from its Berries turning Water black, like the Galls of an Oak.[38]

When this Shrub is transplanted into Gardens, it will not thrive without frequent watering.[39]

The two other Commissioners came up with them just at their Journey's end, and that Evening they arriv'd all together at Mr. Crafords, who lives on the South Branch of Elizabeth-River, over against Norfolk. Here the Commissioners left the Men with all the Horses and heavy Baggage, and cros't the River with their Servants only, for fear of making a Famine in the Town.[40]

Norfolk has most the Ayr of a Town of any in Virginia. There were then near 20 Brigantines and Sloops riding at the Wharfs, and oftentimes they have more. It has all the advantages of situation requisite for Trade and Navigation. There is a secure Harbour for a good number of Ships of any Burthen. Their River divides itself into 3 several Branches, which are all Navigable. The Town is so near the Sea, that its Vessels may sail in and out in a few Hours. Their Trade is chiefly to the West Indies, whither they export abundance of Beef, Pork, Flour and Lumber. The worst of it is, they contribute

[u]*Sic in V and A*   [v]A: in Winter

much towards debauching the Country, by importing abundance of Rum, which like Ginn in Great Britain breaks the Constitutions, vitiates the Morals, and ruins the Industry of most of the Poor People of this Country.[41]

This Place is the Mart for most of the Commodities produc'd in the adjacent Parts of North-Carolina. They have a pretty deal of Lumber, from the Borderers on the Dismal, who make bold with the King's Land thereabouts, without the least Ceremony. They not only maintain their Stocks upon it, but get Boards, Shingles, and other Lumber out of it in great abundance.

The Town is built on[a] a level Spot of Ground upon Elizabeth River, the Banks whereof are neither so high, as to make the Landing of Goods troublesome, or so low as to be in Danger of overflowing. The Streets are strait, and adorn'd with several good Houses, which encrease every Day. It is not a Town of Ordinarys, and Publick Houses, like most others in this Country, but the Inhabitants consist of Merchants, Ship-Carpenters, and other useful Artisans, with Sailors enough to manage their Navigation. With all these Conveniences it lies under two great disadvantages that most of the Towns in Holland do, by having neither good Air, nor good Water. The two Cardinal Vertues, that make a place thrive, Industry and Frugality, are seen here in Perfection, and so long as they can banish Luxury and Idleness, the Town will remain in a happy and flourishing Condition.

The Method of building Wharffs here is after the following Manner. They lay down long Pine Logs, that reach from the Shore to the Edge of the Channel. These are bound fast together by Cross Pieces, notch't into them according to the Architecture of the Log-Houses in North-Carolina. A Wharff built thus will stand several Years, in spight of the Worm, which bites here very much, [12] but may be soon repair'd, in a Place where so many Pines grow in the Neighbourhood.[42]

The Commissioners endeavour'd in this Town to list Three more men to serve as Guides in that dirty Part of the Country, But found that these people knew just enough of that frightful Place—to avoid it.

They had been told that those Netherlands were full of Bogs, of Marshes, and Swamps, not fit for Human Creatures to engage in, and this was Reason enough for them not to hazard their Persons. So they told us flat and plain that we might e'en daggle thro' the mire by our selves for them.[43]

The worst of it was, we cou'd not learn from any body in this Town, what Rout to take to Coratuck Inlet, till at last we had the fortune to meet with a Borderer upon North Carolina, who made us a rough Sketch of that part of the Country. Thus upon seeing how the Land ^lay^, we determin'd to march

[a]A: built upon

directly to Prescot-Landing upon N.W. River, and proceed from thence by Water to the Place where our Line was to begin.

4.   In pursuance of this Resolution we cros't the River this morning to Powder-Point, where we all took Horse, and the Grandees of the Town with great Courtesy conducted us Ten Miles on our way[b], as far as the long Bridge, built over the S. Branch of the River. The Parson of the Parish Mr. Marston, a painful Apostle from the Society made one in this ceremonious Cavalcade.[44]

At the Bridge these Gentlemen, wishing us a good Deliverance, return'd[c], and then a Troop of Light Horse escorted us as far as Prescot Landing upon N.W. River. Care had been taken before hand to provide 2 Periaugas to lie ready at that Place, to transport us to Coratuck Inlet. Our Zeal was so great to get thither at the time appointed, that we hardly allow'd ourselves leisure to eat,[d] which in truth we had the less Stomach to, by reason the Dinner was served up by the Landlord, whose Nose stood on such ticklish Terms, that it was in Danger of falling into the Dish. We therefore made our Repast very short, and then embark't with only the Surveyors, and nine chosen Men; leaving the rest at Mr W. . . .ns, to take care of the Horses and Baggage. There we also left our Chaplain, with the charitable Intent that the Gentiles round about might have time and opportunity, if they pleas'd, of getting themselves and their Children baptiz'd.[45]

We row'd down N.W. River about 18 miles, as far as the Mouth of it, where it empties itself into Albemarle Sound. It was really a Delightful Sight all the way, to see the Banks of the River adorn'd with Myrtle, Laurel, and Bay Trees, which preserve their Verdure the Year round, tho' it must be own'd, that these beautiful Plants, sacred to Venus, and Appollo, grow commonly in a very dirty Soil. The river ^is^ in most Places fifty or sixty Yards wide, without spreading much wider at the Mouth. 'Tis remarkable it was never known to ebb and flow, till the year 1713, when a violent Storm open'd a new Inlet about 5 miles south of the old one; since which convulsion the Old [13] Inlet is almost choak'd up by the Shifting of the Sand, and grows both narrower and shoaller every day.[46]

It was dark before we could reach the Mouth of the River, where our wayward Stars directed us to a miserable Cottage. The Landlord was lately removed Bag and Baggage from Maryland, thro' a strong Antipathy he had to work, and paying his Debts. For want of our Tent[e] we were oblig'd[f] to shelter our selves in this wretched Hovel, where we were almost devour'd by Vermin

---

[b]V: *Here in the margin, in light pencil, someone has written* South   [c]V: *At this point someone has written in the margin* Now [————]   [d]A: time to eat   [e]A: tents   [f]A: forc't

of various kinds. However we were above complaining, being all Philosophers enough to improve such slender Distresses into Mirth and good Humour.[47]

5.   The Day being now come, on which we had agreed to meet the Commissioners of North Carolina, we embark't very early, which we cou'd ^the^ easier do, having no Temptation to stay where we were. We shap't our Course along the South End of Knots Island, there being no passage open on the North.

Farther still to the southward of us, we discover'd two smaller Islands, that go by the Names of Bell's, and Churches Isles. We also saw a small New-England Sloop riding in the Sound a little to the south of our Course. She[g] had come in at the New-Inlet, as all other Vessels have done, since the opening of it. This Navigation is a little difficult, and fit only for Vessels, that draw no more than ten feet Water.

The Trade hither is engrosst by the Saints of New-England, who carry off a great deal of Tobacco without troubling themselves with paying that Impertinent Duty of a Penny a Pound.

It was just noon before we arrived at Coratuck Inlet, which was so shallow, that the Breakers ^fly^ over it[h] with a horrible Sound, and at the same time afford a very wild Prospect. On the north Side of the Inlet[i], the High Land terminated in a Bluff Point, from which a Spit of Sand extended itself towards the South East full half a Mile. The Inlet lies between that Spit and another on the South of it, leaving an Opening of not quite a Mile, which at this day is not practicable for any Vessel whatsoever. And ^as^ shallow as it now is, it continues to fill up more and more, both the Wind and Waves rolling in the Sand from the Eastern Shoals.

About two a Clock in the Afternoon we were join'd by two of the Carolina Commissioners, attended by Mr. S[   ]n[j] their Surveyor. The other two were not quite so punctual, which was the more unlucky for us, because there could be no sport till they came. These Gentlemen it seems had the Carolina Commission in thcir keeping, notwithstanding which, they cou'd not forbear paying too much regard to a Proverb fashionable in their Country, not to make more hast than good Speed.

However that we who were punctual, might not spend our precious time unprofitably, we took the several bearings of the Coast. We also survey'd part of the adjacent High-Land, which had scarcely any Trees growing upon it, but

[g]A: *Here the text of the nineteenth-century copy (pp. 1–28) overlaps A with the older copy to supply a hiatus in the APS MS.*   [h]A: beat over it   [i]A: On the North Side the Inlet
[j]A: Swan

Cedars. Among the Shrubs we were shewed here and there a Bush of Carolina Tea call'd Japon, which is one Species of the Phylarreas[k]. This is an Evergreen the Leaves whereof have some resemblance to Tea, but differ very widely ^both^ in Tast and Flavour.[48] [14]

We also found some few Plants of the Spired-Leaf Silk-grass, which is likewise an Evergreen, bearing on a lofty Stemm a large Cluster of Flowers of a Pale Yellow. Of the Leaves of this Plant the People thereabouts twist very strong Cordage. A Vertuoso might divert himself here very well, in picking up shells of various Hue and Figure, and amongst the rest that Species of Conque Shell which the Indian Peak is made of. The Extremities of these Shells are Blue[l], and the rest white, so that Peak of both these Colours are drill'd out of one and the same Shell, serving the Natives both for Ornament and Money, and are esteem'd by them far beyond Gold and Silver.[49]

The Cedars were of singular use to us in the Absence of our Tent, which we had left with the rest of the Baggage, for fear of overloading the Periaugas. We made a circular Hedge[m] of the Branches of the Tree, wrought so close together, as to fence us against the cold Winds. We then kindled a rouseing fire in the center of it, and lay round it like so many Knights Templars. But as comfortable as this Lodging was, the Surveyors turn'd out about 2 in the Morning, to try the Variation by a Meridian taken from the North Star, and found it to be somewhat less than three degrees West.[50]

The Commissioners of the neighbouring Colony came better provided for the Belly than the Business. They brought not above two men along with them, that would put their Hand to any thing but the Kettle and the Frying Pan. These spent so much of their Industry that way, that they had as little Spirit as Inclination for Work.

At Noon having a perfect Observation, we found the Latitude of Coratuck Inlet to be 36 Degrees and 31 Minutes.

Whilst we were busied about these necessary Matters, our Skipper row'd to an Oyster Bank just by, and loaded his Periauga with Oysters as savoury and well-tasted, as those from Colchester or Walfleet, and had the advantage of them too by being much larger and fatter.[51]

About 3 in the Afternoon the two lagg Commissioners arriv'd, and after a few decent excuses for making us wait, were ready to enter upon Business as soon as we pleas'd. The first Step was, to produce our respective Powers, and the Commission from each Governor was distinctly read, and copies of them interchangeably deliver'd.

It was observ'd by our Carolina Friends, that the Latter Part of the Virginia-

[k]A: Phyllarea   [l]A: the Extremities of these shells is Blue   [m]A: Edge

Commission had something in it a little too lordly and positive; In answer
to which[n] we told them, 'twas necessary to make it thus peremptory, lest
the present Commissioners might go upon as fruitless an Errand, as their
Predecessors. The former Commissioners were ty'd down to act in exact
Conjunction with those of Carolina, and so could not advance one Step
farther, or one Jot faster, than they were pleas'd to permit them.

The Memory of that disappointment therefore induc'd the Government
of Virginia to give fuller Powers to the [15] present Commissioners, by
authorizing them to go on with the Work by Themselves, in case those of
Carolina should prove unreasonable, and refuse to join with them in carrying
the business to[o] Execution; and all this was done lest His Majesty's gracious
Intention shou'd be frustrated a second time.

After both Commissions were consider'd, the first Question was where
the Dividing Line was to begin. This begat a warm debate, The Virginia
Commissioners contending with a great deal of Reason to begin at the End
of the Spitt of Sand, which was undoubtedly the North Shore of Coratuck-
Inlet. But those of Carolina insisted strenuously, that the Point of High Land
ought rather to be the Place of Beginning, because that was fix't and certain,
whereas the Spitt of Sand was ever shifting, and did actually run out farther
now than formerly. The Contest lasted some Hours with great Vehemence,
neither Party receding from their Opinion that Night. But next Morning
Mr. M. . . . .[p] to convince us he was not that obstinate Person, he had been
represented, yielded to our Reasons, and found means to bring over his
Collegues.

Here we began already to reap[q] the Benefit of those Peremptory Words
in our Commission, which in truth added some Weight to our Reasons.
Nevertheless, because positive ^proof^ was made by the Oaths of two credible
Witnesses, that the Spitt of Sand had advanc'd 200 Yards towards the Inlet,
since the Controversy first began, we were willing for Peace-Sake to make
them that allowance. Accordingly we fixt our beginning about that Distance
North of the Inlet, and there order'd a Cedar-Post to be driven deep into the
Sand, for our Beginning; while we continued here we were told, that on the
South Shore, not far from the Inlet, dwelt a Marooner that modestly call'd
himself a Hermit, tho' he forfeited that Name, by suffering a wanton Female
to cohabit with Him.

His Habituation was a Bower cover'd with Bark, after the Indian Fashion,
which in that mild Situation protected him pretty well from the Weather.
Like the Ravens, he neither plow'd nor sow'd, but subsisted chiefly upon

[n]A: and postive. In [order] to which   [o]A: into   [p]A. M——y   [q]A: we began to reap

Oysters, which his Handmaid made a shift to gather from the adjacent Rocks. Sometimes too for change of Dyet, he sent her to drive up the Neighbour's Cows, to moisten their Mouths with a little Milk. But as for Raiment, he depended mostly on his Length of ―――― Beard, and she upon her Length of Hair, part of which she brought decently forward, and the rest dangled behind quite down to her Rump, like one of Herodotus's East Indian Pigmies.[r,52]

Thus did these Wretches live in a dirty State of Nature, and were mere Adamites, Innocence only excepted.[53]

7.   This Morning the Surveyors began to run the Dividing Line from the Cedar-Post we had driven into the Sand, allowing near 3 Degrees for the Variation. Without making this just Allowance[s], we should not have obey'd his Majesty's order in running a Due West Line. It seems the former Commissioners had not been so exact, which gave our Friends of Carolina but too just an Exception to their Proceedings.

The Line cut Dosiers-Island, consisting only of a Flat Sand [16] with here and there an humble Shrub growing upon it. From thence it cros't over a narrow Arm of the Sound into Knots Island, and there split a Plantation belonging to William Harding.[54]

The Day being far spent, we encamp't in this Man's Pasture, tho it lay very low, and the Season now inclin'd People to Aguish Distempers. He suffer'd us to cut Cedar-Branches for our Enclosures, and other Wood for Fireing, to correct the moist Air, and drive away the Damps. Our Landlady in the Days of her Youth, it seems, had been[t] a Laundress in the Temple, and talk't over her Adventures in that Station with as much pleasure as an old Soldier talks over his Battles, and Distempers, and I believe with as many Additions to the Truth.

The Soil is good in many places of this Island, and the Extent of it pretty large. It lyes in the form of a Wedge; the South End of it is several Miles over, but towards the North it sharpens into a Point. It is a plentiful place for Stock by reason[a] of the wide Marshes adjacent to it, and because of its warm Situation. But the Inhabitants pay a little dear for this Convenience by losing as much Blood in the Summer Season by the infinite number of Mosquetas, as all their Beef and Pork can recruit in the Winter.

The Sheep are as large as in Lincolnshire, because they are never pinch't by cold or Hunger. The whole Island was hitherto reckon'd to lye in Virginia, but now our Line has given the greater part of it to Carolina. The principal

---

[r]A: like one of Herodotus's East Indians.   [s]A: without this just allowance   [t]A: Youth, had been   [a]A: for Stock, both by reason

Freeholder here is Mr. White[b], who keeps open House for all Travellers, that either Debt or Shipwreck happen to cast in his way.[55]

8.   By break of Day we sent away our largest Periauga with the Baggage round the South end of Knots Island, with Orders to the Men to wait for us in the Mouth of North River. Soon after we embark't our selves on board the smaller Vessel, with Intent, if possible, to find a Passage round the North End of the Island[c].

We found this Navigation very difficult, by reason of the continued Shoals, and often stuck fast aground: for tho' the Sound spreads many miles, yet it is in most places extremely shallow, and requires a Skilful Pilot to steer even a Canoe safe over it.

It was almost as hard to keep our Temper, as to keep the Channel in this provoking Situation. But the most impatient amongst us strok't down their Choler, and swallow'd their Curses, lest if they suffer'd them to break out, they might sound like Complaining, which was expresly forbid, as the first Step to Sedition.

At a distance we descry'd several Islands to the Northward of us, the largest of which goes by the Name of Cedar Island. Our Periauga stuck so often, that we had a fair chance to be benighted in this wide Water, which must certainly have been our Fate, had we not luckily spied a Canoe, that was giving a Fortune teller a cast from Princess Anne County ^over^ to North Carolina. But, as conjurers[d] are sometimes mistaken, the Man mistrusted we were Officers of Justice in pursuit [17] of a young Wench, he had carry'd off along with him. We gave the Canoe chace for more than an Hour, and when we came up with her threaten'd to make them all prisoners, unless they would direct us into the right Channel.[56]

By the Pilotage of these People we row'd up an Arm of the Sound, call'd the Back-Bay, till we came to the Head of it. There we were stop't by a miry Pocoson full half a Mile in Breadth, thro' which we were oblig'd to daggle on foot, plungeing now and then, tho' we pick't our Way, up to the Knees in Mud. At the End of this charming walk, we gain'd the Terra Firma of Princess Anne County. In that Dirty Condition we were afterwards oblig'd to foot it two Miles, as far as John Heath's[e] Plantation, where we expected to meet the Surveyors, & the men who waited on them.[57]

While we were performing this tedious Voyage, they had carried the Line thro' the firm Land of Knots Island, where it was no more than half a Mile wide. After that they travers'd a large Marsh, that was exceeding miry[f], and

---

[b]A: W——e   [c]A: round the North End of it   [d]A: as all Conjurers   [e]A: H—— (eaths *overwritten later, with pencil*)   [f]A: mighty Miry

extended to an Arm of the Back-Bay. They cross't that water in a Canoe which we had order'd round for that Purpose, and then waded over another Marsh, that reacht quite to the High-Land of Princess Anne. Both these Marshes together make a breadth of five Miles, in which the Men frequently sunk up to the Middle, without muttering the least complaint; on the contrary they turn'd all their Disasters into Merriment.[58]

It was discover'd by this day's Work that Knots Island was improperly so call'd, being in Truth no more than a Peninsula. The N.W. side of it is only divided from the Main by the great Marsh abovementioned, which is seldom totally overflow'd. Instead of that, it might by the Labour of a few Trenches be drain'd into firm Meadow, capable of grazing as many Cattle, as Job in his best Estate was master of. In the miry condition it now lies, it feeds great Numbers in the Winter; tho' when the Weather grows warm, they are driven from thence by the mighty Armies of Mosquetas, which are the Plague of the lower part of Carolina, as much as the Flys were formerly of Egypt[g], and some Rabbi's think these Flys were no other than Mosquetas.[59]

All the People in the Neighbourhood flock't to John Heath's[h] to behold such Rarities as they fancied us to be. The Men left their belov'd Chimney Corners, the good Women[i] their Spining Wheels, and some of more Curiosity than ordinary rose out of their sick Beds to come and stare at us. They look't upon us as a Troop of Knight Errants, who were running this great Risque of our Lives, as they imagin'd, for the Publick Weal, and some of the gravest of them question'd much whether we were not all Criminals condemned to this dirty work, for Offences against the State.

What puzzled them most was, what cou'd make our Men so very light Hearted[j] under such intolerable Drudgery. Ye have little Reason to be merry, my Masters, said one of them with a very solemn Face. I fancy the Pocoson you must struggle with tomorrow, will make you change your Note, and try what Metal[k] ye are made of. Ye are to be sure the first of Human Race, that ever had the Boldness to attempt it, and I dare say will be the last. [18] If therefore you have any Worldly Goods to dispose of, my Advice is, that you make your Wills this very Night, for fear you die Intestate to morrow. But, alas, these frightfull Tales were so far from disheartening the men, that they serv'd only to whet their Resolution.

9   The Surveyors enter'd early upon their Business this Morning, and ran the Line thro' Mr. Eyland's[l] Plantation, as far as the Banks of North River. They

---

[g]A: *The paragraph ends here*] V: *the following text inserted in space at end of paragraph in Byrd's hand.*   [h]A: H——h's   [i]A: and the good Women   [j]A: our men so light hearted
[k]A: Mettle   [l]A: E——d's

past over it in the Periauga, and landed in Gibbs Marsh, which was a mile[m] in Breadth, and tolerably firm. They trudg'd thro' this Marsh without much difficulty[n] as far as the High Land, which promis'd more fertility than any they had seen in these lower parts[o]. But this firm Land lasted not long, before they came upon the dreadful Pocoson, they had been threaten'd with. Nor did they find it one Jot better than it had been painted to them. The Beavers and Otters had render'd it ^quite^ impassable[p] for any Creature but themselves.[60]

Our poor Fellows had much ado to drag their Legs after them in this Quagmire, but disdaining to be baulkt, they cou'd hardly be persuaded from pressing forward by the Surveyors, who found it absolutely necessary to make a Traverse in the Deepest Place to prevent their sticking fast in the Mire, and becoming a certain prey to the Turkey-Buzzards.[61]

This Horrible Days Work ended two Miles to the Northward of Mr. Merchant's[q] Plantation, divided from N.W. River by a narrow Swamp, which is causway'd over. We took up our Quarters in the open Field not not far from the House, correcting by a Fire as large as a Roman Funeral Pile, the Aguish Exhalations arising from the sunken Grounds, that surrounded us.[62]

The Neck of Land included betwixt N. River, and N.W. River, with the adjacent Marsh, belong'd formerly to Governor Gibbs, but since his Decease, to Colonel Bladen in right of his first Lady, who was Mr. Gibb's Daughter. It would be a valuable Tract of Land in any Country but North Carolina, where for want of Navigation and Commerce, the best Estate affords little more than a coarse Subsistence.[63]

[10]   The Sabbath happen'd very opportunely to give some ease to our jaded People, who rested religiously from every work but that of cooking the Kettle. We observed very few corn fields in our Walks, and those very small, which seem'd the stranger to us, because we could see no other Token of Husbandry or Improvement. But upon further Enquiry, we were given to understand, People only made Corn for themselves, and not for their Stocks, which know very well how to get[r] their own Living.[64]

Both Cattle and Hogs ramble into the Neighbouring Marshes and Swamps, where they maintain themselves the whole Winter long, and are not fetch't home till the Spring. Thus these Indolent Wretches, during one half of the Year, lose the Advantage of the Milk[s] of their Cattle, as well as their Dung, and many of the ^poor creatures^ perish[t] in the Mire into the Bargain by this ill Management. [19]

---

[m]A: about a Mile   [n]A: without difficulty   [o]A: in the lower Parts   [p]A: unpassable
[q]A: M——t's   [r]A: knew how to provide for   [s]A: lose one half of the Milk   [t]A: many of them perish

Some who pique themselves ^more^ upon Industry than their Neighbours, will now and then, in complement to their Cattle, cut down a Tree, whose Limbs[a] are loaden with the Moss aforemention'd. The trouble wou'd be too great to climb the Tree in order to gather this Provender, but the shortest way (which in this Country is always counted the best) is to fell it, just like the Lazy Indians, who do the same by such Trees as bear fruit, and so make one Harvest for all. By this bad Husbandry, Milk is so Scarce in the Winter Season, that were a Big-belly'd Woman to long for it, she would lose her Longing. And in truth I believe this is often the Case, and at the same time a very good reason why so many People in this Province[b] are mark't with a Custard-Complexion.[65]

The only Business here is raising of Hogs, which is manag'd with the least Trouble, and affords the Diet they are most fond of. The Truth of it is, the Inhabitants of N. Carolina devour so much Swine's flesh, that it fills them[c] full of gross Humours. For want too of a constant Supply of Salt, they are commonly obliged to eat it Fresh, and that begets the highest taint of Scurvey. Thus whenever a severe Cold happens to Constitutions thus vitiated, 'tis apt to improve into the Yaws, call'd there very justly the country-Distemper. This has all the Simptoms of the Pox, with this Aggravation, that no Preparation[d] of Mercury will touch it. First it siezes the Throat, next the Palate, and lastly shews its spite to the poor Nose, of which 'tis apt in no small time treacherously to undermine the Foundation.[66]

This Calamity is so common, and familiar here, that it ceases to be a Scandal, and in the disputes that happen about Beauty, the Noses have in some Companies much ado to carry it. Nay 'tis said that once after three good Pork years a Motion had like to have been made in the House of Burgesses, that a Man with a Nose shou'd be incapable of holding any Place of Profit in the Province, which extraordinary Motion could never have been intended without some Hopes of a Majority.

Thus considering the foul and pernicious Effects of eating Swines Flesh in a hot Country, it was wisely forbid, and made an Abomination to the Jews, who liv'd much in the same Latitude, with Carolina.[67]

11.   We ordered the Surveyors early to their Business, who were blest with pretty dry Grounds for three Miles together: But they paid dear for it in the next two, consisting[e] of one continuous frightfull Pocoson, which no Creatures[f] but those of the amphibious kind, ever had ventur'd into before.

This filthy Quagmire did in earnest put the Men's Courage to a Tryal, and

---

[a]A: Leaves   [b]A: Colony   [c]A: 'em   [d]A: that often no Preparation   [e]A: which consisted
[f]A: no other Creatures

tho I can't say it made them lose their Patience, yet they lost their Humour for Joking. They kept their Gravity like so many Spaniards, so that a Man might then have taken his Opportunity to plunge up to the Chin, without Danger of being laught at. However, this unusual composure of Countenance could not fairly be call'd complaining.

Their Days Work ended at the Mouth of Northern's Creek, which empties itself into North River; tho' we chose to Quarter a little higher up the River near Mossy Point. This we did for the Convenience of an old house to shelter our Persons and Baggage from the [20] Rain, which threaten'd us hard. We judg'd the thing right, for there fell an heavy shower[g] in the Night, that drove the most hardy of us into the House: Tho' indeed our Ease was not much mended by retreating thither, because that Tenement having not long before been us'd as a Pork-Store, the Moisture of the Air dissolv'd the Salt, that lay scatter'd on the Floor, and made it as wet within Doors as without. However the Swamps and Marshes, we were lately accustom'd to, had made such Beaver and Otters of us, that no body caught the least Cold.

We had encamp'd so early, that we found time in the Evening to walk near half a Mile into the Woods. There we came upon a Family of Mulattos, that call'd themselves free, tho' by the Shyness of the Master of the House, who took care to keep least in Sight, their Freedom seem'd a little Doubtful. It is certain many Slaves shelter themselves in this obscure Part of the World, nor will any of their righteous Neighbours discover them. On the contrary they find their Account in[h] settling such Fugitives on some out-of-the-way-Corner of their Land, to raise Stocks for a mean and inconsiderable Share, well knowing their Condition makes it necessary for them to submit to any Terms.[68]

Nor were these worthy Borderers content to shelter Runaway Slaves, but Debtors and Criminals have often met with the like Indulgence. But if the Government of North Carolina have encourag'd this unneighbourly Policy, in order to encrease their People, it is no more than what ancient Rome did before them, which was made a city of Refuge for all Debtors and Fugitives, and from that wretched Beginning grew up in time to be Mistress of great Part of the World. And considering how Fortune delights in bringing great things out of small, who knows but Carolina may some time[i] or other come to be the Seat of some other great Empire?[69]

12. Every thing had been so soak't with the Rain, that we were oblig'd to lie by a good part of the Morning and dry them. However that time was not lost, because it gave the Surveyors an opportunity of platting[j] off their

[g]A: a heavy Shower [h]A: of [i]A: one time [j]A: plotting

Work, and taking the Course of the River. It likewise help't to recruit the Spirits of the Men who had been a little harrass'd with Yesterday's March. Notwithstanding all this, we cros't the River before Noon, and advanc'd our Line 3 Miles. It was not possible to make more of it, by reason good part of the way was either Marsh or Pocoson. The Line cut two or three Plantations, leaving part of them in Virginia, and part of them in Carolina. This was a Case that happen'd frequently, to the great Inconvenience of the Owners, who were therefore oblig'd to take out two Patents, and pay for a new Survey in each Government.

In the Evening we took up our Quarter in Mr. Ballances[k] Pasture, a little above the Bridge built over N.W. River. There we discharg'd the two Periaugas, which in truth had been very serviceable in transporting us over the many waters in that Dirty and Difficult Part of our Business.[70] [21]

Our Landlord had a tolerable good House, and clean Furniture, and yet we cou'd not be tempted to lodge[l] in it. We chose rather to lye in the open Field for fear of growing too tender. A clear Sky spangled with Stars was our Canopy, which being the last thing we saw before we fell asleep, gave us magnificent Dreams. The Truth of it is, we took so much Pleasure in that natural kind of Lodging, that I think at the foot of the Account, Mankind are great Losers by the Luxury of Feather-Beds, and warm appartments.

The Curiosity of beholding so new and withal so sweet a Method of Encamping, brought one of the Senators of N. Carolina to make us a Midnight Visit. But he was so very clamorous in his Commendations of it, that the Centinel, not seeing his Quality either thro' his habit or Behaviour, had like to have treated him roughly.

After excusing the Unseasonableness of his Visit, and letting us know he was a Parliament Man, he swore he was so taken with our Lodging, that he would set Fire to his House as soon as he got Home, and teach his Wife and Children to lie, like us in the open Field.[71]

[13] Early this Morning our Chaplain repair'd to us with the Men we had left at Mr. Wilsons.[m] We had sent for them the Evening before, to relieve those who had the Labour-Oar from Corotuck-Inlet. But to our great surprise, they petition'd not to be reliev'd, hoping to gain immortal Reputation by being the first of Mankind that ventur'd thro' the great Dismal. But the rest being equally ambitious of the same Honour, it was but fair to decide their Pretentions by Lot. After Fortune had declar'd herself, those which she had excluded, offer'd money to the Happy Persons, to go in their Stead. But

[k]A: B——ces [l]A: lie [m]A: W——ns

Hercules would have as soon sold the Glory of cleansing the Augean Stables, which was pretty near the same sort of work.[72]

No sooner was the Controversy at an end, but we sent them unfortunate Fellows back to their Quarters, whom Chance had condemn'd to remain upon Firm Land, and sleep in a whole Skin. In the mean while the Surveyors carry'd the Line 3 Miles, which was no contemptible days work, considering how cruelly they were intangled with Bryars and Gall Bushes. The Leaf of this last Shrub bespeaks it to be of the Alaternus Family.[73]

Our work ended within a Quarter of a Mile of the Dismal above mention'd, where the Ground began already to be full of Sunken Holes, and Slashes, which had here and there some few Reeds growing in them.[74]

'Tis hardly credible how little the Bordering inhabitants were acquainted with this mighty Swamp, notwithstanding they had liv'd their whole lives within smell of it. Yet as great Strangers as they were to it, they pretended to be very exact in their Account of its Dimensions, and were positive it could not be above 7 or 8 Miles wide, but knew no more of the Matter than Stargazers know[n] of the Distance of the Fixt Stars. At the same time they were simple enough to amuse our Men with Idle Stories of the Lyons[o], Panthers, and Allegators, they were like to encounter in that dreadful Place.[75]

In short we saw plainly there was no Intelligence of this Terra Incognita to be got, but from our own Experience. For that Reason it was resolv'd to make the requisite Dispositions to enter it next Morning. We allotted every one of the Surveyors, for this [22] painful Enterprise, with 12 Men to attend them. Fewer than that cou'd not be employ'd in clearing the way, carrying the Chain, marking the Trees, and bearing the necessary Bedding and Provisions. Nor wou'd the Commissioners themselves have spar'd their Persons on this Occasion, but for fear of adding to the poor men's Burthen, while they were certain they cou'd add nothing to their Resolution.

We quarter'd with our Friend and Fellow-Traveller, William Wilkins, who had been our ^faithfull^ Pilot[p] to Coratuck, and liv'd about a Mile from the place, where the Line ended. Every thing look't so ^very^ clean[q], and the Furniture so neat, that we were tempted to Lodge[r] within Doors. But the Novelty of being shut up so close quite spoil'd our Rest, nor did we breath so free by abundance as when we lay in the open air.

14.   Before nine of the clock this Morning the Provisions Bedding, and other Necessaries were made up into Packs, for the Men to carry on their Shoulders into the Dismal. They were victual'd for 8 Days at full Allowance,

[n]A: do   [o]A: Idle Stories of Lyons   [p]A: had been our Pilot   [q]A: so clean   [r]A: ly

no body doubting but that wou'd be abundantly sufficient to carry them[s] thro' that Inhospitable Place. Nor indeed was it possible for the Poor Fellows to Stagger under more. As it was, their Loads weigh'd from 60 to 70 Pounds, in just proportion to the Strength of those who were to bear them.

T'wou'd have been unconscionable to have saddled them with Burthens heavier than that, when they were to lugg[t] them thro' a filthy Bogg, which was hardly practicable with no Burthen at all.

Besides this Luggage at their Backs they were oblig'd to measure the distance, mark the Trees, and clear the way for the Surveyors every Step they went. It was really a pleasure to see with how much Chearfulness they undertook, and with how much Spirit they went thro' all this Drudgery[a]. For their Greater Safety the Commissioners took care to furnish them with Peruvian Bark, Rhubarb, and Hipocoacanah, in case they might happen in that wet Journey to be taken with Fevers or Fluxes.[76]

Altho' there was no need of Example to inflame Persons already so chearful, yet to enter the People with the better grace, the Author and two more of the Commissioners accompanied them half a Mile into the Dismal. The skirts of it were thinly planted with Dwarf Reeds, and Gall-Bushes, but when we got into the Dismal itself we found the Reeds grew there much taller[b] and closer, and, to mend the matter, were so interlac'd with Bamboo-bryars, that there was no scuffling thro' them without the help of Pioneers. At the same time we found the Ground moist and trembling under our feet, like a Quagmire; Insomuch that it was an easy matter to run a Ten-Foot-Pole up to the Head in it, without exerting any uncommon Strength to do it[c].[77]

Two of the Men whose Burthens were the least cumbersome had orders to march before with their Tomahawks, and clear the way in order to make an Opening for the Surveyors. By their Assistance we made a shift to push the Line half a Mile in 3 Hours. And then reacht a ^small^ piece of firm Land about 100 [23] Yards wide, standing up above the rest like an Island. Here the People were glad to lay[d] down their Loads, and take a little Refreshment, while the happy man whose lot it was to carry the Jugg of Rum began already, like Aesop's Bread Carriers, to find it grow a good deal lighter.[78]

After reposing about an Hour, the Commissioners recommended Vigour and Constancy to their Fellow-Travellers, by whom they were answer'd with 3 cheerful Huzzas, in Token of Obedience. This Ceremony was no sooner over, but they took up their Burthens, and attended the Motion of the Surveyors,

[s]A: that ^'em^ [t]A: drag [a]A: thro' this Drudgery [b]A: grew much taller
[c]V: uncommon Strength to do it *(inserted at end of line in Byrd's hand)*] A: uncommon Strength [d]A: set

who tho' they work't with all their might cou'd reach but one Mile farther[e], the same obstacles still attending them, which they had met with in the Morning.

However small this distance may seem to such as are us'd to travel at their Ease, yet our Poor Men who were oblig'd to work with an unwieldy Load at their Backs, had reason to think it a long[f] way; especially in a Bogg, where they had no firm Footing, but every Step made a deep Impression, which was instantly fill'd with Water. At the same time they were labouring with their Hands to cut down the Reeds which were Ten-feet-high[g], their Legs[h] were hampered with the Bryars. Besides the Weather happen'd to be warm, and the tallness of the Reeds kept off every Friendly Breeze from coming to refresh them. And indeed it was a little provoking to hear the Wind whistling among the Branches of the White Cedars, which grew here and there amongst the Reeds, and at the same time not have the Comfort[i] to feel the least Breath of it.

In the mean time the 3 Commissioners return'd out of the Dismal the same way they went in and having join'd their Brethren, proceeded that night as far as Mr. Wilson's[j].

This worthy Person lives within sight of the Dismal, in the Skirts whereof, his Stocks range and maintain themselves all the Winter, and yet he knew as little of it, as he did of Terra Australia Incognita. He told us a Canterbury Tale of a North-Briton whose Curiosity spurr'd him a long way into this great Desart, as he call'd it, near 20 Years ago, but he having no Compass, nor seeing the Sun for several Days together, wander'd about till he was almost famisht, but at last he bethought himself[k] of a secret his Country-men make use of to Pilot themselves in a Dark day.[79]

He took[l] a fat Louse out of his Collar, and expos'd it to the open day on a Piece of White Paper, which he brought along with him for his Journal. The poor Insect, having no Eye-lids, turn'd himself about, till he found the Darkest Part of the Heavens, and so made the best of his way towards the North. By this Direction he steer'd himself safe out, and gave such a frightfull account of the Monsters he saw, and the Distresses he underwent, that no Mortall[m] since has been hardy enough to go upon the like dangerous Discovery.[80]

18.   The Surveyors pursued their work with all Diligence, but still found the Soil of the Dismal so spungy, that the Water ouz'd up into every footstep

---

[e]A: further   [f]A: longer   [g]A: ten-Foot-high   [h]A: hands   [i]A: and not have the comfort   [j]A: W——n's   [k]A: almost famish't. At last he bethought himself   [l]A: pull'd   [m]A: no Body

they took. To their Sorrow too they found the Reeds and Bryars more firmly interwoven than they did the day before. But the greatest Grievance was, from large Cypresses [24] which the Wind had blown down, and heap't upon one another. On the Limbs of most of them grew sharp Snaggs pointing every way, like so many Pikes that requir'd much pains and caution to avoid.[81]

These Trees being Evergreens, and shooting their Large Tops very high, are easily overset by every Gust of Wind, because their[n] is no firm Earth to steddy their Roots. Thus many of them were laid prostrate, to the great Encumbrance of the way[o]. Such Variety of Difficulties made the Business go on heavily, insomuch that from morning till night the Line could advance no farther than 1 Mile and 31 Poles. Never was Rum, that Cordial of Life found more necessary, than it was in this Dirty Place. It did not only recruit the Peoples Spirits now almost Jaded with Fatigue, but serv'd to correct the Badness of the Water, and at the same time to resist the Malignity of the Air. Whenever the Men wanted to drink, which was very often, they had nothing more to do but to make a Hole, and the Water bubbled up in a Moment. But it was far from being ^either^ clear or well tasted, and had besides a Physical Effect, from the Tincture it receiv'd from the Roots of the Shrubbs and Trees[p] that grow in the Neighbourhood.[82]

While the Surveyors were thus painfully employ'd, the Commissioners discharged the long score they had with Mr. Wilson[q] for the Men and Horses, which had been quarter'd upon him during our Expedition to Coratuck. From thence we marcht in good Order along the East Side of the Dismal and past the long Bridge, that lies over the South Branch of Elizabeth River. At the End of 18 Miles we reach't Timothy Ivy's Plantation[r], where we pitch't our Tent for the first Time, and were furnish't with everything the Place afforded.[83]

We perceiv'd the happy Effects of Industry in this Family[s], in which every one look't tidy and clean, and carry'd in their Countenances the chearfull Marks of Plenty. We saw no Drones there, which are but too common alas in that Part of the World. Tho' in truth the Distemper of Laziness seizes the Men oftener much than the Women. These last spin, weave, and knit[t] all with their own Hands, while their Husbands, depending on the Bounty of the Climate, are sloathfull in every thing, but getting of Children, and in that only Instance make themselves, usefull Members of an Infant-Colony.

There is but little Wool in that Province, tho' Cotton grows very kindly, and so far South is seldom nipp't by the Frost. The Good Women mix this with their Wool for their outer Garments, tho' for want of Fulling that kind of

---

[n]A: there   [o]A: our way   [p]A: from the Shrubbs and Trees   [q]A: W——n   [r]A: Ti——y I——'s   [s]A: happy Effects in this Family   [t]A: Spin, Knit, and Weave

Manufacture is open and sleazy. Flax likewise thrives there extreamly, being perhaps as fine as any in the World, and I question not might with a little Care and Pains be brought to rival that of Egypt, and yet the Men are here so intollerably lazy, they seldom take the trouble to propagate it.[84]

The Line was this day carry'd one Mile[a] and an half, and 16 Poles. The Soil continued soft and miry, but fuller of Trees, [25] especially White Cedars. Many of these too were thrown down and pitch'd in Heaps, high enough for a good Muscovite Fortification.[85] The worst of it was, the Poor Fellows began now to be troubled with Fluxes, occasion'd by bad Water and moist Lodging; but chewing of Rhubarb kept that Malady within Bounds.[86]

In the mean time the Commissioners decampt early in the Morning, and made a March of 25 Miles, as far as Mr Andrew Mead's[b] who lives upon Nansimond River. They were no sooner got under the Shelter of that Hospitable Roof, but it began to rain hard, and continued so to do great part of the Night. This gave them much Pain for their Friends in the Dismal, whose Sufferings[c] spoilt their Tast for the good Chear, wherewith they were entertain'd themselves.[87]

However late that Evening these poor Men had the Fortune to come upon another Terra-firma, which was the luckyer for them, because the lower ground, by the Rain that fell[d], was made a fitter Lodging[e] for Tadpoles than Men.

In our Journey we remarkt that the North Side of this[f] great Swamp, lies higher than either the East or the West, nor were the approaches to it so full of sunken Grounds. We pas't by no less than two Quaker Meeting Houses, one of which had an awkward Ornament on the West End of it, that seem'd to Ape a Steeple. I must own I expected no such Piece of Foppery from a Sect of so much outside Simplicity.

That Persuasion prevails much in the lower End of Nansimond County, for want of Ministers to Pilot the People a decenter way to Heaven.

The ill Reputation of Tobacco planted in those lower Parishes, makes the Clergy unwilling to accept of them, unless it be such, whose abilities are as mean as their Pay. Thus whether the Churches be quite void, or but indifferently filled, the Quakers will have an Opportunity of gaining Proselytes.

'Tis a wonder no Popish Missionaries are sent from Maryland to labour in this neglected Vineyard who we know have Zeal enough to traverse Sea and Land on the Meritorious Errand of making Converts.

---

[a]A: a Mile [b]A: A——w M——ds] V: <A w M ds> [c]A: Suffering [d]A: by Reason of the Rain that fell [e]A: made much a fitter Lodging [f]A: the

Nor is it less strange that some Wolf in Sheep's cloathing arrives not from New-England, to lead astray a Flock that has no Shepherd. People uninstructed in any Religion, are ready to embrace the first that offers. 'Tis natural for helpless Man to adore his Maker in some Form or other, and were there any exception to this Rule, I should suspect it to be among the Hottentots of the Cape of Good Hope, and of North-Carolina.[88]

There fell a great deal of Rain in the Night, accompany'd with a strong Wind [that made us all tremble][g]. The fellow-feeling we had for the poor Dismalites, on account of this unkind Weather, render'd the Down we laid upon uneasy. We fancy'd them half-drown'd in their wet Lodging, with the Trees blowing down about their Ears. These were the Gloomy Images our Fears suggested, tho' 'twas [26] so much uneasiness dear-gain['d][h]. They happened to come of[f][i] much better by being luckily encampt on the dry piece of Ground aforemention'd.

[17]   They were however forc't to keep the Sabbath in spite of their Teeth, contrary to the Dispensation of our good Chaplain had given them. Indeed their short allowance of Provision[j] would have justify'd their making the best of their way, without Distinction of days. 'T'was certainly a Work both of Necessity and Self-preservation to save themselves from starving. Nevertheless the hard Rain had made every thing so thoroughly wet that it was quite impossible to do any Business. They therefore made a Vertue of what they could not help, and contentedly rested in their dry Situation.

Since the Surveyors had enter'd the Dismal, they had laid Eyes on no living Creature: Neither Bird, nor Beast, Insect, nor Reptile came in view. Doubtless the Eternal Shade, that broods over this mighty Bog, and hinders the Sun-beams from blessing the Ground, makes it an uncomfortable Habitation for any thing that has life. Not so much as a Zealand Frog cou'd endure so aguish a Situation.[89]

It had one Beauty however, that delighted the Eye, tho' at the Expence of all the other Senses: the Moisture of the Soil preserves a continual Verdure, and makes every Plant an ever-green; but at the same time the foul Damps ascend without ceasing, corrupt the Air, and render it unfit for Respiration. Not even a Turky-Buzzard will venture to fly over it, no more than the Italian Vultures will over the filthy Lake Avernus, or the Birds[k] in the Holy Land over the Salt Sea, where Sodom and Gomorrah formerly stood[l].[90]

In these sad circumstances the kindest thing we cou'd do for our suffering

[g]A: with a strong Wind that made us all tremble.   [h]V: ['d] *supplied from A; Fields reads* clear-gains] A: dear-gain'd   [i]V: come of[f] *emended*] A: come off   [j]A: Provisions
[k]A: Byrds   [l]A: Gomorra had stood

Friends, was to give them a place in the Litany. Our Chaplain for his Part did his Office, and rubb'd us up with a seasonable Sermon. This was quite a new thing to our Brethren of North Carolina, who live in a climate, where no Clergyman can breath, any more than Spiders[m] in Ireland.[91]

For want of men in Holy Orders both the Members of the Council, and Justices of the Peace are empower'd by the Laws of that Country to marry all those who will not take one another's word. But for the ceremony of Christening their Children, they trust that to chance. If a Parson come in their Way, they will crave a Cast of his office, as they call it, Else they are content their Offspring should remain as Arrant Pagans as themselves. They account it among their greatest advantages, that they are not Priest ridden, not remembring that the Clergy is rarely guilty of Bestriding such as have the misfortune to be poor.[92]

One thing may be said for the Inhabitants of that Province, that they are not troubled with any Religious Fumes, and have the least Superstition of any People living. They do not know Sunday from any other day, any more than Robinson [27] Cruso did[n] which wou'd give them a great Advantage were they given to be industrious. But they keep so many Sabbaths every week, that their disregard of the Seventh Day has no manner of Cruelty in it, either to Servants or Cattle.[93]

[18]   It was with some difficulty we cou'd make our People quit the good Chear they met with at this House, so it was late before we took our Departure, but to make us amends, our Landlord was so good as to conduct us Ten Miles on our Way, as far as the Cypress Swamp, which drains itself into the Dismal. Eight Miles beyond that, we forded the Waters of Coropeak, which tend the same way, as do many others on that side. In six Miles more we reach't the Plantation of Mr. Thomas Spight[o] a Grandee of N. Carolina. We found the good Man upon his Crutches, being crippled with the Gout in both his Knees.[94]

Here we flatter'd ourselves we should by this time meet with good Tydings of the Surveyors, but had reckon'd alas without our Host. On the contrary we were told the Dismal was at least Thirty Miles wide in that Place. However as no body cou'd say this on his own Knowledge, we order'd Guns to be fired, and a Drum to be beaten, but receiv'd no Answer, unless it was from that prating Nymph, Eccho, who like a loquacious Wife, will always have the last Word, and sometimes return three for one.[95]

It was indeed no Wonder our Signal was not heard at that time by the

[m]V: *Some one has written* Snakes *in a light hand (pencil?) above the word* Spiders] *also in A, p. 55.*   [n]A: Crusoe was able to do   [o]A: T——s S ——t

People in the Dismal, because in Truth they had then not penetrated[p] one Third of their way. They had that Morning fallen to work with great Vigour, and finding the Ground better than Ordinary, drove the Line 2 Miles and 38 Poles. This was reckon'd an Herculean day's Work, and yet they would not have stop't there, had not an impenetrable Cedar Thicket checkt their Industry.

Our Landlord had seated Himself on the Borders of this Dismal, for the Advantage of the green Food His Cattle find there all Winter, and for the Rooting that supports his Hogs. This I own is some convenience to his Purse for which his whole Family pay dear in their Persons, for they are devoured by Musketas all the Summer, and have Agues every Spring and Fall, which corrupt all the Juices of their Bodies, give[q] them a cadaverous Complexion, and besides[r] a lazy creeping Habit, which they never get rid of.

19.   We order'd several Men to patrole on the Edge of the Dismal, both towards the North and towards the South, and to fire Guns[s] at proper Distances. This they perform'd very punctually, but cou'd hear nothing in return, nor gain any sort of Intelligence. In the mean time whole Flocks of Women and Children flew hither to stare at us with as much curiosity, as if we had lately landed from Bantam or Morocco.[96]

Some Borderers too had a great Mind to know where the Line wou'd come out, being for the most part apprehensive lest their Lands should be taken into Virginia. In that case they must <submit> have ^submitted^ to some sort of Order and Government; whereas in N. Carolina, every one does what seems best in his own Eyes. There were some good Women, that brought their Children to be Baptiz'd, but brought no Capons along with them to make the [28] Solemnity chearful. In the mean time it was strange, that none came to be marry'd in such a Multitude, if it had been only for the Novelty of having their Hands Joyn'd by one in Holy Orders; Yet so it was, that, tho' our Chaplain christen'd above an Hundred, he did not marry so much as one Couple dureing the whole Expedition. But Marriage is reckon'd a lay contract in Carolina, as I said before, and a Country Justice can tie the ^fatal^ Knot[t] there as fast as an Arch-Bishop.

None of our Visitors could however tell us any News of the Surveyors, nor indeed was it possible that any of them shou'd at that time, They being still Labouring in the Midst of the Dismal.

It seems they were able to carry the Line this Day no farther than one Mile and 61 Poles, and that whole Distance was thro' a miry Cedar Bogg, where the

[p]A: had not then penetrated   [q]A: gives   [r]A: and besides that   [s]A: and fired Guns
[t]A: tie the Knot

Ground trembled under their Feet most frightfully. In many Places too their
Passage was retarded by a great number of fallen Trees, that lay Horsing upon
one another.[97]

Tho' many Circumstances concurr'd to make this an unwholsome
Situation, yet the poor men had no time to be sick, nor can one conceive
a more calamitous Case, than it would have been to be laid up in that
uncomfortable Quagmire. Never were Patients more tractable, or willing
to take Physick, than these honest Fellows, but it was from a Dread of
laying their Bones in a Bogg, that wou'd soon spew them up again. That
Consideration also put them upon more caution about their Lodging.

They first cover'd the Ground with square Pieces of Cypress bark, which
now in the Spring they cou'd easily slip off the Tree for that purpose. On this
they spread their Bedding, but unhappily the Weight and Warmth of their
Bodies made the Water rise up betwixt the Joints of the Bark to their great
Inconvenience. Thus they lay not only moist, but also exceedingly cold[a],
because their Fires were continually going out. For no sooner was the Trash
upon the Surface burnt away, but immediately the Fire was extinguisht[b] by
the Moisture of the Soil; Insomuch that it was great part of the Centinel's
Business, to rekindle it again in a fresh Place every Quarter of an Hour. Nor
cou'd they indeed do their duty better, because Cold was the only Enemy they
had to Guard against in a miserable Morass, where nothing can inhabit.

20.   We could get no Tidings yet of our Brave Adventurers,
notwithstanding we dispatch't Men to the likeliest Stations to enquire after
them. They were still scuffleing in the Mire, and could not possibly forward
the Line this whole day more than one Mile and 64 Chains. Every Step of this
Days work was thro' a Cedar-Bog, where[c] the Trees were somewhat smaller
and grew more into a Thicket.

It was now a great Misfortune to the Men to find their Provisions grow less
as their Labour grew greater. They were all forc't to come to short Allowance,
and consequently to work hard[d] without filling their Bellies. Tho' this was
very severe upon English Stomachs, yet the People were so far from being
discomfitted at it, that they still kept up their good Humour, and [29] merrily
told a young Fellow in the Company, who lookt very plump and wholesome,
that he must expect to go first to Pot, if matters shou'd come to Extremity.

This was only said by way of Jest, yet it made Him thoughtful in earnest.
However for the Present he return'd them a very civil answer letting them
know that dead or alive, he shou'd be glad to be useful to such worthy good

[a]A: exceeding cold   [b]A: but the fire was immediately intirely extinguished   [c]A: tho'
[d]A: work smartly

Friends. But after all, this Humorous saying had one very good Effect, for that Younker, who before was a little inclin'd by his Constitution to be lazy[e], grew on a sudden extreamly Industrious that so there might be less Occasion to Carbonade him for the good of his Fellow-Travellers.

While our Friends were thus embarass't in the Dismal, the Commissioners began to ly under great uneasiness for them. They knew very well their Provisions must[f] by this time begin to fall short, nor cou'd they conceive any likely means of a Supply. At this time of the Year both the Cattle and Hoggs had forsaken the Skirts of the Dismal, invited by the springing Grass on the firm Land. All our hopes were that Providence wou'd cause some wild Game to fall in their way, or else direct them to a wholesome Vegetable for Subsistence. In short they were haunted by so many Frights on this Occasion, that they were in truth more uneasy than the Persons, whose Case they lamented.

We had several Visitors from Edenton in the Afternoon, that came with Mr. Gale, who had prudently left us at Corotuck to scuffle thro' that Dirty Country by our selves. These Gentlemen, having good Noses had smelt out at 30 Miles Distance, the Precious Liquor with which the Liberality of our good Friend Mr. Mead[g] had just before supply'd us. That generous Person had judg'd very right[h], that we were now got out of the Latitude of Drink proper for men in Affliction, and therefore was so good as to send his cart loaden with all sorts of refreshments, for which the Commissioners return'd Him their Thanks, and the Chaplain His Blessing.

21.   The Surveyors and their Attendants began now in good Earnest to be alarm'd with Apprehensions of Famine[i], nor could they forbear looking with some sort of Appetite upon a Dog, that had been the faithful Companion of their Travels.

Their Provisions were now near exhausted. They had this Morning made the last Distribution, that so each might Husband his small Pittance as he pleas'd. Now it was that the fresh colour'd Young Man began to tremble every Joint of Him, having dreamt the Night before, that the Indians were about to Barbacue him over[j] live coals.

The Prospect of Famine determind'd the People at last with one consent to abandon the Line for the Present, which advanced but slowly, and make the best of their way to firm Land. Accordingly they set off very early, and by the help of the Compass, which they carried along with them, steer'd a direct Westerly Course, they marcht from Morning till Night, and computed

[e]A: inclin'd to be lazy   [f]A: knew very well ^their Provisions must^   [g]A: M——d
[h]A: rightly   [i]A: Family   [j]A: upon

their Journey to amount to about 4 Miles which was a great way considering the difficulties of the Ground. It was all along a Cedar-Swamp, so dirty and perplext, that if they had not travel'd for [30] their Lives, they cou'd not have reach't so far.

On their way they espied a Turky-Buzzard, that flew prodigiously high to get above the noisome Exhalations, that ascend from that filthy Place. This they were willing to understand as a good Omen, according to the Superstition of the Ancients, who had great Faith of in[k] the Flight of Vultures.[98]

However after all this tedious Journey, they could yet discover no End of their Toil, which made them very pensive, especially after they had eat the last Morsel of their Provisions. But to their unspeakable comfort, when all was husht in the Evening, they heard the Cattle low, and the Dogs bark very distinctly, which to Men in that distress was more delightfull Musick than Faustina or Farinelli cou'd have made. In the mean time the Commissioners cou'd get no News of them from any of their Visitors, who assembled from every Point of the Compass.[99]

But the good Landlord had Visitors of another kind, while we were there, that is to say, some industrious Masters of Ships, that lay in Nansimond River. These worthy Commanders came to bespeak Tobacco from these Parts, to make up their Loadings, in contempt of the Virginia Law, which positively forbad[l] their taking in any made in North Carolina: Nor was this Restraint at all unreasonable, because they have[m] no Law in Carolina, either to mend the Quality, or lessen the Quantity of Tobacco, or so much as to prevent the turning out of Seconds, all which cases have been provided against by the Laws of Virginia. Wherefore[n] there can be no reason, why the Inhabitants of that Province, shou'd have the same Advantage of Shipping their Tobacco in our Parts, when they will by no means submit to the same Restrictions, that we do.[100]

22. Our Patrole happen'd not to go far enough to the Northward this Morning; if they had the People in the Dismal might have heard the Report of their Guns. For this Reason they return'd without any Tydings which threw us into a great tho' unnecessary Perplexity. This was now the ninth day, since they enter'd into that unhospitable Swamp, and consequently we had reason to believe their Provisions were quite spent.

We knew they workt hard, and therefore would eat heartily, so long as they had wherewithal to recruit their Spirits, not imagining the Swamp so wide as they found it. Had we been able to guess, where the Line wou'd come

[k]V: of in [l]A: forbid [m]A: having [n]A: Therefore

out, we wou'd have sent Men to meet them with a fresh supply. But as we
cou'd know nothing of that, and as we had neither Compass nor Surveyor to
guide a Messenger on such an Errand, we were unwilling to expose him to no
Purpose; Therefore all we were able to do for them, in so great an Extremity,
was to recommend them to a Merciful Providence.

However long we might think the time, yet we were cautious of shewing
our uneasiness, for fear of mortifying our Landlord. He had done his best for
us and therefore we were unwilling he should think us dissatisfy'd with our
Entertainment. In the midst of our concern, we were most agreeably surpriz'd
just [31] after Dinner, with the News that the Dismalites were all safe. These°
blessed Tidings were brought us by Mr. Swan^p the Carolina Surveyor, who
came to us in a very tatter'd Condition.

After very short Salutations, we got about him as if He had been a
Hottentot, and began to enquire into his Adventures. He gave us a Detail of
their uncomfortable Voyage thro' the Dismal, and told us particularly they
had pursued their Journey early that Morning, encouraged by the good Omen
of seeing the Crows fly over their Heads; that after an Hour's march over
very Rotten Ground; they on a sudden began to find themselves among tall
Pines, that grew in the Water, which in many Places was Knee-deep. This
Pine Swamp, into which that of Coropeak drain'd itself, extended near a Mile
in Breadth, and tho' it was exceedingly wet, yet was much harder at Bottom,
than the rest of the Swamp; That about Ten in the Morning they recover'd
firm Land, which they embraced with as much Pleasure, as shipwreckt
Wretches do the Shoar.

After these honest adventurers had congratulated each others Deliverance,
their first Enquiry was for a good House, where they might satisfy the
Importunity of their Stomachs. Their good Genius directed them to Mr
Brinkley's^q, who dwells a little to the Southward of the Line. This Man began
immediately to be very inquisitive, but they declar'd they had no Spirits to
answer Questions till after Dinner.[101]

But pray Gentlemen, said he, answer me one Question at least. What shall
we get for your Dinner? To which they replied, no matter what ^provided it be
but^ Enough^r. He kindly supply'd their Wants as soon as possible, and by the
Strength of that Refreshment, they made a Shift to come to us in the Evening,
to tell their own Story. They all look't very thin and as ragged as the Gibeonite
Ambassadors did in the days of Yore. Our Surveyors told us they had measur'd
Ten Miles in the Dismal and computed the Distance, they had march't since,

---

°A: The   ^PA: S——n   ^qA: B——y's   ^rA: no matter what—Enough.

to amount to about five more: So they made the whole Breadth to be 15 Miles in all.[s,102]

23.   It was very reasonable that the Surveyors and the Men, who had been Sharers in their Fatigue, should now have a little Rest. They were all, except one, in good Health and good Heart, blessed be God, notwithstanding the dreadful Hardships they had gone through. It was really a Pleasure to see the Chearfulness, wherewith they receiv'd the Order to prepare to re-enter the Dismal on the Monday following, in order to continue the Line, from the Place, where they had left off measuring[t], that so we might have the exact Breadth of that Dirty Place. There were[a] no more than two of them, that cou'd be perswaded to be reliev'd on this Occasion, or suffer the other men to share the Credit of that bold Undertaking. Neither wou'd these have suffer'd it had not one of them been ^very^ lame, and the other much Indispos'd.

By the Description, the Surveyors gave of the Dismal we were convinc'd, that nothing but the exceeding dry Season, we had been bless'd with, cou'd have made the passing of it practicable. It is the Source of no less than Five several Rivers which discharge [32] themselves Southward into Albemarle Sound, and of two that run Northerly into Virginia. From thence 'tis easy to imagine, that the Soil must be thoroughly soakt with Water, or else there must be plentiful Stores of it under Ground; to supply so many Rivers; especially since there is no Lake, or any considerable Body of that Element to be seen on the Surface. The Rivers, that Head into it from Virginia, are the South Branch of Nansimond, and the West Branch of Elisabeth, and those from Carolina, are North-West River, North River, Pasquetank, Little River, and Pequimons.[103]

There is one remarkable part of the Dismal lying to the South of the Line, that has few or no Trees growing on it, but contains a large Tract of tall Reeds; These being green all the Year round, and waveing with every Wind, have procur'd it the Name of the Green Sea.[104]

We are not yet acquainted with the precise Extent of the Dismal, the whole haveing never been survey'd: but it may be computed at a medium to be ^about^ 30 Miles long and 10 Miles broad, tho' where the Line cros't it, 'twas compleatly 15 Miles wide. But it seems to grow narrower towards the North, or at least does in many Places. The Exhalations, that continually rise from this vast Body of Mire and Nastiness, infect the Air for many Miles round, and render it very unwholsome for the Bordering Inhabitants. It makes them

---

[s]V: *Insertion at end of line:* A: to be 15 Miles.   [t]A: at which they had left off measuring] V: *erasure, insertion, dash in empty space.*   [a]A: was

liable to Agues, Pleurisies, and many other Distempers, that kill abundance of People, and make the rest look not better than Ghosts. It wou'd require a great sum of Money to drain it, but the Publick Treasure cou'd not be better bestow'd than to preserve the Lives of his Majesty's Liege People, and at the same time render so great a Tract of Swamp very profitable, besides the Advantage of making a Channel to transport by water-carriage Goods from Albemarle Sound into Nansimond, and Elsabeth[b] Rivers in Virginia.[105]

24.   This being Sunday, we had a numerous Congregation, which flock't to our Quarters from all the adjacent Country. The News that our Surveyors were come out of the Dismal encreas'd the Number very much, because it wou'd give them an Opportunity of guessing at least, whereabouts the Line wou'd cut, whereby they might form some Judgment, whether they belong'd to Virginia or Carolina. Those who had taken up Land within the Disputed Bounds, were in great pain, lest it should be found to ly in Virginia, because this being done contrary to an Express Order of that Government, the Patentees had great Reason to fear, they should in that case have lost their Land. But their Apprehensions were now at an End, when they understood that all the Territory, which had been controverted, was like to be left in Carolina.[106]

In the Afternoon those who were to re-enter the Dismal, were furnish't with the necessary Provisions, and order'd to repair the over Night to their Landlord, Peter Brinklys[c], that they might be ready to begin their Business early on Monday Morning. Mr. Irvin[d] was excus'd from the Fatigue, in Complement to [33] his Lungs. But Mr. Mayo and Mr. Swan[e] were Robust enough to return upon that painful Service, and to do them Justice, they went with great Alacrity. The Truth was, they now knew the worst of it, and cou'd guess pretty near at the time, when they might hope to return to Land again.

25.[107]   The Air was chill'd this Morning with a smart North-west Wind, which favour'd the Dismalites in their Dirty March. They return'd by the Path, they had made in coming out, and with great Industry arriv'd in the Evening at the Spot, where the Line had been discontinu'd.

After so long and laborious a Journey, they were glad to repose themselves on the Couches of Cypress-Bark, where their Sleep was as sweet, as it wou'd have been on a Bed of Fin-land Down.[108]

In the mean time we who stay'd behind had nothing to do, but to make the best observations, we cou'd upon that Part of the Country. The Soil of our Landlord's Plantation, tho' none of the best, seem'd more fertile than any thereabouts, where the Ground is near as sandy as the Desarts of Affrica,

[b]A: Elizabeth   [c]A: P——r B——ys   [d]A: I——e   [e]A: Mr. M—— and Mr. S——

and consequently barren. The Road leading from thence to Edenton being
in distance about 27 Miles, lies upon a Ridge call'd Sandy Ridge, which is so
wretchedly poor that it will not bring Potatoes.[109]

The Pines in this Part of the Country are of a Different Species from those
that grow in Virginia. Their bearded Leaves are much longer, and their Cones
much Larger. Each Cell contains a Seed of the Size and Figure of a black-ey'd
Pea, which shedding in November, is very good Mast for Hogs, and fattens
them in a short time.[110]

The smallest of these Pines are full of Cones, which are 8 or 9 Inches
long, and each affords commonly 60 or 70 Seeds. This Kind of Mast has the
Advantage of all other, by being more constant, and less liable to be nipt
by the Frost, or eaten by the Catterpillars[f]. The Trees also abound more
with Turpentine, and consequently yield more Tarr, than either the Yellow
or the White Pine. And for the same reason makes more durable Timber
for Building. The Inhabitants hereabouts pick up Knots of Lightwood
in abundance, which they burn into Tar, and then carry it to Norfolk or
Nansimond for a Market. The Tar made in this Method is the less valuable
because it is said[g] to burn the Cordage, tho' it is full as good for all other uses,
as that made in Sweden and Muscovy.[111]

Surely there is no place in the World where the Inhabitants live with
less Labour, than in N. Carolina. It approaches nearer to the Description of
Lubberland than any other, by the great felicity of the Climate, the easiness of
raising Provisions, and the Slothfulness of the People.[112]

Indian Corn is of so great increase that a little pains will subsist a very
large Family with Bread, and then they may have meat without any pains at
all, by the Help of the Low Grounds, and the great Variety of Mast that grows
on the High-land. The Men for their parts, just like the Indians, impose all the
Work upon the poor Women. They make their Wives rise out of their [warm]
Beds[h], early in the Morning at the same time that they lye and [34] snore, till
the Sun has run one third of his Course, and dispers't all the unwholesome
Damps. Then after Stretching and Yawning for half an Hour, they light
their Pipes, and under the Protection of a Cloud of Smoak venture out into
the open Air; tho' if it happen to be never so little cold, they quickly return
Shivering into the chimney corner. When the Weather is mild, they stand
leaning with both their Arms upon the cornfield fence, and gravely consider
whether they and best go—and take a small Heat at the Hough: but generally
find reasons to put it off till another time.[113]

---

[f]A: by Caterpillars   [g]A: 'tis said   [h]A: out of their warm Beds *(an instance of editorial expansion in A)*

Thus they loiter away their Lives, like Solomon's Sluggard, with their Arms across, and at the Winding up of the Year scarcely have Bread to eat.[114]

To speak the Truth, 'tis a thorough Aversion to Labour, that makes People file off to N. Carolina, where Plenty and a warm Sun confirm them in their Disposition to Laziness for their whole Lives.

26. Since we were like to be confin'd to this place, till the People return'd out of the Dismal, 'twas agreed that our Chaplain might safely take a turn to Edenton, to preach the Gospel to the Infidels there, and christen their Children. He was accompany'd thither by Mr. Little one of the Carolina Commissioners, who to shew his regard for the Church, offer'd to treat Him on the Road with a Fricassee of Rum. They fry'd half a Dozen Rashers of very fat Bacon in a Pint of Rum[i], both which being dish't up together, serv'd the Company at once both for Meat and Drink.[115]

Most of the Rum, they get in this Country, comes from New-England and is so bad, and so unwholsome, that it is not improperly call'd Kill-Devil. It is distill'd there from Forreign Molosses, which if skilfully manag'd yields near Gallon for Gallon. Their Molosses comes from the same Country, and has the Name of Long Sugar in Carolina, I suppose, from the Ropiness of it, and serves all the purposes of Sugar both in their Eating and Drinking.

When they entertain their Friends bountifully, they fail not to set before them a capacious Bowl of Bombo, so call'd from the Admiral of that Name. This is a Compound of Rum and Water in equal Parts, made palatable with the said long Sugar. As good Humour begins to flow, and the Bowl to ebb, they take Care to replenish it with Shear Rum, of which there always is a Reserve under the Table. But such Generous doings happen only, when that Balsam of Life is plenty: for they have often such melancholly times, that neither Land-graves, nor Cassicks can procure one drop for their Wives, when they ly in, or are troubled with the Colick, or Vapours. Very few in this Country have the Industry to plant Orchards, which in a Dearth of Rum, might supply them with much better Liquor.[116]

The Truth is, there is one Inconvenience, that easily discourages lazy People from making this Improvement: Very often in Autumn, when the Apples begin to ripen, they are visited with numerous Flights of Paraqueets that bite all the Fruit to [35] Pieces in a Moment for the Sake of the Kernels.

The Havock they make is sometimes so great, that whole Orchards are laid waste in Spite of all the Noises that can be made, or Mawkins, that can be dress't up, to fright 'em away. These Ravenous Birds visit North-Carolina only during the warm Season, and so soon as the Cold begins to come on, retire

[i]A: very fat Rashers of Bacon in a Pint of Rum

back towards the Sun. They rarely venture so far North as Virginia, except in a very hot Summer, when they visit the most Southern Parts of it. They are very Beautiful, but, like some other pretty Creatures, are apt to be loud and mischievous.[117]

27.   Betwixt this [Plantation] and Edenton[j] there are many Huckleberry Slashes, which afford a convenient Harbour for Wolves, and Foxes. The first of these Wild Beasts is not so large and fierce as they are in other Countries more Northerly. He will not attack a Man in the keenest of his Hunger, but run away from him, as from an Animal more mischievous than himself.[118]

The Foxes are much bolder, and will sometimes not only make a Stand, but likewise assault any one, that would baulk them of their Prey. The Inhabitants hereabouts take the trouble to dig abundance of Wolf-Pits, so deep and perpendicular, that when a Wolf is once tempted into them, he can no more scramble out again, than a Husband who has taken the Leap, can scramble out of Matrimony.

Most of the Houses in this Part of the Country are Log-houses, covered with Pine, or Cypress Shingles 3 feet long[k], and one broad. They are hung upon Laths with Peggs, and their Doors too turn upon wooden Hinges, and have wooden Locks to secure them, so that the Building is finish't without Nails or other Iron-Work. They also set up their Pales without any Nails at all, and indeed more securely than those that are Nail'd. There are 3 Rails mortised into the Posts, the lower of which serves as a Sill with a Groove in the Middle, big enough to receive the End of the Pales: the middle Part of the Pale rests against the Inside of the next Rail, and the Top of it is brought forward[l] to the outside of the uppermost. Such Wreathing of the Pales in and out makes them stand firm, and much harder to unfix, than when nail'd in the ordinary way.[119]

Within 3 or 4 miles of Edenton, the Soil appears to be a little more fertile, tho' it is much cut with Slashes, which seem ^all^ to have a tendency towards the Dismal.

This Town is situate on the North-side of Albermarle Sound, which is there about 5 Miles over. A Dirty Slash runs all along the Back of it, which in the Summer is a foul annoyance, and furnishes abundance of that Carolina Plague, Musquetas. There may be 40 or 50 Houses most of them small and built without Expence. A Citizen here is counted Extravagant, if he has Ambition enough to aspire to a Brick-Chimney. Justice herself is but indifferently Lodged, The Court-House having much the Air of a common

[j]A: Betwixt this Plantation and Edenton (*another instance of editorial expansion in A*)
[k]A: 3 foot long   [l]A: the top is brought forward

Tobacco House. I believe this is the only Metropolis in the Christian or
^Mahometan^ World^m, where there is neither Church, Chappel, Mosque,
Synagogue, or any other Place of Publick Worship of any Sect, or Religion
whatsoever.[120]

What little Devotion there may happen to be, is much more [36] private
than their Vices. The People seem easy without a Minister, as long as they
are exempted from paying Him. Sometimes the Society for propagating the
Gospel has had the Charity to send over Missionaries to this Country, but
unfortunately the Priest has been too lewd for the People, or, which oftener
happens, they too lewd for the Priest. For these Reasons the Reverend
Gentlemen have always left their Flocks as arrant Heathen^n, as they found
them. Thus much however may be said for the Inhabitants of Edenton,
that not a Soul has the least taint of Hypocrisy, or Superstition, acting very
Frankly, and above board in all their Excesses.[121]

Provisions here are extremely cheap, and extremely good, so that People
may live plentifully at a triffleing Expence. Nothing is dear, but Law, Physick,
and strong Drink, which are all bad in their Kind, and the last they get with
so much Difficulty, that they are never guilty of the Sin of suffering it to
sow'r^o upon their Hands. Their Vanity generally lies not so much in having
a handsome Dining Room, as a Handsome House of Office. In this Kind of
Structure they are really extravagant.[122]

They are rarely guilty of Flattering, or making any Court to their Governors,
but treat them with all the Excesses of Freedom, and Familiarity. They are
of Opinion their Rulers wou'd ^be apt to^ grow insolent, if they grew Rich,
and for that reason take care to keep them poorer and more dependant, if
possible, than the Saints in New-England ^us'd to^ do their Governors. They
have very little Coin so they are forced to carry on their Home-Traffick with
Paper-Money. This is the only Cash, that will tarry in the Country, and for that
reason the Discount goes on encreasing between that and real Money, and
will do so to the End of the Chapter.[123]

28.   Our Time passt heavily in our Quarters where we were quite cloy'd
with the Carolina Felicity of having nothing to do. It was really more
insupportable than the greatest Fatigue, and made us even envy the Drudgery
of our Friends in the Dismal: Besides, tho' the Men we had with us were kept
in Exact Discipline, and behav'd without Reproach, yet our Landlord began to
be tired of them, fearing they would breed a Famine in his Family.

Indeed so many keen Stomachs made great Havock amongst the Beef
and Bacon^p, which he had laid in for his Summer Provision, nor cou'd he

---

^mA: in the Christian World   ^nA: Heathens   ^oA: letting it sower   ^pA: Beef and Pork easily purchase more at that time of the Year with the Money we paid him, because People having no certain Market, seldom provide any more of these Commodities, than will barely support their own Occasions. Besides the Weather was now grown too warm to lay in a fresh Stock so late in the Spring. These Considerations abated somewhat of that Chearfulness, with which he bid us Welcome in the Beginning, and made him think the time quite as long, as we did, till the Surveyors return'd.

While we were thus all Hands uneasy, we were comforted with the News, that this Afternoon the line was finish't throughq [37] the Dismal. The Messenger told us it had been the hard work of three days, to measure the Length of only 5 Miles, and mark the Trees as they past along, and by the most exact Survey they found the Breadth of the Dismal in this Place to be completely 15 Miles.[124]

How wide it may be in other Parts, we can give no Account, but believe it grows narrower toward the North. Possibly towards Albermarle Sound it may be something broader, where so many Rivers issue out of it. All we know for certain, is, that from the Place, where the Line enter'd the Dismal, to where it came out, we found the Road round that Portion of it, which belongs to Virginia, to be about 65 Miles. How great the Distance may be from each of those Points, round that Part, that falls within the Bounds of Carolina, we had no certain Information: Tho' tis conjectur'd it cannot be so little as 30 Miles, at which rate the whole Circuit must be about an Hundred. What Mass of Mire and Dirt, is treasur'd up within this filthy Circumference, and what a Quantity of Water must perpetually drain into it from the riseing ground, that surrounds it on every Side?

Without taking the exact level of the Dismal, we may be sure, that it declines toward the Places, where the several Rivers take their Rise, in order to carrying off the constant Supplies of Water. Were it not for such Discharges, the whole Swamp would long since have been converted into a Lake. On the other side this Declension must be very gentle, else it would be laid perfectly dry by so many ^continual^ drains, whereas on the contrary, the Ground seems every where to be thoroughly drench't even in the dryest Season of the Year.

The Surveyors concluded this Days work with running 25 Chains up into the Firm Land, where they waited farther Orders from the Commissioners.

29.   This day the Surveyors proceeded with the Line no more than 1 Mile and 15 Chains, being Interrupted by a Mill Swamp, thro' which they made no difficulty of wading, in order to make their work more exact.[125]

---

qV: through *supplied from catchword, though omitted at beginning of next page*] A: thro'

Thus, like Norway-Mice, these worthy Gentlemen went right forward, without suffering themselves to be turn'd out of the way by any Obstacle whatever.

We are told by some Travellers, that those Mice march in mighty Armies, destroying all the fruits of the Earth, as they go along. But something peculiar to those obstinate little Animals, is, that nothing stops them in their Career, and if a House happen to stand in their way, disdaining to go an Inch about, they crawl up one side of it, and down the other: or if they meet with any River, or other Body of Water, they are so determin'd, that they swim directly over it, without varying one Point from their Course, for the sake of any Safety or Convenience.[126]

The Surveyors were also hinder'd some time by setting up Posts in the great Road, to shew the Bounds between the two Colonies.

Our Chaplain return'd to us in the Evening from Edenton, in Company with the Carolina-Commissioners. He had preach't there in the Court House for want of a consecrated Place, and made no less than 13 of Father Hennepin's Christians.[127]

By the Permission of the Carolina-Commissioners, Mr. Swan [38] was allow'd to go home, as soon as the Survey of the Dismal was finish't; He met with this Indulgence for a Reason, that might very well have excus'd his coming at all; namely that he was lately marry'd.[128]

What remain'd of the Drudgery for this Season was left to Mr. Moseley, who had hitherto acted only in the capacity of a Commissioner. They offer'd to employ Mr. Joseph Mayo as their Surveyor in Mr. Swan's Stead, but He thought it not proper to accept of it, because he had hitherto acted as a Volunteer in behalf of Virginia, and did not care to change Sides, tho' it might have been to his Advantage.[129]

30.   The Line was advanc'd this day 6 Miles and 35 Chains, the Woods being pretty clear, and interrupted with no Swamp, or other wet Ground. The Land hereabouts had all the Marks of Poverty, being for the most part Sandy, and full of Pines. This kind of Ground tho' unfit for ordinary Tillage, will however bring Cotton and Potatoes in Plenty, and consequently Food and Raiment to such as are easily contented, and, like the Wild Irish, find more Pleasure in Laziness, than Luxury.

It also makes a shift to produce Indian-Corn, rather by the Felicity of the Climate, than by the Fertility of the Soil. They, who are more Industrious than their Neigbours, may make what Quantity of Tar they please, tho' indeed they are not always sure of a Market for it.[r]

[r]A: sure of a Market.] V: for it. *added at end of line.*

The Method of burning Tar in Sweden and Muscovy succeeds not well in this warmer part of the World. It seems they kill the Pine-Trees by barking them quite round at a certain Height, which in those cold Countreys brings down the Turpentine into the Stump in a Years time. But experience has taught us, that in warm Climates the Turpentine will not so easily descend, but is either fix't in the upper parts of the Tree, or fryed out by the intense Heat of the Sun.[130]

Care was taken to erect a Post in every Road, that our Line ran thro', with Virginia carv'd on the North-Side of it, and Carolina on the South, that the Bounds might every where appear.

In the Evening the Surveyors took up their Quarters at the House of one Mr. Parker[s], who by the Advantage of a better Spot of Land, than ordinary, and a more industrious Wife, lives comfortably, and has a very neat Plantation.[131]

31. It rain'd a little this Morning, but this happening again upon a Sunday, did not interrupt our Business. However the Surveyors made no Scruple of protracting and platting off their work upon that good day, because it was rather an Amuzement than a Drudgery.

Here the Men feasted on the fat of the Land, and believing the dirtiest part of their work was over, had a more than ordinary Gaiety of Heart. We Christen'd two of our Landlords Children, which might have remain'd Infidels all their Lives, had not we carry'd Christianity home to his own Door.

The Truth of it is, our Neighbours of North-Carolina are [39] not so Zealous as to go much out of their way to procure this benefit for their Children: Otherwise being so near Virginia, they might without exceeding much Trouble make a Journey to the next Clergy-man, upon so good an Errand.

And indeed should the neighbouring Ministers once in two or three Years, vouchsafe to take a turn amongst these Gentiles, to baptize them and their children, 'twou'd look a little Apostolical, and they might hope to be requited for it hereafter, if that be not thought too long to tarry for their Reward.

[April] 1.[t] The Surveyors getting now upon better Ground, quite disengag'd from Underwoods, pusht on the Line almost 12 Miles. They left Sommerton-Chappel almost[a] 2 Miles to the Northward, so that there was now no Place of publick Worship[b], left in the whole Province of North-Carolina.[132]

The high Land of North-Carolina[c], was barren, and cover'd with a deep

---

[s]A: of R——d P——r [t]V: *The new month is recorded at the top right-hand corner of p. 39; in A it is given in bold letters in the center of p. 78, just before the entry for April 1.*
[a]A: near [b]A: so that now there was no Place of Publick Worship [c]A: The high Land we travell'd

Sand; And the Low Grounds were wet and Boggy, insomuch that several of our Horses were mir'd, and gave us F̲r̲e̲q̲u̲e̲n̲t̲ Opportunitys̲ to shew[d] our Horsmanship.

The Line cut W̲i̲l̲l̲i̲a̲m̲ S̲p̲i̲g̲h̲t̲s[e] Plantation in two, leaving little more than his dwelling House and Orchard in Virginia. Sundry[f] other Plantations were split in the same unlucky Manner, which made the Owners accountable to both Governments. Wherever we past, we constantly found the Borderers laid it to Heart, if their Land was taken into Virginia; They chose much rather to belong to Carolina, where they pay no Tribute either to God or to Caesar.[133]

Another reason was, that the Government there is so Loose and the Laws so feebly executed, that like those in the Neighbourhood of Sydon formerly, every one does just what seems good in his own Eyes. If the Governors Hands have been weak in that Province under the Authority of the Lord Proprietors, much weaker then were the hands of the Magistrate, who tho' he might have had Virtue enough to endeavour to punish Offenders, which very rarely happen'd; yet that Virtue had been quite Impotent for want of Ability to put it in Execution.[134]

Besides there might have been some Danger perhaps in venturing to be so rigorous, for fear of undergoing the Fate of an honest Justice in Corotuck Precinct. This bold Magistrate, it seems, taking upon him to order a fellow to the Stocks, for being disorderly in his Drink, was for his intemperate Zeal carry'd thither himself, and narrowly escap'd being whipt by the Rabble into the Bargain.[135]

This easy day's work carried the Line to the Banks of Somerton-Creek, that runs out of Chowan River, a little below the Mouth of Notoway.

2.   In less than a Mile from Somerton Creek the Line was carry'd to Black-Water, which is the Name of the upper Part of C̲h̲o̲w̲a̲n̲[g], running some Miles above the Mouth of Notoway. It must be observ'd that Chowan, after taking a Compass [40] round the most beautiful part of North Carolina, empties itself into Albermarle Sound, a few Miles above Edenton. The Tide flows 7 or 8 Miles higher than where the River changes its Name, and is navigable thus high for any small Vessel. Our Line intersected it exactly half a Mile to the Northward of the Mouth of Notoway.

However in Obedience to His Majesty's Command, we directed the Surveyors to come down the River, as far as the Mouth of Notoway, in order to continue our true West Line from thence.

[d]A: gave us a fair Opportunity to shew   [e]A: W——m S——ts   [f]A: Several   [g]A: Chowan River

Thus we found the Mouth of Notoway to lye no more than half a Minute farther to the Northward, than Mr. Lawson had formerly done. That Gentleman's Observation, it seems, placed it in 36°, 30, and our Working made it out to be 36°, 30½ a very inconsiderable Variance.[136]

The Surveyors cros't the River over against the Middle of the Mouth of Notoway, where it was about 80 Yards wide. From thence they run the Line about half a Mile thro' a dirty Pocoson, as far as an Indian Field. Here we took up our Lodging in a moist Situation, having the Pocoson abovemention'd on one Side of us, and a Swamp on the other.

In this Camp 3 of the Meherin Indians made us a Visit. They told us, that the small Remains of their Nation had deserted their ancient Town, situated near the Mouth of Meherrin River, for fear of the Cataubas, who had kill'd 14 of their People the Year before; and the few that surviv'd that Calamity had taken refuge amongst the English, on the East side of Chowan. Tho' if the complaint of these Indians were true[h], they are hardly used by our Carolina Friends. But they are the less to be pitied, because they have ever been reputed the most false and treacherous to the English of all the Indians in the Neighbourhood.[137]

Not far from the Place, where we lay, I observ'd a large Oak[i] which had been blown up by the Roots, the Body of which was shiver'd into perfect Strings, and was in truth the most violent Effect of Light'ning, I ever saw.

But the most curious Instance of that dreadfull Meteor happen'd at York, where a man was kill'd near a Pine Tree in which the Lightening made a Hole before it struck the Man, and left an exact Figure of the Tree upon his Breast with all its Branches to the wonder of all that beheld it[j], In which I shall be more particular hereafter.[138]

We made another Tryal of the Variation in this Place; and found it some Minutes less than we had done at Corotuck-Inlet[k]; but so small a Difference might happen[l] thro' some defect in one or other of the Observations, and therefore we alter'd not our Compass for the Matter.

3. By the advantage of clear woods the Line was extended 12 Miles and three Quarters, as far as the Banks of Meherin. Tho' the Mouth of this River lyes 15 Miles below the Mouth of Notoway, yet it winds so much to the Northward, that we came upon it, after running this small Distance. [41] During the first 7 Miles, we observ'd the Soil to be poor and sandy, but as we approach't Meherin, it grew better, tho' there it was cut to pieces by sundry

[h]A: be true   [i]A: a very large Oak   [j]A: *Paragraph ends here.* V: *phrase inserted in blank space at end of line.*   [k]A: had done before at Corotuck-Inlet   [l]A: might easily happen

miry Branches, which discharge themselves into that River. Several of our Horses plunged up to the Saddle Skirts, and were not disengaged without Difficulty.

The latter part of our Days work was pretty laborious, because of the unevenness of the way, and because the low Ground of the River was full of Cypress-Snags, as Sharp and Dangerous to our Horses as so many Chevaux de Frize. We found the whole distance from the Mouth of Notoway to Meherin River, where our Line intersected it, thirteen Miles and a Quarter.[139]

It was hardly possible to find a level large enough on the Banks of the River, whereupon to pitch our Tent. But tho' the Situation was on that account not very convenient for us, yet it was for our poor Horses, by reason of the Plenty of small Reeds, on which they fed voraciously.

These Reeds are green here all the Year round, and will keep Cattle in a tolerable good Plight during the Winter: But whenever the Hogs come where they are, they destroy them in a short time, by plowing up their Roots, of which unluckily they are very fond[m].

The River was in this Place about as wide as the River Jordan, that is 40 Yards, and wou'd be Navigable very high for flat Bottom-Boats and Canoes, if it were not choak't up with[n] large Trees brought down by every Fresh. Tho' the Banks were full 20 feet high from the Surface of the Water[o], yet we saw certain Marks of their having been overflow'd.[140]

These narrow Rivers, that run high up into the Country, are subject to frequent Inundations, when the Waters are roll'd down with such Violence as to carry all before them. The Logs that are then floated, are very fatal to the bridges built over these Rivers, which can hardly be contriv'd strong enough to stand against so much Weight and Violence join'd together.

The Isle of Wight County begins about 3 Miles to the East of Meherin River, being divided from that of Nansimond only by a Line of mark't Trees.

4.   The River was here hardly fordable tho' the Season had been very dry. The Banks too were so steep, that our Horses were forced to climb like Mules to get up them. Nevertheless we had the Luck to recover the opposite Shore without Damage.

We halted for half an hour at Charles Andersons, who lives on the Western Banks of the River, in order to christen one of his Children. In the mean time the Surveyors extended the Line 2 Miles and 39 Chains, in which small Distance Meherin River was so serpentine that they cros't it 3 times.[141]

Then we went on to Mr. Kinchin's a Man of Figure and Authority in N. Carolina, who lives about a Mile to the Southward of the Place, where the

---

[m]A: unluckily are they very fond   [n]A: by   [o]A: from the Water

Surveyors left off. By the Benefit of a little pains, and good Management, this worthy Magistrate lives in much Affluence.[142]

Amongst other Instances of his Industry, he had planted a good Orchard, which is not common in that Indolent Climate. Nor is it at all strange, that such improvident People, who take no thought for the Morrow, shou'd save themselves the Trouble to make [42] Improvements, that[p] will not pay them for several Years to come. Tho' if they cou'd trust futurity for any thing, they certainly wou'd for Cyder, which they are so fond of, that they generally drink it before it has done working, lest the Fermentation might unluckily turn it sower.

It is an Observation, which rarely fails of being true, both in Virginia and Carolina, that those, who take care to plant good Orchards, are in their General Characters Industrious People. This held good in our Landlord, who had many Houses built upon this Plantation, and every one kept in decent Repair. His Wife too was tidy, his Furniture clean, his Pewter bright, and nothing seem'd to be wanting to make his Home comfortable.

Mr. Kinchin made us the Compliment of his House, but because we were willing to be as little troublesome, as possible, we order'd the Tent to be pitch'd in his Orchard, where the Blossoms of the Apple Trees, contributed not a little to the sweetness of our Lodging.

5. Because the Spring was now pretty forward, and ^the^ Rattle-Snakes began to crawl out of their Winter-Quarters, and might grow dangerous both to the Men and their Horses, it was determin'd to proceed no farther with the Line till the Fall. Besides the uncommon Fatigue the People had undergone for near 6 Weeks together, and the Inclination, they all had to visit their Respective Familys, made a Recess highly reasonable.[143]

The Surveyors were employ'd great part of the Day, in forming a Correct and Elegant Map of the Line, from Corotuck-Inlet to the Place where they left off.[q] On casting up the Account in the most accurate manner, they found the whole distance, we had run to amount to 73 Miles and 13 Chains. Of this Map they made two fair Copies, which agreeing exactly, were subscrib'd by the Commissioners of both Colonies, and one of them was deliver'd to those on the Part of Virginia, and the other to those on the Part of North-Carolina.

6. Thus we finish't our Spring Campaign, and having taken leave of our Carolina-Friends, and agreed to meet them again the Tenth of September following at the same Mr. Kinchin's in order to continue the Line, we cros't Meherin River near a Quarter of a Mile from the House. About ten Miles

[p]A: which   [q]V: *The following sentence is added in the blank space at the original paragraph end and the indented beginning of the next, as in A.*

from that we halted at Mr. Kindred's Plantation, where we Christen'd two Children.[144]

It happen'd that some of [the] Isle of Wight Militia[r] were exercising in the adjoining Pasture, and there were Females enough, attending that Martial Appearance, to form a more invincible Corps.

Ten Miles farther we past Notoway River at Bolton's ferry, and took up our Lodgings about three Miles from thence, at the House of [Mr.] Richd. Parker[s], an honest Planter, whose Labours were rewarded with Plenty, which in this Country is the constant Portion of the Industrious.[145]

7.   The next Day being Sunday, we order'd Notice to be sent to all the Neighbourhood, that there wou'd be a Sermon at this Place, and an Opportunity of Christening their Children. But the likelihood of Rain got the better of their Devotion, and what perhaps might still be a stronger motive, of their Curiosity. [43]

In the Morning[t] we dispatch'd a Runner to the Notoway Town, to let the Indians know we intended them a Visit that Evening, and our honest Landlord was so kind as to be our Pilot thither, being about 4 Miles from his House.

Accordingly in the Afternoon we marcht in good Order to the Town, where the Female Scouts, station'd on an Eminence for that Purpose, had no sooner spy'd us, but they gave Notice of our Approach to their Fellow-Citizens by continual Whoops and Cries, which cou'd not possibly have been more dismal at the sight of their most implacable Enemy's.

This Signal assembled all their Great Men, who receiv'd us in a Body, and conducted us into the Fort. This Fort was a square piece of Ground, inclos'd with subtantial Puncheons, or strong Palisades, about ten feet high, and leaning a little outwards to make a Scalade more difficult.[146]

Each side of the Square might be about 100 Yards long, with Loopholes at proper Distances, through which they may fire upon the Enemy[a].

Within this Inclosure we found Bark Cabanes[b] sufficient to lodge all their People, in case they should be obliged to retire thither. These Cabanes are no other but close Arbours made of Saplins, arched at the Top, and cover'd so well with Bark[c], as to be proof against all Weather. The Fire is made in the Middle according to the Hibernian Fashion, the Smoak whereof finds no other Vent but at the Door, and so keeps the whole Family warm, at the Expence both of their Eyes and Complexion.[147]

---

[r]A: some of the Isle of Wight Militia   [s]A: House of Mr Parker   [t]A: Evening *(probably copyist error, anticipating* Evening *later in the sentence)*   [a]A: upon their Enemies
[b]A: Within this Enclosure are Cabanes   [c]A: so well cover'd over with Bark

The Indians have no standing Furniture in their Cabanes, but Hurdles
to repose their Persons upon, which they cover with Mats or Deer Skins. We
were conducted to the best Appartments in the Fort, which just before had
been made ready[d] for our Reception, and adorn'd with new Mats, that were
very sweet and clean.[148]

The Young Men had painted themselves in a Hideous Manner, not so
much for Ornament, as Terror. In that frightful Equipage they entertain'd us
with sundry[e] War-Dances, wherein they endeavour'd to look as formidable as
possible. The Instrument they danc't to, was an Indian-Drum, that is a large
Gourd with a Skin stretch't[f] tort over the Mouth of it. The Dancers all sang to
this Musick keeping exact Time with their Feet, while their Head and Arms
were screw'd into a thousand Menacing Postures.[149]

Upon this Occasion the Ladies had array'd themselves in all their Finery.
They were wrapt[g] in their Red and Blue Match-Coats, thrown so negligently
about them, that their Mehogony Skins appear'd in several Parts, like the
Lacedemonian Damsels of old. Their Hair was breeded with white and Blue
Peak, and hung gracefully in a large Roll upon their Shoulders.[150]

This Peak consists of small Cylinders cut out of a Conque-Shell, drill'd
through[h] and strung like Beads. It serves them both for Money, and Jewels,
the Blue being of much greater Value than the White, for the same reason
that Ethiopian Mistresses in France are dearer than French, because
they are more scarce. The Women wear Neck-laces and Bracelets of these
precious Materials, [44] when they have a mind to appear lovely. Tho' their
complexions be a little sad-colour'd, yet their Shapes are very strait and
well proportion'd. Their Faces are seldom handsome, yet they have an Air of
Innocence and Bashfulness, that with a little less dirt wou'd not fail to make
them desirable. Such Charms might have had their full Effect upon Men,
who had been so long depriv'd of female Conversation, but that the whole
Winter's Soil was so crusted upon the Skins of those dark Angels, that it
requir'd a very strong Appetite to approach them. The Bears Oyl, with which
they anoint their Persons all over, makes their Skins soft, and at the same
time protects them from every Species of Vermin, that use to be troublesome
to other uncleanly People.[151]

We were unluckily so many, that they cou'd not well make us the
Complement of Bedfellows, according to the Indian Rules of Hospitality, tho'
a grave Matron whisper'd one of the Commissioners very civilly in the Ear,
that if her Daughter had been but one year older, she shou'd have been at his
Devotion.[152]

---

[d]A: swept out   [e]A: several   [f]A: brac'd   [g]A: had wrapt themselves   [h]A: and drilled thro'

It is by no means a loss of Reputation, among the Indians, for Damsels that are Single, to have Intrigues with the Men: on the contrary they account it an Argument of superior Merit to be liked by a great Number of Gallants. However, like the Ladys that Game, they are a little Mercenary in their Amours and seldom bestow their Favours, out of Stark Love and Kindness. But after these Women have once appropriated their Charms by Marriage, they are from thenceforth faithful to their Vows, and will hardly ever be tempted by an agreeable Gallant, or be provok't by a Brutal or even by a fumbling Husband to go astray.[153]

The little Work that is done among the Indians, is done by the poor Women[i], while the men are quite Idle, or at most employ'd ^only^ in the Gentlemanly Diversions of Hunting and Fishing.[154]

In this as well as in their Wars, they now use nothing but Fire-Arms[j], which they purchase of the English for Skins. Bows and Arrows are grown into disuse, except only amongst their Boys[k]. Nor is it ill Policy, but on the contrary very prudent thus to furnish the Indians with Fire-Arms, because it makes them depend entirely[l] upon the English, not only for their Trade, but even for their subsistance. Besides they were really able to do more mischief while they made use of Arrows, of which they wou'd let silently fly several in a Minute with wonderful Dexterity, whereas now they hardly ever discharge their Firelocks more than once, which they insiduously do from behind a Tree, and then retire as nimbly, as the Dutch Horse us'd to do now and then formerly in Flanders.[155]

We put the Indians to no expence, but only of a little Corn[m] for our Horses, for which in Gratitude we cheer'd their Hearts with what Rum we had left, which they love better than ^they do^ their Wives and Children[n].

Tho' these Indians dwell among the English, and see [45] in what Plenty a little Industry enables them to live, yet they chuse to continue in their stupid Idleness, and to suffer all the Inconveniences of Dirt, Cold, and Want, rather than disturb their Heads with Care, or defile their Hands with Labour.

The whole Number of People belonging to the Notoway Town, if you include Women and Children, amount to about 200. These are the only Indians of any consequence now remaining within the Limits of Virginia. The rest are either removed, or dwindled to a very inconsiderable Number, either by destroying one another, or by the Small Pox, and other Diseases. Tho' nothing has been so fatal to them as their ungovernable Passion for Rum,

[i]A: is done by the poor Indians is done by the poor Women *(copyist's error)* [j]A: they use nothing but Fire Arms [k]A: except amongst their Boys [l]A: entirely depend [m]A: but only a little Corn [n]A: better than their Wives and Children

with which, I am sorry to say it, they have been ^but^ too liberally supply'd[o] by the English that live near them.[156]

And here I must lament the bad Success, Mr. Boyle's Charity has hitherto had, towards converting any of these poor Heathens to Christianity. Many Children of our Neighbouring Indians have been brought up in the College of William and Mary. They have been taught to read and write, and been carefully Instructed in the Principles of the Christian Religion, till they came to be men. Yet after they return'd home, instead of civilizeing and converting the rest, they have immediately Relapst into Infidelity and Barbarism themselves.[157]

And some of them too have made the worst use of the Knowledge, they acquir'd among the English, by employing it against their Benefactors. Besides as they unhappily forget all the good they learn, and remember the Ill, they are apt to be more vicious and disorderly, than the rest of their Country-men.

I ought not to quit this Subject without doing Justice to the great Prudence of Colo. Spotswood in this Affair. That Gentleman was Lieut. Governor of Virginia, when Carolina was engaged in a Bloody-War with the Indians. At that critical Time, it was thought expedient, to keep a watchfull Eye upon our Tributary Savages, who we knew had nothing to keep them to their Duty but their Fears.

Then it was that he demanded of each Nation a competent Number of their great Men's Children, to be sent to the College, where they serv'd as so many Hostages for the good Behaviour of the Rest, and at the same time were themselves principled in the Christian Religion. He also plac'd a School-Master among the Saponi Indians at the Salary of Fifty Pound ℘[p] Annum, to instruct their Children. The Person that undertook that charitable work was Mr. Charles Griffin, a Man of a good Family, who by the Innocence of his Life, and the Sweetness of his Temper[q], was perfectly well qualify'd for that pious undertaking. Besides he had so much the Secret of mixing Pleasure with Instruction, that he had not a Scholar who did not love him affectionately.[158]

Such Talents must needs have been blest with a proportionable Success, had he not been unluckily remov'd to the College, by which he left the good work, he had began, unfinish't. In short all the Pains he had taken among the Infidels had no other Effect but to make them something cleanlier than other Indians are.[159]

The care Colo. Spotswood took to tincture the Indian Children with

[o]A: have been all along too liberally supply'd [p]V and A: *A common sign for* per *in the eighteenth century.* [q]A: and Sweetness of his Temper

Christianity, produce'd the following Epigram, which was not [46] Publish't during his Administration, for fear it might then have look't like Flattery.

> Long had the Furious Priest assay'd in Vain
> With Sword and Faggot Infidels to gain.
> But now the milder Soldier wisely trys
> By gentler Methods to unveil their Eyes.
> Wonders apart, he knew 'twere vain t'engage
> The fixt Preventions of misguided Age.
> With fairer Hopes he forms the Indian Youth
> To early Manners, Probity, and Truth,
> The Lyon's whelp thus on the Lybian Shore ⎫
> Is tam'd and Gentled by the artful Moor ⎬
> Not the Grim Sire, inured to Blood before. ⎭

I am sorry I can't give a Better Account of the State of the poor Indians with respect to Christianity, altho a great deal of Pains has been, and still continues to be taken with them. For my Part I must be of Opinion, as I hinted before, that there is but one way of converting these poor Infidels, and reclaiming them from Barbarity, and that is charitably to intermarry with them, according to the Modern Policy of the most Christian King in Canada, and Louisiana.[160]

Had the English done this at the first Settlement of the Colony, the Infidelity of the Indians had been worn out at this Day, with their Dark Complexions, and the Country had swarm'd with People more than it does with Insects.

It was certainly an unreasonable Nicety, that prevented their entering into so good-natur'd an Alliance. All Nations of Men have the same Natural Dignity, and we all know that very bright Talents may be lodg'd under a very dark Skin. The principal Difference between one People and another, proceeds only from the Different Opportunities of Improvement.[161]

The Indians by no means want understanding, and are in their Figure tall and well proportion'd. Even their copper-colour'd Complexion wou'd admit of Blanching, if not in the first, at farthest in the second Generation.

I may safely venture to say, the Indian Women would have made altogether as Honest Wives for the first Planters, as the Damsels they us'd to purchase[r] from aboard the Ships. 'Tis strange therefore that any good Christian should have refused a wholesome strait Bedfellow, when he might have had so fair a Portion with her, as the Merit of saving her Soul.[162]

[r]A: they purchas'd

8.   We rested on our clean Mats very comfortably tho' alone, and the next Morning went to the Toilet of some of the Indian Ladys, where what with the Charms of their Persons, and the Smoak of their Apartments, we were almost blinded. They offer'd to give us Silk Grass Baskets of their own making, which we modestly refused, knowing that an Indian present, like that of a Nun, is a Liberality put out to Interest, and a Bribe plac'd to the greatest Advantage.[163]

Our Chaplain observ'd with concern, that the Ruffles of some of our Fellow-Travellers were a little discolour'd with Pochoon, [47] wherewith the good Man had been told those Ladies us'd to improve their invisible Charms.[164]

About 10 a Clock we march[s] out of Town in good order, & the War-Captains saluted us with a Volley of Small-Arms. From thence we proceeded over Black-water Bridge to Colo. Henry Harrisons, where we congratulated each other upon our Return into Christendom.[t,165]

Thus ended our Progress for this Season, which we may justly say was attended with all the Success, that could be expected. Besides the punctual Performance of what was committed to us, we had the Pleasure to bring back every one of our Company in perfect Health. And this we must acknowledge to be a singular Blessing, considering the Difficulties and Dangers to which they had been expos'd.

We had reason to fear the many Waters, and sunken Grounds, thro' which we were oblig'd to wade, might have thrown the men into sundry acute distempers, especially the Dismal, where the Soil was so full of Water, and the Air so full of Damps[a], that nothing but a Dutchman could live in them.

Indeed the Foundation of all our Success was the exceeding dry Season. It rain'd during the whole Journey but rarely, and then, as when Herod built his Temple, only in the Night, or upon the Sabbath when it was no Hinderance at all to our Progress.[166]

[*Part the Second.*][b]

[Sept.]   The tenth of September being thought a little too soon for the Commissioners to meet in order to proceed on the Line, on account of Snakes, 'twas agreed to put it off to the twentieth, of the same Month, of which due Notice was sent to the Carolina Commissioners.[167]

19.   We on the part of Virginia, that we might be sure to be punctual arriv'd at Mr. Kinchins ^the place appointed^ on the 19th after a Journey of three days, in which nothing Remarkable happen'd.

---

[s]A: march't   [t]A: Return to Christianity   [a]A: so full of Damp,   [b]V: *This title, centered in midpage, has been erased or scraped away.* A: Part the Second. *Below this title the word* September *is centered and bold.*

We found three of the Carolina Commissioners had taken Possession of the House, having come thither by water from Edenton. By the Great Quantity of Provisions these Gentlemen brought, and the few men they had to eat them, we were afraid they intended to carry the Line to the South Sea.[168]

They had 500 lb. of Bacon and dry'd Beef, and 500 lb. of Bisket, and not above three or four men. The misfortune was, they forgot to provide Horses to carry their good things, or else trusted to the Incertainty of hireing them here, which considering the place was leaving too much to that Jilt Hazard.[169]

On our part we had taken better Care, being completely furnisht with every thing necessary for transporting our Baggage, and Provisions. Indeed we brought no other Provisions out with us, but 1000 lb. of Bread, and had Faith enough to depend on Providence for our Meat, being desirous to husband the publick Money as much as possible.[c,170]

We had no less than 20 men besides the Chaplain, the Surveyors, and all the Servants to be subsisted upon this Bread.[d] However that it might hold out the better, our men had been order'd to provide themselves at Home with Provision[e] for Ten days, in which time we judg'd we should get beyond the Inhabitants, where Forest Game [48] of all sorts[f] was like to be plenty at that time of the Year.

20. This being the day appointed for our Rendezvous, great part of it was spent in the careful fixing our Baggage[g], and assembling our Men, who were order'd to meet us here. We took care to examine their Arms, and made proof of the Powder provided for the Expedition.

Our Provision-Horses had been hinder'd by the Rain from coming up exactly at the Day; but this Delay was the less Disappointment, by reason of the ten days Subsistence the men had been directed to provide for themselves.

Mr. Moseley did not join us till the afternoon, nor Mr. Swan till several Days after.

Mr. Kinchin[h] had unadvisedly sold the Men a little Brandy of his own making, which produced much disorder, causing some to be too cholerick and others too loving; Insomuch that a Damsel, who assisted in the Kitchen, had certainly suffer'd what the Nuns call Martyrdom, had she not capitulated a little too soon.[171]

This outrage would have call'd for some severe Discipline, had she not bashfully withdrawn herself early in the Morning, & so carry'd off the Evidence.

---

[c]A: to husband the publick Money.   [d]A: upon the Road   [e]A: Provisions   [f]A: Sort   [g]A: in carefully fixing our Baggage   [h]A: Our Landlord

21.　We dispatcht away the Surveyors without Loss of Time, who with all their diligence could carry the Line no farther than 3 Miles and 176 Poles, by reason the Low-Ground was one entire Thicket. In that Distance they crost Meherin River the 4th time. In the mean while the Virginia Commissioners thought proper to conduct their Baggage a farther way about, for the Convenience of a clearer Road.

The Carolina-Gentlemen[i], did at length more by Fortune, than forecast, hire a clumsy Vehicle something like a Cart, to transport their Effects as far as Roanoak. This wretched Machine at first setting out, met with a very rude choque, that broke a Case-Bottle of Cherry Brandy[j] in so unlucky a Manner, that not one precious Drop was saved. This Melancholly Beginning forboded an unprosperous Journey and too quick a Return to the Persons most immediately concern'd.[172]

In our way we crost Fountains Creek, which runs into Meherin River, so call'd from the disaster of an unfortunate Indian Trader, who had formerly been drowned in it, and like Icarus left his name to that fatal Stream. We took up our Quarters on the Plantation of John Hill, where we pitch't our Tent with design to tarry, till such time as the Surveyors cou'd work their way to us.[173]

22.　This being Sunday we had an Opportunity of resting from our Labours. The expectation of such a Novelty as a Sermon in these parts, brought together a numerous Congregation. When the Sermon was over, our Chaplain did his part towards making eleven of them Christians.

Several of our men had Intermitting Feavers, but were soon restored to their Health again by proper Remedies. Our chief Medicine was Dogwood Bark, which we used instead of that of Peru, with good Success. Indeed it was given in larger Quantity: but then to make the the Patients amends, they swallowed much fewer Doses.[174] [49]

In the afternoon our Provision Horses arrived safe in the Camp. They had met with very heavy Rains, but, thank God, not a single Bisket receiv'd the least Damage thereby.

We were furnisht by the Neighbours with very lean Cheese, and very fat Mutton, upon which occasion 'twill not be improper to draw one Conclusion from the Evidence of North-Carolina, that Sheep would thrive much better in the Woods than in Pasture Land, provided a careful Shepherd were employed to keep them from straying, and by the help of Dogs, to protect them also from the Wolves.

23.　The Surveyors came to us at Night, tho' they had not brought the Line so far as our Camp, for which reason, we thought it needless to go forward

[i]A: The Carolina Commissioners　[j]A: of ˮCherryˆ Brandy

til they came up with us. They cou'd run no more than 4 Miles and 5 Poles, because the Ground was every where grown up with thick Bushes.

The Soil here appear'd to be very good, tho' much broken betwixt[k] Fountain Creek and Roanoak River. The Line crost Meherin the 5th and last time, nor were our People sorry to part with a Stream, the Meanders of which had given them so much Trouble.[175]

Our Hunters brought us four wild Turkeys, which at that Season began to be fat and very delicious, especially the Hens.

These Birds seem to be of the Bustard kind, and fly heavily. Some of them are exceedingly large, and weigh upwards of 40 Pound; Nay some bold Historians venture to say, upwards of 50. They run very fast, stretching forth their Wings all the time, like the Ostrich, by way of Sails to quicken their Speed.

They roost commonly upon very high Trees, standing near some River or Creek, and are so stupify'd at the Sight of Fire, that if you make a Blaze in the Night near the place where they roost, you may fire upon them several times successfully, before they will dare to fly away.

Their Spurs are so sharp and strong, that the Indians used formerly to point their Arrows with them, tho' now they point them with a sharp white Stone. In the Spring the Turkey Cocks begin to gobble, which is the Language wherein they make Love.[176]

It rain'd very hard in the Night with a Violent Storm of Thunder, and Lightening, which oblig'd us to trench in our Tent all round, to carry off the Water that fell upon it.

24. So soon as the men could dry their Blankets, we sent out the Surveyors, who now meeting with more favourable Grounds, advanc'd the Line 7 Miles and 82 Poles. However the Commissioners did not think proper to decamp that day, believing they might easily overtake the Surveyors the next. In the mean time they ^sent^ out some of their most expert Gunners, who brought four more Wild Turkeys.

This part of the Country being very proper for raising[l] Cattle and Hogs, we observ'd the Inhabitants lived in great Plenty without killing themselves with Labour.

I found near our Camp some Plants of that kind of Rattle-Snake Root, called Star-Grass. The Leaves shoot out Circularly, and grow Horizontally and near the Ground. The Root is in Shape not unlike the Rattle of that Serpent, and is a Strong Antidote against the Bite of it; It is very bitter, and where it meets [50] with any Poison, works by Violent Sweat, but where it meets with

[k]A: between   [l]A: to raise

none, has no Sensible Operation, but that of putting the Spirits into a great Hurry[m], and so of promoting Perspiration.[177]

The Rattle-snake hath an utter Antipathy to this Plant, insomuch that if you smear your hands with the Juice of it, you may handle the Viper safely. Thus much I can say on my own Experience, that once in July, when these Snakes are in their greatest Vigour, I besmear'd a Dog's Nose with the Powder of this Root, and made him trample on a large Snake several times, which however was so far from biteing him, that it perfectly sicken'd at the Dog's Approach, and turn'd its Head from him with the utmost Aversion.[178]

Our Chaplain, to shew his Zeal, made an Excursion of 6 Miles to Christen 2 Children[n], but without[o] the least regard to the good chear at these Solemnities.

25. The Surveyors taking the Advantage of clear Woods, push't on the Line 7 Miles and 40 Poles. In the mean time the Commissioners march't with the Baggage about 12 Miles, and took up their Quarter's near the Banks of the Beaver Pond, (which is one Branch of Fountain's Creek) just by the place where the Surveyors were to finish their day's work.

In our march one of the men kill'd a small Rattle Snake, which had no more than two Rattles. Those Vipers remain in Vigour generally till towards the End of September, or sometimes later, if the Weather continues a little warm. On this consideration we had provided three several sorts of Rattle Snake Root, made up into proper Doses, and ready for immediate use, in case any one of the Men, or their Horses had been bitten.[179]

We cros't Fountain's Creek once more in our Journey this day, and found the Grounds very Rich, notwithstanding they were broken and stony.

Near the place where we encampt, the county of Brunswick is divided from[p] the Isle of Wight. These Counties run quite on the back of Surry and Prince George, and are laid out in very irregular Figures.

As a Proof of the Land mended hereabouts, we found the Plantations began to grow thicker by much, than we had found them lower down.

26. We hurry'd away the Surveyors without Loss of time, who extended the Line 10 Miles and 160 Poles, the Ground proving dry and free from Underwoods. By the way the chain carriers kill'd two more Rattle Snakes, which I own was a little ungrateful, because two or three of the Men had strided over them without receiving any Hurt. Tho one of these Vipers had made bold to strike at one of the Baggage Horses, as he went along, but by good Luck his Teeth only grazed on the hoof, without doing him any Damage.

[m]V: *Following clause added in Byrd's hand in space at end of line]* A: a great Hurry.
[n]A: to Christen a few Children [o]A: with *(copyist error)* [p]A: divided by *(copyist error)*

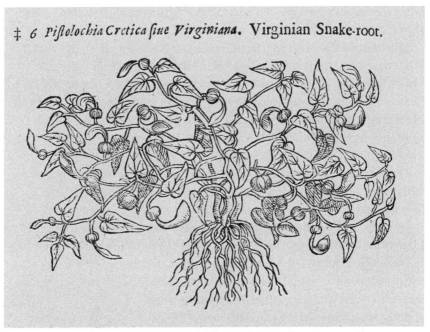

‡ *6 Piſtolochia Cretica ſiue Virginiana.* Virginian Snake-root.

PLATE 4. Virginia Snakeroot. *John Gerarde,* The Herball; or, Generall Historie of Plantes *(London, 1633). This item is reproduced by permission of the Huntington Library, San Marino, California*

However these Accidents were I think so many Arguments[q], that we had very good Reason to defer our coming out till the 20th of September.[180]

We observ'd Abundance of St. Andrews Cross in all the Woods, we past thro', which is the common Remedy used by the Indian [51] Traders to cure their Horses, when they are bitten by Rattle-Snakes. It grows on a strait Stem about 18 Inches high, and bears a Yellow Flower on the Top, that has an Eye of Black in the Middle, with several Pairs of Narrow Leaves shooting out at right Angles from the Stalk over against one another.[181]

This Antidote grows Providentially all over the Woods, and upon all sorts of Soil, that it may be every where at hand in Case a Disaster should Happen, and may be had all the hot Months, while the Snakes are dangerous.[182]

About four a clock in the Afternoon we took up our Quarters upon Caban Branch, which also discharges itself into Fountain-Creek. On our way we observed several Meadows cloath'd with very rank Grass and Branches full of tall Reeds, in which Cattle keep themselves fat good part of the Winter. But Hogs are as injurious to both, as Goats are said to be to Vines, and for that

[q]A: were so many Arguments

Reason it was not lawfull to Sacrifice them to Bacchus. We halted by the way to Christen two Children at a Spring, where their Mothers way laid us for that good Purpose.[183]

27. It was ten of the Clock before the Surveyors got to work, because some of the Horses had straggled a great Distance from the Camp. Nevertheless meeting with Practicable Woods, they advanc't the Line 9 Miles and 104 Poles. We cros't over Pea-Creek about four Miles from our Quarters, and three Miles farther Lizzard-Creek, both which empty their Waters into Roanoak River.

Between these two Creeks a poor Man waited for us with five Children to be baptiz'd, and we halted till the Ceremony was ended. The Land seem'd to be very good by the largeness of the Trees, tho' very stony. We proceeded as far as Pigeon-Roost-Creek, which also runs into Roanoak, and there Quarter'd.

We had not the pleasure of the Company of any of the Carolina Commissioners in this days March, except Mr. Moseleys, the rest tarrying behind, to wait the coming up of their Baggage Cart, which they had now not seen nor heard (tho the wheels made a Dismal Noise) for several days past.

Indeed it was a very difficult Undertaking to conduct a Cart thro' such pathless and perplex't Woods, and no wonder, if the Motion was a little Planetary. We would[r] have pay'd them the Complement of waiting for them, cou'd we have done it at any other Expence, but that of the Publick.[184]

In the stony Grounds we rode over, we found great Quantity of the true Ipocoacanna, which in this part of the World is call'd Indian-Physick. This hath several Stalks growing up from the same Root about a Foot high, bearing a Leaf resembling that of a Straw-Berry. It is not so strong, as that from Brasil, but has the same ^happy^ Effects, if taken in somewhat a larger Dose. It is an excellent Vomit, and generally cures intermitting Fevers, and Bloody Fluxes at once or twice taking. There is abundance of it in the upper part of the Country, where it delights most in a stony Soil intermixt with black Mold.[185]

28. Our Surveyors got early to work, yet cou'd forward the Line but 6 Miles 121 Poles, because of the uneven Grounds[s] in the [52] Neighbourhood of Roanoak, which they crost in this[t] Days work.

In that Place the River is 49 Poles wide, and rolls down a crystal Stream of very sweet water, Insomuch that when there comes to be a great Monarch in this Part of the World, he will cause all the Water for his own Table, to be brought from Roanoak, as the great King's of Persia did theirs from the Nile,

---

[r]A: cou'd *(copyist error, anticipating the* cou'd *in the next clause)*   [s]A: the unevenness of the Grounds   [t]A: that

and Choaspis, because the Waters of those Rivers were light, and not apt to corrupt.[186]

*[a]The same Humour prevails at this day in[b] the Kings of Denmark, who order all the East India ships[c] of that nation to call[d] at the Cape of Good Hope and take in a But of Water from a Spring on[e] the Table Hill and bring ^it^ to Coppenhagen[f] for Their Majestys own Drinking.[187]

The great Falls of Roanoak lie about 20 Miles lower, to which a Sloop of moderate Burthen may come up. There are besides these many smaller Falls above, tho' none that intirely intercept the Passage of the River, as the great ones do, by a Chain of Rocks for 8 Miles together.

The River forks about 36 Miles higher, and both Branches are pretty equal in Breadth where they divide, tho the Southern, now call'd the Dan, runs up the farthest[g]. That to the North runs away near Northwest, and is call'd the Staunton, & heads not far from the Source of Appamatuck River, while the Dan stretches away pretty near West, & runs clear thro the great Mountains.[188]

We did not follow the Surveyors till towards Noon, being detain'd in our Camp, to Christen several more Children. We were conducted a nearer way by a famous Woodsman call'd Epaphroditus Bainton. This Forrester spends all his time in ranging the Woods, and is said to make great Havock among the Deer, and other Inhabitants of the Forrest, not much wilder than Himself.[189]

We proceeded to the Canoe Landing on Roanoak, where we past the River with the Baggage. But the Horses were directed to a Ford about a Mile higher, call'd by the Indians Moni-seep, which signifies in their Jargon, Shallow Water. This is the Ford where the Indian Traders used to cross with their Horses in their way to the Catawba-Nation.[190]

There are many Rocks in the River thereabouts, on which grows a kind of a Water Grass, which the wild Geese are fond of, and resort to it[h] in great numbers.[191]

We landed on the South Side of Roanoak at a Plantation of Colo. Mumfords, where by that Gentleman's special Directions we met with sundry Refreshments. Here we pitch our Tent for the benefit of the Prospect upon an Eminence that over look't a broad Piece of[i] Low Ground very rich, tho' liable to be overflow'd.[192]

By the way one of our men kill'd another Rattle-Snake with 11 Rattles, having a large Grey Squirrel in his Maw, the head of which was already digested, while the Body remain'd stil entire.[193]

---

[a]V: *An asterisk indicates the insertion of the next paragraph, as written in the left margin of p. 52.* [b]A: with [c]A: every E. India Ship [d]A: touch [e]A: from the Table Hill [f]A: and bring it home [g]A: runs the farthest up [h]A: thither [i]A: a large Piece of

PLATE 5. Rattlesnake Charming a Squirrel. *John Lawson,* A New Voyage to Carolina . . . *(London, 1709). This item is reproduced by permission of the Huntington Library, San Marino, California*

The way these Snakes catch their Prey is thus: They Ogle the poor little
Animal till by force of the Charm he falls down stupify'd and senseless on
the Ground. In that condition the Snake approaches, and moistens – first one
Ear, and then[j] the Other with his Spawl, and after that the other Parts of the
Head, to make all Slippery. When that is done, he draws this Member into his
Mouth, and after it by slow Degrees all the rest of the Body.[194]

30.   This being Sunday, we had Divine Service, and a Sermon, at which
several of the Borderers assisted, and we concluded the Duties of the Day[k]
with Christening five Children. Our Devotion[l] being perform'd in the open
Field, like that of Mr. Whitfields Flocks[m], [53] an unfortunate Shower of Rain
had almost dispers't our Congregation.[195]

About four in the Afternoon the Carolina Commissioners made a Shift
to come up with us, whom we had left at Pidgeon-Roost-Creek the Fryday
before, waiting for their Provisions. When their Cart came up they prudently
discharg'd it, and rather chose to hire two Men to carry some part of their
Baggage. The Rest they had been oblig'd to leave behind in the Crotch of an
old Tree, for want of proper Conveniences to transport it any farther.

We found in the low Ground several Plants of the Fern Root, which is said
to be much the strongest Antidote yet discover'd against the Poison of the
Rattle Snake. The Leaves of it resemble those of Fern, from whence it obtain'd
its Name. Several Stalks shoot from the same Root about 6 Inches long, that
ly mostly on the Ground. It grows in a very Rich Soil, under the Protection
of some tall Tree, that shades it from the Meridian Beams of the Sun. The
Root has a faint spicy tast, and is prefer'd by the Southern Indians to all other
Counterpoisons in this Country.[196]

But there is another Sort prefer'd by the Northern Indians, that they call
Seneca Rattle Snake Root, to which wonderful Vertues are ascrib'd in the
Cure of Pleurisys, Feavers, Rhumatisms, and Dropsys; besides it being a
^powerfull^ Antidote[n] against the Venom of the Rattle Snake.[197]

In the Evening the Messenger we had sent to Christanna, return'd with five
Saponi Indians. We cou'd not entirely rely on the Dexterity of our own Men,
which induced us to send for some of the[o] Indians. We agreed with two of the
most expert of them, upon reasonable Terms, to hunt for us the remaining
Part of our Expedition. But one of them falling sick soon after, we were
content to take only the other, whose Hunting Name was Bearskin.[198]

This Indian either by his Skill, or good Luck, supply'd us plentifully all the
way with Meat, seldom dischargeing his Piece in vain.

[j]A: after that   [k]A: the Duties of the Duties of the Day *(copyist error: repetition)*
[l]A: Devotions   [m]A: like Mr. Whitfield's Flocks   [n]A: an Antidote   [o]A: these

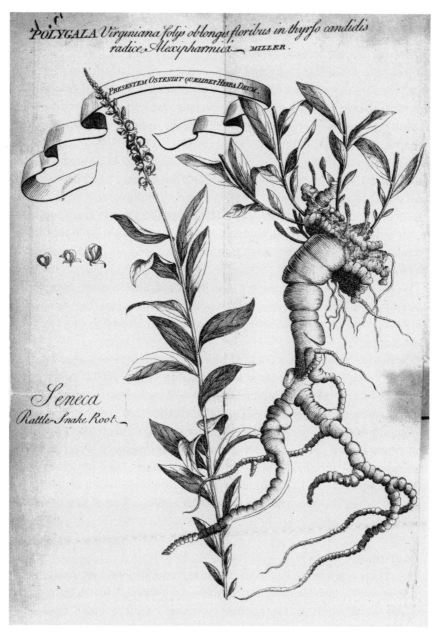

PLATE 6. Seneca Rattlesnake Root. *John Tennent,* An Epistle to Dr. Richard Mead . . .
(Edinburgh, 1742). Permission The Virginia Historical Society

By his Assistance therefore we were able to keep our men to their Business, without suffering them to straggle about the Woods, on pretence of furnishing us with necessary Food.

30. It had rain'd all night, and made every thing so wet, that our Surveyors cou'd not get to their Work before noon. They cou'd therefore measure no more than four Miles and 220 Poles, which according to the best information we cou'd get, was near as high as the uppermost Inhabitant at the time.

We cros't the Indian Trading Path abovemention'd about a Mile from our Camp, and a Mile[p] beyond that, forded Haw-Tree-Creek. The Woods, we past thro' had all the Tokens of Sterility, except a small Poison'd Field, on which grew no Tree bigger than a slender Saplin. The Larger[q] Trees had been destroyed either by Fire, or Caterpillars, which is often the Case in the upland Woods, and the places where such Desolation happens, are call'd Poison'd Fields.

We took up our Quarters upon a Branch of Great Creek, where there was tolerable good Grass for the poor Horses. These poor Animals having now got beyond the Latitude of Corn, were oblig'd to shift as well as they cou'd for them selves.[199]

On our way the men rous'd a Bear which being the first we [54] had seen since we came out, the poor Beast had many Pursuers. Several Persons contended for the Credit of killing Him: tho' he was so poor, he was not worth the Powder. This was some Disappointment to our Woodsmen, who commonly prefer the Flesh of Bears[r] to every kind of Venison. There is something indeed peculiar to this Animal, namely that its fat is very firm, and may be eaten plentifully without rising in the Stomach. The Paw (which when stript of the hair looks like a Human Foot) is accounted a delicious Morsel, by all, who are not shockt at the ungracious Resemblance it bears to a Human Foot.[200]

OCTOBER[s]

1. There was a white Frost this morning on the Ground, occasion'd by a Northwest Wind, which stood our Friend in dispersing all Aguish Damps, and making the Air wholsome, at the same time that it made it cold. Encourag'd therefore by the Weather our Surveyors got to work early, and by the Benefit of clear Woods, and level Grounds drove the Line 12 Miles and 12 Poles.

At a small Distance from our Camp we cros't Great Creek, and about

[p]A: and about a Mile   [q]A: large   [r]A: Bear   [s]V: *Month given at upper left-hand corner of p. 54]* A: *Month given in large, dark letters, centered on journal p. 106.*

7 Miles farther Nut-bush Creek, so call'd from the many Hazle-Trees growing upon it. By good Luck many Branches of these Creeks were full of Reeds, to the great comfort of our Horses. Near five miles from thence, we encampt on a Branch, that runs into Nut-bush Creek, where those Reeds[t] flourish't more than ordinary. The Land, we march't over, was for the most part broken and stony, and in some places cover'd over with Thickets almost impenetrable.

At Night the Surveyors, taking the Advantage of a very clear Sky, made a third Tryal of the Variation, and found it still something less than 3 Degrees, so that it did not diminish by advancing towards the West, or by approaching the Mountains, nor yet by encreasing our distance from the Sea: but remain'd much the same, we had found it at Corotuck-Inlet.[201]

One of our Indians kill'd a large Fawn, which was very welcome, tho' like Hudibras's Horse it had hardly Flesh enough to cover its Bones.[202]

In the low Grounds the Carolina Gentlemen shew'd us another Plant, which they said was us'd in their Country to cure the Bite of the Rattle Snake. It put forth several Leaves in figure like a Heart; and was clouded ^so^ like the common Assa-rabacca, that I conceiv'd it to be of that Family.[203]

2.   So soon as the Horses cou'd be found, we hurry'd away the Surveyors, who advanc't the Line 9 Miles and 254 Poles. About 3 Miles from the Camp, they cros't a large Creek, which the Indians call'd Massamoni, signifying in their Language, Paint-Creek, because of the great Quantity of red Ocre found in its banks. This in every Fresh tinges the Water just as the same Mineral did formerly, and to this day continues to tinge the famous River Adonis in Phoenicia, by which there hangs a celebrated Fable.[204]

Three Miles beyond that, we past another Water with difficulty, call'd Yaypatsco, or Bever-Creek. Those industrious Animals had damm'd up the Water so high, that we had much ado to get over. [55]

'Tis hardly credible how much work of this kind they will do in the Space of one Night[a]. They bite young Saplins into proper Lengths[b] with their Fore-teeth, which are exceeding Strong, and Sharp, and afterwards drag them to the Place, where they intend to stop the Water.

Then they know how to join Timber, and Earth together with so much Skill, that their Work is[c] able to resist the most violent Flood[d], that can happen. In this they are qualify'd to instruct their Betters, it being certain their Damms will stand firm, when the strongest, that are made by men, will be carry'd down the Stream.

We observ'd very broad low Grounds upon this Creek, with a growth of

---

[t]A: on a Branch, where those Reeds   [a]A: do in one Night   [b]A: Length   [c]A: works are
[d]A: Floods

large Trees, and all the other Signs of Fertility, but seem'd subject to be every where overflow'd in a Fresh.

The certain way to catch these sagacious Animals is thus, squeeze all the Juice out of the large Pride of the Beaver, and 6 Drops out of the small Pride. Powder the inward Bark of Sassafras, and mix it with this Juice, then bait therewith a Steel Trap, and they will eagerly come to it, and be taken.[205]

About three Miles and an half farther we came to the Banks of another Creek, call'd in the Saponi Language, Ohimpa-moni, signifying Jumping Creek from the frequent Jumping of Fish during the Spring Season.

Here we encampt, and by the time the Horses were hobbled, our Hunters brought us no less than a Brace and an half of Deer, which made great Plenty, and consequently great content in our Quarters.

Some of our People had shot a great Wild-Cat, which was that fatal moment making a comfortable Meal upon a Fox Squirrel, and an ambitious Sportsman of our Company, claim'd the merit of killing this monster after it was dead.

The Wild-Cat is as big again as any Household-Cat, and much the fiercest Inhabitant of the Woods. Whenever 'tis disabled, it will tear its own Flesh for madness. Altho' a Panther will run away from a Man, a Wild-Cat will only make a surly Retreat, now and then facing about if he be too closely pursued, and will even pursue in his turn, if he observe the least Sign of Fear, or even of caution in those that pretend to follow Him.[206]

The Flesh of this Beast as well, as of the Panther, is as white as Veal, and altogether as sweet and delicious.[207]

3. We got to work early this Morning, and carry'd the Line 8 Miles and 160 Poles. We forded several Runs of excellent Water, and afterwards traverst a large levil of high land full of lofty Walnut, Poplar, and White Oak Trees, which are certain Proofs of a fruitful Soil. This Levil was near two Miles in length, and of an unknown breadth, quite out of Danger of being overflow'd, which is a Misfortune most of the Low Grounds are liable to in those parts.[208]

As we march't along we saw many Buffalo-Tracks, and abundance of their Dung very Fresh, but could not have the Pleasure of seeing them. They either smelt us out, having that sense very Quick, or else were alarmed at the Noise, that so many People must necessarily make in marching along.[209]

At the Sight of a Man, they will Snort and Grunt, cock up [56] their ridiculous short Tails, and tear up the Ground with a sort of Timorous Fury.

These wild Cattle hardly ever range alone, but herd together like those that are tame. They are seldom seen so far North as 40° of Latitude, delighting much in Canes and Reeds[e], which grow generally more Southerly.[210]

---

[e]A: in Reeds and Canes

We quarter'd on the Banks of a Creek, that the Inhabitants call, Tewahominy, or Tuskarooda Creek, because one of that Nation had been kill'd thereabouts, and his Body thrown into the Creek.[211]

Our People had the Fortune to kill a Brace of Does, one of which we presented to the Carolina-Gentlemen, who were glad to partake of the Bounty of Providence, at the same time, that they sneer'd at us for depending upon it.

4.   We hurry'd away the Surveyors about 9 this Morning, who extended the Line 7 Miles and 160 Poles, notwithstanding the Ground was exceedingly uneaven. At the Distance of five Miles we forded a Stream to which we gave the Name of Bl^u^ewing-Creek, because of the great Number of these Fowls, that then frequented it.[212]

About 2½ Miles beyond that, we came upon Sugar-Tree-Creek, so call'd from the many Trees of that kind, that grow upon it. By tapping this Tree in the first warm weather in February, one may get from 20 to 40 Gallons of Liquor very sweet to the tast, and agreable to the Stomach. This may be boil'd into Molosses first, and afterwards into very good Sugar, allowing about 10 Gallons of the Liquor to make a Pound. There's no doubt too but a very fine Spirit may be distill'd from the Molosses, at least as good as Rum. The Sugar Tree delights only in Rich Ground, where it grows very tall, and by the softness and spunginess of the Wood shou'd be a quick Grower.[213]

Near this Creek we discovered likewise[f] several Spice-Trees, the Leaves of which are fragrant, and the Berries, they bear are black when dry, and of a hot tast, not much unlike Pepper.[214]

The low Grounds upon the Creek are very wide, sometimes on one Side, sometimes on the other, tho' most commonly upon the opposite Shore the high-land advances close to the Bank, only on the North-Side of the Line, it spreads itself into a great Breadth of rich low Ground[g] on both sides the Creek for four Miles together, as far as this Stream runs into Hico-River, whereof I shall presently make mention.

One of our Men spy'd three Buffalos but his Piece being loaden only[h] with Goose-shot, he was able to make no effectual Impression on their thick Hides: However this Disappointment was made up by a Brace of Bucks, and as many Wild Turkeys kill'd by the rest of the Company.

Thus Providence was very Bountiful to our Endeavour, never disappointing those that faithfully rely upon it, and pray heartily for their Daily Bread.

5.   This day we met with such uneven Grounds, and thick Underwoods, that with all our Industry we were able to advance the Line but 4 Miles 312 Poles. In this small Distance it [57] intersected a large Stream four

[f]A: we likewise discover'd   [g]A: Grounds   [h]A: only loaden

times, which our Indian at first mistook for the South Branch of Roanoke River: but discovering his Error soon after, he assured us twas a River call'd Hicootomony, or Turky Buzzard River, from the great Number of those unsavory Birds, that roost on the tall Trees growing near its Banks.[215]

Early in the Afternoon to our very great Surprize the Commissioners of Carolina acquainted us with their Resolution to return Home. This Declaration of theirs seem'd the more abrupt, because they had not been so kind as to prepare us by the least Hint of their Intention to desert us.[216]

We therefore let them understand, they appear'd to us to abandon the Business they came about with too much Precipitation, this being but the 15th day since we came out the last time. But altho' we were to be so unhappy as to lose the Assistance of their great Abilities, yet we who were concern'd for Virginia, determin'd by the Grace of God not to do our Work by Halves. But all deserted, as we were like to be, shou'd think it our duty to push the Line quite to the Mountains. And if their Government should refuse to be bound by so much of the Line, as was run without their Commissioners, yet at least it would bind Virginia, and stand as a Direction how far his Majesty's Lands extend to the Southward.[217]

In short these Gentlemen were positive, and the most we could agree upon was to subscribe Plats of our work so far as we had acted together, tho' at the same time we insisted, these Plats should be got ready by Monday noon at farthest, when we on the Part of Virginia intended, if we were alive, to move forward without farther Loss of Time, the Season being then too far advanc't to admit of any unnecessary or complaisant delays.

6.   We lay still this day being Sunday on the Bank of Hico River, and had only Prayers, our Chaplain not having Spirits enough to preach. The Gentlemen of Carolina assisted not at our Publick Devotions, because they were taken up all the Morning in making a formidable Protest against our Proceeding on the Line without them.

When the Divine Service was over, the Surveyors set about making the Plats of so much of the Line, as we had run this last Campaign. Our pious Friends of Carolina assisted in this work with some seeming Scruples, pretending it was a Violation of the Sabbath, which we were the more surpriz'd at, because it happen'd to be the first Qualm of Conscience they had ever been troubled with dureing the whole Journey. They had made no Bones of staying from Prayers to hammer out an unnecessary Protest, tho' Divine Service was no sooner over, but an unusual Fit of Godliness made them fancy that finishing the Plats, which was now matter of necessity, was a Prophanation of the Day. However the Expediency of losing no time, for us who thought it our duty to finish what we had undertaken, made such a Labour pardonable.

In the Afternoon Mr. Fitz-William, one of the Commissioners for Virginia, acquainted his Collegues, it was his Opinion, that by his Majesty's Order they could not proceed farther on the Line, but in Conjunction with the Commissioners of Carolina, for which [58] reason he intended to retire the next Morning with those Gentlemen.

This look't a little odd in our Brother Commissioner, tho' in Justice to Him, as well as to our Carolina Friends[i], they stuck by us as long, as our good Liquor lasted, and were so kind to us, as to drink our good Journey to the Mountains in the last Bottle we had left.

7.   The Duplicates of the Plats cou'd not be drawn fair this day before Noon, when they were countersign'd by the Commissioners of each Government. Then those of Carolina deliver'd their Protest, which was by this time lick't into form, and sign'd by them all. And we have been so just to them, as to set it down at full length in the Appendix, that their Reasons for leaving us may appear in their full Strength.[218]

After having thus adjusted all our Affairs, with the Carolina-Commissioners, and kindly supply'd them with Bread to carry them back, which they hardly deserv'd at our hands, we took leave both of them, and of our Colleague Mr. Fitz-William.

This Gentleman had still a stronger Reason for hurrying him back to Williamsburg, which was, that neither the General Court might lose an able Judge, nor himself a double Salary, not despairing in the least but he shou'd have the whole pay of Commissioner into the Bargain, tho' he did not half the Work. This to be sure was relying more on the Interest of his Friends, than on the Justice of his Cause, in which however he had the misfortune to miscarry[j], when it came to be fairly consider'd.[219]

It was two a Clock in the Afternoon, before these arduous Affairs could be dispatch't, and then all forsaken as we were, we held on our Course towards the West, But it was our misfortune to meet with so many Thickets in this Afternoon's Work, that we cou'd advance no farther than 2 Miles and 160 Poles.

In this small Distance we cros't the Hico the fifth time, and Quarter'd near Buffalo-Creek, so nam'd from the frequent Tokens, we discover'd of that American Behemoth.

---

[i]A: as to our Carolina Friends   [j]A: to miscarry] V: *phrase following inserted at end of line in Byrd's hand.*

Here the Bushes were so intolerably thick, that we were oblig'd to cover the Bread Baggs with our Deer Skins otherwise the Joke of one of the Indians must have happen'd to us in good Earnest, that in a few days we must cut up our House to make Bags for the Bread, and so be[k] forc't to expose our Backs in Compliment ^to^ our Bellys[l].

We computed we had then Bisquet enough left to last us with good Management seven Weeks longer; and this being our chief Dependance, it imported us to be very careful, both in the Carriage, and Distribution of it.

We had now no other Drink, but what Adam drank in Paradise, tho to our comfort we found the Water excellent, by the Help of which we perceiv'd[m] our Appetites to mend, our Slumber to sweeten, the Stream of Life to run cool and peaceably in our Veins, and if ever we dreamt of Women, they were kind.

Our men kill'd a very fat Buck, and several Turkeys. These two kinds of Meat boil'd together, with the Addition of a little Rice[n] or French Barley, made excellent Soupe and what [59] happens rarely in other good things, it never cloy'd; no more than an engaging Wife wou'd do, by being a constant Dish.

Our Indian was very Superstitious in this Matter, and told us, with a Face[o] full of Concern, that if we continued to boil Venison and Turkey together, we shou'd for the future kill nothing, because the Spirit that presided over the Woods, would drive all the Game out of our Sight. But we had the Happiness to find this an Idle Superstition, and tho' his Argument could not convince us, yet our repeated Experience at last with much ado convinc'd him.[220]

We observ'd abundance of Colt's-foot, and Maidenhair in many Places, and nowhere a larger Quantity than here. They are both excellent Pectoral Plants, and seem to have greater Virtues much in this part of the World, than in more Northern Climates, and I believe it may pass for a Rule in Botanicks, that where any Vegetable is planted by the hand of Nature, it has more Vertue than in Places whereto it is transplanted by the Curiosity of Man.[221]

8. Notwithstanding we hurry'd away the Surveyors very early, yet the Underwoods embarrass'd them so much, that they cou'd with Difficulty advance the Line 4 Miles and 20 Poles.

Our Cloaths suffer'd extreamly by the Bushes, and it was really as much as both our hands could do to preserve our Eyes in our Heads. Our poor Horses too could hardly drag their Loads thro'the Saplins, which stood so close together, that it was necessary for them to draw and carry at the same time.[222]

We quarter'd near a Spring of very fine Water as soft as Oyl, and as cold as

[k]A: we must cut up our House, for our Bread to lodge in, and be   [l]A: to Complement our Bellys   [m]A: found   [n]A: together with a little Rice   [o]V: *Lowercase* f *made uppercase with a top stroke.*

Ice, to make us amends for the want of Wine. And our Indian knockt down a very fat Doe just time enough to hinder us from going supperless to Bed.

The heavy Baggage cou'd not come up with us, because of the excessive badness of the Ways. This gave us no small Uneasiness, but it went worse with the poor men, that guarded it. They had nothing in the World with them but dry Bread, nor durst they eat any of that, for fear of inflaming their Thirst, in a place where they could find no Water to quench it.[223]

This was however the better to be endured, because it was the first Fast, any one had kept during the whole Journey, and then, Thanks to the gracious Guardian of the Woods, there was no more than a single Meal lost to a few of the Company.

We were entertain'd this Night with the Yell of a whole Family of Wolves, in which we cou'd distinguish the Treble, Tenor, and Base very clearly. These Beasts of Prey kept pretty much upon our Track, being tempted by the Garbage of the Creatures we kill'd every day: For which we were serenaded with their shrill Pipes almost every Night[p]. This Beast is not so untameable, as the Panther but the Indians know how to gentle their Whelps, and use them about their cabans instead of Dogs.[224]

9.   The Thickets were hereabouts so impenetrable, that we were obliged at first setting off this Morning, to order four Pioneers to clear the way before the Surveyors. But after about 2 Miles of these rough woods, we had the Pleasure to meet with open Grounds, [60] and not very uneaven, by the help of which we were enabled to push the Line about 6 Miles.

The Baggage, that lay short of our Camp last Night, came up about Noon, and the men made heavy Complaints, that they had been half starv'd like Tantalus, in the midst of Plenty, for the Reason abovemention'd.[225]

The Soil, we past over this Day, was generally very good, being cloath'd with large Trees, of Poplar, Hiccory, and Oak. But another certain Token of it's Fertility was, that wild Angelica grew plentifully[q] upon it.

The Root of this Plant, being very warm and aromatick, is coveted by Woodsmen extremely as a dry Dram, that is, when Rum that Cordial for all Distresses is wanting.[226]

Several Deer came into our View as we march't along, but none into the Pot, which made it necessary for us to sup on the Fragments, we had been so provident, as to carry along with us. This being but a temperate[r] Repast, made some of our hungry Fellows call the Place we lodg'd at that Night, Bread and Water Camp.

[p]A: we were serenaded every Night with their Shrill Pipes   [q]A: grew very plentifully
[r]A: moderate

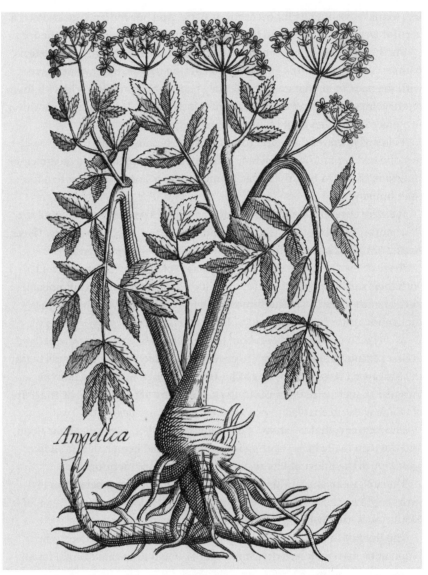

PLATE 7. Angelica. *[Pierre] Pomet,* A Compleat History of Druggs *(London, 1712). This item is reproduced by permission of the Huntington Library, San Marino, California*

A great Flock of Cranes flew over our Quarters, that were exceeding clamorous in their Flight. They seem[s] to steer their Course towards the South (being Birds of Passage) in Quest of warmer Weather. They only took this Country in their way being as rarely met with in this part of the World, as a Highwayman, or a Beggar.

These Birds travel generally in Flocks, and when they roost they place Sentinels upon some of the highest Trees, which constantly stand upon one leg to keep themselves waking.[227,*t]

Nor are these Birds the only Animals that appoint Scouts to keep the main Body from Being surprizd [by the Enemy][a]. For the Babboons whenever they go upon[b] any mischievous Expedition, such as robbing[c] an Orchard, [the first thing] they [do, is to] place Centinels[d] to look out [sharp][e] towards every Point of the Compass, & give Notice of any danger[f]. Then ranking themselves in one[g] File, that reaches from the Mountain where they harbour[h], to the Orchard they intend to rob, some of them toss the Fruit from the Trees[i] to those that stand nearest, these [in an instant][j] throw them to the next, and so from one to tother til the fruit is all secur'd[k] in a few Minutes out of Harms Way. In the mean time[l] if any of the Scouts shou'd [happen to][m] be careless at[n] their Posts, & suffer any Surprize, they are[o] torn to pieces without Mercy. In case of danger these Centinels set up a fearfull cry[p], upon which[q] the rest take the alarm, and scour away to the Mountains as fast as [their legs will carry them[r]].[228]

Our Indian kill'd nothing all day, but a Mountain Partridge, which a little resembled the common Partridge in the Plumage, but was near as large as a Dunghill Hen. These are very frequent towards the Mountains, tho' we had the fortune to meet with very few. They are apt to be shy, and consequently the Noise of so great a Number of People might easily scare them away from our Sight.[229]

We found what we conceiv'd to be good Lime Stone in several Places, and a great Quantity of Blue Slate.[230]

10.   The day began very fortunately by killing a Fat Doe, and two Brace of wild Turkeys, so[s] the Plenty of the Morning made amends for the short

---

[s]A: seem'd   [t]V: *Asterisk indicates place for insertion of marginal addition, the paragraph following. A revisions are here given in square brackets.*   [a]A: surpriz'd by the Enemy. [b]A: are bound on   [c]A: pilfering of   [d]A: the first thing they do, is to place their Centinels [e]A: to look out sharp   [f]A: in Case of Danger   [g]A: a long   [h]A: from their Habitation in the Mountains   [i]A: those that gather the Fruit toss it to   [j]A: these in an instant   [k]A: all is convey'd   [l]A: mean while   [m]A: shou'd happen to   [n]A: in   [o]A: will be   [p]A: yell [q]A: at which   [r]V: they can.] A: their legs will carry them   [s]A: so that

Commons over Night. One of the new men we brought out with us the last time, was unfortunately heard to wish himself at Home, and for that Shew of Impatience was publickly reprimanded at the Head of the men, who were ^all^ drawn up to witness his Disgrace.

He was askt, how he came so soon to be tired of the Company of so many brave Fellows, and whether it was the Danger or the Fatigue of the Journey, that dishearten'd Him? This publick Reproof, from thence forward put an effectual Stop to all Complaints, and not a man amongst us after that pretended so much as to wish himself in Paradise.[61ᵗ]

A small Distance from our Camp, we cros't a pleasant Stream of Water call'd Cocquade Creek, and something more than a Mile from thence our Line intersected the South Branch of Roanoak River, the first time, which we call'd the Dan. It was about [150] 200 Yardsᵃ wide, where we forded it, and when we came over to the West Side we found the Banks lin'd with a Forest of Tall Canesᵇ, that grew more than a Furlong in depth. So that it cost us abundance of time and Labour to cut a Passage thro' them wide enough for our Baggage.

In the mean time we had Leizure to take a full view of this charming River. The Stream, which was perfectly clear, ran down about two Knots, or two Miles anᶜ Hour, when the water was at the lowest. The Bottom was cover'd with a coarse Gravel, spangled very thick with a shining Substance, that almost dazzled the Eye, and the Sand upon either Shore sparkled with the same splendid Particles.[231]

At first Sight the Sun Beamsᵈ giving a Yellow cast to these Spangles, made us fancy them to be Gold-Dust, and consequently that all our Fortunes were made. Such Hopes as these were the less extravagant, because several Rivers lying much about the same Latitude with this, have formerly abounded with Fragments of that tempting Metal.[232] Witness the Tagus in Portugal, the Heber in Thrace, and the Pactolus in lesser Asia; Not to mention the Rivers on the Gold Coast in Africa, which ly in a more Southern Climate.[233]

But we soon found our selves mistaken, and our Gold-Dust dwindled into small Flakes of Ising-Glass. However tho' this did not make the River so rich as we cou'd wish, yet it made it exceedingly Beautiful.[234]

We march't about two Miles and an half beyond this River, as far as Cane Creek, so call'd from a Prodigious Quantity of tall Canes that fring'dᵉ the Banks of it.

On the West Side of this Creek we markt out our Quarters, and were glad to find our Horses [so] fond of the Canes, tho' they scowred them smartly at

Cäne-Reed.

PLATE 8. Canes. *William Salmon, The English Herbal; or, History of Plants (London, 1710). This item is reproduced by permission of the Huntington Library, San Marino, California*

first, and discolour'd their Dung. This beautiful Vegetable grows commonly from 12 to 16 feet High, and some of them as thick as a Man's Wrist.

Tho' these appear'd large to us, yet they are no more than Spires of Grass, if compar'd to those which some curious Travellers[f] tell us grow in the East Indies, one Joint of which will make a Brace of Canoes, if saw'd in two in the middle. Ours[g] continue green thro' all the Seasons during the space of six Years, and the seventh shed their Seed, wither away, and Die. The Spring following they begin to shoot again, and reach their former Stature the second or third Year after.[h,235]

They grow so thick, and their Roots lace together so firmly, that they are the best Guard that can be of the River Bank, which wou'd otherwise be wash't away by the frequent Inundations, that happen in this part of the World.

They would also serve excellently well to plant on the Borders of Fish Ponds and Canals[i], to secure their sides from falling in, tho' I fear they would not grow kindly in a cold Country, being seldom seen here so Northerly as 38 Degrees of Latitude.[236]

11.   At the Distance of 4 Miles and 60 Poles from the place where[j] [62[k]] we encampt, we came upon the River Dan a second time, tho' It was not so wide in this Place[l] as where we crost it first, being not above [100] 150[m] Yards over.

The West Shore continu'd to be cover'd with the Canes abovemention'd, but not to so great a Breadth as before, and 'tis remarkable that these Canes are much more frequent on the West Side of the River, than on the East, where they grow generally very scattering.

It was still a beautiful Stream rolling down its limpid and murmuring waters among the Rocks, which lay scatter'd here and there, to make up the variety of the Prospect.

It was about two Miles from this River to the End of our Days Work, which led us mostly over Broken Grounds and troublesome Underwoods. Hereabout[n] from one of the Highest hills we made the first Discovery of the Mountains on the Northwest of our Course. They seem'd to lye off[o] at a vast Distance, and look't like Ranges of Blue Clouds rising one above another.

We encamp't about two Miles beyond the River, where we made good Chear upon a very fat Buck, that luckily fell in our way. The Indian likewise shot a Wild Turkey, but confest he wou'd not bring it us, lest we shou'd continue to provoke the Guardian of the Forrest, by cooking the Beasts of the Field, and the Birds of the Air together in one Vessel.

[f]A: some Travellers   [g]A: They   [h]V: A: third year   [i]A: of Canals and Fish Ponds
[j]A: from where   [k]V: *Page misnumbered* 64, *verso of* 61 *misnumbered* 62.   [l]A: here
[m]A: 100   [n]A: Hereabouts   [o]A: ly still

This Instance of Indian Superstition I confess is countenanc'd in some
measure by the Levitical Law, which forbad the mixing things of a Different
Nature together in the same field, or in the same Garment, and why then not
in the same Kettle?[237]

But after all, if the Jumbleing of two Sorts of Flesh together be a Sin,
how intolerable an Offence must it be to make a Spanish Oleo, that is a
Hotchpotch of every kind of thing that is eatable, and the good People
of England wou'd have a great deal to answer for, for beating up so many
different Ingredients into a Pudding.[238]

12.   We were so cruelly intangled with Bushes, and Grape-Vines all day,
that we could advance the Line no farther than 5 Miles and 28 Poles.

The Vines grew very thick in these Woods, twineing lovingly round the[P]
Trees almost every where, especially to the Saplins. This makes it evident how
natural both the Soil, and Climate of this Country are to Vines, tho' I believe
most to our own Vines.

The Grapes, we commonly met with were black, tho' there be two or three
kinds of White Grapes that grow wild. The black are very sweet, but small,
because the Strength of the Vine spends itself in Wood, tho' without Question
a proper Culture wou'd make the same Grapes both larger and sweeter. But
with all these Disadvantages I have drunk tolerable good Wine prest from
them, tho' made without Skill. There is then good Reason to believe, it might
admit of great Improvement if rightly managed.[239]

Our Indian kill'd a Bear of two years old, that was feasting on these Grapes.
He was very fat as they generally are, in [63[q]] that Season of the year. In the
fall the Flesh of this Animal has a high Relish, different from that of other
Creatures, tho' inclining nearest to that of Pork, or rather Wild Boar.[240]

A true Woodsman prefers this sort of meat to that of the fattest Venison,
not only for the Haut-gout; but also because the Fat of it is well tasted, and
never rises in the Stomach. Another proof of the goodness of this meat is, that
it is less apt to corrupt, than any other we are acquainted with.

As agreeable as such rich Diet was to the men, yet we who were not
accustom'd to it, tasted it at first with some sort of Squemishness, that
Animal being of the Dog-kind; tho' a little use soon reconcil'd us to this
American Venison. And that its being of the Dog kind might give us less
disgust, we had the Example of that Ancient and polite People the Chinese,
who reckon Dog's Flesh too good for any under the Quality of Mandarin.[241]

This Beast is in truth a very clean Feeder, living while the Season lasts
upon [Acorns[r]], Chesnuts, and Chinkapens, Wild-Hony, and wild Grapes. They

[P]A: to the   [q]V: *Page misnumbered* 60   [r]V: Acrons] A: Acorns are naturally not carnivorous, unless Hunger constrain them to it, after the Mast is all gone, and the Product of the Woods quite exhausted[s].

They are not provident enough to lay up any Hoard, like the Squirrels, nor can they after all live very long upon licking their Paws, as Sir John Mandevil and some[t] Travellers tell us, but are forc't in the Winter Months to quit the Mountains, and visit the Inhabitants.[242]

Their Errand is then to surprise a poor Hog at a Pinch to keep them from starving. And to shew they are not Flesh Eaters by Trade, they devour their Prey very awkwardly.[243]

They don't kill it right out, and feast upon its Blood and Entrails, like other Ravenous Beasts, but having after a fair pursuit seiz'd it with their Paws, they begin first upon the Rump, and so devour one Collop after another, til they come to the Vitals, the poor Animal crying all the while for several Minutes together. However in so doing Bruin acts a little imprudently, because the dismal outcry of the Hog alarms the Neighbourhood, and 'tis odds but he pays the forfeit with his Life, before he can secure his Retreat.

But Bears soon grow weary of this unnatural Diet, and about January, when there is nothing to be got in the Woods, they retire into some cave or hollow Tree, where they sleep away two or three Months very comfortably. But then they quit their Holes in March when the Fish begin to run up the Rivers, on which they are forc't to keep Lent, till some Fruit or Berry comes in Season.[244]

But Bears are fondest of Chesnuts, which grow plentifully towards the Mountains upon very large Trees, where the Soil happens to be rich. We were curious to know how it happen'd that many of the outward Branches of those Trees came to be broke off in that solitary Place, and were inform'd, that the Bears are so discreet, as not to trust their unwieldy Bodies on the smaller Limbs of the Tree, that would not [64] bear their Weight. But after venturing as far as is safe, which they can juge to an Inch, they bite off[a] the End of the Branch, which falling down, they are content to finish their Repast on the Ground. In the same Cautious Manner they secure the Acorns, that grow on the weaker Limbs of the Oak. And it must be allow'd, that in these Instances a Bear carries Instinct a great way, and acts more reasonably than many of his Betters, who indiscreetly venture upon frail Projects that won't bear them.

13. This being Sunday we rested from our Fatigue, and had leisure to reflect on the signal Mercies of Providence.

The great Plenty of Meat, wherewith Bearskin furnish't us in these lonely Woods, made us once more shorten the men's allowance of Bread from 5 to

[s]A: all exhausted   [t]A: some other   [a]A: *Here begins the second section supplied from another MS in the nineteenth century.*

4 Pounds of Bisket a week. This was the more necessary, because we knew not yet how long our Business might require us to be out.

In the Afternoon our Hunters went forth, and return'd triumphantly with three Brace of wild Turkeys. They told us they cou'd see the Mountains distinctly from every Eminence, tho' the Atmosphere was so thick with Smoak, that they appear'd at a greater Distance than they really were.

In the Evening we examin'd our Friend Bearskin, concerning the Religion of his Country, and he explain'd it to us, without any of that Reserve, to which his Nation is Subject.

He told us he believ'd there was one Supreme God, who had several Subaltern Deities under Him. And that this Master-God made the World a long time ago. That he told the Sun, the Moon, and Stars, their Business in the Beginning, which they with good looking after have faithfully perform'd ever since.[245]

That the same Power, that made all things at first, has taken Care to keep them in the same Method and Motion ever since.

He believed that God had form'd many Worlds before he form'd this, but that those Worlds either grew old and ruinous, or were destroyed for the Dishonesty of the Inhabitants.

That God is very just and very good, ever well pleas'd with those men who possess those God-like Qualities. That he takes good People into his safe Protection, makes them very rich, fills their Bellies plentifully, preserves them from Sickness, and from being surprizd, or overcome by their Enemies.

But all such as tell Lies, and cheat those they have Dealings with, he never fails to punish with Sickness, Poverty, and Hunger, and after all that, suffers them to be knock't on the Head and scalp't by those that fight against them.

He believ'd that after Death both good and bad People are conducted by a strong Guard into a great Road in which departed Souls travel together for some time, Til[b] at a certain Distance this Road forks into two Paths, the one extremely Levil, and the other Stony and Mountainous.

Here the good are parted from the Bad, by a flash of Lightening, the first being hurry'd away to the Right, the other to the Left. The Right Hand Road leads to a charming warm Country, where the Spring is everlasting, and every Month is May, [65] and as the year is always in its Youth, so are the People, and particularly the Women are bright as Stars, and never scold.

That in this happy Climate there are Deer, Turkeys, Elks, and Buffalos innumerable, perpetually fat and gentle, while the Trees are loaded with delicious Fruit quite throughout the four seasons.

[b]V: *Lowercase* t *made uppercase with top stroke.*

That the Soil brings forth Corn spontaneously, without the Curse of Labour, and so very wholesome, that None who have the happiness to eat of it, are ever sick, grow old, or dy.

Near the Entrance into this Blessed Land sits a venerable old Man on a Mat richly woven, who examins strictly all that are brought before Him, and if they have behav'd well, the Guards are order'd to open the Chrystal Gate, and let them enter into the Land of Delights.

The left hand Path is very rugged and uneaven, leading to a dead and barren Country, where it is always Winter. The Ground is the whole year round cover'd with Snow, and nothing is to be seen upon the Trees, but Icicles.

All the People are hungry, yet have not a Morsel of anything to eat, except a bitter kind of Potatoe, that gives them the Dry-Gripes, and fills their whole Body, with loathsome Ulcers, that stink and are insupportably painfull.

Here all the Women are old and ugly, having claws like a Panther, with which they fly upon the Men, that slight their Passion. For it seems these haggard old Furies are intolerably fond, and expect a vast deal of Cherishing. They talk much and exceedingly shrill, giving exquisite Pain to the Drum of the Ear, which in that Place of the Torment is so tender that every sharp Note wounds it to the Quick.

At the end of this Path sits a dreadful Old Woman on a monstrous Toad-Stool, whose head is cover'd with Rattle Snakes instead of Tresses, with glaring white Eyes, that strike a Terror unspeakable into all that behold her.

This Hag pronounces Sentence of Woe upon all the miserable Wretches that hold up their hands at her Tribunal. After this they are deliver'd over to huge Turkey-Buzzards, like Harpys, that fly away with them, to the Place above mentioned.

Here after they have been tormented a certain number of Years, according to their several Degrees of Guilt, they are again driven back into this World, to try if they will mend their Manners, and merit a place the next time in the Regions of Bliss.

This was the Substance of Bearskins Religion, and was as much to the purpose as could be expected from a meer State of Nature, without one glimps of Revelation or Philosophy.

It contain'd however the three Great Articles of Natural Religion, The Belief of a God. The Moral Distinction betwixt Good and Evil, and the Expectation of Rewards and Punishments in another World.

Indeed the Indian Notion of a Future Happiness is a little Gross and Sensual, like Mahomet's Paradise. But how can it be otherwise in a People, that are contented with Nature, as they find Her, and have no other Lights but what they receive from purblind Tradition.

14.   There having been great Signs of Rain yesterday Evening, we had taken our Precautions in securing the Bread, and Trenching in our Tent.

The men had also stretch't their Blankets upon Poles, Pent-house fashion, against the Weather, so that nobody was taken unprepar'd. It began to fall heavily about three a Clock in the Morning, [66] and held not up till near Noon. Every thing was so thoroughly soakt, that we laid aside all thoughts of Decamping that Day.

This gave leizure to the most expert of our Gunners to go and try their Fortunes, and they succeeded so well that they return'd about Noon with three fat Deer, and 4 wild Turkeys. Thus Providence took care of us, and however short the Men might be in their Bread, 'tis certain they had Meat at full Allowance.

The Cookery went on merrily all Night long, to keep the Damps from entering our Pores, and in truth the Impressions of the Air are much more powerfull upon empty Stomachs.

In such a Glut of Provisions a true Woodsman, when he has nothing else to do, like our honest Countrymen the Indians, keeps eating on, to avoid the imputation of Idleness; tho' in a Scarcity the Indians will fast with a much better Grace than they. They can subsist several days upon a little Rockahominy, which is parch't Indian Corn reduc'd to powder. This they moisten in the hollow of their Hands with a little Water, and 'tis hardly credible how small a Quantity of it will support them. Tis' true they grow a little lank upon it, but to make themselves feel full, they gird up their Loins very tight with a Belt, taking up a Hole every day. With this slender Subsistence they are able to travel very long Journeys; but then to make themselves Amends, when they do meet with better Chear they eat without ceasing, till they have raven'd themselves into another Famine.[246]

This was the first time, we had ever been detain'd a whole day in our camp by the Rain, and therefore, had reason to bear it with the more Patience.

As I sat in the Tent I overheard a learn'd Conversation between one of our Men and the Indian. He ask't the Englishman what it was that made that rumbling Noise when it Thunder'd?

The Man told him merrily, that the God of the English was firing his great Guns upon the God of the Indians, which made all that roaring in the Clouds, and that the Lightening was only the Flash of those Guns.

The Indian carrying on the Humour, reply'd very gravely, He believ'd that might be the Case indeed, and that the Rain which follow'd upon the

Thunder must be occasion'd by the Indian God's being so scar'd he cou'd not hold his Water.

The few good Husbands amongst us, took some thought of their Backs as well as their Bellies, and made use of this Opportunity to put their Habiliments in repair, which had suffer'd wofully by the Bushes.

The Horses got some rest by reason of the bad weather, but very little Food, the chief of their Forage being a little wild Rosemary, which resembles the Garden Rosemary pretty much in Figure, but not at all in taste or smell. This Plant grows in small Tufts here and there on the Barren Land in these upper Parts, and the Horses liked it well, but the Misfortune was, they cou'd not get enough of it to fill their Bellies.[247]

15.   After the Clouds brake away in the Morning the People dryed their Blankets with all diligence. Nevertheless it was [67] Noon before we were in condition to move forward, and then were so puzzled with passing the River twice in a small Distance, that we could advance the Line in all no farther than one single Mile and 300 Poles.

The first time we pas't the Dan this day was 240 Poles from the Place where we lay, and the second time was one Mile and seven Poles beyond that. This was now the fourth time, we forded that fine River, which still tended Westerly with many short, and returning Reaches.

The Surveyors had much Difficulty in getting over the River, finding it deeper than formerly. The Breadth of it here did not exceed fifty Yards. The Banks were about 20 feet high from the Water, and beautifully beset with Canes.

Our Baggage Horses cros't not the River here at all, but fetching a compass went round the Bent of it. On our Way we forded Sable-Creek, so call'd from the Dark Colour of the Water, which happen'd I suppose, by its being shaded on both Sides with Canes.[248]

In the Evening we quarter'd in a charming Situation near the Angle[c] of the River, from whence our Eyes were carried down both Reaches, which, kept a Strait Course for a great way together.

This Prospect was so beautifull, that we were perpetually climbing up to a neighbouring Eminence, that we might enjoy it in more Perfection.

Now the Weather grew cool, the Wild Geese began to direct their Flight this way from Hudson's Bay, and the Lakes, that lay North-west of us.

They are very lean at their first coming, but fatten soon upon a sort of Grass, that grows on the Shores and Rocks of this River.

The Indians call this Fowl Cohunks, from the hoarse Note it hath, and

[c]V: *Words inserted above the line here, and then erased.*

PLATE 9. Bear Fishing from Pile of Stones. *John Lawson,* A New Voyage
to Carolina . . . *(London, 1709). This item is reproduced by permission of
the Huntington Library, San Marino, California*

begin the year from the Coming of the Cohunks, which happens in the
Beginning of October.

These Wild Geese are guarded from Cold by a Down,[d] that is exquisitely
soft and fine, which makes them much more valuable for their Feathers, than
for their Flesh, which is dark and coarse.[249]

The Men chac't a Bear into the River, that got safe over, notwithstanding
the continual fire from the Shore upon Him. He seem'd to swim but heavily,
considering it was for his Life.

Where the Water is shallow, 'tis no uncommon Thing to see a Bear sitting
in the Summer time on a heap of Gravel in the Middle of the River, not only
to cool himself, but likewise for the Advantage of Fishing, particularly for a
small Shell-fish, that is brought down with the Stream.

In the upper part of James River I have observ'd this several times, and
wonder'd very much at first, how so many heaps of small Stones came to be
piled up in the Water, till at last we spy'd a Bear sitting upon one of them
looking with great attention on the Stream, and rakeing up something with
his Paw, which I take to be the Shell-fish above mention'd.

[d]A: *Here (p. 129) the eighteenth-century hand resumes, after the hiatus supplied in the
ninteenth century from another MS.*

16.   It was Ten a Clock this Morning before the Horses cou'd be found, having hid themselves among the Canes, whereof there was great plenty just at hand. Not far from our Camp we went over a Brook, whose Banks were edg'd on both Sides with these Canes. [68]

But three Miles farther we forded a larger Stream, which we call'd Low Land Creek, by reason of the great Breadth of Low Grounds inclos'd between that and the River.

The high Land we travell'd over was very good, and the low Grounds promis'd the greatest Fertility of any I had ever seen.

At the End of 4 Miles and 311 Poles from where we lay, the Line intersected the Dan the fifth time. We had day enough to carry it farther, but the Surveyors cou'd find no Safe ford over the River.

This oblig'd us to ride two Miles up the River in quest of a Ford, and by the way we traverst several small Indian Fields where we conjectur'd the Sawro's had been used to plant Corn, the Town where they had liv'd, lying seven or eight Miles more Southerly upon the Eastern Side of the River.[250]

These Indian Fields produc'd a sweet kind of Grass almost knee-high, which was excellent Forage for the Horses.

It must be observ'd by the way, that Indian Towns, like Religious Houses, are remarkable for a fruitful Situation; for, being by Nature not very Industrious they choose such a Situation, as will subsist them with the least Labour.

The Trees grew surprizeingly large in this low-Ground[e], and amongst the rest we observ'd a tall kind of Hiccory, peculiar to the Upper Parts of the Country. It is cover'd with a very rough Bark, and produces a Nut with a thick Shell that is easily broken. The Kernel is not so rank, as that of the Common Hiccory, but altogether as oily.[251]

And now I am upon the subject of these Nuts, it may not be improper to remark, that a very great benefit might be made of Nut-Oyl in this Colony. The Walnuts, the Hiccory-Nuts, and Pig-nuts contain a vast deal of Oyl, that might be press'd out in great abundance with proper Machines.

The Trees grow very kindly, and may be easily propagated. They bear plenty of Nuts every year, that are now of no other use in the World, but to feed Hogs.

'Tis certain there is a large Consumption of this Oyl in several of our Manufactures, and in some parts of France, as well as in other Countries it is eaten instead of Oyl-Olive, being tolerably sweet and wholsome.[252]

The Indian kill'd a fat Buck, and the men brought in four Bears; and a

[e]A: in these low Grounds

Brace of Wild Turkeys, so that this was truly a Land of Plenty both for man
and Beast.

17.   We detach't a Party of men this morning early in search of a Ford,
who after all cou'd find none, that was safe; tho' dangerous as it was, we
determin'd to make use of it, to avoid all farther delay. Accordingly we rode
over a narrow Ledge of Rocks, some of which lay below the Surface of the
Water, and some above it.

Those that lay under the Water were as slippery as Ice, and the Current
glided over them so swiftly, that tho' it was only Water, it made us perfectly
drunk. Yet we were all so fortunate as to get safe over to the West Shore, with
no other Damage than the sopping of some of our Bread by the flounceing of
the Horses. [69]

The tedious time spent in finding out this Ford, and in getting all the
Horses over it, prevented our carrying the Line more than 2 Miles & 250 Poles.

This was the last time we cros't the Dan with our Line, which now began
to run ^away^ more Southerly with a very flush and plentifull Stream, the
Description whereof must be left to future Discoveries; tho' we are well
assured by the Indians that it runs thro' the Mountains.

We conducted the Baggage a roundabout way for the Benefit of evener
Grounds, and this carry'd us over a broad Levil of exceeding rich Land, full
of large Trees, with Vines marry'd to them, if I may be allow'd to speak so
Poetically.

We untreed a young Cubb in our March, that made a brave Stand against
one of the best of our Dogs. This and a Fawn were all the Game that came in
our way.

In this day's Journey, as in many others before, we saw beautiful Marble of
several[f] Colours, and particularly that of the Purple kind with white Streaks,
and in some places we came across large pieces of pure Alabaster.

We markt out our Quarters on the Banks of a purling Stream, which we
call'd Casquade Creek, by reason of the Multitude of Water Falls that are in it.
But different from all other Falls that ever I met with the Rocks over which[g]
the water roll'd were soft[h] and would split easily into broad Flakes very proper
for Pavement, and some Fragments of it seem'd soft enough for Hones, and
the Grain fine enough.[253]

Near our Camp we found a prickly Shrub riseing about a foot from the
Ground, something like that which bear the Barberry, tho' much smaller. The

[f]A: many   [g]V: *Erasure and insertion at end of paragraph line and beginning of next*]
A: *paragraph ends with* that are in it. *and new paragraph begins* The rocks over which
[h]A: smooth

Leaves had a fresh agreable smell, and I am perswaded the Ladies would be apt to fancy a Tea made of them provided they were told how far it came, and at the same time were obliged to buy it very dear.[254]

About a Mile to the Southwest of our Camp rose a regular Mount, that commanded a full Prospect of the Mountains, and an extensive View of the Flat Country. But being with respect to the high Mountains no more than a Pimple, we call'd it by that Name.[255]

Presently after Sunset we discover'd a great Light towards the West, too bright for a fire, and more resembling the Aurora Borealis. This all our Woodsmen[i] told us it was a common Appearance in the High Lands, and generally foreboded bad Weather. Their Explanation happen'd to be exactly true, for in the Night we had a violent Gale of Wind, accompany'd with smart Hail, that rattled frightfully amongst the Trees,[j] tho' it was not large enough to do us any Harm.

18.   We crost Casquade-Creek over a Ledge of smooth Rocks, and then scuffled thro' a mighty Thicket, at least three Miles long. The whole was one continued Tract of rich high Land, the woods whereof had been burnt not long before. It was then overgrown with Saplins of Oak, Hiccory, and Locust, interlac'd with Grape Vines. In these fine Lands however, we met with no Water till at the End of three Miles, we luckily came upon a Chrystal Stream, which like some Lovers of Conversation, discover'd every thing committed to its faithless Bosom.

Then we came upon a piece of Rich Low Grounds covered with large Trees, of the extent of half a Mile, which made us fancy ourselves not far from the River, tho' after that we ascended [70] gently to higher Land, with no other Trees growing upon it, except[k] Butter wood, which is one species of white Maple.[256]

This being a dead Levil without the least Declivity to carry off the Water, was moist in many Places, and produc'd abundance of Grass. All our Woodsmen[l] call these flat Grounds, High-Land Ponds, and in their Trading Journeys are glad to halt at such Places for several days together, to recruit their jaded Horses, especially in the Winter Months, when there is little or no Grass to be found in other places.

This High-Land-Pond extended above two Miles, our Palfry's snatching greedily at the Tufts of Grass, as they went along. After we got over this Level, we descended some stony Hills for about half a Mile, and then came upon a large Branch of the River, which we christen'd the Irvin, in honour of our

---

[i]A: Aurora Borealis. Our Woodsmen   [j]A: *Paragraph ends here]* V: *phrase inserted at end of line.*   [k]A: but   [l]A: The Woodsmen

learned Professor. This River we forded[m] with much Difficulty, and some
Danger, by reason of the Hollow-Spaces betwixt the Rocks, into which our
Horses plunged almost every Step.[257]

The Irvin runs[n] into the Dan about four Miles to the Southward of the
Line, and seem'd to roll down its Waters from the N.N.W. in a very full and
Limpid Stream, and the Murmur it[o] made in tumbling over the Rocks, caus'd
the Situation to appear very Romantick, and had [almost][p] made some of the
Company Poetical, tho' they drank nothing but Water.

We encamp't on a pleasant Hill overlooking the River, which seem'd to
be deep every where, except just where we forded. In the mean time neither[q]
that Chain of Rocks, nor any other that we cou'd observe in this Stream, was
so uninterrupted, but that there were several Breaks, where a Canoe, or even
a moderate Flat-bottom'd Boat might shear Clear. Nor have we reason to
believe, there are any other Falls (except the great ones, thirty Miles below
Moniseep-Ford) that reach quite across, so as to interrupt the Navigation
for small Craft. And I have been inform'd that even at those Great Falls, the
Blowing up a few Rocks, wou'd open a Passage at least for Canoes, which
certainly wou'd be an unspeakable Convenience to the Inhabitants of all that
beautiful Part of the Country.

The Indian kill'd a very fat Doe, and came across a Bear, which had been
put to Death, and was half devour'd by a Panther. The last of these Brutes
reigns absolute Monarch of the Woods, and in the keenness of his hunger will
venture to attack a Bear, tho' then 'tis ever by Surprize, as all Beasts[r] of the
Cat-kind ^use to^ come[s] upon their Prey.

Their Play is to take the poor Bears napping, they being very drowsy
Animals; And tho' they be exceedingly strong, yet their Strength is heavy,
while the Panthers are too nimble, and cunning[t] to trust themselves within
their Hugg.[258]

As formidable as this Beast is to his Fellow-Brutes, he never hath the
confidence to venture upon a Man, but retires from him with great respect,
if there be a way open for his Escape. However it must be confess't[a] his Voice
is a little contemptible for a Monarch[b] of the Forrest, being not a great deal
louder, nor more awful, than the Mewing of a Household Cat.*[c]

[m]V: *Inserts* in honour of our learned Professor. This River *at the end of the line extending
into the paragraph indentation. A ends the paragraph at* the Irvin *and begins the next* This
we forded   [n]A: This River   [o]A: the Waters   [p]A: also] V: alsmost *(incomplete revision)*
[q]A: forded it. But neither   [r]A: ^all^ Beasts   [s]A: Cat-kind come   [t]A: too cunning and
nimble   [a]A: I must own   [b]A: Prince   [c]V: *An asterisk directs the insertion of the following
paragraph, written in the margin. Here, as in the previous marginal addition, A reflects
revision.*

Some Authors who have given an Account[d] of the Southern Continent of America, wou'd make the World believe there are Lyons. But in all likelihood they were mistaken, imagining these[e] Panthers to be Lyons. What makes this probable[f] is, that the Northern and Southern Parts of America being join'd by the Isthmus of Darien, if there were Lyons in either they wou'd find their way into the other, the Latitude of each being equally proper for that generous Animal.[259] [71]

In South Carolina they call this Beast a Tyger, tho' improperly, and so they do in some part of the Spanish West Indies. Some of their Authors a little more improperly complement[g] it with the Name of a Leopard[h], But none of these are the Growth of America, that we know of.[i]

The whole Distance the Surveyors advanc'd the Line this Day, amounted to 6 Miles and 30 Poles. Which was no small Journey considering the Grounds, we had[j] traverst were exceeding[k] rough and uneven, and in many Places intolerably intangled with Bushes. All the Hills we ascended[l] were encumber'd with Stones, many of which seem'd to contain a Metallick Substance, and the Vallies we crost were[m] interrupted with miry Branches. From the top of every Hill we cou'd discern distinctly, at a great Distance, three or four Ledges of Mountains rising one above another, and on the highest of all rose a single Mountain very much resembling a Woman's Breast.

19. About four Miles beyond the River Irvin we forded Matrimony Creek, call'd so by an unfortunate marry'd man, because it was exceedingly noisy, and impetuous. However, tho' the Stream was clamorous, yet like those Women, who make themselves plainest heard, it was likewise perfectly clear and unsully'd.[260]

Still half a Mile farther we saw a small Mountain[n] about five Miles to the Northwest of us, which we call'd the Wart, because it appear'd no bigger than a Wart in Comparison of the great Mountains which hid their haughty Heads in the Clouds.[261]

We were not able to extend the Line farther than 5 Miles and 135 Poles, notwithstanding we began our March early in the Morning, and did not encamp till it was almost dark.

We made it the later by endeavouring to Quarter in some convenient Situation either for Grass or Canes: But Night surprizing us, we were oblig'd

[d]A: that have treated [e]A: fancying the [f]A: proves this pretty clearly [g]A: have stil more improperly complemented [h]A: Lyon [i]A: which is nowhere the growth of America, as we know of. [j]A: now [k]A: exceedingly [l]A: The Hills were [m]A: vallies now and then [n]A: a ^small^ Mountain

to Lodge ^at last^ upon High and uneven Ground, which was so overgrown
with Shrubs and Saplins, that we cou'd hardly see ten yards around us.

The most melancholly part of the Story, was, that our Horses had short
Commons. The poor Creatures were now grown so weak that they stagger'd,
when we mounted them. Nor wou'd our own Fare have been at all more
plentiful, had we not been so provident as to carry a Load of Meat along with
us. Indeed the Woods were too thick to shew us any sort of Game, but one
Wild Turkey, which help'd enrich our Soup.

To make us amends, we found abundance of very sweet Grapes, which
with the help of Bread might have furnish't out a good Italian Repast in the
Absence of more savoury Food.

The men's Mouths water'd at the Sight of a Prodigious Flight of wild
Pigeons, which flew high over our Heads to the Southward.

The Flocks of these Birds of Passage are so amazingly great sometimes
that they darken the Sky, nor is it uncommon for them to light in such
Numbers on° the Larger Limbs of Mulberry-Trees, and Oaks as to break them
down.[262]

In their Travels they make vast Havock amongst the [72] Acorns and
Berries of all Sorts, that[p] they wast whole Forrests in a short Time, and leave a
Famine behind them for most other Creatures and under[q] some Trees, where
they light, it is no strange thing to find the Ground cover'd three Inches thick
with their Dung.[289] These wild Pigeons commonly breed[r] in the uninhabited
Parts of Canada, and as the Cold approaches assemble their Armies, and
bend their Course Southerly, shifting their Quarters like many of the winged
Kind according to the ^Season^.[s] But the most remarkable thing in their
Flight, as we are told,[t] is, that they never have been observ'd to return to the
Northern Countries the same way they came from thence, but take quite
another Rout, I suppose for their better Subsistence.[263]

In these long Flights they are very lean, and their Flesh ^is^ far from being
white or tender, tho' good enough upon a March, when Hunger is the Sauce,
and makes it go down better than Truffles and Morels, wou'd do.

20.   It was now Sunday, which we had like to have spent in Fasting as well
as Prayer. For our Men taking no Care for the Morrow, like good Christians
but bad Travellers, had improvidently devour'd all their Meat for Supper.[264]

They were order'd in the Morning to drive up their Horses, lest they shou'd

°A: in   [p]A: insomuch that   [q]A: Creatures. Under   [r]A: Dung. They commonly breed
[s]A: Southerly.] V: *Phrase* shifting their Quarters like many of the winged Kind according
to the Season *inserted at end of sentence/paragraph and carrying over into indentation
space of new paragraph*   [t]A: the Flight of these Pigeons

stray[a] too far from the Camp and be lost, in case they were let alone all day. At their Return they had the very great Comfort to behold a monstrous fat Bear which the Indian had kill'd very seasonably for their Breakfast.

We thought it still necessary to make another Reduction of our Bread, from four to three Pounds a Week to every man, computing that we had still enough in that Proportion to last us three weeks longer.

The Atmosphere was so smoaky all round us, that the Mountains were again grown invisible. This happen'd not from the Hazyness of the Sky, but from the fireing of the Woods by the Indians, for we were now near the Route the Northern Savages take when they go out to War against the Cataubas and other Southern Nations.[265]

On their way the Fires they make in their Camps are left burning, which catching the dry Leaves that ly near, soon put[b] the adjacent Woods into a Flame.[266]

Some of our men in search of their Horses discovered one of those Indian Camps, where not long before they had been a Furring[c] and dressing their Skins.

And now I mention the Northern Indians, it may not be improper to take Notice of their implacable Hatred to those of the South. Their Wars are everlasting without any Peace, Enmity being the only Inheritance among them, that descends from Father to Son; and either Party will march a Thousand Miles to take their Revenge upon such Hereditary Enemies.

These long Expeditions[d] are commonly carry'd on in the following Manner: Some Indian remarkable for his Prowess, that has rais'd himself to the Reputation of a War-Captain, declares his Intention of paying a Visit to some Southern [73] Nation. Hereupon as many of the Young Fellows as have either a strong Thirst of Blood or Glory, list themselves under his Command.

With these Volunteers he goes from one Confederate Town to another, listing all the Rabble he can, till he has gather'd together a competent Number for Mischief.

Their Arms are a Gun and Tomahawk, and all the Provisions they carry from Home is a Pouch of Rockahominy. Thus provided and accouter'd they march toward the Enemies Country, not in a Body, or by a certain Path, but straggling in small Numbers, for the greater convenience of Hunting, and passing along undiscover'd.

So soon as they approach the Grounds on which the Enemy is used to hunt, they never kindle any Fire themselves, for fear of being found out by

[a]A: lest they stray   [b]A: set   [c]A: had been Furring   [d]A: These Expeditions

the Smoak, nor will they shoot at any kind of Game, tho' they shou'd be half-famish't, lest they might alarm their Foes, and put them upon their Guard.

Sometimes indeed while they are still at some distance, they roast either Venison or Bear, till it is very dry, and then having strung it on their Belts, wear it round their Middle, eating very sparingly of it, because they know not when they shall meet with a fresh Supply. But coming nearer they begin to look all round the Hemisphere, to watch if any Smoak ascends, and listen continually for the Report of Guns, in order to make some happy Discovery for their own advantage.[267]

Tis amazing to see their Sagacity in discerning the Track of a Human Foot, even amongst dry Leaves, which to our shorter Sight is quite undiscoverable.[268]

If by one or more of those Signs they be able to find out the Camp of any Southern Indians, they squat down in some Thicket, and keep themselves hush and snug till it is dark. Then creeping up softly, they approach near enough to observe all the Motions of the Enemy. And about two a Clock in the Morning, when they conceive them to be in a Profound Sleep, for they never keep Watch and Ward, pour in a Volley upon them each singling out his Man. The Moment they have discharg'd their Pieces, they rush in with their Tomahawks, and make sure work of all that are disabled.

Sometime when they find the Enemy asleep round their little Fire, they first pelt them with little Stones to wake them, and when they get up, fire in upon them, being in that posture a better Mark than when prostrate on the Ground.

They that are kill'd of the Enemy, or disabled, they Scalp, that is, they cut the Skin all round the Head just below the Hair, and then clapping their Feet to the poor Mortals Shoulders, pull the Scalp off clean, and carry it home in Triumph, being as proud of those Trophies, as the Jews used to be of the Foreskins of the Philistines.[269]

This way of Scalping was practised by the ancient Scythians, who us'd these hairy Scalps, as Towels at Home, and Trappings for their Horses when they went abroad.

They also made Cups of their Enemies Sculls, in which they drank[e] Prosperity to their Country, and Confusion to all their Foes.[270]

The Prisoners, they happen to take alive in these expeditions[f] generally pass their time very scurvily. They put them to all the Tortures that ingenious

[e]A: us'd to drink   [f]A: *Here begins the third section in which a hiatus in the eighteenth-century MS was supplied by a transcription (in a nineteenth-century hand) from V.*

Malice and Cruelty can invent. And (what shews [74] the baseness of the
Indian Temper in perfection) they never fail to treat those with greatest
Inhumanity, that have distinguish'd themselves most by their Bravery, and
if he be a War-Captain, they do him the Honour to roast him alive, and
distribute a Collop to all that had a share in stealing the Victory.*g

Tho who can reproach the poor Indians for this, when Homer makes his
celebrated Hero Achilles drag the Body of Hector at the Tail of his chariot,
for having fought gallantly in defence of his Country. Nor was Alexander the
great with all his fam'd Generosity less inhuman to the brave Tyrians, 2000
of which he order'd to be crucify'd in cold Blood for no other Fault but for
having defended their City most couragiously against Him dureing a Siege of
Seaven Months. And what was stil more brutal he dragg'd [———] alive at the
Tail of his Chariot thro' all the Streets for defending the Town with so much
Vigour.[271]

They are very cunning in finding out new ways to torment their unhappy
Captives, tho' like those of Hell, their usual Method is by Fire. Sometimes
they Barbacue them over live-Coals, taking them off every now and then to
prolong their Misery; at other times, they will stick sharp Pieces of Lightwood
all over their Body's, and setting them afire, let them burn down into the
Flesh to the very Bone. And when they take a Stout Fellow, that they believe
able to endure a great deal, they will tear all the Flesh off his Bones with red
hot Pincers.

While these and such like Barbarities are practising, the Victors are so
far from being toucht with Tenderness and Compassion, that they dance
and sing round these wretched Mortals, shewing all the Marks of Pleasure
and Jollity. And if such Cruelties happen to be executed in their Towns, they
employ their Children in tormenting the Prisoners, in order to extinguish in
them betimes all Sentiments of Humanity.

In the mean time, while these poor Wretches are under the Anguish of
all this inhumane Treatment, they disdain so much as to groan, sigh, or
shew the least Sign of Dismay or Concern, so much as in their Looks; On the
contrary they make it a Point of Honour all the time to soften their Features,
and look as pleas'd as if they were in the actual Enjoyment of some Delight;
And if they never sang before in their Lives, they will be sure to be Melodious
on this sad and Dismal Occasion.

So prodigious a Degree of Passive Valour in the Indians is the more to be
wonder'd at, because in all Articles of Danger, they are apt to behave like
Cowards. And what is still more surprizeing the very Women discover on such

gV: *Asterisk signals insertion of paragraph added in margin, following.*

Occasions, as great Fortitude and Contempt both of Pain and Death, as the Gallantest of their Men can do.[272]

21.   The Apprehensions, we had of losing the Horses in these Copse-Woods, were too well founded, nor were the Precautions, we us'd Yesterday of driveing them up, sufficient to prevent their straying away afterwards, notwithstanding they were securely hobbled.

We therefore order'd the men out early this Morning to look diligently for them, but it was late before any cou'd be found. It seems they had straggled in quest of Forrage, and besides all that, the Bushes grew thick enough to conceal them from being seen at the smallest Distance. One of the People was so bewilder'd in search of his Horse, that he lost Himself, being no great Forrester.

However because we were willing to save time, we left two of our most expert Woodsmen behind, to beat all the adjacent Woods in Quest of Him. [75]

In the mean while the Surveyors proceeded vigorously on their Business, but were so perplext with Thickets at[h] their first setting off, that their Progress was much retarded.

They were no sooner over that Difficulty, but they were oblig'd to encounter another. The rest of their days-Work lay over very sharp Hills, where the dry leaves were so slippery, that there was hardly any hold for their Feet. Such Rubbs as these prevented them from measuring more than 4 Miles and 270 Poles.

Upon the Sides of these Hills, the Soil was rich, tho' full of Stones, and the Trees reasonably large.

The Smoak continued still to veil the Mountains from our Sight, which made us long for Rain, or a brisk Gale of Wind to disperse it. Nor was the loss of this wild Prospect all our Concern, but we were apprehensive lest the Woods shou'd be burnt in the Course of our Line before us, or happen to take fire behind us, either[i] of which would effectually have starv'd the Horses, and made us all Foot-Soldiers. But we were so happy, thank God, as to escape this Misfortune in every Part of our Progress.[273]

We were exceedingly uneasy about our lost man, knowing he had taken no Provision of any kind, nor was it much Advantage towards his Support, that he had taken his Gun along with him, because he had rarely been guilty of putting any thing to Death.

He had unluckily wander'd from the Camp several Miles, and after steering sundry unsuccessful courses, in order to return either to us, or to

[h]A: *Here concludes the nineteenth-century transcription (pp. 139a–c, 140 [blank])*
[i]A: before us, either

the Line, was at length so tired he could go no further. In this Distress he sat himself down under a Tree, to recruit his jaded Spirits, and at the same time indulge a few melancholly Reflections.

Famine was the first Phantom, that appear'd to him, and was the more frightfull because he fancy'd himself not quite Bear enough to subsist long upon licking his Paws.

In the mean time the two Persons we had sent after him, hunted diligently great part of the day without coming upon his Track. They fir'd their Pieces towards every Point^j of the Compass, but cou'd perceive no fireing in return. However advancing a little farther, at last ^they made^ a lucky Shot, that our Straggler had the good Fortune to hear, and he returning the Salute, they soon found each other with ^no small^ Satisfaction^k. But, tho' they light of the Man, they could by no means light of his Horse, and therefore he was oblig'd to be a Foot Soldier all the rest of the Journey.[274]

Our Indian shot a Bear so prodigiously fat, that there was no way to kill Him, but by fireing in at his Ear.

The forepart of the Scull of that Animal, being guarded by a double Bone, is hardly penetrable, and when it is very fat, a Bullet aim'd at his Body is apt to lose its force, before it reaches the Vitals.[275]

This Animal is of the Dog kind, and our Indians as well as Woodsmen are as fond of its Flesh as the Chinese can be of that of the Common Hound.[276]

22.   Early in the Morning we sent back to men to make farther^l [76] Search for the Horse, that was stray'd away. We were unwilling the poor man shou'd sustain such a Damage as wou'd eat out a large Part of his Pay, or that the Publick shou'd be at the Expence of re-emburseing Him for it.

These Forresters hunted over all the neighbouring Woods, and took as much pains, as if the Horse had been their own Property, but all their Diligence was to no Purpose.

The Surveyors in the mean time, being fearful of leaving these men too far behind, advanc'd the Line no farther than One Mile and 230 Poles.

As we rode along we found no less than three Bears and a fat Doe, that our Indian, who went out before us, had thrown in our Course, and we were very glad to pick them up.

About a Mile from the Camp we cros't Miry Creek, so call'd because several of the Horses were mired in its Branches. About 230 Poles beyond that, the Line intersected another River that seem'd to be a Branch of the Irvin, to which we gave the Name of the Mayo, in Complement to the ^other^ of our Surveyors^m. It was about 50 Yards wide where we forded it, being just

---

^jA: <Part> Point   ^kA: with Satisfaction   ^lA: further   ^mA: to one of our Surveyors

below a Ledge of Rocks, which reach't across the River, and made a natural Casquade.[277]

Our Horses cou'd hardly keep their feet over these[n] slippery Rocks, which gave some of their Riders no small Palpitation.

This River forks about a Quarter of a Mile below the Ford, and has some scattering Canes growing near the Mouth of it.

We pitch't our Tent on the Western Banks of the Mayo, for the Pleasure of being lull'd to sleep by the Casquade. Here our Hunters had leisure[o] to go out, and try their Fortunes, and return'd loaden with Spoil.[p] They brought in no less than six Bears exceedingly fat, so that the frying pan had no rest all Night. We had now the[q] Opportunity of trying the Speed of these lumpish Animals by a fair Course it had with the nimblest of our Surveyors.

A Cubb of a year old will run very fast, because being upon his growth, he ^is^ never incumber'd[r] with too much fat, but the old ones are more[s] sluggish, and unwieldy, especially when Mast is plenty. Then their nimblest Gate is only a heavy Gallop, and their Motion is still slower down hill, where they are oblig'd to sidle along very awkwardly, to keep their Lights from riseing up into their Throat.[278]

These Beasts always endeavour to avoid a man, except they are wounded, or happen to be engaged in the Protection of their Cubbs.

By the force of these Instincts, and that of Self Preservation, they will now and then throw off all Reverence for their Maker's Image. For that Reason excess of hunger will provoke them to the same Desperate Attack, for the support of their Being.[279]

A memorable Instance of the last Case is said to have happen'd not long ago in New England, where a Bear assaulted a Man just by his own Door, and rearing himself upon his Haunches, offer'd to take him lovingly into his Hug. But the [77] Man's Wife, observing the Danger her Husband was in, had the Courage to run behind the Bear, and thrust her Thumbs into his Eyes. This made Bruin quit the Man, and turn short upon the Woman to take his Revenge, but she had the presence of mind to spring back with more than Female Agility, and so both their Lives were preserved.[280]

23.   At the Distance of 62 Poles from where we lay, we cros't the South Branch of what we took for[t] the Irvin, nor was it without Difficulty we got over, tho' it happen'd to be without Damage.

Great part of the way after that, was Mountainous, so that we were no sooner got down one Hill, but we were oblig'd to climb up another. Only for

[n]A: those   [o]A: likewise had leisure   [p]A: Spoils   [q]A: an   [r]A: never is encumber'd
[s]A: too   [t]A: what we took to be

the last Mile of our Stage[a], we encounter'd a Locust Thicket that was levil but interlac'd terribly with Bryars, and Grape Vines.

We forded a large Creek no less than five times, the Banks of which were so steep, that we were forc'd to cut them down with a Hough.

We gave it the Name of Crooked Creek, because of its frequent Meanders. The Sides of it were planted with Shrub-Canes extremely inviting to the Horses, which were now quite jaded with clambering up so many Precipices, and lugging thro' so many dismal Thickets notwithstanding wch. we pusht the line this day Four Miles 69 Poles.[b]

The men were so unthrifty this Morning as to bring but a small Portion of their Abundance along with them. This was the more unlucky, because we cou'd discover no sort of Game the whole live-long Day. Woodsmen are certainly good Christians in one respect at least, that they always leave the Morrow to care for itself, tho' for that very reason, they ought to pray more fervently[c] for their Dayly-Bread than most of them remember to do.[281]

The Mountains were still conceal'd from our Eyes by a Cloud of Smoak. As we went along we were alarm'd at the Sight of a great Fire, which shew'd itself to the Northward. This made our small Corps march in closer Order, than we us'd to do, lest perchance we might be way-laid by Indians. It made us look out sharp to see if we cou'd discover any Track, or other Token of these insidious Foresters, but found none. In the mean time we came often upon the Track of Bears, which cant without some Skill, be distinguish't[d] from that of Human Creatures made with Naked Feet. And indeed a Young Woodsman wou'd be puzzled ^to^ find out the Difference, which consists principally in a Bear's Paw's being something smaller than a Man's foot, and in its[e] leaving sometimes the Mark of the[f] Claws in the Impression made upon the Ground.

The Soil where the Locust Thicket grew, was exceedingly rich, as it constantly is, where that kind of Tree is naturally and largely produced.

But the Desolation made there lately either by Fire, or Caterpillars, had been so general, that we could not see a Tree of any Bigness standing within our Prospect. And the Reason why a Fire makes such Havock in these lonely Parts is this.

The Woods are not there burn't every year, as they generally are amongst the Inhabitants. But the dead Leaves and Trash of many years are heap't up together, which being, at length kindl'd by the Indians, that happen to pass that way, furnish Fewel for a Conflagration, that carries all before it. [78]

---

[a]A: our Journey   [b]A: Thickets. (*New paragraph*) The Distance we push't the Line this day was 4 Miles and 69 Poles.   [c]A: frequently   [d]A: discover'd   [e]A: the   [f]A: its

There is a beautiful Range of Hills as levil as a Terrass-Walk, that overlooks the Valley, through which Crooked Creek conveys its Spiral Stream.

This Terrass runs pretty near East and West about two Miles South of the Line, and is almost Parallel with it.

The Horses had been too much harrass'd to permit us to ride at all out of our way, for the pleasure of any Prospect, or the gratification of any Curiosity. This confin'd us to the narrow Sphere of our Business, and is at the same time a just Excuse for not animating our Story with greater Variety.

24.   The Surveyors went out the sooner this Morning, by reason the men lost very little time in cooking their Breakfast. They had made but a spare Meal over Night, leaving nothing but the Hide of a Bear for the Morrow. Some of the keenest of them got up at Midnight to cook that nice Morsel after the Indian Manner.

They first singed the Hair clean off, that none of it might stick in their Throats; Then they boil'd the Pelt into Soup, which had a Stratum of Grease swiming upon it full half an Inch Thick. However they commended[g] this Dish extremely, tho' I believe the Praises they gave it, were ^more^ owing to their good Stomach[h], than to their good Tast.

The Line was extended 6 Miles and 300 Poles, and in that Distance cros't Crooked Creek at least eight times more.

We were forc't to scuffle through a Thicket about two Miles in breadth planted with Locusts and Hiccory Sapplins as close as they cou'd stand together. Amongst these there was hardly a Tree of Tolerable Growth within View. It was a dead Plane of several Miles Extent, and very fertile Soil. Beyond that the Woods were open for about three Miles, but Mountainous. All the rest of our Day's Journey was pester'd with Bushes and Grape Vines, in the thickest of which we were oblig'd to take up our Quarters, near one of the Branches of Crooked Creek.[282]

This Night it was the Men's good fortune to fare very sumptuously.[i] The Indian had kill'd two large Bears, the fattest of which he had taken napping. One of the People too shot a Raccoon which is ^also^ of[j] the Dog-kind, and as big as a small Fox, tho' its Legs are shorter, and when fat, has much a higher relish than either Mutton or Kid. Tis naturally not carnivorous, but very fond of Indian Corn, and Parsimons.[283]

The fat of this Animal is reckon'd very good to asswage Swellings, and Inflammations. Some Old Maids are at the Trouble of breeding them up tame for the pleasure of seeing them play over as many Humourous Tricks as a

[g]A: Thick. They commended   [h]A: Stomachs   [i]A: to fare sumptuously.   [j]A: which is of

Munkey. It climbs up small Trees like a Bear by embraceing the Bodies of them.[284]

Till this Night we had accustom'd our selves to go to Bed in our Night-Gowns, believing we shou'd thereby be better secur'd from the Cold: But upon tryal found we lay much warmer by stripping to our Shirts, and spreading our Gowns over us.

A True Woodsman if he have no more than a single Blanket, constantly pulls[k] all off, and lying on one part of it, draws the other over him, believing it much more refreshing to ly so, [79] than in his cloaths, and if he find himself not warm enough, shifts his Lodging to Leeward of the Fire, in which Situation the Smoak will drive over him, and effectually correct the cold Dews, that wou'd otherwise descend upon his Person, perhaps to his great damage.[l]

25. The Air clearing up this Morning, we were again agreeably surprized with a full Prospect of the Mountains. They discover'd themselves both to the North and South[m] of us, on either side not distant above ten Miles according to our best Computation.[n]

We cou'd now see those to the North rise in four distinct Ledges, one above another, but those to the South form'd only a[o] single Ledge, and that broken and interrupted in many Places. Or rather they were only single Mountains detacht from each other.[p]

One of the Southern Mountains was so vastly high, it seem'd to hide its head in the Clouds, and the West End of it terminated in a horrible Precipice, that we call'd the dispairing Lover's Leap. The next to it towards the East, was lower except at one End, where it heav'd itself up in the form of a vast Stack of Chimneys.[285]

The Course of the Northern Mountains seem'd to tend West South West and those to the Southward very near West. We cou'd descry other Mountains a head of us exactly in the Course of the Line, tho' at a much greater distance. In[q] this Point of View the Ledges on the right and Left, both seem'd to close, and form a Natural Amphi-Theater.

Thus twas our Fortune to be wedg'd in betwixt these two Ranges of Mountains, insomuch that, if our Line had run ten Miles on either Side, it had butted before this day either upon one or the other, both of them now stretching away plainly to the Eastward of us.

It had rain'd a little in the Night, which disperst the Smoak, and open'd this Romantick Scene to us all at once, tho' it was again hid from our Eyes, as we mov'd forwards[r], by the rough Woods we had the Misfortune to be engag'd with. The Bushes were so thick for near four Miles together, that they tore the Deer-Skins to Pieces, that guarded the Bread Bags. Tho' as rough as the Woods were, the Soil was extremely good all the way, being wash't down from the neighbouring Hills into the Plane Country. Notwithstanding all these[s] Difficulties, the Surveyors drove on the Line 4 Miles and 205 Poles.

In the mean time we were so unlucky as to meet with no sort of Game the whole day, so that the men were oblig'd to make a frugal distribution of what little they left in the Morning.

We encamp't upon a small Rill, where the Horses came off as temperatly as their Masters. They were by this time grown so thin by hard Travel, and spare Feeding, that henceforth in pure Compassion we chose to perform the greater Part of the Journey on foot. And as our Baggage was by this time grown much lighter, we divided it after the best Manner, that every Horse's Load might be proportion'd[t] to the Strength he had left. Tho' after all the the prudent Measures we cou'd take, we perceived the Hills began to rise upon us so fast in our Front, that, it wou'd be impossible for us to proceed much farther. [80]

We saw very few Squirrels in the upper parts, because the Wild Cats devour them unmercifully. Of these there are four kinds, The Fox-Squirrel, the Grey, the Flying, and the Ground-Squirrel.[286]

These last resemble a Rat in every thing, but the Tail, and the black, and Russet Streaks that run down the Length of their little Bodies.

26.   We found our way grow still more Mountainous after extending the Line ^300 Poles^ farther. We came then to a Rivulet, that ran with a swift Current towards the South. This we fancy'd to be another Branch of the Irvin, tho' some of these[a] men who had been Indian Traders, judg'd it rather to be the head of Deep River, that discharges its Stream into that of Pedee: but this seem'd a wild Conjecture.

The Hills beyond that River were exceedingly lofty, and not to be attempted by our jaded Palfreys, which could now hardly drag their Legs after them upon level Ground. Besides the Bread began to grow scanty, and the Winter Season to advance apace upon us[b].

We had likewise reason to apprehend the Consequences of being intercepted by deep Snows; and the Swelling of the many Waters between us and Home. The first of these Misfortunes would starve all our Horses, and the other, ourselves, by cutting off our Retreat, and obliging us to winter in

---

[r]A: march't forward   [s]A: those   [t]A: proportionable   [a]A: the   [b]A: upon us apace

those Desolate Woods. These considerations determin'd us to stop short here, and push our Adventures no farther. The last Tree, we markt was a Red Oak, growing on the Bank of the River, and to make the Place more remarkable we blaz'd all the Trees around[c] it.[287]

We found the whole Distance from Corotuck Inlet to the Rivulet where we left off, to be in a Strait Line Two Hundred and Forty One Miles, and Two Hundred and Thirty Poles. And from the Place where the Carolina Commissioners deserted us 72 Miles and 302 Poles. This last part of the Journey was generally very hilly, or else grown up with troublesome Thickets, and underwoods, all which our Carolina Friends had the Discretion to avoid.

We encampt in a dirty Valley near the Rivulet abovemention'd for the Advantage of the Canes, and so sacrificed out own Convenience to that of our Horses.

There was a small Mountain half a Mile to the Northward of us, which we had the Curiosity to climb up in the Afternoon, in order to enlarge our Prospect. From thence we were able to discover, where the two Ledges of Mountains clos'd, as near, as we cou'd guess about 30 Miles to the West of us, and lamented that our present Circumstances wou'd not permit us to advance the Line to that Place, which the Hand of Nature had made so very remarkable[d].

Not far from our Quarters one of the men pickt up a pair of Elks Horns not very large, and discover'd the Track of the Elk that had shed them. It was rare to find any Tokens of those Animals so far to the South, because they keep commonly to the Northward of 37 Degrees, as the Buffaloes for the most part confine themselves[e] to the Southward of that Latitude.

The Elk is full as big, as a Horse, and of the Deer kind. The Stags only have Horns, and those exceedingly large and [81] spreading. Their Colour is something lighter than of the Red Deer, and their Flesh tougher. Their swiftest Speed is a large trot; and in that Motion they turn their Horns back upon their Necks, and cock their Noses aloft[f] in the Air. Nature has taught[g] them this Attitude to save their Antlers from being entangled in the Thickets, which they always retire to. They are very shy, and have the Sense of Smelling so exquisite, that they wind a man at a great distance. For this reason they are seldom seen, but when the Air is moist, in which Case their smell[h] is not so nice.

They commonly herd together, and the Indians say, if one of the Drove happen by some Wound to be disabled from making his Escape, the rest

[c]A: round   [d]A: made so remarkable   [e]A: confine themselves for the most part   [f]A: up
[g]A: thought   [h]A: smelling

will forsake[i] their fears, to defend their Friend, which they will do with
great obstinacy, till they are kill'd[j] upon the Spot. Tho' otherwise they are so
alarm'd at the Sight of a man, that to avoid him, they will sometimes throw
themselves down very high Precipices into the River.[288]

A misadventure happen'd here, which gave us no small perplexity. One
of the Commissioners was so unlucky as to bruise his Foot against a Stump,
which brought on a formal Fit of the Gout.[289]

It must be own'd there cou'd not be a more unseasonable time, nor a more
improper Situation, for anyone to be attack't by that cruel Distemper. The
Joint was so inflam'd, that he cou'd neither draw Shoe or[k] Boot upon it, and
to ride without either, wou'd have expos'd him to so many rude knocks, and
Bruises in those rough Woods, as to be intolerable even to a Stoick.

It was happy inded that we were to rest here the next day being Sunday,
that there might be leisure for trying some Speedy Remedy. Accordingly he
was persuaded to bath his Foot in Cold Water, in order to repel the Humour,
and asswage the Inflamation. This made it less painful, and gave us hopes too
of reducing the Swelling in a short time.

Our men had the fortune to kill a Brace of Bears, a fat Buck, and a Wild
Turkey, all which paid them with Interest for Yesterday's Abstinence. This
constant and seasonable Supply of our daily Wants made us reflect thankfully
on the Bounty of Providence.

And that we might not be unmindful of being all along fed by Heaven in
this great and solitary Wilderness, we agreed to wear in our Hats the *Maosti,*
which is in Indian, the Beard of a Wild Turkey Cock, and on our Breast the
Figure of that Fowl with its Wings extended, and holding in its Claws a Scrowl
with this Motto, *Vice coturnicum,* meaning that we had been supported by
them in the Wilderness in the room of Quails.[290]

27. This being Sunday we were not wanting in our Thanks to Heaven
for the constant Support and Protection, we had been favour'd with. Nor did
our Chaplain fail to put us in mind of our Duty by a Sermon proper for the
Occasion.

We order'd a strict Inquiry to be made into the Quantity of Bread we
had left, and found no more than wou'd subsist us a Fortnight at Short
Allowance. We made a fair Distribution of our whole Stock, and at the same
time recommended to the Men, to manage this their last Stake to the best
advantage, not knowing how long they wou'd be oblig'd to live upon it. [82]

We likewise directed them to keep a watchfull Eye upon their Horses, that
none of them might by missing ^the^ next Morning to hinder our Return.

[i]A: forget [j]A: are all kill'd [k]A: nor

There fell some Rain before Noon, which made our Camp more a Bogg, than it was before. This moist Situation began to infect some of the men with Fevers, and some ^with^ Fluxes[l], which however we soon remov'd with Peruvian Bark, and Ippocoacannah.

In the Afternoon we marcht up again to the top of the Hill to entertain our Eyes a second time with the View of the Mountains, but a perverse Fog arose that hid them from our Sight.

In the Evening we deliberated which way it might be most proper to return. We had at first intended to cross over at the foot of the Mountains to the head of James River, that we might be able to describe that Natural Boundary so far. But on second Thoughts we found many good Reasons against that laudable Design, such as the Weakness of our Horses, the Scantiness of our Bread, and the near approach of Winter. We had Cause to believe the way might be full of Hills, and the farther we went towards the North, the more danger there wou'd be of Snow. Such Considerations as these determin'd us at last to make the best of our way back upon the Line, which was the straitest, and consequently the shortest way to the Inhabitants. We knew the worst of that Course, and were sure of a beaten Path all the way, while we were totally ignorant what Difficulties and Dangers, the other Course might be attended with. So Prudence got the better for once[m] of Curiosity, and the Itch for new Discoveries gave place to Self-preservation.

Our Inclination was the stronger to cross over according to the Course of the Mountains, that we might find out whether James River and Appamattuck River head there, or run quite thro' them. Tis certain that Potomeck passes in a large Stream thro' the Main Ledge, and then[n] divides itself into two considerable Rivers. That which stretches away to the Northward is call'd Cohungaroota*[o] which by a Late Survey has been found to extend above 200 Miles before[p] it reaches its Sources in[q] a Mountain from whence Allegany one of the Branches of Missasipi takes its Rise, and runs Southwest as this River dos Southeast, and that which flows to the Southwest, hath the Name of Sharantow.[291]

The Course of this last Stream is near parallel to the ^blue Ridge of^ Mountains[r], at the distance only of about three or four Miles. Tho' how far it may continue that Course has not yet been sufficiently discover'd: but some Woodsmen pretend to say it runs as far, as the Source of Roanoak: Nay they

---

[l]A: and some Fluxes   [m]A: got the better once   [n]A: there   [o]V: *Asterisk indicating insertion of marginal addition:* which . . . Southeast *(note subsequent A expansion of text)*
[p]A: above the Blue Mountains before   [q]A: to   [r]A: to the Mountains

are so very particular as to tell us that Roanoak, Sharantow, and another Wide
Branch[s] of Messasippi all head in one and the same Mountain[t].

What dependance there may be upon this Conjectural Geography, I won't
pretend to say, tho 'tis certain that Sharantow keeps close to[a] the Mountains,
as far as we are acquainted with its Tendency. We are likewise[b] assur'd that
the South Branch of James River within less than 20 Miles East of the Main
Ledge, makes an Elbow, and runs due Southwest, which is parallel with the
Mountains on this side. But how far it stretches that way before it returns, is
not yet certainly known, no more than where it takes its Rise.

In the mean time, it is strange that our Woodsmen have not had Curiosity
enough to inform themselves more exactly [83] of these particulars, and is
stranger still, that the Government has never thought it worth the Expence
of making an accurate Survey of the Mountains, that we might be Masters
of that Natural Fortification before the French, who in some places have
Settlements not very distant from it.

It therefore concerns his Majesty's Service very nearly, and the Safety of
His Subjects in this part of the World, to take possession of so important a
Barrier in time, lest our good Friends, The French, and the Indians thro' their
Means, prove a perpetual Annoyance to the Colonies.

Another Reason to invite us to secure this great Ledge of Mountains is,
the[c] Probability that very valuable Mines may be discover'd there. Nor wou'd
it be at all extravagant to hope for Silver Mines among the rest, because Part
of these Mountains ly exactly in the same Parallel, as well as upon the same
Continent with New Mexico, and the Mines of St. Barb.[292]

28.   We had given Orders for the Horses to be brought up early, but the
likelyhood of more Rain, prevented our being over hasty in decamping. Nor
were we out in our Conjectures, for about ten a Clock it began to fall very
plentifully.

Our Commissioners Pain began now to abate, as the Swelling encrcas'd.
He made an excellent Figure for a Mountaineer, with one Boot of Leather, and
the other of Flannel. Thus accoutur'd he intended to mount, if the Rain had
not happen'd opportunely to prevent him.

Tho' in Truth it was hardly possible for Him to ride with so slender a
Defense, without exposeing his Foot to be bruis'd and tormented by the
Saplins, that stood thick on either side of the Path. It was therefore a most
seasonable Rain for Him, as it gave more time for his Distemper to abate.[293]

Tho' it may be very difficult to find a certain Cure for the Gout, yet it is not

[s]A: the Easternmost Branch   [t]A: the same River   [a]A: with   [b]A: also   [c]A: a

improbable but some things may ease the Pain, and shorten the Fits of it. And those Medicines are most likely to do this, that Supple the Parts, and clear the Passage thro' the narrow Vessels, that are the Seat of this cruel Disease. Nothing will do this more suddenly than Rattlesnake Oyl, which will even penetrate the Pores of Glass, when warm'd in the Sun.[294]

It was unfortunate therefore that we had not taken out the Fat of those Snakes, we ^had^ kill'd some time before, for the Benefit of so usefull an Experiment, as well as for the Relief of our Fellow Traveller.

But lately the Seneca-Rattle Snake Root has been discover'd in this Country, which being infus'd in Wine, and drank Morning and Evening has in several Instances had a very happy Effect upon the Gout, and enabled Cripples to throw away their Crutches, and walk several Miles, and what is stranger still, it takes away the Pain in half an hour.[295]

Nor was the Gout the only Disease amongst us, that was hard to cure. We had a man in our Company, who had too voracious a Stomach for a Woodsman. He eat as much as any other two, but all he swallow'd stuck by him, till it was carry'd off by a strong Purge. Without this Assistance often repeated, his Belly and Bowels wou'd swell to so enormous a Bulk, that he cou'd [84] hardly breath, especially when he lay down, just as if he had had an Asthma tho' notwithstanding this oddness of Constitution he was a very strong lively Fellow, and us'd abundance of Violent Exercise by which twas wonderfull the Peristaltick Motion was not more vigorously promoted.

We gave this poor Man several Purges, which only eas'd Him for the present[d], and the next day he wou'd grow as burly as ever. At last we gave him a moderate Dose of Ippocoacanah in Broth made very Salt, which turn'd all its Operation downwards. This had so happy an Effect, that from that day forward to the End of our Journey, all his Complaint[e] ceas'd and the Passages continued unobstructed[f].

The Rain continued most of the Day, and some part of the Night, which incommoded us much in our Dirty Camp, and made the men think of nothing but Eating, even at a time when nobody cou'd stir out to make Provision for it.

29.   Tho' we were flatter'd in the Morning with the usual Tokens of a fair Day, yet they all blew over, and it rain'd hard before we cou'd make ready for our Departure.

This was still in favour of our Podagrous Friend, whose Lameness was now grown better, and the Inflamation fallen. Nor did it seem to need above

---

[d]A: for the Present] V: for the <moment> present   [e]A: Complaints   [f]A: remain'd perfectly unobstructed

one day more to reduce it to it's Natural Proportion, and make it fit for the Boot. And effectually The Rain procur'd this Benefit for him, and gave him particular Reason to believe his Stars propitious.[296]

Notwithstanding the falling Weather, our Hunters sally'd out in the Afternoon, and drove the Woods in a Ring, which was thus perform'd. From the Circumference of a large Circle they all march't inwards, and drove the Game towards[g] the Center. By this means they shot a Brace of fat Bears, which came very seasonably, because we had made clean work in the Morning, and were in Danger of dining with St. Anthony, or his Grace Duke Humphry.[297]

But in this Expedition the unhappy man, who had lost himself once before, straggled again so far in Pursuit of a Deer, that he was hurry'd a second time quite out of his knowledge. And Night coming on before he cou'd recover the Camp, he was oblig'd to ly down without any of the Comforts, of Fire, Food, or Covering. Nor wou'd his Fears suffer him to sleep very sound, because to his great disturbance, the Wolves howl'd all that Night, and the Panthers scream'd most frightfully.

In the Evening a brisk North Wester swept all the Clouds from the Sky, and expos'd the Mountains, as well as the Stars to our Prospect[h].

That which was the most lofty to Southward, and ^which^ we call'd[i] the Lovers Leap, some of of our Indian Traders fondly fancy'd was the *Kiawan* Mountain, which they had formerly seen from the Country of the Cherokees.

They were the more positive, by reason of the prodigious Precipice, that remarkably distinguish'd the West End of it.

We seem'd however not to be far enough South for that, tho' 'tis not improbable, but a few Miles farther the Course of our [85] Line might carry us to the most Northerly Towns of the Cherokees.[298]

What makes this the more credible, is, the North West Course, that our Traders take from the Catauba's for some hundred Miles together, when they carry Goods that roundabout way to the Cherokees.

It was a great Pity, that the want of Bread, and the Weakness of our Horses hinder'd us from making the Discovery. Tho' the great service such an Excursion might have been to the Country, would certainly have made the Attempt not only pardonable, but much to be commended.

Our Traders are[j] now at the vast Charge and Fatigue of travelling above five hundred[k] Miles for the Benefit[l] of that Traffique, which hardly quits cost. Wou'd it not then be worth the Assembly's while to be at some Charge to find

---

[g]A: to   [h]A: Stars distinctly to our Prospect   [i]A: and we call'd   [j]*Here begins the CWR.d (C) MS.*   [k]C: <a Thousand> Five Hundred] A: 500   [l]A: benefits

a shorter cut to carry on so profitable a Trade with more advantage, and less hazard and Trouble than they do[m] at present[n]? For I am persuaded it will not then be half the Distance, that our Traders make it now[o], nor half so far as Georgia lies from the Northern Clans of that Nation.

Such a Discovery woud certainly[p] prove an unspeakable Advantage to this Colony, by facilitateing a Trade with so considerable a Nation of Indians, which have 62 Towns, and more than 4000 Fighting Men. Our Traders at that rate would be able to undersell[q] those sent from the other Colonies so much, that the Indians must have reason[r] to deal with them preferably to all others.

Of late the new Colony of Georgia has made an Act obliging us to go 400 Miles to take out a Licence to traffick with these 9, tho' many of their Towns ly out of their Bounds, and we had carry'd on this Trade 80 Years before that Colony was thought of.[299]

30. In the Morning early the man, who had gone astray the day before, found his[s] way to the Camp, by the Sound of the Bells, that were upon[t] the Horses Necks.

At Nine a Clock we began our March back towards the rising Sun, for tho' we had finisht the Line, yet we had not yet near finisht our Fatigue. We had after all 200 good Miles at least to our several Habitations, and the Horses were brought so low, that we were oblig'd to travel on foot great part of the way, and that in our Boots too, to save our Legs from being torn to pieces by the Bushes and Briars. Had we not done this, we must have left all our Horses behind, which cou'd now hardly drag their Legs after them. And with all the favour we cou'd shew the poor Animals, we were forc'd to set seven of them free not far from the foot of the Mountains.

Four men were dispatch't early to clear the Road, that our Lame Commissioners Leg might be in less danger of being bruis'd, and that the Baggage-Horses might travel with less difficulty and more expedition.

As we past along, by favour of a serene Sky, we had still from every Eminence a perfect View of the Mountains as well to the North as to the South. We cou'd not forbear now and then facing[u] about to survey them, as if unwilling to part with a Prospect, which at the same time, like some Rakes, was very wild, and very agreeable.

We encourag'd the Horses to exert the little Strength, they [86] had, and being light, they made a shift to jogg on about eleven Miles. We encampt on Crooked Creek, near a Thicket of Canes. In the front of our Camp rose a very

---

[m]A: it is [n]C: <this round about way> at present [o]C: <at present> now
[p]C: <thoroughly> [q]A: wou'd undersell [r]C: <will> must have reason [s]A: the
[t]A: about [u]V: facing] C: faceing

beautifull Hill, that bounded our View at about a Miles Distance, and all the Intermediate Space was cover'd with green Canes. Tho' to our Sorrow Firewood was scarce, which was now the harder upon us, because a Northwester blew very cold from the Mountains.

The Indian kill'd a stately fat Buck, & we pickt his Bones as clean, as a Score of Turkey-Buzzards cou'd have done.

By the advantage of a clear Night, we made Tryal once more of the Variation, and found it much the same as formerly.[300]

This being his Majesty's Birth-Day, we drank all the Loyal Healths in excellent Water, not for the sake of the drink (like many of our Fellow Subjects) but purely for the sake of the Toast. And because all Publick Mirth shou'd be a little noisy, we fir'd several Volleys of Canes instead of Guns, which gave a loud report.[301]

We threw them into the Fire, where the Air enclosed betwixt the Joints of the Canes, being expanded by the violent Heat, burst its narrow Bounds with a considerable Explosion.

In the Evening one of the men knock't down an Opossum, which is a harmless little Beast, that will seldom go out of your way, and if you take hold of it, will only grin, and hardly ever bite. The Flesh was well tasted and Tender, approaching nearest to[v] Pig, which it also resembled[w] in Bigness. The Colour of its Furr was a Goose Gray, with a Swines Snout, and a Tail like a Rat, but[a] at least a foot long. By twisting this Tail about the Arm of a Tree, it will hang with all its weight, and swing to any thing it wants to take hold of.[302]

It has five Claws on the fore-Feet of equal length, but the hinder feet have only four Claws, and a sort of Thumb standing off at a proper Distance[b].

Their Feet, being thus form'd, qualify them for climbing up Trees to catch little Birds, which they are very fond of.

But the greatest Particularity of this Creature, and which[c] distinguishes it from most others that we are acquainted with, is the *False-Belly* of the *Female,* into which her Young retreat in time of Danger. She can draw the Slit, which is the Inlet into this Pouch so close, that you must look narrowly to find it, especially if she happen to be a Virgin.

Within the *False Belly* may be seen seven or eight[d] Teats, on which the young ones grow from their first Formation, till they are big enough to fall off, like ripe Fruit from a Tree. This is so odd a Method of Generation that I shou'd not have believ'd it, without the Testimony of mine own Eyes. Besides a knowing and credible Person has assur'd me he has more than

[v]A: unto   [w]A: it resembles   [a]C: Tail like a <Rat's tale, the> Rat, but   [b]C: at a ^proper^ Distance   [c]C: ^and^ which   [d]C: six or eight] A: 6 or 8

once observ'd the Embryo-Possums growing to the Teat, before they were completely shaped, and afterwards watcht[e] their daily growth, till they were big enough for Birth. And all this he cou'd the more easily pry into, because the Damm was so perfectly gentle and harmless, that he cou'd handle her just as he pleas'd.[f]

I cou'd hardly perswade myself to publish a thing so contrary [87] to the Course, that Nature takes in the Production of other Animals, unless it were a Matter commonly believ'd in all Countries, where that Creature is produc'd, and had been often observ'd by Persons of undoubted Credit and Understanding.

They say that the Leather-winged Bat produce their Young in the same uncommon Manner. And that Young Sharks at Sea, and Young Vipers ashoar run down the Throats of their Damms, when they are closely pursued.[303]

The frequent crossing of Crooked-Creek, and mounting the Steep Banks of it, gave the finishing Stroke to the foundering of our Horses, and no less than[g] two of them made a full Stop here, and would not advance a foot farther either by fair means or foul.

We had a Dreamer of Dreams amongst us, who warn'd me in the Morning to take care of my self, or I shou'd infallibly fall into the Creek; I thank'd him kindly, and us'd what Caution I cou'd, but was not able it seems to avoid my Destiny, for my Horse made a false Step, and laid me down at my full Length in the Water.

This was enough to bring dreaming into Credit, and, I think it[h] much for the Honour of our Expedition, that it was grac'd not only with a *Priest,* but also with a *Prophet.*

We were so perplext with this Serpentine Creek, as well as in passing the Branches of the Irvin, (which were swell'd since we saw them before) that we could reach but 5 Miles this whole day. In the Evening we pitcht our Tent near Miry Creek[i] (tho' an uncomfortable place to lodge in) purely for the advantage of the Canes.

Our Hunters kill'd a large Doe, and two Bears, which made all other Misfortunes easy. Certainly no Tartar ever lov'd Horseflesh, or Hottentot Guts and Garbage, better than Woodsmen do Bear. The truth of it is, It may be proper food, perhaps for such as Work or Ride it off, but with our Chaplain's

---

[e]C: and ^afterwards^ watcht   [f]C: *Vertical line inserted in continuous text to signal paragraph break.*   [g]C: the foundering our Horses. No less than] A: the foundering of our Horses. No less than.   [h]C: 'twas] A: t'was   [i]V: *The phrase* In the Evening we *added in Byrd's hand at the end of the paragraph line and beginning of next. C and A both end the paragraph with* this whole day. *and begin the next, indented, with* We pitch't

Leave, who lov'd it much, I think it not a very proper Dyet for Saints, because 'tis apt to make them a little too rampant.[304]

And now for the good of Mankind, and for the better Peopling an Infant Colony, which has no want but that of Inhabitants, I will venture to publish a Secret of Importance, which our Indian disclos'd to me. I askt him the reason why few or none of his Country-women were barren? to which curious *Question* he answer'd with a Broad Grin upon his Face, they had an infallible *Secret* for that. Upon my being importunate to know what the secret might be, He inform'd me, that if any Indian-Woman did not prove with Child at a decent time after Marriage, the Husband to save his Reputation with the Women, forthwith enter'd into a Bear-dyet for Six Weeks, which in that time[j] makes him so vigorous, that he grows exceedingly impertinent to his poor Wife, and 'tis great odds but he makes her a Mother in Nine Months.

And thus much I am able to say besides, for the Reputation of the Bear-dyet, that all the Marry'd men of our Company, were joyful Fathers within forty weeks after they got Home, and most of the single men had Children sworn to them within the same time, our Chaplain always excepted, who with much adoe made a shift[k], to cast out that importunate kind of Devil, by Dint of—Fasting and Prayer[l]. [88]

NOVEMBER

1. By the Negligence of one of the Men in not hobbling[m] his Horse, he straggled so far that he cou'd not be found. This stopt us all the Morning long, yet because our Time shou'd not be entirely lost, we endeavour'd to observe the Latitude at 12 a Clock. Though our Observation was not perfect, by reason the Wind blew a little too fresh, However by such a one, as we cou'd make, we found ourselves in 36° 20′ only.

Notwithstanding our being thus delay'd, and the unevenness of the Ground, over which we were oblig'd to walk[n] (for most of us serv'd now in the Infantry) we travell'd no less than 6 Miles, Tho' as merciful[o] as we were to our poor Beasts, another of 'em[p] tired by the way, & was left behind for the Wolves & Panthers to feast upon.

As we march't along, we had the fortune to kill a Brace of Bucks, as many Bears and one wild Turkey. But this was carrying our Sport to Wantonness,

[j]V: *The phrase* for six Weeks, which in that *added in Byrd's hand at the end of the paragraph and beginning of next; in C and A, ending with* dyet *and the new one beginning* This in a short time   [k]C and A: altho' a Widdower, was instructed   [l]C and A: right down Fasting and Prayer   [m]C: hobbleing   [n]C: Ground ^over^ which we were oblig'd to walk <over>   [o]A: serv'd in the Infantry, though as merciful   [p]A: them

because we butcherd more than we were able to transport. We order'd the Deer to be quarter'd and divided among the Horses for the lighter Carriage, and recommended the Bears to our dayly Attendants the Turkey Buzzards.

We always chose to carry Venison along with us rather than Bear, not only because it was less cumbersome, but likewise because the People cou'd eat it without Bread, which was now almost spent. Whereas the other, being richer food, lay too heavy upon the Stomach, unless it were lighten'd by something farinaceous.

This is what I thought proper[q] to remarque for the Service of all those, whose Business or Diversion shall oblige them to live any time in the Woods.

And because I am persuaded that very usefull Matters may be found out by searching this great Wilderness, especially the upper parts of it about the Mountains, I conceive it will help to engage able men in that good Work, If I recommend, a wholesome kind[r] of Food of very small Weight, and very great Nourishment, that will secure them from starving, in case they shou'd be so unlucky, as to meet with no Game. The chief discouragement at present from penetrating far into the Woods, is the trouble of carrying a Load of Provisions. I must own Famine is a frightfull Monster, and for that reason to be guarded against as well as we can. But the common precautions against it are so burthensome, that People can't tarry long out[s], and go far enough from home, to make any effectual Discovery.

The Portable[t] Provisions, I wou'd furnish our Forresters withall, are Glue-Broth, and Rockahomini; one contains the Essence of Bread, the other of Meat.

The best way of making the Glue-Broth is after the following Method.

Take a Leg of Beef, Veal, Venison, or any other Young Meat, because Old Meat will not so easily Jelly. Pare off all the fat, in which there is no Nutriment, and of the Lean make a very strong Broth after the usual Manner, by boiling the Meat to Rags, till all the Goodness be out. After skimming off what fat remains, pour the Broth into a wide stew Pan well tinn'd, & let it simmer over a gentle even Fire, till it come to a Thick Jelly. Then take it off, and set it over Boiling Water, which is an [89] evener Heat, and not so apt to burn the Broth to the Vessel. Over that let it evaporate, stirring it very often, till it be reduc'd, when cold, into a solid Substance like Glue. Then cut it into small Pieces, laying them Single in the Cold, that they may dry the sooner. When the Pieces are perfectly dry, put them into a Canister, and they will be good, if kept dry, a whole East-India Voyage.

This Glue is so strong, that two or three Drams[u] dissolv'd in boiling Water with a little Salt will make half a pint of good Broth, & if you shou'd be faint with fasting or Fatigue, let a small Piece of this Glue melt in your Mouth, and you will find yourself surprizeingly refresht.

One Pound of this cookery wou'd keep a man in good heart above a Month, and is not only nourishing, but likewise very wholsome. Particularly it is good against Fluxes, which Woodsman are very liable to, by lying too near the moist Ground, and guzzling too much cold Water[v]. But as it will be only us'd now and then in times of Scarcity, when Game is wanting, two Pounds of it will be enough for a Journey of Six Months.[305]

But this Broth will be still more heartening, if you thicken every[w] Mess with half a Spoonfull of Rockahominy[a], which is nothing but Indian Corn parch't without Burning and reduced to Powder. The Fire[b] drives out all the watery Parts of the Corn, leaving the Strength of it behind, and this being very dry[c] becomes much lighter for carriage, and less liable to be spoilt by the moist Air.

Thus half a Dozen Pounds of this sprightly Bread, will sustain a Man for as many Months[d], provided he husband it well, and always spare it when he meets with Venison, which as I said before, may be very safely eaten[e] without any Bread at all.

By what I have said, a Man, needs not encumber himself with more than 8 or 10 Pounds of[f] Provisions, tho' he continue half a year in the Woods.

These and his Gun will support him[g] very well during that time, without the least danger of keeping one[h] single Fast. And tho' some of his[i] days may be what the French call *Jours maigres,* yet there will happen no more of those than will be necessary for his health, and to carry of the Excesses of the Days of Plenty, when our Travellers will be apt to indulge their Lawless Appetites too much[j].[306]

2.   The Heavens frown'd this Morning, and threaten'd abundance of Rain, but our Zeal for returning made us defy the Weather, and decamp a little[k] before Noon. Yet we had not advanc't two Miles, before a soaking Shower made us glad to pitch our ^Tent^ as fast as we could. We chose for

[u]C: This Glue is so strong, that <a> ^two or three^ Drams   [v]V: *Phrase* and guzzling too much Water *inserted in Byrd's hand at end of paragraph and beginning of next. C and A end paragraph with* cold Water *and begin next with* But   [w]A: each   [a]C: Rockahomin<i>y   [b]A: Heat   [c]C: and ^this being^ <dry, it> very dry   [d]A: for many Months   [e]C: very safely <eat> eaten   [f]C: Pounds Weight of   [g]C: Gun <with> will support him   [h]C and A: a   [i]C: <their> his   [j]C: <free> much   [k]C: and decamp a little (de *written in left margin before* camp *overwritten on an erasure*)

that purpose a rising Ground half a Mile to the East of *Matrimony-Creek*. This was the first and only time we were catcht in the Rain, during the whole Expedition. It us'd before to be so civil as to fall in the Night, after we were safe in our Quarters, and had trench't our selves in. Or else it came upon us on Sundays, when it was no Interruption to our Progress, nor any Inconvenience to our Persons.

We had however been so lucky in this Particular before, that we had abundant Reason to take our present Soaking patiently, & the Misfortune was the less, because we had taken our Precautions [90] to keep all our Baggage and Bedding perfectly dry.[1]

This Rain was enliven'd with very loud Thunder which was eccho'd back by the Hills in the Neighbourhood in a frightfull Manner. There is Something in the Woods that makes the Sound of this Meteor more awfull, and the Violence of the Lightening more visible. The Trees are frequently shiver'd quite down to the Root, and sometimes perfectly twisted. But of all the Effects of Lightening that ever I heard of, the most amazing happen'd in this Country in the Year 1736.

In the Summer of that year a Surgeon of a Ship whose Name was Davis, came ashoar at York to visit a Patient. He was no sooner got into the House but it began to rain with many terrible claps of Thunder. When it was almost dark there came a dreadfull Flash of Lightening which struck the Surgeon dead as he was walking about the Room, but hurt no other Person, tho' several were near him. At the same [time][m] it made a large Hole in the Trunk of Pine Tree, which grew about Ten Feet from the Window. But what was most surprizing in this Disaster, was, that on the Breast of the unfortunate Man that was kill'd, was the Figure of Pine-Tree as exactly delineated, as any Limner in the World cou'd draw it. Nay the Resemblance went so far as to represent the coulour of the Pine, as well as the Figure. The Lightening must probably have past thro' the Tree first before it struck the Man and by that means have printed the Icon of it on his Breast.

But whatever may have been the Cause, the Effect was certain, & can be attested by a Cloud of Witnesses who had the Curiosity to go and see this wonderfull Phœnomenon.[307]

The worst of it was, we were forc'd to encamp in a barren Place, where there was hardly a blade of Grass to be seen, Even the wild Rosemary fail'd us here, which gave us but too just apprehensions that we shou'd not only be

---

[1]C: *An asterisk at the end of this sentence signals an insertion, probably the ensuing paragraphs about thunder not present in the extant MS, which resumes with* The worst of it was   [m]V *Omits the word* time, *here supplied from A.*

oblig'd to trudge all the way home on foot, but also to lugg[n] our Baggage at our Backs into the Bargain.

Thus we learn't by our own Experience, that Horses are very improper Animals to use in a long Ramble into the Woods[o], and the better they have been us'd to be fed, they are still the worse. Such will fall away a great deal faster, and fail much sooner, than those which are wont to be at their own keeping. Besides Horses that have been accustom'd to a Plane and Champaign-Country will founder presently, when they come to clamber up Hills, and batter their Hoofs against continuall Rocks.[p,308]

We need Welch Runts, and Highland Galloways to climb our Mountains withal, they[q] are us'd to Precipices, and will bite as close as Banstead Down Sheep. But I shou'd much rather recommend Mules, if we had them, for these long and painful Expeditions; tho 'till they can be bred, certainly Asses are the fittest Beasts of Burthen for the Mountains[r]. They are sure-footed, patient under the heavyest Fatigue, and will subsist upon Moss, or Browzing on[s] Shrubs all the Winter. One of them will carry the necessary Luggage of four Men, without any Difficulty, and upon a Pinch will take a Quarter of a Bear, or Venison upon their Backs into the Bargain.[309] [91]

Thus when the Men are light, and disengag'd[t] from every thing but their Guns, they may go the whole Journey on foot with Pleasure. And tho' my Dear Country-men have so great a Passion for riding, that they will often walk two Miles to catch a Horse, in order to ride One, yet if they'll please to take my Word for't, when they go into the Woods upon Discovery, I wou'd advise them by all Means to march a foot[a], for they will then[b] be deliver'd[c] from the great Care and Concern for their Horses, which takes up too large a portion of their time.

Over Night we are now at the trouble[d] of hobbling them out, and often of leading them a Mile or two to a convenient place for Forrage, and then in the Morning[e] we are some Hours in finding them again, because they are apt to stray a great way from the place, where they were turn'd out.[f] Now and then too they are lost for a whole day together, and are frequently so weak and jaded, that the Company must ly still severall[g] days near some Meadow or Highland Pond to recruit them. All these[h] delays retard their Progress intolerably. Whereas if they had only a few Asses, they wou'd abide close by

[n]A: lug all   [o]C: a long <Journey in> Ramble into the Woods   [p]C and A: against Rocks.
[q]C: that   [r]C and A: to take along with us   [s]C and A: of   [t]C and A: discharg'd   [a]A: on foot   [b]C and A: They will then   [c]C: disengaged] A: disengag'd   [d]C: Over Night <they are> we are ^now^ at the trouble   [e]C: and in the Morning ^again^] A: and in the morning   [f]C: *Paragraph break.*   [g]C: must <ly> lie still ^severall days^] A: must ly still severally days   [h]A: those

the Camp, and find sufficient food every where, and in all Seasons of the Year.[i]
Men wou'd then be able to travel safely over Hills and Dales, nor wou'd the
steepest Mountain obstruct their Progress.

They might also search more narrowly for Mines and other Productions of
Nature without being confin'd to level Grounds, in Complement to the Jades
they ride on. And one may foretell without the Spirit of Divination, that so
long as Woodsmen continue to range on Horse-back, we shall be Strangers to
our own Country, and few or no valuable Discoveries will ever be made.

The *French-Coureurs de Bois,* who have run from one End of the Continent
to the other, have perform'd it all on foot, or else in all probability must have
continued full as Ignorant as we are.

Our Country has now been inhabited more than 130 years by the English
and still we hardly know any thing of the Appallachian Mountains, that
are no where above 250 Miles from the Sea. Whereas the French, who are
later comers, have rang'd from Quebec Southward as far as the Mouth of
Messasippi in the Bay of Mexico, and to the West almost as far as California,
which is either way above 2000 Miles.[310]

3. A Northwest Wind having clear'd the Sky, we were now tempted to
travel on a Sunday for the first time for want of more plentifull Forage, tho
some of[j] the more Scrupulous ^amongst us^ were unwilling[k] to do Evil, that
good might come of it, and make our Cattle work a good Part of the Day, in
order to fill their Bellies at Night. However the Chaplain put on his casuistical
Face, and offer'd to take the Sin upon Himself. We therefore consented to
move a Sabbath Day's Journey of 3 or 4 Miles, It appearing to be a Matter of
some[l] necessity.

On the way our unmercifull Indian kill'd no less than two Brace of Deer
and a large Bear. We only prim'd the Deer, being unwilling to be encumber'd
with their whole Carcasses. The rest we consign'd to the Wolves, which in
Return serenaded us great[m] Part of the Night. They are very clamorous in
their Banquets, which we know is the way some other Brutes ^have^ in the
extravagance of their Jollity and Sprightliness, of[n] expressing their thanks to
Providence.[311] [92]

We came to our old Camp in sight of the River Irvin, whose Stream was
swell'd now[o] near four foot with the Rain, that fell the Day before. This made

[i]*In C, Byrd here inserts a horizontal line or dash in the paragraph indentation, canceling
the paragraph break. There is no paragraph break in A or V.* [j]*V: Insertion in Byrd's hand
at end of paragraph and indentation of next.* C and A: Forage. Some of [k]C and A: most
Scrupulous were unwilling [l]C: mere] A: meer [m]A: most [n]C and A: now and then
have of shewing their Joy, and [o]C and A: now swell'd

it impracticable for us to ford it, nor cou'd we guess when the Water wou'd fall enough to let us go over.

This put our Mathematical Professor, who shou'd have set a better Example, into the Vapours, fearing he shou'd be oblig'd to take up his Winter Quarters in that doleful Wilderness. But the rest were not infected with his want of Faith, but preserv'd a Firmness of Mind superior to such little Adverse Accidents.[p] They trusted that the same good Providence, which had most remarkably prosper'd them hitherto[q], wou'd continue its goodness, and conduct them safe to[r] the End of their Journey.[312]

However we found plainly that travelling on the Sunday contrary to our constant Rule had not thriven with us in the least. We were not gainers of any distance by it, because the River made us pay two days for violating one.

Nevertheless by making this Reflection[s], I wou'd not be thought so rigid an Observer of the Sabbath, as to allow of no Work at all to be done, or Journeys to be taken upon it. I shou'd not care to ly still, and be knockt on the head as the Jews were heretofore by *Antiocus,* because I believ'd it unlawfull to stand upon my Defense on this good Day; Nor wou'd I care like a certain New-England Magistrate, to order a Man to the Whipping-Post, for daring to ride for a Midwife on the Lord's day[t].[313]

On the contrary I am for doing all Acts of Necessity, Charity, and Self-Preservation upon a Sunday, as well as other day's of the Week. But as I think our present March cou'd not strictly be justify'd[a] by any of these Rules, it was but just we shou'd suffer a little for it.

I never cou'd learn that the Indians set apart any day of the Week, or the Year, for the Service of God. They pray[b] as Philosophers eat, only when they have a Stomach, without having any set time for it. Indeed these Idle People have very little occasion for a Sabbath, to refresh themselves after hard Labour[c], because very few of them ever Labour at all. Like the wild Irish they had rather want than work, and are all Men of Pleasure, to whom every day is a day of rest.

Indeed in their Hunting they will take a little Pains, but this being only a Diversion, their Spirits are ^rather^ rais'd than depress'd by it, and therefore need at most but a Night's Sleep to recruit them.

4.   By some Stakes we had driven into the River yesterday, we perceiv'd the Water began to fall, but fell so slowly, that we found we must have

[p]C: *Paragraph break canceled with added lines.*   [q]A: either to   [r]A: and conduct them to   [s]A: Observation   [t]C: days] A: Days   [a]A: But as our present March cou'd not be justify'd] C: *as in V.*   [b]A: or the Year. They pray] C: *as in V.*   [c]C: Indeed <they> these ^Idle People^ have

Patience a day or two longer. And because we were unwilling to ly altogether Idle, we sent back some of the men to bring up the two Horses, that tir'd the Saturday before. They were found near the place where we had left them, but seem'd too sensible of their Liberty to come to us. They were found standing indeed, but as motionless as the Equestrian Statue at *Charing-Cross*.[314]

We had great reason to apprehend more Rain by the Clouds [93] that drove over our Heads. The boldest amongst us were not without some Pangs of uneasiness at so very sullen a Prospect. However God be prais'd it all blew over in a few Hours.[d]

If much Rain had fallen, we resolv'd to make a Raft and bind it together with Grape-Vines, to Ferry ourselves[e] and Baggage over the River.[f] Tho' in that Case we expected the Swiftness of the Stream wou'd have carry'd down our Raft a long way before we cou'd have tugg'd it to the opposite Shoar.

One of the young Fellows we had sent to bring up the tired Horses, entertained us in the Evening with a remarkable Adventure, he had met with that day.

He had straggled it seems from his Company in a mist, and made a Cubb of a year old betake itself to a Tree. While he was new priming his piece with intent to fetch it down, the Old Gentlewoman appear'd, and perceiving her Heir apparent in Distress, advanc'd open Mouth'd to his relief.

The Man was so intent upon his Game, that she had approach't very near him[g], before he perceiv'd her. But finding his Danger, he faced about upon the Enemy, which immediately rear'd upon her Posteriors, &[h] put herself in Battle Array.

The Man admiring at the Bear's assurance, endeavour'd to fire upon Her, but by the Dampness of the Priming, his Gun did not go off. He cock't it a second time, and had the same Misfortune. After missing Fire twice, he had the folly to punch the Beast with the muzzle of his Piece, but Mother Bruin, being upon her Guard, seiz'd the Weapon with her Paws, and by main Strength wrencht it out of the Fellows Hands.

The Man, being thus fairly disarm'd, thought himself no longer a Match for the Enemy, and therefore retreated as fast as his Legs cou'd carry him.

The Brute naturally grew[i] bolder upon the flight of her Adversary, and pursued him with all her heavy Speed. For some time it was doubtfull whether fear made one run faster, or Fury the other. But after an even Course

---

[d]V: *Phrase* in a few Hours *added at end of line in Byrd's hand (absent in C and A).*
[e]C: ferry over   [f]C: *Paragraph break canceled.*   [g]A: approach't near him   [h]C: reared <del>herself</del> upon her Posteriors, <and so> to put herself] A: Posteriors, to put   [i]A: grew naturally

of about 50 Yards, the Man had the Mishap to stumble over a Stump, and fell down at his full Length. He now wou'd have sold his Life a Penny-worth: but the Bear apprehending there might be some Trick in the Fall, instantly halted, and look't with much attention on her Prostrate Foe[j].[315]

In the mean while the Man had with great Presence of Mind resolv'd to make the Bear believe he was dead, by lying Breathless on the Ground, in hopes that the Beast wou'd be too generous to kill him over again. To carry on the Farce, he acted the Corps for some time, without dareing to raise his head, to see how near the Monster was to him. But in about two Minutes, to his unspeakable Comfort, he was rais'd from the Dead, by the Barking of a Dog, belonging to one of his Companions, who[k] came seasonably to his Rescue, and drove the Bear from pursuing the Man to take care of her Cubb, which she fear'd might now fall into a second Distress.[316]

5.   We judg'd the Waters were asswag'd enough this Morning to make the River fordable. Therefore about Ten we try'd the Experiment, and every Body got over safe, except one Man, whose Horse slipt from [94] a Rock, as he forded over, and threw him into the River. But being able to swim, he was not carry'd down the Stream very far[l], before he recover'd the North Shoar.

At the Distance of about 6 Miles we past *Cascade Creek,* and 3 Miles farther we came upon the Banks of the Dan, which we cros't with much Difficulty, by reason the Water was risen much higher than when[m] we forded it before.

Here the same unlucky Person happen'd to be duck't a second time, and was a second time sav'd by swimming.[n] My own Horse too plunged[o] in such a Manner, that his Head was more than once under Water: but with much ado recover'd his Feet, tho' he made so low an Obeisance, that the water ran fairly over my Saddle.

We continued our March as far as *Low-Land-Creek,* where we took up our Lodging for the benefit of the Canes, and Winter Grass, that grew upon the rich Grounds thereabouts. On our way thither we had the Misfortune to drop another Horse, tho he carry'd nothing the whole day but his Saddle. We shew'd the same favour to most of our Horses, for fear, if we did not do it, we shou'd in a little time be turn'd into Beasts of Burthen ourselves.

Custom had now made travelling on foot so familiar, that we were able to walk ten Miles with Pleasure. This we cou'd do in our Boots, notwithstanding[p] our way lay over rough Woods, and uneven Grounds.

Our learning to walk in heavy Boots was the same advantage to us, that

[j]C: Postrate Foe   [k]C and A: which   [l]C: A: very far down the stream] C: *as in V*
[m]C: risen <since> ^much higher than^ when   [n]C: *Paragraph break canceled.*   [o]A: Horse plung'd too   [p]C: <'tho> ^notwithstanding^

learning to Dance High-Dances in wooden Shoes[q], is to the French, it made us most exceeding nimble[r] without them.[317]

The Indians, who have no way of travelling but on the Hoof, make nothing of going 25 Miles a day, and carrying their little necessaries at their backs, and sometimes a stout Pack of Skins into the Bargain. And very often[s] they laugh at the English, who can't stir to a next Neighbour without a Horse, and say that 2 Legs are too much for such lazy People, who can't visit their next Neighbour without Six.[t]

For their Parts, they were utter Strangers to all of our Beasts of Burthen or[a] Carriage, before the Sloathfull Europeans came amongst them. They had on no part of the American Continent, or in any of the Islands, either Horses or Asses, Camels, Dromedaries, or Elephants[b] to ease the Legs of the Original Inhabitants, or to lighten their Labour.

Indeed in South America, and particularly in *Chili,* they have an usefull Animal call'd *Paco.* This Creature resembles a Sheep pretty much, only in the Length of the Neck, and figure of the Head, it is more like a Camel. It is very near as high as an Ass, and the Indians there make use of it for carrying moderate Burthens.

The Fleece that grows upon it, is very valuable for the fineness, length, and Glossiness of the Wool[c]. It has one remarkable Singularity that the Hoofs of its fore feet have three Clefts, and those behind no more than one. The Flesh of this animal is something dryer than our Mutton, but altogether as well tasted.

When it is Angry, it has no way of resenting it's wrongs, but by spitting in the Face of those that provoke it: and if the Spawl happen to light on the bare Skin of any Person, it first [95] creates an Itching, and afterwards a Scab, if no Remedy be apply'd. The way to manage these *Pacos,* and make them tractable, is, to bore a hole in their Ears, thro' which they put a Rope, and ^then^ guide them[d] just as they please.

In Chili they weave a beautifull kind of Stuff, with thread made of this Creatures Wool, which has a Gloss Superior to any Camlet, and sold very dear in that Country.[318]

6.   The Difficulty[e] of finding the Horses among the tall Canes made it late before we decampt. We travers'd very hilly Grounds, but to make amends,

[q]A: learning to Dance in Wooden Shoes] C: learning to dance High-Dances in wooden Shoes   [r]C: ^most^ exceedingly nimble] A: most exceedingly nimble   [s]A: sometimes   [t]V: *Phrase inserted at end of paragraph in Byrd's hand (absent in C and A).*   [a]A: and   [b]A: Camels, or Elephants   [c]A: for the fineness of the Wool   [d]C and A: and guide them   [e]*Here ends the C MS.*

it was pretty clear of Underwoods. We avoided crossing the Dan twice by taking[f] a Compass round the Bent of it. There was no passing by the Angle of the River, without halting a Moment to entertain our Eyes ^again^[g] with that charming Prospect. When that pleasure was over, we proceeded to Sable Creek, and encampt a little to the East of it.

The River thereabouts had a charming Effect, its Banks being adorn'd with green Canes, sixteen feet high, which make a Spring all the Year, as well as plenty of Forrage all the Winter.[h]

One of the Men wounded an Old Buck, that was grey with years, and seem'd by the Reverend Marks he bore upon him, to confirm the currant Opinion of that Animals Longevity. The Smart of his Wound made him not only turn upon the Dogs, but likewise pursue them to some Distance with great fury.

However he got away at last, tho' by the blood that issued from his Wound, he cou'd not run far before he fell, and without doubt made a comfortable repast for the Wolves. However the Indian had better Fortune, and supply'd us with a fat Doe, and a Young Bear of two Years old; at that age they are in their Prime, and if they[i] be fat withal, are a[j] Morsel for a Cardinal.[319]

All the Land we travell'd over this day, and the day before, that is to say from the River Irvin to Sable Creek, is exceedingly rich, both on the Virginia Side of the Line, and that of Carolina. Besides whole Forrests of Canes, that adorn the Banks of the River and Creeks thereabouts, the fertility of the Soil throws out such a Quantity of Winter Grass, that Horses and Cattle might keep themselves in Heart all the cold Season without the help of any Fodder. Nor have the low Grounds only this advantage, but likewise[k] the higher Land, and particularly that which we call the Highland Pond, which is two Miles broad and of a length unknown.[320]

I question not but there are 30,000 Acres at least lying all-together as fertile, as the Lands were said to be about Babylon, which yielded, if Heroditus tells us right, an Increase of no less than 2 or 300 for One. But this hath the Advantage of being a higher, & consequently a much healthyer Situation than that. So that a Colony of 1000[l] Families might with the help of Moderate Industry[m] pass their time very happily there.[321]

Besides Grazing and Tillage, which wou'd abundantly compensate ^their Labour^ they might plant Vineyards upon the Hills, in which Situation the richest Wines are always produc'd.

[f]A: fetching   [g]A: Eyes with   [h]V: *Phrase* as well . . . Winter *inserted at end of paragraph in Byrd's hand (absent in A).*   [i]A: he is in his Prime, and if he   [j]A: is   [k]A: also
[l]A: a Thousand   [m]A: might with a Moderate Industry

They might also propagate white Mulberry Trees, which thrive exceedingly in this Climate, in order to the feeding of Silk Worms, and making of Raw Silk.[322] [96]

They might too[n] produce Hemp, Flax, and Cotton in what quantity they pleas'd, not only for their own use, but likewise for Sale. Then they might raise very plentifully Orchards, both of Peaches and Apples, which contribute as much as any Fruit, to the Luxury of Life. There is no Soil or Climate will yield better Rice than this, which is a Grain of prodigious Increase, and ^of^ very[o] wholesome Nourishment. In short every thing will grow plentifully here to supply either the Wants[p] or Wantonness of Man.

Nor can I so much as wish that the more tender Vegetables might grow here, such as Orange, Lemon, and Olive Trees, because then we shou'd lose the much greater benefit of the brisk Northwest Winds, which purge the Air, and sweep away all the Malignant Fevers, which hover over Countries, that are always warm.

The Soil wou'd also want the Advantages of Frost, and Snow, which by their Nitrous Particles contribute not a little to its Fertility. Besides the Inhabitants wou'd be depriv'd of the Variety and Sweet Vicissitude of the Seasons, which is much more delightfull[q] than one dull and constant Succession of Warm Weather, diversify'd only by Rain and Sun-Shine.[323]

There is also another convenience, that happens to this Country by cold Weather, it destroys a great number of Snakes, and other Venomous Reptiles, and troublesome Insects, or at least lays them to sleep for several Months, which otherwise would annoy us the whole year round, & multiply beyond all Enduring.

Tho' Oranges and Lemons are desirable Fruits, and usefull enough in many Cases, yet when the Want of them is supply'd by others more useful, we have no cause to complain.

There is no Climate, that produces every thing, since the Deluge wrencht the Poles of the World out of their place, nor is ^it^ fit it shou'd be so, because, it is[r] the mutual Supply one Country receives from another, which creates a mutual Traffick and Intercourse amongst Men.[324] And in Truth were it not for this Correspondence in order to make up each others Wants, the Wars betwixt Bordering Nations, like those of the Indians and other barbarous People, wou'd be[s] perpetual, and irreconcileable.[325]

As to Olive Trees, I know by Experience they will never stand the Sharpness of our Winters, but their Place may be supply'd by the Plant call'd Sesamum,

---

[n]A: also   [o]A: and very   [p]A: to supply the Wants   [q]A: which is more delightfull
[r]A: because of   [s]A: of the Indians, wou'd be

which yields an infinite quantity of large Seed, from whence a sweet Oyl is prest, that is very wholsom, and in use amongst the People of Lesser Asia. Likewise it is us'd in Egypt, preferably to Oyl Olive, being not so apt to make those that eat it constantly break out in Scabbs as they do in many parts of Italy. This wou'd grow very kindly here, and has already been planted with good Success in North Carolina by way of Experiment.[326]

7.   After crossing the Dan, we made a march of 8 Miles over Hills and Dales, as far as the next Ford of that River. And now we were by Practice become such very able Footmen, that we easily outwalk't our Horses, and cou'd have march't much farther, [97] had it not been in pity to their Weakness. Besides here[t] was plenty of Canes, which was reason enough to make us shorten our Journey. Our Gunners did great Execution as they went along, killing no less than two Brace of Deer, and as many Wild Turkeys.

Tho' Practice will soon make a Man of tolerable Vigour an able Footman, yet as a Help to bear Fatigue I us'd to chew a Root of Ginseng as I walk't along. This kept up my Spirits, and made me trip away as nimbly in my half Jack-Boots as younger men cou'd do in their Shoes.[327] This Plant is in high Esteem in China, where it sells for its Weight in Silver. Indeed it dos not grow there, but in the Mountains of Tartary, to which Place the Emperor of China sends 10,000 Men every Year on purpose to gather it. But it grows so scatteringly there, that even so many hands can bring home no great Quantity.[328] Indeed it is a Vegetable of so many Vertues, that Providence has planted it very thin in every Country, that has the happiness to produce it. Nor ^indeed^ is[a] Mankind worthy of so great a Blessing, since Health and long Life are commonly abus'd to ill Purposes. This Noble Plant grows likewise at the Cape of Good-hope where tis call'd *Kanna* and is in wonderfull Esteem among the Hotentots. It grows also on the Northern Continent of America near the Mountains, but as sparingly as Truth & Publick Spirit. It answers exactly both to the Figure and Vertues of that which grows in Tartary, so that there can be no doubt of its being the same.[329]

Its vertues are, that it gives an uncommon Warmth and Vigour to the Blood, and frisks the Spirits beyond any other Cordial. It chears the Heart even of a Man that has a bad Wife, and makes him look down with great Composure on the Crosses of the World. It promotes insensible Perspiration, dissolves all Phlegmatick and Viscous Humours, that are apt to obstruct the narrow Channels of the Nerves. It helps the Memory, and wou'd quicken even Helvetian dulness. Tis friendly[b] to the Lungs, much more[c] than Scolding itself. It comforts the Stomach, and strengthens the Bowels, preventing

---

[t]A: there   [a]A: Nor is   [b]A: quickens even dulness itself. It is friendly   [c]A: even more

PLATE 10. Chinese Root (Ginseng). *[Pierre] Pomet,* A Compleat History of Druggs *(London, 1712). This item is reproduced by permission of the Huntington Library, San Marino, California*

all Collicks and Fluxes. In one[d] Word it will make a Man live a great while, and very well while he dos live. And what is more, it will even make Old Age amiable, by rendring it chearful, and good humour'd. However 'tis of little use in the Feats of Love, as a great Prince once found, who hearing of its invigorating Quality, sent as far as China for some of it, tho[e] his Ladys cou'd not boast of any Advantage thereby.[330]

We gave the Indian the Skins of all the Deer that he shot himself and the Men the Skins of what they kill'd, and every Evening after the Fires were made, they stretch't them very tight upon Sticks and dry'd them. This by a nocturnal Fire appear'd at first a very odd Spectacle, every thing being dark and gloomy round about. After they are dry'd in this Manner, they may be folded up without Damage, till they come to be dress't according to Art.

The Indians dress them with Deer's Brains, and so do the English here by their Example. For Expeditions sake they often stretch their Skins over Smoak in order to dry them, which makes them smell so disagreeably that a Rat must have a good Stomach to gnaw them in that condition. Nay tis said, while that Perfume continues in a Pair of Leather Breeches, the Person that wears them, will be in no Danger of that Villanous little Insect the French call *Morpion*.[331] [98]

And now I am upon the Subject of Insects, it may not be improper to mention some few Remedies against those that are most Vexatious in this Climate. There are two Sorts without Doors, that are great Nusances, the *Tikes* and the *Horse Flies*. The Tikes are either Deer Tikes, or those that annoy the Cattle. The first kind are long and take a very strong Gripe, being most in remote Woods above the Inhabitants.[332]

The other are round and more gently insinuate themselves into the Flesh, being in all places where Cattle are frequent. Both these Sorts are apt to be troublesome during the Warm Season, but have such an Aversion to Penny Royal, that they will attaque no Part, that is rubb'd with the Juice of that fragrant Vegetable. And a strong Decoction of this is likewise the most effectual Remedy against Seed-Tikes, which bury themselves in your Legs, when they are so small, you can hardly discern them without a *Microscope*.

The *Horse Flies* are not only a great Grievance for Horses, but likewise to those that ride them; These little Vixons confine themselves chiefly to the Woods, and are most in moist[f] Places. Tho' this Insect be no bigger than an ordinary Fly, it bites very smartly, darting its' little Proboscis into the Skin the instant it lights upon it. These are offensive only in the hot Months, and in the Day time, when they are a great Nusance to Travellors: Insomuch that it is no

[d]A: a   [e]A: but   [f]A: in low and moist

Wonder they were formerly made use of for one of the Plagues of Egypt. But Dittany, which is to be had in the Woods, all the while those Insects remain in Vigour, is a sure Defense against them. For this purpose, if you stick a Bunch of it on the Head-Stall of your Bridle, they will be sure to keep a respectfull Distance.[333]

Thus in what part of the Woods soever any thing mischievous or troublesome is found, kind Providence is sure to provide a Remedy. And 'tis probably one great Reason why God was pleas'd to create these, and many other Vexatious Animals, that Men shou'd exercise their Wits and Industry, to guard themselves against them.

Bears Oyl is used by the Indians as a General Defense against every Species of Vermin. Among[g] the rest, they say it keeps both Bugs and Musquetas from assaulting their Persons, which wou'd otherwise devour such uncleanly People. Yet Bears Grease has no strong Smell, as that Plant had, which the Egyptians formerly us'd against Mosquetas, resembling our Palma-Christi, the Juice of which smelt so disagreeably, that the Remedy was worse than the Disease.[334]

Against mosketas in Egypt the[h] Richer Sort us'd to build lofty Towers with Bed Chambers in the Tops of them, that they might rest undisturbed. 'Tis certain that these Insects[i] are no High-Flyers, because their Wings are weak, and their Bodies so light, that if they mount ever so little, the wind blows them quite away from their Course, and they become an easy prey to the Martins, East-India Bats, and other Birds that fly about in continual Quest of them.[335]

8. As we had twice more to cross the Dan over two Fords, that lay no more than 7 Miles from each other, we judg'd the Distance [99] wou'd not be much greater to go round the Bent of it. Accordingly we sent the Indian and two white Men that way, who came up with us in the Evening, after fetching a Compass of about 12 Miles.

They told us that about a Mile from our last Camp they past a Creek fortify'd with steep Cliffs, which therefore gain'd the name of Cliff Creek. Near 3 Miles beyond that they forded a second Creek, on the Margin of which grew abundance of Tall Canes, and this was call'd Hixe's Creek, from one of the Discoverers. Between these two Creeks lies a level of exceeding rich Land full of large Trees, and cover'd with black Mould as fruitfull, if we believe them, as that which is yearly overflow'd by the Nile.[336]

We who march't the nearest way upon the Line, found the Ground rising and falling between the two Fords[j] of the Dan, which almost broke our own

[g]A: Amongst   [h]A: those in Egypt   [i]A: that Mosquetas   [j]A: Branches

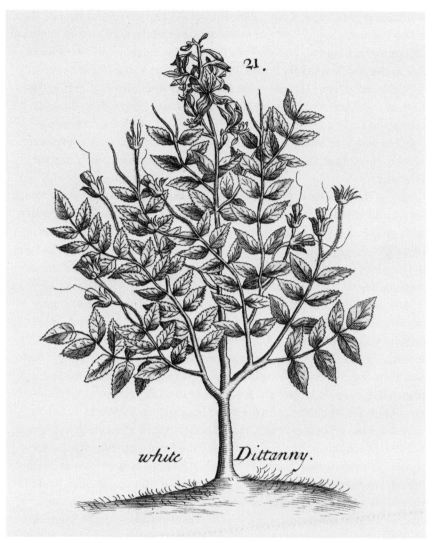

PLATE 11. Dittany. *[Pierre] Pomet, A Compleat History of Druggs (London, 1712). This item is reproduced by permission of the Huntington Library, San Marino, California*

Winds, and the Hearts of our jaded Palfreys. When we had past the last Ford, it was a sensible Joy to find[k] our selves safe over all the Waters, that might cut off our Retreat. And we had the greater Reason to be thankfull, because so late in the Year, it was very unusual to find the Rivers so fordable.

We catch't a large Tarapin in the River, which is one kind of Turtle. The flesh of it is wholesome, and good for consumptive People. It lays a great number of Eggs, not larger but rounder than those of Pigeons. These are soft, but withal so tough, that 'tis difficult to break them, yet are very sweet and invigorating so that some Wives recommend them earnestly to[l] their Husbands.[337]

One of the Men by an Overstrain had unhappily got a Runing of the Reins, for which I gave him every Morning a Little Sweet Gumm dissolv'd in Water, with good Success. This Gumm distils from a large Tree, call'd the Sweet-Gumm Tree, very common in Virginia, and is as healing in its Vertue as Balm of Gilead, or the Balsams of Tolu and of Peru. It is likewise a most agreeable Perfume very little inferior to Ambergris.[338]

And now I have mention'd Ambergris, I hope it will not be thought an unprofitable[m] digression, to give a faithfull Account how it is produced, in order to reconcile the various Opinions concerning it. It is now certainly found to be the Dung of the Sperma-Cete-Whale, which is at first very black and unsavory. But after having been wash't for some Months in the Sea, and blanch'd in the Sun, it comes at length to be of a Grey Coulour, and from a most offensive smell, conracts the finest fragrancy in the World.

Besides the Fragrancy of this Animal Substance tis a[n] very rich & innocent Cordial, which raises the Spirits without stupefying them afterwards, like Opium, or Intoxicating ^them^ like[o] Wine. The Animal Spirits are amazeingly refresh't by this Cordial without the Danger of any ill Consequence. And if Husbands were now and then to dissolve a little of it in their Broth, their Consorts might be[p] the better for it as well as themselves. In the Bahama Islands (where a great Quantity is found, by reason the Sperma-Cete-Whales resort thither continually) it is us'd as an Antidote against the Venomous Fish which abound thereabouts, wherewith the People are apt to Poison themselves.[339]

We are not only oblig'd to that Whale for this rich Parfume, [100] but also for the Sperma Cete itself, which is the Fat of that Fishes Head boil'd and purg'd from all its Impuritys. What remains is of a Balsamick and detersive Quality very friendly to the Lungs, and usefull in many other Cases.[340]

---

[k]A: Joy to us to find   [l]A: recommend them to   [m]A: improfitable   [n]A: it is a
[o]A: intoxicating like   [p]A: wou'd be

The Indian had kill'd a fat Doe in the Compass he took round the Elbow of the River, but was contented to Prime it only, by reason it was too far off, to lugg the whole Carcass upon his Back. This and a Brace of Wild Turkeys, which our Men had Shot, made up all our Bill of Fare this Evening but could only afford a Philosophical Meal to so many craving Stomachs.[341]

The Horses were now so lean, that any thing would gall those that carryd the least Burthen. No wonder then if several of them had Sore Backs, especially now the Pads of the Saddles and Packs were press'd flat with long and constant Use. This would have been another Misfortune, had we not been provided with an easy Remedy for it.

One of the Commissioners believing that such Accidents might happen in a far Journey, had furnish't himself with Plasters of Strong Glue spread pretty[q] thick. We laid on these, after making them running hot, which sticking fast, never fell off till the Sore was perfectly heal'd. In the mean time it defended the part so well, that the Saddle might bear upon it without Danger of further Injury.

We reckon'd our selves now pretty well out of the Latitude of Bears, to the great Grief of most of the company. There was still Mast enough left in the Woods to keep the Bears from drawing so near to the Inhabitants. They like not the Neighbourhood of Merciless Man, till Famine compels them to it. They are all Black in this part of the World, and so is their Dung, but will make Linnen white, being tolerable good Soap without any Preparation, but only drying.[342]

These Bears are of a Moderate Size, whereas within the Polar Circles they are white, and much larger. Those of the Southern parts of Muscovy are of a Russet Colour, but among the *Samoeids* as well as in *Greenland,* and *Nova-Zembla,* they are as white as the Snow, they converse with, and by some Accounts are as large as a moderate Ox.

The Excessive Cold of that Climate sets their Appetites so Sharp, that they will attack a Man without Ceremony, and even climb up a Ships Side to come at him. They range about, and are very mischievous all the time the Sun is above the Horizon, which is something more than Five Months, but after the Sun is set for the rest of the Year, they retire into Holes, or bury themselves under the Snow, and sleep away the Dark Season without any Sustenance at all. Tis pitty our Beggars and Pick-pockets cou'd not do the same.[343]

Our Journey this day was above 12 Miles, and more than half the way terribly hamper'd with Bushes. We tir'd another Horse, which we were oblig'd to leave two Miles short of where we encampt, and indeed several others were

[q]A: very

upon the Careen almost every Step. Now we wanted one of those celebrated Musicians of Antiquity, who they tell us among[r] many other Wonders of their Art, cou'd play an Ayr, which by its Animateing [101] *Briskness,* wou'd make a Jaded Horse caper, and curvet[s] much better than any Whip, Spur, or even than Swearing. Tho' I fear our poor Beasts were so harrast, that it wou'd have been beyond the Skill of Orpheus him self so much as to make them prick up their Ears.

For proof of the Marvellous Power of Musick among the Ancients, some Historians say, that one of those skilfull Masters took upon him to make the great Alexander start up from his Seat, and handle his Javelin, whether he would or not, by the force of a sprightly Tune, which he knew how to play to Him. The King order'd the Man to bring his Instrument, and then fixing himself firmly in his chair, and determining not to stir, he bad him strike up as soon as he pleas'd. The Musician obey'd, and presently rous'd the Heros Spirits with such Warlike Notes, that he was constrain'd in spite of all his Resolution, to spring up and fly to his Javelin with great Martial Fury[t].[344]

We can the easier credit these prophane Stories by what we find recorded in the Oracles of Truth, where we are told the Wonders David perform'd by sweetly touching his Harp. He made nothing of driving the Evil Spirit out of Saul, tho' a certain Rabbi assures us, he could not do so much by his Wife *Michal,* when she happened to be[a] in her Ayrs.[345]

The greatest Instance we have of the Power of Modern Musick, is, that which cures those who in Italy are bit by the little Spider call'd the Tarantula. The whole Method of which is perform'd in the following Manner.[346]

In Apulia tis a common Misfortune for People to be bit by the Tarantula, and most about Taranto and Gallipoli. This is a grey spider not very large, with a narrow Streak of White along the Back. It is no wonder there are many of these Vilainous Insects, because by a Ridiculous Superstition tis accounted great Inhumanity to kill them. They believe, it seems, that if the Spider come to a Violent Death, all those who had been bit by it, will certainly have a Return of their Frenzy every Year as long as they live. But if it dye a Natural Death, the Patient will have a chance to recover in two or three Years.[347]

The Bite of the Tarantula gives no more pain than the Bite of a Mosqueta, and makes little or no inflammation on the Part, especially when the Disaster happens in April or May. But its Venom encreasing with the Heat of the Season[b], has more fatal Consequences in July and August. The Persons who are so unhappy as to be bit in those Warm Months, fall down on the Place

[r]A: amongst   [s]A: curvet and caper   [t]V: *Phrase* with great Martial Fury *inserted at end of line in Byrd's hand; absent in A.*   [a]A: she was   [b]A: Weather

in a few Minutes, and lye senceless for a considerable time, and when they come to themselves, feel horrible Pains, are very sick at their Stomachs, and in a short time break out into foul Sores. But those who are bit in the Milder Months, have much gentler Symptoms. They are longer before the Distemper shews itself, and then they have[c] a small Disorder in their Sences, are a little Sick, and perhaps have[d] some moderate Breakings out.[348]

However in both cases the Patient keeps upon the Bed, not caring to stir, till he is rous'd by a Tune proper[e] for his particular case. Therefore [As soon as][f] the Symptoms discover themselves, a Tarantula-Doctor is sent for, who after viewing [102] carefully the condition of the Person, first trys one Tune, and then another, til he is so fortunate as to hit the Phrenetick turn of the Patient. No sooner dos this happen, but he begins first to Wag a Finger, then a Hand, and afterwards a Foot, til at last he springs up and dances round the Room with[g] a Surprizeing Agility, rolling his Eyes, and looking wild the whole time.[349] This dancing Fit lasts commonly about 25 Minutes, by which time, he will be all in a Lather. Then he sits down, falls a laughing, and returns to his Sences. So plentiful a Perspiration discharges so much of the Venom as will keep off the Return of the Distemper for a whole Year. Then it will visit Him again, and must be remov'd in[h] the same merry Manner. But three dancing Bouts will do the Business, unless peradventure the Spyder, according to the Vulgar Notion, hath been put to a Violent Death[i].[350]

The Tunes play'd to expell this Whimsicall Disorder are of the Jigg-kind, and exceed not 15 in Number. The Apulians are frequently dancing off the Effects of this Poison, and no Remedy is more commonly apply'd to any other Distemper elsewhere, than those sprightly Tunes are to the Bite of the Tarantula in that part of Italy.

It is remarkable that these Spiders have[j] a greater Spight to the Natives of the Place, than they have to Strangers, and Women are oftener bit than Men. Tho' there may be a Reason for the last, because Women are more confin'd to the House, where these Spyders keep, and their coats make them liable to Attacks unseen, whereas the Men can more easily discover, and brush them off their Legs. Nevertheless both Sexes are cur'd the same way, and thereby shews the Wonderfull Effects of Musick.

Considering how far we had walk't, and consequently how hungry we were, we found but short commons when we came to our Quarters. One Brace of Turkeys were all the Game we cou'd meet with, which almost needed a

[c]A: have only   [d]A: and have   [e]A: Proper Tune   [f]V: Therefore as soon as soon as *amended from A.*   [g]A: dances round with   [h]A: remov'd again in   [i]A: put to Death [j]A: this Spider has

Miracle to enable them to suffice so many Voracious Appetites. However they just made a Shift to keep Famine, and consequently Mutiny out of the Camp. At Night we lodg'd upon the Banks of Buffalo Creek, where none of us cou'd complain of loss of Rest, for having eat too heavy and Luxurious a Supper.[351]

10.   In a Dearth of Provisions our Chaplain pronounc'd it lawfull to make bold with the Sabbath, and send a Party out a Hunting. They fired the Dry Leaves in a Ring of five Miles circumference, which burning inwards drove all the Game to the Center, where they were easily kill'd.

'Tis really a pitiful Sight, to see the extreme Distress, the poor Deer are in, when they find themselves surrounded with this Circle of Fire. They Weep and Groan, like a Human Creature, yet can't move the compassion of those hard hearted People, who are about to murder them. This unmerciful Sport is call'd Fire Hunting, and is much practis'd by the Indians, and Frontier-Inhabitants, who sometimes in the Eagerness of their Diversion [103] are punisht for their cruelty and are hurt by one another, when they shoot across at the Deer which are in the middle.[352]

What the Indians do now by a Circle of Fire, the Ancient Persians perform'd formerly[k] by a Circle of Men: And the same is practis'd at this day in Germany upon extraordinary Occasions, when any of the Princes of the Empire have a Mind to make a General Hunt, as they call it. At such times they order a vast Number of People to surround a whole Territory. Then marching inwards in close Order, they at last force all the Wild Beasts into a Narrow Compass, that the Prince and his Company may have the Diversion of slaughtering as many as they please with their own hands.[353]

Our Hunters massacred two Brace of Deer after this unfair way, of which they brought us one Brace whole, and only the Primings of the rest. So many were absent on this Occasion, that we who remain'd, excus'd the Chaplain from the Trouble of spending his Spirit by Preaching to so thin a Congregation.

One of the men, who had been an old Indian Trader, brought me a Stem of Silk Grass, which was about as big as my little Finger. But being so late in the Year, that the Leaf was fallen off, I am not able to describe the Plant.

The Indians use it in all their little Manufactures, twisting a Thread of it, that is prodigiously strong. Of this they make their Baskets, and the Aprons which[l] their Women wear about their Middles for Decency Sake. These are long enough to wrap quite round them, and reach down to their Knees, with a Fringe on the under part by way of Ornament.

They put on this modest Covering with so much Art, that the most

[k]A: formerly perform'd   [l]A: that

impertinent Curiosity can't in the Negligentest of their Motions or Postures make the least discovery. As this Species of Silk-Grass is much stronger than Hemp, I make no doubt, but Sail-Cloath and Cordage might be made of it, with considerable Improvement.[354]

11.   We had all been so refresht by our day of rest, that we decampt earlier than Ordinary, and past the several Fords[m] of Hico-River. The Woods were thick great Part of this Days Journey, so that we were forc'd to scuffle hard to advance 7 Miles, being equal in fatigue to double that distance of clear and open Grounds.

We took up our Quarters upon Sugar-Tree-Creek, in the same Camp we had lain, when we came up, and happened to be entertain'd at Supper with a Rarity we had never had the fortune to meet with before dureing the whole Expedition[n].

A little wide of this Creek, one of the men had the Luck to meet with a Young Buffalo of two Years Old. It was a Bull, which[o] notwithstanding he was no older, was[p] as big as an ordinary Ox. His Legs were very thick, and very short, and his Hoofs exceeding broad. His Back rose into[q] a kind of Bunch a little above the Shoulders, which I believe contributes not a little to that creature's enormous Strength[r]. His Body is vastly deep from the Shoulders[s] to Brisket, sometimes 6 feet in those that are full grown.[355] [104]

The portly figure of this Animal is disgrac'd by a shabby little Tail not above 12 Inches long[t]. This he cocks up on End, whenever he's in a Passion, and instead of lowing or bellowing, grunts[a] with no better grace than a Hog.[356]

The Hair growing on his Head and Neck is long and shagged, and so soft ^that^ it will spin into Thread not unlike Mohair, which might be wove into a sort of Camblet. Some People have Stockings knit of it, that would have serv'd an Israelite during his forty-Years march thro' the Wilderness.[357]

It's Horns are short and strong, of which the Indians make large Spoons, which they say will split and fall to pieces when ever Poison is put into them. It's Colour is a dirty Brown, and it's Hide so thick, that it is scarce penetrable. However it makes very spungy Sole Leather by the ordinary Method of Tanning, tho' this fault might by good[b] contrivance be mended.

As thick as this poor Beast's Hide was, a Bullet made shift to enter it, and fetch him[c] down. It was found all alone, which seldom Buffalos are[d].

---

[m]A: past all the Fords   [n]V: *Phrase* dureing . . . Expedition *inserted in Byrd's hand at end of paragraph; not in A.*   [o]A: yet   [p]A: he was   [q]A: in   [r]A: that Animal's Natural Strength   [s]A: Shoulder   [t]A: not above 12 Feet long   [a]A: of lowing and bellowing, it grunts   [b]A: some   [c]A: it   [d]A: which Buffalos seldome are

They usually range about in Herds, like other Cattle, and tho' they differ something in figure, are certainly of the same Species. There are two Reasons for this Opinion, The Flesh of both has[e] exactly the same taste, and the mixt Breed betwixt both they say will generate. All the Difference, I cou'd perceive between the Flesh of Buffalo, and common Beef[f], was, that the Flesh[g] of the first was much Yellower than that of the other, and the Lean something tougher.[358]

The Men were so delighted with this new Dyet, that the Gridiron and Frying-Pan had no more rest all Night, than a poor Husband subject to Curtain Lectures. Buffalos may be easily tamed, when they are taken Young. The best way to catch them, is, to carry a Milch Mare into the Woods, and when you find a Cow and a Calf, to kill the Cow, and than having catch't the Calf, to suckle it upon the Mare. After once or twice sucking her, it will follow Her Home, and become as gentle as another Calf.[359]

If we cou'd get into a Breed of them, they might be made very usefull not only for the Dairy, by giving of an Ocean of Milk, but also for drawing vast and cumbersome Weights by their prodigious Strength. These with the other Advantages, I mention'd before[h], wou'd make this sort of Cattle more profitable to Owner, than any other we are acquainted with, tho' they woud need a World of Provender[i].

12.   Before we marcht this Morning, every man took care to pack up some Buffalo-Steaks in his Wallet, besides what he cramm'd into his Belly. When Provisions were Plenty, we always found it Difficult to get out early, being too much embarrast with a long-winded Breakfast.

However by the Strength of our Beef, we made a shift to walk about 12 Miles, crossing Blewing, and Tewaw-homini Creeks. And because this last Stream receiv'd its Appellation from the Disaster of a Tuskaruro Indian, t'will not be straggleing much out of the way, to say something of that particular Nation. [105]

These Indians were heretofore very numerous and powerfull, making within time of Memory, at least a Thousand fighting men. Their Habitation before the War with Carolina, was on the North Branch of Neus River, commonly call'd Connecta-Creek, in a pleasant and fruitfull Country. But now the few that are left of that Nation, live on the North Side of Moratuck, which is all that Part of Roanoak below the great Falls towards Albemarle-Sound.[360]

---

[e]A: hath   [f]A: and that of Common Beef   [g]A: Fat   [h]A: other Advantages wou'd
[i]V: *phrase* tho' . . . Provender *inserted in Byrd's hand at end of paragraph; absent in A.*

Formerly there were seven Towns of these Savages, lying not far from each other, but now their Number is greatly reduc'd.

The Trade, they have had the Misfortune to drive with the English, has furnish't them constantly with Rum, which they have used so immoderately, that what with the Distempers, and what with the Quarrels it begat[j] amongst them, it has prov'd a double Destruction.

But the greatest Consumption of these Savages happen'd by the War about Twenty Five years ago, on Account of some Injustice the Inhabitants of that Province had done them about their Lands.[361]

It was on that Provocation they resented their Wrongs a little too severely upon Mr. Lawson, who under Colour of being Surveyor Genll. had encroach't too much upon their Territories, at which they were so enrag'd, that they way-laid him, and cut his Throat from Ear to Ear, but at the same time releas'd the Baron-de-Graffenried, whom they had seiz'd for Company, because it appear'd plainly he had done them no Wrong.[362]

This Blow was followed by some other Bloody Actions on the Part of the Indians, which brought on the War, wherein many of 'em were cut off, and many were oblig'd to flee for Refuge to the Senecas, so that now there remain[k] so few, that they are in Danger of being quite exterminated by the Cataubas, their mortal Enemies.[363]

These Indians have a very odd Tradition amongst them, that many Years ago, their Nation was grown so dishonest, that no man cou'd keep any of his Goods, or so much as his loving Wife to himself. That however their God, being unwilling to root them out for their crimes, ^did them the honour to^[l] send a Messenger from Heaven to instruct them, and set them a perfect Example of Integrity, and kind Behaviour towards one another.

But this holy Person with all his Eloquence and Sanctity of Life, was able to make very little Reformation amongst them. Some few Old Men did listen a little to his Wholsome Advice, but all the young fellows were quite incorrigible. They not only neglected his Precepts, but derided and Evil Entreated his Person. At last takeing upon Him to reprove some Young Rakes of the Conechta-Clan very sharply for their impiety, they were so provok'd at the Freedom of his Rebukes, that they tied him to a Tree, and shot him with Arrows thro' the Heart.[m] But their God took instant Vengeance on all who had a Hand in that Monstrous Act, by Lightening from Heaven, & has ever since visited their Nation with a continual Train of Calamitys, nor will he ever leave

[j]A: it has begat   [k]A: remains   [l]V: *Phrase* did . . . to *inserted in V, absent in A.*   [m]A: thro' the Heart with Arrows

off punishing, & wasting their People, till he shall have blotted every liveing Soul of them out of the World.[364] [106]

Our Hunters shot nothing this whole day but a straggling Bear, which happen'd to fall by the Hand of the very Person, who had been lately disarm'd, and put to flight, for which he declar'd War against the whole Species.

13.   We pursued our Journey with all Diligence, and forded Ohimpamony Creek about Noon, and from thence proceeded to Yaypatsco, which we cou'd not cross without difficulty. The Beavers had dammed up the Water much higher than we found it at our going up, so that we were oblig'd to lay a Bridge over a part that was shallower than the rest, to facilitate our Passage.

Beavers have more of Instinct, that Half-Brother[n] of Reason, than any other Animal, especially in matters of Self-Preservation. In their Houses they always contrive a Sally-Port, both towards the Land, and towards the Water, that so they may escape by one, if their Retreat shou'd happen to be cut off at the other.

They perform all their Works in the Dead of Night, to avoid Discovery, and are kept diligently to it by the Master-Beaver, which by his Age or Strength has gain'd to himself an Authority over the Rest. If any of the Gang happen to be lazy, or will not exert himself to the utmost in felling of Trees, or dragging them to the place where they are made use of, this Superintendant will not fail to chastize him with the Flat of the Tail, wherewith he is able to give unmercifull Strokes.

They lie snug in their Houses all day, unless some unneighbourly Miller chance to disturb their repose, by demolishing their Damms for supplying[o] his Mill with Water.

'Tis rare to see one of them, and the Indians for that Reason have hardly any way to take them, but by laying Snares near the place, where they damm up the Water. But the English Hunters have found out a more effectual Method, by using the following Receipt. Take the Large Pride of the Beaver, squeeze all the Juice out of it, then take the small Pride, and squeeze out about 5 or 6 Drops; Take the inside of Sassafras Bark, Powder it, and mix it with the Liquor, and place this Bait conveniently for your Steel-Trap.[365]

The story of their biteing off their *Testicles* to compound for their Lives, when they are pursued, is a Story taken upon trust by Pliny, like many others. Nor is it the Beavers Testicles that carry the Perfume, but they have a Pair of Glands just within the Fundament as sweet as Musk, that perfume their Dung, and communicate a strong scent to their Testicles, by being plac'd near them.[366]

[n]A: Younger Brother   [o]A: for the better supplying

Tis true several Creatures have strange Instincts for their Preservation, as the Egyptian Frog we are told by Elian will carry a whole Joint of Reed across its Mouth, that it may not be swallow'd by the Ibis.[367]

And this long-neckt fowle, will give itself a Clyster with its Beak, whenever it finds itself too costive or feaverish.[368] The Dogs of that Country lap the Water of the Nile in a full Trot, that [107] they may not be snapt by the Crocodiles.[369] Both Beavers and Wolves we know when one of their Legs is catch't in a Steel Trap, will bite it off, that they may escape with the rest. The Flesh of the Beavers is tough and dry, all but the Tail, which like the Parrots Tongue, was one of the far fetcht Rarities with which *Heliogabulus* us'd to furnish his Luxurious Table.[370]

The Furr of these Creatures is very valuable, especially in the more Northern Countries, where it is longer and finer. This the Dutch have lately contriv'd to mix with their Wool, and weave into a sort of Drugget, that is not only warm, but wonderfully light and soft. They also make Gloves and Stockins of it, that keep out the Cold almost as well as the Furr itself, and don't look quite so Savage.[371]

There is a deal of Rich low Ground on Yapatsco Creek, but I believe, liable to be overflow'd in a fresh. However it might be proper enough for Rice, which receives but little Injury from Water.

We encampt on the Banks of Massomony-Creek, after a Journey of more than 11 Miles. By the way we shot a fat Doe, and a wild Turkey, which fed us all plentifully. And we have reason to say, by our own happy Experience, that no man need to despair of his daily Bread in the Woods, whose Faith is but half so large as his Stomach.

14.   Being at length happily arriv'd within 20 Miles of the uppermost Inhabitants, we dispatch't two Men who had the ablest Horses, to go before, and get a Beef kill'd, and some Bread bak'd, to refresh their Fellow Travellers upon their arrival. They had likewise Orders to hire an express to carry a Letter to the *Governour,* giving an Account that we were all return'd in Safety. This was the more necessary, because we had been so long absent, that many now began to fear we were by this time scalp't, and barbacu'd by the Indians.[372]

We decampt with the rest of the People about ten a clock, and marcht near 12 Miles. In our way we crost Nut-bush Creek, and 4 Miles farther we came upon a beautifull Branch of Great Creek, where we took up our Quarters. The Tent was pitcht on an Eminence, which[p] overlookt a wide piece of low Grounds cover'd with Reeds and water'd by a Chrystal Stream gliding thro'

[p]A: that

the middle of it. On the other side of this delightfull Valley, which was about half a Mile wide, rose a Hill that terminated the View, and in the figure of a Semicircle closed in upon the opposite Side of the Valley. This had a most agreeable Effect upon the Eye, and wanted nothing but Cattle grazing in the Meadow, and Sheep and Goats feeding on the Hill, to make it a Compleat Rural *Landscape.*

The Indian kill'd a Fawn, which being upon its growth was[q] not fat, but made some amends by being tender. He also shot an Otter, but our People were now better fed than to eat such Coarse Food. The truth of it is, the Flesh of this Creature has a rank Fishy taste. And for that reason might be a a proper Regale for the *Samoeids*[r], who drink the Czar of *Muscovy*'s Health, and toast their Mistresses, in a Bumper of Train-Oyl.[373]

The Carthusians, to save their Vow of eating no Flesh, pronounce [108] this Amphibious Animal to be a Fish, and feed upon it as such, without wounding their Consciences.[374]

The Skin of the Otter is very soft, and the Swedes make Caps and Socks of it, not only for Warmth, but also because they fancy it strengthens the Nerves, and is good against all Distempers of the Brain.[375]

The Otter is a great Devourer of Fish, which are its Natural Food, and whenever it betakes itself to a Vegetable Dyet, it is as some high-spirited Wives obey their Husbands, by pure Necessity. They dive after their Prey, tho' they can't continue long under Water, but thrust their Noses up to the Surface now and then for Breath. They are great Enemies to Weirs set up in the Rivers to catch Fish, devouring or biteing to pieces all they find there. Nor is it easy either to fright them from this kind of Robbery, or to destroy them. The best way, I cou'd ever find, was, to float an old Wheel just by the Weir, and so soon as the Otter has taken a large Fish, he will get upon the Wheel to eat it at his Ease, which may give you an Opportunity of fireing upon him from the Shoar.[376]

One of our People shot a large Grey Squirel with a very Bushy Tail, a singular Use of which our merry Indian discover'd to us. He said whenever this little Animal has occasion to cross a Run of Water, he launches a Chip or Piece of Bark into the Water, on which he embarks, and holding up his Tail to the Wind, sails over very safely. If this be true, 'tis probable Men learn't at first the Use of Sails, from these ingenious little Animals, as the Hottentots learn't the Physical Use of ^most of their^[s] Plants, from the Baboons.[377]

About three Miles from our Camp, we past *Great-Creek,* and then after traversing[t] very barren Grounds for 5 Miles together, we cros't the Tradeing Path, and soon after had the pleasure of reaching the uppermost Inhabitant.

[q]A: 'twas   [r]A: <Samaids> Samoieds   [s]A: use of their   [t]A: travelling

PLATE 12. Squirrel Using Tail as a Sail. *Olaus Magnus,* Historia de gentibus septentrionalibus . . . *(Rome, 1555). This item is reproduced by permission of the Huntington Library, San Marino, California*

This was a Plantation belonging to Colonel Mumford, where our Men almost burst themselves with Potatoes and Milk. Yet as great a Curiosity as a House was to us Forresters, yet stil we chose to lye in the Tent, as being much the cleanlier, and sweeter Lodging.

　The Tradeing Path[a] abovemention'd receives its Name from being the Route the Traders take with their Caravans, when they go to traffick with the Cataubas, and other Southern Indians. The Catauba's live about 250 Miles beyond Roanoke River, and yet our Traders find their Account in transporting Goods from Virginia to trade with them at their own Towne[b].[378]

　The Common Method of carrying on this Indian Commerce, is as follows. Gentlemen send for Goods proper for such a Trade from *England,* and then either venture[c] them out at their own Risk to the Indian Towns, or else credit some Traders with them of Substance and Reputation, to be paid in Skins at a certain Price agreed betwixt them.

[a]A: Indian Path　[b]V: *Phrase* at their owne Towne *added at end of line, absent in* Λ.
[c]A: and then venture

The Goods for the Indian Trade consist chiefly in Guns, Powder, Shot, Hatchets, (which the Indians call Tomahawks,) Kettles, red & blue Planes, Duffields, Stroudwater Blankets, and [109] some Cutlary Wares, Brass Rings, and other Trinkets.

These Wares are made up into Packs, and carry'd upon Horses, each Load being from 150 to 200 Pounds, with which they are able to travel about 20 Miles a day, if Forrage happen to be[d] plentifull.

Formerly an Hundred Horses have been employ'd in one of these Indian *Caravans,* under the Conduct of 15 or 16 Persons only, but now the Trade is much impair'd, insomuch that they seldom go with half that Number.

The Course from Roanoak to the Cataubas is laid down nearest SW, and lies thro' a fine Country[e], that is water'd by several beautiful Rivers.

Those of the greatest Note are, first *Tar River,* which is the upper Part of *Pamptico,* Flat River, Little River, and Eno River, all three Branches of *Neuse.*

Between Eno and Saxapahaw River, are the Haw old Fields, which have the Reputation of containing the most fertile high-land in this part of the World, lying in a Body of about 50, 000 Acres[f].[379]

This Saxapahaw is the upper Part of Cape-Fair River, the falls of which lye many Miles below the Trading Path.

Some Mountains overlook this Rich Spot of Land, from whence all the Soil washes down into the Plane, and is the Cause of its exceeding Fertility. Not far from thence the Path crosses *Aramanchy* River, a Branch of Saxapahaw, and about 40 Miles beyond that, *Deep-River,* which is the N. Branch of *Pedee.* Then 40 Miles beyond that, the Path intersects the *Yadkin* which is then half a Mile over, & is suppod'd to be the South Branch of the same *Pedee.*

The Soil is exceedingly rich on both sides the *Yadkin,* abounding in rank Grass, and prodigious large Trees, and for plenty of Fish, Fowl and Venison is inferior to no part of the Northern Continent. There the Traders commonly ly still for some days to recruit their Horses Flesh, as well as to recover their own Spirits.

Six Miles farther is Crane Creek so nam'd from its being the Rendezvous of great Armies of Cranes, which wage a more cruel War at this day with the Frogs and the Fish, than they us'd to do with the Pigmies in the Days of Homer.[380]

About threescore Miles more bring you to the first Town of the Cataubas call'd Nauvasa, situated on the Banks of *Santee River.* Besides this Town there are five others belonging to the same Nation, lying all on the same Stream within the Distance of 20 Miles.

These Indians were all call'd formerly by the general Name of the *Usherees,* and were a very numerous and powerfull People, but the frequent Slaughter made upon them by the Northern Indians, and what has been still[g] more destructive by far, the Intemperance and Foul Distempers introduc'd among them by the Carolina Traders, have now reduc'd their Number to little more than 400 Fighting Men, besides Women & Children. It is a charming Place where they live, the Air very wholesome, the Soil fertile, & the Winters ever mild and serene.[381]

In Santee River, as in several others of Carolina, a smaller kind of Allegator is frequently seen, which parfumes the Water with a musky Smell. They seldome exceed Eight Feet in Length in these Parts, whereas near the Equinoctial they come up to twelve [110] or Fourteen.[382] And the heat of the Clymate don't only make them bigger, but more fierce and voracious. They watch the Cattle there, when they come to drink and cool themselves in the River, & because they are not able to drag them into the Deep Water, they make up by Stratagem, what they want in Force. They swallow great Stones, the Weight of which being added to their Strength, enables them to tug a moderate Cow under Water, and as soon as they have drown'd her, discharge the Stones out of their Maw, and then feast upon the Carcase. However as fierce, and as strong as these Monsters are, The Indians will surprize them napping, as they float upon the Surface, get astride upon their Necks, then whip a short piece of Wood like a Truncheon into their Jaws, & holding the Ends with their two hands, hinder them from diving by keeping their Mouths open, and when they are almost spent, they will make to the Shoar where their Riders knock them on the Head and eat them. This amphibious Animal is a smaller kind of Crocodile, haveing the same Shape exactly, only the Crocodile of the Nile is twice as long, being when full grown from 20 to Thirty Feet. This enormous Length is the more to be wonder'd at, because the Crocodile is hatcht from an Egg very little larger than that of a Goose. It has a long Head, which it can open very wide, with very sharp[h] & strong Teeth. Their Eyes are small, their Legs short, with Claws upon their Feet. Their Tail makes half the Length of their Body, and the whole is guarded with hard impenetrable Scales except the Belly which is much softer and smoother. They keep much upon the Land in the day time, but towards the Evening retire into the Water, to avoid the Cold Dews of the Night. They run pretty fast

[g]A has still been   [h]A: with sharp

right forward, but are very awkward and slow in turning, by reason of their unwieldy Length. It is an Error that they have no Tongue, without which they cou'd hardly swallow their Food, but in eating they move the upper Jaw only contrary to all other Animals. The way of catching them in Egypt, is, with a strong Hook[i] fixt to the End of a Chain, and baited with a Joynt of Pork, which they are very fond of. But a live Hog is generally tyed near, the Cry of which allures them to the Hook. This Account of the Crocodile will agree in most particulars with the Allegator, only the Bigness of the last cannot intitle it to the Name of *Leviathan,* which Job gave formerly to the Crocodile, and not to the Whale, as some Interpreters wou'd make us believe.[383]

So soon as the Catauba Indians are inform'd of the Approach of the Virginia-Caravans, they send a Detatchment of their Warriours to bid them Welcome, and escort them safe to their Town, where they are receiv'd with great Marks of Distinction. And their Courtesys to the Virginia-Traders, I dare say, are very sincere, because they sell them better Goods, and better Penny-worths than the Traders of Carolina. They commonly reside among the Indians, till they have barter'd their Goods away[j] for Skins, with which they load their Horses, and come back by the same Path they went.[384] [111]

There is generally some Carolina ^Trader^ that constantly lives[k] among the Cataubas, and pretend[l] to exercise a dictatorial Authority over them. These petty Rulers don't only teach the honester Savages all sorts of Debauchery, but are unfair in their dealings, and use them with all kinds of Oppression. Nor has their Behaviour been at all better to the rest of the Indian Nations among whom they reside, by abusing their Women, and Evil-intreating their Men: And by the way this was the true Reason of the fatal War, which the Nations round about made upon Carolina, in the Year 1713.[385]

Then it was that all the Neighbour[m] Indians, grown weary of the Tyranny and Injustice, with which they had been abus'd for many Years, resolv'd to endure their Bondage[n] no longer, but enter'd into a General Confederacy against their Oppressors of Carolina.

The Indians open'd the War by knocking most of those little Tyrants on the Head, that dwelt amongst them, under pretence of regulating their Commerce. And from thence carry'd their Resentment so far, as to endanger both *North* and *South Carolina.*[386]

16.   We gave Orders that the Horses shou'd pass Roanoak River at Monisep-Ford, while most of the Baggage was transported in a Canoe.

We landed at the Plantation of Cornelius Keith where I beheld the

---

[i]A: is a strong Hook   [j]A: barter'd away their Goods   [k]A: Traders that live   [l]*Thus in V and A.*   [m]A: Neighbouring   [n]A: Burden

wretchedest Scene of Poverty I had ever met with in this happy Part of the World. The Man, his Wife, and six small Children[o] liv'd in a Penn, like so many Cattle, without any Roof over their Heads, but that of Heaven, and this was their airy Residence in the Day time.[p,387]

But then there was a Fodder Stack not far from this Inclosure[q] in which the whole Family shelter'd themselves anights, and in bad weather.

However 'twas almost worth while to be as poor as this Man was, to be as perfectly contented. All his Wants proceeded from Indolence, and not from Misfortune. He had good Land, as well as good Health, and good Limbs to work it, and besides had a Trade very usefull to all the Inhabitants round about. He cou'd make, and set up Quern-Stones very well, and had proper Materials for that purpose just at Hand, if he cou'd have taken the pains to fetch them.[r,388]

There are no other kind of Mills in those remote Parts, and therefore if the Man would have workt at his Trade, he might have liv'd very comfortably. The poor Woman had a little more Industry, and spun Cotton enough to make a thin covering for her own, and her Children's Nakedness.

I am sorry to say it, but Idleness is the general character of the Men in the Southern Parts of this Colony, as well as in North Carolina. The Air is so mild, and the Soil so fruitfull, that very little Labour is requir'd to fill their Bellies, especially where the Woods afford such Plenty of Game. These advantages discharge the Men from the Necessity of killing themselves with Work. And then for[s] the other Article of Raiment, a very little of that will suffise in so temperate a Climate. But so much as is absolutely necessary, falls to the good Womens Share to provide. They all spin, weave, and knit, whereby they make a good Shift to cloath the whole [112] Family, and, to their Credit be it recorded, many of them do it very compleately, and thereby reproach their Husbands Laziness, a ^better^ Spirit[t] of Industry in themselves.

From hence we mov'd forward to Colo. Mumfords other Plantation, under the care of Miles Riley, where by that Gentleman's Directions we were again supply'd with many good things. Here it was we discharg'd our Worthy Friend, and Fellow-Travellour Mr. Bearskin, who had so plentifully supply'd us with Provisions dureing our long Expedition. We rewarded Him to his Hearts content, so that he return'd to his Town loaden both with Riches, and the Reputation of haveing been a great Discoverer.

17.　This being Sunday we were seasonably put in mind how much we

---

[o]A: six Children　　[p]V: *Phrase* and . . . time *inserted at end of line; absent in A.*　　[q]A: Airy-Dwelling　　[r]V: *Phrase* if . . . them *inserted at end of line; absent in A.*　　[s]A: And for　　[t]A: a Spirit

were oblig'd to be thankfull for our happy return to the Inhabitants. Indeed we had great reason to reflect with Gratitude on the signal Mercies we had receiv'd. First that we had day by day been fed by the Bountifull hand of Providence, in the desolate Wilderness, Insomuch that[a] if any of our People wanted one[b] single Meal during the whole Expedition it was intirely owing to their own imprudent[c] Management.

Secondly that not one Man of our whole Company had any Violent Distemper, or bad Accident befall him, from one End of the Line to the other. The very worst that happen'd, was that one of them gave himself a smart cut on the Pan of his Knee with a Tomahawk, which we had the good Fortune to cure in a short time without the help of a Surgeon.[389]

As for the Misadventures of Sticking in the Mire and falling into Rivers and Creeks, they were rather Subjects of Mirth than Complaint, and serv'd only to diversify our Travels with a little farcicall Variety.

And lastly that many uncommon Incidents have concurr'd to prosper our Undertaking. We had not only a dry Spring before we went out, but the preceeding Winter, and even a Year or two before, had been much dryer than Ordinary. This made not only the Dismal, but likewise most of the Sunken Grounds near[d] the Sea Side, just hard enough to bear us, which otherwise had been quite unpassable[e].

And the whole time we were upon the Business, which was in all about Sixteen Weeks, we were never catch't in the Rain, except once. Nor was our Progress Interrupted by bad Weather above 3 or 4 days at most. Besides all this we were surpriz'd by no Indian Enemy, but all of us brought our Scalps back safe upon our Heads.

This cruel Method of Scalping of Enemies is practis'd by all the Savages in America, and perhaps is not the least proof of their Original from the Northern Inhabitants of Asia. Among the Ancient Scythians it was constantly us'd, who carry'd about these hairy Scalps as Trophies of Victory. They serv'd them ^too^ as Towels[f] at home and Trappings for their Horses abroad. But these were not content with the Skins of their Enemy's Heads but also made use of their Sculls for Cups to drink out of upon high Festival days, & made greater Ostentation of them, than if they had been made of Gold, or the purest crystal.[390] [113]

Besides the Duties of the Day, we Christen'd one of our Men, who had been bred a Quaker. The Man desir'd this of his own meer Motion, without being tamper'd with by the Parson, who was willing every one shou'd go to Heaven

---

[a]A: Providence Insomuch that in the Desolate Wilderness, if [b]A: a [c]A: Improvident [d]A: by [e]A: had been unpassable [f]A: serv'd them as Towels

his own way. But whether he did it by the Conviction of his own Reason, or to get rid of some Troublesome Forms and Restraints, to which the Saints of that Perswasion are subject, I can't positively say.[391]

18.   We proceeded over a Levil Road 12 Miles, as far as George Hixe's Plantation in the South Side Meherin River, our Course being for the most part North-East. By the way we hired a Cart to transport our Baggage, that we might the better befriend our jaded Horses.

Within 2 Miles of our Journey's End this day we met the Express We[g] had sent the Saturday before to give Notice of our Arrival. He had been almost as expeditious, as a carrier-Pigeon, rideing in 2 Days no less than 200 Miles.

All the Grandees of the Sappony-Nation did us the Honour to repair hither to meet us, and our worthy Friend and Fellow Travellor *Bearskin* appear'd among the gravest of them, in[h] his Robes of Ceremony. Four Young Ladies of the first Quality came with them, who had more the Air of Cleanliness, than any Copper-Colour'd Beauties I had ever seen: Yet we resisted all their Charms, notwithstanding the long Fast we had kept from the Sex, and the Bear Dyet we had been so long engag'd in. Nor can I say the Price, they set upon their Charms, was at all Exorbitant. A Princess for a Pair of Red Stockings, can't surely be thought buying Repentance much too dear.

The Men and something great and venerable in their Countenances, beyond the common Mien of Savages, and indeed they all had the Reputation of being the Honestest as well as the bravest Indians, we have ever been acquainted with.

This People is now made up of the Remnant of several other Nations, of which the most considerable are the Sapponys, the Occaneches, and Steukenhocks, who not finding themselves separately numerous enough for their Defense, have agreed to unite into one Body, and all of them now go under the Name of the Sapponys.[392]

Each of these was formerly a distinct Nation, or rather a several Clan or Canton of the same Nation, speaking the same Language, and using the same Customs. But their perpetual Wars against all other Indians, in time reduc'd them so low, as to make it necessary to join their Forces together.[393]

They dwelt formerly not far below the Mountains upon Yadkin River, about 200 Miles West and by South from the Falls of Roanoak. But about 25 Years ago they took Refuge in Virginia, being no longer in condition to make Head, not only against the Northern Indians, who are their implacable Enemies, but also against most of those to the South. All the Nations round about bearing in mind the Havock these Indians us'd[i] formerly to make among their

[g]V <I> We   [h]A: drest in   [i]A: Havock they us'd

Ancestors in the Insolence of their Power, did at length avenge it Home upon them, and made them glad to apply to this Government for Protection.

Colo. Spotswood our then Lieut. Governor, having a good [114] Opinion of their Fidelity & Courage, settled them at Christanna ten Miles North of Roanoak, upon the belief that they wou'd be a good Barrier on that Side of the Country against the Incursion of all Forreign Indians, and in Earnest[j] they wou'd have serv'd well enough for that Purpose, if the White People in the Neighbourhood, had not debauch't their Morals, and ruin'd their Health with Rum, which was the Cause of many disorders, and ended at last in a barbarous Murder committed by one of these Indians, when he was drunk, for which the poor Wretch was executed when he was sober.

It was matter of great Concern to them however that one of their Grandees shou'd be put to so ignominious a Death. All Indians have as great an Aversion to hanging, as the Muscovites, tho' perhaps not for the same cleanly reason. These last believing, that the Soul of one that dies ^in this Manner^[k] being forc'd to sally out of the Body at the Postern, must needs be defiled. The Sappony's took the Execution so much to Heart, that they soon after quitted their Settlement, and remov'd in a Body to the Cataubas.[394]

The Daughter of the *Tetero King* went away with the Sapponys, but being the last of her Nation, and fearing she shou'd not be treated according to her Rank, poison'd herself, like an Old Roman, with the Root of the Trumpet Plant. Her Father dy'd 2 Years before, who was the most intrepid Indian, we have been acquainted with. He had made himself terrible to all other Indians by His Exploits, and had escaped so many Dangers, that he was esteem'd invulnerable. But at last he dy'd of a Pleurisy, the last Man of his Race and Nation, leaving only that unhappy Daughter behind him, who would not long survive Him[l].[395]

The most uncommon Circumstances in this Indian visit, was, that they all come on Horse-back, which was certainly intended for a Piece of State, because the Distance was but 3 Miles, and 'tis likely they had walkt afoot twice as far to catch their Horses. The Men rode more awkwardly than any Dutch Sailor, and the Ladies bestrode their Palfrys a-la-mode de France, but were so bashfull about it, that there was no persuading them to mount, till they were quite out of our[m] Sight.

The French Women use to ride a straddle, not so much to make them sit firmer in the Saddle, as from the hopes the same thing might peradventure befall them, that once happen'd to the *Nun of Orleans,* who escaping out of a

[j]A: and indeed [k]A: this Way [l]V: *Phrase* who . . . Him *inserted at end of line; absent in* A.
[m]A: their

Nunnery, took Post *en Cavalier,* and in ten Miles hard rideing had the good
Fortune to have all the Tokens of a Man break out upon her.[396]

This piece of History ought to be the more credible, because it leans upon
much the same Degree of Proof as the Tale of Bishop Burnets two Italian
Nuns, who according to his Lordship's Account underwent the same happy
Metamorphosis probably by some other Violent Exercise.[397]

19.   From hence we dispatcht the Cart with our Baggage under a Guard,
and cros't *Meherin River,* which was not 30 Yards [115] wide in that Place.
By the help of Fresh Horses, that had been sent us, we now began to mend
our Pace, which was also quicken'd by the strong Inclinations, we had to get
Home.[398]

In the Distance of 5 Miles we forded *Meherin* Creek, which was very near
as broad as the River. About 8 Miles farther we came to *Sturgeon*-Creek, so
call'd from the Dexterity an *Occaneechy* Indian shew'd there in catching one
of those Royal Fish, which was perform'd after the following Manner.[399]

In the Summer time tis no unusual thing for Sturgeons to sleep on the
Surface of the Water, and one of them, having wander'd up into this Creek in
the Spring, was floating in that drowsy Condition. The Indian abovemention'd
ran up to the Neck into the Creek[n] a little below the Place where he discover'd
the Fish, expecting the Stream wou'd soon bring his Game down to Him. He
judg'd the Matter right, and as soon as it came within his Reach, he whip't a
running Noose over his Jole. This waked the Sturgeon, which being strong in
its own Element, darted immediately under Water, and dragg'd the Indian
after Him. The Man made it a point of Honour to keep his Hold, which he
did to the apparent Danger of being drown'd. Sometimes both the Indian
and the Fish disappear'd for a Quarter of a Minute, & then rose at some
Distance, from where they dived. At this rate they continued flouncing about,
sometimes above, and sometimes under Water for a considerable time,
till at last the Hero suffocated his Adversary, and haled his Body ashoar in
Triumph.[400]

About six Miles beyond that we past over *Wicco-quoi Creek,* named so
from the Multitude of Rocks over which the Water tumbles in a Fresh with
a bellowing Noise. Not far from where we went over, is a Rock much higher
than the rest, that strikes the Eye with agreeable Horror, and near it a very
Talkative *Eccho,* that like a fluent Help-meet, will return her good Man seven
Words for one, & after all be sure to have the last. It speaks not only the
Language of Men, but also of Birds & Beasts, and often a single Wild Goose is
cheated into[o] the Belief, that some of his Company are not far off, by hearing

[n]A: ran into the Creek up to the Neck   [o]A: with

his own cry multiply'd, & 'tis pleasant to see in what a flutter the poor Bird is, when he finds himself disappointed.

On the Banks of this Creek are very broad low Grounds in many Places, and abundance of good high Land, tho' a little subject to Floods.

We had but two Miles more to Capt. Embrys, where we found the House-keeping much better than the House. Our Bountifull Landlady had set her Oven, and all her Spits, Pots, Gridirons, and Saucepans to work, to diversify our Entertainment, tho' after all it prov'd but a Mahometan Feast, there being nothing to drink but Water. The worst of it was, we had unluckily out rid the Baggage, and for that Reason were oblig'd to Lodge very sociably in the same Apartment with the Family, where reckoning Women and Children, we muster'd[p] in all no less than nine Persons, who all pigg'd loveingly together.[401] [116]

20.   In the Morning Colo. Bolling, who had been surveying in the Neighbourhood, and Mr. Walker, who dwelt not far off, came to visit us. And the last of these Worthy Gentlemen, fearing that our drinking so much Water might incline us to Pleurisys, brought us a kind Supply both of Wine and Cyder.[402]

It was Noon before we cou'd disengage ourselves from the Courtesies of this Place, and then the two Gentlemen abovemention'd were so good as to accompany us that days Journey, tho' they cou'd by no means approve of our *Lithuanian* Fashion of Dismounting now and then, in order to walk part of the way on foot.[403]

We cros't Nottoway River not far from our Landlords House, where it seem'd[q] to be about 25 Yards over. This River divides the Country of *Prince-George* from that of *Brunswick.* We had not gone 8 Miles farther before our Eyes were bless'd with the Sight of *Sapponi-Chappel,* which was the first House of Prayer, we had seen for more than two Calender Months.

About 3 Miles beyond that, we past over Stony Creek, where one of those that Guarded the Baggage kill'd a Polcat, upon which he made a comfortable Repast. Those of his Company were so Squeamish, they cou'd not be persuaded at first to tast, as they said, of so unsavory an Animal: but seeing the Man smack his Lips with more pleasure than usual, they ventur'd at last to be of his Mess, and instead of finding the Flesh rank, and high-tasted, they own'd it to be the sweetest Morsel, they had ever eat in their Lives.

The ill-Savour of this little Beast lys altogether in its Urine, which Nature has made so detestably ill-scented, on purpose to furnish a helpless Creature with something to defend itself. For as some Brutes have Horns and Hoofs, and others are arm'd with Claws, Teeth, and Tuskes for their Defence, and as some spit a sort of Poison at their Adversaries, like the *Paco,* and others dart Quills at their Pursuers, like the *Porcupine,* and as some have no Weapons to help themselves but their Tongue, and others none but their Tails, so the poor *Polcat*'s safety lies altogether in the irresistable Stench of its Water, insomuch that when it finds itself in Danger from an Enemy, it moistens its bushy Tail plentifully with this Liquid Ammunition, and then with great fury sprinkles it like a Shower of Rain, full into the Eyes of its Assailant, by which it gains time to make its Escape.[404]

Nor is the Polcat the only Animal that defends itself by a Stink. At the *Cape of Good Hope* is a little Beast call'd a Stinker, as big as a Fox, and shap't like a Ferret, which being pursued, has no way to save himself, but by Farting and Squittering. And then such a Stench ensues, that none of its Pursuers[r] can possibly stand it.[405]

At the End of 30 good Miles we arriv'd in the Evening at Colo. Bollings, where first from a primitive Course of Life, we began to relapse into Luxury. This Gentleman lives within Hearing of the Falls of Appamatuck River, which are very Noisy, whenever a Flood happens to roll a greater Stream than ordinary over the Rocks[s]. [117]

The River is navigable for Small Craft as high as the Falls, and at some distance from thence fetches a Compass, and runs near paralel with James River almost as high as the Mountains.

While the Commissioners fared sumptuously here, the poor Chaplain and two Surveyors stop't Ten Miles short, at a poor Planters House in Pity to their Horses, where they made a Saint *Anthony*'s Meal, that is, they supt upon the Pickings of what stuck in their Teeth ever since Breakfast. But to make them amends, the good Man laid them in his own Bed, where they all three nestled together in one Cotton Sheet, and one of Brown Osnabrugs, made still something Browner by two Months copious Perspiration.[406]

21.   But those worthy Gentlemen were so alert[a] in the Morning after their light Supper, that they came up with us before Breakfast, & honestly paid their Stomachs all they ow'd them[b].

We made no more than a Sabbath days Journey from this, to the next Hospitable House, namely, that of our great Benefactor Colo. *Mumford.* We had already been much befriended[c] by this Gentleman, who besides sending Orders to his Overseers at *Roanoak,* to let us want for Nothing, had in the

---

[r]A: none of his Followers   [s]V: *Phrase to . . . Rocks inserted at end of paragraph line; absent in A.*   [a]A: were alert   [b]A: all their arrears   [c]A: been befriended

Beginning of our Business been so kind, as to recommend most of the Men to us, who were[d] the faithfull Partners of our Fatigue.

Altho' in most other *Atchievements,* those who command are apt to take all the *Honour* to themselves, of what perhaps was more owing to the Vigour of those who were under them: Yet I must be more just, and allow these brave Fellows their full Share of Credit for the Service we perform'd, & must declare, that it was in a great Measure owing to their Spirit and indefatigable Industry, that we overcame many[e] Obstacles in the Course of our Line, which till then had been esteem'd unsurmountable.

Nor must I at the same time omit to do Justice to the Surveyors, and particularly to Mr. Mayo, who besides an eminent degree of Skill, encounter'd the same Hardships, and underwent the same Fatigue, that, the forwardest of the Men did, and that with as much Chearfulness, as if Pain had been his Pleasure, and Difficulty his real Diversion.

Here we discharg'd the few Men, we had left, who were all as Ragged as the *Gibeonite Ambassadors,* tho' at the same time their Rags were very honourable, by the Service they had so Vigorously[f] perform'd in making them so[g].[407]

22. A little before Noon we all took leave, and disperst to our Several Habitations, where we were so happy as to find ^all^ our[h] Familys well. This crown'd all our other Blessings, and made our Journey as prosperous, as it had been painfull.

Thus ended our Second Expedition, in which we extended the Line within the Shadow of the *Chariky Mountains,* where we were oblig'd to set up our Pillars, like *Hercules,* and return Home.[408]

We had now upon the whole been out Sixteen Weeks, including going, and returning, and ^had^ travell'd[i] at least Six Hundred Miles, and no small part of that Distance on foot. Below towards the Sea-Side, [118] our Course lay through *Marshes, Swamps,* and great Waters; and above, over steep *Hills,* craggy *Rocks,* and Thickets hardly penetrable. Notwithstanding this Variety of Hardship, we may say without Vanity, that we faithfully obey'd the King's Orders, and perform'd the Business effectually, in which we had the Honour to be employ'd.

Nor can we by any Means reproach ourselves with having put the Crown to any exorbitant Expence in this difficult Affair, the whole Charge, from Beginning to End, amounting to no more than One Thousand Pounds. But let no one concern'd in this painfull Expedition complain of the Scantiness of his Pay, so long as His Majesty has been Graciously pleas'd to add to our Reward the Honour of his *Royal Approbation,* and to declare, notwithstanding the Desertion of the *Carolina Commissioners,* that the Line by us run, shall hereafter stand as the true *Boundary* betwixt the *Governments* of *Virginia* and *North-Carolina.*

APPENDIX

To the Foregoing Journal, containing[j] the Second Charter to the Proprietors of *Carolina,* confirming and enlarging the First, and also several other Acts to which it refers. These are plac'd by themselves at the End of the Book, that[k] they may not interrupt the Thread of the Story, and the Reader will be more at liberty whether he will please to read them or not, being something dry and unpleasant.

[119]

The second *Charter* granted by King *Charles* 2d.

To the Proprietors of Carolina.

Charles by the Grace of God &c: Wheras by our *Letters Patents,* bearing date the four and twentieth day of March in the fifteenth Year of our Reign, we were graciously pleas'd to grant unto our right trusty, and right well beloved[l] Cousin and Councellor Edward Earl of Clarendon, our high Chancellor of England, our right trusty and right intirely beloved Cousin and Counsellor George Duke of Albemarle, Master of our Horse, our right trusty, and well beloved William[m], now Earl of Craven[n], our Right-trusty and well beloved Counsellor, Anthony Lord Ashley, Chancellor of our Exchequer, our right-trusty and well beloved Counsellor Sir George Carterett[o] Knight and Baronet, vice-Chamberlain of our houshold, our right trusty and well beloved, Sir John Colleton[p], Knight and Baronet, and Sir William Berkley[q], Knight, all that Province, Territory, or Tract of Ground, called Carolina, scituate, lying and being within our Dominions of America, extending from the North End of the Island, called Luke Island, which lyes in the Southern Virginia Seas, and within Six and thirty Degrees of the Northern Latitude[r]; and to the West as far as the South Seas; & so respectively as far as the River of Mathias, which bordereth upon the Coast of Florida, & within one and thirty Degrees of the Northern Latitude[s], and so west in a direct Line as far as the South Seas

---

[j]A: Journals, refering to [k]A: by themselves, that [l]V: and right well beloved] A: & well beloved [m]A: right trusty and well beloved Councellor William [n]*In both V and A the name of John Lord Berkeley is omitted.* [o]A: Cartaret [p]A: right Trusty and right well beloved Sir John Colleton [q]A: Berkeley [r]A: Degrees of Northern Latitude [s]A: Degrees of Northern Latitude

aforesaid. Now, know ye, that we at the humble request of the said Grantees in the aforesaid Letters Patents named, and as a further[t] mark of our especial favour towards them we are graciously pleas'd to enlarge our said Grant unto them according to the Bounds & limits hereafter specifyed, & in favour to the pious & noble purpose of the said Edward Earl of Clarendon, George Duke of Albemarle, William Earl of Craven, John Lord Berkley, Anthony Lord Ashley, Sir George Carterett[a], Sir John Colleton and Sir William Berkley[b], we do give & grant to them their Heirs and Assigns, all that Province, Territory, or tract of Ground[c], scituate, lying, & being within our Dominions of America aforesaid, extending North and Eastward, as far as the North end of Carahtuke[d] River, or Inlet, upon a streight westerly line, to Wyonoake[e] Creek, which lyes within or about the Degrees of thirty six, and thirty Minutes Northern Latitude[f], & so West in a Direct line, as far as the South Seas; & south and westward; as far as the Degrees of twenty nine inclusive Northern Latitude, & so west in a direct line, as far as the South Seas; together with all and singular parks, harbours, Bays, rivers, & inlets belonging unto the Province or Territory aforesaid. And also, all the Soil, lands, fields, Woods, Mountains, farms, Lakes, Rivers, Bays, and Inlets, scituate, lying or being[g] within the Bounds or limits last before mention'd; with the fishing of all sorts of fish, Whales, Sturgeons, and all other Royal fishes in the Sea, Bays, Inlets, and Rivers, within the Premises, and the fish therein taken; together with the royalty of the Sea, upon the Coast within the limits aforesaid, and moreover all Veins, Mines and Quarries, as well discover'd as not discover'd, of Gold, Silver, Gems & precious Stones, and [120] [all] other whatsoever[h]; be it of Stones, Metal, or any other thing found or to be found within[i] the Province Territory, Inlets and limits aforesaid.

And furthermore, the Patronage & Avowsons of all the Churches and Chappels, which as the Christian Religion shall encrease within the Province Territory Isles and limits aforesaid, shall happen hereafter to be erected; together with License and Power[j] to build & found Churches & Chappels & Oratories in fit and convenient places, within the said Bounds and Limits, and to cause them to be dedicated and consecrated, according to the Ecclesiastical Laws of our Kingdom of England; together with all and singular the Like, and as ample Rights, Jurisdictions and Priviledges, Prerogatives, Royalties, Liberties, Immunities[k], and Franchises of what kind soever,

---

[t]A: farther [a]A: Cartaret [b]A: Berkeley [c]A: Land [d]A: Corahtucke [e]A: Wyenoke
[f]A: thirty Minutes of Northern Latitude [g]A: situate lying and being [h]V: *Copyist provided* all *as catchword but omitted it from next page*] A: and all other whatsoever
[i]A: found in [j]A: Power and License [k]A: Immunities, Liberties

within the Territory, Isles, Inlets, and Limits aforesaid. To have, hold, use, exercise, & enjoy[l] the same as amply, fully, and in as ample a Manner, as any Bishop of Durham, in our Kingdom of England, ever heretofore had, held, enjoy'd or used, or of right ought, or cou'd hold, use, or enjoy[m]; and them the said Edward Earl of Clarendon, George Duke of Albemarle, William Earl of Craven, John Lord Berkley, Anthony Lord Ashley, Sir George Carteret, Sir John Colleton, and Sir William Berkley[n], their Heirs and Assigns[o]; We do by these Presents, for us, our Heirs and Successors, make, create, and constitute, the true and absolute Lords and Proprietors of the said Province, or Territory, and of all other the Premises, saveing always the Faith, Allegiance, and Sovereign Domininon due to Us, our Heirs, and Successors for the same; to have, hold, possess, and enjoy, the said Province, Territory, Inlets, and all and singular other the Premises, to them the said Edward Earl of Clarendon, George Duke of Albemarle, William Earl of Craven, John Lord Berkley, Anthony Lord Ashley, Sir George Carteret, Sir John Colleton, & Sir William Berkley[p], their Heirs and Assigns for ever, to be holden of Us, Our Heirs, & Successors, as of our Mannor of East-Greenwich, in Kent[q], in free & common Soccage, & not in Capite, nor by Knights Service, yielding and paying yearly to Us Our Heirs, & Successors, for the same the fourth part of all Gold and Silver Oar[r], which within the Limits hereby granted, shall from time to time happen to be found, over and besides the yearly Rent of twenty Marks, and the fourth part of the Gold & Silver Oar[s], in and by the said recited Letters Patents reserv'd and payable,

And that the Province, or[t] Territory hereby granted and described, may be dignify'd with as large Titles and Priviledges as any other Parts of our Dominions, and Territories, in that Region, Know ye, that we, of our[a] further Grace certain knowledge & meer Motion, have thought fit to annex the same Tract of Ground and Territory, unto the same Province of Carolina and out of the fulness of our Royal Power & Prerogative, We do for Us, our Heirs and Successors, annex & unite the same to the said Province of Carolina, and forasmuch as we have made and ordain'd, the said Edward Earl of Clarendon, George Duke of Albemarle, William Earl of Craven, John Lord Berkley, Anthony Lord Ashley, Sir George Carteret, Sir John Colleton, and Sir William Berkley, their Heirs and Assigns, the true Lords[b] and Proprietors of all the Province and Territory aforesaid. Know ye therefore moreover that we

[l]A: use, enjoy and exercise   [m]A: cou'd have, hold, use, or enjoy   [n]A: Berkeley . . . Berkley
[o]A: their Heirs and their Assigns   [p]A: Berkley . . . Berkley   [q]A: East-Greenwich, in the
County of Kent   [r]A: Ore   [s]A: Ore   [t]A: Province and   [a]A: We out of our   [b]A: true and
absolute Lords

reposing especial Trust & Confidence in their Fidelity, Justice, and provident Circumspection[c] for Us, our Heirs, and Successors, do grant full and absolute Power [121] by Vertue of these Presents, to them the said Edward Earl of Clarendon, George Duke of Albemarle, William Earl of Craven, John Lord Berkley, Anthony Lord Ashley, Sir George Carteret, Sir John Colleton, and Sir William Berkley, and their Heirs & Assigns, for the good & happy Government of the said whole Province or Territory, full Power and Authority to erect, constitute, & make several Counties, Baronies, & Colonies, of & within the said Provinces, Territories, Lands, and Hereditaments, in & by the said recited Letters Patents, & these Presents granted[d], or mention'd to be granted, as aforesaid, with several and distinct Jurisdictions, Powers, Liberties, and Priviledges, and also to ordain, make, and enact, and under their Seals, to Publish any Laws and Constitutions whatsoever, either appertaining to the Publick State of the said whole Province or Territory, or of any distinct or particular[e] County, Barony, and Colony, within the same[f], or to the private Utility of particular Persons, according to their best discretion, by & with the Advice, Assent & Approbation of the Freemen of the said Province or[g] Territory, or of the Freemen of the County, Barony, or Colony, for which such Law and Constitution shall be made, or the great or part of them, or of their Delegates or Deputies, whom for the enacting of the said Laws, when as often as need shall require, We will that the said Edward Earl of Clarendon, George Duke of Albemarle, William Earl of Craven, John Lord Berkley, Anthony Lord Ashley, Sir George Carteret, Sir John Colleton, & Sir William Berkley[h], their[i] Heirs or Assigns, shall from time to time, assemble in such Manner and Form as to them shall seem best, and the same Laws duly to Execute[j] upon all People within the said Province or Territory, County, Colony, or Barony the Limits[k] thereof for the time being, which shall be constituted under the Power & Government of them, or any of them, either sailing towards the said Province or Territory of Carolina[l], or returning from thence towards[m] England, or any other of Our, or foreign Dominions, by Imposition of Penalties, Imprisonments, or other Punishment. Yea, if it shall be needfull, and the Quality of the Offence require it by takeing away Member & Life, either by them the said Edward Earl of Clarendon, George Duke of Albemarle, William Earl of Craven, John Lord Berkley, Anthony Lord Ashley, Sir George Carteret, Sir John Colleton, & Sir William Berkley[n] and their Heirs,

[c]A: Fidelity, Justice, Wisdom, and provident Circumspection   [d]A: Patents ^and these Presents^ granted   [e]A: of any particular   [f]A: of or within the same   [g]A: Province and   [h]A: Berkely . . . Berkeley   [i]A: and their   [j]A: Laws to execute   [k]A: Barony, in the Limits   [l]A: Province ^or^ Territory of Carolina   [m]A: returning thence towards   [n]A: Berkeley

or by them or their Deputies, Lieutenants, Judges, Justices, Magistrates, or
Officers whatsoever, as well as within the said Province as at Sea, in such
Manner & form, as unto the said Edward Earl of Clarendon, George Duke of
Albemarle, William Earl of Craven, John Lord Berkley, Anthony Lord Ashley,
Sir George Carteret, Sir John Colleton, & Sir William Berkley[o] and their Heirs
shall seem most convenient: Also, to remit release pardon and abolish,
whether before Judgment or after, all Crimes and Offences whatsoever,
against the said Laws, and to do all and every[p] other thing and things which
unto the compleat establishment of Justice, unto Courts, Sessions & forms of
Judicature, and Manners of proceedings therein, do belong, altho' in these
Presents, express mention is not made thereof; & by Judges, to him or them
delegated to award Process hold Pleas & determine in all the said Courts &
Places of Judicature, all Actions, Suits, & Causes whatsoever as well Criminal
as Civil, real, mixt, personal, or of any other kind or Nature whatsoever:
Which Laws so as aforesaid to be publish'd. Our Pleasure is & we do enjoyn,
require and command, shall be absolutely firm & available in Law; and that
[122] all the Liege People of Us, Our Heirs and Successors, within the said
Province or Territory, do observe & keep them inviolably, in those Parts, so far
as they concern them, under the Pains & Penalties therein express'd, or to be
express'd; provided nevertheless, that the said Laws be consonant to Reason,
and as near as may be conveniently, agreeable to the Laws & Customs of this
our Realm of England.

And because such Assemblies of freeholders, cannot be suddenly call'd
as there may be Occasion to require the same, We do therefore by these
presents, give & Grant unto the said Edward Earl of Clarendon, George Duke
of Albemarle, William Earl of Craven, John Lord Berkley, Anthony Lord
Ashley, Sir George Carteret, Sir John Colleton, and Sir William Berkley[q], their
Heirs, & Assigns, by themselves or their Magistrates, in that Behalf, lawfully
authorized, full Power and Authority from time to time, to make & ordain
fit and wholesome Orders & Ordinances, within the Province or Territory
aforesaid, or any County, Barony, or Province of[r] or within the same, to
be kept and observ'd as well for the keeping of the Peace, as for the better
Government of the People there abiding, & to Publish the same to all whom
it may concern, which Ordinances we do, by these presents, streightly charge
and command to be inviolably observ'd within the same Province, Counties,
Territorys, Baronys, & Provinces, under the Penalties therein express'd; so
as such Ordinances be reasonable & not repugnant or contrary, but as near

[o]A: Berkeley   [p]A: all ^and every^   [q]A: Berkly . . . Berkley   [r]A: any County, Barony, or
Colony of

as may be agreeable to the Laws & Statutes of this our Kingdom of England: and so as the same Ordinances do not extend to the binding, charging, or taking away of the right or Interest of any Person or Persons in their Freehold, Goods, or Chattels whatsoever.

And to the End the said Province or Territory, may be the more happily encreas'd by the Multitude of People resorting thither, & may likewise be the more strongly defended from the Incursions of Savages and other Enemies, Pirates & Robbers, Therefore, We for Us, Our Heirs, and Successors, do give and grant by these Presents, Power, License and Liberty[s] unto all the Liege People of Us, Our Heirs and Successors in our Kingdom of England, & elsewhere, within any other our Dominions, Islands, Colonies, or Plantations (excepting those who shall be especially forbidden,) to transport themselves & Families unto the said Province or Territory, with convenient Shipping, & fitting Provisions; & there to settle themselves, dwell and Inhabit; any Law, Act, Statute, Ordinance, or other thing to the contrary in any wise notwithstanding.

And we will also, and of our especial Grace, for Us, Our Heirs and Successors, do streightly enjoyn, ordain, constitute, and command, that the said Province or Territory, shall be of our Allegiance, & that all and singular the Subjects and Leige People of Us, Our Heirs, & Successors, transported, or to be transported, into the said Province, and the Children of them, and such as shall descend from them, there born, or hereafter to be born, be, and shall be Denizens & Liege People of Us, our Heirs, and Successors of this our Kingdom of England, and be in all Things, held, treated, and reputed as the Leige faithfull People of Us, Our Heirs and Successors, born within this our said Kingdom, or any other of our Dominions, and may inherit, or otherwise purchase & receive, take, hold, buy, & possess any Lands, [123] Tenements, or Hereditaments[t], within the said Places, & them may occupy, & enjoy, sell, alien, and bequeath: as also all Liberties, Franchises, & Priviledges[a] of this our Kingdom, and of other our Dominions aforesaid, may freely and quietly have, possess, and enjoy, as our Liege People born within the same, without the Molestation, vexation, grievance or Trouble of Us, our Heirs and Successors, any Act, Statute, Ordinance ^or^ Provision to the Contrary notwithstanding.

And furthermore, that our Subjects of this our said Kingdom of England, & others our Dominions, may be the rather encouraged to undertake this Expedition, with ready & chearfull Means, Know Ye, that We, of our Especial Grace, certain Knowledge & meer Motion, do give & Grant, by Vertue of these

[s]A: Power, Liberty & License   [t]A: and Hereditaments   [a]A: Liberties, Priviledges, and Franchises

presents[b], as well to the said Edward Earl of Clarendon, George Duke of
Albemarle, William Earl of Craven, John Lord Berkley, Anthony Lord Ashley,
Sir George Carteret, Sir John Colleton, & Sir William Berkley and their Heirs,
as unto all others, that shall from time to time, repair to the said Province
or Territory, with a Purpose to inhabit there or to trade with the Natives
thereof: full Liberty and License to lade & freight in every Port whatsoever of
Us, our Heirs & Successors, and into the said Province of Carolina, by them,
their Servants & Assigns, to transport all & singular, their goods, Wares, and
Merchandizes; as likewise all Sorts of Grain whatsoever, & any other thing
whatsoever necessary for their Food & Cloathing, not prohibited by the
Laws and Statutes of our Kingdom & Dominions[c], to be carry'd out of the
same without any let or molestation of Us our Heirs & Successors, or of any
other our Officers or Ministers whatsoever, saving also to Us, our Heirs and
Successors, the Customs & other Duties & Payments due for the said Wares &
Merchandizes, according to the several Rates of the Places from whence the
same shall be transported.

We will also, & by the Presents for Us, our Heirs & Successors, do give and
grant Licence by this our Charter unto the said Edward Earl of Clarendon,
George Duke of Albemarle, William Earl of Craven, John Lord Berkley,
Anthony Lord Ashley, Sir George Carteret, Sir John Colleton and Sir William
Berkeley, their Heirs & Assigns, and to all the Inhabitants & Dwellers in
the Province or Territory aforesaid, both present and to come, full Power
& absolute Authority to import or unlade by themselves or their Servants,
Factors, or Assigns, all Merchandizes & Goods whatsoever, that shall arise of
the Fruits & Commodities of the said Province or Territory, either by Land or
Sea[d], into the Ports of us, our Heirs & Successors, in our Kingdom of England,
Scotland, or Ireland, or otherwise, to dispose of the said Goods, in the said
Ports, and if need be, within one year next after the unlading, to lade the
same Merchandizes & Goods again, into the same, or other Ships, & to export
the same into any other Countrys, either of our Dominions or forreign, being
in Amity with Us, our Heirs, and Successors, so as the rest of the Customs,
Subsidies, & other Duties for the same to Us, our Heirs & Successors, as the
rest of our Subjects of this our Kingdom of England, for the time being, shall
be bound to pay. Beyond which we will not that the Inhabitants of the said
Province or Territory, shall be any way charged. Provided, nevertheless, and
our Will & Pleasure is, and we have further, for the Considerations aforesaid,
of our Special Grace, certain Knowledge, & meer Motion, given & granted,

[b]A: grant, by these presents   [c]A: by the Laws of our said Dominions   [d]A: whether by
Land or Sea

& by these Presents for Us, our Heirs and Successors, do give and grant[e], unto the said Edward Earl of Clarendon, [124] George Duke of Albemarle, William Earl of Craven, John Lord Berkley, Anthony Lord Ashley, Sir George Carteret, Sir John Colleton, & Sir William Berkley, & their Heirs & Assigns, full & free License, Liberty, Power, & Authority, at any time or times, from & after the Feast of St. Michael the Arch Angel, which shall be in the Year of our Lord Christ, One Thousand, six Hundred, Sixty & Seven; as well to import or bring into any our Dominions from the said Province of Carolina, or any part thereof, the several Goods & Commodities herein after mention'd; that is to say, Silks, Wines, Currants, Raysons, Capers, Wax, Almonds, Oyl and Olives, without paying or answering to us our Heirs & Successors, any Custom, Impost, or other Duty, for, or in respect[f] thereof, for and during the time and space of seven Years to commence & ^be^ accompted from, and after the first Importation of four Tons of any the said Goods in any one Bottom Ship or Vessel, from the said Province or Territory, into any of our Dominions; as also to export and carry out of any of our Dominions into the said Province or Territory, Custom-free, all sorts of Tools, which shall be usefull or necessary for the Planters there, in the Accommodation & Improvement of the Premises, any thing before in these Presents contain'd, or any Law, Act, Statute, Prohibition, or any other Matter or Thing, heretofore had, made, enacted or provided in any wise notwithstanding.

And furthermore of our more Ample & especial Grace, certain Knowledge and mere Motion, We do for Us, our Heirs, an Successors, grant unto the said Edward Earl of Clarendon, George Duke of Albemarle, William Earl of Craven, John Lord Berkley, Anthony Lord Ashley, Sir George Carteret, Sir John Colleton, & Sir William Berkeley[g], their Heirs[h] & Assigns, full & absolute Power & Authority to make erect and Constitute within the said Province, or Territory, & the Isles[i] & Inlets aforesaid, such & so many Sea Ports, Harbours, Creeks and other Places for discharge & unladeing of Goods & Merchandizes out of Ships, Boats and other Vessels[j], & for lading of them in such and so many places & with such Jurisdictions Priviledges & Franchises, unto the said Ports belonging, as to them shall seem most Expedient, & that all & Singular, the Ships, Boats, & other Vessels, which shall come[k] for Merchandizes and Trade into the said Province or Territory, or shall depart out of the same, shall be laden and unladen at such Ports only, as shall be erected & constituted by the said Edward Earl of Clarendon, George Duke of Albemarle, William Earl of

[e]A: by these presents, do give and grant, for Us our Heirs, & Successors   [f]A: for & in respect   [g]A: Berkley . . . Berkley   [h]A: & their Heirs   [i]A: & Isles   [j]A: Ships, Vessels & Boats   [k]A: that shall come

Craven, John Lord Berkley, Anthony Lord Ashley, Sir George Carteret, Sir John Colleton, & Sir William Berkeley[l], their Heirs & Assigns, and not elsewhere, any use, Custom, or anything to the contrary in any wise notwithstanding.

And we do further will, appoint & ordain, & by these presents for Us, our Heirs, and Successors do grant unto the said Edward Earl of Clarendon, George Duke of Albemarle, William Earl of Craven, John Lord Berkley, Anthony Lord Ashley, Sir George Carteret, Sir John Colleton, & Sir William Berkley, their Heirs & Assigns, that they, the said Edward Earl of Clarendon, George Duke of Albemarle, William Earl of Craven, John Lord Berkley, Anthony Lord Ashley, Sir George Carteret, Sir John Colleton, & Sir William Berkley, their Heirs & Assigns, may from time to time, for Ever, have and enjoy [125] the Customs & Subsidies, in the Ports, Harbours, Creeks, & other Places within the Province aforesaid[m], payable for the Goods, Merchandizes, & Wares there Laded, or to be Laded or unladed, the said Customs to be reasonably assess'd to upon any Occasion by themselves, & by & with the Consent of the free People, or the greater Part of them, as aforesaid, to whom we give Power by these Presents, for Us, our Heirs & Successors, upon just Cause, & in due proportion to assess, & impose the same.

And further of our especial Grace certain Knowledge & meer Motion, we have given, granted, & confirm'd, by these Presents for Us, our Heirs & Successors do give, grant, & confirm unto the said Edward Earl of Clarendon, George Duke of Albemarle, William Earl of Craven, John Lord Berkley, Anthony Lord Ashley, Sir George Carteret, Sir John Colleton, & Sir William Berkley, their Heirs & Assigns, full & absolute Power & Authority, that they the said Edward Earl of Clarendon, George Duke of Albemarle, William Earl of Craven, John Lord Berkley, Anthony Lord Ashley, Sir George Carteret, Sir John Colleton, & Sir William Berkley, their Heirs & Assigns, from time to time, hereafter for ever, at his & their Will & Pleasure, may Assign, alien, grant, demise, or enfeoff, the Premises or any Part or Parcell thereof to him or them, that shall be willing to purchase the same; & to such Person or Persons as they shall think fit, to have & to hold to them the said Person or Persons, their Heirs & Assigns in fee Simple or in Fee Tayle[n] or for the Term of Life or Lives, or Years to be held of them the said Edward Earl of Clarendon, George Duke of Albemarle, William Earl of Craven, John Lord Berkley, Anthony Lord Ashley, Sir George Carteret, Sir John Colleton, & Sir William Berkley, their Heirs & Assigns, full & absolute Power & Authority, that they the said Edward Earl of Clarendon, George Duke of Albemarle, William Earl of Craven, John Lord Berkley, Anthony Lord Ashley, Sir George Carteret, Sir

[l]A: William Berkley   [m]A: within the said Province   [n]A: Fee Tail

John Colleton, & Sir William Berkley, their Heirs & Assigns, by such rents & services, and Customs, as shall seem fit to the said the said Edward Earl of Clarendon, George Duke of Albemarle, William Earl of Craven, John Lord Berkley, Anthony Lord Ashley, Sir George Carteret, Sir John Colleton, & Sir William Berkley, their Heirs & Assigns, full & absolute Power & Authority, that they the said Edward Earl of Clarendon, George Duke of Albemarle, William Earl of Craven, John Lord Berkley, Anthony Lord Ashley, Sir George Carteret, Sir John Colleton, & Sir William Berkley, their Heirs & Assigns, & not of Us, our Heirs & Successors: And to the same Person or Persons, & to all & every one of them, We do give & grant by these Presents, for Us, our Heirs and Successors Licence, Authority, & Power, that such Person or Persons may have and take the Premises, or any Parcell thereof, of the said Edward Earl of Clarendon, George Duke of Albemarle, William Earl of Craven, John Lord Berkley, Anthony° Lord Ashley, Sir George Carteret, Sir John Colleton, & Sir William Berkley, their Heirs & Assigns, full & absolute Power & Authority, that they the said Edward Earl of Clarendon, George Duke of Albemarle, William Earl of Craven, John Lord Berkley, Anthony Lord Ashley, Sir George Carteret, Sir John Colleton, & Sir William Berkley, their Heirs & Assigns, & the same to hold to themselves, their Heirs or Assigns, in what Estate of Inheritance soever, in Fee Simple, or in Fee Tayle or otherwise, as to them the said Edward Earl of Clarendon, George Duke of Albemarle, William Earl of Craven, John Lord Berkley, Anthony Lord Ashley, Sir George Carteret, Sir John Colleton, & Sir William Berkley, their Heirs & Assigns, full & absolute Power & Authority, that they the said Edward Earl of Clarendon, George Duke of Albemarle, William Earl of Craven, John Lord Berkley, Anthony Lord Ashley, Sir George Carteret, Sir John Colleton, & Sir William Berkley, their Heirs & Assigns shall seem expedient. The Statute in the Parliament of Edward, Son of King Henry, heretofore King of England, our Predecessor, commonly call'd the Statute of Quia Emtores Terrar; or any other Statute, Act, Ordinance, Use, Law, Custom, or any othe Matter, Cause, or thing heretofore published or provided to the contrary in any wise notwithstanding.

And because many Persons born & Inhabiting in the said Province for their Desert & Services may expect, & be capable of Marks of Honour & Favour, which in respect of the great Distance cannot conveniently be conferred by us; our Will & Pleasure therefore is, & We do by these Presents, give and grant unto the said Edward Earl [126] of Clarendon, George Duke of Albemarle, William Earl of Craven, John Lord Berkley, Anthony Lord Ashley, Sir George Carteret, Sir John Colleton, & Sir William Berkley, their Heirs & Assigns, full

°*The remainder of the Appendix is missing from the A manuscript.*

& absolute Power & Authority, that they the said Edward Earl of Clarendon, George Duke of Albemarle, William Earl of Craven, John Lord Berkley, Anthony Lord Ashley, Sir George Carteret, Sir John Colleton, & Sir William Berkley, their Heirs & Assigns, full Power & Authority to give & confer unto & upon such of the Inhabitants of the said Province or Territory, as they shall think, do or shall merit, such Marks of Favour, & Titles of Honour, as they shall think fit, so as their Titles or Honours be not the same as are enjoy'd by, or conferr'd upon any of the Subjects of this our Kingdom of England.

And further also, we do by these Presents, for Us, our Heirs & Successors, give and grant, Licence to them the said Edward Earl of Clarendon, George Duke of Albemarle, William Earl of Craven, John Lord Berkley, Anthony Lord Ashley, Sir George Carteret, Sir John Colleton, & Sir William Berkley, their Heirs & Assigns, full & absolute Power & Authority, that they the said Edward Earl of Clarendon, George Duke of Albemarle, William Earl of Craven, John Lord Berkley, Anthony Lord Ashley, Sir George Carteret, Sir John Colleton, & Sir William Berkley, their Heirs & Assigns, full Power & Authority, Liberty and Licence to erect raise & Build in the said Province or Places aforesaid or any Part or Parts thereof, such & so many Forts, Fortresses, Castles, Cities, Burroughs, Towns, Villages, or any other Fortifications whatsoever; & the same or any of them to fortify & furnish with Ordnance, Powder, Shott, Armour, & all other Weapons, Ammunition & Habiliments of War, both defensive & Offensive, as shall be thought fit and convenient for the safety & Welfare of the said Province, & Places, or any Part thereof; and the same, or any of them, from time to time, as occasion shall require, to Dismantle, Disfurnish, Demolish, & pull down; and also to Place, Constitute, & Appoint in, or over all, or any of the said Castles, forts, fortifications Cities Towns & Places aforesaid, Governors Deputy Governors, Magistrates, Sheriffs, & other Officers, Civil and Military as to them shall seem meet; and to the said Cities, Burroughs, Towns, Villages, or any other place, or Places within the said Province or Territory, to grant Letters or Charters of Incorporation with all Liberties, Franchises & Priviledges requisite, or usual, or to, or within this our Kingdom of England granted, or belonging: And in the same Cities, Burroughs, Towns & other Places, to constitute, erect & appoint, such & so many Markets, Mart, & Fairs, as shall in that behalf thought fit and necessary; and furthermore also, to Erect & make in the Province or Territory aforesaid, or any part thereof, so many Mannors with such Signories to them as shall seem meet & convenient, & in every of the said Mannors to have & to hold a Court-Baron with all things whatsoever, which to a Court Baron do belong, & to have & to hold views of franck pledge, & Courts Leet, for the conservation of the Peace, and better Government of those Parts, with such Limitations,

Jurisdiction & Precincts, as by the said Edward Earl of Clarendon, George Duke of Albemarle, William Earl of Craven, John Lord Berkley, Anthony Lord Ashley, Sir George Carteret, Sir John Colleton, & Sir William Berkley, their Heirs & Assigns, full & absolute Power & Authority, that they the said Edward Earl of Clarendon, George Duke of Albemarle, William Earl of Craven, John Lord Berkley, Anthony Lord Ashley, Sir George Carteret, Sir John Colleton, & Sir William Berkley, or their Heirs, shall be appointed for that purpose, with all things whatsoever, which to a Court leet or View of Franck Pledge, do belong, the same Courts to be holden by Stewards, too be deputed & authorized by the said Edward Earl of Clarendon, George Duke of Albemarle, William Earl of [127] Craven, John Lord Berkley, Anthony Lord Ashley, Sir George Carteret, Sir John Colleton, & Sir William Berkley, their Heirs & Assigns, full & absolute Power & Authority, that they the said Edward Earl of Clarendon, George Duke of Albemarle, William Earl of Craven, John Lord Berkley, Anthony Lord Ashley, Sir George Carteret, Sir John Colleton, & Sir William Berkley, their Heirs, by the Lords of the Mannors & Leets, for the time being, when the same shall be erected.

And because that in so remote a Country, & scituate amongst so many barbarous Nations, the Invasions as well of Salvages, as other Enemies, Pirates, & Robbers may probably be fear'd; Therefore we have given, & for Us, our Heirs & Successors do give Power by these Presents, unto the said Edward Earl of Clarendon, George Duke of Albemarle, William Earl of Craven, John Lord Berkley, Anthony Lord Ashley, Sir George Carteret, Sir John Colleton, & Sir William Berkley, their Heirs & Assigns, full & absolute Power & Authority, that they the said Edward Earl of Clarendon, George Duke of Albemarle, William Earl of Craven, John Lord Berkley, Anthony Lord Ashley, Sir George Carteret, Sir John Colleton, & Sir William Berkley, their Heirs & Assigns, by themselves, or their Captains, or other Officers to Levy, Muster, & train up all sorts of Men, of what Condition soever, or wheresoever born, whether in the said Province, or elsewhere, for the time being; And to make War & pursue the Enemies aforesaid, as well by Sea, as by Land; yea even without the Limits of the said Province, and by Gods Assistance, to Vanquish, and take them, & being taken, to put them to Death by the Law of War, & to save them at there pleasure: and to do all & every other thing which to the Charge & Office of a Captain General of an Army do belong, or hath accustom'd to belong, as fully & freely as any Captain General of an Army hath had the same.

Also our Will & Pleasure is, & by this our Charter, We do give & grant unto the said Edward Earl of Clarendon, George Duke of Albemarle, William Earl of Craven, John Lord Berkley, Anthony Lord Ashley, Sir George Carteret, Sir John Colleton, & Sir William Berkley, their Heirs & Assigns, full & absolute

Power & Authority, that they the said Edward Earl of Clarendon, George
Duke of Albemarle, William Earl of Craven, John Lord Berkley, Anthony
Lord Ashley, Sir George Carteret, Sir John Colleton, & Sir William Berkley,
their Heirs & Assigns, full Power & Liberty & Authority in case of Rebellion,
Tumult or Sedition (if any should happen which God forbid) either upon
the Land within the Province aforesaid, or upon the main Sea, in making
a Voyage thither, or returning from thence, by him & themselves, their
Captains, Deputies or Officers, to be authorized under his or their Seals for
that purpose: To whom also for Us, our Heirs & Successors, we do give & grant
by these Presents, full Power & Authority to exercise Martial Law against
Mutinous & Seditious Persons of those Parts; such as shall refuse to submit
themselves to their Government, or shall refuse to serve in the Wars, or
shall fly to the Enemy, or forsake their Colours or Ensigns or be Loyterers or
Stragglers, or otherwise howsoever offending against law, Custom, or Military
Discipline, as freely & in as ample manner & form as any Captain General of
an Army, by Vertue of his Office, might, or hath accustom'd to use the same.

And our further Pleasure is, & by these presents, for Us, our Heirs &
Successors, We do grant unto the said Edward Earl of Clarendon, George
Duke of Albemarle, William Earl of Craven, John Lord Berkley, Anthony Lord
Ashley, Sir George Carteret, Sir John Colleton, & Sir William Berkley, their
Heirs & Assigns, full & absolute Power & Authority, that they the said Edward
Earl of Clarendon, George Duke of Albemarle, William Earl of Craven, John
Lord Berkley, Anthony Lord Ashley, Sir George Carteret, Sir John Colleton, &
Sir William Berkley, their Heirs & Assigns, & to the Tenants & Inhabitants of
the said Province, or Territory, both present & to come, & to every of them,
that the said Province or Territory, & the Tenants & Inhabitants thereof, shall
not from henceforth, be held or reputed any member or part of any Colony
whatsoever, in America or elsewhere; now transported or made, nor shall be
depending on or subject to their Government in any thing, but be absolutely
seperated & divided from the same; And our Pleasure is, by these Presents,
that they [128] be Seperated, and that they be Subject immediately to our
Crown of England, as depending thereof for ever. And that the Inhabitants of
the said Province or Territory.

And in case it shall happen, that any doubts or questions shou'd arise
concerning the true Sence & Understanding of any word, clause, or sentence,
contain'd in this our present Charter, We will, ordain, and command, that at
all times, & in all things such as Interpretations be made thereof, & allow'd
in all & every of our Courts whatsoever, as lawfully may be adjudged most
advantageous & favourable to the said Edward Earl of Clarendon, George
Duke of [129] Albemarle, William Earl of Craven, John Lord Berkley, Anthony

Lord Ashley, Sir George Carteret, Sir John Colleton, & Sir William Berkley, their Heirs & Assigns, full & absolute Power & Authority, that they the said Edward Earl of Clarendon, George Duke of Albemarle, William Earl of Craven, John Lord Berkley, Anthony Lord Ashley, Sir George Carteret, Sir John Colleton, & Sir William Berkley, their Heirs & Assigns, although Express mention &c.

Witness our self at Westminster, the thirtieth day of June, in the Seventeenth Year of our Reign.

Per ipsum Regem.

At the Court of St. James's the 1st Day of March 1710.

Present

The Queen's most Excellent Majesty in Council.

Upon reading this day at the Board a Representation from the Rt. Honble. the Lords Commissioners for trade & Plantations in the Words following. In pursuance of your Majesty's Pleasure Commissioners have been appointed on the part of your Majesty's Colony of Virginia, as likewise on the part of the Province of Carolina, for the settling the Bounds between those Governments; And they have met several times for that purpose, but have not agreed upon any one point thereof, by reason of the triffleing delays of the Carolina Commissioners, & of the many difficulties by them rais'd in relation to the proper Observations & survey they were to make. However the Commissioners for Virginia, have delivered to your Majesty's Lieut. Governor of that Colony, an account of their proceedings, which Account has been under the Consideration of your Majesty's Council of Virginia, & they have made a Report thereon to the said Lieut. Governor, who haveing lately transmitted unto us a Copy of that report, we take leave humbly to lay the Substance thereof before your Majesty, which is as follows.

That the Commissioners of Carolina, are both of them persons engag'd in Interest to obstruct the settling the Boundarys between that Province and the Colony of Virginia; for one of them has for several Years been Surveyor General of Carolina, has acquired to himself great profit by surveying Lands within the controverted Bounds, & has taken up several Tracts of Land in his own name, & sold the same to others, for which he stands still oblig'd [to] obtain Patents from the Government of Carolina; The other of them is at this time Surveyor General, & hath the same Prospect of Advantage by making future surveys within the said Bounds. That the Behaviour of the Carolina Commissioners has tended visibly to no other End, than to protract and defeat the Settling this Affair: and particularly Mr. Moseley

has us'd so many Shifts & Excuses to disappoint all Conferences with the
Commissioners of Virginia, as plainly show his Aversion to proceed in a
Business that tends so manifestly to his disadvantage. His prevaricating on
this occasion has been so undiscreet and so unguarded, as to be discover'd
in the presence of the Lieut. Governor of Virginia. He started so many
objections to the powers granted to the Commissioners of that Colony, with
design to render their Conferences ineffectual, that his Joint Commissioner
could hardly find an excuse for him. And when the Lieut. Governor had
with much adoe prevail'd with [130] the said Mr. Moseley, to appoint a time
for meeting the Commissioners of Virginia, & for bringing the necessary
Instruments to take the Latitude of the Bounds in dispute which Instruments
he owned were ready in Carolina, he not only fail'd to comply with his own
appointment, but, after the Commissioners of Virginia had made a Journey
to his House, and had attended him to the Places proper for observing the
Latitude, he wou'd not take the trouble of carrying his own Instrument,
but contented himself to find fault with the Quadrant produc'd by the
virginia Commissioners, tho' that Instrument had been approv'd by the best
Mathematicians, and is of universal Use. From all which it is evident how
little hopes there are of settling the Boundarys, abovemention'd in concert
with the present Commissioners of Carolina. That tho' the Bounds of the
Carolina Charter are in express words limitted to Weyanoak Creek, lying in or
about 36° 30′ of Northern Latitude, yet the Commissioners for Carolina have
not by any of their Evidences pretended to prove any such Place as Weyanoak
Creek, the amount of their Evidence reaching no further than to prove which
is Weyanoak River, & even that is contradicted by affadavits taken on the
part of Virginia, by which affadavits it appears that before the Date of the
Carolina Charter to this day, the place they pretend to be Weyanoak River
was, & is still called Nottoway River. But supposing the same had been call'd
Weyanoak River, it can be nothing to their purpose, there being a great
difference between a River & a Creek. Besides, in that Country there are
divers Rivers & Creeks of the same Name, as Potomeck River, & Potomeck
Creek, Rappahannock River, & Rappahannock Creek, & several others, tho'
there are many Miles distance between the mouths of these Rivers, and
the mouths of these Creeks. It is also observable, that the Witnesses on the
Part of Carolina are all very Ignorant Persons & most of them of ill Fame &
Reputation, on which Account they had been forced to remove from Virginia
to Carolina; Further, there appeared to be many contradictions in their
Testimonys; whereas on the other hand the Witnesses to prove that the Right
to those Lands is in the Government of Virginia, are Persons of good Credit,
their knowledge of the Lands in question is more ancient than any of the

Witnesses for Carolina, & their Evidence fully corroborated by the concurrent Testimony of the Tributary Indians. And that right is further confirm'd by the Observations lately taken of the Latitude in those parts; by which 'tis plain, that the Creek proved to be Weyanoak Creek by the Virginia Evidences, & sometimes call'd Wiccocon, answers best to the Latitude described in the Carolina Charter, for it lyes in 36° 40', which is ten Minutes to the Northward of the Limits describ'd in the Carolina grant; Whereas Nottoway River, lyes exactly in the Latitude of 37° and can by no construction be suppos'd to be the Boundary described in their Charter; So that upon the whole Matter, if the Commissioners of Carolina, had no other view than to clear the just right of [131] the Proprietors, such undeniable Demonstrations wou'd be sufficient to convince them, but the said Commissioners give too much cause to suspect that they mix their own private Interest with the Claim of the Proprietors, & for that reason endeavour to gain time in order to obtain Grants for the Land already taken up, and also to secure the rest on this occasion we take Notice, that they proceed to survey the Land in dispute, not withstanding the assurance given by the Government of Carolina to the contrary by their letter of the 17th of June, 1707 to the Government of Virginia, by which letter they promised that no lands shou'd be taken up within the controverted bounds till the same were settled.

Whereupon we humbly propose, that the Lords Proprietors be acquainted with the foregoing complaint of the triffleing delays of their Commissioners, which delays 'tis reasonable to believe, have proceeded from the self-Interest of those Commissioners, and that therefore your Majesty's pleasure be signify'd to the said Lords Proprietors that by the first Opportunity they send Orders to their Governour or Commander in Chief of Carolina for the time being, to issue forth a new Commission to the purport of that lately issued, thereby constituting two other Persons, not having any personal Interest in, or claim to any of the Land lying within the Boundarys, in the room of Edward Moseley & John Lawson. The Carolina Commissioners to be appointed being strictly required, to finish their Survey, and to make a return thereof in conjunction with the Virginia Commissioners, within six months, to be computed from the time, that due notice shall be given by Your Majesty's Lieut. Governor of Virginia to the Governor or Commander in Chief of Carolina, of the time & place, which your Majesty's said Lieut. Governor shall appoint for the first meeting of the Commissioners one part & the other: In order whereunto we humbly offer, that directions be sent to the said Lieut. Governor, to give such Notice accordingly; & if after Notice so given, the Carolina Commissioners shall refuse or neglect to Join with those on the part of Virginia in making such survey as likewise a Return thereof within the time before mention'd; that then and in such Case the Commissioners on the Part of Virginia be directed, to draw up an Account of the proper Observations and Survey which they shall have made for ascertaining the Bounds between Virginia & Carolina, and to deliver the same in writing under their hands and seals to the Lieut. Governor and Council of Virginia, to the end the same may be laid before your Majesty for your Majesty's final Determination therein, within, with regard to the Settleing of those Boundaries; the Lords Proprietors haveing by an Instrument under their Hands, submitted the same to Your Majesty's royal determination, which Instrument dated in March 1708, is lying in this Office:

And lastly we humbly propose, that your Majesty's further Pleasure be signify'd to the said Lords Proprietors, and in like manner to the Lieut. Governor of Virginia, that no Grants be pass'd by either of these Governments of any of the Lands lying within the [132] controverted Bounds, until such Bounds shall be ascertain'd and settled as aforesaid, whereby it may appear whether those Lands do of Right belong to your Majesty or to the Lords Proprietors of Carolina.

Her Majesty in Council approveing of the said Representation is pleas'd to order, as it is hereby ordered, that the Rt. Honble. the Lords Commissioners for Trade & Plantations do signifye her Majesty's Pleasure herein to her Majesty's Lieut. Governor, or Commander in Chief of Virginia for the time being, and to all Persons to whom it may belong, as propos'd by their Lordships in the said Representation, and the Rt. Honble. the Lords Proprietors of Carolina are to do what on their part does appertain.

Edw. Southwell

Proposals for determining the controversy relating to the Bounds between the Governments of Virginia and North Carolina, most humbly offered for His Majesty's Royal Approbation, and for the Consent of the Rt. Honble. the Lords Proprietors of Carolina.

For as much as the dispute between the said two Governments about their true Limits, continues still, notwithstanding the several meetings of the Commissioners, and all the proceedings of many Years past, in order to adjust that affair, & seeing no speedy Determination is likely to ensue, unless some Medium be found out; in which both Party's may incline to acquiesce, wherefore both the underwritten Governors having met, and consider'd the prejudice both to the King & the Lord Proprietors Interest by the continuance of this contest, and truly endeavouring a Decision, which they Judge comes nearest the Intention of Royal Charter granted to the Lords Proprietors, do with the advice & consent of their respective Councils propose as follows.

That from the mouth of Corotuck River or Inlet & setting the Compass on the North Shoar thereof a due West Line be run & fairly mark'd, & if it happen to cut Chowan River between the mouths of Nottoway River, and Wicocon Creek, then shall the same direct Course be continued toward the Mountains and be ever deem'd the sole divideing line between Virginia & Carolina.

That if the said West Line cuts Chowan River to the Southward of Wicocon Creek, then from point of Intersection the Bounds shall be allow'd to continue up the middle of the said Chowan River to the middle of the Enterance into the said Wicocon Creek, and from thence a due West Line shall divide the said two Governments.

That if a due West Line shall be found to pass through Islands or to cut out small slips of Land, which might more conveniently be included in one Province or the other by Natural Water Bounds, In such Cases the Persons appointed for runing the Line, shall have power to settle Natural Bounds, provided the Commissioners of both Sides agree thereto, and that all [133] such Variations from the West Line be particularly noted in the Maps or Plats, which they shall return, to be put upon the Records of both governments, all which is humbly submitted by

Charles Eden A. Spotswood

Order of the King and Council upon the foregoing Proposals.
At the Court of St. James's, the 28th day of March 172[7].
Present
The King's most Excellent Majesty in Council.

Whereas it has been represented to his Majesty at the board, that for adjusting the disputes, which have subsisted for many Years past between the Colonys of Virginia and North Carolina, concerning their true Boundarys, the late Governors of the said Colonys did some time since agree upon certain Proposals for regulating the said Boundarys for the future, to which Proposals the Lords Proprietors of Carolina have given their Assent. And whereas the said Proposals were this day presented to his Majesty as proper for his Royal Approbation,

His Majesty is thereupon pleas'd with the Advice of his Privy Council, to approve of the said Proposals, a copy whereof is hereunto annext, and to order as it is hereby order'd, that the Governor or Commander in chief of the Colony of Virginia, do settle the said Boundarys in conjunction with the Governor of North Carolina, agreeable to the said Proposals.

Edward Southwell.

The Lieut. Governour of Virginia's Commission in obedience to His Majesty's Order.

George the Second by the Grace of God of great Britain, France, and Ireland King, Defender of the Faith, to our trusty and well beloved William Byrd, Richard Fitz-William, and William Dandridge Esqrs. members of our Council of the Colony and Dominion of Virginia, Greeting, Whereas our late Royal Father of Blessed memory was graciously pleas'd by Order in his Privy Council, bearing date the 28 day of March 1727, to approve of certain Proposals agreed upon by Alexander Spotswood Esqr. late Lieut. Governor of Virginia, on the one part, and Charles Eden Esqr. late Lieut. Governour of the Province of North Carolina, for determineing the Controversy relating to the Bounds between said two Governments, & was farther pleased to direct and order, that the said Boundary's shou'd be laid out & settled agreeable to the said Proposals: Know ye therefore that reposing special trust and confidence in your Ability & Provident circumspection [we] have assign'd, constituted and appointed, and by these presents do assign, constitute, and appoint you & every of you, jointly & severally, our Commissioners for & on behalf of our Colony and Dominion of Virginia to meet the Commissioners appointed or to be appointed on the part of the Province of North [134] Carolina, and in conjunction with them to cause a Line or Lines of Division to be run and markt to divide the said two Governments according to the proposals above mentioned, & the Order of our late Royal Father, Copy's of both of which you will herewith receive. And we do farther give and grant unto you, and in case of the Death or absence of any of you, such of you as shall be present, full Power and Authority, to treat & agree with the said Commissioners of the Province of North Carolina on such rules and methods as you shall judge most expedient, for the adjusting and finally determining all disputes or controversies which may arise touching any Islands or other small Slips of Land which may happen to be intersected or cut off by the dividing Line aforesaid, and which may with more conveniency be included in the one Province or the other by natural water bounds agreeable to the Proposals aforemention'd, and generally to do and perform all matters and things requisite for the final determination and settlement of the said Boundarys, according to the said Proposals. And to the end our Service herein may not be disappointed through the refusal or delay of the Commissioners for the Province of North Carolina to act in Conjunction with you in settling the Boundarys aforesaid, we do hereby give & grant unto you, or such of you as shall be present at the time and place appointed for running the dividing Line aforesaid, full Power and Authority to cause the said Line to be run and mark'd out, conformable to the said Proposals, having due regard to the doing equal Justice to Us, and to the Lords Proprietors of Carolina, any refusal disagreement, or opposition of the said Commissioners of North Carolina notwithstanding; And in that case we do hereby require you to make a true report of your proceedings to our Lieut. Governour, or Commander in Chief of Virginia, in order to be laid before us for our approbation, and final determination herein. And in case any Person or Persons whatsoever shall presume to disturb, molest, or resist you, or any of the Officers or Persons by your direction, in running the said Line, and executing the Powers herein given you, we do by these presents Give and Grant unto you, or such of you as shall be attending the service aforesaid, full Power & Authority by Warrant under your or any of your hands and Seals, to order and command all and every the Militia Officers in our Counties of Princess Anne, Norfolk, Nansemond, & Isle of Wight, or other the adjacent Counties together with the Sheriff of each of the said Counties, or either of them, to raise the Militia & Posse of each of the said several Counties, for the removeing all force and opposition, which shall or may be made to you in the due Execution of this our Commission, & we do hereby will and require, as well the Officers of the said Militia, as all other Officers & loving Subjects within the said Counties, & all others whom it may concern, to be Obedient aiding & assisting unto you in all & singular [135] the Premises, And we do in like manner command & require you to cause fair Maps & descriptions of the said Divideing Line, and the remarkable Places through which it shall pass, to be made and return'd to our Lieut. Governor or Commander in Chief of our said Colony for the time being, in order to be enter'd on Record in the proper Offices within our said colony. Provided that you do not by colour of this our Commission, take upon you or determine any Private Man's property, in or to the Lands which shall by the said dividing Line be included within the limits of Virginia, nor of any other matter or thing, that doth not relate immediately to the adjusting, settling, & final Determination of the Boundary aforesaid, conformable to the Proposals herein before mention'd, and not otherwise. In Witness whereof we have caused these presents to be made. Witness our trusty and well beloved William Gooch Esqr., our Lieut. Governor & Commander in Chief

of our Colony & Dominion of Virginia, under the Seal of our said Colony, at
Williamsburgh the 14th day of December 1727 in the first Year of our Reign.

William Gooch

The Governour of North Carolina's Commission
in Obedience to His Majesty's Order.

Sir Richard Everard Baronet, Governor Captain Generall, Admirall, and
Commander in Chief of the said Province, To Christopher Gale Esqr. Chief
Justice, John Lovick Esqr. Secretary; Edward Moseley Esqr. Surveyor General
& William Little Esqr. Attorney General, Greeting, Whereas many disputes
& differences have formerly been between the Inhabitants of this Province,
and those of his Majesty's colony of Virginia, concerning the Boundaries
and Limits between the said two Governments, which having been duly
considered, by Charles Eden Esqr. late Governor of this Province, and
Alexander Spotswood Esqr. late Governor of Virginia, they agree[d]P to certain
proposals for determining the said controversy, & humbly offer'd the same
for his Majesty's Royal Approbation, and the Consent of the true & absolute
Lords Proprietors of Carolina: and his Majesty having been pleas'd, to signify
his Royal approbation of these proposals (consented unto by the true and
absolute Lords Proprietors of Carolina) and given directions for adjusting &
settling the Boundarys as near as may be to the said Proposals.

I therefore reposing especial trust and confidence in you the said
Christopher Gale, John Lovick, Edward Moseley and William Little to be
Commissioners on the part of ^the^ true and absolute Lords Proprietors, and
that you, in conjunction with such Commissioners, as shall be nominated for
Virginia, use your utmost Endeavours and take all necessary care in adjusting
and settling the said Boundarys, by drawing such a distinct Line or Lines of
Division between the said two Provinces, as near as reasonable you can to the
Proposals made by the two former Governours, and the Instructions herewith
given you. Given at the Council Chamber in Edenton, under my hand, and the
Seal of the Colony, the 21st day of [136] February Anno Dom: 1727, and in the
first year of the Reign of our sovereign Lord, King George the Second.

Richard Everard

PA: agreed

The Protest of the Carolina Commissioners, against
our proceeding on the Line without them

We, the underwritten Commissioners for the Government of N. Carolina in conjunction with the Commissioners on the part of Virginia, having run the Line for the division of the two Colonys, from Corotuck Inlet to the South Branch of Roanoak River, being in the whole about 170 Miles, and near 50 Miles, without the Inhabitants, being of Opinion we had run the Line as far as would be requisite for a long time, judged the carrying it farther wou'd be a needless charge and trouble. And the Grand Debate which had so long subsisted between the two Governments, about Wyanoke River or Creek being settled at our former meeting in the Spring; when we were ready on our parts to have gone with the Line to the utmost Inhabitants, which if it had been done, the Line at any time after might have been continued at an easy expence by a Surveyor on each side; and if at any time hereafter, there shou'd be occasion to carry the Line on further that we have now run it, which we think will not be in an Age or two, it may be done in the same easy Manner without the great Expence that now attends it. And, on a Conference of all the Commissioners we have communicated our sentiments thereon, and declar'd our Opinion that we had gone as far as the Service required, and thought proper to proceed no farther; to which it was answer'd by the Commissioners for Virginia, that they should not regard what we did, but if we desisted, they wou'd proceed without us. But we conceiving by his Majesty's Order in Council, they were directed to act in conjunction with the Commissioners appointed for Carolina, & having accordingly run the Line jointly so far, and Exchanged Plans, thought they cou'd not carry on the Bounds singly: but that their proceedings without us wou'd be irregular& invalid, and that it wou'd be no Boundary, and thought it proper to enter our Dissent thereto. Wherefore for the reasons aforesaid, in the name of His Excellency the Lord Palatine, and the rest of the true and absolute Lords Proprietors of Carolina, we do hereby dissent and Disallow of any farther proceeding with the Bounds without our Concurrence, and pursuant to our Instructions do give this our Dissent in writing.

October 7, 1728.   Edward Moseley.   C. Gale.
                     Will. Little.   J. Lovick.

The Answer of the Virginia Commissioners to the foregoing protest.

Whereas on the 7th of October last a paper was deliver'd to us by the Commissioners of N. Carolina, in the Stile of a [137] Protest, against our carrying any farther without them the dividing Line between the 2 Governments, we the underwritten Commissioners on the part of Virginia having maturely considered the reasons offer'd in the said Protest why those Gentlemen retir'd so soon from that Service, beg leave to return the following answer:

 They are pleas'd in the first place to alledge by way of Reason that having run the Line near 50 Miles beyond the Inhabitants, it was sufficient for a long time, in their Opinion, for an Age or two. To this we answer that by breaking off so soon, they did but imperfectly obey his Majesty's Order, assented to by the Lords Proprietors. The plain meaning of that Order, was, to ascertain the Bounds betwixt the two Governments as far toward the Mountains as we cou'd, that neither the King's Grants may hereafter encroach on the Lords Proprietors, nor theirs on the Rights of his Majesty. And tho' the distance toward the great Mountains be not precisely determin'd, yet surely the West Line shou'd be carry'd as near them as may be that both the King's Lands and those of their Lordships may be taken up the faster, and that his Majesty's Subjects may as soon as possible extend themselves to that Natural Barrier. This they will certainly do in a few Years, when they know distinctly in which Government they may enter for the Land, as they have already done in the more northern Parts of Virginia. So that 'tis strange the Carolina Commissioners, shou'd affirm, that the distance only of 50 Miles above the Inhabitants, wou'd be sufficient to carry the Line for an Age or two, especially considering that two or three days before the date of their Protest, Mr. Mayo had enter'd with them for 2000 Acres of Land, within 5 Miles of the Place where they left off. Besides if we reflect on the richness of the Soil in those parts, & the convenience for Stock, we may foretell without the Spirit of Divination, that there will be many Settlements higher than those Gentlemen went in less than ten Years, and perhaps in half that time.

Another reason mention'd in the Protest for their retiring so soon from the Service, is, that their going farther wou'd be a needless Charge and Trouble. And they alledge that the rest may be done by one Surveyor on a Side in an easy manner, whenever it shall be thought necessary.

To this we answer, that Frugality for the Publick is a rare vertue, but when the publick Service must suffer by it, it degenerates into a Vice. And this will ever be the Case when Gentlemen Execute the orders of their Superiors by halves. but had the Carolina Commissioners been sincerely frugal for the government, why did they carry out provisions sufficient to support them and their Men for ten weeks when they intended not to tarry half that time? This they must own to be true, since they brought 1000 lb. of Provisions along with them. Now after so great an Expence in their preparations, it had been no mighty Addition to their Charge, had they endured the Fatigue 5 or 6 Weeks longer. It wou'd at most have been no more than they must be at, whenever they finish their Work, [138] even tho' they shou'd fancy it proper to trust a matter of that consequence to the Management of one Surveyor. Such a one must have a Number of Men along with him, both for his assistance and Defense, and those Men must have Provisions to support them.

These are all the reasons these Gentlemen think fit to mention in their Protest, tho' they had in truth a more powerfull argument for retiring so abruptly, which because they forgot, it will be neighbourly to help them out. The Provisions they intended to bring along with them, for want of Horses to carry them were partly Drop't by the way, & what they cou'd bring was husbanded so ill that after 18 days, (which was the whole time we had them in our Company,) they had no more left, by their own confession, than two Pounds of Biscuit for each Man to carry them home. However tho' this was an unanswerable Reason for Gentlemen for leaving the Business unfinish't, it was none at all for us, who had at that time Bread sufficient for 7 Weeks longer. Therefore lest their want of Manag^em^ent, might put a Stop to his Majesty's Service, & frustrate his Royal intentions, we judg'd it our Duty to proceed without them, and have extended the Dividing Line so far West, as to leave the great Mountains on each hand to the Eastward of us. And this we have done with the same fidelity & exactness as if the Gentlemen had continued with us. Our Surveyors (whose Integrity I am perswaded they will not call in Question) continued to act under the same Oath, which they had done from the beginning. Yet not withstanding all this, if the government of N. Carolina, shou'd not hold itself bound by that part of the Line, which we made without the Assistance of its Commissioners, yet we shall have this benefit in it at least, that his Majesty will know how far his Lands reach towards the South, & consequently where his Subjects may take it up, & how far they may be granted without Injustice to the Lords Proprietors. To this we may also add, that, haveing the Authority of our Commission, to act without the Commissioners of Carolina in Case of their disagreement or Refusal, we thought ourselves bound upon their Retreat to finish the Line without them, lest his Majesty's Service might suffer by any [dis]honour or neglect on their part.[409]

William Dandridge W. Byrd

THE NAMES OF THE COMMISSIONERS TO DIRECT THE RUNNING OF
THE LINE BETWEEN VIRGINIA AND NORTH CAROLINA.

William Byrd.
Richd. Fitz William.
William Dandridge. } Commissioners for Virginia
   Esqrs.

Christopher Gale
John Lovewick
Edward Moseley } Commissioners for Carolina
Wm. Little
   Esqrs.

[139]

Alexr. Irvin
William Mayo } Surveyors for Virginia

Edward Moseley } Surveyors for N. Carolina
Samuely Swann

The Revd. Peter Fountain, Chaplain.

NAMES OF THE MEN EMPLOY'D ON THE PART OF VIRGINIA TO
RUN THE LINE BETWEEN THAT COLONY AND N. CAROLINA

On the first Expedition	On the 2d. Expedition
1. Peter Jones	Peter Jones
2. Thomas Jones	Thomas Jones
3. Thomas Short	Thomas Short
4. Robert Hix	Robert Hix
5. John Evans	John Evans
6. Stephen Evans	Stephen Evans
7. John Ellis	John Ellis
8. John Ellis Junr.	John Ellis Junr.
9. Thomas Wilson	Thomas Wilson
10. George Tilman	George Tilman
11.Charles Kimbal	Charles Kimball
12. George Hamilton	George Hamilton
13. Robert Allen	Thomas Jones Junr.
14. Thomas Jones Junr.	James Petillo
15. James Petillo	Richd. Smith
16. Richard Smith	Abraham Jones
17. John Rice	Edward Powell
	William Pool
	William Calvert
	James Whitlock
	Thomas Page

ACCOUNT OF THE EXPENCE OF RUNNING THE LINE
BETWEEN VIRGINIA AND N. CAROLINA

To the Mens Wages in currant money	£277	10	0
To Sundry Disbursements for Provisions &c.	174	1	6
To paid the Men for 7 Horses lost	44	0	0
	£495	11	6

The sum of £495 11 6 Currant Money reduc't at 15 *P*Cent to Sterling amounts to	430	8	10
To paid to Colo. Byrd	142	5	7
To paid to Colo. Dandridge	142	5	7
To paid Mr. Fitz William	94	0	0
To paid the chaplain, Mr. Fontain	20	0	0
To paid to Mr. William Mayo	75	0	0
To paid to Mr. Alexr. Irvin	75	0	0
To paid for a Tent and Marquis	20	0	0
	£1000	0	0

This Summ was discharg'd by a Warrant out of His Majesty's Quitrents from the Lands in Virginia.

NOTES

1. Byrd makes much of the early designation of all North American lands claimed by the British as "Virginia," as if the primacy of foundation infused Virginia with a fundamental superiority to the other colonies. The notion had a well-established precedent, for Captain John Smith opened his account of the 1606 voyage to the New World with a similarly all-encompassing chorographical assertion:

> But this Virginia is a Country in America betweene the degrees of 34. and 45. of the North latitude. The bounds thereof on the East side are the great Ocean: on the South lyeth Florida: on the North nova Francia: as for the West thereof, the limits are unknowne.
> —*The Generall Historie of Virginia, New-England, and the Summer Isles . . .* (London, 1624), 21 (*Hayes*, 182), in *Smith*, II, 100

2. Byrd's phrasing is curiously similar to a passage in Fayrer Hall's *Short Account of the First Settlement of the Provinces of Virginia, Maryland, New-York, New-Jersey, and Pennsylvania, by the English* (London, 1735), 3:

> The famous Sir *Walter Raleigh* having proposed to other great Men of his Time to join with him in an Expedition for the Discovery of Parts then unknown in the *West-Indies*, obtained Letters Patent from Queen *Elizabeth*, of ever glorious Memory, bearing Date the 25th of *March*, 1584.

See also John Smith, *Generall Historie* (1624):

> The most famous, renowned, and ever worthy of all memory, for her courage, learning, judgement, and vertue, Queene Elizabeth granted her Letters Patent to Sir Walter Raleigh for the discovering and planting new Lands and Countries.
> —*Smith*, II, 63

3. Philip Amadas and Arthur Barlow were ship captains previously employed by Raleigh (*Smith*, II, 63; Hall, *Short Account*, 3). Richard Hakluyt published Barlow's report to Raleigh as "The first voyage made to the coasts of *America*, with two barks, where in were Captaines M. *Philip Amadas*, and M. *Arthur Barlowe*, who discovered part of the Countrey now called *Virginia, Anno 1584*." Barlow's phrasing contains a few parallels with Byrd's:

> We manned our boats, and went to view the land next adjoyning, and to take possession of the same, in the right of the Queenes most excellent Majestie, as rightfull Queene, and Princesse of the same, and after delivered the same over to your use, according to her Majesties grant, and letters patents, under her Highnesse great Seale. Which being performed, according to the ceremonies used in such enterprises, we viewed the land about us.
> —*The Principal Navigations, Voyages, Traffiques, and Discoveries of the English Nation* (London, 1599), 246

4. Possibly Byrd's own invention; no source for this anecdote has been discovered.

5. *Santer to the holy land:* To saunter is "to wander or travel about aimlessly or unprofitably; to travel as a vagrant," or "to walk with a leisurely and careless gait; to stroll. Also,

to travel by vehicle in a slow and leisurely manner" *(OED)*. Byrd might well have had John Ray's apposite derivation of *santer* in mind:

> To *Santer* about; or go *Santering* up and down. It is derived from *Saincte terre, i.e.* The Holy Land, because of old time when there were frequent Expeditions thither: many idle persons went from place to place, upon pretence that they had taken or intended to take the Cross upon them, and to go thither. It signifies to idle up and down, to go loitering [about].
> —*A Collection of English Words Not Generally Used,* 2d ed. (London, 1691), 111

Byrd also used the word "santer" in a letter to John Boyle: "No grave santerer at Wills can be better informed." Byrd to John Boyle, Baron Boyle of Broghill, Feb. 12, 1727/8, *Correspondence,* I, 372.

6. Twice in the *Dividing Line* Byrd criticizes the first Anglo-Virginians for neglecting the opportunity to cement friendship with the Indians by the personal and social bonds of marriage. Miscegenation as a means of peacemaking between colonists and indigenous people was not an uncommon notion. Typical was Beverley's observations on the marriage of Pocohantas and John Rolfe:

> Intermarriage had been indeed the Method proposed very often by the *Indians* in the Beginning, urging it frequently as a certain Rule, that the *English* were not their Friends, if they refused it. And I can't but think it wou'd have been happy for that Country, had they embraced this Proposal: For, the Jealousie of the *Indians,* which I take to be the Cause of most of the Rapines and Murders they committed, wou'd by this Means have been prevented, and consequently the Abundance of Blood that was shed on both sides wou'd have been saved; the great Extremities they were so often reduced to, by which so many died, wou'd not have happen'd; the Colony, instead of all these Losses of Men on both Sides, wou'd have been encreasing in Children to its Advantage, the country wou'd have escaped the *Odium* which undeservedly fell upon it, by the Errors and Convulsions in the first Management; and, in all Likelihood, many, if not most, of the *Indians* would have been converted to Christianity by this kind Method; the Country would have been full of People, by the Preservation of the many *Christians* and *Indians* that fell in the Wars between them.
> —*Beverley,* book 1, 25–26

Cf. *Lawson,* 236–237. At the same time, Virginia passed strict laws to prevent any "abominable mixture and spurious issue" in 1691, 1696, and 1705 (*Hening,* III, 86–88).

Nonetheless, the notion of intermarriage had political currency. Governor Spotswood wrote to the Board of Trade in November 1716, concerning troubles with the Indians, candidly acknowledging that no hostilities were ever committed by the Indians "except where the English have given the first provocation." He commented,

> And as to gaining a nearer friendship by intermarriages as the custom of the French is, the inclinations of our people are not the same with those of that Nation, for notwithstanding the long intercourse between the inhabitants of this country and the Indians, and their living among one another for so many years, I cannot hear of one Englishman that has an Indian wife, or an Indian marryed to a white woman.
> —Spotswood to Board of Trade, *CSP,* XXIX, 282, no. 522

In 1721, the Board of Trade sent George I a comprehensive report on the state of the North American colonies, stressing the importance of "cultivating a good understanding with the native Indians," observing that the French had always been so careful

> to gain the natives to their intrest, that they have spared no pains, no cost nor artifice to attain this desirable end; wherein it must be allowed, that they have succeeded, to the great prejudice of your Majesty's subjects in those parts. . . . For this purpose their missionaries are constantly imploy'd, frequent presents are made to the Sachems or Kings of the several nations, and incouragement given for intermarriages between the French and natives, whereby their new empire may in time be peopled without draining France of its inhabitants.
> —Board of Trade report to the king on plantations, Sept. 8, 1721, *CSP,* XXXII, 442– 443, no. 656

The Board of Trade reminded the king it had recommended such a measure to him when it drew up the instructions for the governor of Nova Scotia, proposing then

> that proper incouragement should be given to such of your Majesty's subjects as should intermarry with the native Indians; and we conceive it might be for your Majesty's service, that the said instructions should be extended to all the other British Colonies.

There is a strong likelihood that Byrd was familiar with this important summary of the state of the colonies as well as the other sources listed above.

7. Compare with Catesby: "The Indians have healthful constitutions, and are little acquainted with those diseases which are incident to Europeans" (*Catesby,* 149).

A "sprightly lover" is spirited, animated, brisk, and sportive. Byrd might have been echoing usages such as that of the English poet John Dryden, who describes the contest for Helen of Troy between the charms of the "sprightly Lover" Paris and the "Nauseous Bed" of King Menelaus, in *Cleomenes,* in *The Dramatick Works of John Dryden Esq;* (London, 1717), VI, 305 (*Hayes,* 988, 2003).

8. The saying here employed is a common English proverb indicating a futile undertaking; for instance, in 1736 John Stirling employed it to illustrate the rhetorical use of proverbs: "You wash the Black-moor white, i.e. you labour in vain." John Stirling, *A System of Rhetoric in a Method Entirely New* (London, 1736), 7.

9. Gordon Sayre has observed that French officials offered a generous bounty (three thousand livres) to men who married native women, but in practice the bounty was never actually granted. The Jesuit fathers would allow French men to marry only Christianized Indian women, and generally the cultural exchange went the opposite way. Contact with Indians "had the effect of easing the transition of Frenchmen into Indian life and away from the colony, rather than solidifying the Frenchification of the Indians." After 1684 the policy was reversed and intermarriage prohibited. Gordon Sayre, "Native American Sexuality in the Eyes of the Beholders, 1535–1710," in Merril D. Smith, ed., *Sex and Sexuality in Early North America* (New York, 1998), 41.

10. Byrd is mistaken about the date, for the "Virginia Charter" incorporating the Plymouth and London Companies was actually signed April 10, 1606. The charter was granted

to Thomas Hanham, Rawleigh Gilbert, William Parker, George Popham, "and others of the Town of *Plimouth, etc.* to plant where they shall see fit and convenient, between 38 and 45 Degrees of Northern Latitude" (*Oldmixon*, I, 26) (*Hayes,* 995). After their first expedition was intercepted by the Spanish fleet, Popham sent out a second ship, and, after an encouraging report, the proprietors sent out two ships with a hundred men under the command of Captain George Popham and Captain Gilbert. The colony settled at the mouth of the Kennebec River in the summer of 1607; they built a fort there, but, after the death of Captain Popham in 1608, the settlement was abandoned. See also Daniel Neal, *The History of New England* (London, 1720), 18 (*Hayes,* 46).

Lord Chief Justice Popham (ca. 1531–1607), educated at Balliol College, Oxford, and called to the bar in the Middle Temple, is best known for presiding over the capital trials of Sir Walter Raleigh and Guy Fawkes.

11. Byrd here refers to the relocation of the English Dissenting exiles (later known as the Plymouth Brethren) in Leiden under the leadership of the Reverend John Robinson. After an uncomfortable time in England, they sailed from Plymouth in the *Mayflower* on September 6, 1620. Compare Byrd's summary with Ogilby:

> In all probability *New England* would have been but thinly peopled to this day, had not a great Tide of People, possess'd with an aversion to the Church-Government of *England,* and fled into *Holland* for *Liberty of Conscience,* eagerly taken hold of this opportunity to make themselves Masters of their own Opinions, and of a Place where they might erect a Government suitable thereunto: and though at first there were some Exceptions taken, as if this Countrey was to be made a Receptacle of Sectaries, and such as condemn'd the Ecclesiastical Government of the Nation . . . at last there was little notice taken who went, perhaps upon consideration, that the vast resort of People thither would be of greater advantage to the Plantations, than their different Opinions, at so remote a distance, could be prejudicial, so long as they acknowledg'd Obedience to the King and Civil Power.
> —John Ogilby, *America: Being the Latest, and Most Accurate Description of the New World* (London, 1671), 142 (*Hayes,* 2030)

An allusion to 1 Kings 11:1: "But King Solomon loved many strange women." Byrd's source could have been the biblical passage itself, or perhaps the commentary of Josephus, who noted that Achaias prophesied God would rend the government from Solomon "because *Solomon* hath offended God, and addicted himself to the love of strange Women, and the service of foreign Gods" ([Flavius] Josephus, *The Works of Josephus,* trans. Arnauld d'Andilly [London, 1701], 218 [*Hayes,* 1227]). Byrd's diaries report his frequent early morning discipline of reading Josephus in the original Greek (*Hayes,* 1610). An alternate source may be Algernon Sidney, who maintained that locating all civic power in a king brings about civil and religious decay: "When *Solomon's* heart was drawn away by strange Women, he fill'd the Land with Idols, and opprest the People with intolerable Tributes." *Discourses concerning Government,* 2d ed. (London, 1704), 95 (*Hayes,* 2049).

12. While Switzerland certainly is a relatively small country (less than sixteen thousand square miles), Byrd is probably here alluding to the Baron de Graffenreid's continuing schemes to seat emigré "Switzers" in North Carolina, as reported in the *Virginia Gazette,* Oct. 15–22, 1736:

> We are informed by private Letters from London, That his Majesty has granted a
> large Tract of Land behind the Two *Carolinas* to the *Swiss,* who are to send over their
> People at their own Expence; and they have assured the Government, in a few Years
> they will send at their own Expence, above 100,000 of their People. By Agreement
> they are not to settle themselves within 150 Miles of the Sea.

Byrd himself had hoped to benefit by seating Swedish immigrants on his own lands.

13. Byrd contrasted Virginia's royal mandate with the implicit disloyalty of the New England colony, populated by fractious Dissenters, Presbyterians, Independents, and Puritans who "thought themselves persecuted at home." He eyed New England with suspicion because, as he believed, its foundation lay in disruption of the English social, political, and ecclesiastical order. Byrd implies the New England colonists were the same people who had deposed and executed the royal martyr Charles I. To clinch this argument he invokes the names of the leaders of the parliamentary era, John Hampden (ca. 1595–1643), John Pym (1584–1643), and Oliver Cromwell (1599–1658).

14. Byrd's figures are excessively high. Books in Byrd's library offer more conservative population counts. In 1708 Oldmixon estimated the Boston population at ten to twelve thousand, and the fleet three or four hundred sail (*Oldmixon,* I, 44). In Oldmixon's 1741 edition the population estimate rose to twenty-four thousand, and the fleet to "near 600 Sail of Ships" ([London, 1741], I, 196–197). In 1720 Neal numbered Boston's population between nineteen and twenty thousand, and ships between three and four hundred (Neal, *History of New-England,* 588, 590). An "Account of the Number of Inhabitants" commissioned by the selectmen of Boston in 1742 numbered "16,382 Souls, including 1,374 Negroes, 1,719 houses" (*The Annals of Europe for the Year 1742* [London, 1745], 416). Even after Byrd's death Boston's population remained well below his estimates. The 1765 census counted 15,520 people (excluding Indians, blacks, mixed-race, and "French neutrals") and 1,676 houses; see Evarts B. Greene and Virginia D. Harrington, *American Population before the Federal Census of 1790* (New York, 1932), 21–22.

The number of ships in Boston for certain dates may be found by consulting the records of the Board of Trade. For example, Richard Coote, first earl of Bellomont, appointed governor of Massachusetts, New Hampshire, and New York in 1697, wrote to the Board of Trade in 1700 that he had examined the registers of all the vessels belonging to these provinces "and found there then belong'd to the town of Boston, 25 ships from 100 ton to 300; ships about a 100 ton and under, 39; brigantines 50; ketches 13 and sloops 67; in all 194 vessels" (*CSP,* XVIII, 676, no. 953).

15. The charter establishing the colony of Connecticut and incorporating New Haven was signed April 23, 1662. Byrd's comment that Charles II granted Massachusetts the privilege of "chusing their own Governors" suggests a lingering resentment that Virginia's governors were imposed upon the colony by the Board of Trade on behalf of the crown.

16. *Quo warranto:* a legal document, specifically, a prerogative writ of the King's Bench "by which a person or persons were called upon to show by what warrant he or they held, claimed, or exercised an office or franchise" *(OED).* By this legal process the king, whose prerogative was thus administered, could revoke earlier grants and charters. *Boyd* (p. 6) notes that the process was initiated in June 1683, but the Court of King's Bench did not render its final judgment until October 23, 1684.

17. Sir Edmund Andros (1637–1714) had been appointed governor in 1674 of the proprietary colony of New York by Charles II's brother James, duke of York. According to the terms of New York's charter, there was to be no legislative body, the better to consolidate revenues for the proprietor. Among the tactics Andros devised in pursuit of profits for the duke were measures favoring Dutch traders. This diminished New York merchants' trade with England, and the merchants' complaints brought about Andros's recall in 1681. Andros retained James's favor nonetheless, and, soon after his patron was crowned James II, Andros was appointed governor of New England, a dominion then consisting of Massachusetts, Maine, New Hampshire, Plymouth, and part of Rhode Island. Once again Andros was instructed to rule without a legislature, to collect quitrents, and to establish a limited liberty of conscience, which really meant promoting the growth of the Church of England. None of these measures suited the colonists, who had been used to self-government, relative freedom from heavy taxation, and protection of their community-based congregations. Andros enforced his program with a heavy hand, imprisoning those who protested, ruling with an administrative coterie of outsiders, and increasing revenue with land seizures and exorbitant fees and rents. When James II was displaced by William and Mary by the Glorious Revolution, Andros was finished in New England. Byrd's phrase, "they laid unhallowed Hands upon Him," no doubt reflects his own political preference for popular submission to authority as well as his own advocacy of Andros in the 1690s. Andros became governor of Virginia in 1692. Commissary Blair and Francis Nicholson (whom Andros had supplanted) complained to the Board of Trade that Andros had neglected both the church and the College of William and Mary. Byrd prepared a defense of Andros when he appeared before an ecclesiastical court at Lambeth, but, as it turned out, Commissary Blair's presentation was so convincing, Byrd did not even get to address the court. A copy of his brief is in the Huntington Library. See "Andros, Sir Edmund (1637–1714)," *ODNB;* Louis B. Wright, "William Byrd's Defense of Sir Edmund Andros," *WMQ,* 3d Ser., II (1945), 47–62; and Kevin R. Hardwick, "Narratives of Villainy and Virtue: Governor Francis Nicholson and the Character of the Good Ruler in Early Virginia," *Journal of Southern History,* LXXII (2006), 39–74.

18. Byrd's history of Nova Scotia assumes British right to North American territory based on John and Sebastian Cabot's claim for Henry VII of England on their 1497 voyage to Newfoundland. The French claimed the region in 1603 and in 1604 established a fort at Port Royal. According to John Oldmixon, "The *English* always took *Acadia* to be part of North *Virginia;* and indeed the first *Virginia*-Company thought all was their own, which shou'd be discover'd Northward, and was not planted by any other European Nation" (*Oldmixon,* I, 20). According to the doctrine of prior claim, the English declared the French colonies invalid despite the de facto claim of present possession. Possession shifted back and forth until the French territories in what is now Canada came under British rule at the close of the Seven Years' War with the Treaty of Paris, February 10, 1763.

19. The second Treaty of Breda (July 31, 1667) returned Acadia to France, Surinam to the Dutch, and the New Netherlands to England. From these territories, already claimed by right of conquest, emerged New York, the Jerseys, Pennsylvania, and Delaware.

20. The Treaty of Utrecht (March–April 1713) brought to an end the War of the Spanish Succession. France ceded the territories claimed by the Hudson's Bay Company (Prince Rupert's Land, Acadia, and Newfoundland) to Britain.

21. Byrd represents the Dutch settlement of New Amsterdam as an encroachment on the British title to Virginia. The Dutch had claimed the right of discovery for lands along the Hudson River after Henry Hudson first visited the harbor in 1609; by 1613 the Dutch had established trading posts. The United New Netherlands Company (1614) governed the region, and then the Dutch West India Company (1622). Meanwhile, the English claimed all islands along the Atlantic seaboard, including Long Island. In 1664, James, duke of York (later James II), purchased the English title to this region from the earl of Stirling and decided to extend his claim forcibly, even though the English and Dutch were not then at war. Four British warships entered the harbor of New Amsterdam on August 27, 1664, and demanded surrender. The Dutch leader Peter Stuyvesant saw that the Dutch were outnumbered and complied with English demands; the Second Anglo-Dutch War ensued. British title was affirmed by the Treaty of Breda in 1667. Six years later, in 1673, a Dutch fleet took New York again and held it for eight months, but the Treaty of Westminster returned the title to England in 1674.

Comparison with Oldmixon indicates close parallels in terms, phrasing, and historical interpretation:

> The *English,* who sail'd from *Holland* to the *West-Indies,* and settled *Plimouth*-Colony, intended to take Possession of the Territories lying on the Coast of the Bay form'd by *Newhaven* Colony, and *Long-Island:* but the Master of the Ship being a *Dutchman,* was brib'd by some of his Countrymen to betray them and land them further *Eastward;* which he did accordingly, and prevented their settling in *Nova Belgia;* where the *Hollanders* had begun to plant, but had been driven thence by Sir *Samuel Argall,* Governour of *Virginia.* They then apply'd themselves to King *James* I. who gave them leave to build some Cottages, for the Convenience of their Ships touching there for fresh Water and Provisions, in their Voyage to *Brazil.* Under this Pretence, they incroach'd by little and little, so much, that they built Towns, fortify'd them, planted, and became a flourishing Settlement.
> —*Oldmixon,* I, 118

There is no evidence to confirm the Oldmixon / Byrd allegation that the Dutch treacherously bribed captains of the vessels carrying English Dissenters to deliver them to the less desirable region of Massachusetts, allowing the Dutch to take possession of more attractive territory to the south.

22. Dutch supremacy in the East Indies allowed their sugar trade to prosper, and the Dutch cornered the market for nutmeg and other spices.

23. Compare Byrd's phrasing with [Sir William Berkeley], *A Discourse and View of Virginia* (London, [1663]), 6:

> Another impediment, and an important one too has been the dis-membering of the Colonie, by giving away and erecting divers Principalities out of it, as *Maryland* to my Lord *Baltimore,* and part of *Florida* to my Lord of *Arundell,* these Grants will in the next Age be found more disadvantagious to the Crown then is perceptible in this.

Charles I married Henrietta Maria of France in 1625. The queen's devout Roman Catholic faith in combination with her strong interest in the political life of Britain made her a frequent target of Protestant complaint. It was claimed she exerted a "too too powerfull influence" (Sir Philip Warwick, *Memoires of the Reign of King Charles I* [London, 1701], 141). It was widely believed that Charles had consented to measures favoring Catholics as part of the marriage settlement. Relaxing strictures against Catholics drew howls of protest from Protestants, who charged the king with favoring his queen's preferences over the good of the people. Frequently figuring in anti-Catholic rhetoric, the topos of the queen's undue influence reappeared when English Protestants campaigned against a Catholic king (during the Exclusion Crisis and after the Glorious Revolution drove the Catholic James II from the throne). For this purpose even the writings of a Cromwellian general could be employed for their Protestant vigor, as in a tract by Edmond Ludlow republished in 1691 asserting that in his marriage Charles I had broken his oath to protect his people:

> Besides the General Articles upon that *Marriage,* he agreed to *Private Articles* in favour of *Papists* (viz.), *that those who had been imprisoned, as well* Ecclesiasticks *as* Temporal, *should be released: That* Papists *should be no more molested for their* Religion, *etc,*
>
> Hereby a *Toleration* (little less) was instantly granted to *Papists,* who without fear of Laws, fell to their Practice of *Idolatry,* and scoffed at *Parliaments,* at Law and all; Their Numbers, Power and Insolence daily increased in all parts of the Kingdom, especially in the City of *London,* which seem'd to be overflowed with Swarms of Locusts.
> —Edmond Ludlow, *A Letter from Major General Ludlow to Sir E. S., Comparing the Tyranny of the First Four Years of King Charles the Martyr, with the Tyranny of the Four Years Reign of the Late Abdicated King* ("Amsterdam," 1601), 6

The fact that the king and queen did not get along well—Charles banished nearly all of Henrietta Maria's Catholic courtiers—had no influence on the propagandists whatever. Byrd's reference to the king's "complaisance" probably referred to the tradition of anti-Catholic rhetoric; however, the possibility that Byrd's reference was ironic cannot be ruled out. For more on the queen's life and influence, see Erin Griffey, ed., *Henrietta Maria: Piety, Politics, and Patronage* (Aldershot, 2008); Michelle A. White, *Henrietta Maria and the English Civil Wars* (Aldershot, 2006); C. V. Wedgwood, *The King's Peace: 1637–1641* (New York, 1955).

24. The Gunpowder Plot of 1605 was a failed attempt by Roman Catholics to assassinate James I. The conspiracy was revealed by an anonymous letter, and one of the conspirators, Guy Fawkes, was discovered on November 5 in the cellars of the House of Lords with enough gunpowder to level the building. The event was memorialized with bonfires, fireworks, and anti-Catholic demonstrations.

25. *Suffering the same Martyrdom, the Romish Popish priests do in Sweden.* It was rumored that the Protestant nation of Sweden protected its church by castrating any Roman Catholic priests who dared try converting their people. Byrd probably encountered the rumor in the anonymous 1700 tract (probably written by Daniel Defoe) entitled *Reasons Humbly Offer'd for a Law to Enact the Castration of Popish Ecclesiastics, as the Best Way to Prevent the Growth of Popery in England* (London, 1700). Aping the more extreme tactics of anti-Papist writers of an earlier era, the author stresses sexual misconduct among Roman Catholic priests, monks, and nuns. Prohibited from exercising the natural order of propagating the species in marriage, they turned to fornication, adultery, and sodomy.

Priestly celibacy, or the appearance thereof, benefits the church by increasing the confessional (and seductive) power of priests over susceptible women. Moreover, maintaining an abundant supply of priests untrammeled by marriage frees them for service in missionary proselytizing, assassination, conspiracy, and "Rebellions against Princes and States, at the Commands of their Superior." Therefore, the author recommended

> that the best way to rid this Kingdom of Popish Priests, and to prevent the growth of Popery, is to make a Law, that all of them who shall be discover'd in *England,* except such as are thought fit to be allowed to Foreign Ambassadors, shall be Guelded, as they are in *Sweden;* where since the same was enacted into a Law, and practis'd upon a few of them, that Kingdom hath never been infested with Popish Clergy, or Plots, nor their Women reproach'd with want of Chastity.
> —*Reasons Humbly Offer'd,* 9–10

The treatment could not be considered cruel, since the operation was rarely fatal, and indeed more priests have been executed in England than were ever gelded in Sweden. Nor would it be an unreasonable imposition, the author declared with an outrageous pun, for priests who have taken vows of chastity "have no occasion for those Seminary Vessels" (11).

26. A northern Swedish province, as Edmund Bohun's *Geographical Dictionary* explains:

> *Dalecarle, Dalecarlia,* or *Dalecarne,* a great Province in the Kingdom of *Sweden,* towards the Mountains of *Savona,* and *Norway,* which bounds it on the West; on the North it hath *Helsinga; Gestricia* on the East, and *Vermelandia* on the South: a vast Country, but has never a City or good Town in it.
> —*A Geographical Dictionary* . . . (London, 1688), 107 (*Hayes* 12)

Dalecarlia was the site of the peasant uprising against the Danes, led by Gustavus Vasa, who established Swedish independence, becoming king of Sweden (1523–1560). As a rebel against tyranny Vasa provided numerous English writers with a precedent for English liberties. Still, it is not clear whether Byrd's reference compares the liberty of Virginia favorably with that of the old country. Perhaps he merely means to note a preference for fertile over rocky farmland, and a southern over a northern climate. Byrd owned several books about Sweden, notably the Abbot Vertat [Vertot], *History of the Revolutions in Sweden, Occasioned by the Change of Religion, and Alteration of the Government in That Kingdom* (London, 1696) (*Hayes* 154, 2139), and he was very interested in accommodating "Switzer" emigrants on his land.

27. When in 1664 the British supplanted the Dutch, Charles II granted the land west of the Hudson to his brother James, duke of York, who in turn granted it to two men who had been loyal to the monarchy during the Civil War and the Interregnum, Lord Berkeley and Sir George Carteret. The New Jersey proprietors hoped to profit from quitrents and trade, and to encourage emigration they legislated religious freedom in the colony with the 1665 Concession and Agreement. However, the profit was slow to develop, and the proprietors sold their rights to new proprietors. Berkeley sold his interest in West Jersey on March 18, 1674, to William Penn and four other Quakers. In 1676 the Quintipartite Deed of Revision adjusted the boundaries between the proprietary land held by Carteret

and that of Penn et al. The proprietors of West Jersey then purchased East Jersey from Carteret's widow. This was confirmed in 1680 by "The Duke of York's Second Grant." On April 15, 1702, the two proprietary provinces reverted to the crown and became New Jersey again, when, as Byrd explains, the proprietors "made a formal surrender of the Dominion to the Queen."

28. I.e., 1680/1.

29. Byrd's scandalous attribution to Penn of "much Wordly Wisdom"—a phrase proverbially denoting one watchful for opportunities for profit, without reference to moral wisdom—cannot be found in any historical records or texts. Byrd's rhetorical question about how a Quaker could have had such influence with "a Popish Prince" may be answered. Charles II owed sixteen thousand pounds to Penn's father, an admiral who had served him well, and the grants were meant to repay the debt. This fact was well known in Byrd's day, though Byrd elected to provide a "secret history" explanation, tentatively grounded in late-seventeenth-century history, specifically the troubles associated with the royal succession. By the end of his reign it had become clear that Charles II was a Roman Catholic, as was his heir and brother, James. For a short while it appeared that Charles's illegitimate son Monmouth, a Protestant, might become the next king, but the movement to proclaim him heir was treated as a rebellion and put down with extraordinarily harsh measures. The English, unwilling to accept a Roman Catholic as king of a Protestant nation, eventually replaced the last Stuart king (James II) with a suitably Protestant monarch, the Dutch prince William of Orange, who reigned with his wife, the English princess Mary. The Monmouth-related anecdote inserted into *The History of the Dividing Line* probably originated with Whig resentment against Penn, who had supported James II's campaign to bring in religious tolerance and so acted on behalf of the king on several occasions. There was no shortage of negative interpretations of Penn's cooperation among contemporary historians. Abel Boyer charged Penn with covertly supporting James II when he met with opposition from Oxford's Magdalen College:

> *William Penn,* the Head of the *Quakers,* or as some then thought, an ambitious, crafty *Jesuit,* who under a phanatical Outside promoted King *James*'s Designs, was industriously employ'd.
> —[Abel Boyer], *History of King William the Third* (London, 1702), I, 114

Laurence Echard repeated the charge:

> Yet before he made *Magdalen*-College feel the Weight of his Displeasure, *William Penn,* who with a Jesuitical Conscience promoted King *James*'s Designs, was industriously employ'd.
> —Laurence Echard, *The History of England . . .* (London, 1718), III, 833

Byrd refers to this text in his *Commonplace Book* (§547), though the title does not appear in Byrd's library. Byrd's anecdotal interest in the Monmouth Rebellion is reflected in his *Commonplace Book,* where he records anecdotes about Colonel Kirke (§23, §408) and Chancellor Jeffreys of the Bloody Assizes (§382).

The notion that Quakers were secret allies of the Catholics was a common argument in anti-Quaker literature. Anglican polemicists argued that toleration of Dissenters would be the first step on the slippery slope leading to the return of Papism. Thus, the Quakers' principled opposition to tithes, the Test Act, and penal laws was misrepresented as a covertly Papist strategy to destroy Protestantism and the established church. Byrd owned a copy of a tract by the prolific anti-Quaker polemicist Francis Bugg, *The Quakers Set in Their True Light, in Order to Give the Nations a Clear Sight of What They Hold concerning Jesus of Nazareth, the Scriptures, Water Baptism, the Lords Supper, Magistracy, Ministry, Laws, and Government* (London, 1696), which—typically for anti-Quaker propaganda—links Quakers and Jesuits as equivocators and allies (16–17) (*Hayes* 2188).

30. Although Pennsylvania's reputation for treating fairly with the Indians was well established in Byrd's day, seventeenth- and eighteenth-century historians made similar claims for other colonies. Daniel Neal maintained the Plymouth community observed the same principles:

> One Instance of the Civility and Justice of the Planters to [the Indians] was this, that nothwithstanding the Patent which they had for the Country from the Crown of *England*, they fairly purchased of the Natives, the several Tracts of Land which they afterwards possessed.
> —*History of New-England*, I, 134, citing Cotton Mather, *Magnalia Christi Americana . . .* (London, 1702), I, 22 (*Hayes* 2)

31. The Virginia Commissioners of 1710, Philip Ludwell and Nathaniel Harrison, reported to the Board of Trade that their North Carolina counterparts, Edward Moseley and John Lawson, postponed and missed meetings for more than six months. Ludwell and Harrison took testimonies from ancient colonists and Indians concerning the charter's landmark, "Wayanoake River," while Moseley and Lawson did the same. Inevitably, the two sets of testimonies conflicted. Ludwell and Harrison reported that Moseley forgot the dates of agreed-on meetings, failed to bring surveying instruments, and generally made the proceedings impossible to complete. Moreover, in their report to the Virginia Council, forwarded to the Board of Trade, Ludwell and Harrison accused Moseley and Lawson of blocking the survey in an effort to preserve their own interests:

> For one of those Gentlemen has been for several years last past Surveyor Generall of that Province, and has acquired to himself great profit by Surveying Land within the Contraverted bounds, and has taken up severall tracts of land in his own name and sold the same to others, for wch he stands still obliged to obtaine patents from the Government of Carolina. The other of them is at this time, Surveyor Generall, and hath at the same prospect of advantage by makeing future Surveys within the said Bounds. That the whole behaviour of the Carolina Commrs. hath tended visibly to no other end than to protract and Defeat the Settleing this affair, and particularly Mr. Mosely has used so many Shifts and excuses to disappoint all Conference with the Commissrs. of Virga., as plainly shew his Aversion to proceed in a business that tends so manifestly to his disavantage. His prevaricateing on this occasion hath been so indiscreet and unguarded, as to be discovered in the presence of her Majties. Lieut. Governr.
> —"A Journal of the Proceedings of Philip Ludwell and Nathaniel Harrison Commissioners Appointed for Setling the Boundary between Her Majestys Colony

and Dominion of Virginia and the Province of Carolina, Board of Trade and Plantations Journals, CO 5, 1316, f. 174r–183

Parts of the Ludwell and Harrison report were incorporated into the Board of Trade's correspondence with the Privy Council as the 1728 commission was being prepared, giving rise to the clause empowering Virginia's commissioners to complete the survey if those of North Carolina refused.

32. The Board of Trade received the "Proposals for determining the bounds between Virginia and N. Carolina" signed by Spotswood and Eden in February 1716. The Board of Trade was unable to forward the proposals to the Privy Council until August 31, 1726, because the Carolina Proprietors had not yet assented to them. On March 28, 1727, an order of the King in Council directed "the Governors of Virginia and N. Carolina . . . to settle the boundary according to the proposal submitted." *CSP*, XXIX, 16, no. 45.i, XXXV, 139, no. 279, 240, no. 494.

33. The Barbados Assembly commissioned surveyor William Mayo (1684–1744) to develop a comprehensive map of the island. On July 21, 1720, the legislature declared the map "legal evidence in all disputes respecting the bounds of the parishes" (*The History of Barbados* . . . [1848; New York, 1971], 7). In 1721 Mayo was in London, where a presentation copy gained Mayo the approval and thanks of the Royal Society. Mayo took up residence in Henrico County in 1726, surveying, acquiring land, and serving as justice of peace. Moving to Goochland County just before the expedition, Mayo was appointed justice of peace there.

Alexander Irvin (d. 1731), educated at Edinburgh, was professor of mathematics at the College of William and Mary in 1728–1729 and, later, professor of natural philosophy.

Byrd does not name the expedition's chaplain. He was Peter Fontaine (1691–ca. 1757), one of the sons of a Huguenot minister who emigrated to Ireland. Peter Fontaine was educated at Trinity College, Dublin, ordained by the bishop of London in 1715, and arrived in Virginia in 1716. He had an especially close relationship with Byrd and served as a minister in Westover Parish for nearly forty years.

34. Son of a prominent Virginian who moved to North Carolina, Samuel Swann II (1704–1774) was a young man in his twenties at the time of the expedition. It is possible that he learned elements of surveying from his father, but he does not appear to have been a professional surveyor; in the *Secret History* Byrd called him "a young Man of much Industry, but no Experience." Later in life he followed his father's example, representing Perquimans in the North Carolina Assembly from 1725 to 1734.

35. Colonel John Allen of Surry County (ca. 1674–1742), the first surveyor appointed for Virginia, was highly qualified; he served as surveyor of Isle of Wight and Surry Counties and attended Ludwell and Harrison on the 1710 survey (*DVB*, I, 77; *Council*, III, 340). But he withdrew from the expedition because of his wife's illness; the Executive Council acknowledged his withdrawal on February 27, 1728:

> This Board having received information that Mr Allen one of the Surveyors
> appointed for running the dividing line between this Colony and No. Carolina
> declines going on that service being hindred by the dangerous indisposition of
> his wife the Governor with the advice of the Council was pleased to nominate and

appoint Mr Alexander Irwin Professor of the Mathematicks in the College of William and Mary in the room of the said Mr Allen, and in case he shall refuse to undertake the same, then Mr Drury Stith is appointed for that service.

—*Council,* IV, 167

See also Thad W. Tate, "The Colonial College, 1693–1782," in Susan H. Godson, Ludwell H. Johnson, Richard B. Sherman, Thad W. Tate, and Helen C. Walker, *The College of William and Mary: A History* (Williamsburg, Va., 1993), I, 69–70.

36. *Widdow Allen:* Katherine Baker Allen, widow of Arthur Allen II (d. 1725). Boyd identified her maiden name as Bray, noting she later married Arthur Smith, Jr., and still later an unnamed man of the Stith family, and died in 1774 (*Boyd,* 33, citing "Bray Family," *WMQ,* 1st Ser., XIII [1905], 266–269). Both here and in the *Secret History* Byrd compares Mrs. Allen to the ideal set forth in Proverbs 31. Possibly Byrd was thinking of the *Athenian Oracle's* account of Solomon's definition of a good wife:

> The truth is, he gives such a character of a *good wife* as is not easily found, in the following instances; "The *heart* of her *husband* does *safely trust in* her—she'll do him *good* and not evil ALL HER Days—she WORKS WILLINGLY with her HANDS— she RISETH while 'tis yet NIGHT—with the FRUIT of her HANDS she PLANTS a *Vineyard*—she lays her HANDS to the SPINDLE, (is a *Spinster* more than in *Title*)— she stretcheth out her HAND to the POOR—she openeth her Mouth with WISDOM, and in her Tongue is the law of KINDNESS (No *Fool, Gossip,* or *Scold*)—she looks well to the way of her HOUSEHOLD, and eats not the Bread of IDLENESS["]—*such* she is—but *where* is she? For Solomon himself, who had *try'd* as many as most, says after all, *Who can find a vertuous Woman?* He that has her; let him e'en make much of her, for he'll hardly e'er get such another.
>
> —*The Athenian Oracle . . . ,* 3d ed. (London, 1728), I, 520

37. Weather historians do not record a severe storm in the region in 1726. Perhaps Byrd is referring to the "Great Gust" that raged across the Chesapeake on August 23, 1724. This tropical storm featured high winds and nearly a week of very heavy rain, severely damaging crops. Governor Hugh Drysdale wrote the Board of Trade that the storm had "almost wholly destroy'd all the tobacco then on the ground," adding that "the country suffers very much for want of corn." David M. Ludlum, *Early American Hurricanes, 1492–1870* (Boston, 1963), 20–21; *CSP,* XXXIV, 318, no. 487.

Thomas Godwin (b. 1680), planter in Isle of Wight and Nansemond Counties and sheriff of Nansemond. His plantation was named Cherry Grove. *Council,* IV, 235, 273, 319; John Bennett Boddie, *Seventeenth Century Isle of Wight County, Virginia* (Baltimore, 1994), 465.

38. *Scour:* to purge or evacuate *(OED).* The plant is commonly known as Spanish moss *(Tillandsia usneoides).*

Kind of Myrtle: probably the waxberry *(Morella cordifolia)* or wax myrtle *(Morella cerifera),* members of the bayberry family used to make candles known for their pleasant scent and also used medicinally. Beverley described how colonists extracted wax from the berries, noting that myrtle-wax candles are neither greasy nor prone to melt in hot weather and yield a pleasant smell when snuffed (*Beverley,* book 2, 22).

39. The gall bush *(Ilex coriaciae),* also known as bay-gall or ink-berry holly, is a peren-

nial shrub of the holly family, growing in moist soil and stream banks to a height of ten to fifteen feet. The berries yield an inky juice, black as that of the oak gall, a growth caused by insect secretions, and "largely used in the manufacture of ink and tannin, as well as in dyeing and in medicine" *(OED)*.

40. Major William Crawford (or Crafford), a planter on the south branch of the Elizabeth River below Norfolk. He was burgess for Lower Norfolk in 1688, and for Norfolk in the sessions of 1696, 1714, 1716, 1718, 1720–1722, 1723–1726, 1736–1740, 1742–1747. In 1725 he was appointed sheriff. Lyon Gardiner Tyler, ed., *Encyclopedia of Virginia Biography* (New York, 1915), I, 219; *Council,* IV, 86.

41. The borough of Norfolk was chartered in 1736, one of only three chartered corporations in colonial Virginia. The others were the College of William and Mary (1693) and the city of Williamsburg (1722). Rogers Dey Whichard, *The History of Lower Tidewater Virginia* (New York, 1959), I, 255.

42. Shipworm *(Teredo navalis)* is a saltwater bivalve that attacks untreated wood in ship hulls and wharf pilings. Beverley observed:

> In the Month of *June* Annually, there rise up in the Salts, vast Beds of Seedling-Worms, which enter the Ships, Sloops, or Boats where-ever they find the Coat of Pitch, Tar, or Lime worn off the Timber; and by degrees eat the Plank into Cells like those of an Honey-Comb.
> —*Beverley,* book 2, 5

Wood treated with pitch or tar resists the worm, hence Byrd's comment about the convenient supply of pines.

43. *Netherlands:* literally, "lowlands." The Low Countries were the western Europe lands below sea level. Here Byrd uses the term figuratively for any low, damp, swampy ground, with an oblique jest at the expense of Holland.

To *daggle* means "to clog with mud, to wet and soil a garment, etc., by trailing it through mud or grass" *(OED)*. The word also appears in Byrd's *Commonplace Book,* §380.

44. Richard Marsden (ca. 1675–1742), a minister who moved through the southern colonies, accused of various disreputable activities, most of which involved fraudulent occupation of parishes without license or assignment, and flight to escape debt. Marsden qualified as a Church of England lay reader in April 1700, and on October 22 he was ordained a minister and assigned to a parish in Maryland. Instead, he appeared in Charleston, South Carolina, without episcopal authorization, and served at Saint Philip's Church until he was discharged in 1707. John Clement, "Clergymen Licensed Overseas by the Bishops of London, 1696–1710 and 1715–1716," *Historical Magazine of the Protestant Episcopal Church,* XVI (1947), 323, and "Anglican Clergymen Licensed to the American Colonies, 1710–1744," XVII (1948), 238. The most complete account is Fleming H. James, "Richard Marsden, Wayward Clergyman," *WMQ,* 3d Ser., XI (1954), 578–591.

Gideon Johnston, the church's commissary for South Carolina, charged Marsden with issuing "sham bills," embezzling books from the provincial library, practicing both medicine and law, excommunicating political enemies, and committing numerous mercantile frauds. He even bilked the captain of the ship who gave him passage to England to escape his South Carolina debts. In London he met an ailing Barbados rector and traveled to the Caribbean to supply his parish—unofficially—until the minister's recovery and return. Soon Marsden flew from Barbados, leaving behind more debt, resulting from "some very foul practices." Frank J. Klingberg, ed., *Carolina Chronicle: The Papers of Commissary Gideon Johnston, 1707–1716* (Berkeley, Calif., 1946), 44–49; James, "Richard Marsden, Wayward Clergyman," 581, 582.

In 1714 Marsden was running a school in Chester, Pennsylvania, supported by a stipend from the SPG but returned to England when the society cut its budget. There he served briefly as chaplain to the duke of Portland and attended him to Jamaica when the duke took up his position as governor. Marsden prospered until the death of his patron in 1726.

Once more he popped up in Virginia in 1727, and served—again without the authorization of the bishop of London—in Lynnhaven Parish, Princess Anne County, 1728–1729. In 1727 the newly arrived Governor Gooch wrote to the bishop of London, informing him that he had recommended three clergymen to livings, including one Mr. Marsden, noting that

> the latter indeed had not your Lordship Certificate But as he had several
> Testimonials of his Doctrine, good Life and Conversation, and as he told me he was
> known to your Lordship, and I had good reason to believe he was hurried out of
> England by misfortunes truly so, I did venture to send him to a Parish.
> —William Gooch to bishop of London, Oct. 18, 1727, in G. MacLaren Brydon, ed.,
> "The Virginia Clergy: Governor Gooch's Letters to the Bishop of London, 1727–1749,"
> *VMHB*, XXXII (1924), 219

Commissary Blair also wrote to the bishop about Marsden, "a man of figure and good sense" with "ample testimonials of his good behaviour" where he had served as minister. Blair related Marsden's account to the bishop: compelled to flee England suddenly because of bankruptcy proceedings, he had not time for "waiting on your Lordship and bringing your letters as he should have done. He promised to write to your Lordship for it" (James, "Richard Marsden, Wayward Clergyman," *WMQ*, 3d Ser., XI [1954], 585). A remarkably plausible liar, Marsden had once again shown up for a job without the necessary papers. Serving in Lynnhaven Parish in 1728 placed him in the neighborhood just at the time of the first part of the Dividing Line expedition. Just barely, because before very long Marsden once again absconded to escape debt. The governor wrote to the bishop of London on June 29, 1729, "Mr Marsden to whom in a former letter I acquainted your Lordship I had given a Parish, about Moneth since run away above £400 in Debt by borrowing Money and drawing Bills in England." Brydon, ed., "The Virginia Clergy," *VMHB*, XXXII (1924), 227.

Marsden was not finished yet. He resurfaced in the Cape Fear district of North Carolina in 1729, claiming falsely "to hold a commission as itinerant missionary and inspector of clergy." There he "effectively usurped" the parish of the Reverend John Lapierre. In 1733 he was acting as parish priest in Cape Fear, according to a complaint by Lapierre, the incumbent, in a letter to the bishop of London. Marsden had been

> formerly a preacher in Charlestown in Sth. Carolina who declined appearing
> before Commissary Johns[t]on and the rest of the Clergy to shew his credentials:
> afterwards my lord Portlands chappelain in Jamaica. Then an incumbent in virginy

in a parrish called princess Ann and of late a traficant to Lisbon and Sometimes after his return promoted by a few gentlemen to be minister of Cape fear without any popular Election.

Still, in 1732 Governor George Burrington praised Marsden's effective ministry. Clement, "Clergymen Licensed Overseas by the Bishops of London, 1696–1710," *HMPEC,* XVI (1947), 335; James, "Richard Marsden, Wayward Clergyman," *WMQ,* 3d Ser., XI (1954), 585–589; Robert J. Cain et al., eds., *The Church of England in North Carolina: Documents, 1669–1741,* CRNC, X (Raleigh, N.C., 1999), 331, 347–348, 350, 382, 500–501.

Church historian Edgar Pennington states that Marsden at last gained an SPG appointment as missionary to southwestern North Carolina and in 1738 was assigned to Saint James Parish, Wilmington. However, the official papers of the SPG tell another story: the society did at last accept him on May 19, 1738, but his appointment was "cancelled for misconduct before he was established Missionary under Society's seal." His subsequent retreat from South Carolina was more than his usual flight to escape debtors' prison. South Carolina Commissary Alexander Garden informed the bishop of London in 1739 that Marsden had defrauded English merchants in Lisbon of a cargo worth fifteen hundred pounds by uttering worthless bills of exchange and several other frauds for which he had been arrested in Chester, England, though he escaped from that jail. Still more scandalously, he was married bigamously in Jamaica. Moreover, in his later career he posed as commissary, solicited contributions in Ireland for the SPG by presenting forged papers, and performed other criminal activities. At last Commissary Johnston conceded Marsden "might have done a great deal of good . . . had he been an honest man." Edward Legare Pennington, *The Church of England and the Reverend Clement Hall in Colonial North Carolina* (Hartford, Conn., 1937), 33; C. F. Pascoe, *Two Hundred Years of the S.P.G.* . . . (London, 1901), 850; Cain, ed., *The Church of England in North Carolina,* 390, 395, 501, 583; James, "Richard Marsden, Wayward Clergyman," *WMQ,* 3d Ser., XI (1954), 590–591.

What did Byrd mean by calling Marsden "a painful Apostle from the Society"? It may be that Byrd met Marsden during one of those periods of indefatigable service that endeared him to his parishioners. But, if Byrd knew anything of Marsden's debt and disgrace, and Byrd treats fleeing debtors scornfully elsewhere in the Dividing Line histories, then the passage would have to be a sly, ironic dig. Byrd would then have known that Marsden was neither "painful"—that is, taking pains to do his duty—nor in fact an "Apostle from the Society." The solution to the puzzle depends on what Byrd might have known when he wrote this passage, in 1728 or afterward. Regrettably, the extent and timing of Byrd's knowledge of Marsden cannot be discovered with any degree of assurance.

45. Noses in danger of falling off were stock satirical images, indicating an advanced stage of venereal disease.

W . . . ns: perhaps Willis Wilson, militia captain and justice of the peace for Norfolk County, as Boyd suggests (*Boyd,* 39), or Captain James Wilson, as Fields suggests (*Fields,* 323), but more likely Captain [John] Wilkins, mentioned in the *Secret History.*

46. The bay *(Laurus nobilis)* was sacred to Apollo, and its leaves were used to crown Olympic victors, poets, and emperors (*Pliny* 5.15.38–40). Many New World botanists conflated shiny-leaved native evergreens with European trees; thus, the magnolia *(Magnolia virginiana)* came to be known as sweetbay. The Mediterranean shrub myrtle *(Myrtus com-*

munis) was sacred to Venus; as with laurel or bay, New World species bearing the name myrtle are not in fact related.

During the hurricane of September 17, 1713, a storm surge breached the barrier islands, opening inlets into Currituck Sound. The conflation of the word *shoal,* "a place where the water is of little depth; a shallow; a sand-bank or bar" with *shallow* (less deep) appears to be common maritime usage. However, the word *shoaller* is not recorded in the *OED.*

47. In the *Secret History* entry for this day Byrd identifies this host as "Andrew Dukes."

48. *Japon:* yaupon or yaupon holly *(Ilex vomitoria);* this plant, also called cassena, was well known for its medicinal effects, both vomiting and purging. Lawson mentioned it as the only such medicine the Indians use, in "vast Quantities," every other day whenever they can procure it. They "keep their Stomachs clean," and the diuretic effect further "carries off a great deal, that perhaps might prejudice their Health, by Agues, and Fevers." Their freedom from these distempers Lawson credited to "this Plant alone." It grows "chiefly on the Sand-Banks and Islands, bordering on the Sea of *Carolina. . . .* All the Savages on the Coast of *Carolina"* use yaupon and sell it to Indians in the west. The Spanish in Florida "prefer it above all Liquids, to drink with Physick, to carry the same safely and speedily thro' the Passages, for which it is admirable, as I myself have experimented" *(Lawson,* 90–91, 221).

Between 1729 and 1735 the *Philosophical Transactions* featured extracts from Mark Catesby's "Essay towards the Natural History of Carolina and the Bahama Islands." Catesby reported on the cassena, from which the Indians extracted their "beloved Decoction" for its purifying effect. Catesby's account did not differ substantially from Lawson's, but Catesby goes on to state (mistakenly) that cassena, or yaupon, is "the same Plant as the Paraguay Tea, which comes from *Buenos Ayres."* By "*Paraguay* Tea" Catesby meant the Argentinian drink *Yerba Maté (Ilex paraguariensis).* The similarity lies primarily in the presence of caffeine in the young leaves of both plants. "A Continuation of an Essay towards a Natural History of Carolina and the Bahamas," *Philosophical Transactions,* XXXIX (1735–1736), 257–258.

49. It is unclear which variety of silkgrass Byrd calls "Spired-leafed"—probably the most common species in the region, narrow-leafed silkgrass *(Pityopsis graminifola)* or the pine-leafed silkgrass *(Pityopsis pinifolia).*

Vertuoso: one who has "a general interest in arts and sciences, or one who pursues special investigations in one or more of these; a learned person; a scientist, savant, or scholar" *(OED).* The term was applied to collectors of empirical data of natural philosophy and to collectors of antiquarian material culture. The term was used to ridicule superficial and obsessive specialization—see Thomas Shadwell's 1676 farce *The Virtuoso*—but practitioners of the New Science used the term uncritically. See R[obert] B[oyle], *The Christian Virtuoso: Shewing, That by Being Addicted to Experimental Philosophy, a Man Is Rather Assisted, than Indisposed, to be a Good Christian* (London, 1690); and Eusebius Renaudot, *A General Collection of Discourses of the Virtuosi of France, upon Questions of All Sorts of Philosophy, and Other Natural Knowledg* (London, 1664). Both books were in Byrd's library (*Hayes* 927, 1038, 2260). On Byrd's use of the term, see *Commonplace Book,* 52–53.

Conque, peak: Byrd here describes the beads made from shells. The word "conch" initially denoted any shellfish, including bivalves such as mussels and oysters. Only later was the term limited to the large marine gastropods such as the queen conch *(OED)*. By "peak" Byrd means *wampumpeak,* the Algonquian term for beads produced from quahog, whelk, or periwinkle shells, abbreviated as *peak* or (more frequently) *wampum.* These beads were used for personal decoration, exchange of goods, and marking diplomatic occasions. See Gunther Michelson, "Iroquoian Terms for Wampum," *International Journal of American Linguistics,* LVII (1991), 108–116; Wilbur R. Jacobs, "Wampum, the Protocol of Indian Diplomacy," *WMQ,* 3d Ser., VI (1949), 596–604.

Compare Byrd's description with Beverley's on the riches of the Indians, who before the English arrived had nothing

> except *Peak, Roenoke,* and such like trifles made out of the *Cunk* shell. These
> past with them instead of Gold and Silver, and serv'd them both for Money, and
> Ornament. . . .
>   *Peak* is of two sorts, or rather of two colours, for both are made of one Shell, tho
> of different parts; one is a dark Purple Cylinder, and the other a white. . . . The dark
> colour is the dearest, and distinguish'd by the name of *Wampom Peak.*
> —*Beverley,* book 3, 58

50. *Knights Templars:* Members of "a military and religious order, consisting of knights *(Knights Templars, Knights,* or *Poor Soldiers of the Temple),* chaplains, and men-at-arms, founded ca. 1118, chiefly for the protection of the Holy Sepulchre and of Christian pilgrims visiting the Holy Land: so called from their occupation of a building on or contiguous to the site of the Temple of Solomon at Jerusalem. They were suppressed in 1312" *(OED).* London's Middle Temple, where Byrd studied law, occupied buildings once belonging to the order.

Byrd's comparison of the members of the expedition sleeping on the ground around a fire may allude to the order's vow of poverty, or it may refer to the recumbent memorial sculptures of knights in many English churches, or perhaps it echoes a line in Samuel Butler's *Hudibras* tracing the squire Ralpho's ancestry through a line of "cross-legg'd Knights" (canto I, l. 471)—that is, knights whose stone effigies decorate their tombs (*Hayes* 843, 885, 990, 999).

BL (March 6): "By an Observation att 3 In afternoone 36 Deg's 31 Minutes found the Variation 3 degs: West by a Meridian from the North Starr att Midnight."

51. Colchester and Wellfleet, in Essex, have supplied the English with oysters since Roman times.

52. Byrd quotes Luke 12:24, a passage usually cited to illustrate Providence: "Consider the ravens: for they neither sow nor reap; which neither have storehouse nor barn; and God feedeth them: how much more are ye better than the fowls?"

Herodotus placed the pygmies in northern Africa, Aristotle in Egypt, and Strabo in the farthest parts of the continent. It was Pliny who located them in the East Indies. Byrd's source was probably Johannes Jonstonus, who described the pygmies of India thus:

> Their haire hangs as farr and somtime below their knees, and they wear their beards
> longer than any men. And so soon as their long beard is grown, they use no clothing,
> but they let their haire fall backwards much below their knees, and their beard

covers their foreparts. Then when they have covered their whole bodies with haire, they girt themselves about with them instead of garments.

—*An History of the Wonderful Things of Nature* (London, 1657), 326

These specific details are absent in other accounts of pygmies.

53. The Adamites were an early Christian sect dedicated to regaining the innocence of Adam's prelapsarian state through practices such as nudity and simplicity. In Byrd's day, the term often appeared as a dismissive reference to the profusion of Dissenting sects.

54. William Harding (d. 1746) was a planter at Little Fresh Pond, Knott's Island, whose lands the survey placed in North Carolina. John Anderson Brayton, comp., *"By a Line of Marked Trees": Abstracts of Currituck County, North Carolina* (Memphis, Tenn., 2000), I, 87, 107, 108, 117; J. Bryan Grimes, ed., *Abstracts of North Carolina Wills* (Baltimore, 1967), 150.

55. Mr. White: Capt. Solomon White, who in 1717 patented 2,136 acres in Princess Anne County, in Lynhaven Parish, in "Corotock and Knott's Island," then considered part of Virginia. He also owned land in Norfolk County (*C&P*, III, 156, 201). He was an officer in the Princess Anne militia (Lloyd DeWitt Bockstruck, *Virginia's Colonial Soldiers* [Baltimore, 1988], 219).

56. According to the "Surveyors' Journal or Field Book," "Malburns or Cedar Island N 7° 20 W."

Cast: "A 'lift' in a conveyance, given to one to put him forward on his way" *(OED)*. *Conjurer:* "One who conjures spirits and pretends to perform miracles by their aid" *(OED)*. Just who this fortune-teller or conjurer might have been remains unclear; perhaps he was indeed a Virginia or North Carolina teller of fortunes or some other sort of charlatan. It is curious to note that, in early works about North America, the term *conjurer* denoted Native American religious practitioners, consistent with the usual labeling of non-Christian priests and practitioners as frauds; see, for instance, *Beverley,* book 1, 6; *Lawson,* 23–24.

57. For the origin of the term *pocosin,* see William Wallace Tooker, "The Adopted Algonquian Term 'Poquosin,'" *American Anthropologist,* n.s., I (1899), 162–170.

John Heath: There were Heaths throughout the region; James and John Heath each had land on the west side of the North River, just south of Richard Eisland's plantation. The "Surveyors' Journal or Field Book" entry for March 9 lists "John Heaths House S 64° E" and "James Heaths S 70° 30' E."

58. The "Surveyors' Journal or Field Book" here mentions Jones's Point on "Notts Island" and Morses Point on the mainland.

59. Byrd's estimate is no doubt hyperbolic, for Job's livestock extended to "seven thousand sheep, and three thousand camels, and five hundred yoke of oxen, and five hundred she asses, and a very great household; so that this man was the greatest of all the men of the east" (Job 1:3).

The third plague visited upon Egypt was of flies (Exod. 8:20–32). Many early modern commentators agreed that stinging insects such as gnats must have been an effective torment. Thomas Moffett, in his *Insectorum Sive Minimorum Animalium Theatrum* (London, 1634), 34, commented:

Origines in Exodum, his animaculis Deum tertiò Pharaonis pervicaciam correxisse author est: quae (inquit) pennis per aëra suspenduntur, sed quasi invisibilia, atque stimulo tam subtiliter et cito cutem perforant, ut quam muscam volitantem non videas, pungentem sentias. Sic fere omnes reliqui antiqui interpretes Originê secuti σχιπᾶς interpretantur. Unicus Tremelius, *(Hebraicae* linguae et sacri codicis interpres fidelissimus) aliter sentit, qui colluviem animalium interpretatur, ac si culices atque muscae omnimodae venenatae, et molestae, veluti conjuratione facta, agminatim venissent, et per examina à Deo ad conterendam Aegyptii superbiam immissae fuissent.

This passage is translated in *The Theater of Insects; or, Lesser Living Creatures* (London, 1658) (credited to "Tho. Mouffet"), published and paginated with Edward Topsell, *History of Four-Footed Beasts and Serpents* (London, 1658), 955:

> *Origen* upon *Exodus,* saieth that with these little creatures God did the third time take down the proud heart of *Pharoah:* the which are hung in the air by the wings, but yet as it were invisible, and do so subtilly and quickly pierce the skin, that the fly which you cannot perceive flying, you may feel stinging. So all the ancient interpreters following *Origen,* expound the word σχιπᾶς. Only Tremellus (a very faithful interpreter of the Hebrew Text, and of sacred Writ) is of another minde, who thinks this plague to be a swarm of such kinde of creatures, as if the Gnats and all other venemous and stinging flies joyning all their forces and coming together in troops and swarms, had agreed as being sent by God to break the pride of the *Aegyptians.*

Both versions of Muffett's book were in Byrd's library (*Hayes* 794, 924). I have not been able to locate a rabbinical commentary of the sort Byrd mentions; it may well be a fanciful reference.

60. The Journal of the North Carolina Commissioners identifies Eyland as Richard Eisland (Robert J. Cain, ed., *Records of the Executive Council, 1664–1734,* CRNC, VII [Raleigh, N.C., 1988], 567). The name is sometimes spelled Eisland, Island, and Iland, and other variants. Richard Eiland, Jr. (ca. 1681–1733), was a planter on the west side of the North River. The Eiland plantation was just to the north of John Heath's; Richard Eiland, Jr., married Elizabeth Heath, daughter of James Heath. In 1731 he represented Currituck in the North Carolina Assembly. In his will, dated March 7, 1733, he left five hundred acres of land to his children, excluding the home plantation, which went to his wife during her life, and property on the shore that he ordered sold to pay debts. The extent to which the boundary split the plantation may be seen in the language of Eiland's will: "the major part lying in Princess Ann Co. in Virginia, the lesser part in Corotuck, North Carolina." Worth S. Ray, ed., *Ray's Index and Digest to Hathaway's North Carolina Historical and Genealogical Register* (Baltimore, 1997), 75. Thanks to Diane Eiland for help with this investigation.

BL (March 9): "Cross'd the East Branch of North River & then Cross't Gibbs Marsh, then Interrupted by a Beaver Dam & Otter Holes so made a Traverse round & allow'd for crossing of this dangerous place advanceing 2 Miles."

61. *Traverse:* in surveying, the process of continuing a line "by measuring the lengths and azimuths of a connected series of straight lines," used to supply a hiatus in the survey *(OED).* The surveyors stopped their observations on one side of the pocosin, and started again on the other side, an option that they chose not to take in the Great Dismal Swamp.

62. The Merchant (or Marchant) family owned a large plantation in the disputed re-

gion. In 1696, Virginia's Executive Council charged Christopher Merchant (d. 1698) with improperly collecting customs in Virginia; he had been collecting in Currituck Precinct for North Carolina. The permeability of the boundary is evident in the fact that his son, Willoughby Merchant (ca. 1680–1727), was justice of the peace in Princess Anne County, Virginia, and sheriff in 1726.

Boyd thought the planter Byrd mentions was Willoughby Merchant, but he was dead a year before the expedition. Rather, it was Willoughby's eldest son Christopher Merchant, justice of Currituck Precinct Court in 1728, mentioned in Byrd's report to the Board of Trade. The survey established that the Merchant plantation lay in North Carolina. *DNCB,* IV, 255; Mattie Erma Edwards Parker, ed., *North Carolina Higher-Court Records, 1670–1696,* CRNC, II (Raleigh, N.C., 1968), 818; *Boyd,* 53; *Fields,* 323.

63. Martin Bladen (1680–1746) was a British army officer, Whig politician, and member of Parliament, comptroller of the Royal Mint, and influential member of the Board of Trade from 1717 until his death. He married Mary, daughter of Colonel John Gibbs of Currituck (who once claimed the governorship of North Carolina, disputing the appointment of Philip Ludwell); hence Bladen owned property in the region. See "Bladen, Martin (1680–1746)," *ODNB,* and *Boyd,* 52.

64. *BL* (March 10): "Sunday Instead of a Sermon our Chaplain Baptized all the Children in the Neighbourhood for there was no Clergy in this part of the Country."

Here and in several places below Byrd emphasizes the duty of honoring (especially resting on) the Sabbath. An act of the Virginia Assembly in 1657/8, *"The Sabboth to bee kept holy,"* specified that no trade could be carried on and no journeys made "except in case of emergent necessity." Violators could be placed in the stocks and fined one hundred pounds of tobacco (*Hening,* I, 434). Byrd's diaries reveal that his concern for keeping the Sabbath on the expedition was consistent with his usual practice at home.

65. The term *complexion* refers to both the "natural colour, texture, and appearance of the skin" and to the physiological "'temperament' or bodily constitution" signaled by variations in the appearance of skin *(OED).* Skin color was a common diagnostic sign. It was a commonplace of early modern medicine that maternal emotions physically affected the human fetus, and Byrd cannot resist making a milk-related joke: the paucity of milk to satisfy the cravings of pregnant women in the region produced offspring with a "custard" complexion, i.e., unhealthily yellow.

66. *Yaws:* An infectious tropical disease (treponematosis) generically related to syphilis but transmitted by skin contact, yaws produces inflammatory lesions and sometimes bone destruction. In the eighteenth century its etiology was unknown; it was thought to result from poor diet (especially excessive consumption of pork), as a complication of other diseases left untreated, or through sexual contact. Its similarity to syphilis frequently provoked ribald jests.

67. The term *latitude* initially indicated measurement of the globe, but by extension it came to denote a "locality as marked or defined by parallels of latitude; . . . regions, climes, parts of the world" *(OED).* On the stubborn adherence of Byrd and Beverley to "the preconception that climates remained constant at given latitudes around the world," see James D. Drake, "Appropriating a Continent: Geographical Categories, Scientific Metaphors, and the Construction of Nationalism in British North America and Mexico," *Journal of World History,* XV (2004), 331. Claims for the significance of shared latitudes were

quite common. See, for example, Robert Ferguson's description of the flourishing province of Carolina, "parallel with *Jerusalem* in *Palestine*," in *The Present State of Carolina, with Advice to the Setlers* (London, 1682), 4.

68. Virginia's 1666 law governing taking up patents for land stipulated a preliminary survey and a declaration in court of the number of people imported to the new land. "Importing" meant settling people on the land to clear trees, plant crops, and tend livestock, a process known as "seating." The act defined seating as establishing possession by building a house and keeping livestock on the land for one year, or clearing at least one acre, planting a crop, and tending it for one year. The people "imported" were brought by the proprietor to the county in which the claim was registered (*"An act for seating and planting,"* Hening, II, 244; see also definitions of seating in the 1720 act, *Hening*, IV, 81–83; *Beverley*, book 4, 14–15.

In his comment about the plight of fugitives, Byrd notes that unscrupulous landowners could easily exploit runaway indentured servants and slaves by importing them to isolated seated lands. This reproduced virtually the same condition they had escaped but without any recourse even to the limited protection of Virginia laws regulating treatment of servants and slaves. However, a Virginia law of 1643 provided stiff penalties for persons who "enter into covenants" with runaway servants and freemen under contract with other employers (*Hening*, I, 253).

69. Carolina legislation of 1669 delayed lawsuits to recover old debts from emigrants for five years after their arrival (William L. Saunders, ed., *The Colonial Records of North Carolina* [Raleigh, N.C., 1886–1890], I, 183; *Boyd*, 58). Though Byrd complains of this statute, Virginia also exempted emigrants from England from prosecution for debt in 1643 (*Hening*, I, 257), a policy reaffirmed in 1663 and 1683. The Carolina law was disallowed by the Privy Council in 1707, and the Virginia law in 1718 (*Colonial Records*, I, 717; *Boyd*, 58).

Contrary to Byrd's assertion, Rome was not a refuge for debtors. Though the Roman historian Lucan wrote that Romulus first populated the city with criminals, there was no toleration of debt (*Pharsalia* 7.437–438). In fact, Roman histories are filled with stories of the high interest and severe conditions imposed by creditors and of revolts by debtors. It is hard to conceive that any knowledgeable person would suggest Rome relaxed debt laws to promote immigration. Jonathan Swift, for instance, maintained that, during the turbulent times when consular government was first established,

> many of the poorer Citizens had contracted numerous Debts, either to the richer sort among themselves, or to Senators and other Nobles: and the Case of Debtors in *Rome* for the first four Centuries, was, after the set time for Payment, no Choice but either to pay or be the Creditor's Slave. In this Juncture the Commons quit the City · in Mutiny and Discontent, and will not return but upon condition to be acquitted of all their Debts.
> —[Jonathan Swift], *A Discourse of the Contests and Dissensions between the Nobles and Commons in Athens and Rome* (London, 1701), 28 (*Hayes* A3)

Byrd might have been indulging in playfully learned misdirection.

70. *Mr. Balance:* William Ballance (d. ca. 1732), who patented 950 acres near the Northwest River in Norfolk County in 1697. William's sons included Samuel, William, and Richard. Samuel Ballance inherited his father's plantation just south of the Northwest

River; after the 1728 survey, he appears in the Norfolk County, Virginia, list of tithables. William and Richard each inherited half of their father's Currituck plantation in Albemarle Precinct. Their names also appear in Virginia documents after the 1728 survey. There was also a Robert Ballance living in the region; his relation to William Ballance and his family is unclear. *C&P,* III, 13; "The Ballance Families of Virginia and North Carolina," *High Tides: Hyde County Historical Journal,* XX, no. 1 (Spring 1999), 3–43.

71. *Parliament Man:* The phrase originally denoted a member of the British Parliament, and by extension a member of any other legislature (*OED,* citing Byrd for the second definition). But it is more likely that Byrd used the term to refer in a sarcastic fashion to a politician without the proper gravitas or social status. The origin of this usage lies in the Tory characterization of their Whig opponents as men of obscure origin, the unrepentant heirs of the regicidal parliamentary or Cromwellian era. For Byrd, then, the appellation "Parliament Man" would have been a term of abuse indicating the inappropriate rise to power of unqualified men. Thus, the drunken Carolinian "Senator" was a crude, self-important upstart, lacking any respect for proper authority and aligned with the most vulgar forms of democratic culture. This is not to say that Byrd's political alignment was Whig or Tory; his use of the term simply reinforces his continuing satirical distinction between the patrician elite of Virginia's Executive Council and the rude gentry of Carolina.

72. *Mr. Wilson:* probably Captain James Wilson, Jr., in 1706 captain of horse in the Norfolk County Militia, and appointed sheriff of Norfolk County in 1712. He owned land above the bridge over the southern branch of the Elizabeth River as well as land in the Blackwater region. *Council,* III, 305; *C&P,* III, 156, 213–214, 293–294; *Fields,* 324.

Cleaning the Augean stables was the fifth of the twelve labors of the Greek hero Hercules. King Augeus owned more livestock than any other Greek, and Hercules was required to clean up after them in a single day. This he did in epic fashion by diverting the course of a river. In Byrd's time proverbial references to the Augean stables indicated extreme dirtiness and difficulty.

73. *Alaternus:* While there are many varieties of buckthorn in North America, Byrd here refers to a European genus, the Italian buckthorn *(Rhamnus alaternus).* Byrd is mistaken in identifying the gallbush as a buckthorn; as noted above, it is actually a North American species of holly *(Ilex coriaciae).*

Bryars: The word "briar" may indicate any "prickly, thorny bush or shrub in general; formerly including the bramble" *(OED).* The plant that made traveling difficult could have been wild rose, raspberry, briar root, or any such plant.

74. *Slash:* "An open tract or clearing in a forest, esp. one strewn with debris resulting from felling or logging, high wind, or fire" *(OED).*

75. *BL* (March 13): "It is Incredible how little the bordering Inhabitants were acquainted with this frightfull Swamp. Tho many had lived all their lives within the smell of It."

76. *Peruvian Bark:* the name given to both the vegetable source and the extracted medicine now known as quinine, used widely as a febrifuge. Jesuit missionaries, observing its use by the indigenous people of Peru, brought the bark to Europe by the mid-seventeenth century; it first appeared in the *London Pharmacopoeia* in 1677. Byrd's use of the bark as a febrifuge reflects the medical knowledge of his day, corroborated by all the medical books in his library; see, for instance, Nicolas Lemery, *A Course of Chymistry: Containing an Easie*

Method of Preparing Those Chymical Medicines Which Are Used in Physick (London, 1720), 350–355 *(Hayes 706, 724).*

Rhubarb: The medicinal use of rhubarb *(Rheum officinale)* originated in China and traveled to Europe via Russia, Barbary, and the Levant. The herbalist Nicholas Culpeper observed that the root "gently purgeth choler from the Stomach and Liver, opens stoppings, withstands the Dropsie, Hypochondriack Melancholy." *Pharmacopoeia Londinensis; or, The London Dispensatory* (Boston, 1720), 11. See also [Nicolas] Lemery, *New Curiosities in Art and Nature; or, A Collection of the Most Valuable Secrets in All Arts and Sciences* (London, 1711), 340–342. Cotton Mather recommended "a *Tea* made of *Rhubarb,* and sweetened with a Syrup of *Marshmallows*" as a purgative after a bout of measles, in *A Letter, about a Good Management under the Distemper of the Measles* (Boston, 1713).

Hipocoacannah: ipecacuanha, commonly known as ipecac, is a powerful emetic, derived from the root of a Brazilian shrub *(Cephaelis ipecacuanha).*

77. *BL* (March 14): "the Ground was Wett & Boggy, full of tall Reeds, every where interlaced with Strong Bamboe Bryars wch hamper'd the feet very much."

Pioneer: "A person who goes before others to prepare or open up the way" *(OED).*

Bamboo bryars: probably bamboo vine *(Smilax pseudochina),* a prickly member of the greenbriar family.

Quagmire: "A piece of wet and boggy ground, too soft to sustain the weight of men or the larger animals" *(OED).*

78. *Aesop's Bread Carriers:* The "Life of Aesop," in Sir Roger L'Estrange, *Fables of Aesop and Other Eminent Mythologists* (London, 1692), I, 2–3 *(Hayes 1930),* relates this story:

> It was *Aesop*'s Fortune to be sent to *Ephesus,* in Company with other Slaves to be sold. His Master had a great many Burdens to Carry, and *Aesop* begg'd of his Companions not to over Charge him. They found him a Weakling, and bad him please himself. The Parcel that he Pitch'd upon was a Panyer of Bread; and twice as heavy as any of the rest. They called him a thousand Fools for his pains, and so took up their Luggage, and away they Trudg'd together. About Noon, they had their Dinner deliver'd out of *Aesop*'s Basket, which made his Burden Lighter by one half in the Afternoon, than it had been in the Morning: And after the next Meal he had Nothing left him to Carry, but an Empty Basket. His Fellow-Slaves began Now to Understand, that *Aesop* was not so Arrant a Fool as they took him for; and that they Themselves had not half the Wit they Thought they had.

79. *Desart:* In Byrd's era, any "uninhabited and uncultivated tract of country" or "any wild, uninhabited region, including forest-land" was considered desert land. The modern sense of the word—"a desolate, barren region, waterless and treeless, and with but scanty growth of herbage"—had not yet come into use *(OED).*

80. On the anatomy of lice, see R[ober]t Hooke, "Of a Louse," in *Micrographia; or, Some Physiological Descriptions of Minute Bodies* (London, 1665), 211:

> On either side behind the head (as it were, being the place where other Creatures ears stand) are placed its two black shining goggle eyes . . . looking backwards, and fenced round with several small *cilia* or hairs that incompass it, so that it seems this Creature has no very good foresight: It does not seem to have any eye-lids, and

therefore perhaps its eyes were so placed, that it might the better cleanse them with its fore-legs; and perhaps this may be the reason, why they so much avoid and run from the light behind them, for being made to live in the shady and dark recesses of the hair, and thence probably their eye having a great aperture, the open and clear light, especially that of the Sun, must needs very much offend them.

While the scientifically observed optical anatomy of the louse was well known, it has not been possible to identify a source for this scientific curiosity used in jest, once more at the expense of Scotland.

81. *BL:* (March 15): "Another great hindrance was Cypresses blown down which lye Cross one another with their sharp snags pointing Every way required great caution to gett over these Evergreen Trees have [   ] heads are Easily overset in the Bog being no firm Earth for their Roots to shoot in."

Cypress: the bald cypress *(Taxodium distichum)* is a large tree found in or at the edge of wetlands. Its root system throws up "knees," woody growths rising above the surface of the soil or water. Cypress knees as well as fallen trees probably added to the difficulty of passage.

A *pike* was an infantry weapon "consisting of a long wooden shaft with a pointed steel head" *(OED)*.

82. The "Physical Effect" was laxative or cathartic — "physical" in the sense of the processes induced by physick; compare with *BL* (March 16): "The water was found purgative from a strong tincture from the Juniper Roots."

83. The names *Ives, Ivy, Ivie* seem to have been interchangeable. The Ivy family settled in lower Norfolk County as early as the 1650s and was active there and in Princess Anne and Surry up to the time of the expedition. In 1704, both Timothy Ives and Timothy Ives, Jr., were listed in the quitrent rolls for Norfolk County: Louis des Cognets, Jr., ed., *English Duplicates of Lost Virginia Records* (1958; Baltimore, 1990), 194; Annie Laurie Smith, *The Quit Rents of Virginia, 1704* (Baltimore, 1975), 481; *C&P,* III, 173. See also W. Mac Jones, "Notes on the Ivey Family," *WMQ,* 2d Ser., VII (1927), 181–192.

84. *Fulling:* "The process of cleansing and thickening cloth by beating and washing." *Sleazy:* "Of textile fabrics or materials: Thin or flimsy in texture; having little substance or body" *(OED)*. Flax was one of the many potential crops recommended by colonial developers; John Oldmixon, for instance, observed that Virginians "might also manufacture Flax, Hemp, Cotton, and even Silk; the first three Commodities thriving there as well as in any Country in the World." *Oldmixon,* I, 319.

85. Byrd might have been thinking of the Russian use of palisades or perhaps Adam Olearius's description of the use of wood in Moscow buildings:

'Tis true, that, the Palaces of great Lords, and the Houses of some rich Merchants excepted, which are of Brick or Stone, all the rest are of Wood, and made up of beams, and cross-pieces of Firr laid one upon another. They cover them with barks of trees, upon which they sometimes put another covering of Turfes. The carelesness of the *Muscovites,* and the disorders of their house-keeping are such, that there hardly passes a moneth, nay not a week, but some place or other takes fire, which, meeting with what is very combustible, does in a moment reduce many houses, nay, if the wind be any thing high, whole streets into ashes. Some few days before

our arrival, the fire had consumed the third part of the City; and about 5 or 6 years since, the like accident had near destroy'd it all. To prevent this, the *Strelits* of the Guard, and the Watch, are enjoyn'd, in the night time to carry Pole-axes, wherewith they break down the houses adjoyning to those which are a-fire, by which means they hinder the progress of it, with much better success than if they attempted the quenching of it. And that it may not fasten on other more solid structures, the doors and windows are very narrow, having shutters of Lattin, to prevent the sparks and flashes from getting in. Those who have their houses burnt, have this comfort withall, that they may buy houses ready built, at a market for that purpose, without the white-Wall, at a very easy rate, and have them taken down, transported, and in a short time set up in the same place where the former stood.
—Adam Olearius, *The Voyages and Travells of the Ambassadors Sent by Frederick Duke of Holstein, to the Great Duke of Muscovy, and the King of Persia*, 2d ed. (London, 1669), 43 (*Hayes* 194)

Byrd also wrote an entry in his Commonplace Book about the wooden buildings of Russia, possibly after reading Olearius; see *Commonplace Book, §80*.

86. Cf. *BL* (March 19): "Several of the Men was troubled with fluxes & small Fevers by the badness of the Water and Moisture of their Lodging but the Chewing a Little Rhubarb relieved them Effectually." Rhubarb was used generally as a purgative; in this case, the Dismalites suffering from flux (diarrhea, perhaps a symptom of dysentery) used rhubarb to clear the bowels.

87. Andrew Meade (d. 1745), planter and Indian trader, came to Virginia from County Ballintobber, Ireland, around 1685 and settled in Nansemond County,

where he became conspicuous and prosperous. He was engaged in trade with the Indians up the Roanoke River, in Virginia and North Carolina, and also in the lumber trade, and became a man of wealth. He built a handsome family mansion and storehouses. The mansion stood on an eminence just back of the town of Suffolk, and had an avenue of trees, which led from it to the church in Suffolk, of which he was a vestryman.
—P. Hamilton Baskervill, *Andrew Meade of Ireland and Virginia* . . . (Richmond, Va., 1921), 23–24

Meade also served in the House of Burgesses, as a judge, and senior colonel of the militia. This is probably not the same Mead the "Surveyors' Journal and Field Book" mentions on March 28, west of the Dismal Swamp.

88. See Hugh Jones: "The common nominal Christians live there not much better than heathens." Jones recommended missionary assistance not only for Indians and Negroes, "but for the christening and recovery to the practical profession of the gospel great numbers of English, that have but the bare name of God and Christ; and that too frequently in nothing but vain swearing, cursing, and imprecations." *Jones,* 105.

Hottentots: The doctrine of natural religion asserts that human beings are so constructed that they may discover the existence of a supreme being using only the divine gift of reason, even without the benefit of revelation. At the same time, as if discovering the exception that proves the rule, early modern authors declared the Hottentots—the

Cape Khoikoi, the indigenous people of the Cape of Good Hope—were so base they were even devoid of natural light. Byrd extracted several passages about the Hottentots from the accounts of travelers in his Commonplace Book (*Commonplace Book,* 174, 268–272). The notion that the Hottentots were devoid of religion recurs frequently; for instance, in John Maxwell, "An Account of the Cape of Good Hope" in the *Philosophical Transactions:*

> By all that I have seen and heard of them and other Nations, they are the most Lazy and Ignorant part of Mankind; by virtue of which two most excellent Qualifications, there are no manner of Arts practised among them, no Plowing or Sowing, no going to Sea in so much as a Boat, no use of Iron or Money, no Notion of God, Providence, or of a future State, no Tradition of Creation or a Flood, no Prayers or Sacrifices, no Magical Rites; nor, in fine, any Notion of any Invisible Being capable of doing them either good or harm.
> —*Philosophical Transactions,* XXV (1706–1707), 2425

From accounts such as this emerged a common metaphor applied to any person or persons existing in a spiritually or culturally benighted condition. On the European construction of the Cape Khoikoi, see Linda E. Merians, *Envisioning the Worst: Representations of "Hottentots" in Early-Modern England* (Newark, Del., 2001).

The comparison here depends on the reader's recognition of the proverbial use of the word "Hottentot" to indicate spiritual darkness. Without such recognition, the magnitude of the insult is lost.

89. Byrd viewed swamps as barren because they could not be turned to human use, and noxious because their "foul Damps" spread disease. He asserts hyperbolically that it is even hostile to animals, such as a "Zcaland Frog." Zealand, or Zelandt, a province of the United Netherlands consisting of five islands at the mouth of the Schelde River, was notoriously subject to flooding; see Bohun's *Geographical Dictionary* (*Hayes* 12).

90. Here and in his letters about the 1728 expedition to Lord Orrery and John Perceval (*Correspondence,* I, 374, 404), Byrd called the Dismal Swamp "Avernus," referring to Virgil, *Aeneid* 6.237–242:

> spelunca alta fuit vastoque immanis hiatu,
> scrupea, tuta lacu nigro nemorumque tenebris,
> quam super haud ullae poterant impune volantes
> tendere iter pinnis: talis sese halitus atris
> faucibus effundens supera ad convexa ferebat
> *unde locum Grai dixerunt nomine Aornum.*
> —Virgil, *Eclogues, Georgics, Aeneid I–VI,* ed. H. Rushton Fairclough, rev. G. P. Goold (Cambridge, Mass., 1999), 548

The Dryden translation (ll. 338–347) renders the passage thus:

> Deep was the cave; and downward as it went
> From the wide Mouth, a rocky rough Descent;
> And here th' access a gloomy Grove defends;
> And there th' unnavigable Lake extends.
> O're whose unhappy Waters, void of Light,

No Bird presumes to steer his Airy Flight;
Such deadly Stenches from the depth arise,
And steaming Sulphur, that infects the Skies.
From hence the *Grecian* Bards their Legends make,
And give the name *Avernus* to the Lake.
—*The Works of Virgil . . . , Translated into English Verse, by Mr. Dryden* (London, 1697),
422 (*Hayes* 806)

Strabo related that natives of the region believed "that all birds that fly over the lake
fall down into the water, being killed by the vapours that rise from it, as in the case of
all the Plutonia" (*The Geography of Strabo* 5.4.5, trans. Horace Leonard Jones [London,
1917–1932]). Plutonia, openings through which subterraneous gases or mephitic vapors
emerged, were viewed as entrances to the underworld, and thus the name.

An early editor of Byrd's manuscripts once noted, "Buzzards cannot smell" (Thomas
H. Wynne, ed., *History of the Dividing Line and Other Tracts: From the Papers of William
Byrd, of Westover in Virginia, Esquire* [Richmond, Va., 1866], I, 50), but this is not good ornithology, for buzzards would starve without the ability to detect by scent while in flight the
carrion on which they feed.

Salt Sea: Dead Sea. The River Jordan flows into the Dead Sea without further outlet.
It gets its name from the intense salinity of the water that makes it impossible for fish or
plants to survive. Early modern geographers associated it with the doomed biblical cities
of the plain; Bohun's *Geographical Dictionary* identifies it as "a lake of Judaea where formerly the Cities of *Sodom* and Gomorrah were consumed" (26, s.v. *Asphaltites*). The myth
that birds cannot overfly the Dead Sea might have originated with Tacitus: "The last is a
lake of great size: vast circumference; it is like the sea, but its water has a nauseous taste;
and its offensive odour is injurious to those who live near it. Its waters are not moved by
the wind, and neither fish nor water-foul can live there" (*Annals 5.6*, in Tacitus, *The Histories; The Annals,* trans. John Jackson [London, 1925–1937], II, 185). English travel writer
Henry Maundrell reported: "It is a common tradition, that birds, attempting to fly over
this Sea, drop down dead into it. . . . The former report I saw actually confuted, by several
birds flying about, and over the Sea, without any visible harm" (*A Journey from Aleppo to
Jerusalem at Easter A.D. 1697* [Oxford, 1703], 83 [*Hayes* 124]). Edward Wells, too, asserted
"the Bituminous Smell it sends forth" is toxic, but curiously he refers to Maundrell (*An
Historical Geography of the New Testament,* 2d ed. [London, 1712], 80 [*Hayes* 2077]). The
story persisted; in 1735, Benjamin Martin reported:

> *Asphaltos,* this is that slimy bituminous Substance, of a purple Hue, which is found
> in the *Lake of Sodom,* or *Dead-Sea,* in the *Land of Palestine;* from whence its Waters
> are said to stink to that Degree, that no Fish can live in them, nor the Birds in the Air
> fly over it, and live.
> —*The Philosophical Grammar; Being a View of the Present State of Experimented
> Physiology or Natural Philosophy* (London, 1735), 213–214

91. Byrd's comments about the absence of clergy in North Carolina are not strictly
factual. As Boyd noted, "Prior to 1728 the Society for the Propagation of the Gospel had
sent to North Carolina thirteen ministers and one schoolmaster." Boyd counters Byrd's

description of North Carolina as overrun with Dissenters and irreligious men by pointing out that "three of four North Carolina boundary commissioners were churchmen, Moseley, Gale and Little, and also Swann, the Surveyor" (*Boyd*, 72).

The proverbial absence of snakes in Ireland is so well known that somebody saw fit to "correct" both the Virginia Historical Society and the American Philosophical Society manuscripts, noting in pencil the word "Snakes" written above "Spiders." However, both manuscripts clearly say "Spiders." Byrd might have been thinking of this passage in Guy Miège's description of Ireland:

> The Wonder of this Country is, that it breeds no venemous Creature, and that no such will live here, brought from any other Places, nor does the Wood of its Forests breed either Worms or Spiders.
> —*The Present State of Great Britain and Ireland* (London, 1723), III, 7 (*Hayes* 223)

Additionally, most of this passage is repeated (without crediting Miège) by John Fransham, *The World in Miniature; or, The Entertaining Traveller* (London, 1741), II, 255 (*Hayes* A14).

92. North Carolina designated marriage a civil contract in 1669; the 1715 Vestry Law authorized magistrates to perform marriage ceremonies where no ministers were resident. Boyd notes it was not until 1741 that "the right was confined to the clergy of the Church of England and magistrates" (*Boyd*, 72).

Cast of his office: A specimen or taste of the service or task to be performed by one in his position. In John Dryden's *Amphitryon,* Mercury offers a song to Phaedra with these words: "In the mean while, here's a Cast of my Office for thee" (*The Dramatick Works of John Dryden, Esq.* [London, 1717], VI, 215 [*Hayes* 988, 1003]). Another instance Byrd might have known occurred in Bishop Robert Sanderson's sermon to the magistrates at the 1625 assizes:

> If *lastly,* thou art in any place or office of *service,* or *trust,* or *command,* or *attendance* about the Courts: rejoyce not as if it were now in thy power to do a friend a *courtesie,* or a foe a *spite.* Do not shew a *cast of thy Office,* for the promise or hope of a *reward,* in helping a *great Offender* out of the Briars.
> —*Thirty-six Sermons . . .* (London, 1686), 148–149 (*Hayes* 1143)

93. Virginia legislated Sabbath observance in 1657/8 (*Hening*, I, 434), and North Carolina in 1715 (*Boyd*, 72). Byrd's ironic phrase, "no manner of Cruelty," suggests there could be no real cruelty in depriving Carolinian servants and cattle of a day of rest by treating the Sabbath like any other working day, because they do so little on ordinary working days anyway.

Robinson Cruso: the industrious hero of Daniel Defoe's novel, *The Life and Strange Surprizing Adventures of Robinson Crusoe . . .* (London, 1719) (*Hayes* 2083). The shipwrecked Crusoe of necessity did not observe the Sabbath, there being no calendar or community of coreligionists on his island, whereas the Carolinians fail to observe the Sabbath from mere sloth and lack of piety.

94. Thomas Speight (1670–1737), a prominent planter of Perquimans County, North Carolina. In 1696–1702 he claimed 1,386 acres, importing more than two dozen persons, and in 1712–1715 he expanded his holdings by purchasing another 411 acres from Epaphro-

ditus Benton and continued to buy and sell land in North Carolina until his death. He apparently also owned land in neighboring Nansemond County, Virginia, having purchased 104 acres in the Upper Parish in 1719. Speight was appointed justice of the peace for Perquimans Precinct in 1724, represented Perquimans in the North Carolina Assembly in 1725, and was named associate justice of the General Court in 1726. *NCHGR*, II (1901), 136; William S. Price, Jr., ed., *North Carolina Higher-Court Minutes, 1709–1723*, CRNC, V, (Raleigh, N.C., 1977), 72, and *1724–1730*, CRNC, VI (1981), 141, 164, 231; *C&P*, III, 215.

95. The notion that the voice of Echo was empty of meaning is a conventional topos of classical and neoclassical poetry. Byrd is possibly echoing one of the poet Giles Fletcher's Lucianic dialogues in which sea nymphs mock a suitor so musically untalented that "prating Eccho scorn'd for to repeate" his tunes. *Licia, or Poemes of Love . . .* [Cambridge, 1593], 58.

96. *Bantam or Morocco:* two distant and exotic seaports, the former on the island of Java in the Sunda Strait, the latter in the Maghreb (North Africa) on the Mediterranean. Historian N. I. Matar has observed that Muslim ambassadors to the Court of Saint James's

> arrived in pomp and enjoyed the protection of the monarch and therefore could and did practise their religious observances openly, abide by their dietary rules, and appear in their national dress with its conspicuous turban. . . . As these ambassadors . . . continued their visits to England throughout the seventeenth century, the public celebration of their arrivals grew wider: not only did the king and his court become familiar with them, but the general population too (especially in London). Furthermore, as people became curious about them, coverage of their visits increased and publications proliferated to provide detailed descriptions of their activities, diet, clothes, and attitude.

Matar tells of the extraordinary impression of the 1637 visit of Moroccan ambassador Al-kaid Jaurar bin Abdella, who not only displayed great wealth and exotic costumery to the public but also brought with him 366 British subjects freed from slavery. Subsequent ambassadors might not have demonstrated such largesse, but there was always grand spectacle (N. I. Matar, "Muslims in Seventeenth-Century England," *Journal of Islamic Studies,* VIII [1997], 63–82, esp. 73). Byrd might have witnessed such spectacles or read accounts of the arrival of Moroccan ambassadors in 1682, 1691, 1700, 1706, 1709, and later.

97. *Horsing:* originally, the "covering" of a mare by a stallion and, by extension, the diagonal, stacking items such as chairs or timber.

98. The ancient Greeks and Romans interpreted natural phenomena as omens. Aelian refers to the founding legend of Rome:

> And when Romulus on the Palatine Hill, divining by the flight of twelve Vultures, had received a favourable augury, following the number of the birds he decreed that the rulers of Rome should be preceded by a number of rods *[fasces]* equal to that of the birds seen on that occasion.
> • —*On the Characteristics of Animals* 10.22, trans. A. F. Schofield (London, 1958)

See also Livy 1.6.4–1.7.1 (*Hayes* 1486), Lucan, *Pharsalia* 7.437–440 (*Hayes* 1512), and Plutarch's *Life of Romulus.* Byrd owned Latin editions of Plutarch's *Lives* and *Works* (*Vitae parallelae* and *Opera: Hayes* 1781, 1780). The story also occurs in any number of intervening texts, such as Echard's *Roman History,* which tells how Romulus and Remus, competing for preeminence, were told by their grandfather

> to go apart, and observe the Flying of Birds; and the most Fortunate of the two
> should be counted the Founder of the Colony. They both took their Station upon
> their own Hills, and *Remus* first had a Flight of six Vultures; but *Romulus* having or
> pretending to have, double the number, both were saluted by the title of *King.*
> —Laurence Echard, *The Roman History . . .* (London, 1702), I, 6 (*Hayes* 2136)

99. In the *BL* (March 21) version the description is simpler: "In the Evening they heard Dogs bark & Cattle low which was Musick in their Ears." Faustina and Farinelli were two prominent figures on the London stage. Faustina Bordoni (1699–1758), a great Italian soprano, is probably best known for her rivalry with soprano Francesca Cuzzoni (1698–1770). Composer and impresario George Frederick Handel engaged first Cuzzoni and then Faustina to sing at the Royal Academy of Music. Soon after Faustina arrived in 1726, rival claques emerged, and tension mounted in the audiences. The climax came on June 6, at the end of the 1727 season, during a production of Giovanni Battista Bononcini's opera *Astianatte.* Applause and hissing gave way to catcalls and curses, brawling erupted in the audience, and, to the scandalized delight of the public, on stage the "Rival Queens" lashed out with their fists and pulled each other's hair, all the while using shocking language. The battle of the sopranos reappeared in London satires for many years. The other singer Byrd named was the Italian male soprano and castrato, Carlo Broschi, called Farinelli (1705–1782). He first came to London in 1734, where he sang at Lincoln's Inn Fields in a company rivaling Handel's, featuring operas by Farinelli's teacher Niccolo Porporà. In 1737, he left England to become official singer to Philip V of Spain and later retired to Italy.

100. Tobacco was a staple crop for North Carolina as well as Virginia. However, North Carolina's trade was severely restricted by the lack of serviceable ports, forcing it to transport its tobacco to Virginia, where tariffs and surcharges reduced the profits. In 1679 the Virginia Act placed strict restrictions on the flow of North Carolina tobacco through Virginia ports, making a bad situation worse. The result was an increase in smuggling. W. Neil Franklin explains:

> As early as 1677 we have reference to a tobacco trade with New England. This was
> done by the vessels of New England, drawing very little water, penetrating the
> sounds, inlets, and rivers of the eastern coast, evading the few customs officials,
> storing the tobacco on board, and returning to New England, the Carolina tobacco
> finding its ultimate destination in Scotland.
> —"Agriculture in Colonial North Carolina," *North Carolina Historical Review,* III
> (1926), 553–554

See also Franklin, ed., "Act for the Better Regulation of the Indian Trade: Virginia, 1714," *VMHB,* LXII (1964), 141–151; Stacy L. Lorenz, "'To Do Justice to His Majesty, the Merchant, and the Planter': William Gooch and the Virginia Tobacco Inspection Act of 1730," *VMHB,* CXVIII (2000), 345–392.

This is the trade in defiance of the Navigation Acts that Byrd mentions, complaining of the presence in North Carolina's inland waters of small ships illegally taking on uninspected, untaxed tobacco; the captains of these ships acted "in contempt of the Virginia

Law." Byrd appears less concerned with the equity of trade laws between colonies than with the undercutting of Virginia tobacco profits incurred by illegitimate traders. As a prominent tobacco producer and trader himself, his perspective is not impartial. Nor is his account of North Carolina smuggling strictly accurate, for tobacco smuggling was not unknown in Virginia waterways. Indeed, North Carolina laws against smuggling did exist, though apparently little enforced.

101. Peter Brinkley, eldest son of Jacob Brinkley (who emigrated to Virginia in 1684), a planter in Perquimans Precinct, west of the Great Dismal Swamp. The entry for March 28 states, "John Brinkly's bore N $\frac{1}{10}$ of a mile & Peter Brinkly's SW about the same distance." Peter Brinkley married Anne Eley and had a large family. Freddie L. Brinkley, *The Brinkley and Allied Families of Nansemond County, Virginia, and Gates County, North Carolina: A Family History* (Pasadena, Md., 1994), 17–18.

102. When during the exodus from Egypt Moses dispatched men to scout out the situation in Canaan, the Gibeonites used deception to persuade Joshua to ally himself with them:

> They did work wilily, and went and made as if they had been ambassadors, and took old sacks upon their asses, and wine bottles, old, and rent, and bound up. And old shoes and clouted upon their feet, and old garments upon them; and all the bread of their provision was dry and mouldy. And they went to Joshua unto the camp at Gilgal, and said unto him, and to the men of Israel, We be come from a far country: now therefore make ye a league with us.
> —Josh. 9:4–6

103. Byrd's hydrological terminology is confusing, for he tends to describe the path of rivers running *away* from his position, whether up- or downstream. Thus later in *The History of the Dividing Line* he mentions the Staunton "runs away near Northwest," and "the Dan stretches away pretty near West, & runs clear thro the great Mountains." This subjective description suits a traveler following the rivers upstream. Thus, when Byrd numbers the "Rivers, that Head into" the swamp, he does not mean rivers moving *into,* but *out of* the swamp. The headwaters of nearly all these rivers do in fact lie within the boundaries of the Dismal drainage area. The Perquimans, however, starts up to the west of the Dismal watershed. See Robert Q. Oaks, Jr., and Donald R. Whitehead, "Geologic Setting and Origin of the Dismal Swamp, Southeastern Virginia and Northeastern North Carolina," in Paul W. Kirk, ed., *The Great Dismal Swamp* (Charlottesville, Va., 1979), 1–24.

104. Though Byrd has just declared there is "no Lake, or any considerable Body" of water in the Great Dismal Swamp, he describes a treeless expanse of reeds, the "Green Sea," which might have been Lake Drummond. It is not clear why Byrd did not mention this lake, though many accounts extant in his time declared that North Carolina governor William Drummond had discovered the lake that bore his name as early as 1665.

105. Some time after the expedition Byrd laid out the benefits of draining the swamp, floating the idea of chartering a company to drain it. The projected public benefits of the undertaking included transforming land of no value to the crown into a source of quitrents; making the surrounding country more wholesome by "correcting and purifying the air"; transforming bog into "the fittest soil in the world for the producing of hemp," the raw materials for the cordage so vital to transatlantic shipping; and the creation of canals

to promote shipping between northern and southern rivers. Byrd called for a crown grant of the entire area to a limited company, free from quitrents, for the economic benefits he projected would accrue to the crown indirectly, through duties on the resulting trade. He conceived that the Dismal could be drained in ten years for the sum of four thousand pounds, to be raised by twenty subscriptions only. Byrd proposed that several prominent figures "be invited to encourage this subscription"—George Hamilton, first earl of Orkney (nonresident governor of Virginia from 1704 to 1737), Sir Charles Wager (first lord of the Admiralty from 1733 to 1742), Sir Jacob Acworth (surveyor of the navy from 1715 to 1749), and Martin Bladen (the most influential member of the Board of Trade from 1717 to 1746). Byrd's proposal was not published in his lifetime, and no evidence of a concerted attempt to bring his plan to fruition remains in his extant correspondence. But it is interesting to note the proposal's description of the Dismal as a noxious, barren wilderness is virtually identical to the description in *The History of the Dividing Line*. Published posthumously in 1789, Byrd's "Description of the Dismal Swamp, in Virginia, with Proposals for and Observations on the Advantages of Draining It" appeared in *Columbian Magazine*, III (1789), 230–234. In 1837 Edmund Ruffin published it from manuscript with a brief editorial preface, "Proposal to Drain the Dismal Swamp," *Farmer's Register*, IV (1837), 521–524. See Kirk, ed., *The Great Dismal Swamp;* Charles Royster, *The Fabulous History of the Dismal Swamp Company: A Story of George Washington's Times* (New York, 1999), 5–7.

106. Cf. *BL* (March 24): "This being Sunday Wee had a very large Congregation some out of Curiosity & some out of Devotion & to have their Children Christned, for the Inhabitants of North Carolina have the Misfortune not to have a Minister in their whole Country wch is the Reason many are not Baptized till Men & Women & some not att all—but by the laws of the Country a Justice of the Peace may Marry."

107. Here Byrd's copyist has mistakenly written the year "1729," an error probably involving the application of the Old Style practice of beginning the new year on that date.

108. Compare with Beverley's description of Indian travel: "In their Travels, a Grass-plat under the covert of a shady Tree, is all the lodgings they require, and is as pleasant and refreshing to them, as a Down Bed and fine *Holland* Sheets are to us" (*Beverley,* book 3, 12). There may also be an echo here of the Roman Stoic philosopher Seneca's description of contentment:

> Place me in the midst of sumptuous furnishings and the trappings of luxury; I shall not think myself one whit happier because I have a soft mantle, because my guests recline on purple. Change my mattress; I shall be not a whit more wretched if my wearied neck must rest on a handful of hay, if I shall sleep on a cushion of the Circus with the stuffing spilling out through its patches of old cloth.
> —Seneca, *De tranquillitate animi (On the Happy Life)* 25.2, in *Moral Essays*, trans. John W. Basore (London, 1932), II, 165–167

Byrd owned five copies or editions of the *Opera* of Seneca (*Hayes* 1741, 1755, 1796, 2542, 2536) as well as a translation, *Seneca's Morals* (*Hayes* 2373), and the tragedies.

109. This formation is known today as the Suffolk Sand Ridge.

110. Catesby identifies four kinds of Carolina pines, pitch pine *(Pinus rigidus)*, richland pine (probably longleaf pine, *Pinus palustris*), short-leaved pine *(Pinus echinata),* and

swamp pine (probably slash pine, *Pinus eliottii*): Catesby, 154. Byrd's description fits the longleaf variety.

111. Two commodities essential for maritime commerce and naval maintenance were pitch and tar, obtained by heating or partially burning resinous wood, especially pine. The fire or kiln produced charcoal at the same time that it drove the heavy sap outward for collection. Wooden ships required continual caulking and preventive coating; pitch applied to ropes made them water-resistant and long-lasting as well as more easy to grip.

Evidently the Atlantic colonies competed for this market. In 1717 Byrd proposed to the Board of Trade several strategies for encouraging the production of naval stores in Virginia, acknowledging the same objections to tar produced in the Virginia manner. The fact "that it burns the cordage, arises from it's being made of the knots of the pine, and not of the trunk. When it is made there after the methods of Norway and Sweden, it will be as good as any." Byrd to Board of Trade, CO 5, 1318, 1; CO 323, 7, and 324, 10; CSP, XXIX, 506–507, 273.

112. Byrd here adapts the traditional satirical term "Lubberland" to mock the supposed indolence of Carolinians. Medieval European folklore described an imaginary land of plenty where rivers flowed with beer and wine, fruit fell from the trees into the waiting mouths of the people, the walls of buildings were made of pudding, and roast pigs or fowl leapt off the spit and ran to the table calling, "Come eat me." In France, this land was called *Cockaigne,* in Germany *Schlaraffenland,* in Holland *Luilikkerland,* Italy *Cuccagna,* in Spain *Cucaña*—and in England it was called *Lubberland.* From its earliest instances in medieval satirical poetry, the imaginary region functioned as a satirical tool to be used against both idleness and gluttony. In England the term *Lubberland* first appeared in the Elizabethan era. For a history of the imaginary land of plenty, see Herman Pleij, *Dreaming of Cockaigne: Medieval Fantasies of the Perfect Life* (New York, 2001). For the ancient origins of the tradition, see Campbell Bonner, "Dionysiac Magic and the Greek Land of Cockaigne," American Philological Association, *Transactions and Proceedings,* XLI (1910), 175–185. For Lubberland's lasting presence in folk tradition, see Frederick B. Jonassen, "Lucian's 'Saturnalia,' the Land of Cockaigne, and the Mummer's Plays," *Folklore,* CI (1990), 58–68. For Lubberland's arrival in the New World, see J. A. Leo Lemay, *New England's Annoyances: America's First Folk Song* (Newark, Del., 1985), 21–35.

113. *Take a small Heat at the Hough:* undertake a brief effort at weeding with a hoe. Byrd's spelling of this gardening tool is idiosyncratic; *hough* as an alternate spelling for "hoe" is not recorded in the *OED.*

114. Byrd's reproof echoes the biblical language of Proverbs: "The sluggard will not plow, by reason of the cold" (Prov. 20:4). It is a severe charge, for, according to the Christian teaching to which Byrd refers, sloth is much more than a minor defect of personality. Rather, it is a serious vice with moral ramifications. This text is the basis for much commentary and sermonizing; in Christian homiletics the sluggard most often appears making the feeble excuse of avoiding work because the weather is cold, and sleeping away the day. The crucial early statement of English Protestantism, John Foxe's *Actes and Monuments,* explained:

> Item, where we read in the scripture, the slouthful man reprehended, Pro. 6. why slepest thou O sluggard, thy poverty and beggery is comming upon thee like an

armed man. etc. And agayne in the same booke of Proverbs. The slouthfull man
(sayth the scripture) for colde would not go to the plough, therfore he shal beg in
sommer, and no man shall geve him. etc.
—John Foxe, *Actes and Monuments* . . . (London, 1586), 413 (*Hayes* 2389)

The sluggard reproved is a central image of Christian teaching about the doctrine of
stewardship as set forth in the parable of the talents, which emphasizes God's expectation
that people will improve their talents, recognizing that everything they have—property,
wealth, and "talent" (*techne,* skill) in the modern sense—is given in trust and therefore
must be developed. The influential *Whole Duty of Man* explains that people must work to
improve their earthly and spiritual condition alike:

> The *second* part of *diligence,* is *industry,* or *labour,* and this also we owe to our Souls,
> for without it they will as little prosper as that vineyard of the sluggard, which
> *Solomon* describes, *Prov.* 24.30. For there is a husbandry of the Soul, as well as of the
> estate, and the end of the one, as of the other, is the increasing, and *improving* of its
> riches.
> —[Richard Allestree], *The Whole Duty of Man* . . . (London, 1659), 165 (*Hayes* A25);
> Matt. 25:14–30

Industry is not limited to pious seeking of material prosperity. It is always necessary
to work for one's subsistence; the sluggard neglects himself and those who depend on
his efforts. Thus, taking as its epigraph the proverb from Solomon, an essay in Richard
Steele's *Guardian* explained:

> It has been observed by Writers of Morality, that in order to quicken Human
> Industry, Providence has so contriv'd it, that our daily Food is not to be procured
> without much Pains and Labour.

The industry required of humankind is common even to "Brute Creation." All must labor
to procure subsistence for themselves and their dependents.

> The Preservation of their Being is the whole Business of it. An Idle Man is therefore a
> kind of Monster in the Creation. All Nature is busie about him; every Animal he sees
> reproaches him.
> —*Guardian,* no. 157, in *The Guardian* (London, 1714), II, 397–398 (*Hayes* 867)

Thus Byrd's habitual railing against the lack of industry among North Carolinian colonists has a traditional Anglican background.

115. *BL* (March 26): "Mr. Fountain took a turn to Eden Town Metropolis of No: Carolina to preach a Sermon & Christen Children it being a place where the Gospel is Little
preach'd and as Little practiced."

William Little (1691–1734), North Carolina attorney general, chief justice, and boundary commissioner.

116. Admiral John Benbow (ca. 1653–1702) was in 1698 named commander in chief in
the West Indies. He sailed against Caribbean pirates in 1700, and against the French in
1702; the king ordered Virginia to contribute five hundred pounds to his campaign (Percy
Scott Flippin, *The Financial Administration of the Colony of Virginia,* Johns Hopkins Uni-

versity Studies in Historical and Political Science, XXXIII, no. 2 [Baltimore, 1915], 70). Benbow engaged the French under Ducasse near Port Royal, and, when four captains deserted, he engaged the enemy single-handed. Later he died of wounds inflicted during this battle.

Byrd's etymology is no doubt a species of joke. The punch made with rum, sugar, water, and nutmeg is actually called *bumbo* or *bombo* (the latter is the word Byrd uses in the *Secret History*).

Land-graves, nor Cassicks: The Proprietors of Carolina, with the aid of John Locke's constitution, projected a political structure for Carolina paralleling the English monarchy. At the head was the senior proprietor, named the *palatine,* a ruler "having a jurisdiction within a given territory such as elsewhere belongs to the sovereign alone" *(OED).* Landgraves and caciques were analogous to higher-ranking members of the nobility, sitting in the upper house of the Carolina legislature. Locke took the term *landgrave* from an order of high-ranking German counts, and *caciques* from indigenous Caribbean chiefs or princes. Locke's *Fundamental Constitutions of Carolina* clearly projected a new hereditary aristocracy in the colonies:

> There shall be just as many *Landgraves* as there are *Counties,* and twice as many *Cassiques,* and no more. These shall be the hereditary *Nobility* of the Province, and by right of their *Dignity* be Members of *Parliament.* Each *Landgrave* shall have four *Baronies,* and each *Cassique* two *Baronies, hereditarily* and *unalterably annexed* to, and setled upon the said *Dignity.*
> —[John Locke], *The Fundamental Constitutions of Carolina* [London, 1670], 3

It should be noted that Byrd mentions the Carolinian orders of nobility in the midst of a discussion of providing rum punch for the grandees' wives. Rum is hardly an appropriately genteel drink for women of rank; hence we may see Byrd's satirical wit at play.

117. *Mawkins (malkins):* scarecrows. *Fields* (327) notes that the *OED* provides another definition: "an untidy, female, esp. a servant or country wench; a slut, slattern, *occas.* a lewd woman." If Byrd was aware of the double meaning, it might well have amused him.

The Carolina parakeet *(Conuropsis carolinensis)* was once widespread along the Atlantic from Florida to Virginia but is now extinct. According to John Lawson the birds arrived in the early summer, "when Mulberries are ripe, which Fruit they love extremely. They peck the Apples, to eat the Kernels, so that the Fruit rots and perishes. They are mischievous to Orchards" *(Lawson,* 142). Catesby observed, "The orchards in autumn are visited by numerous flights of them; where they make great destruction for their kernels only; for the same purpose they frequent Virginia; which is the furthest north I ever heard they have been seen" *(Catesby,* 64).

118. Compare Catesby: "The wolves in America are like those of Europe in shape and color, but are somewhat smaller; they are more timorous and not so voracious as those of Europe; a drove of them will fly from a single man, yet in very severe winter there has been some instances to the contrary" *(Catesby,* 157).

119. *Pale:* A fence made of upright strips fastened (usually with nails) to horizontal rails supported by posts.

120. Byrd's censure of Edenton is not entirely accurate. In 1702, the recorder of deeds

in Chowan County registered the transfer of a parcel of Edward Smithwick's land to the church wardens of Chowan Parish:

> "Seventy yards square of land for to build and arect *[sic]* a church, and the church to stand in the middle of said land, for the use of said Parish, forever, the said land to be on the road or the highway from Thomas Gylliams in the woods, joining on the old field of the Edward Smithwick"; April 7, 1702
> —*NCHGR*, I (1900), 87.

The church in Chowan Parish, North Carolina, was built on this land, one mile south of Edenton on the Yoppim Road to Sandy Point. Construction began in 1702, though it still had only a sand floor in 1708. There is evidence of use, though not on a regular basis, well before 1728. Pennington, *Church of England*, 15; J. R. B. Hathaway, "The First Church Built in North Carolina and Its Location Etc.," *NCHGR*, I (1900), 256–267.

The construction of Saint Paul's Church, in Edenton proper, did not begin until 1736. The process was slow—the building was usable in 1760, but the interior woodwork was not finished until 1774. "St. Paul's Church, Edenton, N.C.," *NCHGR*, I (1900), 600–609.

Thus, strictly speaking, Byrd was correct in stating Edenton had no church, but the small church about one mile up Yoppim Road was convenient enough to residents of Edenton. Many eighteenth-century worshipers had much farther to travel. Byrd might have been aware of the long delay in carrying out the plans for a church at Edenton. The considerable sum of six hundred pounds had been set aside, but opposition from the commissioners hindered the building, as Governor Everard wrote the bishop of London in 1729 (Pennington, *Church of England*, 29).

121. The first missionary the Society for Promoting Christian Knowledge sent to North Carolina was Daniel Brett. He was "not a man of high qualities; and after about six months, he disappeared from the scene" (Pennington, *Church of England*, 14).

122. This from a gentleman whose "Necessary House" at Westover had five seats and a fireplace!

123. Technically, paper money is a promissory note issued by a government payable to the bearer on demand. In the early eighteenth century, as John J. McCusker explains, money was "divided into two sorts, imaginary and real" (quoting Alexander Justice in 1770). In the British colonies of North America, "real" money consisted of minted coins, the hard currency of various governments; the colonies did business with Spanish coins (piastre, piece of eight, pistole, doubloon), Portuguese (escuso, crusado, moidore), Dutch (stuiver, gulden, rijksdaalder), and German (mark, thaler)—and, much less frequently, English coins. *Money and Exchange in Europe and America, 1600–1755: A Handbook* (Chapel Hill, N.C., 1978), 3, 6–12. On commodity prices and "Proclamation Money" (paper money issued by colonial governments), see Franklin, "Agriculture in Colonial North Carolina," *North Carolina Historical Review*, III (1926), 539–574.

The *OED* notes that the term "pistole," originally indicating the Spanish coin (a gold double-escudo), was also used to denote any coins resembling the the Spanish issue, including the French louis d'or and Irish and Scottish coins. In the *Secret History*, Byrd mentions that the reason John Allen ("Capricorn") had for withdrawing from the expedition must have been serious, since he would have been unlikely to deprive himself deliberately of five pistoles.

The supply of coins was very limited. Byrd's "paper Money" is probably not printed bills, but notes. The discount he mentions is a differential between the face value of coin and the stipulated value of the note and is therefore best understood as a discount granted to the purchaser or receiver of the note to adjust for inconvenience of transforming the paper to cash, the risk of fraud, and the very real risk that the issuer might not remain solvent.

124. *BL:* "this Evening the Surveyers finish'd their Line through the *Dismal,* haveing not been able to Measure five Miles in Less then three Days, this mad *[sic]* the whole distance cross this dismal swamp to be 15 Miles in that part where it is supposed to be broadest while the length from North to South is computed to be about 30 Miles."

125. The word *swamp* in early American writing indicates wet, low-lying ground, and specifically "a tract of rich soil having a growth of trees and other vegetation, but too moist for cultivation" *(OED).* The compound term *mill swamp* (not listed in the *OED*) usually describes the soggy terrain resulting from the overflow from the stream dammed to provide water power for a flour mill; in 1753, the Burgesses used "the Mouth of *John Blair* Esq; his Mill-Swamp" as one of the landmarks in laying out the boundary of James City County. *The Journal of the House of Burgesses, MDCCLIII* (Williamsburg, Va., 1753), 63.

126. *Norway mice:* lemmings. See W[illiam] Derham, *Physico-Theology; or, A Demonstration of the Being and Attributes of God, from His Works of Creation,* 4th ed. (London, 1716), 56 (Hayes 1985). Byrd used the same comparison in a letter to Lord Perceval: "This service took me up 16 weeks by reason of the very difficult ways we had to go through. Like Norway mice we went strait forwards through thick and thin." Byrd to John Perceval, Viscount Perceval, June 10, 1720, *Correspondence,* I, 404.

127. *Father Hennepin's Christians:* Father Louis Hennepin (1640–1705), a member of La Salle's first continental expedition in 1678 and historian of an expedition to discover the source of the Mississippi in 1680. After returning to Europe, he published *Nouvelle découverte d'un tres grand pays situé dans l'Amérique entre le Nouveau Mexique et la mer Glacial* (Utrecht, 1697), which was in Byrd's library (Hayes 1399), as was the English translation of 1698. Hennepin complained of the Indians' lack of seriousness:

> These poor blind Creatures look upon all our Mysteries of Faith as Tales and Dreams. They have Naturally a great many Vices, and are very much addicted to several Superstitions which have no meaning at all in 'em: They have many barbarous and brutal Usages amongst them: They would suffer themselves to be Baptiz'd six times a Day for a Glass of *Aqua vitae,* or a Pipe of Tobacco: They frequently offer their Infants to the Font, but that without any manner of Motive or Zeal. Those, whom one had Converted in a whole Winter, as it happen'd I had instructed a few, while I was at the Fort of *Frontenac,* do not discover any greater knowledge of matters of Religion than the rest; which has occasion'd many dreadful Alarms of Conscience to several of our Fraternity, in the beginning of their Mission amongst the People of *Canada.* They observ'd that those few which they had instructed, and admitted to the Holy Baptism, some relaps'd into the former Indifference, and seem'd rather to Prophane than Adore.
> —L[ouis] Hennepin, *A New Discovery of a Vast Country in America* . . . (London, 1698), II, 56.

According to many Protestant writers, the evangelism of Roman Catholic missionaries was opportunistic and superficial. John Callender, for instance, objected to complaints about New England methods of converting Indians, asserting that Roman Catholics "make such Christians among the *Indians,* as knew no more of the Gospel, than to make the *Sign of the Cross,* or who desired *Baptism* only, for the sake of the *new Shirt,* with which their Conversion was to be rewarded" (*An Historical Discourse on the Civil and Religious Affairs of the Colony of Rhode-Island and Providence Plantation in New-England in America . . .* [Boston, 1739], 83). Thus, with the phrase "Father Hennepin's Christians" Byrd satirizes the benighted Carolinians' willingness to have their children baptized—a willingness that indicated little or no significant religious conviction on their part.

128. Swann was married to Jane Jones, daughter of North Carolina chief justice Frederick Jones (*DNCB,* V, 488). *Boyd* misidentified her as Mildred Lyon, daughter of John Lyon of Cape Fear (100).

129. Byrd's suggestion that the Carolina Commissioners nominated the younger Mayo to take Swann's place and that he declined the offer is more than a little disingenuous. Byrd had already attempted unsuccessfully to have Joseph Mayo named the second surveyor for Virginia at the beginning of the expedition when John Allen withdrew. Fitzwilliam strenuously expressed displeasure at the younger Mayo's presence as a volunteer.

130. The best pitch and tar came from Sweden, until the supply was interrupted by the Great Northern War (1700–1721) between Charles XII of Sweden and Peter the Great of Russia; see John J. Murray, "Robert Jackson's 'Memoir on the Swedish Tar Company,' December 29, 1709," *Huntington Library Quarterly,* X (1946–1947), 419–428. The quality of colonial pitch and tar was decidedly inferior, as Virginia governor Sir Edmund Andros explained to the Board of Trade: "I understand that the tar is much hotter and more burning than that of Sweden and no ways fit for ropes. It casts very black on wood and scorches much." June 5, 1698, *CSP,* XVI, 264–265, no. 550.

South Carolina agents and merchants optimistically reported to the Board of Trade in 1716: "Any quantity of tarr and pitch (upon due encouragement) may be had from South Carolina. . . . The pitch is as good as any imported into Great Brittaine, tarr but little inferiour to that of Stockholm, and is capable of being improved to the greatest perfection" (*CSP,* XXIX, 258, no. 477). London ropemakers provided a certificate that Carolina tar was suitable for cordage (*CSP,* XXIX, 267, no. 487).

131. *Mr. Parker:* Richard Parker, Jr. (d. 1751), planter in Surry County and vestryman of Nansemond Parish. The journal of the North Carolina Commissioners records that on March 30 the Line was run just to the north of Richard Parker's house, west of the Dismal "and 515 Chain west of the road that leads from Perquimmons to the White Marsh in Virginia." Cain, ed., *Records of the Executive Council, 1664–1734,* CRNC, VII, 567.

132. *BL* (April 1): "Sommerton Chapple was left near 2 Miles in Virginia, so that now they have as few places of Worship as Ministers." Built in 1692 on land near Somerton donated by Captain Hugh Campbell, the chapel of upper Nansemond Parish came to be called Somerton Chapel. Its location in Virginia was not really in doubt; Campbell had petitioned the Virginia government to support readers at three locations on the land he planned to donate—on the Blackwater River in Isle of Wight County, on the North River in Norfolk County, and Somerton in Nansemond County. See George Carrington Mason, "The Colonial Churches of Nansemond County, Virginia," *WMQ,* 2d Ser., XXI (1941),

50–51. Still, Byrd's assertion that there was no place of public worship left in North Carolina when the Line passed below Somerton Chapel was not strictly true, since (as we have seen) the church on Yoppin Road, just outside Edenton in Chowan Parish, had been active for more than twenty years.

133. William Speight (ca. 1674–ca. 1749) of the Upper Parish, Nansemond County, Virginia. His lands had long been in both jurisdictions: in 1711 and 1719 he patented land in Virginia (*C&P*, III, 118, 215); in 1716 he witnessed a lease for a tract of land in Chowan Precinct, North Carolina (Margaret M. Hofmann, *Chowan Precinct, North Carolina, 1696 to 1723* [Three Rivers, Mass., 2000], 147). In 1726 he paid quitrents to North Carolina (Cain, ed., *Records of the Executive Council, 1664–1734*, CRNC, VII, 551). In 1728 as a resident of Nansemond County he sold property in Virginia that was registered in a North Carolina document (*NCHGR*, II [1901], 444). In 1735 he sold lands on Horse Pen Branch, North Carolina (*NCHGR*, I [1900], 109, III [1902], 128).

The journal of the North Carolina Commissioners reported that on April 1 the Line crossed Sommerton Road 1.5 miles south of the Chapel and Meherrin Ferry Road "near William Speights whose plantation was Split by the Line Posts marked being put up on the main Roads where the Line Crost them" (Cain, ed., *Records of the Executive Council, 1664–1734*, CRNC, VII, 567–568). Records of the Speight family in the documents of both provinces suggest he preferred to remain Virginian, but he also served as a vestryman in Saint Paul's Parish in Chowan Precinct, North Carolina.

Tribute: An allusion to Matt. 22:15–22: "Then saith he unto them, Render therefore unto Caesar that which is Caesar's, and render unto God, that which is God's."

134. *Sydon:* an ancient Phoenician city. With Solomon's alliance by marriage with Sydon, the worship of strange gods gained entry into Israel:

> Because that they have forsaken me, and have worshipped Ashtoreth the goddess of the Zidonians, Chemosh the god of the Moabites, and Milcom the god of the children of Ammon, and have not walked in my ways, to do that which is right in mine eyes, and to keep my statutes and my judgments, as did David his father.
> —1 Kings 11:33

135. Byrd implies that maintaining law and order in the rough and tumble of early North Carolina was difficult, especially during the last years of proprietary government and during the transition to royal control. Historian Donna J. Spindel has characterized this period as a time when "colonists attacked tax collectors, verbally and physically abused lawmen, and resisted arrest." *Crime and Society in North Carolina, 1663–1776* (Baton Rouge, La., 1989), 64.

No extant records precisely match Byrd's anecdote of wild proceedings in the court at Currituck. However, it is distinctly possible that Byrd here is alluding—with deliberate obscurity—to the case of Thomas Swann of Pasquotank Precinct, prosecuted in October 1725 for seditious words and actions the previous month in Currituck Precinct Court. Swann spoke abusively to Justice John Woodhouse, calling him a pitiful fellow and a rascal, and he menaced the court with a drawn sword, exposing the sitting court to public contempt, "the better to move and instigate other's to mutiny and Sedition and to oppose and obstruct the present Government." Swann went so far as to wound Woodhouse with his sword. In 1726 Swann obtained William Little as his attorney, and, by the time the case came to court in October 1727, Little had risen to the office of attorney general. At this juncture Little informed the General Court that he would not prosecute Swann, adding that the governor had assented to dismissing the case. Cain, ed., *North Carolina Higher-Court Minutes, 1724–1730*, CRNC, VI, 180, 453–454.

The indictment does not specify why Swann had been called before the Currituck justices in the first place, but his alleged behavior reported in the indictment suggests extreme drunkenness and disorderly conduct. The possibility that Byrd was alluding to this particular case is enhanced by the fact that William Little, at first the attorney acting in Thomas Swann's defense and then the official of the court who quashed the prosecution, was also one of the North Carolina commissioners on the expedition and the defendant was related to one of North Carolina's surveyors. Such an ironic passage would be especially satisfying to Byrd, since it would reflect badly on the disorderly Carolina populace, the ineffectual local courts, and the corrupt colonial officials, all with one blow.

136. John Lawson (1674–1711), the naturalist, North Carolina surveyor general, and cartographer, had been a member of the 1710 boundary commission, which, despite its failure, was accurate in this measurement. Lawson did not discuss the boundary or the location of the mouth of the Nottoway River in his accounts of his travels.

137. *BL* (April 2): "Here some of the Meherrin Indians came to visit us who are now removed from their Town att the Mouth of Meherrin River for fear of the Cataubas, who cutt off 14 of them last year, the rest take refuge now amongst the English on the East Side of Chowan."

On the Meherrin response to colonization and their history at the time of the Dividing Line expedition, see Shannon Lee Dawdy, "The Meherrin's Secret History of the Dividing Line," *North Carolina Historical Review*, LXXII (1995), 386–415. Byrd's distrust of the Meherrin can be traced to skirmishes with Anglo-Virginians in the wake of Bacon's Rebellion, seemingly at odds with their alliance with Virginia during the rebellion itself. Still more troubling was the rumor of Meherrin support for King Hancock's southern Tuscarora in the war of 1711, a rumor supported by the discovery of clothing taken from the German Protestants killed in North Carolina in Meherrin possession. *Council*, III, 291; Dawdy, "The Meherrin's Secret History," 403–406.

138. *Meteor:* In early modern usage, a meteor denoted "any atmospheric or meterological phenomenon" *(OED)* and thus included lightning.

139. *Cheveaux de Frize:* defensive battle devices consisting of rows of large, pointed timbers fastened together in a row, used to stop cavalry charges. In the *Virginia Gazette,* Sept. 24–Oct. 1, 1736, there is a reference to the Russian army's resourceful use of these devices in attacking a Tartar fortress: "Their Ladders being too short to scale the Precipice, they clapp'd *Cheveaux de Frize* upon one another, and clamber'd up, in spite of the Shower of Darts and Arrows which the Tartars pour'd on them."

140. It has not been possible to identify a source for Byrd's measurement of the Jordan. Descriptions are variable; most travelers compare the Jordan to more familiar rivers, as when Jean de Thévenot described the river as "perhaps half as broad as the *Seine* at *Paris*," in *The Travels of Monsieur de Thevenot into the Levant* (London, 1687), 193 *(Hayes* 100). The Seine averages around 400 feet in width, making Thévenot's comparison 200 feet, or 67 yards.

Sir Thomas Browne noted that Bellonius and other authorities observed "the River *Jordan,* not far from *Jericho,* is but such a Stream as a Youth may throw a Stone over it, or about eight fathoms broad." "Observations upon Several Plants Mention'd in Scripture," 25, in *The Works of the Learned Sir Thomas Brown, Kt.* (London, 1686). Henry Maundrell, in *A Journey from Aleppo to Jerusalem,* explained that the Jordan has two banks. The first marked the flood stage, about a furlong (220 yards) from the regular banks, where the Jordan is notably smaller: in "breadth it might be about twenty yards over" (81–82). Edward Wells deferred to Maundrell in *An Historical Geography of New Old Testament,* 37 (*Hayes* 2078).

141. *Charles Anderson:* Carolus Anderson (ca. 1694–1753), who had patented land in Virginia on the south side of the Meherrin River. The "Surveyors' Journal or Field Book" entry for April 4 noted, "At 15 Chains from the West side of Meherrin Carolus Anderson's bore S. 1 Chain." This means the Dividing Line placed his lands in North Carolina. In the *Secret History* Byrd comments that Anderson's given name Carolus is "learned," for it is the Latin form of "Charles." However, this was not an affectation but a family name. Indeed, Carolus Anderson himself was probably illiterate, for he signed his will with an X. *NCHGR,* I (1900), 165.

142. William Kinchen (d. 1736) owned land in Isle of Wight County, Virginia; between 1702 and 1726 he took out patents for 510 acres. Kinchen was a vestryman at the church near Smithfield from 1724 to 1736 and served as justice of the peace in 1726 and sheriff in 1729. The line placed his house in North Carolina by a mile. The fact that he continued to participate in the political life of Virginia confirms the success of the Virginia Commissioners' negotiations to make variances when the line split properties. Kinchen also appears in a few North Carolina records, including a petition to relocate the seat of the government of Bertie Precinct, and his 1736 will identifies him as "William Kitching, of Perquimans." He was married to Elizabeth Ruffin, daughter of Robert Ruffin of Surry County. Boddie, *Seventeenth Century Isle of Wight County,* 230; *C&P,* III, 61, 320; Hugh Drysdale, "The Present State of Virginia with Respect to the Colony in General," *VMHB,* XLVIII (1940), 145; Cain, ed., *Records of the Executive Council, 1664–1734,* CRNC, VII, 299; *NCHGR,* I (1900), 56; *Boyd,* 111.

143. *BL* (April 5): "The Commissrs. considering the great Fatigue already undergone & the Danger of Rattle Snakes in this advanced Season determined to proceed no further on the Line till the Autumn."

144. Samuel Kindred, who patented 670 acres on Horse Meadow Branch, Isle of Wight County in 1724 and 1727. *C&P,* III, 283, 339.

145. Bolton's Ferry crossed the Nottoway River near Buckhorn Swamp Creek, on the east side docking on the property of John Simmons; hence it was also sometimes called Simmons' Ferry.

146. Byrd uses terms from the construction of early modern European fortifications. A *puncheon* is a piece of roughly dressed timber, used as an upright in framing. A *palisade* is a fence or wall made of pales (stakes) fixed in the ground. A *scalade* is an attack by scaling walls of a fortified place, using ladders *(OED).*

147. Byrd's description bears a close resemblance to Smith's account of Indian accommodations a hundred years earlier:

> Their houses are built like our Arbors, of small young springs bowed and tyed,
> and so close covered with Mats, or the barkes of trees very handsomely, that
> notwithstanding either winde, raine, or weather, they are as warme as stooves.

However, unlike Byrd, Smith reported that the smoke in the arbors was provided with a more efficient exit. Though dwellings were "very smoaky, yet at the toppe of the house there is a hole made for the smoake to goe into right over the fire." See Smith, *Generall History*, in *Smith*, II, 116; cf. *A Map of Virginia*, in *Smith*, I, 161–162. See also Samuel Clarke, *A True and Faithful Account of the Four Chiefest Plantations of the English in America . . .* (London, 1670), 7; Clarke reproduced Smith verbatim and without acknowledgment. Byrd's description also closely resembles Banister, whose account might also have been influenced by Smith:

> Their houses are of bark bore up by small saplins bent archwise after the manner of
> an arbour, and are very close and warm in the winter.
> —*Banister*, 383

A still closer analogue, however, is the version Beverley expanded from Banister:

> The manner the *Indians* have of building their Houses, is very slight and cheap;
> when they would erect a *Wigwang*, which is the *Indian* name for a House, they
> stick Saplins into the ground by one end, and bend the other at the top. . . . Their
> Chimney, as among the true Born *Irish*, is a little hole in the top of the House, to let
> out the Smoak, having no sort of Funnel, or anything within, to confine the Smoke
> from ranging through the whole Roof of the Cabbins, if the vent will not let it out
> fast enough. The Fire is always made in the middle of the Cabbin.
> —*Beverley*, book 3, 11

There remains a curious disagreement between Byrd and Beverley: the former says there is not and the latter says there is a smoke hole in the Indian and Irish houses. Beverley's illustration of Indian dwellings (table 3, book 3) distinctly shows smoke holes.

148. Again, Byrd's description of the furniture follows the same sequence as Smith's description, which Byrd's paragraph closely resembles:

> Against the fire they lie on little hurdles of Reeds covered with a Mat, borne from the
> ground a foote and more by a hurdle of wood. On these round about the house they
> lie . . . some covered with mats, some with skins.
> —*Generall History*, in *Smith*, II, 116; *Map of Virginia*, in *Smith* I, 162

149. *Tort*—i.e., "taut." In *Generall Historie*, Smith also described a drum fashioned by stretching a skin over the mouth of "a great deepe platter of wood" tightened at the corners with "a small rope they twitch them together till it be so *tought and stiffe, that they may beat upon it as upon a drum*." *Smith*, II, 120 (emphasis added); *Map of Virginia*, in *Smith* I, 167.

150. A *matchcoat* was originally a coat of furs worn by Indians. Smith's glossary of indigenous Chesapeake words defines *Matchcores* as "Skins, or garments" (*Map of Virginia*, in *Smith*, I, 136; *Generall Historie*, in *Smith*, II, 130). Later, in the Indian trade matchcoats were heavy wool coats supplied by traders; duffield matchoats were sometimes awarded

as prestige items. Colonial governments attempted to monitor the movement of treaty nations by issuing striped matchcoats, without which travel beyond specified boundaries was forbidden.

Spartan women were legendary for their virtue, simplicity, and patriotism. Their usual clothing was modest but practical: they wore a *peplos* (tunic) slit along the leg to allow freedom of movement; see Sarah B. Pomeroy, *Spartan Women* (Oxford, 2002), 25. Byrd might have had in mind the occasion when Spartan women went out to fight a besieging army, won, and met their men on the way back. As the Jesuit scholar François Pomey explained, the men at first thought the women were an enemy force until "the Women shewed both by Words and by Deeds, that they were their Wives (Modesty forbids a plainer Explanation)." *The Pantheon . . .* (London, 1722), 127.

151. Byrd's reference to "Ethiopian" mistresses is obscure; it may refer to an as-yet-unidentified discussion of miscegenation. On the exoticism of Africans in Europe, Shelby T. McCloy has observed:

> Throughout most of the eighteenth century there was miscegenation in France, as also in the colonies. Until the 1760's there appears to have been little if any racial feeling, the Negro being regarded as a curiosity from a far-off land. A taste for the exotic was paramount in Europe during the age of the Rococo, and the Negro appears to have carried an attraction even as did the "learned" Chinese and the simple or "natural" American Indians.
> —"Negroes and Mulattoes in Eighteenth-Century France," *Journal of Negro History,* XXX (1945), 287–288

Solomon's mistress, the Queen of Sheba, was often identified as Ethiopian, and the *Song of Song*'s praise of her dark beauty became a common topos of exotic beauty in early modern writing.

Sad-colour'd: "dark or deep in color; sorrowful; deplorable" *(OED).*

152. The practice mentioned here, providing an honored guest with an overnight companion, is known to ethnographers as sexual hospitality. Though first-contact European colonists wrote of the practice, it is not certain how widely the custom was practiced, nor among which Indian nations, nor how long it persisted after first contact.

153. *Ladys that Game:* Byrd draws a parallel between the conduct of Indian and European women. In Byrd's day the word "game" meant "to play, sport, jest; to amuse oneself," most often appearing in conjunction with card play and gambling. The word also meant "to indulge in amorous play" *(OED)* and sometimes indicated prostitution. This sense would appear to fit Byrd's view of indigenous sexuality at the same time that it allows him to assume a rakish tone.

154. A standard charge of early writers on native customs. In the early seventeenth century George Percy reported, "I saw Bread made by their women which doe all their drugerie. The men takes their pleasure in hunting and their warres" ("Observations Gathered out of a Discourse of the Plantation of the Southerne Colonie in *Virginia* by the *English,* 1606," in Samuel Purchas, *Purchas His Pilgrimes* [London, 1625], IV, 1689 [*Hayes* 83]). Similarly, Smith, in *Generall Historie,* observed: "The men bestow their times in fishing, hunting, warres, and such manlike exercises, scorning to be seene in any woman-like exercise,

which is the cause that the women be verie painefull and the men often idle" (*Smith*, II, 116; *A Map of Virginia*, in *Smith*, I, 162). See also *Banister:* "The women plant and tend the corn, dress skins, tote, that is carry burdens, and do all drudgery both at home and abroad: the men do little or nothing but hunt" (382). John Ogilby also explained: "The drudgery of all laborious sorts of Work, and the management of all domestick Affairs, lies wholly upon the *Indian* Women, who are made meer Slaves by their Husbands" (*America: Being the Latest, and Most Accurate Description of the New World* [London, 1671], 158).

155. Byrd alludes to the retreat of the Dutch cavalry in the Battle of Fleurus (July 1, 1690), during the War of the Grand Alliance (1689–1697). The duc de Luxembourg commanded the army of the Spanish Netherlands for France, and Prince Georg Friedrich of Waldeck commanded the army of the League of Augsburg, a coalition formed in 1686 of European countries opposed to France and called the Grand Alliance after England joined in 1689. The Battle of Fleurus was a shattering defeat for the alliance, partly because twenty-five thousand Spanish and Brandenburgh troops failed to reinforce the Dutch in time, and partly because of the retreat of the Dutch horse in the face of a far stronger French cavalry charge and infantry gunfire. The Dutch cavalry's losses were terrible: more than fourteen hundred killed and as many wounded. British commentators held the Dutch conduct in contempt.

156. In a meeting of the Council in Williamsburg, April 24, 1703, the Nottoway themselves petitioned for protection against rum:

> Complaint being made by the Nattoway Indians that the Inhabitants of this Colony carrying Rum into their Town may prove of very dangerous consequence, by reason that many of their men getting drunk therewith may at such times be made an easie prey to any strange Indians who shall invade them.
>
> His Excellcy by advice of her Majtys honble Council doth hereby strictly forbid and prohibit all Persons whatsoever to carry any Rum or other strong Liquor into the said Nattoway Town upon pain of suffering such punishmts as may justly be inflicted on them for their offending in a matter of such pernicious consequences.
> —*Council*, II, 316

The Council's decree became law shortly thereafter. In the "Act for prevention of misunderstandings between the tributary Indians, and other of her majesty's subjects of this colony and dominion," Article 13 contains these strict regulations:

> That if any person or persons shall . . . sell, or offer to sale, any rum, or brandy, within any town of the tributary Indians, or to any Indian, upon any land belonging to any such town; every such person or persons so offending, and being thereof lawfully convicted before any justice of the peace of the country where the offence shall be committed, shall forfeit and pay ten shillings current money, for every quart of rum, or brandy sold, or offered for sale, as aforesaid.
> —*Hening*, III, 468

The law was not strictly or consistently enforced. Byrd's diaries reveal that on at least one occasion he himself supplied rum to Nottoway visitors at Westover. *LD*, 510 (Mar. 23, 1721).

157. *Mr. Boyle's Charity:* Robert Boyle (1627–1691), the preeminent natural philoso-

pher of his day, left a great part of his estate to charitable purposes. He directed his executors that after bequests and legacies the residual of his estate should go to charity, and he especially recommended "the laying of the greatest part of the same for the advance or propagation of the Christian religion amongst infidels." With the help of Boyle's nephew, Virginia Commissary James Blair, the executors settled two forty-five-pound per annum allowances on Harvard College and on the Society for the Propagation of the Gospel in Foreign Parts, and the remainder to the College of William and Mary, especially the Indian School. His will is reproduced in an appendix in *The Works of the Honourable Robert Boyle* (London, 1744), I, 103 (*Hayes 1944*). For an account of the way the College of William and Mary became "the preferred beneficiary," see Herbert Lawrence Ganter, "Some Notes on 'The Charity of the Honourable Robert Boyle, Esq., of the City of London, Deceased,'" *WMQ*, 2d Ser., XV (1935), 12–14.

158. The Saponi, the Tutelo, and the Monaca (once the primary group) all belonged to the Monacan Confederacy, a loosely knit alliance of related Siouan peoples who originally lived along the rivers in what later became North and South Carolina and Virginia. On the Monacan Confederacy, see James Mooney, *The Siouan Tribes of the East*, U.S., Bureau of American Ethnology, *Bulletin*, no. 22 (Washington, D.C., 1894), 23; and Jay Hansford C. Vest, "From Nansemond to Monacan: The Legacy of the Pochick-Nansemond among the Bear Mountain Monacan," *American Indian Quarterly*, XXVII (2003), 781–806. The Saponi were the main participants in Governor Spotswood's program at Fort Christanna.

159. For more about Griffin, see Tate, "The Colonial College, 1693–1782," in Godson, Johnson, Sherman, Tate, and Walker, *The College of William and Mary: A History*, I, 53, 55, 59.

With the collapse of the Virginia Indian Company and the withdrawal of governmental support, the fort languished. Griffin then went to the Indian School at William and Mary; see "Brunswick County and Fort Christiana," *WMQ*, 1st Ser., IX (1900–1901), 216–218.

160. *The Most Christian King in Canada:* Byrd here refers to the French king Louis XIV. The early colonizers of New France hoped for the assimilation and conversion of the native peoples. However, as mentioned earlier, the official bounty of three thousand livres offered to Frenchmen who married native women was never actually granted, as Gordon Sayre has pointed out, because Jesuit clergy would allow marriages only with Christianized Indian women. In practice, the French-Indian cultural exchange generally went in the opposite direction: contact with Indians "had the effect of easing the transition of Frenchmen into Indian life and away from the colony, rather than solidifying the Frenchification of the Indians." After 1684, the official policy was reversed and intermarriage banned. Gordon Sayre, "Native American Sexuality in the Eyes of the Beholders, 1535–1710," in Smith, ed., *Sex and Sexuality in Early North America*, 41.

161. In considering the early colonists' judgment of the worth of the Indians as a people, Byrd adapts the arguments of the physician-philosopher Nehemiah Grew, whose 1721 *Cosmologia Sacra* was in his library, and Byrd might have known Grew from meetings of the Royal Society. Grew warns against judging individuals by commonly accepted external characteristics:

We are also to consider the Difference between Worth, and Merit, strictly taken. That is, a Man's Intrinsick; This, his Current Value. . . . Likewise, that the difference

between Men, is oftentimes more by Education, and Opportunities of Improvement, than by Nature. And where it is by Nature, we are the rather to remember, That it is the Divine Benignity, which hath distinguished us from others, and not our selves.
—*Cosmologia Sacra; or, A Discourse of the Universe as It Is the Creature and Kingdom of God* (London, 1701), 75 (*Hayes* 1140)

162. Colonists contracted for the services of felons transported from England for the duration of their sentence. The term "damsels"—an archaic word for a lady of noble birth—is comically inappropriate for transported women, who were usually thieves or prostitutes. Byrd's use of the word "purchase" emphasizes the latter sort.

163. Another satirical jab at Roman Catholicism, this passage echoes a phrase in [Pierre Lambert de Saumery], *The Devil Turn'd Hermit; or, The Adventures of Astaroth Banish'd from Hell* (London, 1741). The demon fell out of favor with a convent of nuns for failing to deliver promised gifts of sugar, coffee, and tea. They influenced his favorite, "a pretty young girl" in their charge, to abandon him as well, and Astaroth tells the narrator, "Her present gallant has been much more generous, and you know that nuns will never do any thing but for interest, but will sacrifice honour and conscience for ready money" (103).

164. *Pochoon:* puccoon (or, variously, pocones, pochone, pohcoon, poughkone, pecoon, poccoon, puckoon, *OED*), a plant producing red coloring, originally either bloodroot *(Sanguinaria canadensis)* or Carolina puccoon *(Lithospermum canescens)*. The dye, as applied to the skin, was quite striking, and was described by many early travelers. In his *Generall Historie,* Smith noted:

> *Pocones* is a small roote that groweth in the mountaines, which being dryed and beate in powder turneth read. And this they use for swellings, aches, annointing their joynts, painting their heads and garments. They account it very precious and of much worth.
> —*Smith,* II, 110

Banister recorded that the Indians

> pulverize the roots of a kind of Anchusa or yellow Alknet which they call Puccoon and a sort of wild Angelica, and mixing them together with Bears oyl make a red ointment, which after they have bathed they anoint themselves cap-a-pe; this supples their skin, renders them nimble and active, and withall so closeth up the pores that they loose little of their strength by perspiration.
> —*Banister,* 379–380

Puccoon also deters lice and fleas. Beverley repeats Banister's words verbatim (*Beverley,* book 3, 52). See also *Oldmixon,* 308. Wright (*Prose Works,* 222) speculated that the plant might be pokeweed *(Phytolacca americana),* but modern ethnobotany does not support this identification.

165. Henry Harrison, a prominent planter in Surry County, was appointed sheriff in 1712, justice of the peace in 1726, burgess in 1715, 1718, 1720–1722, 1723–1726, and member of the Executive Council in 1731. Harrison, his brother Nathaniel, and several others took up twenty thousand acres in Henrico, Surry, and Prince George Counties between

1719 and 1721. *Council,* III, 394, 515, 526, 548, IV, 234; H. R. McIlwaine, ed., *Journals of the House of Burgesses of Virginia, 1712–1714* . . . (Richmond, Va., 1912), viii–xi.

166. *Herod:* Byrd's reference is to Josephus, *Antiquities of the Jews* 15.11 (*Hayes* 8, 153, 1227, 1610, 1742, 1826). *Fields* (329) notes that Byrd made a similar observation in his manuscript essay "Religion" (Virginia Historical Society, Mss2 B9964 a 7).

167. On July 16, Byrd had written Fitzwilliam suggesting the starting date be postponed. Fitzwilliam was apparently not amenable, for only Byrd and Dandridge signed the letter that went to the North Carolina Commissioners.

168. *To the South Sea:* That is, directly across the continent to the Pacific. Contemporary maps often featured such speculative east-west colonial boundaries reaching to the westernmost parts of the continent. See Margaret Beck Pritchard and Henry G. Taliaferro, *Degrees of Latitude: Mapping Colonial America* (Williamsburg, Va., 2002).

169. *The Jilt Hazard:* Hazard (taking a risk, or chance) is proverbially undependable. Hazard is a mode of fortune, upon which it is never safe to rely. English poets personified Fortune as an elusive, undependable, fickle woman, often called a jilt.

170. Earlier in September Byrd reported to Governor Gooch about acquiring supplies for the Virginia party: "I have desird Maj. Bolling to furnish us with 1200 lb. of biscuit, that is, 200 of white, & 1000 of brown, & have agreed with an Indian trader to employ his horses to carry it." Byrd to Governor William Gooch, Sep. 5, 1728, *Correspondence,* I, 388.

171. *What the Nuns call Martyrdom:* any compromise with the virtue of chastity, especially loss of virginity. Byrd may be referring to a controversy at the abbey of Fontevraud, reported by Pierre Bayle in a volume that was in Byrd's library. The abbé, Robert d'Arbrissel, had been accused of "lying with his Nuns, not indeed with a design of enjoying them, but only that he might have the greater temptations to struggle with." Bayle quoted a letter written by one of the abbé's accusers:

> It is reported that you permit some of the women to live in too familiar a way with you; and that you do not blush to lie frequently with, and among them, in the night. If you now do, or have ever done this, you have found out a new, unheard of, but fruitless kind of martyrdom.

Another complained that the abbé chose only the most beautiful women whenever he would thus expose himself to temptation. After considering the historical accuracy of the charge, Bayle paused to consider the matter from the women's point of view:

> Is it not morally certain, that a woman, who consents to let a man come and lie in the same bed with her, is very much disposed not to refuse him any favour? Does not the proximity of a man's body inflame such a disposition in her? Does not such a proximity awake thoughts and desires from which she otherwise would be exempted, were she to lie alone?

Those "holy ramblers, those seekers after alluring opportunities" are morally responsible for any loose desires they may awaken in the young nuns. Truly, Bayle concluded, in the case of temptations of the flesh, flight is better than confrontation. *A General Dictionary, Historical and Critical* (London, 1734–1741), V, 280–283 (*Hayes* 1999).

172. *Case-Bottle:* "A bottle, often square, made to fit into a case with others," or "A bottle protected by a case" *(OED).*

173. *Fountains Creek:* the unfortunate Indian trader for whom the creek was named was John Fontain, or Fountain, a free black trader active in the early eighteenth century. This is probably the John Fountain who, with several colleagues, had been accused in 1704 of stirring up trouble between South Carolina Indians, allegedly encouraging the Tuscarora to "cut off the Inhabitants" of North Carolina. Charges were dismissed for lack of evidence, though suspicions lingered (*Council,* II, 381, 390, 402, 405). Pace Wright (*Prose Works,* 225), the creek was *not* named for John Fontaine, brother to the expedition's chaplain and a member of Spotswood's expedition of 1716.

Icarus: son of the Greek inventor Daedalus. Escaping from Crete on wings of his father's making, Icarus flew too close to the sun and perished in the sea when the wax holding feathers in the wings melted. The part of the Aegean where Icarus fell is still known as the Icarian Sea.

174. The expedition's supply of Peruvian bark must have run out during the expedition, for, when several of the men came down with "Intermitting Feavers," they were treated with alternate (though "proper") remedies. The bark of the dogwood *(Cornus officinalis* or *Cornus alba)* was widely used in Indian remedies. The Cherokee chewed the bark for headache and used the root bark both for breaking fevers and as a stimulant, and medical historians record its use well into the twentieth century "as a quinine substitute," that is, to reduce fever. Substituting dogwood for Peruvian bark was standard practice among Anglo-Virginians, too. John Mitchell, the Virginia physician and botanist, sent samples of dogwood to his former botany professor, Dr. Charles Alston of Edinburgh, because, as he explained, its bark was generally used as a quinine substitute. *NAE;* John K. Crellin and Jane Philpott, *Herbal Medicine Past and Present* (Durham, N.C., 1990), 197–199; Edmund Berkeley and Dorothy Smith Berkeley, *Dr. John Mitchell: The Man Who Made the Map of North America* (Chapel Hill, N.C., 1974), 27.

175. *BL* (September 23): "The Ground through which the Line pass'd was so Intolerable full of Bushes that they could carry it only 4 M. 5 poles, This Days work cut Meherrin River the 5th Time & Last our people was glad to gett rid of a River whose Meanders had given them so much trouble."

176. The bustard is one of a genus of birds in Europe and Asia remarkable for size and running power; the great bustard *(Otis tarda)* is the largest European bird. Byrd's suggestion of a connection was incorrect; the North American turkey *(Meleagris gallopavo)* is not in fact related to the bustard.

It was Smith in the *Generall Historie* who mentioned pointing arrows with turkey spurs: "Another sort of arrowes they use made of Reeds. These are peeced with wood, headed with splinters of christall, or some sharp stone, the spurres of a Turkey, or the bill of some bird." *Smith,* II, 117; *A Map of Virginia,* in *Smith,* I, 163.

177. John Clayton described "Ague-grass" or "Star-grass" in a letter published in the *Philosophical Transactions.* This plant, now known as colicroot or star grass *(Aletris farinose),* was used by the Catawba and other Indian nations. An alternative possibility is star grass that Boyd identified as a member of the "Hypoxidae" (*Boyd* 152), probably *Hypoxis stellatis* or other varieties. Byrd's description resembles this plant, which does have grass-like radiating leaves near the ground. However, the root is a round bulb typical of the lily family, in no way resembling a snake's rattle.

178. At least seventy years before the period of Byrd's writing, the method of killing

rattlesnakes used by Captain Silas Taylor of Virginia, "attested by two credible persons in whose presence it was don," was reported to the Royal Society:

> The Wild *Penny-royal* or *Ditany* of *Virginia,* groweth streight up about one foot high, with the leaves like *Penny royal,* with little blue tufts at the joyning of the branches to the Plant, the colour of the Leaves being a reddish green . . . the Leaves of it bruised are very hot and biting upon the Tongue: and of these, so bruised, they took some, and having tyed them in the cleft of a long stick, they held them to the Nose of the *Ratle-Snake,* who by turning and wriggling laboured as much as she could to avoid it: but she was killed with it, in less than half an hour's time, and, as was supposed, by the scent thereof; which was done *Anno* 1657 in the Month of *July,* at which season, they repute those creatures to be in the greatest vigour for their poison.

Byrd must have been aware of Taylor's experiments with rattlesnakes, recorded in the *Philosophical Transactions;* Taylor's accounts were reproduced in Charles Owens's *Natural History of Serpents,* also in Byrd's library. "Of the Way of Killing *Ratle-Snakes,*" Royal Society, *Philosophical Transactions,* I (1665–1666), 43. Charles Owen reproduced this report in *An Essay towards a Natural History of Serpents* (London, 1742), 92 (*Hayes* A28).

179. *BL* (September 25): "Wee kill'd a Rattle-Snake wth 2 Rattles Wee provided 3 sorts of Rattle-Snake Root, In case our Men should be bitt——."

180. *BL* (September 26): "on their Way the Chain Carriers kill'd 2 Large Rattle Snakes, over which 3 several [per]sons step'd without Hurt—one of these Vipers struck with great Fury att a Horse but grazed his teeth only on its Hoof without Hurt."

181. Saint Andrew's cross *(Hypericum hypericoides)* is another traditional Indian remedy for snakebite *(Plants; NAE).*

182. Byrd is here drawing on the expanded third edition of John Tennent's *Every Man His Own Doctor; or, The Poor Planter's Physician* (Williamsburg, Va., 1736): "The readiest Cure I know, is St. *Andrew's Cross,* which grows providentially all over the Woods, during the whole Season that the *Snakes* are mischievous" (62). Tennent proclaimed the doctrine of providential remedies as a central premise to his book: "Providence has been so good, as to furnish almost every Country with Medicines proper for the Distempers incident to the Climate" (7).

Byrd probably also knew this doctrine from some of the same sources Tennant drew upon. The notion that Providence supplies localized antidotes to poisons is very old. Writing of the snakes of India, Aelian observed:

> Now these snakes are injurious to man and all other animals. But the same land produces herbs that counteract their bites, and the natives have experience and knowledge of them, and have observed which drug is an antidote to which snake, and come to one another's aid with all possible speed and in their effort to arrest the very violent and rapid spread of the poison throughout the body. And the country produces these drugs in generous abundance to help when needed.
> —Aelian, *On the Characteristics of Animals* 12.32, trans. Schofield

Pliny celebrated the generous indulgence of nature (the earth): "When a serpent has stung a man . . . she produces medicinal herbs, and is ever fertile for man's benefit" (*Pliny* 2.63.155). The argument was Christianized in early modern natural philosophy;

294 } Notes to Pages 127–128

William Derham, in his *Physico-Theology,* likewise sees divine providence in antidotes to the viper's poison:

> But although the infinitely wise Creator hath put it in the Power of such vile Animals
> to chastise us, yet hath he shewed no less Wisdom and Kindness in ordering many,
> if not most of them so, as that it shall be in the Power of Man, and other Creatures to
> obviate or escape their Evils.
> —*Physico-Theology,* 56 (see also 420–422 on local medicines)

Derham mentions vegetable and mineral antidotes and adds that many venomous animals "carry their Cure, as well as Poison, in their own Bodies." The principle that plants may be found locally to combat local problems is a corollary of the early modern Christian conviction that the natural world is designed for human benefit.

183. *BL* (September 26): "on our Way wee saw several Meadows & Branches full of tall Reeds, in which Cattle will keep themselves fat great part of the Winter, but the Hoggs do great damage by rooting them up."

Byrd's comparison of the destruction to pasture by hogs and destruction to grapevines by goats is problematic. Contrary to his assertion that goats were never sacrificed to Bacchus, they were in fact *always* the sacrificial animal of choice for Dionysus or Bacchus. Classical scholar John Potter explained the goat was sacrificed precisely because it was inimical to Bacchus for eating the grape vines; see *Archaeologia Graeca; or, The Antiquities of Greece* (London, 1706), I, 228 (*Hayes* 132). This tradition is preserved in Virgil's *Georgics,* Horace's *Odes,* Ovid's *Metamorphoses,* in the works of numerous other Roman writers, and in studies by early modern classical scholars. Despite Byrd's familiarity with classical sources, he seems to have got the story backward—or, perhaps, he was proffering an elaborately obscure erudite joke.

184. The cart's motion was "Planetary" because it followed an erratic course, like the planets. The word *planet* came originally from the Greek term for wandering stars, distinguishing them from the fixed stars *(OED).*

185. The plant Byrd called "the true Ipocoacanna" was "Indian Physick" (*Gillenia stipulata* or *Porteranthus trifoliatus*), which later came to be called "American Ipecac." Though a reliable emetic, it is not in fact related to the Brazilian shrub ipecacuanha *(Cephaelis ipecacuanha).*

186. Herodotus reported that the water of the Choaspis was boiled and carried to the king in silver vessels (*Herodotus* 1.188). Pliny elaborated: "The kings of Parthia drink only of the Choaspes and the Eulaeus; water from these rivers is taken with them even into distant regions" (*Pliny* 31.21.35). According to Athenaeus, "large numbers of four-wheeled mule-carts carrying boiled water of this sort in silver vessels" were transported for the Persian king (*Deipnosophistae* 2.45b, in S. Douglas Olson, ed. and trans., *The Learned Banqueteers* [Cambridge, Mass., 2006–2012], I, 55).

According to the Roman grammarian Solinus, the River Choaspis "is of so sweete tast, that as long as it runneth wythin the borders of Persia, the Kinges of Persia reserved it only for their owne drinking: and when they should go a progresse any whither, they carryed of the water of it with them" (*The Excellent and Pleasant Worke of Iulius Solinus Polyhistor,* trans. Arthur Golding [London, 1587], sig. Aav). Nicolas Venette, the French physician whose work Byrd extracted at length in his commonplace book, also noted that the wise kings of Persia had healthful water brought to them "du fleuve de'*Eulée* ou de *Choaspe*" (*De la genération de l'homme ou tableau de l'amour conjugal* [Cologne, 1696], 267). Montaigne moralized this story in his essay "Of Vanity:

> *Nature* has plac'd us in the World free and unbound, we imprison our selves in certain streights, like the Kings of *Persia,* who oblig'd themselves to drink no other Water but that of the River *Choaspes,* and foolishly quit claim to their right of Usage in all other streams; and as to what concern'd themselves, dried up all the other Rivers of the World.
>
> —*Essays of Michael Seigneur de Montaigne,* trans. Charles Cotton, 4th ed. (London, 1711), III, 260–261 (*Hayes* 847, 1443, 2447)

187. In his account of the Cape of Good Hope, Peter Kolb on several occasions praised the purity of the springs on Table Mountain. Byrd, whose writing of ginseng and Hottentots demonstrates his interest in South Africa, drew this observation from Kolb, who observed,

> I have been assur'd by several Commanders of *Danish* Ships, that every *Danish* Royal Ship, returning from the *Indies,* is charg'd to touch at the *Cape,* and take in a large Cask of the *Cape*-Spring Water for His *Danish* Majesty; this water being look'd upon at the Court of *Denmark* as the brightest, the sweetest and the most salubrious Water in the World.
>
> —Peter Kolben, *The Present State of the Cape of Good-Hope* . . . (London, 1731), II, 22 (*Hayes* 128)

A lengthy review of Kolb, with extracts and commentary, was published in *Present State of the Republick of Letters,* VII (1731), including this passage (370).

188. Byrd here describes the *upstream* geography of these rivers.

189. Epaphroditus Benton appears in both Virginia and North Carolina records as a planter and operator of a ferry over the Chowan River. He patented and sold land in both colonies. *C&P,* III, 25, 41, 334; des Cognets, ed., *Virginia Duplicates of Lost Virginia Records,* 68; Hofmann, *Chowan Precinct, North Carolina, 1696 to 1723,* 82, 191, 223; *NCHGR,* II (1901), 293.

190. The Indian Trading Path, also known as the Occaneechi Path, led through the Piedmont from Fort Henry south and west to the lands of the Cherokee and the Catawba.

191. Either water grass *(Bulbostylis barbata)* or southern water grass *(Luziola fluitans)* *(Plants).*

192. Colonel Robert Mumford (or Munford) was a prominent planter in Prince George County, where he was also justice of the peace, colonel of the militia, and burgess in 1720–1722. In his youth he had worked for Byrd and was instrumental in recruiting the Virginia men for the 1728 expedition. See section "Dramatis Personae," below.

193. *BL* (September 28): "Wee killd a Large Rattle Snake with a Squirrel in His Maw, our Chain-Carriers kill'd another."

194. This popular myth of natural history is exceedingly common, so much so that it is not necessary to credit Byrd as an eyewitness, though doubtless he saw plenty of squirrels

and plenty of snakes. Among travelers in Virginia and Carolina, the myth nearly always appears as an account at second hand. For instance, Indians told John Lederer:

> The Indians . . . told me that it was usual in these Serpents, when they lie basking
> in the Sun, to fetch down those Squirrels from the tops of trees, by fixing their
> eye steadfastly upon them; the horrour of which strikes such an affrightment into
> the little beast, that he has no power to hinder himself from tumbling down into
> the jaws of his enemy, who takes in all his sustenance without chewing, his teeth
> serving him onely to offend withal.
> —*Lederer,* 15–16

195. *Mr. Whitfield's Flocks:* George Whitefield (1714–1770), the great Methodist preacher, was known for preaching in England to very large crowds out of doors. Forbidden to preach in New England and South Carolina, Whitefield did preach in Virginia and North Carolina in 1739 and returned to Virginia twice more in 1746 and 1755. In Williamsburg, he met with an unusually warm reception from Commissary Blair, who invited him to preach in Bruton Parish Church, with Governor Gooch and several members of Council in attendance. Blair even entertained Whitefield as a guest in his own home. The *Virginia Gazette* for Dec. 14–21, 1739, reported:

> *Williamsburg—*On *Sunday* morning last, the Rev. Mr. Whitefield preach'd at
> our Church, on these words, *What think ye of Christ?* There was a numerous
> Congregation, and 'tis thought there wou'd have been many more, if timely Notice
> had been given of his preaching.

Byrd's diary does not mention Whitefield's visit to Williamsburg. He had been in Williamsburg himself on official business earlier that week, dining with Blair on the tenth and breakfasting on the eleventh, returning to Westover on the twelfth. On Sunday, December 16, the day Whitefield preached in Williamsburg, Byrd notes in his diary that he "went not to church" (that is, he did not attend the church at Westover). Thus, Byrd was almost certainly not present for Whitefield's preaching, and he left no record of his feelings about missing the opportunity to hear the sermon.

Colonial newspapers reported outdoor preaching only with Whitefield's next visit in 1740, when he preached in each of the colonies, sometimes to large crowds, fifteen thousand one evening in the spring of 1740 on Society Hill in Philadelphia. Although it is not possible to determine what newspapers Byrd read, it should be noted that both London and colonial newspapers reported so regularly on Whitefield's outdoor preaching in England that the news would have been difficult to avoid. Whitefield himself noted the efficacy of the newspapers, as he passed through North Carolina after his visit to Williamsburg. He rested at the house of one Colonel O——, who was delighted to learn the identity of his guest.

> Upon which he was so rejoiced that he could not tell how to express his satisfaction.
> His wife also seem'd most anxious to oblige, and they were only concerned that they
> could do no more for us. The honest old man told us, that his son-in-law, who lived
> about three miles off, ever since he heard of me in the *News,* wished that I would
> come thither. This is not the first time, by many, that I have found the advantage

of the things my adversaries have inserted in the public papers: they do but excite people's curiosity, and serve to raise their attention, while all men of seriousness and candour naturally infer that some good must be doing where such stories and falsities are invented.

—*George Whitefield's Journals* (London, 1960), 373

On the importance of newspaper coverage to Whitefield's mission, see Frank Lambert, *"Pedlar in Divinity": George Whitefield and the Transatlantic Revivals, 1737–1770* (Princeton, N.J., 1994), 52–94, 103–110. Churchmen wrote anti-Whitefield tracts and letters to newspapers, but a good many reports were less hostile. One example will suffice. The *American Weekly Mercury* (Philadelphia) for July 5–12, 1739, reprinted an item from a London paper:

> *London, May 7:* Yesterday Morning at Seven o'Clock the Rev. Mr. Whitefield preach'd to about 20000 People in Moorfields; and in the Evening at Six o'Clock to about 50000 on Kennington-Common, where were about eighty Coaches, etc among whom were many Gentlemen and Persons of Distinction; and to morrow Evening at Six o'Clock he is to preach on Kennington-Common again.

It should be noted here that Byrd's reference to Whitefield's outdoor preaching provides internal evidence for a writing-revision period extending at least to 1739 or 1740.

196. *Fern Rattlesnake Root:* Probably rattlesnake fern *(Botrychium virginianium),* taking its name from the resemblance of the sporangia to a snake's rattle. Byrd's description matches this plant, and not—as Boyd (158) maintains—*Prenanthes serpentaria.*

197. *Seneca Rattlesnake Root:* This plant *(Polygala senega)* had long been used medicinally by Native Americans as an antitoxin, a tonic, a stimulant, an antispasmodic, and an aid for digestive complaints *(Plants; NAE).* Its efficacy in the diseases Byrd lists here was championed by Virginia doctor John Tennent and adopted by British pharmacopeias.

Pleurisy: Inflammation of the pleura (the membrane around the lungs), characterized by pain in the chest or side, with fever, loss of appetite, etc.; usually caused by chill. In Byrd's time the term was used generally for chest and lung complaints.

Dropsy: A morbid condition characterized by the accumulation of watery fluid in the serous cavities or the connective tissue of the body.

198. The "messenger" was Charles Kimball, who in fact held the government post of interpreter to several tributary Indian nations, including the Saponi. The *BL* manuscript says only that "Sapponi Indians arrived In our Camp & offer'd their Service to attend us Wee agree'd with Two to Kill Deer, Turky &c for us."

199. Here Byrd again uses the term *latitude* metaphorically for geographical region. Passing out of the "Latitude of Corn" simply means leaving the region of agricultural cultivation, so the horses could no longer be furnished with grain or other provender.

200. Pliny remarked on the resemblance of the bear's paw to the human hand. Byrd's observations on the taste of bear meat closely resemble Lawson, who declared:

> I prefer their Flesh before any Beef, Veal, Pork, or Mutton; and they look as well as they eat, their fat being white as Snow, and the sweetest of any Creature's in the World. If a Man drink a Quart thereof melted, it will never rise in his stomach.

Lawson also noted that in the spring, during the herring run the meat is "nought," that is, unpleasantly flavored, and he also reported that the "Paws of this Creature are held as the best bit about him" (*Lawson*, 116). Catesby too noted that in the spring bear meat

> is also very rank and unsavory, but at all other times is wholesome, well tasted, and I think excelled by none; the fat is very sweet, and of the most easy digestion of any other. I have myself, and have often seen others eat much more of it, than possibly we could of any other fat without offending the stomach.
> —*Catesby*, 156

201. *BL* (October 1): "Wee made an Observation in a Clear Night & found the Variation 2 d: 30 m: so that it did not dimish *[sic]* by our approach to the Mountains, nor by our advanceing towards the West or by our distance from the Sea."

202. The skeletal horse of Hudibras, the mock-epic knight in English satirist Samuel Butler's *Hudibras*:

> His strutting Ribs on both side show'd
> Like Furrows he himself had plow'd:
> For underneath the Skirt of Pannel,
> 'Twixt every two there was a Channel.
> —*Hudibras* . . . (London, 1710), canto 1, part 1, ll. 445–448

Governor Spotswood gave Byrd a copy of *Hudibras* in 1710, and Byrd had several other copies (*Hayes* 843, 885, 990, 999), one of which might have been the copy William Mayo read aloud on the expedition, to the discomfort of the chaplain, as Byrd describes in *The Secret History;* and *SD*, 230.

203. Probably wild ginger *(Asarum canadensis)*, which grows in the Virginia–North Carolina region. Lawson included wild ginger in his list of Carolina herbs: "Asarum wild in the Woods, reckon'd one of the Snake-Roots" (*Lawson*, 78). However, among the many medicinal uses of *Asarum* listed in the *Native American Ethnobotany* database, treating snakebite is conspicuously missing. Wild ginger is not related to ginger *(Zingiber officinale)*, which has tall, reedy leaves. Nor is it the same as Asarabacca *(Asarum europaeum)*, a medicinal plant also known as hazelwort or European wild ginger. The plants resemble each other only very slightly *(Plants; NAE)*.

As a practical dispenser of physic, Byrd must have known asarabacca as a purgative and emetic used in the treatment of agues, dropsies, ailments of the liver and spleen, and greensickness; see Nich[olas] Culpeper, *Pharmacopoeia Londinensis; or, The London Dispensatory* (London, 1653), esp. 4, 14 (*Hayes* 713). The plant appears in many of his medical books, including Thomas Willis, *Dr. Willis's Practice of Physick* . . . (London, 1681), 91 (*Hayes* 631); Gideon Harvey, *The Family-Physician, and the House-Apothecary,* 2d ed. (London, 1678), 57–58 (*Hayes* 764); [George Bate], *Pharmacopœia Bateana; or, Bate's Dispensatory,* 5th ed. (emended by William Salmon) (London, 1720), 583 (*Hayes* 663, 760); Nich[olas] Culpeper, *The English Physician Enlarged* . . . (London, 1718), 22–24 (*Hayes* 722); [Nathan Bailey], *Dictionarium Rusticum, Urbanicum and Botanicum* . . . (London, 1726), s.v. *asarabacca;* Philip Miller, *The Gardener's Dictionary* (London, 1733) (*Hayes* 1838); [Pierre] Pomet, *A Compleat History of Druggs* (London, 1712), 279. The eminent physician John Radcliffe (celebrated in Byrd's *Commonplace Book,* §396) included powdered leaves of asarabacca as a component of his "Cephalick Snuff," in *Dr. Radcliffe's Practical Dispensatory* (London, 1730), 157 (*Hayes* 681).

204. *BL* (October 2): "wee forded a Creek call'd Massa-Mony and Indian Name for Paint Creek from Red Oher found on its Banks." The "celebrated fable" concerns the death of Thammuz, beloved of Ishtar, the story that by syncretism became merged with the legend of Venus and Adonis. Byrd must have known the story from his reading of Lucian's *De Dea Syria:*

> There is also another Wonder in this Country of *Byblis,* and that is, a certain River runneth out of Mount *Libanus* into the Sea, the Name whereof is *Adonis:* Now this River, every Year, is turned into Blood, and being so discoloured, falleth into the Sea; a considerable part whereof it tinctures of a Purple Colour, thereby signifying to the *Byblians,* the Time when to begin their Mourning. They also further relate, how that at that very time *Adonis,* being wounded on *Libanus,* and his Blood running into the Water, changed the Colour of the River, and giveth the Denomination to the Current. Which Things are reported by the Vulgar; But a certain *Byblian* of Credit related to me another Cause of this Accident, which was this: The River *Adonis* (said he) passeth through Mount *Libanus,* which consists of a very red Mold; so that strong Winds, arising at that time of the Year, carry the Earth into the River, and turns it into a reddish Colour: which the *Byblian* assured me was the true Cause of that Accident, and not the Blood they talk of. However, admitting this Relation to be true, yet the arising of this Wind always at such a certain time, seemeth to me to be something extraordinary.
> —*The Works of Lucian,* (London, 1711), I, 244

Byrd, whose diaries record frequent reading in the works of Lucian and whose library included a remarkably large number of editions and translations of that author (*Hayes* 984, 1353, 1484, 1496, 1522, 1555), must have been struck by the parallel between the Adonis and the Massimony when he observed the river stained with red ochre. However, he might have recalled the legend as it was related in any of a number of intervening sources.

205. *Pride:* This usage (for testicles, "cods," or scent sacs) is not registered in the *OED.* See note 365, below.

206. Catesby observes of the wildcat, "This beast is about three times the size of a common cat" (*Catesby,* 156), and Lederer comments on its ferocity: "This creature is something bigger then our English Fox . . . fierce, ravenous, and cunning" (*Lederer,* 16).

Of panthers, Catesby reported, "They rarely attack a man, but fly from him" (*Catesby,* 156).

207. Lawson reported that the flesh of the panther "looks as well as any Shambles-Meat whatsoever"—that is, as good as meat prepared by a butcher—adding that "a great many People eat him, as a choice Food" (*Lawson,* 118). Catesby also praised panther meat: "Their flesh is white, well tasted, and is much esteemed by the Indians and white people" (*Catesby,* 156). However, Lederer asserted "their flesh, though rank as a Dogs, is eaten by the Indians" (*Lederer,* 17).

208. Catesby divided Carolina soil into three categories: rice land (low, wet ground suitable only for cultivating rice); "*Oak* and *Hiccory-land*" (so called because these trees "grow mostly on good Land"); and pine barrens. For Catesby as for Byrd, the perpetual

criterion is utility. *The Natural History of Carolina, Florida, and the Bahama Islands,* rev. ed. (London, 1771), I, iii.

209. Catesby observed that the thick hair hanging over the buffalo's eyes severely limited its vision, adding, "But this obstruction of sight is in some measure supplied by their good noses, which is no small safeguard to them" (*Catesby,* 157).

210. "They range in droves" (*Catesby,* 157).

211. Compare with the entry in the "Surveyors' Journal or Field Book" entry for October 3: "Tuskerooda Creek call'd so by the Saponi Indians, who kill'd a Tusk and flung him into this Creek. the Indian Name is Heewahomony."

212. *Bluewing Creek:* A tributary of the Hicootomony River (now called Hyco River), Blue Wing Creek was named for the blue-winged teal *(Anas discors).* Lawson described the birds: "The Blue-Wings are less than a Duck, but fine Meat. These are the first Fowls that appear to us in the Fall of the Leaf, coming then in great Flocks, as we suppose, from *Canada,* and the Lakes that lie behind us" (*Lawson,* 148).

213. *Sugar-Tree:* Byrd describes the sugar maple *(Acer saccharum).* Banister noted that the Indians get one pound of sugar from ten pounds of sap (*Banister,* 375), and Beverley followed Banister: "The *Indians* make One Pound of Sugar, out of Eight Pounds of the Liquor" (*Beverley,* book 2, 21). Byrd's recipe calls for a higher proportion of sap to sugar.

214. *Spice Trees:* the spicebush or benjamin bush *(Lindera benzoin),* a shrub or small tree that grows in bottomlands and near streams. The leaves are aromatic, especially when crushed, and the red berries black when dried *(Plants).*

215. The turkey buzzard, also known as the turkey vulture *(Cathartes aura),* is the most common vulture in North America. These birds tend to nest communally, often in cliffs, treetops, and riverbanks and are sometimes seen circling in groups high in the air.

216. The *BL* manuscript dates the Carolina Commissioners' announcement to the following day, on Sunday morning.

217. The terms of the commission given to the Virginia Commissioners explicitly authorized the survey to continue should their North Carolina counterparts refuse to participate or continue.

218. The proverbial expression, to "lick something into shape," originated with the ancient belief that bear cubs are born a shapeless lump of flesh, which the mother slowly licks until it assumes its proper form (*Pliny* 8.14.126; Aelian, *On the Characteristics of Animals* 2.19, 2.33, 6.3). On the history of this notion, see Sir Thomas Browne, *Pseudodoxia Epidemica; or, Enquiries into Very Many Received Tenents, and Commonly Presumed Truths* (London, 1646), 116–117 (*Hayes* 1928).

219. In the *Secret History* Byrd declares that Fitzwilliam returned to Williamsburg to make himself available to act as a justice in General Court, a remunerative assignment for which his position on Council qualified him. He did not succeed in obtaining this benefit, nor did he receive full payment for his part in the expedition.

220. I have encountered no other prohibition against mixing meats among early accounts of Indian customs. Indeed, the contrary seems to occur frequently. Lahontan, for instance, reported a ceremonial feast along the Ohio River that featured "Broth made of several sorts of Meat." *Lahontan,* I, 106 (*Hayes* 73, 160).

221. Both coltsfoot *(Tussilago farfara)* and maidenhair fern *(Adiantum capillus-veneris)* were used medicinally as *pectorals,* that is, a medicine for chest complaints. Coltsfoot,

an introduced plant that quickly spread throughout the eastern seaboard, took its name from the Latin *tussis,* or cough (Crellin and Philpott, *Herbal Medicine Past and Present,* I, 170). The plant was well known to European herbalists; Nicholas Culpeper outlined its use:

> The fresh Leavs, or Juyce, or a Syrup made therof is good for a hot dry Cough, for wheesings and shortness of breath. The dry Leavs are best for those that have thin Rhewms, and Distillations upon the Lungs, causing a Cough, for which also the dried Leavs taken as Tobacco, or the Root, is very good.
> —*The English Physitian; or, An Astrologo-Physical Discourse of the Vulgar Herbs of This Nation* (London, 1652), 36–37 (*Hayes* 722)

Coltsfoot was not a native species, and charting its western invasive migration during Byrd's era would be difficult or impossible. If it had not spread beyond the inhabitants, Byrd possibly mistook another member of the Aster family for coltsfoot.

The maidenhair fern grows on the banks of streams and in moist rocky places everywhere in the Virginia–North Carolina region. It was another staple of English herbal medicine; Culpeper noted: "The Decoction of the Herb Maidenhair being drunk, helpeth those that are troubled with the Cough, shortness of breath." *The English Physitian,* 132.

Byrd's "Rule in Botanicks"—that plants have stronger medicinal virtues in their native habitat—should be weighed against the botanical efforts of the New Science and with Byrd's own advocacy of New World medicines in his letters to English correspondents. Explorers and investigators routinely sent seeds and live plants back to England, where they were grown and tested in several major herb gardens and discussed in meetings of the Royal Society. Banister and Catesby actively supported the collecting project, and Byrd and his father also sent plants home to England. Indeed, in his botanical correspondence with Sir Hans Sloane, Byrd repeatedly stressed the efficacy of American medicinal plants, especially ginseng, and recommended them for export.

222. *BL* (October 8): "our Cloths suffer'd very much by the Bushes and it was as much as our Hands could do to preserve our Eyes in our Heads our poor Horses had much had enough to do to Drag the bagage thro' the saplins wch obliged them to draw as well as carry."

223. The *BL* manuscript, however, says that the fresh water at the camp site was what "the poor Men wanted that was behind with the heavy baggage, but they comforted themselves with that cordial for all Distresses a dram of Rum." By the time this passage was revised for *The History of the Dividing Line,* the rum seems to have disappeared.

224. Lawson explains, "The Wolf of *Carolina,* is the Dog of the Woods. The *Indians* had no other Curs, before the Christians came amongst them. They are made domestick" (*Lawson,* 119). See also Catesby: "Wolves were domestic with the Indians, who had no other dogs before those of Europe were introduced" (*Catesby,* 157).

225. *Tantalus:* mythical Greek king, best known for the manner of his punishment in Tartarus after death. The son of Zeus by a nymph, Tantalus had stolen ambrosia from the gods and brought it back to his realm, along with other divine secrets. He compounded this offense by offering the gods a meal consisting of the body of his son Pelops. For these crimes he was thrust into the lowest regions of punishment and placed waist-deep in a body of water overhung by grape vines. If he bent down to slake his thirst, the water re-

ceded; if he reached up for the fruit, the vines lifted it just beyond his reach. The story proverbially indicates impossible satisfaction.

226. The *BL* manuscript also makes the connection: "Wee found the land for the most part exceeding good, a never failing proof of which, was, that Angelica grow plentyfully in It."

Three species of Angelica grow in the Virginia–North Carolina region: hairy angelica *(Angelica venenosa),* filmy angelica *(Angelica triquinata),* and purple-stemmed angelica *(Angelica atropurpurea).* The Royal Society correspondent John Clayton remarked that it "grows generally on a rich sandy Ground." "A Letter fron the Revd. Mr. John Clayton . . . to Dr. Grew," *Philosophical Transactions,* XLI (1739–1741), 155. Modern botanists agree that the preferred habitat of angelica is moist ground *(Plants),* which is often rich soil as well. Angelica is an aromatic medicinal plant, the root and seeds of which were used in many preparations. According to Chambers's *Cyclopaedia,* the plant owes its name to

> its great Virtue as an Alexipharmic or Counterpoison. . . . It is reputed cordial, stomachick, cephalick, aperitive, sudorifick, vulnerary, resists Poison, etc. tho the chief Intention wherein it is now prescribed among us, is, as a Carminative.
> —Ephraim Chambers, *Cyclopaedia; or, An Universal Dictionary of Arts and Sciences* (London, 1728), I, 88 *(Hayes* 1833)

The effect of a "cordial" is "stimulating, 'comforting,' or invigorating the heart; restorative, reviving, cheering." An "alexipharmic" counters poisons *(OED).* Cf. John Ray, *Historia plantarum* (London, 1686), I, 434 *(Hayes* 786, 1917). Other authorities recommended angelica as a cordial; in *The English Physitian* Culpeper wrote that the candied stalks and roots "warm and comfort a cold Stomach" (4).

Though all Byrd's medical books include angelica in recipes for many ailments, I have not found any published reference to the effect of the plant as a "dry dram." Perhaps by this phrase Byrd means consuming in the field the raw or dried ingredients of medicinal plants ordinarily used to make a cordial. This may be the case, for John Pechey declared, "The Root of it is allow'd by all Physicians to be very cordial and Alexipharmick" *(The Compleat Herbal* [London, 1707], 5 *[Hayes* 758]). Pierre Pomet said spirit of angelica "chears the Heart, and revives the Spirits to a Miracle" *(Compleat History of Druggs,* I, 39–40 *[Hayes* 650]).

227. The ancients esteemed the intelligence and social organization of cranes; Aristotle explained the cranes' use of sentinels:

> When they settle down, the main body go to sleep with their heads under their wing, standing first on one leg and then on the other, while their leader, with his head uncovered, keeps a sharp look out, and when he sees anything of importance signals it with a cry.
> —*Aristotle,* I, 958; *History of Animals* 9.614.b28–b30 958. Cf. *Pliny* 10.30.58–60; Aelian, *On the Characteristics of Animals* 3.13.

228. Leo Africanus noted the "wonderfull witte and subtletie" of African apes in the organization of their raids on people's crops:

> They live upon grasse and corne, and go in great companies to feede in the corne fieldes, and one of their companie which standeth centinell or keepeth watch and

ward upon the borders, when he espieth the husbandman comming, he crieth out and giveth as it were an alarme to his fellowes, who every one of them flee immediately into the next woods, and betake themselues to the trees.
—*A Geographical Historie of Africa,* trans. John Pory (London, 1600), 343

The compiler of histories Thomas Salmon drew on Leo Africanus:

They have large Monkeys or Baboons in the *Hottentot* Countries; but these are Animals so well known every where, that they need not a particular Description. They frequently rob the *Dutch* gardens at the *Cape* in Troops; which, 'tis said, they manage with a great deal of Artifice, setting their Centinels at every Avenue, to prevent Surprize, and planting a Line of their Camrades, from the Orchard, or Garden, to the Hills: That they toss the Fruit from one to the other, and thereby make a surprizing Dispatch in pilfering a Garden. When their Centinels discover any Person approaching, they set up a great Cry, and alarm the rest, who immediately take to their Heels.
—*Modern History; or, The Present State of All Nations,* XXXVI (London, 1735), 146

229. *Mountain Partridge:* In Byrd's day the terms partridge and quail were often inter-changeable, making it difficult to narrow the possibilities to one specific bird. It seems likely, however, that Byrd's "Mountain Partridge" was the bobwhite *(Colinus virginianus).* The bobwhite is about the size of a domestic chicken. The name "Dunghill Hen" refers to the range of domestic poultry, everywhere in the barnyard including the manure pile. In John Ray's publication of the seventeenth-century ornithologist Francis Willughby, for in-stance, the common domestic fowl appears under this heading: "The Dunghill Cock and Hen," in *The Ornithology of Francis Willughby* . . . (London, 1678), 154 (*Hayes* 790).

230. One of the key purposes of exploration was discovery of things of use in devel-oping the land. Limestone, a sturdy but workable stone, is useful in constructing foun-dations and walls, and slate is useful for roofing, flooring, and paving. Most early mod-ern exploration and colonial development narratives mentioned similar resources; see, for instance, Beverley: "They have besides in those upper Parts . . . Slate for Covering, and Stones for Building, and Flat-Paving in vast Quantities, as likewise Pibble-Stones" (*Beverley,* book 2, 9).

231. *BL* (October 10): "the Stream of this beautifull River ran about 2 Miles an Hour with water as clear as Crystal, the Bottome of It was gravelly & spangled very thick with small Flakes of Mother of Perle that dazzel'd our Eyes & the Sand on Either shore sparkled wth the same shining Substance."

The story of the company's dreams of wealth was added later, a passage that bears a striking resemblance to Beverley's description of gold fever among the Jamestown colo-nists:

They found . . . a fresh Steam of Water springing out of a small Bank, which wash'd down with it a yellow sort of Dust-Isinglass, which being cleansed by the fresh streaming of the Water, lay shining in the Bottom of that limpid Element, and stirr'd up in them an unseasonable and inordinate Desire after Riches.
—*Beverley,* book 1, 17

232. It was commonly believed that mineral deposits were to be found distributed in those parts of the world sharing the same latitudes. This notion might have evolved from the theory of the growth of minerals, which began with Aristotle's proposition that minerals were formed from wet or dry exhalations from the earth. Scholastic and early modern writers credited this theory, right up to the corpuscular operations of the Cartesian mechanical theory of matter. Byrd could have read about the growth of minerals in any number of sources; his library was well stocked with physiotheological works and other premodern geographic and geological texts. For a detailed account of the theory of the growth of minerals, see David R. Oldroyd, *Thinking about the Earth: A History of Ideas in Geology* (Cambridge, Mass., 1996), esp. 17. My account of this theory relies on Oldroyd.

By extension, it apparently seemed natural that certain minerals should be produced by certain climatic regions, and thence that parallel minerals should grow in parallel latitudes. Byrd would have encountered the parallel latitude theory in writers such as John Smith, for instance, who declared, "Onely this is certaine, that many regions lying in the same latitude, afford Mines very rich of divers natures" (*Smith*, I, 145, 156, II, 102, 111). Others as well shared Smith's optimism. In 1622, Patrick Copland compared Virginia's potential to the rich resources of Japan:

> *Iapan* (I say) lying under the same latitude that *Virginia* doth, aboundeth with all things for *profit* and *pleasure,* being one of the mightiest and opulentest Empires in the world, having in it many rich Mines of Gold and Silver.
> —*Virginia's God Be Thanked; or, A Sermon of Thanksgiving for the Happie Successe of the Affayres in Virginia* . . . (London, 1622), 12

Similarly, in 1650, Edward Williams compared Virginia with China:

> To conclude, what ever else China may presume to boast of: Whether Nitre, Allum, Quicksilver, Rhubarb, and China Root, of which some wee have already discovered: If wee consider the parallell in Latitude, the equality of temperate Climate, the parity in soile, and its fertility, the similitude in brave Navigable Rivers, the unanimous congruity and consent in divers knowne Commodities, wee shall have an ample basis to ground conjectures upon, that what ever singularity of Nature that Nation may imagine her selfe Victorious over others will be found equall in this Garden of the World, this aemulous Rivall of China, Virginia.
> —*Virginia: More Especially the South Part Thereof, Richly and Truly Valued* . . . (London, 1650), 19

Thus Byrd, like other explorers, expected it would be possible to find similar deposits of precious metals in parallel locations. Reflecting on lessons learned on the expedition, Byrd recommends in *The History of the Dividing Line* that explorers should use surefooted mountain ponies to "search more narrowly for Mines and other Productions of Nature without being confin'd to level Grounds."

233. Byrd justifies the expectation of finding gold with a remarkable flood of learned ancient and modern parallels. It was Aristotle who first noted that the river Oxus (Amudarya) in Bactria and the Theodorus (Tagus) in Iberia carried gold downstream and deposited it on the banks. Pliny also described the way gold washed down in the detritus of rivers such as Spain's Tagus, Italy's Po, Thrace's Maritza, Asia Minor's Sarabat, and India's

Ganges. The geographer Strabo also mentioned gold dust washing downriver: "The Pactolus River flows from Mt. Timolus; in early times a large quantity of gold-dust was brought down in it, whence, it is said, arose the fame of the riches of Croesus and his [forefathers]. But the gold-dust has given out" (*The Geography of Strabo,* trans. Jones, 3.2.3–4, 13.4.5; see also Aristotle, *On Marvelous Things Heard* 833b19–833b21, 1277; *Pliny* 33.21.66). Byrd might have drawn on the Greek originals for these references, or he might have drawn on more recent texts quoting these ancient sources, such as Father Jerom Merolla da Sorrento's travels. On arriving in Lisbon, Merolla da Sorrento commented:

> The Waters here are a proportionable mixture of Salt and Sweet, the latter being
> plentifully pour'd out by the River *Tagus,* so famous for its Golden Sands, and not
> unlike the *Lydian Pactolus,* according to *Juvenal* and others.
> —Jerom Merolla da Sorrento, *A Voyage to Congo, and Several Other Countries, Chiefly
> in Southern-Africk,* in Awnsham Churchill and John Churchill, comps., *A Collection of
> Voyages and Travels* (London, 1704–1732), I, 656 (*Hayes* 79)

The notion that gold dust could be suspended in water had scriptural sanction, for a tradition recorded by Pierre Bayle claims that Moses ground the golden calf to powder and cast it into a river:

> Moses melted down the gold again, and divided it into very minute particles, which,
> thrown into the water, became imperceptible, like those which are said to be found
> in the Tagus and Pactolus.
> —*A General Dictionary,* I, s.v. Aaron

And Robert Boyle, in his "Hydrostatical Paradoxes," wrote of gold suspended in river water:

> 'Tis well known, that *European* traders yearly bring great quantities of gold from
> the coast of *Guinea,* which is wash'd, or pick'd out of the sand. And, even in *Europe,*
> there are rivers whose sand is inrich'd by grains of gold. For this, the *Tagus,* that runs
> by *Lisbon,* and *Pactolus* were famous among the ancients.
> —*The Philosophical Works* (London, 1725), II, 325 (*Hayes* 140, 1944)

Byrd might also have read about African gold in William Bosman's African travels, which locate three sources of river-borne gold: mines in the hills, "at, and about some Rivers and Water-falls; whose violence washeth down great Quantities of Earth, which carry the Gold with it," and on the seashore where "there are little Branches or Rivulets into which Gold is driven from Mountainous Places, as well as to the Rivers." William Bosman, *A New and Accurate Description of the Coast of Guinea . . .* (London, 1705), 80 (*Hayes* 112).

234. Byrd's account of the disappointment of not finding gold bears a curious resemblance to similar passages in Smith's works. In *The Generall Historie,* Smith reported that spring floods "wash from the rocks such glistering tinctures, that the ground in some places seemeth as guilded, where both the rocks and the earth are so splendent to behold, that better judgements then ours might have beene perswaded, they contained more then probabilities." Several pretenders to the refiner's skill attempted to find gold ore in "the washings from the mountaines," where "shining stones and spangles" in the rivers

promised well. But the projectors, "flattering themselves in their owne vaine conceits to have beene supposed what they were not," were ultimately disappointed. Both the event and the authors' moralizing are remarkably similar to Byrd's version. *Smith*, II, 102, 111.

Mica, sometimes called isinglass, occurs either as sparkling fragments intermixed with soil or as deposits of shiny, easily separated semitransparent layers, serviceable as a substitute for glass panes. Note that Lederer, traveling fifty years earlier beside the Pamunkey River, also discovered a deposit of "Isinglas," which he "peeled off in flakes about four inches square" (*Lederer*, 17).

235. Pliny reported that the reed or bamboo of India grows so large that "sometimes a single section between two knots will make a canoe that will carry three people," and again that "a single length between knots, if we can believe it, will actually serve as a boat" (*Pliny* 7.2.21–23, 16.65.162).

236. The term "cane" indicates a very wide range of wetland plants, including reeds, rushes, cattails, and other large grasses. Byrd's canes were probably giant cane or switch cane *(Arundinaria gigantea),* a wetland plant native to the Southeast *(Plants).*

237. *BL* (October 10): "the Indian begg'd Earnestly of our Cook that He would not make a Soup of Venison & Turky so together for fear of spoiling his Luck & causing a famine, but wee would not Humour his Superstition to Convince him there was nothing in it." Again, the *BL* manuscript reports on the following day that "the Indian" would not bring a turkey he'd shot to camp, "least wee should offend the God that presides over Hunting, by boiling the beasts of the forest & the fowls of the Air together."

Biblical proscriptions included mixing different crops in the field and mixing different kinds of thread in weaving material for clothing. Jewish dietary laws (kashrut) originating in Deuteronomy and Leviticus do not in fact forbid the mixing of different kinds of meat in one container.

238. *Oleo:* "a dish of Spanish and Portuguese origin, composed of pieces of meat and fowl, bacon, pumpkins, cabbage, turnips, and other ingredients stewed or boiled together and highly spiced; by extension, Any dish containing a great variety of ingredients, a hotchpotch" *(OED).*

239. The possibility of viniculture was a frequent topic with early explorers and projectors. In his *Generall Historie,* Smith wrote:

> Of vines great abundance in many parts that climbe the toppes of the highest trees in some places, but these beare but few grapes. Except by the rivers and savage habitations, where they are not overshadowed from the sunne, they are covered with fruit, though never pruined or manured. Of those hedge grapes we made neere twentie gallons of wine, which was like our French Brittish wine, but certainly they would prove good were they well manured.
> —*Smith*, II, 108–109; c.f. *Map of Virginia,* in *Smith*, I, 152

(Smith's editor Barbour explains that "French Brittish" meant Breton.) Beverley also offered comments on the possibilities of making good wine from native grapes:

> The *French* Refugees at the *Monacan* Town have lately made a sort of Clarret, tho' they were gather'd off of the wild Vines in the Woods. I was told by a very good Judge, who tasted it, that it was a pleasant, strong, and full body'd Wine. From

which we may conclude, that if the Wine was but tolerably good, when made of the wild Grape, which is shaded by the Woods, from the Sun, it would be much better, if produc'd of the same Grape cultivated in a regular Vineyard.
—*Beverley*, book 2, 18–19

In a letter to Lord Orrery, Byrd suggested that with a little industry the colonists could make something of the native vines: "The wanton vine twined round every tree, reproaching the laziness of our people who will not improve them." Byrd to Charles Boyle, earl of Orrery, May 26, 1729, *Correspondence*, I, 396.

240. Catesby: "A young bear fed with autumn's plenty, is a most exquisite dish" (*Catesby*, 156). See also Charles Carter, *The Complete Practical Cook; or, A New System of the Whole Art and Mystery of Cookery* (London, 1730): "A young Bear is certainly as good Meat as the World affords, no Flesh is sweeter, of a better Relish or finer Colour" (198).

241. *Dog-kind:* The dietary squeamishness Byrd mentions alludes to the categorization of bears in the zoological category, "the Dog-kind." In Byrd's day various pre-Linnaean systems of zoological classification had been devised, separating animals into groups according to key morphological and behavioral features. Byrd might have encountered this approach in any number of scientific texts; the most likely influence was Bishop Wilkins, the Royal Society's expert in scientific language, who lucidly explained the prevailing system: "Beasts, may be distinguished by their several shapes, properties, uses, food, their tameness or wildness, etc." Vivaparous animals were divided into three classes: whole-footed, cloven-footed, and clawed. Animals with claws were divided into the rapacious and not rapacious. Rapacious animals, in turn, were divided into the "Cat-kind, having a roundish head," and the "Dog-kind, whose heads are more oblong." John Wilkins, *An Essay towards a Real Character, and a Philosophical Language* (London, 1668), 156 (*Hayes* 93).

In Byrd's era the term *venison* denoted meat taken from any game animal, not restricted to deer, as in the modern usage. His assertion that the Chinese reserved dog meat for their elite is not traceable to early modern accounts of travelers to China, who rather asserted the contrary. See, for instance, Gaspar da Cruz, "A Treatise of *China,* and the Adjoyning Regions," in Purchas, *Purchas His Pilgrimes,* Third Part (London, 1625), 179: "It is a meate which the base people doe eate" (II, 179).

242. Pliny and Aelian were the principal circulators of this myth, which eventually achieved proverbial status (*Pliny* 8.14.128; Aelian, *On the Characteristics of Animals* 6.3). Byrd must have misremembered Mandeville's fictional narrative of his travels to Jerusalem, for no reference to bears occurs in Mandeville's fabulous history, *The Voyages and Travels of Sir John Mandevile . . .* ([London], 1704).

243. Compare with Catesby on bears: "Vegetables are their natural food, such as fruit, roots, etc. on which they subsist wholly until cold deprives them of them. It is then only they are compelled by necessity, and for want of such food, to prey upon hogs and other animals" (*Catesby*, 156).

244. Catesby: "In March when herrings run up the creeks, and shallow waters to spawn, bears feed on them" (*Catesby*, 156).

245. Byrd's account of Bearskin's creation myth closely resembles Smith's report on the religion of the tidewater "Salvages" in his *Generall History:*

There is one chiefe God that hath been from all eternitie, who as they say when he first purposed to make the world, made first other gods of a principall order, to be as instruments to be used in the Creation and government to follow: And after the Sunne, Moone, and Starres, as pettie gods; and the instruments of the other order more principall.

—*Smith*, II, 78

246. Compare with T[homas] A[my], *Carolina; or, A Description of That Country, and the Natural History Thereof* (London, 1682), 13–14: "The *Indians* in *Carolina* parch the ripe Corn, then pound it to a Powder, putting it in a Leathern Bag: When they use it, they take a little quantity of the Powder in the Palms of their Hands, mixing it with Water, and sup it off: with this they will travel several days." Similarly, Banister observed: "Instead of bread they usually carry Rocka hominy, that is Indian corn parched and beaten to flower" (*Banister*, 376). Cf. Beverley: "Sometimes also in their Travels, each Man takes with him a Pint or Quart of *Rockahomonie*, that is, the finest *Indian Corn*, parched, and beaten to powder" (*Beverley*, book 3, 18).

247. *Wild rosemary:* Probably bog rosemary *(Andromeda polifolia)*, not related to the European herb rosemary *(Rosmarinus officinalis)*. The leaves resemble rosemary, but without the scent *(Plants)*.

248. *Fetching a compass:* a nautical term for making a circuit, or taking a roundabout course.

249. Probably the Canada goose *(Branta canadensis)*; many of the earliest colonists wrote of goose migrations. James Mooney has identified *Cohunks* as a Saponi word, in *The Siouan Tribes of the East*, 47.

250. The Sawro—variously known as the Cheraw, Sara, Saraw, Suala, Keyawee, Xuala— originally lived far south along the Blue Ridge in the Carolinas. Not long after Lederer encountered them in 1670, they settled on the Dan River in the region of the Virginia–North Carolina border. But the incursions of the northern Indians forced them to move southeast, joining their North Carolina allies, the Keyauwee. But there they encountered the hostility of the colonists, who declared war against the Cheraw and their allies. With the end of the Yamassee War, the remaining Cheraw apparently joined the Catawba to the south (Mooney, *Siouan Tribes of the East*, 56–61).

251. Byrd here describes either shagbark hickory *(Carya ovata)* or southern shagbark hickory *(Carya caroliniae-septentrionalis)*, both of which grow in the region *(Plants)*.

252. The pignut hickory *(Carya glabra)* produces a sweet nut. Byrd here lists members of the walnut family capable of producing comestible oil in the appropriate mill or press. In 1682, Robert Ferguson observed:

The *Indian-Natives* get a sweet Oyl out of the *Hickery Nutt*, which is much of the nature of our *English Walnutt;* but not so racy, nor the Kernal so plump and pleasant . . . which Oyl may be much more improved, and substituted in lieu of *Oyl Olives.*
—*The Present State of Carolina*, 11

Boyd erred in transcribing this term as "Nig-nuts," which he identified as "the fruit of the brown hickory" (*Boyd*, 208).

253. Slate, a relatively soft and easy-to-split sedimentary stone, was used for paving.

Hones or whetstones, fashioned from dense, fine-grained stone, were used for sharpening metal edges.

254. Wright identifies this phrase as a version of the proverbial saying, "Dear-bought and far-fetched are dainties for ladies" (*Prose Works,* 253).

255. Stephen Conrad Ausband suggests this eminence is one of the hills now known as "Mountain Hill," near the Dan River. *Byrd's Line: A Natural History* (Charlottesville, Va., 2008), 101.

256. Identifying this tree is difficult, since the name *butter-wood* is no longer in use. There is a butternut tree *(Juglans cinerea),* also known as white walnut, but it is not a member of the maple family. Its bark is a pale gray, much lighter than that of its relatives, the hickory, pignut, and black walnut. It may be that Byrd meant this tree, for there is no white maple in the maple family. It may be that he was describing the tree now known as chalk maple *(Acer leucoderm)* or the silver maple *(Acer saccharinum),* both of which grow in the region and can have a whitish or silvery cast to their leaves.

257. Alexander Irvin, appointed surveyor to the Virginia expedition. A graduate of Edinburgh University, Irvin was professor of mathematics at the College of William and Mary.

258. "Panther" was a name often given to the large North American cat now known as puma or cougar *(Felis concolor).*

259. Early accounts of exploration frequently placed lions and tigers in South America; see, for instance, Herman Moll on the wildlife of Amazonia: "There are also divers sorts of wild Beasts, as . . . some few Lions, Tigers, and Bears in the mountainous Tracts." *A System of Geography; or, A New and Accurate Description of the Earth . . .* (London, 1701), 210 (seond numbering).

260. Cf. *BL* (October 19): "wee crost Matrimony Creek so call'd from its being a Little Noisy."

261. *The Wart:* Ausband has identified this peak as the one now known as Chestnut Knob (*Byrd's Line,* 99).

262. Banister, Lawson, and Catesby all agree: "I cannot omit (though it be allmost incredible) to relate, that here are some years such clouds of pidgeons, they darken the air, the wind of their wings is like the noise of great waters, and they sit so thick, where they roost that their weight break down great limbs of trees" (*Banister,* 355). "I saw such prodigious Flocks of these Pigeons . . . that they had broke down the Limbs of a great many large Trees all over those Woods, whereon they chanced to sit and roost" (*Lawson,* 141). "Of these there come in winter to Virginia and Carolina, from the North, incredible numbers; insomuch that in some places where they roost . . . they often break down the limbs of oak with their weight" (*Catesby,* 61).

263. *Dung.* Lawson and Catesby: "But they seem to me to be a Wood-Pigeon, that build in Trees, because of their frequent sitting thereon, and their Roosting on Trees always at Night, under which their Dung commonly lies half a Foot thick, and kills every thing that grows where it falls" (*Lawson,* 142); "and leave their dung some inches thick under the trees they roost on" (*Catesby,* 61).

Breeding. Catesby: "The only information I have had from whence they come, and their places of breeding, was from a Canadian Indian, who told me he had seen them make their nests in rocks by the sides of rivers and lakes far north of the St. Lawrence River, where he said he shot them. It is remarkable that none are ever seen to return, at least this way, and what other route they may take is unknown" (*Catesby*, 61).

264. Byrd humorously alludes to Matt. 6:25–34, ironically mocking the company's *improvidence* with Matthew's injunction to trust Providence:

> Therefore I say unto you, Take no thought for your life, what ye shall eat, or what ye shall drink; nor yet for your body, what ye shall put on. Is not the life more than meat, and the body than raiment? Behold the fowls of the air: for they sow not, neither do they reap, nor gather into barns; yet your heavenly Father feedeth them. Are ye not much better than they? Which of you by taking thought can add one cubit unto his stature? And why take ye thought for raiment? Consider the lilies of the field, how they grow; they toil not, neither do they spin: And yet I say unto you, That even Solomon in all his glory was not arrayed like one of these. Wherefore, if God so clothe the grass of the field, which to day is, and to morrow is cast into the oven, shall he not much more clothe you, O ye of little faith? Therefore take no thought, saying, What shall we eat? or, What shall we drink? or, Wherewithal shall we be clothed? (For after all these things do the Gentiles seek:) for your heavenly Father knoweth that ye have need of all these things. But seek ye first the kingdom of God, and his righteousness; and all these things shall be added unto you. Take therefore no thought for the morrow: for the morrow shall take thought for the things of itself. Sufficient unto the day is the evil thereof.

Byrd's allusive satirical jab is particularly clever, especially immediately following his extended digression on those abundant "fowls of the air," the pigeons.

265. *Northern Savages:* warriors from the Five Nations of the Iroquois Confederacy, traditional enemies of the Catawba.

266. The *BL* manuscript does not mention smoke at all: "Woods had been so full of Mists & foggs for several Days past that Wee had quite lost sight of the Mountains." By the time Byrd polished his report to the Board of Trade, he noted that the atmosphere was smoky, not misty, suggesting a later revision.

If the air was smoky, the fires probably did not result from carelessness or accident of hostile Indians, as Byrd would have it. Rather, fires in that region were in all probability part of the long-established practice of forest burning to promote a balanced forest economy. Indeed, Omer C. Stewart has declared, Indian burning in North America "was almost universal" ("Burning and Natural Vegetation in the United States," *Geographical Review*, XLI [1951], 319). Erhard Rostlund and other agricultural historians have explained that the Indians set fires to keep down undergrowth, which both increased the food supply for deer and other game and made access to game easier for hunters. Therefore, Rostlund declares, "the open, parklike appearance of the woodlands" noted by Smith and other early writers, "the most common type of forest in the ancient Southeast, was mostly the work of man" ("The Myth of a Natural Prairie Belt in Alabama: An Interpretation of Historical Record," Association of American Geographers, *Annals*, XLVII [1957], 408). Stephen Adams explains that burning cleared the land to improve habitats for hunting and gathering, even creating openings in upland forests that "may have encouraged buffalo to migrate into Virginia" (*The Best and Worst Country in the World: Perspectives on the Early Virginia Landscape* [Charlottesville, Va., 2001], 35). Kenneth H. Garren has observed that the practice of burning "passed from Indians to the early white settlers to the extent that a law of North Carolina in 1731 required the burning of pastures and rangelands each March" ("Effects of Fire on Vegetation of the Southeastern United States," *Botanical Review*, IX [1943], 617).

267. *look all round the Hemisphere:* to watch "that half of the heavens seen above the horizon" *(OED)*.

268. Beverley: "For the *Indians* are very artful in following a track, even when the Impressions are not visible to other People, especially if they have any advantage from the looseness of the Earth, from the stiffness of the Grass, or the stirring of the Leaves, which in the Winter Season lye very thick upon the ground" (*Beverley*, book 3, 19).

269. Byrd refers to Saul's demand of David that he gather a hundred foreskins of the enemy in lieu of dowry for his daughter Michal:

> And Saul said, Thus shall you say to David, The king desires not any dowry, but an hundred foreskins of the Philistines, to be avenged of the king's enemies. But Saul thought to make David fall by the hand of the Philistines. Wherefore David . . . slew of the Philistines two hundred men and brought their foreskins, and they gave them in full tale to the king, that he might be the king's son in law. And Saul gave him Michal his daughter to wife.
> —1 Sam. 18:25, 27

270. Herodotus, reporting the war customs of the Scythians, explained that warriors carried the heads of slain enemies to the king to claim a reward:

> He scalps the head by making a cut round it by the ears, then grasping the scalp and shaking the head out. Then he scrapes out the flesh with the rib of an ox, and kneads the skin with his hands, and having made it supple he keeps it for a napkin, fastening it to the bridle of the horse which he himself rides, and taking pride in it; for he is judged the best man who has most scalps for napkins. . . .
> The heads themselves, not of all but of their bitterest foes, they treat in this wise. Each saws off all the part beneath the eyebrows, and cleanses the rest. If he be a poor man, then he does but cover the outside with a piece of raw hide, and so makes use of it; but if he be rich, he covers the head with the raw hide, and gilds the inside of it and so uses it for a drinking-cup.
> —Herodotus 4.64–65

Following Herodotus, Pliny reported the Scythian cannibals living north of the Dnieper drink from human skulls "and use the scalps with the hair on as napkins hung round their necks" (*Pliny* 7.2.12).

271. *Achilles:* Homer, *Iliad* 22. The name belonging in the blank space is Batis (also known as Vatis), the commander of a Persian garrison in Gaza. Alexander the Great, enraged at his resistance, ordered him to be dragged behind his chariot, in mock emulation of Achilles. Quintus Curtius, *History of Alexander* 4.6.26–29.

272. Though purporting to describe the "Northern Indians," Byrd's words very closely resemble Lawson's account of Saponi war customs:

Those Captives they did intend to burn, few Prisoners of War escaping that Punishment. The Fire of Pitch-Pine being got ready, and a Feast appointed, which is solemnly kept at the time of their acting this Tragedy, the Sufferer has his Body stuck thick with Light-Wood-Splinters, which are lighted like so many Candles, the tortur'd Person dancing round a great Fire, till his Strength fails, and disables him from making them any farther Pastime. Most commonly, these Wretches behave . . . with a great deal of Bravery and Resolution, esteeming it Satisfaction enough, to be assur'd, that the same Fate will befal some of their Tormentors, whensoever they fall into the Hands of their Nation.

—*Lawson,* 47

Indeed, Byrd's passage contains detail specifically belonging to the Virginia–North Carolina region, particularly the use of pitch pine splinters. "Lightwood" is a term used primarily in the Southeast, and the pitch pine grows in a more southerly climate than the northerly home country of the Five Nations.

273. The phrase "wild Prospect" has intrigued Byrd scholars, suggesting a proto-Romantic appetite for sublime landscape. Byrd used the phrase again in *A Progress to the Mines:* "There is a very wild prospect both upward and downward." *Prose Works,* 341.

Byrd of course predates Edmund Burke's *Philosophical Enquiry into the Origin of Our Ideas of the Sublime and Beautiful* (1757) by three decades, so Byrd probably used the phrase literally, as if to say simply, from here one can see a great deal of uncultivated landscape.

274. *Light:* "To come to or arrive in a place; to lodge in some position; to arrive at a point" *(OED).*

275. It is not clear where Byrd came up with the idea that bears have a double skull. It was not ancient zoology, for Pliny declared that only humans have double-crowned skulls. Pliny also insisted that the bear's head is his weakest part, and indeed bears have the weakest skulls among all the animals. *Pliny* 8.54.130, 11.48.133.

276. Here Byrd repeated his observation about bears belonging to the "Dog-kind," as well as his reference to the canine cuisine of China.

277. That is, William Mayo.

278. A tenet of early modern folk zoology was that bears do not have a breastbone, thereby imperiling their internal organs. Also, allegedly, the momentum of a downhill run could force their lights (lungs) to rise in their throats, or, as Byrd puts it in *SH*, "lest their Guts shou'd come out of their Mouths." I have not found a print source for this notion, but the widespread influence of this belief may be seen in a letter of Sir Thomas Browne, the great questioner of received knowledge, who advised his son to dissect a bear should the chance arise: "When the wether proves cold and fitt for dissections if you have opportunity, take notice of a beare: tis commonly sayd that a beare hath no breast bone, and that hee cannot well runne downe a hill, his heart will so come up toward his throat." Sir Thomas Browne to Edward Browne, June 28, 1679[?], in Simon Wilkin, ed., *The Works of Sir Thomas Browne* (London, 1852), III, 457–458.

279. Byrd uses a traditional biblical circumlocution: human beings were created in God's image (Gen. 1:26). By divine favor humans are at the top of the food chain as well

as ordinarily excluded from the circle of natural prey. In fact, the black or brown bears of Virginia rarely attack (or eat) people.

280. No source for this anecdote has been found.

281. Here Byrd repeats his jesting allusion to Matthew, connecting it with an allusion to the Lord's Prayer (Matt. 6:9–13, Luke 11:1–4).

282. *Dead Plane:* The word *dead* in the eighteenth century denoted "flat." Alternately, *dead* could be used as an intensifier meaning "unrelieved, unbroken; absolute; complete" *(OED),* and thus Byrd is describing a completely flat expanse of land, an extremely level plain.

283. Catesby: "The raccoon is somewhat smaller, and has shorter legs than a fox" *(Catesby,* 158).

284. John Josselyn also mentioned using raccoon fat as a salve in *New England's Rarities Discovered:*

> The *Raccoon* liveth in hollow trees, and is about the size of a *Gib Cat;* they feed upon Moss, and do infest our *Indian* Corn very much; they will be exceeding fat in Autumn; their flesh is somewhat dark, but good food roasted.
>
> Their Fat is excellent for Bruises and Aches.
>
> —*New-Englands Rarities Discovered: In Birds, Beasts, Fishes, Serpents, and Plants of That Country* (London, 1672), 17

Compare Lawson on raccoons: "The *Raccoon* is of a dark-gray Colour; if taken young, is easily made tame, but is the drunkenest Creature living, if he can get any Liquor that is sweet and strong. They are rather more unlucky than a Monkey." *Lawson,* 121.

285. Compare Byrd's description with Robert Fallam's journal: "It was a pleasing tho' dreadful sight to see the mountains and Hills as if piled one upon another" (Clarence Walworth Alvord and Lee Bidgood, *The First Explorations of the Trans-Allegheny Region by the Virginians, 1650–1674* [Cleveland, Ohio, 1912], 188). Boyd identifies the chimneys as Pilot Mountain in Surry County, North Carolina. *Boyd,* 232.

286. Byrd here replicates Lawson's list of the four kinds of squirrel *(Lawson,* 124).

287. Compare Byrd's description with the October 26 entry in the "Surveyors' Journal or Field Book":

> The Last Line Tree is a Red Oak, by the East side of the River, and the Trees around it are blazed each on the Side pointing to the Oak.
>
> Here the Surveyors made an End by Order of the Commissioners, having run the Line, from Currituck, in conjunction with the Carolina Surveyors 168 Miles 62 Chs. 50 L, and from the Place they departed at, to the End, 72 Miles 75 Chs. Links: In all 241 Miles 57 Chs. 50 Links.

Boyd located the point at which the survey ended as Peter's Creek, on the border of the present Stokes County, North Carolina *(Boyd,* 234).

288. Byrd's description of the "Elk" is complicated by the fact that the North American moose *(Alces alces)* is the same species as the "Elk" of Europe and Asia, whereas the large North American deer now known as elk, or wapiti *(Cervus canadensis),* bears the same name. In Byrd's era the range of the North American elk extended farther south than it

does now, and elk sightings in the region would not have been impossible. Though Byrd used the term "moose" elsewhere in *The History of the Dividing Line,* he might have been conflating the two species in his description, especially in his description of the animal's management of its horns in the forest, which appears to draw on Paul Dudley's communication to the Royal Society concerning the moose:

> When a Moose goes through a Thicket, or under the Boughs of Trees, he lays his Horns back on his Neck, not only that he may make his way the easier, but to cover his Body from the Bruise, or Scratch of the Wood.
> —"A Description of the Moose-Deer in America. By the Honourable Paul Dudley, Esq; F. R. S. Communicated by John Chamberlayne, Esq;" *Philosophical Transactions,* XXXI (1720–1721), 166–167

Most New World deer species were larger than the European and Asian red deer *(Cervus elaphus),* and early modern writers often misidentified the new species, causing a great deal of confusion. Lederer complained about this confusion when describing rich Piedmont meadows that attracted

> numerous herds of Red Deer (for their unusual largeness improperly termed Elks by ignorant people) to feed. The right Elk, though very common in *New Scotland, Canada,* and those Northern parts, is never seen on this side of the Continent: for that which the *Virginians* call Elks, does not at all differ from the Red Deer of *Europe,* but in his dimensions, which are far greater: but yet the Elk in bigness does as far exceed them.
> —*Lederer,* 35

But the deer Lederer saw were not red deer; Lawson observed that some take the elk "for the red Deer of *America;* but he is not" (123). Catesby agreed, acknowledging that what he called the "Stag of America" does resemble the European red deer, but is much larger. "The Moose or Elk," Catesby noted, is "rarely south of the latitude of 40" (*Catesby,* 157–158). Clarifying the species was a continuing concern; see Samuel Dale, "A Letter from Samuel Dale, M. L. to Sir Hans Sloane, Bart. President of the Royal Society, Containing the Descriptions of the Moose-Deer of New-England, and a Sort of Stag in Virginia; with Some Remarks Relating to Mr. Ray's Description of the Flying Squirrel of America," *Philosophical Transactions,* XXXIX (1735–1736), 384–389.

289. BL (October 28): "Mr. Dandrige was siezed with a formal Fitt of the Gout, so that wee postpon'd our Departure till the next Day." The attack was "formal" in the sense that its symptoms conformed fully to the classical pattern of the disease.

290. *Vice coturnicum:* in place of quails. The tag appears to underscore Byrd's pious acknowledgment that Providence was benevolently involved in the feeding of the company in the wilderness. The motto refers specifically to the way the children of Israel in the wilderness were fed with manna and quails—and just so the survey party were fed with biscuits and game birds. Byrd's description of the Order of Maosti, however, is complicated by the fact that the scriptural passage to which the motto refers emphasizes not so much the gifts God provided to the children of Israel as their dissatisfaction and ungrateful grumbling. After God had provided the hungry travelers making their exodus through the wilderness with manna, they soon tired of this diet, and, forgetting how help-

less they had been before God interceded, complained vociferously: whereupon God supplemented the manna diet with showers of fowl. At first this miracle might have appeared to be another extension of divine mercy, but there was judgment pending. The quails were so numerous that they covered the camp, decayed, and brought disease to punish the impious complainers (Num. 11:33).

The story of the miracle of quails—or the plague of quails—was most often brought forward to exemplify the consequences of human ingratitude. Josephus, one of Byrd's favorite authors, stressed the scorn and chiding of the hungry children of Israel when Moses assured them that God would provide for them. The quails were delivered,

> but it was not long before God took Vengeance upon the *Hebrews* for the Offences they had Committed against *Himself* and *Moses:* For they were visited with a Plague that cost them a great many Lives. The place where this Judgment befel them is call'd *Cabrothaba,* or the *Graves of Lust.*
> —*The Works of Flavius Josephus,* trans. Roger L'Estrange, 4th ed. (London, 1725), 75; Flavius Josephus, *The Jewish Antiquities* 3.13

Byrd himself referred to the plague of quails in his discussion of airborne contagion in *A Discourse concerning the Plague:*

> when the children of *Israel,* being cloy'd with the bread of Heaven, lusted after flesh in the wilderness, God was pleas'd to indulge their disorderly inclinations with a mighty flight of Quails: but they either eat too greedily of 'em, or else great part of that immense number (which we are told lay round about the camp two cubits thick upon the ground, for several miles together) must have dy'd, and with their stench have corrupted the air, and so brought the Plague amongst the people.
> —[Byrd], *A Discourse concerning the Plague, with Some Preservatives against It* (London, 1721), 4

The story of the plague of quails intrigued biblical commentators and religious historians with cautionary tales teaching the impropriety and danger of scoffing at Providence. It provided satirists with a topos of catastrophic discontent, the plague of quails a common emblem of turbulence and complaint—and of apparent blessings turning out to be curses. Thus, John Dryden, inveighing against the grumbling ingratitude of the English people in his "Satyre against Sedition," wrote:

> We loath our Manna, and we long for Quails;
> Ah, what is man, when his own wish prevails!
> —*Poems on Various Occasions; and Translations from Several Authors* (London, 1701), 25 (*Hayes* 984)

Thus Byrd was probably inviting his reader to see through the surface narrative in which the Order of Maosti celebrates heroic achievements to a submerged satirical meaning.

291. The "Cohungaroota" is probably the Potomac River, and "Sharantow" the Shenandoah River, which joins the Potomac at Harper's Ferry. It is not clear what "recent survey" followed the river to its source.

292. *St. Barb:* the silver-rich region of Santa Barbara, Chihuaha, Mexico, which the

Spanish began colonizing in 1547. For the notion that mineral deposits were likely to be found in differing places in the same latitude, see above, note 232.

293. *BL* (October 29): "Wee were stop'd once more by a smart Rain, but what Wee Imagin'd to be a disappointment prov'd a real service by giving Mr. Dandridge time to recover so farr as to be able to draw on his Boot the day following."

294. On the contemporary understanding of capillary narrowness in victims of gout, see George Cheyne, *An Essay of the True Nature and Due Method of Treating the Gout* . . . (London, 1722), 2 (*Hayes* 691):

> The smallest Vessels of the *Gouty* Person must be in their natural Conformation narrower and more stiff, than those of the Other, who is free from the *Gout,* in respect of their common Stature and Size. For thereby the Crude and Gross Humours, which are confin'd, or pass with Pain, in the *Gouty* Person, will easily flee off by Perspiration, and the other Drains of the Body, in the Person free from the *Gout.*

295. Byrd alludes to John Tennent's campaign to promote the medicinal uses of Seneca rattlesnake root *(Polygala senega).* In 1736 Tennent published *An Essay on the Pleurisy,* advertised in the *Virginia Gazette* as providing "a Remedy almost absolutely certain." Soon after, the *Virginia Gazette* published an essay in letter form, addressed by Tennent to the eminent English physician Dr. Richard Mead, concerning the effectiveness of *"Rattle-Snake Root"* in cases of *"Pleurisies* or *Peripneumonies"* and gout. Tennent's remedy operated by thinning the blood, counteracting the coagulation caused by snake venom—and similarly countering the thickening of the blood in cases of pleurisy and peripneumonia (*Virginia Gazette,* Sept. 24–Oct. 1, and Oct. 1–8, 1736). Byrd and Governor Gooch provided Tennent letters of introduction when he brought his remedy to London. Though he did not meet with the success for which he hoped, *Polygala senega* entered the British and Continental materia medica, where it remained for more than a century.

296. *Podagrous:* gouty, from *podagra,* or gout in the foot *(OED).*

297. *Dining with St. Anthony; Dining with Duke Humphrey:* Proverbially to dine with Saint Anthony—or with Duke Humphrey—is to go without food. John S. Farmer and W. E. Henley, eds., *Slang and Its Analogues Past and Present* (London, 1903), VI, 94.

298. Douglas L. Rights identifies these formations as Pilot and Sauratown Mountains, more than twenty miles south of the line:

> Lover's Leap, as they called what is probably Pilot Mountain, was thought by some of the Indian traders to be "Kiawan" or "Katawa Mountain," which they had formerly seen on their trading journeys to the Cherokees. . . . Colonel Byrd was right in insisting on their location further south. He was also correct in his belief that a continuation of the dividing line would lead to the Cherokee country reached by trading parties at that time only by the circuitous journey over the old Trading Path by way of the Catawbas.
>
> —"The Trading Path to the Indians," *North Carolina Historical Review,* VIII (1931), 403–426

Ausband, however, maintains it is the mountain now known as Moore's Knob (*Byrd's Line,* 99).

299. George II signed the charter establishing the colony of Georgia on June 9, 1732. The recent act to which Byrd referred was the "Act for Maintaining the Peace with the Indians in the Province of Georgia," the very first bylaw enacted by the "Trustees for establishing the Colony of Georgia in America," at a meeting in Fleet Street, London, on March 21, 1733. The act stipulated that a commissioner or commissioners for the Indian trade would be empowered to issue licenses and hold the bond of traders. The act further stipulated that, after June 24, 1735, any unlicensed

> Person or Persons whatsoever . . . shall directly or indirectly Visit frequent haunt Trade to Traffick or Barter with any Indian or Indians within the said Province of Georgia all and every Offender or Offenders shall for every such Offence Forfeit One hundred pounds Sterling Money of Great Britain.

Licenses to trade were issued by a commissioner in Savannah, about five hundred miles (as the crow flies) from Williamsburg. Allen D. Candler, ed., *The Colonial Records of the State of Georgia* (Atlanta, 1904), I, 32.

300. *BL* (October 30): "Wee took the Variation the 3d. time . . . and found it continued much the same as before." This return-journey observation was not logged in the "Surveyor's Journal," which concludes at the last surveyed point.

301. George II, who reigned from 1727 to 1760, was born at Schloss Herrenhausen, Hanover, on November 10, 1683.

302. Byrd was familiar with contemporary anatomical work on the opossum; part of his account appears to be a condensed version of Edward Tyson's Royal Society experiments. "Carigueya, seu Marsupiale Americanum; or, The Anatomy of an Opossum, Dissected at Gresham-College, by Edw. Tyson, M.D., Fellow of the College of Physicians, and of the Royal Society, and Reader of Anatomy at the Chyrurgeons-Hall, in London," *Philosophical Transactions*, XX (1698), 109, 110.

However, Byrd undertakes a major diversion when it comes time to regale his readers with an account of the extraordinary marsupial characteristics of the opossum—the longstanding folk tradition of extrauterine fetal development, ubiquitous in early sketches of the opossum, such as the Reverend John Clayton's 1694 report to the Royal Society: "A Continuation of Mr. John Clayton's Account of Virginia," *Philosophical Transactions*, XVIII (1694), 122.

What makes Byrd's retention of this folk embryology the more remarkable is that the very specimens Tyson dissected had been provided by Byrd himself. Tyson opened his disquisition in the *Philosophical Transactions* by acknowledging, "This *Animal* was brought from *Virginia*, and presented to the *Royal Society*, by *Will. Bird*, Esq;"

303. Early modern natural philosophers counted bats among the birds, though the bat's mammalian characteristics were perplexing. Robert Boyle, in his "Essay [concerning] . . . Final Causes," maintained God designed bats "to act sometimes like a bird . . . and on some occasions like a terrestrial animal . . . [or] mouse." In the matter of generation, "the batt differs from other birds":

> Since the female was not, like them, to be oviparous; but, like mice and other quadrupeds, that bring forth their young ones alive, she is not only furnished with an uterus fitted for that purpose, but in regard she does not . . . exclude, together

with the foetus, a competent stock of aliment to nourish it, till it can shift for itself, the batt is furnished with dugs, to give suck.
—*The Works of the Honourable Robert Boyle* (London, 1744), IV, 545 (*Hayes* 1944)

The account of the shark's sheltering its young originates with Aelian, who declared, "The Shark brings forth its young through its mouth in the sea and takes them back again and then disgorges them by the same channel alive and unharmed" (*On the Characteristics of Animals* 2.55, trans. Schofield). Curiously, Tyson cited the Roman poet Oppianus, whose poetic survey of the world of fish, the *Halieutics,* "tells us, that upon any Storm or Danger, if pursued, the *Young Ones run* into the *Mother's Belly;* and when the Fright and Danger is over, they *come out* again." William Derham (acknowledging Tyson) adduced the phenomenon as an instance of parental care in the animal kingdom: "How carefully will they lead them about in places of Safety, carry them into places of Retreat and Security, yea, some of them admit them into their own Bowels?" See Tyson, "Carigueya, seu Marsupiale Americanum," *Philosophical Transactions,* XX (1698), 124–125; Derham, *Physico-Theology,* 209. On the other hand, vipers displayed the reverse of the care shown by such animal parents—they supposedly gnawed their way out of their mother's belly; *Herodotus* 3.9; *Pliny* 10.82.169–170; Aelian, *On the Characteristics of Animals* 1.24, 15.16. Sir Thomas Browne dismisses this tradition in *Pseudodoxia Epidemica,* 142–143, and *Works,* 113 (*Hayes* 1928, 210).

The term *Dog-fish* refers to any one of small sharks of several species, such as the spotted cat shark *(Scyliorhinus canicula)* and the spiny dogfish shark *(Squalus acanthius).*

304. Byrd probably read of the Tartars' horseflesh diet in Giles Fletcher, "A Treatise of *Russia* and the adjoyning Regions," collected in Samuel Purchas, *Purchas His Pilgrimes* (1625): "For their chiefe victuall is Horse-flesh, which they eate without Bread, or any other thing with it" (III, 441). Byrd owned a copy of Purchas (*Hayes* 83), and there is evidence of his familiarity with the text: this passage occurs only a few pages after Fletcher's account of the peculiar tyrannies of Russian tsar Ivan Vasilowich, which Byrd found interesting enough to transcribe it into the *Commonplace Book* (§22). Another possible source is Patrick Gordon: "Their ordinary Food is Horse-flesh, which they greedily tear and eat up like so many Ravenous Vultures." *Geography Anatomiz'd* . . . (London, 1708), 255.

The Hottentots, according to travelers to the Cape of Good Hope, found offal useful for clothing as well as dining. William Dampier, for instance, noted that the women wound "green," or fresh guts, around their legs, wearing them for months and eating them on journeys. Dampier reported that the families of Hottentots who worked for the Dutch camped near their doors waiting for table scraps—guts and garbage. See *A New Voyage round the World* . . . (London, 1717), I, 538, 541 (*Hayes* 58). The phrase "guts and garbage" appeared in John Maxwell's "Account of the Cape of Good Hope" published in *Philosophical Transactions.* Maxwell reported that, when Hottentots slaughter a sheep or cow, "they Eat the Guts and Garbidge, either slightly broil'd or quite raw." *Philosophical Transactions,* XXV (1706–1707), 2427.

305. Glue-broth takes its name from the gelatin glue "obtained by boiling the hides and hoofs of animals to a jelly" *(OED).* Byrd's recipe, somewhat simplified, closely resembles the instructions "To Make Portable Broth," in Nicolas Lémery, *New Curiosities in Art and Nature,* 240:

Take Four Legs of Beef, Four Cocks, Four Necks of Mutton, Four Knuckles of Veal, a sufficient Quantity of Mace, and Sweet Herbs, with Marygolds, boil them in Ten Gallons of Water till the whole become like Rags, then pour out your Liquor through a Gelly-bag into clean glaz'd Pans, and when it is cold take off the Fat, and put it again upon the Fire in an Earthen Vessel, and let it boil once more; then put to it two Pounds of Hartshorn Shavings, and boil them till the Broth be hard enough to cut with a Knife, which you must try by putting some of it in a cold Place; then take it off, and strain it again into glaz'd Earthen Pans, that it may be about Three Inches deep in the Bottom; when it is perfectly cold cut it with a Knife into Slices of an Inch thickness, and lay it upon a Frame, and let it stand in the Wind to dry; for if you set it in the Sun it will melt. . . . When you would use this Glue take such a Quantity as you please, cut it in pieces with a Knife, and boil it in an Earthen Vessel with a Crust of Bread or Bisquet, and season it with Salt or Spice according to your Palate.

On the use of "portable soop" in healthy diet, see also Edward Strother, *An Essay on Sickness and Health* (London, 1725), 49. Portable soup was used in long ocean voyages and cross-country expeditions such as later undertaken by Lewis and Clark.

306. *Jours maigres:* literally, lean days. The term was used in the Roman Catholic Church to indicate fasting days on which meat should not be eaten. On such days soup *not* containing meat juices was acceptable fare.

307. The story appeared in Benjamin Franklin's *Pennsylvania Gazette,* August 12, 1736:

We hear from Virginia, that not long since a Flash of Lightning fell on a House there, and struck dead a Man who was standing at the Door. Upon examining the Body they found no Mark of Violence, but on his Breast an exact and perfect (tho' small) Representation of a Pine Tree which grew before the Door, imprest or printed as it were in Miniature. This surprizing Fact is attested by a Gentleman lately come from thence, who was himself an Eye-witness of it; and 'tis added that great Numbers of People came out of Curiosity, to view the Body before it was interr'd.
—Leonard W. Labaree et al., eds., *The Papers of Benjamin Franklin* (New Haven, Conn., 1959–), II, 160

It has not been possible to identify Franklin's source, the "Gentleman lately come" from Virginia. It is tempting to speculate the story made its way to Philadelphia through the relationship between Franklin and Williamsburg publisher William Parks; Franklin re-published published Tennent's *Every Man His Own Doctor* in 1734 and 1736 (*Papers of Franklin,* II, 155).

Several colonial newspapers republished the story, all giving it the same dateline, "*Philadelphia, August* 12." The York lightning story that appeared in the *New-York Weekly Journal,* Aug. 23, 1736, repeats Franklin's story nearly word for word. The story appeared without any substantive changes in the *Boston Evening-Post,* Aug. 30, 1736; *Boston Weekly Post-Boy,* Aug. 30, 1736; and the *New England Weekly Journal* (Boston), Aug. 31, 1736.

Clearly Byrd's account features more detail than the newspaper story. He does not claim to have seen the victim with his own eyes, so we must assume he got his information more directly from Virginia witnesses or storytellers, or, perhaps, he added some of these details on his own initiative.

308. Lederer, in his account of his second expedition westward in 1670, also observed that in mountainous country his company found "very little sustenance for Man or Horse; for these places are destitute both of Grain and Herbage" (*Lederer*, 20). Like Byrd, Lederer offered advice, "Instructions to such as shall march upon Discoveries into the North-*American* Continent" (*Lederer*, 38–41). Byrd might not have drawn specifically on Lederer's advice, but the passage could have influenced Byrd's decision to compile his own set of instructions to future discoverers.

A Plain and Champaign-Country: level, open terrain.

309. *Welch Runts, and Highland Galloways:* "Runt" is a term applied to small Welsh cattle or sheep, or generally to any small horse. The "Galloway," now extinct, was a Scottish breed of small, strong horses related to the Highland pony.

Banstead Down: a region in Surrey with steep terrain, known for sheep grazing. Byrd might have been thinking of Pope's lines, "To Hounslow Heath I point, and Banstead Down; / Thence comes your mutton, and these chicks my own." *Second Satire of the Second Book of Horace.*

310. *Our Country has now been inhabited more than 130 years:* If Byrd was calculating from the arrival of the Jamestown colonists in 1607, the period of settlement from that point to the 1728 date of the Dividing Line expedition would number only 121 years. Byrd's "more than 130 years" may be considered additional evidence of composition or revision well beyond 1728.

311. The prime cuts of animals butchered for meat are those "of the best or highest quality." Byrd's usage, not recorded in the *OED*, in context may be taken to mean selecting only the best cuts of meat and leaving the rest.

312. *Our Mathematical Professor:* Alexander Irvin.

313. Antiochus IV (Antiochus Epiphanes), Seleucid king of Syria, attempted the Hellenization of Judaism, which together with his profanation of the Temple, inspired the rebellion of the Maccabees. According to Josephus (1.7.3), Pompey took advantage of the fact that the Jews would fight only defensively on the Sabbath, filling in the valley before Jerusalem and bringing in his war machines.

Daring to ride for a Midwife: I have not been able to discover any source for this anecdote. Contrary to Byrd's assertion, however, the Sabbath laws of all colonies made specific exceptions for just this circumstance; see, for instance, New York's "Act against the Prophanation of the Lords Day, called, Sunday":

> It shall be lawful for the Post, or any other person imployed in his Majesties Service, or for any person imployed to bring a Physitian or a Midwife, to travel upon the Lords day, any thing contained herein to the contrary in any way notwithstanding.
> —*The Laws of Her Majesties Colony of New York . . .* (1710), 24

Byrd's story no doubt springs from popular traditions ridiculing Puritan strictness.

314. Edward I (1239–1307) built a memorial at Charing Cross for his wife, Eleanor of Castile. In 1647 it was demolished by the Puritans, who considered it idolatrous. After the Restoration, Hubert Le Seuer's bronze statue of Charles I on horseback was erected on a tall stone pedestal designed by Grinlin Gibbon.

315. *Penny-worth:* an English idiom with several senses; in this case, a very small

amount, no more than a penny could purchase. See below, note 384, for a different use of the idiom.

316. The notion that bears are uninterested in dead bodies can be found as far back as Aelian: "When Bears have sniffed at hunters who have fallen on their face and knocked the breath out of themselves, they leave them for dead, and it seems that these creatures are disgusted by a dead body" (*On the Characteristics of Animals* 5.4.9). In Aesop's fable "Of the Tanner, that bought of a Hunter the skin of a Bear, that was never yet caught," a hunter escapes death by a similar pretense: *"The Hunter, knowing that this wild beast did not prey upon dead carcasses, stopping his breath, counterfeited himself dead. When the Bear, smelling with his nose put to him, could not perceive him to breathe, either at the nose, or the breast, he went his way from him."* Charles Hoole, ed., [*Aesop's Fables English and Latin]* (London, 1700), 118.

317. The French fascination with dance was a staple of English satire on French triviality; no precise source for Byrd's analogy has been located, but a brief article of "news" appeared in the English newspaper the *Bee:*

> We hear that on *Monday* next a Set of *French Dancing-Masters* are to meet at a Place near *Whitehall,* in order to compose a new sort of *English* Country Dance, which is to be danced in a sort of Shoes called *Sabots.*
> —*Bee; or, Universal Weekly Pamphlet,* I (London, 1733), 230

318. *Paco:* Byrd based his description of the alpaca largely on accounts of South America collected in Awnsham and John Churchill's anthology of travel narratives:

> Among other Qualifications belonging peculiarly to the Sheep of *Peru,* this is very remarkable, that they are able to carry a Burden from 50 to 70 pounds weight with ease, just as Camels do, whom they resemble much in shape, except that they have no such bunches on their Backs. They are able (If the *Spaniards* may be believed) to carry a Man four or five Leagues a day. When they are tired, they lie down upon the ground, and are not to be raised again by beating, or any other way, but must be unloaded. If their Riders force them by beating, or otherwise, beyond what they can bear, they turn their Heads, and blow their stinking Breaths into their Faces. It is a very useful Creature (especially those call'd *Pancos*) they eat and drink very little, sometimes they don't drink in four or five days.
> —*An Account of a Voyage to the Coast of Chili . . . in the Years 1642, and 1643, under the Command of Mr. Henry Brewer, Their General,* in *A Collection of Voyages and Travels,* I, 511 (*Hayes 79*)

A plate on page 511 shows "The Figure of a Camel-Sheep, with a *Chilese* and his Wife," clearly showing the triple-cloven forefeet and singly-cloven hindfeet. As Alfonso de Ovalle describes them:

> These Sheep have their upper Lip split, with which they do as it were spit at those who vex them; and the Children, who use to do it, when they see them ready to spit, run away; for they know, and 'tis a common Truth, that wherever their Spitting falls, it causes a Scab, and having a very long Neck, about Three Foot long, they use these Defensive Arms the better.
> —*An Historical Relation of the Kingdom of Chile,* in *Purchas his Pilgrimes,* III, 144

The earliest mention of the paco seems to be José de Acosta, in *The Naturall and Morall Historie of the East and West Indies* (London, 1604), 321. Acosta stresses their ability to carry heavy burdens and to survive on minimal rations. Byrd had access to Acosta in a slightly condensed form in Samuel Purchas, *Purchas His Pilgrimes* (London, 1625), III, 968 (*Hayes* 83). See also Garcilasso de la Vega ("el Inca"), *The Royal Commentaries of Peru* (London, 1688), 329 (*Hayes* 84, 2044).

The animal is called the *Paco Llama* in Captain Edward Cook's *Voyage to the South Sea, and round the World, Perform'd in the Years 1708, 1709, 1710, and 1711* (London, 1712), 206 (*Hayes* 125). See also [Thomas] Salmon, *Modern History; or, The Present State of All Nations*, XXIX (London, 1737), 188–190.

319. Byrd here follows the Protestant tradition of mocking the Roman Catholic Church, whose princes (cardinals, archbishops) were allegedly much given to luxury.

320. Byrd here describes the rich land he purchased from his North Carolina counterparts; see his "Journey to the Land of Eden."

321. Herodotus praised the black, fertile soil of Assyria; it commonly produced grain harvests of two-hundredfold, and sometimes three. *Herodotus* 1.193.

322. Byrd echoes earlier writers who cataloged the potential riches that might spring from developing new crops in Virginia and Carolina. On the history of the silk promotion, see Warren M. Billings, "Sir William Berkeley and the Diversification of the Virginia Economy," *VMHB*, CIV (1996), 436–438; Charles E. Hatch, Jr., "Mulberry Trees and Silkworms: Sericulture in Early Virginia," *VMHB*, LXV (1957), 3–61.

323. According to early modern understanding of weather, the air contained infusions of certain chemicals, inferred from the likeness of thunder and lightning to chemically induced explosions. By condensation, potentially explosive mineral substances such as sulphur and nitre—"Etherial Gunpowder"—are borne aloft. As Robert Hooke noted, "The Atmosphere about the Earth doth abound with a spirituous Nitre, or Nitrous Particles, which are every where carried along with it" (Robert Hooke, "A Discourse of the Nature Of Comets," in *The Posthumous Works of Robert Hooke* [London, 1705], 169 [*Hayes* 796]).

Those nitrous particles not consumed by explosion—thunder and lightning—were returned to the earth in precipitation. Nitre, either sodium carbonate or sodium or potassium nitrate (saltpeter), was both a component in explosive recipes and a key nutritive ingredient in certain soils. It is an easy logical step to conclude that a region where nutritive particles are preserved by cold at the same time they continue to accumulate what the snow brings will increase in fertility. The Virginia climate, with its "Nore winds," ensured the soil was particularly well suited to the cultivation of tobacco. Byrd's belief in the beneficial transference of chemicals from air to earth is clear in a letter he wrote to his friend John Boyle in 1727: "We have had the most delightfull winter here that I ever saw in any country, just frost enough to fertilize our ground, and purify the air" (Byrd to John Boyle, Baron Boyle of Broghill, Feb. 2, 1726/7, *Correspondence*, I, 361).

324. The notion that climatic variations were caused by the tilt of the earth's axis began with ancient philosophers and was extended in the seventeenth century by theorists concerned with reconciling natural phenomena with scriptural history. They proposed that the earth had lost its perpetual spring when the Deluge upset its equilibrium and tilted its axis, thus causing seasonal change and differing climates. In 1681, Thomas Burnet surveyed scriptural and classical texts to establish a consensus that paradise enjoyed a per-

petual spring. The shock of the flood disrupted not only the surface of the earth but also its polar alignment. The antediluvian earth was smooth, "perfectly uniform and regular, having the same Center of its magnitude and gravity." Before the disaster the axis of the earth was "parallel to the Axis of the same Ecliptick, both its Poles being equally inclin'd to the Sun." The "Ecliptick" is the imaginary circle of the celestial sphere in which the sun appears to revolve. The earth's orientation, once parallel but now askew, has become irregular, "standing oblique and inclin'd to the Sun or the Ecliptick."

> This change and obliquity of the Earth's posture has a long train of consequences depending on it; whereof that was the most immediate, that it alter'd the form of the year, and brought in that inequality of Seasons which hath since obtain'd.
> —Thomas Burnet, *The Theory of the Earth: Containing an Account of the Original of the Earth, and of All the General Changes Which It Hath Already Undergone, or Is to Undergo, till the Consummation of All Things,* 2d ed. (London, 1691), 184–186, 194–195 (*Hayes* 94)

Byrd also owned a copy of the Latin original, *Telluris Theoria Sacra: Orbis Nostri Originem et Mutationes Generales* (London, 1681) (*Hayes* 118).

Many other possible sources could be cited, for the works of late-seventeenth- and early-eighteenth-century natural philosophers were filled with speculations about the cause of the Deluge and alteration of the earth's axis, and Byrd owned many of these works. For a succinct discussion of this subject, see François Ellenberger, *History of Geology,* II, *The Great Awakening and Its First Fruits* (Rotterdam, 1999), 26–28; my discussion of Byrd's geology is indebted to Ellenberger's historical analysis.

325. Byrd here echoes an argument from the Cambridge Platonist Henry More's 1653 *Antidote to Atheism.* More's list of the benefits of the arrangement of the earth's axis— steady and parallel to the earth—includes the navigational art of "Dialling" and thus the opportunity for international commerce. Byrd owned a copy of More's Latin works, *Opera Omnia* (London, 1675–1679) (*Hayes* 1219), but it is likely he was referring to John Ray's recapitulation of More:

> For thus there is an orderly measuring of our time for Affairs at home, and an opportunity of Traffick abroad with the most remote Nations of the World, and so there is a mutual Supply of the several Commodities of all Countries, besides the enlarging our Understandings by so ample Experience we get both of Men and Things.
> —*The Wisdom of God Manifested in the Works of the Creation* (London, 1701), 201–202 (*Hayes* 1851)

326. *Herodotus* 1.193 noted the use of sesame oil in Assyria and Babylonia. Strabo also related that the Syrians used sesame oil: *Geography* 16.1.13, 16.4.27; cf. *Pliny* 15.7.25. Sir Hans Sloane, noting the dependence of humankind upon grains, observed, "Some in *Barbary* feed on Palm Oil, others on that drawn from Organ or Erguen Nuts, many on Oil Olive, or that from Walnuts or *Sesamum,* which last is much used in *Egypt* and the *East-Indies*" (*A Voyage to the Islands Madera, Barbados, Nieves, S. Christophers, and Jamaica . . .* [London, 1707], I, 21).

327. *Half Jack-Boots:* A jackboot is a "large strong boot the top of which came above

the knee, serving as defensive armour for the leg, worn by cavalry soldiers in the 17th and 18th centuries." The *OED* does not provide a definition of the half jackboot, but it is presumably a stout riding boot the top of which does not reach the knee.

328. Seventeenth-century missionaries to Asia brought accounts of the traditional medicine ginseng *(Panax ginseng)* back to Europe. Pierre Jartoux, a Jesuit missionary to China, is credited with bringing the traditional Asian medicine to the attention of Western natural historians. The Royal Society published Jartoux's essay on the discovery in the *Philosophical Transactions,* almost certainly a major source for Byrd's account of the plant in *The History of the Dividing Line:* "The Description of a Tartarian Plant, Call'd Gin-Seng; with an Account of Its Vertues," *Philosophical Transactions,* XXVIII (1713), 241. See also Jartoux's letter of Apr. 12, 1711, in *Travels of the Jesuits into Various Parts of the World* (London, 1743), II, 424–437. John H. Appleby, in "Ginseng and the Royal Society," *Notes and Records of the Royal Society of London,* XXXVII (1982–1983), notes that interest in ginseng peaked during several periods, including 1666–1692, 1711–1724, and 1736–1743, and twice more after Byrd's death (121).

The medicinal value of ginseng seems to have been a lifelong cause for Byrd. As early as 1710 he noted in his diary that his daughter "began to take drops of ginseng" (Dec. 23, 1710, *SD,* 275). As soon as it appeared that ginseng grew on the Virginia mountainsides, he began to take a serious interest, comparing Jartoux's illustration with samples gathered in the mountains. In 1730 he wrote praising ginseng to his friends the earl of Orrery and Lord Perceval (Byrd to Charles Boyle, earl of Orrery, June 18, 1730, *Correspondence,* I, 429–430, Byrd to [John Perceval, Viscount Perceval], Aug. 20, 1730, I, 435–437).

329. Lord Perceval responded skeptically to Byrd's praise for ginseng, softening his rejection of the drug by sending Byrd "a picture of the kanna root that grows among the Hottentots," together with a description extracted from Peter Kolb's 1715 account of South Africa, translated from Latin into English and published in 1731 (Perceval to Byrd, Dec. 28, 1730, *Correspondence,* I, 440). Perceval's summary of Kolb predates the publication of the English translation: Peter Kolben, *The Present State of the Cape of Good-Hope* . . . (London, 1731) *(Hayes* 128).

According to Kolb, the plant "is in such Esteem among the *Hottentots* for its great Vertues that they almost adore it. What greatly enflames the Value of this Root, is its Scarcity; for 'tis very rarely found. They look upon it as the greatest Chearer of the Spirits, and the noblest Restorative in the World." Kolb cited Father Tachart and Erasmus Francisci to identify kanna and ginseng as the same plant, with the same medicinal effects, as Francisci explained:

> So small a Quantity as a Penny-weight gives wonderful Relief in Sinkings of the
> Spirits: And on such Occasions the Dose is rarely larger. It wonderfully fortifies the
> Nerves, and warms a cold Constitution. But then the Dose must be somewhat larger.
> 'Tis dangerous to Temperaments that abound with Choler, or are very sanguine;
> for to the Blood and Spirits of such it gives the most furious Action. It is excellent
> for Broken Constitutions, and in all Consumptive Cases. In short, it is, in a Sort, a
> Catholicon for all Constitutions but the very cholerick and the very sanguine; [a]nd
> is of so great Value in *China,* that a Pound of it is rarely sold there for less than three
> Pounds of Silver.

Kolb added that the Hottentots, when they could get kanna, often used it to excess, moving beyond a rise of spirits to intoxication and jovial delirium. Kolben, *The Present State of the Cape of Good-Hope*, I, 210, 212.

Despite the certainty of early modern botanists that kanna is identical with ginseng, the South African plant kanna *(Sceletium tortuosom)*—also known as canna, channa, kaugoed, and ningim (the Japanese name for ginseng)—is a completely different plant.

330. I have not been able to identify the prince who sent to China for ginseng as a sexual stimulant. Such anecdotes might have circulated orally, or this might have been an addition of Byrd's own devising.

331. Beverley, discussing the use Indians make of various parts of the deer, pointed out, "They eat not the Brains with the Head, but dry, and reserve them to dress their Leather with" *(Beverley,* book 2, 14). Francis Jennings has noted that skins dressed in the Indian manner were as much as three times more valuable on the market than ordinary skins *(The Invasion of America: Indians, Colonialism, and the Cant of Conquest* [Chapel Hill, N.C., 1975], 92).

Morpion: Crab-louse. A[bel] Boyer, *The Royal Dictionary Abridged* (London, 1715), s.v. *Morpion (Hayes* 2365).

332. *Tikes:* ticks.

333. *Vixons:* The term *vixen* originally denoted a female fox, and then an ill-tempered, quarrelsome woman, though the use of the word to indicate peevishness or difficulty of character was not always gendered in the early eighteenth century. However, the *OED* lists no usage such as Byrd's, denoting a general nuisance of indeterminate gender.

334. Egyptians, according to Herodotus, anointed themselves with disagreeable-smelling castor-bean oil *(Herodotus* 3.94). The castor-bean plant *(Ricinus communis)* is also known as palma Christi; John Josselyn explained that the palma Christi "is thought to be the plant, that shaded Jonah *the Prophet,* Jonas 4.6." *An Account of Two Voyages to New-England* (London, 1674), 74.

Banister wrote that the plant was a nostrum much used in the Caribbean and also described an Indian ointment of puccoon, angelica, and bear's oil that "keeps lice and fleas and other like troublesom vermin from coming near them" *(Banister,* 380). Beverley reproduced Banister's passage nearly verbatim *(Beverley,* book 3, 52).

335. Mosquitoes were known in Britain as gnats *(OED);* Byrd here draws on the account of Egyptian gnats (κώνωπες) in *Herodotus:* "Gnats are abundant; this is how the Egyptians protect themselves against them: those who dwell higher up than the marshy country are well served by the towers whither they ascend to sleep, for the winds prevent the gnats from flying aloft" (2.95).

East-India Bats: Lawson also uses the same term: "*East-India* Bats or Musqueto Hawks. . . . are so call'd, because the same sort is found in the *East Indies.* They appear only in the Summer, and live on Flies, which they catch in the Air, as Gnats, Musquetos, etc." *(Lawson,* 144). The bird formerly known as the mosquito hawk is now known as the nighthawk *(Chordeiles minor).*

336. The richness of Egyptian lands nourished by the annual flood is proverbial and is mentioned by Herodotus, Plutarch, Pliny, and countless other authorities.

337. Pierre Pomet observed that the meat of the tortoise (also known as terrapin or land turtle) is "proper for Diseases of the Breast, and Consumptions in the hecktick Fever;

and [is] very restorative being eaten in Substance, or else the Broth of the Flesh" (*Complete History of Druggs* [London, 1737], I, 291 [*Hayes* 650]). John Josselyn also declared the meat of the "Land *Turtle*" "good for the Ptisick and Consumptions" (*New England's Rarities Discover'd* . . . [London, 1672], 34).

The notion that turtles supplied various remedies is ancient; Pliny listed traditional medicinal uses of tortoise or turtle: powdered tortoise shell reputedly kindles sexual desire, tortoise blood clarifies the sight, and uncooked tortoise eggs counteract stomach pain (*Pliny* 33.14.33–35). I have not discovered a source for Byrd's claim for the aphrodisiac power of turtle eggs.

338. *Running of the Reins:* a urinary tract discharge. Byrd's word "overstrain" literally indicates an injury caused by some kind of excessively strenuous exercise, and such discharges were understood to be the result of kidney injury or disease — or gonorrhea. George Bate's *Pharmacopeia Bateana* (229) recommended the medicinal use of a similar resin, Balm of Tolu: "It provokes Sweat powerfully, purifies the Blood, and is an excellent thing against the Gonorrhaea, or any Reliks of the *French* Pox" (*Hayes* 663, 760). Thus, it is not possible to rule out an obscurely bawdy reference.

Sweet-Gumm Tree: The sweet gum *(Liquidambar styraciflua)* grows best in bottomlands with rich, moist soil. Compare Byrd's wording with Lawson:

> The sweet Gum-Tree, so call'd, because of the fragrant Gum it yields in the Springtime, upon Incision of the Bark, or Wood. It cures the Herpes and Inflammations; being apply'd to the Morphew and Tettars. 'Tis an extraordinary Balsam, and of great Value to those who know how to use it.
> —*Lawson*, 95

This tree was familiar to English botanists; specimens grew in Edward Morgan's garden near Westminster Palace and at the bishop of London's Garden at Fulham. James Petiver, "Botanicum Hortense III. Giving an Account of Divers Rare Plants, Observed This Summer, A.D. 1713, in Several Curious Gardens about London . . . ," *Philosophical Transactions*, XXVIII (1713), 217–218.

Balm or *balsam:* "an aromatic oily or resinous medicinal preparation, usually for external application, for healing wounds or soothing pain" *(OED)*. The scriptural Balm of Gilead is proverbial; Jeremiah famously demanded, "Is there no Balm in Gilead?" (Jer. 8:22). Pliny declared, "But every other scent ranks below balsam" (*Pliny* 12.54.111). There were several New World balsams. In his *Compleat Herbal of Physical Plants* (London, 1694), John Pechey discusses the pleasing scent and medicinal virtues of the "True, Natural Balsam-Tree," from the Middle East as well as "Peruvian Balsam" and "Balsam of Tolu," from South America (211–214) (*Hayes* 758).

339. The origin of ambergris (a fragrant waxy substance found floating in tropical seas or washed ashore and now understood to be a morbid intestinal secretion of the sperm whale) was controversial in Byrd's era. In his *Cyclopaedia*, Ephraim Chambers observed, "There is a great Variety of Opinions among Naturalists with regard to its Origin and Production; To rehearse 'em all, would make a Volume." Rather than filling an entire volume, Chambers summarized the principal theories: (1) excrement of certain birds swallowed by whales and excreted as ambergris; (2) "the Excrement of a Cetaceous Fish," found both in their entrails and in the sea; (3) a wax or gum dropped into the sea from a tree; (4) a

substance springing from undersea springs; (5) "a Sea-Mushroom"; (6) "a Vegetable Production" from the roots of a seaside tree; (7) a "spongious kind of Earth" or bituminous matter condensed by the action of the sea water; (8) honeycombs falling into the sea. *Cyclopaedia,* I, 75 (Hayes 1833).

340. *Spermaceti oil:* a waxy substance secreted in the head of the sperm whale. Spermaceti was widely believed to have "detersive" and restorative powers: "DETERSIVE *Medicines,* are such as are used to cleanse the Body from sluggish, viscous, and glutinous Humours." John Harris, *Lexicon Technicum; or, An Universal English Dictionary of Arts and Sciences,* 2d ed. (London, 1708).

On the origin and medicinal uses of spermaceti, see Nicolas Culpeper's *Pharmacopoeia Londinensis:*

> *Sperma Ceti, Flos Salis, Flos Maris,* Sperma Ceti. What it is Authors can scarcely determine; however it is gathered from the Sea, upon which it flotes like Froth. Some, as *Valerius Cordus,* affirm it to be the Seed of a Whale, and give great Reasons for the same. *Schroder* says it is false, because it is found in places where Whales are never taken. Some call it . . . *Flos Salis* of *Dioscorides,* but that is an Error, for the *Sal Veterum,* or Salt of the Ancients, was of a Red or Saffron Colour, salt Taste, and Liquid; whereas this of ours is purely white, absolutely fresh, and of a fat solid Body, not fluid, if it be good; if it be rancid, yellowish, or unsavoury, it is naught: There is a counterfeit sort, which is dissolved in Water whereas the true, *Weckerius* saith, *non nisi Oleo resolvitur.* But what it is, or whether Authors agree or no, is no great matter to us, whilst we know what we aim at and intend, and truly understand the Virtues of the same. This of ours is excellent against Cacoetick Ulcers, Phagedaen's, running Sores of the Ears, defects of the Eyes: It resolves, moistens, and is Anodyne, being much used by some to dissolve congealed Blood within, coming from Falls, Bruises, and the like. It eases pains of the Bowels in Children, and the Cholick, is Pectoral, and is oft given in Coughs, Phthisick, Asthma's, and Tartarous Diseases of the Lungs. Some use it outwardly to anoint the marks of Small Pox, to fill them with Flesh. Dose inwardly à .i. ad *ii. [i.e., 1 scruple to 2 drams]. It is best given mixt with Oil of Sweet Almonds new drawn, and White Sugar.
> —William Salmon, *Pharmacopoeia Londinensis; or, The New London Dispensatory,* 6th ed. (London, 1702), 404

The origin of spermaceti intrigued many authors; Samuel Dale's *Pharmacologia seu Manuductio ad Materiam Medicam* (London, 1693) enumerates the theories of its origin. According to the review in *Philosophical Transactions,* which Byrd might have consulted, Dale "affirms it to be an Unctuous Matter to be found in the Brain of a sort of *Whale,* and solves the Reason of its being found floating upon the Sea, as well as in its Natural place." *Philosophical Transactions,* XVII (1693), 934.

Spermaceti was a commodity sometimes shipped from Virginia. For instance, on August 13, 1737, the ship *Katherine* sailed for London from York River with a cargo of "248 Hogsheads of Tobacco, 5800 Staves, a Box of Deer Skins, and a Cask of Sperma Ceti." *Virginia Gazette,* Aug. 12–19, 1737.

341. *Philosophical meal:* a scantily provisioned meal, ostensibly requiring the philosophical virtues of moderation, self-denial, and contentment.

342. No source for the use of bear dung in laundering linen has been identified, but using other dung in a similar fashion was an English folk practice. Christopher Merret reported to the Royal Society on this practice in Lincolnshire:

> They also gather up Hogs-dung and steep it in Water, and having well stirred it, strein it, and so use it to wash Cloaths, which, when bleached in the Summer, will become white and sweet; hence the Proverb, *Linconshire, Where the Hogs sh——— Soap, and the Cow sh———fire.*
> —"An Account of Several Observables in Lincolnshire, Not Taken Notice of in Camden, or Any Other Author, by Mr. Christopher Merret, Surveyor of the Port of Boston," *Philosophical Transactions,* XIX (1695–1697), 349

343. Polar bears were common features in northern travel narratives, and Byrd could have drawn on any number of sources for general information. As for the attack on boats, Constantin de Renneville told of the pursuit of a swimming polar bear in shallow water. After it had been shot and secured with a rope,

> she threw herself with such a Fury upon the Sloop, stood upright upon her Paws, and made such desperate Efforts, that she had almost got into the Sloop; which so frighted the Sloop's Crew, that they row'd away for fear they should all have been devour'd.

On another occasion, when sailors landed to measure the variation of the compass, "a white Bear ran towards the Ship, and would certainly have boarded her if they had not seen her betimes, and prevented her by discharging Muskets at her, and so forc'd her back again." *A Collection of Voyages Undertaken by the Dutch East-India Company* (London, 1703), 4, 22.

344. "*Timothy* a Musician could excite *Alexander the Great* to Arms with the *Phrygian* Sound, and allay his Fury with another Tone, and excite him to Merriment" (Derham, *Physico-Theology,* 135). The tale, originating in Quintus Curtius, was best known in Byrd's era in John Dryden's poem "Alexander's Feast; or, The Power of Music, an Ode in Honour of Saint Cecilia's Day." Byrd owned several copies of Quintus Curtius's history of Alexander (*Hayes* 832, 1421, 1639, 2472, 2505), Derham's *Physico-Theology* (*Hayes* 1095), and numerous volumes of Dryden's poetry and other works (*Hayes* 807, 849, 874, 970, 984).

345. David's wife, Michal, was King Saul's younger daughter. As a princess, she had "ayrs"—strong ideas about her majesty—and chided her husband for lack of proper dignity because he played the harp and danced before the Ark. Afterward she proved to be barren (2 Sam. 7:15–22). The rabbi to whom Byrd refers has not been identified, though it might have been Salomon (Shlomo) Yitzhaki, also known as Rashi. His commentaries were absorbed by early modern Christian biblical scholars, such as the Jesuit commentator Juan de Pineda. Referring to Michal's punishment, Pineda cited the explanation of *"reb. Salom."* This citation in turn appears in later commentaries, such as Zachary Bogan, *A View of the Threats and Punishments Recorded in the Scriptures* (Oxford, 1653), 426–427. According to Bogan, "some say *David* never after that time us'd her as his *wife*"—and he cites "Pineda l. 7 de reb. Salom. c.4." Though Bogan's treatise was not in Byrd's library catalog, similar commentary or annotation could have been found in any number of the Bibles, biblical commentaries, and books of divinity Byrd did own.

346. Byrd's description of tarantism in several places closely resembles that provided by Richard Mead, *A Mechanical Account of Poisons in Several Essays* (London, 1702) (ESTC N00061) (*Hayes* 705): "The Influence of Musick on the *Mind,* will appear to be so much the more powerful and certain" (69–70).

347. Giorgio Baglivi asserted, "The Poison of the *Tarantula* renews it self infallibly every Year, especially about the same time when the Patient receiv'd it." He does not, however, link this "anniversary Return" to the death of the offending spider. "A Dissertation of the . . . Tarantula," in *The Practice of Physick, Reduc'd to the Ancient Way of Observations* (London, 1723), 329, 337.

348. Dr. Mead mentioned the seasonal changes in the toxic strength of Tarantula venom:

> In the Winter it lurks in Holes, and scarcely is seen; and if it does Bite then, it is not Venomous, neither does it induce any ill Symptoms.
> But in the Hot Weather, altho' the Pain of its Bite is at first no greater than what is caused by the Sting of a Bee, yet the Part quickly after is discoloured with a Livid, Black, or Yellowish Circle, and raised to an inflam'd Swelling.
> —Mead, *A Mechanical Account of Poisons,* 57

Baglivi likewise observed that in the summer "their Poison is then exalted by the scorching Beams of the Sun" (*The Practice of Physick,* 326).

349. Mead: "For at the first sound of the *Musical Instrument,* altho' the Sick lye, as it were, in an Apoplectick Fit, they begin by Degrees to move their Hands and Feet, till at last they get up, and fall to Dancing with wonderful Vigour" (58).

350. Mead: "At this Sport they usually spend Twelve Hours a Day, and it continues Three or Four Days; by which time they are generally freed from all their Symptoms, which do nevertheless Attack 'em again about the same time the next Year; and if they do not take Care to prevent this Relapse by Musick, they fall into a *Jaundice,* want of Appetite, universal Weakness, and such like Diseases; which are every Year increased, if Dancing be neglected, till at last they prove incurable" (*A Mechanical Account of Poisons,* 58).

351. *Short Commons:* "Insufficient rations, scant fare" *(OED).*

352. In 1691 Virginia's "Act for a Free Trade with Indians" required any colonist who went hunting far from the "English plantations" to obtain a license from the governor's office. This measure was enacted "for the future prevention of such mischeifes as have frequently happened at huntings, commonly called fire huntings, and other huntings remote from the plantations." *Hening,* III, 69.

353. Byrd's description of Indian fire-hunting has been adduced as an ethnographic source; see Gregory A. Waselkov, "Evolution of Deer Hunting in the Eastern Woodlands," *Mid-Continental Journal of Archaeology,* III (1978), 17–18. Waselkov adduces several other colonial accounts as corroboration. Although Byrd's version is not identical with Beverley's, it is close enough to suggest that Byrd might have borrowed the scene rather than documenting something he had actually witnesed:

> A Company of them wou'd go together back into the Woods, any time in the Winter, when the Leaves were fallen, and so dry, that they wou'd burn; and being come to the Place design'd, they wou'd Fire the Woods, in a Circle of Five or Six Miles

Compass; and when they had completed the first Round, they retreated inward, each at his due Distance, and put Fire to the Leaves and Grass afresh, to accelerate the Work, which ought to be finished with the Day. This they repeat, till the Circle be so contracted, that they can see their Game herded all together in the Middle, panting and almost stifled with Heat and Smoak; for the poor Creatures being frighten'd at the Flame, keep running continually round, thinking to run from it, and dare not pass through the Fire; by which Means they are brought at last into a very narrow Compass. Then the *Indians* let flie their Arrows at them. . . . By this means they destroy all the Beasts, collected within that Circle.

Beverley followed this with an account of a similar hunting method among the Tartars, as described in a Chinese voyage by the Jesuit father Verbiast (*Beverley*, book 2, 39). Indian fire-hunting occurs in Lawson, who described the practice among the Sewee in the "Canes Swamps" (*Lawson*, 10).

Xenophon recorded the Persian practice of driving game, *Cyropaedia* 1.4.14. On ancient and early modern circle, or ring, hunting, see Thomas T. Allsen, *The Royal Hunt in Eurasian History* (Philadelphia, 2006), esp. 25.

354. *Silk Grass:* The plant Byrd mentions is either narrow-leaved silk grass *(Pityopsis graminafolia)* or Carolina silk grass *(Pityopsis aspera),* both native to the region. Silk grass features in the earliest reports of potentially marketable commodities in Virginia, beginning with the 1610 colonizing prospectus, *A True and Sincere Declaration of the Purpose and Ends of the Plantation Begun in Virginia* (London, 1610), 19. Cf. Ralph Hamor, *A True Discourse of the Present Estate of Virginia . . .* (London, 1615), 34; John Smith, *The Generall Historie of Virginia, New England, and the Summer Isles* (London, 1624), 163, and *Smith*, II, 324; William Bullock, *Virginia Impartially Examined . . .* (London, 1649), 8; Edward Williams, *Virginia, More Especially the South Part Thereof, Richly and Truly Valued . . .* (London, 1650), 16; Samuel Clarke, *A True, and Faithful Account of the Four Chiefest Plantations of the English in America . . .* (London, 1670), 8. On June 11, 1697, three members of the Virginia Council sent the Board of Trade "An account of the present state and government of Virginia," informing them that "There is also a plant called silk-grass of which several fine things might be made" (*CSP*, XV, no. 1396, 641–642).

The colonists' interest in silk grass no doubt sprang from observing Indian crafts. Beverley reported that Virginia Indians used "Baskets made of Silk grass" for domestic utensils (*Beverly*, book 3, 63), and Byrd earlier in the narrative mentions Nottoway women offering gifts of silk grass baskets. John Gerard reports that silk grass from Virginia was grown in English gardens as early as the 1630s (*The Herball; or, Generall Historie of Plantes* [London, 1633], 899 [*Hayes* 791–792]). Botanists and natural philosophers were interested in the fibers. Robert Boyle directed Virginia correspondents to report "How the Silk-Grass is prepared" in his guide for Royal Society fieldwork, *General Heads for the Natural History of a Country Great or Small . . .* (London, 1692), 103. The English natural philosopher Robert Hooke described silk grass fibers as "a sort of long and very fine Flax brought out of *America,* which is very flexible and yet very strong, and not subject to shrink or stretch" (*The Posthumous Works of Robert Hooke . . .* [London, 1705], 459 [*Hayes* 796]).

355. *As big as an ordinary Ox:* This seems to be the standard comparison; cf. Catesby: "These creatures, though not so tall, weigh more than our largest oxen" (*Catesby*, 157).

356. Catesby noted the buffalo has "a tail a foot long, bare of hairs, except that at the end is a tuft of long hair" (*Catesby*, 157).

357. *Camblet:* originally an oriental fabric made with silk and camel hair. Later imitations combined silk with other fibers such as wool and hair. Catesby noted only that the Indians "also work the long hairs into garters, aprons, etc." (*Catesby*, 157).

358. Catesby on crossbreeding: "They have been known to breed with tame cattle." Catesby on the quality of buffalo meat: "Their flesh is very good, of a high flavor, and differs from common beef, as venison from mutton. The bunch on their back is esteemed" (*Catesby*, 157).

359. *Curtain-Lecture:* "A reproof given by a wife to her husband in bed" (Samuel Johnson, as quoted by *OED*).

360. *Connecta Creek:* Wright identifies this stream as Contentnea Creek, noting the name was probably a corruption of "Cotechney," the nearby Tuscarora town where Lawson was held prisoner. *Prose Works*, 302.

361. *Twenty Five years ago:* Lawson died in 1711; thus, the writing or revision of this part of the manuscript can be assigned to 1736 or later.

362. At the time of his death, Lawson was North Carolina's surveyor general and was traveling with Christoph von Graffenreid (1661-1743), the projector of a Swedish settlement. Encroachments on Tuscarora lands, raids by unofficial North Carolina militias, and slave-taking had embittered the Tuscarora, and their execution of Lawson was the first act of their war on the settlers.

363. Byrd's language suggests sympathy with the Tuscarora anger at encroachment. Though he does not condone the slaughter of Lawson, he does acknowledge the colonists' major share in provoking the war.

364. There appears to be no other report of this allegedly Tuscarora myth. This factor, together with the obvious analogy to the Incarnation and Crucifixion of Jesus, suggests it may be Byrd's own invention as an etiology of Tuscarora restiveness. *Fields* (340) suggests this passage draws on the martyrdom of Saint Sebastian.

365. Byrd's term "pride" is obscure; he employs it to indicate one of the animal's internal organs, a usage not found in *OED*, which lists only one distant parallel, a medieval usage of *pride* to indicate a deer's spleen. Alternately, "pride" could denote something of which the beaver would be proud—something that "causes a feeling of pride in those to whom it belongs" *(OED)*. But, if we accept the latter suggestion, it still does not clarify precisely what part Byrd would have considered most worthy of a beaver's esteem.

366. Byrd's discussion of beavers combines traditional folk science and observation. He might have encountered the notion of the "Master-Beaver" in Pierre Pomet's discussion of the medicinal use of castoreum: "Amongst the *Beavers* some are accounted Masters, some Servants" (*Compleat History of Druggs*, 246 [*Hayes* 650]).

Castoreum, the secretion of the beaver's anal glands, was much prized as a component in medicine and perfumery. Debate about whether castoreum came from the animal's testicles dates back to the ancient Greeks (*Pliny* 32.13.26–27). The legend that beavers would castrate themselves to escape hunters, as Sir Thomas Browne observed, goes back as far as the ancient Egyptians and was promulgated by Aesop, Aristotle, Aelian, Pliny, and Juvenal. Browne also listed the authorities who denied the legend, including

Pliny, Dioscorides, and many others. Browne, *Pseudodoxia Epidemica,* 112–114 *(Hayes 1928).*

367. In his *Varia Historia* 1.3, Aelian praises the cleverness of the Egyptian frog, but the frog's enemy is the water snake, not the ibis:

> If a frog encounters a water snake that lives in the Nile, it bites off a piece of reed, which it carries at an angle and holds tightly, doing its best not to lose its grip. The water snake cannot swallow the frog, reed and all, because its mouth cannot open as wide as the length of the reed. As a result the frogs by their skill overcome the strength of the water snakes.
> —Aelian, *Historical Miscellany* 1.3, trans. N. G. Wilson (Cambridge Mass., 1997), 29

368. *Clyster:* "A medicine injected into the rectum, to empty or cleanse the bowels, to afford nutrition, etc.; an injection, enema" *(OED).* *Costive:* "Suffering from hardness and retention of the faeces; 'bound' or confined in the bowels; constipated" *(OED).* Enemas were standard remedies for both constipation and fever. Pliny was fascinated by the notion that humans learned methods of dealing with illness and promoting health from animals:

> A somewhat different display has also been made in that same country of Egypt by the bird called the ibis, which makes use of the curve of its beak to purge itself through the part by which it is most conducive to health for the heavy residue of foodstuffs to be excreted. Nor is the ibis alone, but many animals have made discoveries destined to be useful for man as well.
> —*Pliny* 8.41.97

See also Aelian, *On the Characteristics of Animals* 2.35, and 5.46. Byrd notes this legend of natural history in his *Commonplace Book,* §522.

369. "It is known that the dogs by the Nile lap up water from the river as they run, so as not to give the greed of the crocodiles its chance" *(Pliny* 8.41.148–149; see also Aelian, *On the Characteristics of Animals* 6.75, *Historical Miscellany* 1.4). The story also appears in Aesop's fable, "A Dog and a Crocodile," in Sir Roger L'Estrange, *Fables and Storyes Moraliz'd: Being a Second Part of the Fables of Aesop . . . ,* 2d ed. (London, 1708), II, 187 *(Hayes* 1931).

370. Indians considered the tail of the beaver a delicacy, according to Smith's *Generall Historie:* "His taile somewhat like the forme of a Racket, bare without haire, which to eat the Salvages esteeme a great delicate" *(Smith,* II, 110; *A Map of Virginia,* in *Smith,* I, 155; see also *Lahontan,* I, 105).

Heliogabalus: name adopted by Varius Avitus Bassianus, Roman emperor (218–222 C.E.), whose gormandizing excesses were proverbial. His most famous delicacy was the tongue of the peacock, not of the parrot. According to his ancient biographer, Aelius Lampridius, Heliogabalus "frequently ate camels-heels and also cocks-combs taken from the living birds, and the tongues of peacocks and nightingales, because he was told that one who ate them was immune from the plague." *Antoninus Elagabalus* 20.5–6, in David Magie, trans., *Scriptores Historiae Augusti* (London, 1922–1932), II, 147.

371. *Drugget:* cloth woven from wool, or wool mixed with other fibers, usually silk or linen.

372. *Express:* an express-messenger.

373. *Train-oyl:* "Oil obtained by boiling from the blubber of whales, esp. of the right whale; formerly also applied to that obtained from seals, and from various fishes" *(OED).* Sir Hans Sloane noted the dependence of northern people upon this oil: "Most in *Groenland* feed on large Draughts of Train Oil." *A Voyage to the Islands Madera, Barbados, Nieves, S. Christophers and Jamaica, with the Natural History of the Herbs* (London, 1707), I, xxi. See also *Atlas Geographus; or, A Compleat System of Geography, Ancient and Modern,* I (London, 1711), on the people of Samoeida: "Their food is Train-Oil and Honey, with raw Flesh and Fish" (172).

374. The source for Byrd's comments about the reclassification of the fish-eating otter as the dietary equivalent of fish is Thomas Topsell:

> I hear that the *Carthusian* Fryers or Monks (whether you will) which are forbidden to touch all manner of flesh, of other four-footed Beasts, yet they are not prohibited the eating of Otters.
> —*The History of Four-Footed Beasts and Serpents* (London, 1658), 446 (*Hayes* 794)

Lahontan, too, commented:

> The Animals that we meet with there most commonly are Beavers, Otters, and Sea-Calves, all of 'em being very numerous. Those who love Meat are indebted to the Doctors, who perswaded the Popes to Metamorphose these terrestrial animals into Fish; for they are allow'd to eat of 'em in the time of *Lent.*
> —*Lahontan,* 221

375. Byrd again probably draws on Topsell, though conflating Swedish export of furs and German use of otterskin for caps:

> Otter is far more pretious then the skin of the Beaver; and for this cause the *Swetian* Merchants do transport many into *Muscovia* and *Tartaria* for clokes and other garments.
> Thereof also in *Germany* they make caps, or else line other caps with them, and also make stockingsoles; affirming that they be good and wholesome against the Palsie, the Megrim, and other pains of the head.
> —*History of Four-Footed Beasts and Serpents,* 446

Topsell got his information about Lapland from Johannes Scheffer's *Laponia: id est, regionis Lapponum et gentis nova et verissima descriptio* (Frankfort, 1673). Though Byrd had a copy of Scheffer's history of Lapland in Latin (*Hayes* 204), the proximity of other passages drawing on Topsell suggests this too came from the same source.

376. "For in the hunting of fish it must often put his nose above the water to take breath." Topsell, *History of Four-Footed Beasts and Serpents,* 445.

377. This is almost certainly not a Saponi legend. The earliest report of sailing squirrels occurs in the northern history of the sixteenth-century Swedish bishop Olaus Magnus, and the story trickled down through many retellings. First appearing in 1607, Edward Topsell's *History of Four-Footed Beasts and Serpents* cited Magnus Olaus as the source for his repetition of the tale:

The admirable wit of this Beast appeareth in her swimming or passing over the Waters, for when hunger or some convenient prey of meat constraineth her to passe over a river, she seeketh out some rinde or small bark of a Tree which she setteth uppon the Water, and then goeth into it, and holding up her tail like a sail, letteth the winde drive her to the other side, and this is witnessed by *Olaus Magnus* in his description of *Scandinavia,* where this is ordinary among Squirrels, by reason of many rivers, that otherwise they cannot passe over, also they carry meat in their mouth to prevent famine whatsoever befall them, and as Peacocks cover themselves with their tails in hot Summer from the rage of the Sun, as under a shadow, with the same disposition doth the Squirrel cover her body against heat and cold.
—*History of Foure-Footed Beastes and Serpents,* 509–510

The likelihood that Topsell was Byrd's source is confirmed by the fact that the squirrel passage in the *Dividing Line* follows immediately after the passage on otters unmistakably drawn from Topsell.

The notion that people discovered medicinal plants by observing animals is found in *Pliny* 25.40.94. Byrd was probably influenced by Willem Ten Rhyne's *Account of the Cape of Good Hope and the Hottentotes, the Natives of That Country:*

If we are oblig'd to the Brutes for the discovery of several wholesome Remedies; as to the *Dogs* for *Emetics;* to the *Egyptian* Bird *Ibis* for *Clysters,* or *Phlebotemy* to the *Sea-horse,* for the use of *Ditany* or *Garden Ginger* to the *Goats,* of the *Swallow-wort* to the Swallows, of *Fennel* to the *Snake,* of the *narrow small row leav'd Plantin* to the *Toads,* of the *Rue* to the *Weesel,* of the *Origanum* to the *Stork,* of the *Ground-Ivy* to the *Wild Boar,* and of the use of the *Artichoak* to the *Stag,* what wonder is it, if these *Hottentotes,* tho' never so brutish, have their own way of curing Distempers?
—Willem ten Rhyne, "An Account of the Cape of Good Hope and the Hottentotes, Native of that Country," in Awnsham Churchill and John Churchill, *A Collection of Voyages and Travels* (London, 1704), IV, 183

Ten Rhyne, however, does not name baboons as the exemplary beasts. Byrd's assertion that Hottentots learned physick from baboons may be his own humorous invention.

378. *The Tradeing Path:* also known as the Occaneechi Path, the Path to the Catawba, and similar names, this was a network of trails used by Indians for trade and war long before the arrival of the Europeans. The colonists' trade with Indian nations was carried out along a route leading from settled regions—Petersburg, Occaneechee Islands on the Roanoke—through the Piedmont to the interior territory of the Catawbas, Cherokee, and other nations. The trading path appears on Edward Moseley's 1733 map of North Carolina and the 1751 Fry and Jefferson map of Virginia. On the path's route and its history, see William P. Cumming, *The Southeast in Early Maps* (Chapel Hill, N.C., 1998); Gladys Rebecca Dobbs, *The Indian Trading Path and Colonial Settlement Development in the North Carolina Piedmont* (Chapel Hill, N.C., 2007); Warren Hofstra, "'The Extention of His Majesties Dominions': The Virginia Backcountry and the Reconfiguration of Imperial Frontiers," *Journal of American History,* LXXXIV (1997–1998), 1281–1312; James H. Merrell, *The Indians' New World: Catawbas and Their Neighbors from European Contact through the Era of Removal* (Chapel Hill, N.C., 1989).

379. Earlier travelers such as Lederer, Thomas Batts and Robert Fallam, Lawson, and Catesby observed many tracts clear of trees and open meadows that they called "old fields," attributing their origin to the "industry of Indians." Hugh Jones explained that the Indian women who clear trees to make room for planting corn "cut the bark round; so that they die and don't shade the ground, and decay in time" (*Jones*, 55). The Reverend John Clayton noted, "'Old fields' is a common expression for land that has been cultivated by the Indians and left fallow, which are generally overrun with what they call broom grass" ("John Clayton's Transcript of the Journal of Robert Fallam," in Alvord and Bidgood, *The First Explorations of the Trans-Allegheny Region*, 189). See also Erhard Rostlund, "The Myth of a Natural Prairie in Alabama," Association of American Geographers, *Annals*, LXVII (1957), 397; Stephen Adams, *The Best and Worst Country in the World: Perspectives on the Early Virginia Landscape*, 37.

380. On the war between the cranes and pygmies, see Homer, *Iliad* 3.6 (*Hayes* 995, 1524, 1527, 1543, 1550, 1559). See also *Pliny* 7.2.26–27, 10.28.58.

381. The Ushery (so named by Lederer in 1670), or Usheree, are generally thought to be identical with the Catawba. See Douglas Summers Brown, *The Catawba Indians: The People of the River* (Columbia, S.C., 1966), 19, 42; R. P. Stephen Davis, Jr., "The Cultural Landscape of the North Carolina Piedmont at Contact," in Robbie Ethridge and Charles Hudson, eds., *The Transformation of the Southeastern Indians, 1540–1760* (Jackson, Miss., 2002), 140.

382. *Equinoctial:* the equator, so called from the celestial equator; when the sun is on the celestial equator, "the nights and days are of equal length in all parts of the world" *(OED)*.

383. A philological debate sprang up in the seventeenth century, originating with Samuel Bochart (1599–1667), minister to the Protestant church at Caen, tutor to the earl of Roscommon, and accomplished biblical scholar. In 1663 he was the first to identify the crocodile as the biblical Leviathan (Samuel Bochart, *Hierozoicon sive Bipertitum Opus de Animalibus Sacrae Scripturae* [London, 1663], II, 769–791).

Though Bochart's learned treatise does not appear in the catalog of Byrd's library, he might have seen the book elsewhere, or he might have encountered Bochart's argument in any number of later works. Theological treatises, biblical commentaries, and religious works concerned with philological matters all drew on Bochart's discovery. Bernard Lamy's *Apparatus Biblicus,* for instance, notes that the Hebrew words *"Leviathan* and *Thannis* both signify either *Dragons,* or *Whales.* But *Bochart* plainly shews that it must be understood in that place of *Job,* of the *Crocodile"* ([Bernard] Lamy, *Apparatus Biblicus; or, An Introduction to the Holy Scriptures* [London, 1723], 416). See also Simon Patrick, *The Books of Job, Psalms, Proverbs, Ecclesiastes, and the Song of Solomon, Paraphras'd* (London, 1710), I, 109. *The Athenian Oracle* (London, 1703) credits "the very Learned Mr. *Bochart*" for the fact that the most learned commentators "have left the received Opinion concerning *Leviathan,* whom they rather believe the *Crocodile* than the *Whale*" (II, 474.)

Just as Herodotus and Pliny supplemented the work of early travel writers, so did Bochart supplement writers interested in portraying exotic climes. In 1693, Patrick Gordon declared,

In the Famous River of *Nile,* are abundance of *Crocodiles,* those terrible and devouring Animals, which *Bochartus* . . . endeavours to prove to be the same with the Creature mentioned in the Book of *Job* under the Name of *Leviathan,* though commonly and hitherto taken for the Whale.

—[Pat[rick] Gordon, *Geography Anatomiz'd; or, The Geographical Grammar,* 5th ed. (London, 1708), 314

And finally, in characteristic eighteenth-century fashion, some authors brought the translation to square with anatomic discoveries. In 1740, Gilbert Nelson described a collection of animal skeletons, explaining that Bochart had proven the hippopotamus to be the *"Behemoth* in Job," and the crocodile "is the Leviathan" (G[ilbert] Nelson, *The Wonders of Nature throughout the World Display'd, Both for Diversion and Instruction* [London, 1740], 62).

384. *Pennyworth:* "Money's worth, value for one's money; a (sufficient) return for one's payment or trouble; a bargain" *(OED).*

385. The Tuscarora War of 1711–1713.

386. The Catawba allied themselves with the English in the Tuscarora War, but several years later they fought against them in the Yamassee War of 1715.

387. *Cornelius Keith:* This is a puzzling reference, for Virginia records reveal that a certain Cornelius Keith in 1721 had been in partnership with Byrd. He was one of four men (the others were William Byrd, James Terry, and Jonathan Kembro) who petitioned and were allowed to take up five thousand acres in New Kent County. In 1724 Cornelius and Eliza Keeth were parishioners at Bristol Parish (*Council,* IV, 5; Churchill Gibson Chamberlayne, ed., *Vestry Book and Register of Bristol Parish, Virginia, 1720–1789* [Richmond, Va., 1898], 327). If the same person, it is possible that Keith disappointed or angered Byrd at some time after 1721; if so, this portrait could have been a matter of satirical revenge.

388. *Quern-Stones:* hand-operated grindstones used for milling grain. The lower stone is stationary, and the upper turned by hand. A rather primitive tool, it was still useful for farmers with no access to large, water-driven gristmills.

389. *Pan of his Knee:* the patella, or kneecap.

390. On the Scythian practice of scalping, see note 270, above.

391. In the *Secret History* Byrd identifies the "convert" as Thomas Page. As a Quaker in Virginia, Page would indeed have suffered under some legal restraints, including being barred from public office and having to pay stiff penalties for not paying tithes or supporting the militia.

392. After the Tuscarora War, the Saponi and their Siouan allies the Tutelo (Totero), Occaneechi, Keyauwee, Eno, Shakori, and Stuckaho (Stuckanox) were officially incorporated as the Saponi Nation.

393. *Nation, canton,* and *clan* are standard terms in the vocabulary of political geography. Byrd's description of Indian society using the words *nation* and *canton* is probably drawn from Lahontan, who explained the structure of the Five Nations:

> These *Barbarians* are drawn up in five Cantons, not unlike those of the *Swisses.* Tho' these Cantons are all of one Nation, and united in one joynt interest, yet they go by different names. . . . Their Language is almost the same. . . . Every year the five Cantons send Deputies to assist at the Union Feast, and to smoak the great *Calumet,* or Pipe of the five Nations.
> —*Lahontan,* 23 (*Hayes* 83, 160)

Byrd, like other writers of his time, was not very clear about the details of Indian social structures and used various terms interchangeably. Elsewhere in *The History of the Dividing Line* he distinguishes between subgroups of the Tuscarora using the term *clan*—the "Northern Clans of that Nation," the "Connechta-clan."

394. *Postern:* a back door; figuratively an entrance (or exit) other than the principal or honorable one *(OED)*. Byrd's comment about the Muscovite aversion to hanging very probably comes from Pierre Martin de La Martinière:

> 'Tis but lately that the *Muscovites* have hang'd their Criminals; the reason why they would not permit any such Executions before, was out of a foolish fancy, that when the Man was strangled, his Soul departed downwards, and that defil'd it.
> —*A New Voyage to the North: Containing, a Full Account of Norway; the Laplands, both Danish, Swedish, and Muscovite; of Borandia, Siberia, Samojedia, Zembla, and Iseland* (London, 1706), 156

395. The Tottero (or Tutelo or Tetero) were a Siouan nation; they allied themselves with the Saponi in the late-seventeenth century.

Trumpet Plant: the thorn apple, or jimsonweed *(Datura stramonium).* The latter name is a corruption of "Jamestown weed," after soldiers gathered it for salads in Jamestown in 1676 (*Beverley,* book 2, 23). Clayton reported on the hallucinatory effects in *Philosophical Transactions:* "Several of them went to gather a Sallad in the Fields, and lighting in great Quantities on an Herb called *Iames-town-weed,* they gathered it; and by eating thereof in plenty, were rendered apish and foolish" ("A Letter from the Revd Mr. John Clayton (Afterwards Dean of Kildare in Ireland) to Dr. Grew, in Answer to Several Queries relating to Virginia . . . ," *Philosophical Transactions,* XLI [1739–1741], 160). The alkaloid poison of *Datura stramonium* is strongest in the leaves, flowers, and seeds; to achieve a fatal result, the princess would have had to consume a great deal of the root.

396. Ever since Pliny asserted that transformation of females to males "is not an idle story" (*Pliny* 7.4.36), the notion continued to fascinate. Early modern discussions of anatomy usually drew on Galen's theory of genital identity between men and women:

> It was the opinion of *Galen* in his 14. book *de usu partium,* and the 11. chap. that women had all those parts belonging to Generation which men have, although in these they appear outward at the *Peritoaeum* or *interfoeminiam,* in those they are for want of heat reteined within.

> The ancients have thought a woman might become a man, but not on the contrary side a man become a woman. For they say that the parts of generation in women ly hid, because the strength of their naturall heate is weaker then in men in whom it thrusteth those parts outward.
> —Helkiah Crooke, *Mikrokosmographia: A Description of the Body of Man . . .* (London, 1631), 216, 249

Crooke cited numerous authorities who had reported examples of women whose genitalia "opened" into male genitalia, usually through exercise, swift movement, and excessive heat, but he casts doubt on the theory. See also Ambroise Paré's chapter "Of the

Changing of Sexe," in section "Of Monsters and Prodigies," in *The Workes of That Famous Chirurgion Ambrose Parey* (London, 1665), 650–651.

Byrd exhibited considerable curiosity about sexual anatomy. His *Commonplace Book* records extensive reading in Nicolas Venette's popular handbook of sexual matters, *De la génération de l'homme ou tableau de l'amour conjugal* (Cologne, 1696) (*Hayes* 1405, 1469); see *Commonplace Book*, 73–77, 248, 273–292. In the matter of dramatic sex changes, Venette explained:

> Si les parties naturelles des femmes estoient toutes semblables à celles des hommes, et qu'il n'y eust seulement de différence que dans le renversement de ces mesmes parties, on auroit raison de dire que la femme est un homme imparfait, et que le froideur de son sexe est cause que ses parties sont demeurées au dedans, au lieu de sortir au dehors comme celles des hommes.
> —*De la génération de l'homme*, 17–18

> If women's natural parts are exactly like those of men, and if there is only the difference in the turning back of these parts, one could say that woman is an imperfect man, and that the coolness of her sex is the reason that her parts remain inside, instead of emerging without, like those of men.

Venette next adduced examples of women who became men when a dramatic increase of heat associated with achieving sexual maturity caused "les parties amoureuses" to emerge, as occurred with a young Italian woman who became a man in the time of the Emperor Constantine.

> Ce peut estre aussi quelque effort violent qui fait sortir ce mêmes parties; témoin *Marie Germain* dont parle *Paré*, qui ayant fait un grand effort en sautant fossé, devint homme à la mesme heure par la sortie des partes naturelles.
> —*De la génération de l'homme*, 618

> This can also happen when some violent effort causes the same parts to surface, as seen in Marie Germain, according to Paré, who, making a great effort leaping over a ditch, became a man at the same time upon the emergence of the natural parts.

Venette acknowledged that the work of modern anatomists has made it difficult to sustain Galen's theory, and eventually he concluded that essential differences between male and female constitution meant such extraordinary changes were in fact impossible (18, 622).

For a modern survey of the history of how hermaphroditism was understood, see Thomas Laqueur, *Making Sex: Body and Gender from the Greeks to Freud* (Cambridge, Mass., 1990), 122–141. See also Jane A. C. Rush, "Book-ends: The Role of the Eunuch and the Hermaphrodite in Nicolas Venette's *Tableau de l'amour considéré dans l'estat du mariage*," *Journal of European Studies*, XXXV (2004), 195–214.

Thus much for the physiological context; I have not been able to find a source of Byrd's reference to the Nun of Orleans. The jesting tone of the anecdote is, no doubt, Byrd's own addition.

397. Bishop Gilbert Burnet relates the tale of two Italian nuns in the narrative of his European travels:

I have now given you an account of all that appeared most remarkable to me in *Rome*. I shall to this add a very extraordinary piece of *Natural History* that fell out there within these *two years,* which I had first from those two learned Abbots, *Fabretti* and *Nazari,* and that was afterwards confirmed to me by *Cardinal Howard,* who was one of the *Congregation* of *Cardinals* that examined and judged the matter. There were *two Nuns* near *Rome,* one as I remember was in the *City;* and the other not far from it, who, after they had been for some years in a *Nunnery,* perceived a very strange change in Nature, and that their Sex was altered, which grew by some degrees to a total alteration in one; and tho the other was not so entire a change, yet it was visible she was more *Man* than *Woman;* upon this the matter was looked into: That which naturally offereth it self here, is, *that these two had been alwayes what they then appeared to be; but that they had gone into a Nunnery in a disguise, to gratifie a brutal Appetite.* But to this, when I proposed it, answer was made, that as the *Breasts* of a *Woman,* that remained still, did in a great measure shake off that Objection, so the proofs were given so fully, of their having been real *Females,* that there was no doubt left of that, nor had they given any sort of Scandal in the change of their *Sex;* And if there had been any room left to suspect a Cheat or Disguise, the proceedings would have been both more severe and more secret; and these persons would have been Burnt, or at least put to Death in some terrible manner. Some *Physicians* and *Chirurgeons* were appointed to examine the matter, and at last, after a long and exact inquiry, they were judged to be absolved from their *vows,* and were dismissed from the Obligation of a *Religious* Life, and required to go in *mens habit.* One of them was a *Valet de Chambre* to a *Roman Marquess,* when I was there: I heard of this matter only two dayes before I left *Rome,* so that I had not time to inquire after it more particularly; but I judged it so extraordinary, that I thought it was worth communicating to so curious an *Inquirer* into *Nature.*

—G[ilbert] Burnet, *Some Letters, Containing an Account of What Seemed Most Remarkable in Travelling through Switzerland, Italy, Some Parts of Germany, etc. in the Years 1685 and 1686* (Amsterdam, 1688), 179–180

398. Wright's *Prose Works* mistranscribes this width as eighty yards.

399. *Royal Fish:* Very rare in England, sturgeon caught there were reserved for the king as far back as the fourteenth century.

400. *Jole:* the head of a fish, and (in cookery) the head and shoulders of certain fish, such as the salmon, sturgeon, and ling *(OED).*

Compare with Banister's description of the Virginia method of catching sturgeon: "The English and Indians catch Sturgeons; we with Harping Irons, and they by clapping a wyth over their tails, which will sometimes pull them under water; and then he is accounted a Cockkarous or a brave fellow that keeps his hold, till with swimming wading and diving he has tired the Sturgeon, and got him ashore" (*Banister,* 354). Beverley's appropriation of Banister is obvious:

The *Indian* Way of Catching Sturgeon, when they come into the narrow part of the Rivers, was by a Man's clapping a Noose over their Tail, and by keeping fast his hold. Thus a Fish finding itself intangled, wou'd flounce, and often pull him under Water, and then that Man was counted a *Cockarouse,* or brave *Fellow,* that wou'd not let go;

till with Swimming, Wading, and Diving, he had tired the Sturgeon, and brought it ashore.

—*Beverley,* book 2, 33

Byrd's account appears to be an expanded version of Banister and Beverley.

401. *A Mahometan Feast:* a feast without alcoholic drinks, which are prohibited by the Qur'an. The parallel between Indians and Muslims occurred to other writers; William Strachey noted that the Indians have no wine: "Their drinck is, as the Turkes, cliere water; for albeit they have grapes . . . yet they have not falne upon the use of them." *The Historie of Travaile into Virginia Britannia,* ed. R. H. Major (London, 1849), 74.

402. Robert Bolling, who was appointed surveyor of Charles City County in 1726, and not Colonel John Bolling (1700–1757), as Boyd would have it; Drysdale, "The Present State of Virginia," *VMHB,* XLVIII (1940), 143; *Boyd,* 311.

403. *Lithuanian Fashion:* probably a reference to Polish king Jan Sobietski's tactic of dismounting the Lithuanian cavalry in 1673 to defeat the Turkish army at Kamieniec, as described by Edward Bohun:

Yet *Zobietsky,* then Marshal, but now King of *Poland,* with much lesser Forces . . . battered down their Brest-Work with his Cannon; and the next day dismounting his Cavalry to second the *Lithuanian* Foot, (which had been beaten off) in Person at the head of his Men stormed their Camp; took it, slew or took Prisoners thirty one thousand five hundred *Turks,* (and the rest hardly escaped) *Solyman* their General being slain.

—Bohun, *A Geographical Dictionary* (1693), 101 (*Hayes* 12)

404. *Polcat* or *polecat:* a small dark-brown carnivorous quadruped of the *Mustelidae,* or weasel family. The European polecat is *Putorius foetidus,* the American *Putorius nigripes.* The fetid scent they give off when alarmed is secreted by scent glands under the tail, not in its urine. Edward Tyson reported to the Royal Society that he observed in polecats

that just at the extream of the *Rectum,* were placed two *bags,* filled with a crasse, and whitish liquor; whose *stink* was so very great, that I could not well endure the room, till I had removed them; and then the whole body seemed very inoffensive.

—"*Tajacu, seu Aper Mexicanus Moschiferus,* or the Anatomy of the *Mexico Musk-Hog,*" *Philosophical Transactions,* XIII (1683), 377

The notion that the porcupine shoots its quills is another ancient folktale (*Pliny* 8.43.125).

405. *Stinker:* the South African striped polecat *(Ictonyx striatus)* actually does squirt a foul-smelling secretion at enemies, causing blindness if it gets in the eyes. The offensive material is not urine or feces, as Byrd reports—"squittering" is to squirt or splatter, or to void thin excrement—but rather the secretion of anal glands. Byrd's source for this digression is Peter Kolb:

In the *Hottentot* Countries there is an Animal the *Dutch* call *Stinkbingsem,* i.e. *Stink-box* or *Stink-Breeches.* 'Tis the most farting, fizzling, stinking Animal under the Sun. Stinking is the grand Defence Nature has given this Creature against all its Enemies; and, for the most Part, it farts and stinks 'em out of the Field. 'Tis shap'd like a

Ferret; and is of the Size of a midling Dog. When his Pursuer, whether Man or Beast, is come pretty near him, he pours out from his Tail so horrid a Stench, that neither Man nor Beast can endure it. A Man that is surpris'd with this Stench, is almost knock'd down by it before he can get out of it. And a Dog, or any other Animal that runs into it, is strangely confounded and madded by it.

—Peter Kolben, *The Present State of the Cape of Good-Hope* . . . (London, 1738), II, 133

Thomas Salmon offers a version of Kolb's account in *Modern History; or, The Present State of All Nations,* III (London, 1739), 35 (incidentally, this is the same page as Salmon's borrowing of Kolb on baboons' raiding orchards, noted above). The anonymous author, Officer of the Fleet, of *A Voyage to the South-Seas, and to Many Other Parts of the World, Performed from the Month of September in the Year 1740, to June 1744, by Commodore Anson* (London, 1744) (ESTC T144348), repeats the passage almost word for word in his account of the Cape of Good Hope (604–605).

406. *A Saint Anthony's Meal:* see note 297, above.

Osnabrugs (Osnabrigs, Osnaburg): coarse linen of the sort originally made in Osnabrück, Germany.

407. *Gibeonite Ambassadors:* See note 102, above.

408. *Pillars of Hercules:* In classical geography, the rock formations on either side of the straits where the Mediterranean Sea opens into the Atlantic Ocean—Calpe (Gibraltar) on the European side and Abilix (Ximeria) on the African side—were known as the Pillars of Hercules. The pillars marked the bounds of the inhabited world as well as the end of the travels of Hercules (Strabo, *Geography* 3.5.5).

409. Wright, in *Prose Works,* notes, "The sense of the word 'honor' is not clear; perhaps the scribe wrote 'honor' instead of 'humor'" (334).

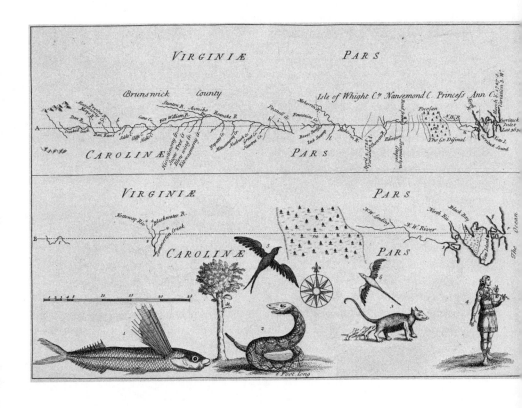

The Secret History of the Line

INTRODUCTION

Byrd's *Secret History of the Line* blends seemingly incongruous elements: accurate transcriptions of official letters, grave reflections on current events, comic anecdotes, scandalous revelations, and a pervasively libertine tone. Still, a degree of seriousness may be discerned in Byrd's approach, despite all the levity, ribaldry, and personal satire. *The Secret History* conceals its agenda within a bawdy, picaresque, satirical narrative. Byrd's satire targets the backward people and venal dignitaries of North Carolina, and especially the drunken, lascivious, and irascible commissioners—as Byrd saw them. His norm is the ideal, imagined Virginia, as in *The History of the Dividing Line*—law-abiding, loyal to the crown, industrious, devout but not to the point of enthusiasm, and well governed by the king's appointed officers and his Council, upright men of the patrician class.

The title of *The Secret History* is significant, not because Byrd wished to keep the narrative "hidden from public eye," as some critics have presumed, though Byrd surely meant it to be seen only by a very few readers. Rather, Byrd consciously participated in a specific tradition of history writing. Secret histories implicitly promised to provide readers with an account of hidden motives and currents of action, revelations of surprising things not known to the general public but momentous and extraordinary. This approach presupposed a gap between public explanations of events and the real story. Official explanations masked greed, corruption, and folly. Secret histories also provide amusement in the form of scandal, banter, mock-serious polemics, satire, lampoon, and ridicule. Certain narrative techniques enhanced the aura of secrecy, as in the case of the anonymous *Secret History of the Most Renown'd Q. Elizabeth, and the E. of Essex,* which purports to reveal a clandestine affair between Elizabeth I and her favorite courtier. The book was so scandalous, or pretended to be, that it could be published only abroad—or pretend to be. The title page bore a false place of imprint (Cologne) and a fantastical publisher (printed for Will with the Wisp, at the sign of the Moon in the Ecliptick). Such spurious politicoromantic secret histories abounded, blurring distinctions between fiction and history, whereas authors of such fictional personal histories as *Robinson Crusoe* or *Fanny Hill: Memoirs of a Woman of Pleasure* pretended their novels were just as real as ostensibly factual historical relations.[1]

---

1. See, for instance, Douglas Anderson, "Plotting William Byrd," *WMQ*, 3d Ser., LVI (1999), 703; Person of Quality, *The Secret History of the Most Renown'd Q. Elizabeth, and the E. of Essex* (Cologne [London], 1680?).

Authors of secret histories often claimed the moral high ground, either seriously or satirically, by insisting their purpose was to expose vice and folly for the common good. Byrd owned a copy of *The Secret History of the Reigns of K. Charles II, and K. James II,* which claimed to follow the example of the Roman historian Suetonius, who made public "the Vices and Miscarriages of the Twelve *Caesars,* with the same freedom with which they were by them Committed." This secret history of the Stuart kings claimed the same lofty purpose, "as well to Vindicate, as to Inform," exposing hidden truths by exposing "the Two Last Reigns upon the Stage, and then let all the World judg of the Furberies and Tyranny of those Times," all the better to highlight "the Integrity, Sincerity, and Sweetness" of the reign of William and Mary. The truth of the Stuarts' "more secret Transactions"—that is, disturbing political machinations—was observable in the consequences.[2]

Thus, Byrd's title signaled his readers what to anticipate, confident they would be sufficiently familiar with the subgenre to expect full disclosure of devious politics and shocking personal actions as well as factual detail needed for a full understanding of historical proceedings. Indeed, Byrd also explicitly named one episode of *The History of the Dividing Line*—the apocryphal tale of a scandal concerning William Penn—a "Secret History." A great deal of Byrd's reportage reproduces the cynical tone characteristic of secret histories, as when he notes that Governor Alexander Spotswood was "overreach't" in assenting to the "unequal Proposals" that eventually yielded more land to North Carolina than Byrd might have preferred.

Together with the political issues of the period, Byrd's *Secret History* focuses on personality, employing satirically exaggerated character sketches of

2. [John Phillips], *The Secret History of the Reigns of K. Charles II, and K. James II* ([London], 1690), sig. A2r–v (*Hayes* 2093). Among the other secret histories in Byrd's library, *The Secret History of the Most Renown'd Q. Elizabeth, and the E. of Essex* was also published by the fantastical publisher "Will with the Wisp" and claimed to reveal undercover negotiations for a marriage between Queen Elizabeth and Catherine de Medici's last unmarried son. Royal intrigue was a topic of perennial interest; Byrd owned a copy of Claude Vanel, *The Royal Mistresses of France; or, The Secret History of the Amours of All the French Kings . . .* (London, 1695) (*Hayes* 2454), and a copy of *The Memoirs of Philip de Comines* (London, 1723) (*Hayes* 240, 241), which, as Kevin Hayes has pointed out, includes "the secret history of Louis XI. out of a book called the scandalous chronicle." This is devoted mostly to political and military scandals, with a few titillating passages added for good measure.

D. Jones, *The Secret History of White-Hall, from the Restoration of Charles II. down to the Abdication of the Late K. James* (London, 1697) (*Hayes* 50, 882), offers "new Discoveries of State-Mysteries" in the form of fictional letters from an Englishman who served as interpreter for the French minister of state (sig. A4v). On Byrd's collection of secret histories, see *Hayes,* 64.

his colleagues. Byrd was a devotee and accomplished practitioner of the Theophrastian art of satirical character writing. Real frictions developed in the expedition, real differences of opinion, and real clashes of personality, and satirical characters typically begin with a factual foundation. Local historian Manly Wade Wellman shrewdly observes:

> No man of the expedition seems to have enjoyed the life of a camping explorer to any great extent, and tempers grew short with many arguments between the two sets of commissioners. The redoubtable William Byrd, who was keeping a journal of the boundary's tracing, soon found he could admire almost no person in the company except himself.[3]

The cast of *The Secret History* may be viewed as a set of serial character sketches, each one emphasizing the way the subject was characteristically marked by folly or vice. Byrd was not well pleased with the North Carolina commissioners, the "Flower & Cream of the Council of that Province," as he sarcastically describes them. They were as arrogant and sure of their status as any Virginia gentleman, but with far less reason. All heavy drinkers, crude, profane, and lecherous, they were continually in trouble with their governor—not because they asserted the liberties of Englishmen like the Virginian councillors, but because they were borderline criminals and rebels. Byrd hinted at nearseditious activities, as when Plausible and Puzzlecause returned from Edenton, "where they had been to recover the great Fatigue of doing nothing & to pick up new Scandal against their Governour."

Byrd provided the commissioners with comic names denoting reprehensible qualities, and the men live up (or down) to their names. According to Byrd, the senior North Carolina commissioner, Christopher Gale ("Judge Jumble") rose to his position as chief justice through family connections, not legal expertise. His wealth came through shady practices, including consorting with pirates. The North Carolina councillors holding offices in the judiciary were always in danger of prosecution. Jumble and Puzzlecause, hurrying to join the second leg of the expedition despite the governor's orders to remain in Edenton for General Court, "seem'd afraid of being pursued, & arrested," and soon a chance visitor's resemblance to the governor put them "into a Panick." All Judge Jumble does during the entire progress of the expedition is to travel with the company and drink to excess whenever possible. He lacks the gravitas of a senior judge, and the nickname Byrd assigns him is apt, for "jumble" denotes a

3. Manly Wade Wellman, *The County of Warren, North Carolina, 1586–1917* (Chapel Hill, N.C., 1959), 11.

For Byrd's interest in Theophrastus and other writers in the literary tradition of the "Character," see *Commonplace Book*, 38–39.

"confused or disorderly mixture or assemblage," precisely fitting Byrd's view of the disorder and muddle of North Carolina and its government.[4]

William Little ("Puzzlecause") was North Carolina's attorney general. The name Byrd attaches to him is appropriately insulting, for it denotes legal chicanery, rumored to be Little's specialty. In legal terminology a "cause" denotes a legal issue or the facts of a case. To "puzzle" a cause is to instill confusion and perplexity in people unable to understand or follow a deliberately overcomplex argument concerning legal matters. Puzzlecause displays his legal sophistry by drawing up a statement "concerning the quarrel betwixt Firebrand & Meanwell" for the timid Orion, who could neither tell the truth for fear of the one, nor lie for fear of the other. Byrd asserts Puzzlecause "had degenerated from a New-England Preacher, for which his Godly Parents design'd him, to a very wicked, but awkward Rake." Thus he stresses the contradiction between Little's public pose of seriousness and his brutish private conduct.

The portrait of Edward Moseley ("Plausible") is a little more complex. Byrd alleges he is as smooth-tongued as a Jesuit, stressing his ability to twist words into equivocation, retaining just enough truth in his lies to appear trustworthy and believable. Moseley's dubious record in the previous survey attempt, however, forced him to be on his best behavior.

The fourth commissioner, John Lovick ("Shoebrush"), earned his name from Byrd's low opinion of his obscure origins and easy manners. He was a "merry good humour'd man," but his manners were servile. There is no evidence that Lovick had really been Governor Hyde's "Valet de Chambre," as Byrd claimed, though he did arrive in North Carolina in Hyde's retinue in 1713. Byrd's characterization highlighted Lovick's vulgar obsequiousness, his unknown origins, and the absence of good family connections (until he married Governor Charles Eden's widow, Penelope). The ironic insult is compounded by mockery of Shoebrush's mismatched clothing.

Virginia commissioner Richard Fitzwilliam ("Firebrand") is the chief target of Byrd's satire. His character-name reveals a choleric temperament, and in *The Secret History* Firebrand is vain, greedy, headstrong, jealous, conspiratorial, given to sudden rages, and obsessed with compelling others to treat him with the respect he believed due to him. Fitzwilliam possessed no qualifications for his position as commissioner, having spent little time in Virginia and none at all on the frontier. He held a place on the Executive Council in respect for his position as surveyor general of Customs and, Byrd implies, got himself appointed to the Virginia commission for the stipend alone—or, perhaps, for

---

4. The definitions supporting analysis of Byrd's nicknames here and in the following discussion draw on the *OED*.

the stipend and the opportunity to order around a large company of inferiors. Firebrand bullies anybody less powerful or independent, compels his subordinates to make obeisance to him, favors the weak in order to enjoy their gratitude, and attempts to use his authority to punish anybody who falls short of flattering him. In the satirical scheme of the expedition, his alliance with the Carolinians makes perfect sense.[5]

The Secret History abounds with ribald humor, sometimes blatant and obvious, and at other times more subtle. A favorite pastime for Byrd is the extended double entendre. One such joke occurs in his description of the decorum of the Reverend Peter Fontaine in the midst of the cruder company. When the surveyors drew up their plat or map charting the progress of the first part of the survey, Fontaine apparently commented on one feature of their draftsmanship, the "Prick't" or dotted line, but with extreme modesty substituted the less suggestive word "Pipp't." The joke hinges on the chaplain's reluctance, unsurprising in such a company, to risk the phallic double entendre, instead calling attention to the very usage he hoped to avoid. Byrd (as "Steddy") claims to be displeased with the "low Wit" of the company, but after all it is Byrd himself who takes care to record every such jest. Moreover, there is really no way for readers to distinguish the jokes of Byrd's companions from those invented by Byrd himself. In this way he manages to have his cake and eat it too. Thus Byrd works both sides of *The Secret History*'s bawdy joking—as the writer recording the jokes and the characterized narrator affecting disapproval.

In the same way Byrd works both sides of the playfully crude libertine activities of the surveying party. Byrd portrays himself (as "Steddy") struggling to maintain or restore order. Steddy intervenes to avert abuses of all sorts, and he voices his disapproval of such barbarity. At the same time, readers will observe that the author relates the stories of abuse with a droll, rakish delight. Nonetheless, it should be stressed that the bawdy humor of *The Secret History* is a literary posture. Byrd affected a rakish tone, considering this sort of joking amusing and acceptable for gentlemen. Libertine humor is a literary artifice, not necessarily a spontaneous expression of moral or psychological character.[6]

The most remarkable literary invention of *The Secret History* is Byrd's fic-

5. For a detailed discussion of Fitzwilliam, see Appendix 1: Dramatis Personae.

6. It is constructive to note that Byrd's bawdy passages are rhetorically devised and indicate a sense of what he imagined would be acceptable to his audience. That is to say, they provide evidence for participation in a culture of misogynistic humor, but they do not reliably indicate the extent of what some historians have concluded were Byrd's "exploitative habits and invidious attitudes." See Douglas Anderson's incisive analysis of the logic by which Kathleen Brown draws her conclusions about Byrd's libertinism, in "Plotting William Byrd," *WMQ*, 3d Ser., LVI (1999), 701–702.

tionalized self-portrait in Steddy, his narrative persona. Steddy's first-person narrative frames the expedition, comprehending both day-to-day occurrence of the official project and behind-the-scenes wrangling, dishonesty, faction, temper, and opportunism. As the account progresses, Byrd enriches the description of the sequence of events with a pattern of contrasts. While the official report of the survey and *The History of the Dividing Line* offered a public history of the Dividing Line survey, *The Secret History* highlights episodes hidden from the public eye, mostly the unbridled licentiousness, gluttony, and laziness of the Carolina commissioners and their ally in the Virginia company, Firebrand. Byrd invites his readers to compare these unruly figures with the mature restraint, guidance, and equanimity of his alter-ego, Steddy. At the same time it must be acknowledged that Byrd is not always able to maintain his separation of the two strains, for it is Steddy, after all, who elects to relate the very scandals about which he affects disapproval. Indeed, Steddy does not separate himself entirely from the unruly company, nor does his reserved stance keep his amusement in check on occasion. Thus, while *The Secret History* rests on a framework of actual events as they unfolded, it is advisable to read the satirical, risqué narration with caution. Everything is mediated through literary artifice, so that no representation of character is entirely reliable—not the targets of Byrd's satire, and not the characterization of Byrd as Steddy endeavoring to bring order out of chaos.

The Secret History of the Line

The Governour & Council of Virginia in the Year 1727 receiv'd an Express Order from his Majesty, to appoint Commissioners, who in Conjunction with others to be nam'd by the Government of North Carolina, shou'd run the Line betwixt the two Colonies. The Rule these Gentlemen were directed to go by, was a paper of Proposals formerly agreed on between the 2 Governors, at that time Spotswood and Eden. It would be a hard thing to say of so wise a Man as Mr. Spotswood thought himself, that he was overreach't, but it has appear'd upon Tryal that Mr. Eden was much better informed how the land lay than he.[1]

However since the King was pleased to agree to these unequal Proposals, the Government of Virginia was too Dutifull to dispute them. They therefore appointed Steddy & Merryman, Commissioners on the part of Virginia to execute that order, and Astrolabe & Capricorn to be the Surveyors. But Merryman dying, Firebrand & Meanwell made interest to fill his Place. Most of the Council inclined to favour the last, because he had offered his Services before he knew that any pay wou'd belong to the Place. But Burly, one of the Honble Board, perceiving his Friend Firebrand would lose it if it came to the vote, proposed the Expedient of sending 3 Commissioners, upon so difficult and [2] hazardous an Expedition. To this a Majority agreed, being unwilling to be thought too frugal of the Publick-Money. Accordingly, they were both join'd with Steddy in this Commission. When this was over Steddy proposed that a Chaplain might be allow'd to attend the Commissioners, by reason they should have a Number of Men with them sufficient for a small Congregation and were to pass thro' an ungodly Country where they shou'd find neither Church nor Minister. That besides it would be an Act of great Charity to give the Gentiles of that part of the World an Opportunity to Christen both them & their Children. This being unanimously consented to, Dr. Humdrum was named upon Steddy's recommendation.[2]

Of all these proceedings Notice was dispatched to Sir Richard Everard Governour of North Carolina, desiring him to name Commissioners on the part of that Province, to meet those of Virginia the Spring following. In consequence whereof that Government named Jumble, Shoebrush, Plausible, and Puzzlecause, being the Flower & Cream of the Council of that Province. The next Step necessary to be taken, was for the Commissionrs. on both Sides to agree upon a day of meeting at Coratuck Inlet, in order to proceed on this Business, and the 5th of March was thought a proper time, because then Mercury & the Moon were to be in conjunction.[3]

It was desired by Sir Richard that the Commissioners might meet on the Frontiers some [3] time in January to settle Preliminarys. And particularly that it might be previously agreed that the present Possessors of Land in either Government should be confirmed in their Possession, tho' it shou'd not happen to fall within the Government that granted it. This the Governor of Virginia disagreed to, not thinking it just that either the King or the Lords Proprietors should grant away Land that did not belong to them. Nor was this proposal made on the part of Carolina purely out of good Nature, but some of the Council of that Province found their own Interest concern'd; and particularly the Surveyor General must in Justice have returned some of his Fees, in case the People shou'd lose the Land he survey'd for them as belonging to the Proprietors, when in truth it belong'd to the King.

Soon after the Commissioners for Virginia wrote the following letter to the worthy Commissioners of N. Carolina:

Gentlemen,

We are sorry we can't have the Pleasure of meeting you in January next, as is desired by your Governor. The Season of the Year in which that is proposed to be done, & the distance of our Habitation from your Frontiers, we hope will make our Excuse reasonable. Besides, his Majesty's Order marks out our Business so plainly that we are perswaded that there can be no difficulty in the Construction of it. After [4] this, what imaginable Dispute can arise amongst Gentlemen who meet together with Minds averse to Chicane, and Inclinations to do equal Justice both to His Majesty and the Lords Proprietors, in which disposition we make no doubt the Commissioners on both Sides will find each other.

We shall have full powers to agree at our first meeting on what Preliminarys shall be thought necessary, which we hope you will likewise be, that an affair of so great Consequence may have no Delay or Disappointment.

It is very proper to acquaint you in what Manner we intend to come provided, that so you Gentlemen who are appointed in the same Station may if you please do the same Honour to your Government. We shall bring with us about 20 Men furnish't with Provisions for 40 Days. We shall have a Tent with us & a Marquis for the Convenience of Ourselves & Servants. We shall be provided with as much Wine & Rum as just enable us, and our Men to drink every Night to the Success of the following Day. And because we understand there are many Gentiles on your Frontiers, who never had an Opportunity of being Baptized, we shall have a Chaplain with us to make them Christians. For this Purpose we intend to rest in our Camp every Sunday that there may be leizure for so good a work. And whoever of your Province shall be desirous of Novelty may repair on Sundays [5] to our Camp and hear a Sermon. Of this you may please to give publick Notice, that the Charitable Intentions of this Government may meet with the happier Success.[4]

Thus much, Gentlemen, we thought it necessary to acquaint you with and to make use of this first Opportunity of Signifying with how much Satisfaction we receiv'd the News that such able Commissioners are appointed for that Government, with whom we promise ourselves we shall converse with prodigious Pleasure, & execute our Commissions to the full content of those by whom we have the Honour to be employ'd.

We are, Gentlemen, Your most humble Servants,

    Firebrand, Steddy, Meanwell

      Williamsburgh

      the 16th of Decemr., 1727.[5]

To this Letter the Commissioners of Virginia the latter End of January receiv'd the following Answer:

    Gentlemen:

We have the Honour of your Favour from Williamsburgh, dated the 16th of December, in which you Signify, that the Proposals already agreed on are so plain, that you are perswaded there can no difficulty arise about the Construction of them. We think so too; but if no dispute shou'd arise in construing them, yet the Manner of our Proceeding in the Execution we thought had better be previously [6] concerted, and the End of the Meeting we propos'd was to remove every thing that might ly in the way to retard the Work, which we all seem equally desirous to have amicably concluded. We assure you Gentlemen we shall meet you with a hearty disposition of doing equal Justice to either Government. And as you acquaint us you shall come fully empower'd to agree at our first Meeting, to settle all necessary Preliminarys, we shall endeavour to have our Instructions as large. Your Governor in his last Letter to ours, was pleas'd to mention our conferring with you by Letters, about any Matters previously to be adjusted. We therefore take leave to desire by this Messenger, you will let us know after what Manner you purpose to run the Line, whether you think to go thro' the Great Swamp, which is near 30 Miles thro', & thought not passable, or by taking the Latitude at the first Station to run a due West Line to the Swamp, & then to find the said Latitude on the West Side the Swamp, & continue thence a due West Line to Chowan River. Or to make the 2d. Observation upon Chowan River and run an East Line to the Great Swamp. We shall also be glad to know what Instruments you intend to use to observe the Latitude, & find the Variation with, in Order to fix a due West Line. For we are told the last time the Commissioners met their Instruments varied Severall Minutes, which we hope will not happen again, [7] after we have been at the trouble of meeting in so remote a place, and with such Attendance & Equipage as you intend on your part. We are at a loss, Gentlemen, whether to thank you for the Particulars you give us of your Tent, Stores, and the Manner you design to meet us. Had you been silent, we had not wanted an Excuse for not meeting you in the same Manner; but now you force us to expose the Nakedness of our Country, & tell you, we can't possibly meet you in the Manner our great respect to you, wou'd make us glad to do, whom we are not emulous of outdoing, unless in Care & Diligence in the Affair we came about. So all we can answer to that Article, is, that we will endeavour to provide as well as the Circumstances of things will admit; And what we want in necessaries we hope will be made up in Spiritual Comfort we expect from your Chaplain, of whom we shall give Notice as you desire; & doubt not of making a great many Boundary Christians. To conclude, we promise, to make ourselves as agreeable to you as possibly we can; & we beg leave to assure you that it is a Singular Pleasure to us, that you Gentlemen are nam'd on that Part, to see this business of so great concern & consequence to both Governments determin'd which makes it to be undertaken on our parts more cheerfully, being assur'd your Characters are above any Artifice or Design.

We are [8]

    Your most obedient humble Servants,

      Plausible.   Jumble

      Puzzlecause   Shoebrush.

This Letter was without date they having no Almanacks in North-Carolina, but it came about the beginning of January. However the Virginia-Commissioners did not return an Answer to it, til they had consulted their Surveyor honest Astrolabe, as to the Mathematical Part. When that was done, they reply'd in the following Terms.[6]

    Gentlemen.

We shou'd have return'd an Answer sooner, had not the cold Weather, & our remote Situation from one another prevented our Meeting. However we hope 'tis now time[a] enough to thank you for that favour, & to assure you, that tho' we are appointed Commissioners for this Government we incline to be very just to yours. And as the fixing fair Boundarys between us will be of equal Advantage to both, you shall have no reason to reproach us with making any Step either to delay or disappoint so usefull a Work. If the Great Swamp you mention should be absolutely impassable[b], we then propose to run a due West Line from our first Station thither, & then survey round the same

[a]*Here begins the Huntington Library fragment of the Secret History (H).*   [b]H: <~~Difficulty~~>, shou'd be absolutely impassable

til we shall come on^c our due West Course on the other Side, & so proceed til we shall be again interrupted. But [9] if you shall think of a more proper Expedient, we shall not be fond of our own Opinion. And though we can't conceive that taking^d the Latitude will be of any Use in running this Line, yet we shall be provided to do it with the greatest exactness. In performing which we shall on our part use no graduated Instrument, but our accurate Surveyor Astrolabe^e tells us he will use a Method that will come nearer the Truth. He likewise proposes to discover as near as possible the just Variation of the Compass, by means of a true Meridian to be found by the North Star. We shall bring with us 2 or 3 very good Compasses, which we hope will not differ much from yours, though if there should be some little Variance^f, 'twill be easily reconciled by two such skillfull Mathematicians as Astrolabe and Plausible.⁷

In short Gentlemen we are so conscious of our own disposition to do right to both Colonys, & at the same time so verily persuaded of yours, that we promise to our selves an intire harmony & good Agreement. This can hardly fail, when Justice & Reason are laid down on both Sides as the Rule and Foundation of our Proceeding. We hope the Season will prove favourable to us, but be that as it will we intend to preserve fair Weather in our Humour, believing that even the Dismal may be very tolerable in good Company. We are [10] without the least Artifice or design,

Gentlemen,

Your most humble Servants,

S. F. M.

It was afterwards agreed by the Commissioners on both Sides to meet on the North Shoar of Coratuck Inlet, on the 5th day of the following March in order to run the Dividing Line. In the mean time, those on the Part of Virginia divided the trouble of making the necessary preparations. It fell to Steddy's Share to provide the Men^g that were to attend the Surveyors. For this purpose, Mr. Mumford recommended to him 15 able Woodsmen, most of which had been Indian Traders. These were order'd to meet him^h at Warren's Mill, arm'd with a Gun and Tomahawk, on the 27th of February, & furnisht with Provisions for ten Days. Astrolabeⁱ came on the 26th in order to attend Steddy^j to the Place of Rendezvous.⁸

The next day they^k crost the River, having first recommended all they left behind^l to the Divine Protection. Steddy carry'd with him 2 Servants, & a

---

^cH: come into ^dH: the takeing ^eH: Astrolabe] *All character names in H are overwritten in spaces which are heavily erased.* ^fH: Variation ^gH: It fell to ^Steddy to^ have to provide the Men ^hH: These <I> were ordered to meet ^<me> him^ ⁱH: Mr. ——— came ^jH: to ^attend Steddy^ ^kH: <we> they ^lH: all they left ^behind^

Sumpter Horse for his Baggage[m]. About 12 a Clock he[n] met the Men at the New-Church near Warren's Mill. He[o] drew them out to the Number of 15, & finding their Arms in good Order, He[p] caus'd them to be muster'd by their Names as follows:

Peter Jones	Tho: Jones	John Ellis
James Petillo	Charles Kimball	John Evans
Tho. Short	George Hamilton	Robert Hix [11]
Tho: Wilson	Steven Evans	Tho: Jones Junr.
George Tilman	Robert Allen	John Ellis, Junr.[q,9]

Here, after drawing out this small Troop, Steddy made them the following Speech:

Friends & Fellow-Travellers:

It is a Pleasure to me to see that we are like to be so well attended in this long & painfull Journey. And what may we not hope from Men who list themselves not so much for Pay, as from an Ambition to serve their Country. We have a great distance to go, & much work to perform, but I observe too much Spirit in your Countenances to flinch at either. As no care shall be wanting on my Part to do every one of you Justice, so I promise myself that on yours, you will set the Carolina Men, whom we are to meet at Corotuck, a constant Pattern of Order, Industry, & Obedience.

Then he march't his Men in good Order to Capricorn's Elegant Seat, according to the Route before projected[r], but found him in dolefull Dumps for the illness of his Wife. She was really indisposed, but not so dangerously as to hinder a vigorous Man from going upon the Service of his Country. However he seem'd in the midst of his Concern to discover a Secret Satisfaction, that it furnish't him with an Excuse of not going upon an Expedition, that he fancy'd wou'd be both dangerous & difficult[s]. Upon his refusing to go for the reason abovemention'd, Steddy wrote to the [12] Governor how much he was disappointed at the Loss of one of the Surveyors, & recommended Astrolabe's Brother to supply his Place. At the same time he dispatch't away an Express to Young Astrolabe to let him know he had nam'd him to the Governor[t] for his Service. But not knowing how it would be determin'd he cou'd promise him nothing, tho' if he would come to Norfolk at his own Risque, he shou'd there be able to resolve him. This was

---

[m]H: <I> ^Steddy^ carried with him 2 Servants & a Sumpter horse for his Baggage
[n]H: <I> ^he^   [o]H: <I> ^he^   [p]H: <I> ^he^   [q]*H has minor variation in names:* Thomas Jones, Charles Kimbal, Geo: Hamilton, Tho. Jones Junr.   [r]H: before had projected
[s]H: ^both difficult and^ dangerous   [t]H: to young Astrolabe to let him know he had named him to the Governor

the best Expedient he could think of for the Service at that Plunge, because Capricorn had in the bitterness of his Concern, taken no Care to acquaint the Governor[a] that he was prevented from going. However Dr. Arsmart who had been to visit Mrs. Capricorn, let the Governor know that he was too tender a Husband to leave his Spouse to the Mercy of a Physician. Upon this Notice, which came to the Governor before Steddy's Letter, it was so managed that the learned Orion was appointed to go in his room. This Gentleman is Professor of the Mathematics in the College of William and Mary[b], but has so very few Scholars, that he might be well enough[c] spared from his Post for a short time. It was urg'd by his friends that a Person of his Fame for profound Learning wou'd give a grace to the Undertaking and be able to silence all the Mathematicks of Carolina. These were unanswerable reasons, [13] and so he was appointed. The Revd. Dr. Humdrum came time enough to bless a very plentiful Supper at Capricorn's. He treated his Company handsomely[d], and by the help of a Bowl of Rack Punch his grief[e] disappeared so entirely, that if he had not sent for Arsmart, it might have been suspected[f] his Lady's Sickness was all a Farce. However to do him Justice, the Man would never be concerned in a Plot that was like to cost him 5 Pistoles.[10]

28.   The Table was well spread again for Breakfast, but, unfortunately for the poor Horses, the Key of the Corn-loft was mislaid; at least the Servant was instructed to say as much.[g] We march't from hence in good Order to the Widdow Allen's, which was 22 Miles. She entertain'd us elegantly, & seem'd[h] to pattern Solomon's Housewife if one may judge by the neatness of her House, & the good Order of her Family. Here Firebrand & Meanwell had appointed to meet Steddy[i] but fail'd; however the Tent was sent hither under the Care of John Rice, of the Kingdom of Ireland, who did not arrive till 12 a Clock at night. This disorder at first setting out, gave us but an indifferent Opinion[j] of Firebrand's Management.[11]

29.   From hence Steddy sent a Letter to the Governor[k], with an Account of his March to that Place, & of the Steps he had taken about Astrolabe's Brother. At Ten in the Morning he thank't the clean Widdow for all her Civilitys, & march't under the Pilotage of Mr. Baker to Colo. Thomas Godding's. [14] By

---

[a]H: in the ^bitterness of his Concern, taken no care to^ acquainted the Governor
[b]H: in the Colledge ^of William and Mary^   [c]H: <very well> ^well enough^   [d]H: <[We were] handsomely entertained> He treated his company handsomely   [e]H: <the Colo's> ^his^ Greif   [f]H: it might have ^been^ suspected that   [g]H: the kea of the Corn-loft was mislaid, ^at least the Servant was instructed to say as much.^   [h]H: & and seemed *[sic]*
[i]H: Here Firebrand & Meanwell had appointed to meet ^Steddy^   [j]H: at our <first> setting out, gave <me> ^us But^ an indifferent Opinion   [k]H: <I> From hence Steddy sent a letter to the Govr.

the way Steddy[l] was oblig'd to be at the Expence of a few Curses upon John Rice, who was so very thirsty that he call'd[m] at every house he past by. The Cavalcade arrived[n] at Colo. Godding's about 4 a Clock after a pleasant Journey of 30 Miles. But Steddy found himself exceedingly fatigued with the March. In passing thro'[o] the upper part of the Isle of Wight, Mr. Baker remarkt the Dismal Footsteps made by the Hurricane[p] which happen'd in August 1626. The Violence of it did not extend in Breadth above a Quarter of a Mile, but in that Compass levell'd all before it. Mr. Baker's House was so unlucky as to stand in its way, which it laid flat to the Ground and blew some of his Goods above 2 Miles. Colo. Godding was very hospitable both to Man & Beast, But the poor Man had the Misfortune to be deaf[q], which hinder'd him from hearing any Parts of the Acknowledgments[r] that were made to him; he prest every body very kindly to eat, ^entreating 'em^ not to be bashfull, which might be a great Inconvenience to Travellors. The Son & Heir of the Family offer'd himself as a Volunteer over Night, but dreamt so much of Dangers and Difficulties, that he declar'd off in the Morning.[12]

MARCH

1. About 9 in the Morning the Colo. was so kind as to set all his Guests over the South Branch of Nansemond River[s], which shorten'd their Journey 7 or 8 Miles, & from thence his Son conducted [15] them[t] into the great Road. Then they past[u] for several Miles together by the North Side of the Great Dismal, and after a Journey of 25 Miles, arriv'd in good Order at Majr. Crawford's over against Norfolk Town. Just before they got hither[a], the Lag Commissioners overtook them, and all the Men[b] were drawn up to receive them. Meanwell was so civil as to excuse his not meeting[c] Steddy at Mrs. Allens as had been agreed; but Firebrand was too big for Apology. It was agreed[d] to leave the Men & the heavy Baggage at Major Crawfords (having made the necessary Provision for it[e]) & pass over to Norfolk only with the Servants & Portmantles, that the Town's Men might not be frighten'd

[l]H: By the way ^Steddy^ [m]H: who being ^was so^ very thirsty ^that he^ call'd [n]H: <We> The ^Cavalcade^ arriv'd [o]H: But <I> ^Steddy^ found <my>himself exceedingly fatigued with the <marching> March. <We past> In passing thro' [p]H: the dismal footsteps <of> made ^by^ the Hu[rri]cane [q]H: but <we were very unlucky in> ^the poor Man had the misfortune to be^ deaf [r]H: from hearing <great part of our Acknowledgments> ^any part of the Acknowledgements^ [s]H: to set <us all over> ^his Guests over the South Branch of^ Nansemond River [t]H: <us> them [u]H: <We> ^Then they^ passt [a]H: <we> they got hither [b]H: and ^all^ the Men [c]H: ^Meanwell^ was so civil as to excuse his not meeting ^Steddy^ [d]H: Firebrand ^was too big^ for Apology. It was [e]H: Provision for them

from entertaining them[f]. Here they divided their Quarters, that as little trouble might be given, as possible, and it was Steddy's Fortune, after some Apprehensions of going to the Ordinary, to be invited by Colo. Newton. To shew his regard to the Church, he took the Chaplain along with him.[g] Mrs. Newton provided a clean Supper without any Luxury about 8 a Clock, and appear'd to be one of the fine Ladies of the Town, and like a true fine Lady, to have a great deal of Contempt for her Husband.[13]

2.   This Morning old Colo. Boush made Steddy a visit[h] with the tender of his Service. There was no Soul in the Town knew[i] how the Land lay [16] betwixt this Place & Corotuck-Inlet, til at last Mr. William Wilkins, that lives upon the Borders, drew a rough Sketch that gave a general Notion of it[j]. The light given by this Draught determin'd the Commissioners to march[k] to the Landing of Northwest River, and there embark in a Periagau in order to meet the Commissioners of Carolina at Currituck[l]. It was really a pleasure[m] to see 12 or 14 Sea Vessels, riding in the Harbour of this City, & several Wharfs built out into the River to land goods upon. These wharfs were built with Pine Logs let into each other at the End, by which those underneath are made firm by those which lye over them. Here the Commissioners were supply'd[n] with 2 Caggs of Wine, & 2 of Rum, 178 lb. of Bread, & several other conveniencys. Our good Landlord entertained Steddy, and the Chaplain at Dinner, but Firebrand refused[o], because he was not sent to in due form. In the Evening the Commissioners were invited to an Oyster and a Bowl by Mr. Sam Smith, a plain Man worth 20000 Pounds.[14] He produced his 2 Nieces, whose Charms were all invisible. These Damsels seem'd discontented that their Uncle shew'd more distinction to his Housekeeper than to them. We[p] endeavour'd to hire 2 or 3 Men here to go along with us, but might for the same Price[q] have hired

---

[f]H: that <we might not fright the Townsmen from> ^the Townsmen might not be frightened from^ entertaining <us> ^them^   [g]H: Here <we> ^they^ divided their Quarters that <might be as little troublesome> ^as little trouble might be given^ as possible, and it was <my> ^Steddy's^ fortune, after some apprehensions <what wou'd become of me to be entertain'd> ^of going to the Ordinary to be invited^ by Colo Newton <and> To shew <my> ^his^ Regard to the Church he took the Chaplain along with him.   [h]H: This morning ^old^ Colo Boush made ^Steddy^ a Visit   [i]H: no Soul in the Town <could tell us> ^knew^ how   [j]H: a rough ^sketch^ which gave us some ^a general^ notion of it   [k]H: the light <we> given receiv'd from him ^by the Draught^ determin'd us ^the Commissioners^ to march   [l]H: at our Rendezvous ^Coratuck^   [m]H: It was ^really^ a pleasure   [n]H: Here <we> ^the Commrs^ were supply'd   [o]H: Our ^good^ Landlord entertain'd <the Parson and me> ^Steddy & the Chaplain^ at dinner, but ^Firebrand^ refus'd   [p]*Here Byrd's revision of the manuscript (from first to third person) breaks off in both H and A.*   [q]H: but [———] might for the same Price *(erasure, not filled in)*

them to make a Trip to the Other World. They look't upon us, as Men devoted, like Codrus and the 2 Decii, to certain destruction[r] for [17] the Service of our Country. The Parson & I return'd to our Quarters in good time & good order, but my Man Tom broke[s] the Rules of Hospitality by getting extreamly drunk in a Civil House[t].[15]

3[d]. This being Sunday, we were edify'd at Church by Mr. Marston with a good Sermon. People cou'd not attend their Devotion for staring at us, just as if we had come from China or Japan. In the mean time Firebrand and Astrolabe not having quite so much regard for the Sabbath, went to the NW Landing to prepare Vessels for our Transportation to Corotuck. I wrote to the Governor an Account of our Progress thus far, with a Billet-douce to my Wife. The Wind blew very hard at S.W. all day. However in the Evening Steddy order'd the Men & Horses to be set over the South Branch to save time in the Morning. My Landlady gave us Tea, & sweeten'd it with the best of her Smiles. At Night we spent an hour with Colo. Boush who stir'd his Old Bones very cheerfully in our Service. Poor Orion's Horse & Furniture were much disorder'd with the Journey hither. His Instrument wou'd not traverse, nor his Ball rest in the Socket. In short all his Tackle had the air of Distress. Over against the Town is Powder-Point where a Ship of any Burden may lye close to, and the Men of War are us'd to careen.[16]

4. About 8 a Clock in the Morning we crost the River to Powder-Point, where we found our Men ready to take Horse. Several of the Grandees of [18] the Town, and the Parson among the rest, did us the Honour to attend us as far as the great Bridge over South River. Here we were met by a Troop under the command of Captain Wilkins, who escorted us as far as his Father's Castle near the Dismal. We halted about a quarter of an Hour and then proceeded to N.W. Landing. Here Firebrand had provided a Dinner for us, serv'd up by the Master of the House, whose Nose seem'd to stand upon very ticklish Terms. After Dinner we chose Ten able Men & embarkt on board 2 Periaugas under the command of Capt. Wilkins, which carry'd us to the Mouth of NW River. By the way we found the Banks of the River lined with Myrtles & Bay-Trees, which afforded a Beautifull Prospect. These beautifull plants dedicated to Venus & Apollo grow in wet Ground, & so does the Wild Lawrell, which in some Places is intermixt with the rest. This River is in most places about 100 Yards over, & had no Tide til the Year 1713. When a violent Tempest open'd a

---

[r]H: Devoted ^like Codrus & the 2 Decii^ to certain Destruction   [s]H: my Man ^Tom^ [————] broke *(the space after the erasure and overwriting suggests Byrd might have initially given a surname)*   [t]*Here the Huntington (H) fragment breaks off, resuming after four missing pages.*

new Inlet about 5 Miles to the Southward of the old one, which is now almost clos'd up and too shallow for any Vessel to pass over. But the new Inlet is deep enough for Sloops. We were 4 Hours in rowing to the Mouth of the River, being about 18 Miles from the Landing. Here we took up our Lodging at one Andrew Dukes, who had lately remov'd, or rather run [19] away, hither from Maryland. We were forc't to lie in Bulk upon a very dirty Floor that was quite alive with Fleas & Chinches, and made us repent that we had not brought the Tent along with us. We had left that with the rest of the heavy Baggage at Capt. Wilson's, under the Guard of 7 Men. There we had also left the Revd. Dr. Humdrum with the hopes that all the Gentiles in the Neighbourhood would bring their Children to be Christen'd, notwithstanding some of them had never been Christen'd themselves. Firebrand had taken care to Board his man Tipperary with Capt. Wilson, because by being the Squire of his Body he thought him too much a Gentleman to diet with the rest of the Men we left behind. This Indignity sat not easy upon their Stomachs, who were all honest house-keepers in good Circumstances.[17]

5.   At break of Day we turn'd out, properly speaking, and blest our Landlord's Eyes with half a Pistole. About 7 we embark't, & passed by the South End of Knot's Island, there being no Passage on the North. To the Southwards at some Distance we saw Bells and Churches Islands. About Noon we arrived at the South Shoar of old Coratuck Inlet, and about 2 we were joined by Judge Jumble & Plausible, two of the Carolina Commissioners; the other two, Shoebrush and Puzzlecause, lagg'd behind, which was the more unlucky because we cou'd enter on [20] no Business for want of the Carolina Commission, which these Gentlemen had in their keeping. Jumble was Brother to the late Dean of York, and if his Honour had not formerly been a Pirate himself, he seem'd intimately acquainted with many of them. Plausible had been bred in Christ's Hospital and had a Tongue as Smooth as the Commissary, and was altogether as well qualify'd to be of the Society of Jesus. These worthy Gentlemen were attended by Bo-otes, as their Surveyor, a young Man of much Industry, but no Experience.[18] We had now nothing to do but to reconnoiter the Place. The High Land ended in a blouf Point, from which a Spit of Sand extended itself to the South-East about half a Mile. The Inlet lys between this Spit & another on the South Side, leaving a Shoal Passage for the Sea not above a Mile over. On the East are shoals that run out 2 or 3 Miles, over which the Breakers rise Mountains high with a Terrible Noise. I often cast a longing Eye towards England, and sighed. This Night we lay for the first time in the Woods, and, being without the Tent, we made a Bower of the Branches of Cedar, with a large Fire in Front, to guard us from the North-Wester, which blew very smartly. At Night Young Astrolabe came to

us, & gave great jealousy to Orion. His Wigg was in such stiff Buckle [21] that if he had seen the Devil the Hair wou'd not have stood on end. This Night we found the Variation to be 8° West, by a due Meridian taken from the North Star.[19]

6. We were treated at Breakfast by the Commissioners of Carolina, who coming from home by water, were much better provided for the Belly than the Business. At Noon we found the Latitude to be 36° 31′, according to Astrolabe, but Orion, to prove his Skill in the mathematics by flat Contradiction, wou'd needs have it but 36° 30′. Capt. Wilkins furnished us with excellent Oysters, as savory & well tasted as those in England.

About 3 a Clock Messrs. Shoebrush & Puzzlecause made a Shift to come to us, after calling at every House where they expected any Refreshment; After the necessary Complements, & a Thousand Excuses for making us wait for them so long, we began to enter upon business. We had a tough dispute where we shou'd begin; whether at the point of high Land, or at the End of the Spit of Sand, which we with good reason maintain'd to be the North Shoar of Coratuck-Inlet, according to the Express Words of his Majesty's Order. They had no Argument to support our beginning at the High-Land, but because the former Commissioners for Virginia submitted to it. But if what they did was to [22] be a Rule for us, then we ought to allow no Variation of the Compass, because those Gentlemen allowed of none. This Controversy lasted til Night, neither Side receding from its Opinion. However, by the lucky advice of Firebrand, I took Plausible aside and let him know the Government of Virginia had look't upon him as the Sole Obstacle to the settling the Bounds formerly, and if we shou'd break off now upon this frivolous Pretence, he wou'd surely bear the Blame again. At the same time I shew'd him a Representation made to the late Queen by Colo. Spotswood greatly to his disadvantage.[20] This worked so powerfully upon his Politicks that he without loss of time soften'd his Brethren in such a Manner, that they came over to our Opinion. They were the rather perswaded to this by the Peremptory Words of our Commission, by which we were directed to go ^on^ with the Business tho' the Carolina Commissioners shou'd refuse to join with us therein. However by reason of some Proof that was made to us by the Oaths of two Credible Persons, that the Spit of Sand was advanced about 200 Yards to the Southward since the year 1712, when the Proposals between the Governours Eden & Spotswood were agreed upon[u], we thought it reasonable to allow for so much. And accordingly made our Beginning from thence. Upon the high-Land we found one kind of Silk Grass, and plenty of

[u]H: Governours Spotswood & Eden were agreed ^upon^

[23] Japon, which passes for Tea in North Carolina[v], tho' nothing like it. On the Sands we saw Conque-Shells in great Number, of which the Indians make both their Blue & white Peak, both Colours being in different Parts of the same Shell.[21]

7.   We drove down a Post at our Place of beginning, & then crossed over to Dosier's Island, which is nothing but a flat Sand with Shrubs growing upon it. From thence we past[w] over to the North End of Knot's Island, our Line running thro' the Plantation of Wm. Harding. This man had a Wife born & bred near Temple Bar, and still talk't[a] of the Walks in the Temple with Pleasure. These poor People bestow'd their Wood & their Water upon us very freely. We found Shoebrush[b] a merry good humour'd man, and had learnt a very decent behaviour from Governour Hyde, to whom he had been Valet de Chambre, of which he still carried the Marks by having his Coat, Wastcoat & Breeches of different Parishes[c]. Puzzlecause had degenerated from a New-England Preacher, for which his Godly Parents design'd him, to a very wicked, but awkward Rake[d]. I had almost forgot to mention a Marooner who had the Confidence to call himself an Hermit[e], living on the South Shoar of Coratuck near the Inlet. He has no other Habitation but a green Bower or Harbour with a Female Domestick as wild & as dirty as himself. His Diet is chiefly Oysters, which he has just Industry enough to gather from the Neighbouring Oyster Banks; [24] while his Concubine makes a Practice of driving up the Neighbour's Cows[f] for the Advantage of their Milk. Orion seem'd[g] to be grievously puzzled about Plotting off his Surveyor's Work, and chose rather to be oblig'd to the Carolina Commissioners than to Mr. Mayo, for their Instruction, which it was evident to every Body that he wanted. The Truth of it is, he had been much more discreet to loiter on at the College, & receive his Sallary quietly (which he owes to his Relation to the pious Commissary[h]) than to undertake a Business which discover'd he knew very little of the Matter[i].[22]

8.   We quitted our Camp about 7 & early dispatch't away the large Periauga, with the Heavy Baggage & most of the men round the South End of Knott's Island. About 9 we embarked ourselves on board the lesser Periauga, under the pilotage of Capt. Wilkins, & steered our Course towards the North

[v]H: for Tea in ^North^ Carolina   [w]H: From thence ^we^ past   [a]H: and ^still^ talkt
[b]H: found ^Shoebrush^   [c]H: Chambre ^after which he still carryd the Marks by having his Coat Waistcoat and Breeches of different various hues^   [d]H: Puzzlecause had degenerated to ^a very wicked but^ awkward Rake   [e]H: a Marooner who ^had the Confidence to^ call<'d> himself an Hermit   [f]H: while his concubine ^makes a practice of^ drive<s>ing up the Neigbours Cows   [g]H: Orion seemd   [h]H: to the ^pious^ Commissary   [i]H: to undertake a business which discover'd he knew very little of the matter.

End of the Island. This Navigation was so difficult by reason of the perpetual Shoals, that we were often fast aground, but Firebrand[j] swore us off again very soon. Our Pilot wou'd have been a miserable Man if one half of that Gentleman's Curses had taken effect. It was remarkable[k] to see how mild & unmov'd the poor man was under so much heavy displeasure insomuch that the most passionate Expression that escap't him was, O, forever & after! which was his form of Swearing[l]. We had been benighted in that wide Water, had we not met a Canoe that [25] was carrying a Conjurer from Princess Anne to Carolina. But, as all Conjurers are sometimes mistaken, he took us at first for Pyrates, & what was worse for him, he suspected afterwards that we were Officers, that were in pursuit of him & a Woman that past for his Wife. However at last being undeceiv'd in both these points, they suffer'd us to speak with them and directed us in the Course we were to steer. By their Advice we rowed up a Water call'd the Back Bay, as far as a Skirt of Pocosin a quarter of a Mile in Breadth. Thro' this we waded up to the Knees in Mud & got safe on the firm Land of Princess Anne County. During this Voyage, Shoebrush[m] in champing a Biscuit, forc't out one of his Teeth, which an unlucky Flux had left loose in his Head. And tho' one of his Feet was inflam'd with the Gout, yet he was forc't to walk 2 Miles as well as the rest of us to John Heath's, where we took up our Quarters. Amongst other Spectators came 2 Girles to see us, one of which was very handsome, & the other very willing. However we only saluted them, & if we committed any Sin at all, it was only in our Hearts. Capt. White a Grandee of Knott's Island[n], & Mr. Moss, a Grandee of Princess-Ann made us a visit and helped to empty our Liquor. The Surveyors & their Attendants came to us at Night, after wading thro' a Marsh near 5 Miles in Breadth, which stretches from the West Side of Knott's Island to the high-Land of Princess-Ann. In this Marsh several of the men [26] had plung'd up to the Middle; however they kept up their good Humor, & only made Sport of what others wou'd have made a Calamity.[23]

9.   In the Morning we walk't with the Surveyors to the Line, which cut through Eyland's Plantation, & came to the Banks of North River. Hither the Girles above-mention'd attended us, but an Old Woman came along with them for the Security of their Vertue. Others rose out of their Sick Beds to see such Raritys as we were. One of our Periaugas set the Surveyors & 5 Men over North River. They landed in a miry Marsh, which led to a very deep Pocoson. Here they met with Beaver Dams & Otter-holes, which it was not practicable to pass in a direct Line, tho' the Men offer'd to do it[o] with great Alacrity. But

[j]H: ^Firebrand^   [k]H: remarquable   [l]H: O for ever & after! which was his form of ———
Swearing   [m]H: Shoebrush   [n]H: Not's Island   [o]H: to do ^it^ with

the Surveyors were contented to make a Traverse. While they were struggling
with these difficultys, we Commissioners went in State[p] in the other Periauga
to N.W. River, and row'd up as high as Mr. Merchant's. He lives near half
a Mile from the River, having a Causeway leading thro' a filthy Swamp[q] to
his Plantation. I encampt in his Pasture with the Men, though the other
Commissioners indulg'd themselves so far as to lie in the House. But it seems
they broke the Rules of Hospitality[r], by several gross Freedoms they offer'd to
take with our Landlord's Sister. She was indeed a pretty Girl, and therefore it
was prudent to send her out of harm's Way[s]. I was the more concern'd at this
unhandsome Behaviour[t], because the [27] People were extremely civil to us,
& deserv'd a better treatment. The Surveyors came to us at night, very much
jaded with their dirty Work, & Orion[u] slept so sound that he had been burn't
in his Blanket, if the Centry had not been kinder to him than he deserv'd.[24]

10.   This being Sunday, we rested the Men & Surveyors, tho' we cou'd not
celebrate the Sabbath as we ought for want of our Chaplain. I had a Letter
from him informing me that all was well, both Soul & Body, under his Care.
Capt. Wilkins went home to make his Wife a Visit, and brought me a Bottle of
Milk, which was better than a Bottle of Tokay. Firebrand took all occasions to
set Orion above Astrolabe[v], which there was no reason for, but because he had
the Honour to be recommended by him. I halted as bad as old Jacob, without
having wrestled with anything like an Angel.[25]

The Men were concern'd at it, and had observ'd so much of Firebrand's
sweet Temper[a], that they swore they wou'd make the best of their way home
if it pleas'd God[b] to disable me from proceeding on the Business. But I walk't
about as much as I cou'd, & thereby made my hip very pliable. We found
Capt. Willis Wilson here, whose Errand was to buy Pork, which is the Staple
Commodity of North Carolina, & which with Pitch & Tar makes up the whole
of their Traffick. The Truth of it is, these People live so much upon Swine's
Flesh, [28] that it don't only incline them to the Yaws, & consequently to the
Downfall of their Noses[c], but makes them likewise extremely hoggish in their
Temper, & many of them seem to Grunt rather than Speak in their ordinary
Conversation.[26]

---

[p]H: we Commissioners went ^in State^   [q]H: a Causway leading thro a filthy Swamp
[r]H: But it seems *inserted at the end of line in paragraph indentation.*   [s]H: a pretty Girle,
and therefore it was prudent to send her out of Harms way   [t]H: this ^unhandsome^
Behaviour   [u]H: and Orion   [v]H: Firebrand took all Occasions set Orion up above
Astrolabe.   [a]H: Firebrands Sweet Temper   [b]H: pleas'd G[od] *(hole in paper)*   [c]H: it
dont only incline th[em] to the [Yaws] & consequently ^to the^ down fall of their Noses
(pp. 21–22 of H are torn, stained, and sometimes illegible)

11.   We order'd the Surveyors early to their Business, with 5 of the Men to attend them. They had a tiresome day's work of it, wading thro' a deep Pocoson near 2 Miles over, in which they frequently plung'd up to the Middle. In the mean time, we Commissioners row'd up the River in our Periauga much more at our ease, & drop't Anchor at Mossy-Point near a deserted Pork-Store belonging to Capt. Willis Wilson. After the Men had swept out a Cartload of Dirt, we put our Baggage into it for fear of Rain. Then we sent our Periauga in quest of the Surveyors; & Firebrand believing nothing cou'd be ^well^ done without him, went in it himself attended by Puzzlecause, tho' he did no other good but favour us[d] with his Room instead of his Company. In the mean while Shoebrush[e] & I took a walk into the Woods, and call'd at a Cottage where a Dark Angel surpriz'd[f] us with her Charms. Her Complexion was a deep Copper, so that her fine Shape & regular Features made her appear like a statue en Bronze done by a masterly hand. Shoebrush was smitten at the first Glance, and examin'd all her neat Proportions with a Critical [29] Exactness. She struggled just enough to make her Admirer more eager, so that if I had not been there, he wou'd have been in Danger of carrying his Joke a little too far.

The Surveyors found us out in the Evening very much fatigued, & the Men were more off their mettle than ever they had been in the whole Journey, tho' without the least Complaint. I took up my Lodging in the Camp, but was driven into the House about Midnight ^without my Breeches^, like Monsr. Broglie, by a smart Shower of Rain. Here we all lay in Bulk the rest of the Night upon a dirty & wet Floor without taking Cold.[27]

12.   Complaint was made to me this Morning, that the Men belonging to the Periauga had stole[g] our People's Meat while they slept. This provoked me to treat them a la Dragon, that is to swear at them furiously, and by the good Grace of my Oaths, I might have passed[h] for an Officer in his Majesty's Guards. I was the more out of Humour, because it disappointed us in our early March, it being a standing Order to boil the Pot over-Night, that we might not be hinder'd in the morning. This Accident, & the Necessity of drying our Bed-Cloaths kept us from decamping til near 12 a Clock. By this delay the Surveyors found time to plot off their Work, and to observe the Course of the River. Then they [30] past it over against Northern's Creek, the Mouth of which was very near our Line. But the Commissioners made the best of their way to the Bridge, and going ashoar walkt to Mr. Balance's plantation.

[d]H: & Firebrand believing nothing coud be well done without him, went in it ^himself^ attended by Puzzlecause, tho' he did no other but favour ——— us   [e]H: Shoebrush
[f]H: Angil ——— surprizd us   [g]H: stol'n   [h]H: past

I retir'd early to our Camp at some distance from the House, while my
Colleagues tarry'd within Doors, & refresh't themselves with a cheerful Bowl.
In the Gaiety[i] of their Hearts, they invited a Tallow-faced Wench that had
sprain'd her Wrist to drink with them, and when they had rais'd her in good
Humour, they[j] examined all her hidden Charms, and play'd a great many gay
Pranks. While Firebrand who had the most Curiosity, was ranging over her
sweet Person, he pick't off several Scabs as big as Nipples, the Consequence
of eating too much Pork. The poor Damsel was disabled from making any
resistance by the Lameness of her Hand; all she could do, was to sit stil, &
make the Fashionable Exclamation of the Country, "Flesh alive & tear it," &
by what I can understand she never spake so properly in her Life. One of the
representatives of North Carolina made a Midnight Visit to our Camp, & his
curiosity was so very clamorous that it waked me, for which I wish't his Nose
as flat as any of his Porcivorous Countrymen.[28]

13.   In the Morning our Chaplain came to us, & with him some Men we
had sent for, to relieve those who had waded thro' the Mire from Coratuck.
But they beg'd they might not be reliev'd, believing they shou'd gain immortal
Honour by going through the [31] Dismal. Only Petillo desired to be excus'd,
on the Account of his Eyes. Old Ellis Petition'd to go in the Room of his Son,
and Kimball was depriv'd from that Favour by Lot. That griev'd him so, that
he offer'd a Crown to Hambleton to let him go in his room, which the other
wou'd not listen to for ten times the Mony. When this great Affair was settled,
we dismist all the Men to their Quarters at Capt. Wilson's, except the Nine
Dismalites. Of these we sent 5 with the Surveyors who ran the Line to the
Skirts of the Dismal, which began first with Dwarf Reeds, & moist, uneven
Grounds. We discharged our Periaugas and about Noon our good Friend Capt
Wilkins conducted us to his own House, & entertain'd us hospitably. We made
the necessary Disposition for entering the Dismal next Morning with 9 of our
Men, & 3 of Carolina, so many being necessary to attend the Surveyors, and
for carrying the Bedding & Provisions. The Men were in good Spirits but poor
Orion began to repent, & wish he had slept in a whole Skin at the College,
rather than become a Prey to the Turkey-Buzzard. These reflections sunk his
courage so low, that neither Liquor nor Toast cou'd raise it. I hardly knew
how to behave my self in a Bed, after having lain a Week in the open Field, &
seeing the Stars twinkle over my head.[29]

14.   This Morning early the Men began to make up the Packs they were
to carry on their Shoulders into the Dismal. They were victual'd for 8 Days,
[32] which was judg'd sufficient for the Service. These Provisions with the

[i]H: gaity   [j]*Here the Huntington fragment ends.*

Blankets & other Necessaries loaded the Men with a Burthen of 50 or 60 lb. for Each. Orion helpt most of all to make these Loads so heavy, by taking his Bed, and several Changes of Raiment, not forgetting a Suit for Sundays along with him. This was a little unmercifull, which with his peevish Temper made him no Favorite. We fixt them out about ten in the Morning, & then Meanwell, Puzzlecause, & I went along with them, resolving to enter them fairly into this dreadfull Swamp, which nobody before ever had either the Courage or Curiosity to pass. But Firebrand & Shoebrush chose rather to toast their Noses over a good Fire, & spare their dear Persons. After a March of 2 miles thro' a very bad way, the Men sweating under their Burthens, we arriv'd at the Edge of the Dismal, where the Surveyors had left off the Night before. Here Steddy thought proper to encourage the Men by a short harangue to this Effect: "Gentlemen, we are at last arriv'd at this dreadfull Place, which til now has been thought unpassable. Tho' I make no doubt but you will convince every Body, that there is no difficulty which may not be conquer'd by Spirit & Constancy. You have hitherto behav'd with so much Vigour, that the most I can desire of You, is to persevere unto the End; I protest to You, the only reason we don't share in your Fatigue, is, the fear of adding to your Burthens; [33] (which are but too heavy already,) while we are sure we can add nothing to your Resolution. I shall say no more, but only pray the Almighty to prosper your Undertaking, & grant we may meet on the other Side in perfect Health & Safety." The Men took this Speech very kindly, and answered it in the most cheerfull manner, with 3 Huzzas.

Immediately we enter'd the Dismal, 2 Men clearing the way before the Surveyors to enable them to take their Sight. The Reeds which grew about 12 feet high, were so thick, & so interlaced with Bamboe-Briars, that our Pioneers were forc't to open a Passage. The Ground, if I may properly call it so, was so spungy, that the Prints of our Feet were instantly fill'd with Water. Amongst the Reeds here & there stood a white Cedar, commonly mistaken for Juniper. Of this Sort was the Soil for about half a Mile together, after which we came to a piece of high land about 100 Yards in Breadth. We were above 2 hours scuffling thro' the Reeds to this Place, where we refresh't the poor Men. Then we took leave, recommending both them & the Surveyors to Providence. We furnish't Astrolabe with Bark & other Medicines, for any of the People, that might happen to be Sick, not forgetting 3 Kinds of Rattle-Snake Root made into Doses in case of Need. It was 4 a Clock before we return'd to our Quarters, where we found our Collegues under some Apprehension that we were gone with the People quite thro' the Dismal. During my Absence Firebrand was so very carefull in sending away the Baggage, [34] that he forgot the Candles. When we had settled Accounts with our Landlord, we rode away to Capt. Wilson's, who treated us with Pork upon Pork. He was a great Lover of Conversation, & rather than it should drop, he wou'd repeat the same Story over & over. Firebrand chose rather to litter the Floor, than lie with the Parson, & since he cou'd not have the best Bed, he sullenly wou'd have none at all. However it broil'd upon his Stomach so much, that he swore enough in the Night, to bring the Devil into the Room, had not the Chaplain been there.[30]

15.   We sent away the Baggage about 8 a Clock under the Guard of 4 Men. We paid off a long reckoning to Capt. Wilson, for our Men & Horses, but Firebrand forgot to pay for the washing of his Linnen, which saved him 2 Shillings at least. He & his Flatterer Shoebrush left us to our selves, intending to reach Capt. Meade's, but losing their way, they took up at Mr. Pugh's, after riding above 50 Miles, & part of the way in the dark. How many Curses this Misadventure cost them I cant say, tho' at least as many as they rode Miles. I was content to tarry to see the Men fixt out & jog on fair & softly along with them, & so were Meanwell and Puzzlecause. One of our Men had a Kick on the Belly by a Horse, for which I order'd him to be instantly Blooded, and no ill Consequence ensued. We left Astrolabe's Negro Sick behind us. About 11 we set off, & call'd at an Ordinary 8 Miles off, not far from the great Bridge. Then we proceeded 8 Miles farther to honest Timothy Ives's [35] who supply'd us with every thing that was necessary. He had a tall, straight Daughter of a Yielding Sandy Complexion, who having the Curiosity to see the Tent, Puzzlecause gallanted her thither, & might have made her free of it, had not we come seasonably to save the Damsel's Chastity. Here both our Cookery and Bedding were more cleanly than ordinary. The Parson lay with Puzzlecause in the Tent to keep him honest, or peradventure, to partake of his Diversion if he should be otherwise.[31]

16.   We march't from hence about 9 always giving our Baggage the Start of us. We call'd at John Ives's for a Tast of good Water, which is as rare in these Parts as good Doctrine. We saw several pretty Girls here as wild as Colts, tho' not so ragged, but drest all in their own Industry. Even those cou'd not tempt us to alight but we pursued our Journey with Diligence. We past by Mr. Oshield's and Mr. Pugh's, the last of which has a very good Brick House, & arrived about 4 at Capt. Meade's. Here amongst other Strong Liquors we had plenty of strong Beer, with which we made as free as our Libertines did with the Parson. The Carolina Commissioners did not only persecute him with their Wit, but with their Kisses too, which he suffer'd with the Patience of a Martyr. We were no sooner under the Shelter of that hospitable House,

368 } The Secret History of the Line

but it began to rain & so continu'd to do great part of the Night, which put us in some Pain for our Friends in the Dismal. The journey [36] this Day was 25 miles, yet the Baggage Horses perform'd it without faltering.[32]

17.   It rain'd this Morning til 10 a Clock, which fill'd us all with the Vapours. I gave myself a thorough wash and scrubb'd off a full Week's dirt, which made me fitter to attend the Service which our Chaplain perform'd. I wrote to the Governor a particular Account of our Proceedings, & had the Complaisance to shew the Letter to my Colleagues. These worthy Gentlemen had hammer'd out an Epistle to the Governor containing a kind of Remonstrance against paying the Burgesses in Mony, & prevailed with our Landlord to deliver it. At night we had a religious Bowl to the ^pious^ Memory of St. Patrick, & to shew due Regard to this Saint several of the Company made some Hibernian Bulls: But the parson unhappily out-blunder'd all, which made his Persecutors merry at his Cost.[33]

18.   It was not possible to get from so good a House before 11 a Clock, nor then neither for our Servants. When Firebrand ask't his Man why he lagg'd behind, he exprest himself with great Freedom of his Master, swearing he cared for no Mortal but his dear-self, & wishing that the Devil might take him, if he ever attended him again in any of his Travels. We made the best of our way to Mr. Tho. Speight's, who appear'd to be a Grandee of North-Carolina. There we arriv'd about 4, tho' the Distance cou'd not be less than 25 Miles. Upon our Arrival our poor Landlord made a Shift to crawl out upon his Crutches, [37] having the Gout in both his Knees. He bid us welcome, & a great Bustle was made in the Family about our Entertainment. We saw two truss Damsels stump about very Industriously, that were handsome enough upon a March. Our Landlord gave us much Concern, by affirming with some Assurance, that the Dismal cou'd not be less than 30 Miles in Breadth. All our Comfort was, that his Computation depended wholly on his own wild Conjecture. We order'd guns to be fired & a Drum to be beaten, to try if we cou'd be answer'd out of the Desart, but we had no Answer, but from that prating Slut Echo. The Servants ty'd the Horses so carelessly that some of them did our Landlord much damage in his Fodder. I was the more concern'd at this, because the poor Man did all he could to supply our Wants.[34]

Firebrand and the Parson lay single while some were oblig'd to stow 3 in a Bed. Nor cou'd lying soft & alone cure the first of these of swearing outrageously in his Sleep.

19.   We dispatch't Men to the North & South to fire Guns on the Edge of the Dismal by way of Signal, but cou'd gain no Intelligence of our People. Men, Women, and Children flockt from the Neighbourhood, to stare at us with as much Curiosity as if we had been Morocco-Embassadors.[35] Many

Children were brought to our Chaplain to be christen'd, but no Capons, so
that all the good he did that way was gratis. Majr. Alston & Capt. Baker made
us a Visit & din'd with us. My Landlord's Daughter Rachel offer'd her Service
to wash my Linnen, & regal'd me with a Mess [38] of Hominy toss't up with
Rank Butter & Glyster Sugar. This I was forc't to eat, to shew that nothing
from so fair a hand cou'd be disagreeable. She was a smart Lass, & when I
desired the Parson to make a Memorandum of his Christenings, that we
might keep an Account of the good we did, she asked me very pertly, who was
to keep an Account of the Evil? I told her she shou'd be my Secretary for that,
if she wou'd go along with me. Mr. Pugh & Mr. Oshield help't to fill up our
House, so that my Landlady told us in her Cups, that now we must lie 3 in a
Bed.[36]

20.   No News yet of our Dismalites tho' we dispatch't Men to every Point
of the Compass to enquire after them. Our Visitors took their Leave, but
others came in the Evening to supply their Places. Judge Jumble who left us
at Coratuck, return'd now from Edenton and brought 3 Cormorants along
with him. One was his own Brother, the 2d. was Brother to Shoebrush, & the
3d., Capt. Genneau, who had sold his Commission & spent the Money. These
honest Gentlemen had no business, but to help drink out our Liquor, having
very little at Home. Shoebrush's Brother is a Collector, and owes his Place to
a Bargain he made with Firebrand. Never were understrappers so humble, as
the N. Carolina Collectors are to this huge man. They pay him the same Court
they would do if they held their Commissions immediately from his Will &
Pleasure. Tho' the Case is much otherwise, because their Commissions are
as good as his, being granted by the same Commissioners of his Majesty's
Customs. However he expects a World of Homage from them, calling them
his Officers. Nor is he content with [39] homage only, but he taxes them, as
indeed he does all the other Collectors of his Province with a hundred little
Services.[37]

At Night the Noble Captain retired before the rest of the Company, & was
stepping without Ceremony into our Bed, but I arriv'd just time enough to
prevent it. We cou'd not possibly be so civil to this free Gentleman, as to make
him so great a Compliment, much less let him take Possession, according to
the Carolina Breeding without invitation. Had Ruth or Rachel my Landlord's
Daughters taken this Liberty; we shou'd perhaps have made no Words: but in
truth the Captain had no Charms that merited so particular an Indulgence.[38]

21.   Several Persons from several parts came to see us, amongst which
was Mr. Baker & his Brother the Surveyor of Nansimond, but cou'd tell us no
Tydings from the Dismal. We began to be in Pain for the Men who had been
trotting in that Bogg so long, & the more because we apprehended a Famine

amongst them. I had indeed given them a Warrant to kill anything that came in their way in case of Necessity, not knowing that no living Creature cou'd inhabit that inhospitable Place. My Landlord thought our Stay here as tedious as we did, because we eat up his Corn & Summer Provisions. However the Hopes of being well paid render'd that Evil more supportable. But Complaint being made that the Corn grew low, we retrench't the poor Men's Horses to one Meal a day.[39]

In the Evening Plausible & Puzzlecause return'd to us from Edenton, where they had been to [40] recover the great Fatigue of doing nothing & to pick up new Scandal against their Governour.[40]

22. Our disagreeable Carolina Visitors were so kind as to take their Leave, so did Mr. Oshield and Capt. Foot, by which our Company & my Landlord's Trouble were considerably lessen'd. We went out several Ways in the Morning, & cou'd get no intelligence. But in the Afternoon Bootes brought us the welcome News that the Surveyors & all the People were come safe out of the Dismal. They landed if one may so call it, near 6 Miles North of this Place, about ten this Morning not far from the House of Peter Brinkley. Here they appeas'd their hungry Stomachs, & waited to receive our Orders. It seems the Distance thro' the Desart where they past it was 15 Miles. Of this they had mark't & measur'd no more than ten: but had travers'd the remainder as fast as they cou'd for their Lives. They were reduced to such Straights that they began to look upon John Ellis's Dog with a longing Appetite, & John Evans who was fat & well-liking, had reason to fear that he wou'd be the next Morsel. We sent Astrolabe's Horses for him & his Brother; & Firebrand ordered Peter Jones with an Air of Authority to send his Horse for Orion, but he let him understand very frankly that nobody shou'd ride his Horse but himself, so not finding his Commands obey'd by the Virginians, he try'd his Power amongst the Carolina-Men, who were more at his Devotion, & sent one of their Horses for his Friend, to save his own; he also sent him a Pottle-Bottle of Strong Beer particularly, without any regard to Astrolabe, tho' the Beer belong'd [41] to the other Commissioners, as much as to him. We also sent Horses for the Men, that they might come to us & refresh themselves after so dreadfull a Fatigue. They had however gone thro' it all with so much Fortitude, that they discover'd as much Strength of Mind as of Body. They were now all in perfect Health, tho' their moist Lodging for so many Nights, & drinking of standing Water tinged with the Roots of Juniper, had given them little Fevers & slight Fluxes in their Passage, which as slight Remedies recover'd. Since I mention'd the Strong Beer, it will be but just to remember Capt. Meads generosity to us. His Cart arriv'd here Yesterday with a very handsome Present to the Commissioners of Virginia. It brought them 2 Doz. Quart Bottles of excellent

Madeira Wine, 1 Doz. Pottle Bottles of Strong Beer, & half a Dozen Quarts of Jamaica Rum. To this general Present was added a particular one to Meanwell, of Naples Biscuit from Mrs. Mead. At the same time we receiv'd a very Polite Letter, which gave a good Grace to his Generosity, & doubled our Obligation. And surely never was Bounty better timed, when it enabled us to regale the poor Dismalites, whose Spirits needed some Recruit. And indeed we needed Comfort as well as they, for tho' we had not shared with them in the Labours of the Body yet we made it up with the Labour of the Mind, and our Fears had brought us as low, as our Fatigue had done them. I wrote a Letter of thanks to our generous Benefactor, concluding with a Tender of the Commissioners Service & the Blessing of their Chaplain.[41]

23.   The Surveyors described the Dismal to us in the following Manner. That it was in many places [42] overgrown with tall Reeds interwoven with large Briars in which the Men were frequently intangled. And that not only in the Skirts of it, but likewise towards the Middle. In other Places it was full of Juniper Trees, commonly so call'd, tho' they seem rather to be white Cedars. Some of these are of a great Bigness: but the Soil being soft & boggy, there is little hold for the Roots, & consequently any high Wind blows many of them down. By this means they lye in heaps, horsing upon one another, and bristling out with Sharp Snags, so that the Passage in many Places is difficult & Dangerous. The Ground was generally very quaggy, & the Impressions of the Men's feet were immediately fill'd with Water. So if there was any hole made it was soon full of that Element, & by that Method it was that our People supply'd themselves with drink. Nay if they made a Fire, in less than half an Hour, when the crust of Leaves & Trash were burnt thro', it wou'd sink down into a Hole, & be extinguish't. So replete is this Soil with Water, that it cou'd never have been passable, but in a very dry Season. And indeed considering it is the Source of 6 or 7 Rivers, without any Visible Body of Water to supply them, there must be great Stores of it under Ground. Some part of this Swamp has few or no Trees growing in it: but contains a large Tract of Reeds, which being perpetually green, & waving in the Wind, it is call'd the Green Sea. Gall-Bushes grow very thick in many Parts of it, which are evergreen Shrubs, bearing a Berry which dies a Black Colour like the Galls of the Oak, & from thence they receive their Name.[42]

Abundance of Cypress Trees grow likewise in this [43] Swamp, and some Pines upon the Borders toward the firm Land, but the Soil is so moist & miry, that, like the Junipers a high Wind mows many of them down. It is remarkable that towards the Middle of the Dismal no Beast or Bird or even Reptile can live, not only because of the Softness of the Ground, but likewise because 'tis so overgrown with Thickets, that the Genial Beams of the Sun can never penetrate them. Indeed on the Skirts of it, Cattle & Hogs will venture for the Sake of the Reeds, & Roots, with which they will keep themselves fat all the Winter. This is a great Advantage to the Bordering Inhabitants in that particular, tho' they pay dear for it by the Agues & other distempers occasion'd by the Noxious Vapours that rise perpetually from that vast Extent of Mire & Nastiness. And a vast Extent it is, being computed at a Medium 10 Miles Broad, & 30 Miles long, tho' where the Line passt it, 'twas compleatly 15 Miles broad. However this dirty Dismal is in many Parts of it very pleasant to the Eye, tho' disagreeable to the other Sences, because there is an everlasting Verdure which makes every Season look like the Spring. The way the Men took to secure their Bedding here from Moisture, was by laying Cypress Bark under their Blankets, which made their Lodging hard, but much more wholesome.[43]

It is easy to imagine the hardships the poor Men underwent in this intolerable Place, who, besides the Burdens on their Backs, were oblig'd to clear the way before the Surveyors, & to measure & mark after them. However they went thro' it all not only [44] with Patience, but cheerfulness. Tho' Orion was as peevish as an old Maid all the way, & the more so, because he cou'd perswade nobody to be out of Humour but himself. The Merriment of the Men, & their Innocent Jokes with one another, gave him great Offence; whereas if he had had a Grain of good Nature, he shou'd have rejoiced to find, that the greatest difficultys cou'd not break their Spirits, or lessen their good Humour. Robin Hix took the Liberty to make him some short replys, that discompos'd him very much, particularly one hot day when the poor Fellow had a Load fit for a Horse upon his Back, Orion had the Conscience to desire him to carry his great Coat. But he roundly refus'd it, telling him frankly he had already as great a Burden as he cou'd stagger under. This Orion stomach't so much, that he complained privately of it to Firebrand as soon as he saw him, but said not one Syllable of it to me. However I was informed of it by Astrolabe, but resolved to take no Notice, unless the Cause was brought before us in Form, that the Person accus'd might have the English Liberty of being heard in his turn. But Firebrand said a Gentleman shou'd be believ'd on his bare word without Evidence, and a poor Man condemned without Tryal, which agreed not at all with my Notions of Justice. I understood all this at 2d. hand, but Meanwell was let into the Secret by the Partys themselves, with the hopes of perverting him into their Sentiments, but he was Stanch, & they were not able to make the least Impression upon him. This was a grievous Baulk, because if they cou'd have [45] gain'd him over, they flatter'd themselves they might have been as unrighteous as they pleased by a Majority. As it happens to Persons disappointed it broiled upon our Gentlemen's Stomacks so much, that they were but indifferent Company, and I observ'd very plain, that Firebrand joked less a days & swore more a nights ever after. After these Misfortunes, to be formally civil was as much as we cou'd afford to be to one another. Neither of us cou'd dissemble enough to put on a gay outside when it was cloudy within. However, these inward uneasinesses helpt to make the rest of our Sufferings the more intollerable. When People are join'd together in a troublesome Commission, they shou'd endeavour to sweeten by Complacency & good Humour all the Hazards and Hardships they are bound to encounter; & not like marry'd people make their Condition worse by everlasting discord. Tho' in this indeed we had the Advantage of marry'd People, that a few Weeks wou'd part us.

24. This being Sunday the People flock't from all Parts, partly out of Curiosity, & partly out of Devotion. Among the Female part of our Congregation, there was not much Beauty, the most fell to Majr. Alston's Daughter, who is said to be no Niggard of it. Our Chaplain made some Christians, but cou'd perswade nobody to be marry'd, because every Country Justice can do that Jobb for them. Major Alston & Captain Baker dined with us. In the Afternoon I equip't the Men with Provisions, & dispatch't them away [46] with Astrolabe & Bootes, to the Place where they were to return into the Dismal, in order to mark and measure what they had left unfinish't. Plausible & Shoebrush took a turn to Edenton, & invited us to go with them, but I was unwilling to go from my Post, & expose the Men to be ill treated that I left behind. Firebrand had a Flirt at Robin Hix, which discover'd much Pique & no Justice, because it happen'd to be for a thing of which he was wholly Innocent.[44]

25. The Air was chill'd with a N. Wester which favour'd our Dismalites who enter'd the Desart very early. It was not so kind to Meanwell who unseasonably kick't off the Bed Cloathes, & catch't an Ague. We kill'd the time, by that great help to disagreeable Society, a Pack of Cards. Our Landlord had not the good Fortune to please Firebrand with our Dinner, but surely when People do their best, a reasonable Man wou'd be satisfied. But he endeavour'd to mend his Entertainment by making hot Love to honest Ruth, who wou'd by no means be charm'd either with his Perswasion, or his Person. While the Master was employ'd in making Love to one Sister, the Man made his Passion known to the other; only he was more boisterous, & employ'd force, when he could not succeed by fair Means. Tho' one of the Men rescu'd the poor Girl from this violent Lover; but was so much his Friend as to keep the shamefull Secret from those, whose Duty it wou'd have been to punish such Violations of Hospitality. Nor was this the only one this disorderly fellow was guilty of, for he broke open a House where our Landlord kept the Fodder

for his own use, upon the belief that it was better than what he allow'd us. This was in Compliment to his Master's horses, I hope, and not in blind Obedience to [47] any order he receiv'd from him.

26.   I perswaded Meanwell to take a Vomit of Ipocoacana which workt very kindly; I took all the Care of him I could, tho' Firebrand was so unfriendly as not to step once up Stairs to visit him. I also gave a Vomit to a poor Shoemaker that belong'd to my landlord, by which he reap't great benefit. Puzzlecause made a Journey to Edenton, & took our Chaplain with him to preach the Gospel to the Infidels of that Town, & to baptize some of their Children. I began to entertain with my Chocolate, which everybody commended, but only he that commends nothing that don't belong to himself. In the Evening I took a solitary walk, that I might have Leizure to think on my absent Friends, which I now grew Impatient to see. Orion stuck as close to his Patron Firebrand as the Itch does to the fingers of many of his Country Folks.

27.   Tho' it threaten'd Rain ^both^ Yesterday & today, yet Heaven was so kind to our Friends in the Dismal as to keep it from falling. I perswaded Meanwell to take the Bark, which He did with good effect, tho' he continued very faint & low-Spirited. He took Firebrand's Neglect in great Dudgeon. And amidst all his good Nature cou'd not forbear a great deal of Resentment; but I won his Heart entirely by the tender Care I took of him in his illness. I also gain'd the Men's Affection by dressing their Wounds, & giving them little Remedys for their Complaints. Nor was I less in my Landlords Books, for acting the Doctor in his Family. Tho' I observ'd some Distempers in it, that were past my Skill to cure. For his [48] Wife & Heir Apparent were so inclin'd to a cheerfull Cup, that our good Liquor was very unsafe in their keeping. I had a long time observ'd that they made themselves happy every day, before the Sun had run one third of his course, which no doubt gave some uneasiness to the Old Gentleman: but Custome that reconciles most Evils, made him bear it with Christian Patience.[45]

As to the Young Gentleman, he seem'd to be as worthless as any homebred Squire I had ever met with, & much the worse for having a good Opinion of himself. His good Father intended him for the Mathematicks, but he never cou'd rise higher in that Study than to gage a Rum Cask. His Sisters are very sensible Industrious Damsels, who tho' they see Gentlemen but seldom, have the Grace to resist their Importunitys, & tho' they are innocently free, will indulge them in no dangerous Libertys. However their cautious Father, having some Notion of Female Frailty, from what he observ'd in their Mother, never suffers them to lie out of his own Chamber.

28.   I had a little Stiffness in my Throat, I fancy by lying alone for

Meanwell being grown restless by his Indisposition chose to ly by Himself. The Time past heavily, which we endeavour'd to make lighter by Cards & Books. The having nothing to do here was more insupportable than the greatest Fatigue, which made me envy the Drudgery of those in the Dismal. In the Evening we walk't several ways just as we drew in the day, but made a Shift to keep within the Bounds of Decency in our behaviour. However I observ'd Firebrand had something that broil'd upon his Stomach, which tho' he seemed to stiffle in the Day, [49] yet in the Night it burst out in his Sleep in a Volley of Oaths & Imprecations. This being my Birth day, I adored the Goodness of Heaven, for having indulged me with so much Health, and ^very^ uncommon Happiness, in the Course of 54 Years in which my Sins have been many, & my Sufferings few, my Opportunitys great, but my Improvements small. Firebrand & Meanwell had very high Words, after I went to Bed, concerning Astrolabe, in which Conversation Meanwell show'd most Spirit, & Firebrand most Arrogance & ill Nature.

29. I wrote a Letter to the Governor which I had the Complaisance to show to my Colleagues to prevent Jealousies & Fears. We receiv'd Intelligence that our Surveyors & People finisht their business in the Dismal last Night, & found it no more than 5 Miles from the Place where they left off. Above a Mile before they came out, they waded up to the Knees in a Pine Swamp. We let them rest this day at Peter Brinkley's, & sent Orders to them to proceed the next Morning. Bootes left them & came to us with intent to desert us quite, & leave the rest of the Drudgery to Plausible, who had indulged his Old Bones hitherto. Our Parson return'd to us with the Carolina Commissioners from Edenton, where he had preach't in their Court house, there being no Place of Divine Worship in that Metropolis. He had also Christen'd 19 of their Children, & pillag'd them of some of their Cash, if Paper Money may be allow'd that Appellation.

30. This Morning all the ill-humour that Firebrand had so long kept broiling upon his Stomach broke out. First he insisted that Young Astrolabe might go no longer with the Surveyors to be a Spy upon Orion. [50] I told him that Volunteers were always employ'd upon the Side, that he was very useful in assisting Orion, who had reason to be satisfy'd with having his defects so well supply'd. Then he complain'd of the Rudeness of Robin Hix to Orion, & proposed he might be punisht for it. To this I answer'd, that if Orion had any Accusation to make against Robin Hix, it had been fair to make it openly before all the Commissioners, that the Person accus'd might have an Opportunity to make his Defence, & ought not to whisper his Complaints in private to one Gentleman, because it look't like suspecting the Justice of the rest. That Word whispering touch't him home, & made him raise his Voice, &

roll his Eyes with great Fury, & I was weak enough to be as loud & Cholerick
as he. However it was necessary to shew that I was not to be dismay'd either
with his big looks or his big Words, and in Truth when he found this, he
cool'd as suddenly as he fired. Meanwell chimed in with my Sentiments in
both these Points, so that we carry'd them by a fair Majority. However to
shew my good Humour, & love of Peace, I desired Young Astrolabe to concern
himself no more with the Surveying Part, because it gave uneasiness, but only
to assist his Brother in protracting, & plotting of the Work. After this Storm
was over Firebrand went with Shoebrush to Mr. Oshields for some Days, and
his going off was not less pleasing to us than the going off of a Fever.

31.   This was Sunday, but the People's Zeal was not [51] warm enough
to bring them thro' the Rain to Church, especially now their Curiosity was
satisfy'd. However we had a Sermon & some of the nearest Neighbours came
to hear it. Astrolabe sent word that he had carry'd the Line 7 Miles Yesterday
but was forced to wade up to the Middle thro' a Mill Swamp. Robins sent his
Mate hither to treat with my Landlord about shipping his Tobacco; they role
it in the Night to Nansimond River, in Defiance of the Law against bringing
of Tobacco out of Carolina into Virginia: but t'were unreasonable to expect
that they shou'd obey the Laws of their Neighbours, who pay no regard to
their own. Only the Masters of Ships that load in Virginia shou'd be under
some Oath, or regulation about it. Sunday seem'd a Day of rest indeed, in the
absence of our Turbulent Companion, who makes every day uneasy to those
who have the Pain of his Conversation.[46]

April 1.   We prepar'd for a March very early, & then I discharg'd a long
Score with my Landlord, & a short One with his Daughter Rachel for some
Smiles that were to be paid for in Kisses. We took leave in form of the whole
Family, & in 8 miles reach't Richard Parkers, where we found Young Astrolabe
and some of our Men. Here we refresht ourselves with what a neat Landlady
cou'd provide, & Christen'd 2 of her Children, but did not discharge our
reckoning that way. Then we proceeded [52] by Somerton Chappel (which
was left 2 Miles in Virginia) as far as the Plantation of William Speight, that
was cut in Two by the Line, taking his Tobacco House into Carolina. Here
we took up our Quarters, and fared the better for a Side of fat Mutton sent
us by Captain Baker. Our Lodging was exceedingly Airy, the Wind having a
free Circulation quite thro' our Bed-Chamber, yet we were so hardy as to take
no Cold, tho' the Frost was sharp enough to endanger the Fruit. Meanwell
entertain'd the Carolina Commissioners with several Romantic Passages of
his Life, with Relation to his Amours, which ^is a subject^ he is as fond of, as
a Hero to talk of Battles he never fought.[47]

2.   This Morning early Capt. Baker came to make us a Visit, & explain'd

to us the Reason of the Present of Mutton which he sent us Yesterday. It seems the Plantation where he lives is taken into Virginia which without good Friends might prejudice him in his Surveyor's Place of Nansimond County. But we promised to employ our Interest in his Favour. We made the best of our way to Chowan River, crossing the Line several times. About a Mile before we came to that River we crost Somerton Creek. We found our Surveyors at a little Cottage on the Banks of Chowan over against the Mouth of Nottoway River. They told us that our Line cut Blackwater River, [53] about half a Mile to the Northward of that Place, but in Obedience to his Majesty's order in that Case, we directed them to continue the Line from the Middle of the Mouth of Nottoway River. Accordingly, the Surveyors past Chowan there, & carried the Line over a miry Swamp more than half a Mile thro', as far as an Indian Old Field.

In the mean time our Horses and Baggage were ferry'd over the River, a little lower, to the same Field, where we pitch't our Tent, promising ourselves a comfortable Repose: but our Evil Genius came at Night & interrupted all our Joys. Firebrand arriv'd with his most humble Servant Shoebrush, tho' to make them less unwelcome, they brought a present from Mr. Oshields, of 12 Bottles of Wine, & as many of Strong Beer. But to say the Truth we had rather have drunk Water the whole Journey to have been fairly quit of such disagreeable Company.

Our Surveyors found by an Observation made this Night, that the Variation was no more than 2° 30′ Westerly, according to which we determined to proceed in the rest of our Work toward the Mountains. Three of the Meherin Indians came hither to see us from the Place where they now live about 7 Miles down the River, they being lately removed from the Mouth of Meherin. They were frighten'd away from thence by the late Massacre committed upon 14 of their Nation by the [54] Catawbas. They are now reduced to a small Number and are the less to be pity'd because they have always been suspected to be very dishonest & treacherous to the English.[48]

3. We sent away the Surveyors about 9 a Clock & follow'd them at 10. By the way Firebrand & Shoebrush having spy'd a House that promised good Cheer, filed off to it, & took it in Dudgeon that we wou'd not follow their Vagarys. We thought it our Duty to attend the Business in hand, & follow the Surveyors. These we overtook about Noon, after passing several miry Branches, where I had like to have stuck fast. However this only gave me an Opportunity to show my Horsemanship, as the fair spoken Plausible told me. After passing several Dirty Places & uneven Grounds, we arriv'd about Sun Set on the banks of Meherin, which we found 13¼ Miles from the Mouth of Notoway River. The County of Isle of Wight begins about 3 Miles to the East

of this River, parted from Nansimond by a dividing Line only.⁴⁹ We pitch't our Tent, & flatter'd ourselves we shou'd be secure from the disturber of our Peace one Night more: but we were mistaken for the Stragglers came to us after it was dark with some Danger to their Necks, because the Low-Grounds near the River were full of Cypress Snaggs as dangerous as so many Chevaux de Frise. But this deliverance from Danger was not enough to make Firebrand good Humour'd, because we had not been so kind as to rejoice at it.⁵⁰

4.   Here we call'd a Council of War, whether we shou'd proceed [55] any farther this Season, and we carry'd it by a Majority of Votes to run the Line only about 2 Miles beyond this Place. Firebrand voted for going on a little longer, tho' he was glad it was carry'd against him. However he thought it gave him an Air of Industry to vote against leaving off so soon, but the Snakes began to be in great Vigour, which was an unanswerable Argument for it.

The River was hardly fordable & the banks very steep, which made it difficult for our Baggage Horses to pass over it. But thank God we got all well on the other Side without any Damage. We went to a House just by the River-Side, belonging to a Man, who learnedly call'd himself Carolus Anderson, where we christen'd his Child. Then we proceeded to Mr. Kinchen's a Man of Figure in these Parts, & his Wife a much better Figure than he. They both did their utmost to entertain us & our People in the best Manner. We pitch't our Tent in the Orchard, where the Blossoms of the Apple Trees mended the Air very much. There Meanwell & I lay, but Firebrand & his Flatterers stuck close to the House. The Surveyors crost this River 3 times with the Line in the Distance of 2½ Miles, & left off about half a Mile to the Northward of this Place.⁵¹

5.   Our Surveyors made an Elegant Plat of our Line from Corotuck Inlet to the Place where they left off, containing the Distance of 73 Miles & 13 poles. Of this exact Copys were made, & being carefully examin'd were both sign'd, by the Commissioners of each Colony. This Plat was chiefly made by Astrolabe, but one of the Copys was taken by Plausible; but Orion was content with a Copy which the Parson took for him. [56] However he deliver'd me the Minutes which he had kept of our Proceedings by Order of the Commissioners. The poor Chaplain was the common Butt at which all our Company aim'd their profane Wit, & gave him the Title of Dean Pipp, because instead of a Prick't Line, he had been so maidenly as to call it a Pipp't Line. I left the Company in good time, taking as little Pleasure in their low Wit, as in their low liquor which was Rum Punch. Here we discharg'd 6 of the Men, that were near their own Habitations.⁵²

6.   We paid our Scores, settled our Accounts, & took leave of our Carolina Friends. Firebrand went about 6 miles with us as far as One Corker's, where

we had the Grief to part with that sweet-temper'd gentleman, & the Burr
that stuck to him Orion. In about ten Miles we reach't a Muster-field near
Mr. Kindred's House, where Capt. Gerald was exercising his Company. There
were Girles enough come to see this Martial Appearance to form another
Company, & Beauty's enough among them to make Officers of. Here we call'd
& Christen'd 2 Children, and offer'd to marry as many of the Wenches as had
got Sweethearts, but they not ripe for Execution. Then we proceeded ten
Miles farther to Bolton's Ferry, where we past Nottoway River at Mr. Symonds'
Quarter. From hence we intended to proceed to Nottoway Town to satisfy
the Curiosity of some of our Company, but loseing our Way, we wandered
to Richard Parkers Plantation, where we had formerly met with very kind
Entertainment. [57] Our Eyes were entertain'd as well as our Stomachs by the
Charms of pretty Sally the eldest Daughter of the Family.[53]

7.   This being Sunday we had a Sermon to which very few of the
Neighbours resorted, because they wanted timely Notice. However some
good Christians came & amongst them Molly Izzard the smartest Damsel
in these Parts. Meanwell made this Girle very vain by saying sweet things to
her, but Sally was more engaging, whose wholesome Flesh & Blood, neither
had nor needed any Ornament. Nevertheless in the Afternoon we cou'd find
in our Hearts to change these fair Beauty's, for the Copper Colour'd ones of
Nottoway Towne.[54] Thither we went having given Notice by a Runner that
we were coming, that the Indians might be at home to entertain us. Our
Landlord shew'd us the Way, and the Scouts had no sooner spy'd us, but they
gave Notice of our Approach, to the whole Town, by perpetual Whoops & Crys,
which to a Stranger sound very dismal. This call'd their great Men to the Fort,
where we alighted, & were conducted to the best Cabins. All the Furniture
of those Appartments was Hurdles cover'd with clean Mats. The Young Men
had painted themselves in a Hideous Manner, not for Beauty, but Terrour, &
in that Equipage entertain'd us with some of their War Dances. The Ladies
had put on all their Ornaments to charm us, but the whole Winter's Dirt was
so crusted on their Skins, that it requir'd a strong Appetite to accost them.
Whatever [58] we were, our Men were not quite so nice, but were hunting after
them all Night. But tho' Meanwell might perhaps want Inclination to these
sad-colour'd Ladys, yet Curiosity made him try the difference between them
& other Women, to the disobligation of his Ruffles, which betray'd what he
had been doing. Instead of being entertain'd by these Indians, we entertain'd
them with Bacon & Rum, which they accepted of very kindly, the Ladys as
well as the Men. They offer'd us no Bedfellows, according to the good Indian
fashion, which we had reason to take unkindly. Only the Queen of Weyanoke
^told Steddy that^ her Daughter had been at his Service if she had not been

too young. Some Indian Men were lurking all Night about our Cabin, with the felonious intent to pilfer what they cou'd lay their hands upon, & their Dogs slunk into us in the Night, & eat up what remain'd of our Provisions.[55]

8.   When we were drest, Meanwell & I visited most of the Princesses at their own Appartments, but the Smoke was so great there, the Fire being made in the middle of the Cabbins, that we were not able to see their Charms. Prince James's Princess sent my Wife a fine Basket of her own making, with the Expectation of receiving from her some Present of ten times its Value. An Indian Present like those made to Princes, is only a Liberality put out to Interest, & a bribe placed to the greatest Advantage. I cou'd discern by some of our Gentlemen's Linnens, discolour'd by the Soil of the Indian Ladys, that they had been [59] convincing themselves in the Point of their having no furr. About Ten we march't out of the Town, some of the Indians giving us a Volley of small Arms at our departure. We drank our Chocolate at one Jones's, about 4 Miles from the Town, & then proceeded over Black-Water Bridge to Colo. Henry Harrison's, where we were very handsomely entertain'd, & congratulated one another upon our Return into Christendom.[56]

9.   We scrubb'd off our Indian dirt, & refresht ourselves with clean Linnen. After a plentifull Breakfast, we took our Leave, & set our Faces towards Westover. By the way we met Boller Cocke & his Lady, who told me my Family was well, Heaven be prais'd.[57]

When we came to the New Church near Warren's Mill, Steddy drew up his Men, & harangued them in the following Manner. "Friends & Fellow-Travellers, It is a great Satisfaction to me, that after so many difficultys & Fatigues, you are return'd in safety to the Place where I first Join'd you. I am much oblig'd to you for the great readiness & Vigour you have shew'd in the business we went about, & I must do you all, the Justice to declare, that you have not only done your Duty but also done it with Cheerfulness & Affection. Such a Behaviour, you may be sure, will engage us, to procure for you the best Satisfaction we can from the Government. And besides that you may depend upon our being ready at all times to do you any manner of Kindness. You are now blessed be God, near your own [60] dwellings, & I doubt not, willing to be discharg'd. I heartily wish you may every one find your Friends & your Familys in perfect Health, & that your Affairs may have suffer'd as little as possible by your Absence." The Men took this Speech very kindly, & were thankfull on their Part for the affectionate Care we had taken of them during the whole Journey. Upon the whole Matter it was as much as we cou'd do to part with dry Eyes. However they filed off to Prince George Court, where they entertain'd their Acquaintance with the History of their Travels, and Meanwell with the 2 Astrolabes past over the River with me to Westover, where I had the Pleasure of meeting all my Family in perfect Health, nor had they been otherwise since I left them. This great Blessing ought to inspire us all with the deepest Sentiments of Gratitude, as well as convince us of the Powerfull Effect of sincere and hearty Prayers to the Almighty in all our undertakings.[58]

Thus ended our Progress for this Season, & it shou'd be remember'd that before we parted with the Commissioners of N. Carolina we agreed to meet again at Kinchins on the 10th of September, to continue the Line from thence toward the Mountains; upon this Condition nevertheless, that if the Commissioners on either Side shou'd find it convenient to alter the Day, they shou'd give timely Notice to the other. I had been so long absent from home, that I was glad to rest my self for a few Days, & therefore went not down to Williamsburgh 'til the 17th of [61] April. And then I waited upon the Governor to give an Account of my Commission, but found my Reception a little cooler than I thought my Behaviour in the Service had deserv'd. I must own I was surpriz'd at it, 'til I came to understand, that several Storys had been whisper'd by Firebrand & Orion to my Disadvantage. Those Gentlemen had been so indiscreet as to set about several ridiculous Falshoods, which cou'd be prov'd so, by every Man that was with us, particularly that I had treated Orion not only without Ceremony, but without Justice, denying him any Assistance from the Men, & supporting them in their rudeness to him. And because they thought it necessary to give some Instance of my unkindness to that worthy Gentleman, they boldly affirm'd, that I wou'd not send one of the Men from Capt. James Wilson's to Norfolk Town for his Horse, which he had left there to be cur'd of a sore back. The Father of Lies cou'd not have told one more point Blank against the Truth than this was, because the Author of it knew in his own Conscience, that I had order'd one of the Men to go upon this Errand for him, tho' it was more than 50 Miles backward & forward, & tho' his own Servant might as well have gone, because he had at that time nothing to hinder him, being left behind at Wilsons, where the Men were, and not attending upon his Master. And this I cou'd prove by Meanwell who wrote the Order I sign'd for this Purpose, & by Dr. Humdrum who receiv'd it, & thereupon [62] had sent one of the Men to Norfolk for him. Nor were these Gentlemen content with doing this wrong to me, but they were still more & more unjust to Astrolabe, by telling the Governor, that he was ignorant in the Business of Surveying, that he had done nothing in running of the Line, but Orion had done all; which was as Opposite to Truth, as Light is to darkness, or Modesty to Impudence. For in Fact Astrolabe had done all, & Orion had done nothing, but what expos'd not only his awkwardness in the Practice, but his Ignorance in the Theory: nor was this a bare untruth only with regard to Astrolabe, but there was Malice in it, for they had so totally prepossest the Commissary with his being Ignorant in the Art of Surveying, that, contrary to his promise formerly given, he determined not to make him Surveyor of Goochland, nor had he yielded to it at last, without the interposition of the Governor. So liable is Humane Nature to prepossession, that even the Clergy is not exempt from it.

They likewise circulated a great many other ridiculous Stories in the Gaiety of their Hearts, which carry'd a keener Edge against themselves than Steddy, & therefore merited rather my Contempt, than resentment. However it was very easy when Meanwell & I came to Town,[59] not only to disprove all their Slander, but also to set every thing in a true light with Regard to them selves. We made it as clear as Noon Day, that all the Evidence they had given was as much upon ^the^ Irish, as their Wit & their Modesty. The Governor was soon [63] convinced, & exprest himself very freely to those Gentlemen & particularly to Orion, who had with great Confidence impos'd upon him. He was also so fully perswaded of Astrolabe's Abilities, that he perfectly constrain'd the Commissary to appoint him Surveyor of Goochland, to the Mortification of his Adversaries.[60]

As soon as I cou'd compleat my Journal, I sent it to Firebrand for his Hand if he found it right, but after many Days he return'd it to me unsign'd, tho' he cou'd make no Objection. I gave myself no further Trouble about him, but desir'd Mr. Banister to give it to the Governor, subscrib'd by Meanwell & me. Upon his asking Firebrand why he would not grace the Journal with his Hand, his Invention cou'd find no other Reason, but, because it was too Poetical. However he thought proper to sign this Poetical Journal at last, when he found it was to be sent to England without it.[61]

Sometime in June Plausible made me a Visit, & let me know in the Name of his Brother Commissioners of N. Carolina, that it was their common Request, that our Meeting to continue the Line might be put off to the 20th of September, & desir'd me to communicate their Sentiments to the other Commissioners for Virginia. I beg'd he wou'd make this request in Writing by way of Letter, lest it might be call'd in question by some Unbelievers. Such a Letter he wrote, & a few days after I shew'd it to Firebrand & let him know Meanwell & I had agreed to their Desire, & intended to write them an Answer accordingly. But he believing this Alteration of the Day to have been made in Compliment to me, [64] (because he knew I had always been of this Opinion), immediately sent away a Letter; or rather an Order to the Commissioners for Carolina, directing them to stick to their first day of meeting, being the Tenth of September, & to disown their Order to Plausible to get it put off. A Precept from so great a Man, three of these worthy Commissioners had not the Spirit to disobey, but meanly swallow'd their own Words, & under their Hands deny'd they had ever desired Plausible to make any such Motion. The Renegade Letter of these Sycophants was afterwards produced by Firebrand to the Governour & Council of Virginia. In the meantime, I sent them an Epistle sign'd by Meanwell & myself, that we, in compliance with their Desire deliver'd by Plausible had agreed to put off our meeting to the 20th of September. This servile Temper in these 3 Carolina Commissioners, shew'd of what base Metal they were made, & had discover'd itself in another pitifull Instance not long before.

Firebrand despairing of a good Word from his Virginia Colleagues, with great Industry procured a Testimonial from his Carolina Flatterers, as well for himself as his Favorite Orion. And because the Complement might appear too gross if addrest to himself it was contriv'd that the Gentlemen abovemention'd shou'd join in a Letter to the Commissary (with whom by the way they had never before corresponded) wherein without Rhyme or Reason, they took care to celebrate Firebrand's Civility and Orion's Mathematics.

This Certificate was soon produced by the good Commissary to our Governour, who could not but see [65] thro' the shallow Contrivance. It appear'd ridiculous to him, but most abject & monstrous to us, who knew them to be as ill Judges of the Mathematicks, as a deaf Man cou'd be of Musick. So that to be sure it was a great Addition to the Character of our Professor, to have the honour of their Testimonials. And tho' we shou'd allow Men of their Education to be Criticks in Civility, yet at first these very men complain'd of Firebrand's haughty Carriage, tho' now they have the meanness to write to the Commissary in Commendation of his Civility. These are such Instances of a poor Spirit as none cou'd equal but themselves in other Passages of their behaviour. And tho' the Subject be very low, yet I must beg leave to mention another Case, in which not only these, but all the Council of N. Carolina discover'd a Submission below all Example. They suffer'd this Firebrand to come in at the head of their Council, when at his first Admission he ought to have been at the Tail. I can't tell whether it was more pretending in him to ask this precedence or more pitifull in them to submit to it. He will say perhaps that it befitted not a Gentleman of his Noble Family & high Station, to sit below a Company of Pyrates, Vagabonds, & Footmen; but surely if that be their Character, he ought as little to sit among them at all. But what have they to say in their Excuse for Prostituting the Rank in which the Lords Proprietors had placed them, since the Person to whom they made this Complement has no other Title to the Arms he bears, and the Name he goes by, but the Courtesy of Ireland. And then for his Office, he is at most but a Publican & holds not his Commission from his [66] Majesty, but from

the Commissioners of the Customs.[62] So they had no other Reason to give
this Man Place but because their own worthlessness flew in their Faces.
Sometime in July I receiv'd a Letter from Firebrand in which he accus'd me
of having taken too much upon me in our last Expedition, by pretending
to a Sole Command of the Men. That then the Number of our Men was too
great, & brought an unnecessary Charge upon the Publick, that 9 or 10 wou'd
be sufficient to take out with us next time, of which he wou'd name 3. This
was the Sum & Substance of his Letter, tho' there were Turns in it & some
Raillery which he intended to be very ingenious, & for which he belabour'd
his poor Brains very much. I did not think this Epistle worth an Answer, but
fancy'd it wou'd be time enough to dispute the Points mention'd therein, at
our next Council. It happen'd in August upon the News of some disturbance
among the Indians, that the Governour call'd a small Council compos'd only
of the Councellors in the Neighbourhood, judging it unnecessary to give
us the Trouble of a Journey, who liv'd at a greater Distance. At this Council
assisted only Firebrand, the Commissary, and 3 other Gentlemen.[63] Neither
Meanwell nor I were there, nor had any Summons or the least Notice of
it. This Firebrand thought a proper Occasion to propose his Questions
concerning the Reduction of the Number of our Men, & the day when we were
to meet the ^Carolina^ Commissioners. He was seconded by his Friend the
Commissary, who surpriz'd the rest of the council into their Opinion, there
being nobody to oppose them, nor any so just as to put off the Question,
til the 2 Commissioners that were absent might be heard in a matter that
concern'd them. However these unfair & short-sighted Politicks were [67] so
far from prospering, that they turn'd to the Confusion of him that contriv'd
them. For having quickly gain'd Intelligence of this proceeding, I complained
of the Injustice of it in a Letter I wrote to the Governor, and he was so much
convinc'd by my Reasons, that he wrote me word, he wou'd call a general
Council the Week following, to overhawle that Matter again. Indeed he had
been so prudent at the little Council as to direct the Clerk not to enter what
had been there determin'd upon the Council Books, that it might not stand
as an Order but only as Matter of Advice to us Commissioners. Upon Receipt
of this Letter I dispatcht an Express to Meanwell, acquainting him with
this whole Matter, & intreating him to call upon me in his way to the next
Council. When he came we consulted what was fittest for us to do after such
Treatment; & upon weighing every Circumstance we resolv'd at last that since
it was not possible for us to agree with Firebrand, we would absolutely refuse
to go with him upon the next Expedition lest his Majesty's Service might
suffer by our perpetual Discord. Full of this Resolution we went down to
Williamsburgh, & begg'd the Governor, that he wou'd be pleas'd to dispence

with our serving any more with Firebrand in running the Line; because he was a Person of such uneasy Temper, that there were no hopes of preserving any Harmony amongst us. The Governor desir'd we wou'd not abandon a Service in which we had acquitted ourselves so well, but finish what we had began, tho' he own'd we were join'd by a Gentleman too selfish & too arrogant to be happy [68] with him. I reply'd that since he did me the Honour to desire me to make another Journey with him, I wou'd do it, but hoped I might have 20 Men & have the Sole command of them to prevent all Disputes upon that Chapter. He thought what I ask't was so reasonable, that if I wou'd propose it to the Council, I might easily carry it.

According to the Governor's Advice, Meanwell & I yielded to put it to the Council, & when it was met, & our Business enter'd upon, I deliver'd myself in the following Terms, "I humbly conceive that the Business of running the Line towards the Mountains will require at least 20 Men, if we intend to follow it with Vigour. The Chain-carriers, the Markers, & the Man who carrys the Instrument after the Surveyor must be constantly reliev'd. There must be 5 in Number always upon Duty, & w[h]ere the Woods are thick, which will frequently be the Case, there shou'd be 2 more Men to clear the way & open the Prospect to the Surveyors. While this Number is thus employ'd, their Arms must be carry'd, & their Horses led after them by as great a Number. This will employ at least 10 Men constantly, and if we must have no more, who must then take care of the Baggage & Provisions which will need several Horses, & in such Pathless Woods, each Horse must be led by a carefull Man, or the Packs will soon be torn off their Backs. Then besides all these, some Men shou'd be at Leizure to hunt & keep us in Meat, for which our whole dependance must be upon the Woods. Nor ought we in an Affair [69] of so much Consequence be ty'd down to so small a Number of Men, as will be exactly requisite for the dayly business, some may be sick, or Lame, or otherwise disabled. In such an Exigence must we return Home, for want of Spare Hands to supply such Misfortunes? Ought we not to go provided against such common Disasters as these? At this rate we shou'd lose more in the length of Time, than we shou'd save by the Shortness of our Number, which wou'd make our Frugality, as it often happens, an extravagant Expence to us. Nor wou'd it be prudent or safe to go so far above the Inhabitants, without a competent Number of Men for our Defence. We shall cross the Path, which the Northern Indians pass to make War upon the Catauba's, & shall go thro' the very Woods that are frequented by those Straggling Savages, who commit so many Murders upon our Frontiers. We ought therefore to go provided with a Force sufficient to secure us from falling into their hands. It may possibly be objected, that the Carolina Men will encrease our Number, which is certain, but they will very little encrease our Force. They will bring more Eaters than Fighters, at least they did so the last time, and if they shou'd be better provided with Arms now, their Commissioners have so little Command over the Men, that I expect no good from them if we shou'd be so unfortunate as to be attack't. From all which I must conclude, that our safety, our Business & the Accidents that attend, it will [require] at least 20 Men. And, in [order] to make this number more usefull, there ought to be no confusion [70] [in the]ᵏ Command. We are taught both by reason & Experience, that when any Men in Arms are sent on an Expedition, they ought to be under the Command of one Person only. For shou'd they be commanded by several claiming equal Power, the Orders given by so many might happen to be contradictory, as probably they wou'd happen to be in our Case. The Consequence of which must follow, that the Men wou'd not know whom to obey. This must introduce an endless distraction, & end in defeating the Business you are sending us about. It were ridiculous to say the Command ought to rest in the Majority, because then we must call a Council every time any Orders are to be issued. It wou'd be still more absurd to propose, that such Persons claiming equal Power, shou'd command by Turns, because then one Commander may undo this day, what his Colleague had directed the day before, & so the Men will be perplext with a Succession of Jarring Orders. Besides, the preference, & distinction which these poor Fellows might have Reason to shew to one of these Kings of Brentford, may be punish't by the other, when it comes to his turn to be in Power.⁶⁴ This being the Case, what men of Spirit or Common Sense wou'd list themselves under such uncertain Command, where they cou'd not know whom to please, or whom to obey? For all which Reasons Sirs I must conclude, that ^the^ Command of the Men ought to rest in One Person, & if in One, then without Controversy in him who has the Honour to be first in Commission." [71]

The Council as well as the Governor, was convinc't by these Arguments, & unanimously voted 20 Men were few enough to go out with us, & thought it reasonable that the Command of them shou'd be given to me, as being the first in Commission. Firebrand oppos'd each of these Points with all his Eloquence, but to little purpose no Body standing by him, not so much as his new Ally the Commissary. He seem'd at first to befriend him with a Distinction which he made between the day of Battle, & a Day of Business: but having no Second, he ran with the Stream. However in pure Compassion to

---

ᵏA: *This leaf is torn at the upper corner, partially obscuring several words here interpolated conjecturally.*

poor Firebrand, for fear he shou'd want somebody to run of his Errands for him, it was agreed he shou'd have 3 Men to fetch & carry for him.

I had the same success in getting the day of Meeting which the Carolina Commissioners desired might be put off till the 20th of September, notwithstanding Firebrand produced Letters from Messrs. Jumble & Shoebrush that they had not desired their Colleague Plausible to procure our Rendezvous to be deferr'd. I confronted these Letters with that Epistle I had from Plausible which flatly contradicted them. Thus it was evident there was a Shamefull untruth on one Side or the other; but if we consider the Characters of the Men, and the Influence of Firebrand over those two, whose Brothers were collectors, one may guess where it lies, especially since this was not the first time their Pens had been drawn in his service. However these Letters did no Service. But the Governor declared he wou'd write [72] to Sir Richard Everard, that we should meet the Commissioners of his Government on the 20th of September with 20 Men. How much the Pride of Firebrand was mortify'd by so intire a Defeat in every one of his Points, may be easily guest by the loud Complaint he made afterwards, how inhumanely the Council had treated him, and by the Pains he took with the Governor to get the Order of Council soften'd with relation to the Command. But remembering how unjustly he had reproach't me with having taken too much upon me in our former Trip, I insisted upon the Order of Council in the fullest Extent. Upon seeing me so Sturdy he declar'd to the Governor, he could not go on such dishonourable Terms, & swore to others he wou'd not, but Interest got the better of his Oath & Honour too, and he did vouchsafe to go at last, notwithstanding all the Disgraces which he thought had been put upon him. From hence we may fairly conclude, that Pride is not the strongest of his Passions, tho' strong enough to make him both ridiculous & detestable.[65]

After these necessary Matters were settled, I ordered 1000 lb of Brown Biscuit, & 200 lb of White to be provided, & 6 Baggage Horses to carry it, at the rate of 3 Baggs containing 200 lb upon each Horse. As for Meat I intended to carry none, but to depend entirely upon Providence for it. But because the Game was not like to be plentiful till we got above the Inhabitants, I directed all the Men to [73] find themselves with 10 days' Provision. I augmented my Number of men to 17, which, together with 3 which Firebrand undertook to get, made up the Complement of 20. For these I provided Ammunition after the Rate of 2 lb of Powder a Man, with Shot in proportion. On the 16th of September Meanwell & Astrolabe came to my house in order to set out with me the day following toward the Place of Rendezvous.

September 17.   About 10 in the Morning I having recommended my

Wife & Family to the Protection of the Almighty past the River with Messrs.
Meanwell & Astrolabe to Mr. Ravenscroft's Landing. He was so complaisant
as to accompany us as ^far as^ the New-Church, where 8 of our Men were
attending for us, namely, Peter Jones, George Hamilton, James Petillo,
Thomas Short, John Ellis Junr., Richard Smith, George Tilman, & Abraham
Jones. The rest were to meet us at Kinchin's, which lay more convenient to
their Habitations. Only I had order'd 3 of them who were absent to convoy the
Bread Horses thither, the nearest Road they cou'd go, namely, Thomas Jones,
Thomas Jones Junr., & Edward Powel, to the last of which the Bread Horses
belong'd.[66]

We proceeded with the 8 Men abovemention'd to Colo. Henry Harrisons,
where our Chaplain Dr. Humdrum was arriv'd before us. We were
handsomely entertain'd, & after Dinner furnish't ourselves with several small
Conveniences out of the Store. Then we took a turn to the Cold Bath, where
the Colo. refreshes himself every Morning. This is about 5 Feet Square, & as
many deep, [74] thro which a pure Stream continually passes, & is covered
with a little House just big enough for the Bath & a Tireing Room. Our
Landlord who us'd formerly to be troubled both with the Gripes & the Gout,
fancys he receives benefit by plunging every day in cold Water. This good
House was enough to spoil us for Woodsmen, where we drank Rack-Punch
while we sat up, & trod on Carpets when we went to Bed.[67]

18.   Having thanked the Colo. for our good Cheer, we took leave about
ten, not at all dismay'd at the likelihood of Rain. We travelled after the Rate
of 4 Miles an hour, passing over Blackwater Bridge, & 10 Miles beyond that
over another call'd Assamousack Bridge. Then we filed off to Richard Parker's
Plantation, where we had been kindly us'd in our return home. We found the
distance 24 Miles going a little astray for want of a Guide, & there fell a sort
of Scots Mist all the way. We arriv'd about 5 a Clock & found things in much
disorder, the good Woman being lately dead, & those that surviv'd sick. Pretty
Sally had lost some of her Bloom by an Ague, but none of her good humour.
They entertain'd us as well as they cou'd, and what was wanting in good cheer
was made up in good humour.[68]

19.   About 10 this Morning we wish't Health to Sally & her Family, & forded
over Notoway River at Bolton's Ferry, the Water being very low. We call'd
upon Samuel Kindred again who regaled us with a Beef Steak, & our Men
with Syder: Here we had like to have listed a Mulatto Wench for Cook to the
Expedition, [75] who formerly liv'd with Colo. Ludwell. After halting here
about an Hour, we pursued our Journey, & in the way Richard Smith shew'd
me the Star-Root, which infallibly cures the Bite of the Rattlesnake. Nine
miles from thence we forded over Meherin River near Mr. Kinchin's, believing

we shou'd be at the Place of meeting before the rest of the Commissioners. But we were mistaken, for the first Sight my Eyes were blest, with was that of Orion, & finding the Shadow there I knew the Substance cou'd not be far off.[69]

Three Commissioners on the Part of N. Carolina came that Night, tho' Jumble & Puzzlecause were order'd by their Governor to stay behind, lest their Genl. Court might be delay'd. But they came notwithstanding, in ^the strength of^ their Interest with the Council, but seem'd afraid of being pursued, & arrested. They put on very gracious Countenances at our first greeting: but yet look't a little Conscious of having acted a very low part in the Epistles they had written. For my part I was not Courtier enough to disguise the Sentiments I had of them & their Slavish proceeding, & therefore cou'd not smile upon those I despis'd. Nor could I behave much better to Firebrand & his Echo Orion, nevertheless I constrain'd myself to keep up a stiff Civility. The last of these Gentlemen, remembering the just Provocation he had given me, thought it necessary to bring a Letter from the Governor recommending him to my Favour & Protection. This therefore had the Air of confessing his former Errors, which made me after some gentle Reproofs, assure him, he shou'd have no Reason to complain of my Treatment. Tho' I carry'd fair weather to Firebrand, yet Meanwell cou'd not, [76] but all Ceremony, Notice, & Conversation seem'd to be cancell'd betwixt them. I caus'd the Tent to be pitch't in the Orchard, where I & my Company took up our Quarters, leaving the House to Firebrand & his Faction.

20.   This Morning Meanwell was taken a-Purging & vomiting for which I dosed him with Veal Broth, & afterwards advis'd him to a Gallon of warm Water, which finish't his Cure. We herded very little with our Brother Commissioners & Meanwell frankly gave Jumble to understand, that we resented the impertinent Letters he & some of his Collegues had writ to Virginia. He made a very lame Apology for it, because the Case would not bear a good one. He & his Brethren were lamentably puzzled how to carry their Baggage & Provisions. They had brought them up by Water near this Place, & had depended on fortune to get Horses there to carry them forward. I believe too they rely'd a little upon us to assist them: but I was positive not to carry one Pound Weight. We had Luggage enough for our own Horses, & as our Provisions lighten'd, the shortness of their Provenders wou'd require them to be lighten'd too. I was not so complaisant to these worthy Gentlemen as Firebrand for he brought a Tent for them out of the Magazine at Williamsburgh, to requite the dirty work they had been always ready to do for him. At last they hir'd something like a Cart to carry their Lumber as far as it cou'd go toward Roanoke River.

In the Evening 6 more of our Men join'd us, namely, Robert Hix, John

Evans, Stephen Evans, Charles Kimball, Thomas Wilson, & William Pool, but [77] the 3 Men that conducted the Bread Horses, came not up as yet, which gave me some Uneasiness tho' I concluded they had been stop't by the rain. Just after Sunset Capt. Hix and Capt. Drury Stith arriv'd & made us the Complement to attend us as far as Roanoke.[70] The last of these Gentlemen, bearing some Resemblance to Sir Richard Everard put Messrs. Jumble & Puzzlecause into a Panick lest the Knight was come to put a stop to their Journey. My Landlord had unluckily sold our Men some Brandy, which produced much disorder, making some too Cholerick, and others too loving. So that a Damsel who came to assist in the Kitchen wou'd certainly have been ravisht if her timely consent had not prevented the Violence.[71] Nor did my Landlady think her self safe in the hands of such furious Lovers, and therefore fortify'd her Bedchamber and defended it with a chamber pot charged to the brim with female ammunition.[72] I never cou'd learn who the Ravisher was; because the Girl had walk't off in the Morning early, but Firebrand & his Servant were the most suspected, having been engaged in those kind of Assaults once before. In the morning Meanwell joined us.[1]

21.   We sent away the Surveyors about 9 who could carry the Line no more than 3½ Miles because the Low Grounds were cover'd with Thickets. As soon as we had paid a very exorbitant Bill, and the Carolina Men had loaded their vehicle & dispos'd of their Lumber, we mounted, & conducted our Baggage about 10 Miles. [78] We took up our Quarters at the Plantation of John Hill, where we pitch't our Tent with design to rest there 'til Monday. This Man's House was so poorly furnish't, that Firebrand & his Carolina Train cou'd not find in their Hearts to lodge in it, so we had the Pleasure of their Company in the Camp. They perfumed the Tent with their Rum Punch, & hunted the poor Parson with their unseemly Jokes, which turn'd my Stomach as much as their Fragrant Liquor. I was grave & speechless the whole Evening, & retired early; by all which, I gave them to understand, I was not fond of the Conversation of those whose Wit, like the Commons at the University & Inns of Court is eternally the same.[73]

22.   This being Sunday we had a large Congregation, & tho' there were many Females, we saw no Beauty bright enough to disturb our devotions. Our Parson made 11 Christians. Mr. Hill made heavy Complaint that our Horses did much Damage to his Corn-Field. Upon which I order'd those that were most Vicious that way to be ty'd up to their good Behaviour. Among these, Humdrum's and Astrolabe's were the greatest Trespassers. After Church I

---

[1]*Although this sentence logically should appear in the next day's entry, it appears in the MS before the break.*

gave John Ellis a Vomit for his Ague with good Success, & was forc'd myself to soften my Bowels with Veal Broth for a Looseness. I also recommended Warm Water to Capt. Stith for the Cholick, which gave him immediate Ease.

In the Afternoon our 3 Men arrived with the 6 Bread-Horses, having been kept so long behind by the Rain, but thank God it had receiv'd no Damage. [79] I took a walk with Plausible, & told him of the Letters his Collegues had writ to falsify what he had told me concerning their Request, to put off the time of our Meeting. He justify'd his own Veracity, but shew'd too much Cold Blood in not been Piqued at so flagrant an Injury. Firebrand & his Followers had smelt out a House about half a Mile off, to which they sent for the Silver Bowl, & spent the Evening by themselves both to their own Satisfaction and ours. We hoped to be rid of them for all Night, but they found the way to the Camp just after we were gone to Bed, & Firebrand hindered us from going to sleep so soon, by his Snoring & swearing.[74]

23.   We continu'd in our Camp, & sent the Surveyors back to the Place where they left off. They cou'd run the Line no more than 4 Miles by reason ^that it^ was overgrown with Bushes. I sent several of the Men out a Hunting & they brought us 4 Wild Turkeys. Old Capt. Hix killed 2 of them, who turn'd his Hand to every thing notwithstanding his great Age, disdaining to be thought the worse for Threescore & ten. Beauty never appear'd better in Old Age, with a Ruddy Complexion, & Hair as white as Snow. It rain'd a little in the Evening but did not hinder our Rum-Commissioners from stepping over to John Hill's to swill their Punch, leaving the Tent clear to us. After Midnight, it rain'd very hard with a Storm of Thunder & Lightening, which oblig'd us to trench in our Tent to cast off the Water. The Line crossed Meherin 5 times in all.

24.   So soon as the Men could dry their Blankets, we [80] sent away the Surveyors who made a Shift to carry the Line 7 Miles. But we thought it proper not to decamp believing we might easily overtake the Surveyors before tomorrow Night. Our Shooters kill'd 4 more Wild Turkeys. Meanwell and Captain Stith pretended to go a-hunting, but their game was eight fresh-colored wenches, which were not hard to hunt down. The Neighbours supply'd us with pretty good Cheese & very fat Mutton. I order'd a View of John Hill's Damage in his Cornfield, & paid him for 6 Barrels on that Account.[75]

Firebrand instructed one of the 3 Men which he listed on the Publick Service to call him Master, thereby endeavouring to pass him on the Carolina Commissioners for his Servant, that he might seem to have as many Servants as Steddy, but care was taken to undeceive them in this Matter & expose his Vanity. The Carolina Men liv'd at Rack & Manger without any sort of

Oeconomy, thereby shewing they intended not to go very far with us, tho' we took care to set them a better example. Our Chaplain had leave to go home with Robert Hix, who lived no more than 6 Miles from this Place to Christen his Child, & the Old Captain went along with them. We had the comfort to have the Tent to ourselves, the Knights of the Rum-Cask retiring in the Evening to the House, & wasting the Liquor & double refin'd Sugar as fast as they cou'd.[76]

25.   Our Surveyors proceeded to run little more than 7 Miles. Firebrand & his Gang got out this Morning [81] before us, on pretence of providing our Dinner; but they outrid the Man that carry'd the Mutton, & he not knowing the way was lost, so that instead of having our Dinner sooner, we run a hazard of having none at all. We came up to them about 4 a Clock & thank't them for the prudent care they had taken. This was a Sample of these Gentlemen's Management, whenever they undertook any thing. We encampt near Beaver Pond Creek, & on our way thither Peter Jones kill'd a small Rattlesnake. The Surveyors made an End very near where we lay. Orion was exceedingly awkward at his Business, so that Astrolabe was oblig'd to do double Duty. There being no house at hand to befriend us, we were forced to do Pennance at the Tent with the Topers.

26.   This Morning we dispatch't the Surveyors early, & they ran about 10½ Miles. By the way the Men that were with him kill'd 2 large Rattlesnakes. Will Pool trod upon one of them without receiving any hurt, & 2 of the Chain Carriers had march't over the other, but he was so civil as to bite neither of them: however one of these Vipers struck at Wilson's horse, and misst him. So many Escapes were very providential, tho' the Danger proves, that my Argument for putting off our Business was not without Foundation. We march't upon the Line after the Surveyors, & about 4 a Clock encampt upon Cabin Branch, which is one of the Branches of Fountain's Creek. Before we set off this Morning, we christen'd 2 Children. One of them was brought by a modest Lass, who, being [82] asked how she liked Captain Stiff? reply'd not at all, nor Capt. Limber neither, meaning Orion. We saw Abundance of Ipocoacanna in the Woods, & the Fern Rattlesnake-Root, which is said to be the strongest Antidote against the Bite of that Viper. And we saw St. Andrew's-Cross almost every Step we went, which serves for the same Purpose. This Plant grows on all kinds of Soil, every where at hand during the Summer Months, when the Snakes have Vigour enough to do Mischief. Old Capt. Hix entertain'd us with one of his Trading Songs, which he quaver'd out most melodiously & put us all into a good humour.[77]

27.   We sent away the Surveyors before 10 a Clock & follow'd with the Baggage at 11. But Firebrand thought proper to remain with 3 of the Carolina

Commissioners til their Cart came up, & took it ill that we tarry'd not with
them likewise. But I cou'd not complement away our Time at that Rate. Here
they made broad Hints to carry some of their Luggage for them, I wou'd put
not such hardships upon our Men, who had all enough to carry of their own,
so we left them there, to make the best Shift they cou'd, & follow'd the Line
with all Diligence. We past Pea-hill-Creek, & sometime after Lizzard Creek,
which empties itself into Roanoke River. Here we halted 'til our Chaplain
baptized 5 Children. Then we proceeded to Pigeon-Roost Creek, where we
took up our Quarters, having carry'd the Line above 9 Miles. [83]

28.   We hurry'd away the Surveyors, who cou'd run no more than 6 Miles
because of the uneven Grounds near Roanoke River. We did not follow with
the Baggage till 10, being staid to christen 6 Children, & to discourse a very
civil Old Fellow, who brought us 2 fat Shoats for a present. The name of our
Benefactor was Epaphroditus Bainton, who is young enough at 60 Years of
Age to keep a Concubine, & to walk 25 miles in a day. He has forsworn ever
getting on a Horses back, being once in Danger of breaking his Neck by a
Fall. He spends most of his time in hunting & ranging the Woods, killing
generally more than 100 Deer in a Year. He pretends to Skill in the Vertues
of many Plants, but I cou'd learn nothing of that kind from him. This Man
was our Guide to Majr. Mumford's Plantation, under the care of Miles Riley,
where we were regaled with Milk, Butter, & many other Refreshments. The
Majr. had order'd some Wine to be lodged here for us, & a fat Steer to be at
our Service: but the last we refus'd with a great many thanks. From hence
we continu'd our Journey to the Canoe-Landing upon Roanoke River, where
Young Mumford & Mr. Walker met us. Here we ferry'd over our Baggage
& our Persons, ordering the men with the Horses to the Ford near a mile
higher, which leads to the Trading Path. Here my old Friend Capt. Hix
took his Leave committing us to our kind Stars. We were [84] set ashore at
another Plantation belonging to Major Mumford, under the Management of
a Man they called Natt. Here was another fat Steer ordered for us, which we
thankfully accepted of for the Sake of the Men. We pitch't the Tent near the
House, which supply'd all our Wants. Poor Miles Riley receiv'd a kick from
one of the Horses, for which I order'd him to be instantly blooded, & hindered
all bad Consequences. I interceded with Plausible in behalf of the Virginians
whose land was left by the Line in Carolina, & he promis'd to befriend them.
George Hamilton kill'd a Snake with 11 Rattles having a Squirrell in his Belly,
which he had charm'd, & only the head of it was digested. Also the Chain-
carriers kill'd another small one the same day.[78]

29.   Being Sunday we had a Sermon, but 'twas interrupted with a Shower
of Rain which dispers'd our Congregation. A little before Noon the Carolina

Baggage came up, & the Servants bless'd us with the News that their Masters wou'd come in the Evening. They also inform'd us they lay last Night at John Youngs, & had hired him & his Brother to assist them upon the Line. That for want of Horses to carry their Luggage, they had left some of it behind. Our Chaplain Baptiz'd 5 Children, & I gave Thomas Wilson a Vomit that work't powerfully, & carry'd off his Feaver. I wrote to the Governor a full & true account of all our proceedings, & sent the Letter by Mr. Mumford, who took his Leave this Evening. About 4 in the Afternoon [85] Firebrand & his Carolina Guards came to us, as likewise did some of the Sapponi Indians. I had sent Charles Kimball to Christanna to perswade 2 of their most able Huntsmen to go the Journey to help supply us with Meat. I had observ'd that our Men were unfortunate Gunners, which made me more desirous to have some that had better luck. Out of 5 which came I chose Bearskin & another, who accepted the Terms I propos'd to them. From this time forward the Carolina Men & their Leader, honour'd us with their Company only at Dinner, but Mornings & Evenings they had a distinct Fire to our great Comfort, at which they toasted their Noses. Indeed the whole time of our being together, our dear Collegue acted more like a Commissioner for Carolina, than Virginia, & not only herded with them perpetually, but in every Instance join'd his Politicks with theirs in their Consultations. No wonder then they acted so wisely in their Conduct, & managed their Affairs with such admirable Prudence. It rain'd the whole Night long & held not up till break of day.[79]

30.   The Tent & Baggage was so wet, that we cou'd not get them dry til 12 a Clock, at which Hour we sent the Surveyors out & they carry'd the Line about 4½ Miles, which we computed, was as high as any Inhabitants. But we mov'd not till 2 with the Baggage. We past over Haw-Tree Creek, 2 Miles from our Camp, marching over poison'd fields. By the way a very lean Boar crost us, & several claim'd the Credit [86] of killing it, but all agreed 'twas Stone dead before Firebrand fired, yet he took the Glory of this Exploit to himself, so much Vanity he had, that it broke out upon such Paltry Occasions. Before we set off this Morning, Orion came to me with a Countenance very pale & disorder'd, desiring that Astrolabe might have Orders never to concern himself, when it was his turn to survey, because when he needed to be reliev'd, he chose rather to be beholden to Bootes, than to him. I cou'd by no means agree to this Request, telling him that none was so proper to assist one Virginia Surveyor, as the other. I let him know too, that such a Motion savour'd more of Pique & Peevishness than Reason. However I desir'd him to ask the Opinion of the other Commissioners, if he was not satisfy'd with mine: but he found it proper to ask no more Questions. Puzzlecause had a sore Throat, which incommoded him ^very much^ indeed, for he

could not swallow so much as Rum-Punch without Pain. But I advis'd him
to part with 12 Ounces of Blood, which open'd the Passage to his Stomach. I
recommended the Bark to Bootes for an Ague, & gave one of the Carolina Men
a dose of Ipocoaccanna for the same Distemper as I did to Powell one of our
own men.[80]

October 1.   We sent out the Surveyors early & by the benefit of clear
Woods & even Ground they carry'd the Line 12 Miles & 12 Poles. One of
our Baggage-Horses being missing, we decampt not til Noon, which gave
Firebrand & his Crew an Opportunity to get the Start of us about an hour.
However we came up with the Surveyors [87] before them. We forded over
Great-Creek not far from the Place where we encampt, & past Nutbush
Creek about 7 Miles from thence. And 5 Miles further we quarter'd near a
Branch which we call'd Nutbush Branch, believing it ran into the Creek of
that Name. One of the Indians kill'd a Fawn, which with the addition of a
little Beef made very Savory Soupe. The Surveyors by the help of a clear Night
took the Variation & found it something more than 2° 30′, so that it did not
diminish by approaching the Mountains, or by advancing toward the West,
or encreasing our Distance from the Sea, but continued much the same we
found it at Coratuck.

2.   The Surveyors got out about 9 a clock, & advanc't the Line about
9 Miles. We follow'd with the Baggage at 11, & past at 3 Miles distance from
our Camp, Mossamony Creek, an Indian Name signifying Paint-Creek, from
red Earth found upon the Banks of it, which in a fresh tinges the Water of that
Colour. Three Miles farther we got over Yapatsco, or Bever Creek with some
difficulty, the Bevers having rais'd the Water a great way up. We proceeded
3¼ Miles beyond this, & encampt on the West Side of Ohimpamony Creek, an
Indian Name which signifys Fishing Creek. By the way Firebrand had another
Occasion to shew his Prowess, in killing a poor little Wild Cat, which had
been crippled by 2 or 3 before. Poor Puss was unhappily making a Meal on a
Fox Squirrel when all these misfortunes befell her. Meanwell had like to have
quarrell'd with Firebrand & his Carolina Squadron for not halting for me on
the West Side of Yapatsco, having been almost mired in crossing that Creek,
[88] while they had the Fortune to get over it at a better Place. The Indians
kill'd 2 deer & John Evans a third, which made great Plenty & consequently
great Content in Israel.[81]

3.   We hurry'd away the Surveyors by 9, who ran something more than
8½ Miles. We follow'd them at 11, & crost several Branches of Excellent Water.
We went thro' a large Level of very rich high-Land, near 2 Miles in Length & of
unknown Breadth. Our Indian kill'd one Deer, & William Pool another; & this
last we graciously gave to the Carolina Men, who deserv'd it not, because they

had declar'd they did not care to rely upon Providence. We encampt upon
Tewahominy or Tuscaruda Creek. We saw many Buffalo Tracks, & abundance
of their Dung, but the Noise we made drove them all from our Sight.
The Carolina Commissioners with their Leader lagg'd behind to stop the
Craveings of their Appetites, nor were we ever happy with their Conversation,
but only at Dinner, when they play'd their Parts more for Spite than Hunger.[82]

4.   The Surveyors got to work a little after 9, & extended the Line near
8 Miles, notwithstanding the Ground was very uneven. We decampt after
them about 11, & at 5 Miles Distance crost Blewing Creek, & 3 Miles beyond
that, we forded Sugar-Tree Creek, & pitch't our Tent on the West Side of it.
This Creek receiv'd its Name from many Sugar Trees, which grow in the Low-
Grounds of it. By tapping the Sugar-Tree in the Spring, a great Quantity of
Liquor flows out of it, which may be boil'd up into good Sugar. It grows very
tall, & the Wood of it is very soft & Spungy. Here we also found abundance of
Spice-Trees, whose Leaves are fragrant, & the Berry they bear is black, [89]
when dry, & hot like Pepper. Both these Trees grow only in a very rich Soil. The
Low-Ground upon this Creek is very wide, sometimes on one Side, sometimes
on the other, but on the opposite Side the high land advances close to the
Creek. It ought to be remember'd, that the Commissioners of Carolina, made
a Complement of about 2000 Acres of Land lying on this Creek to Astrolabe,
without paying any Fees. Robert Hix saw 3 Buffalos, but his Gun being loaden
only with Shot cou'd do no Execution. Bootes shot one Deer, & the Indians
killed 3 more, & one of the Carolina men 4 Wild Turkeys. Thus Providence was
very plentifull to us, & did not disappoint us who rely'd upon it.[83]

5.   This day our Surveyors met with such uneven Ground & so many
Thickets, that with all their Diligence they cou'd not run the Line so far as
5 Miles. In this small Distance it crost over Hico-otto-mony Creek no less
than 5 times. Our Indian Ned Bearskin inform'd us at first, that this Creek
was the South Branch of Roanoke River, but I thought it impossible, both by
reason of its Narrowness & the small Quantity of Water that came down it.
However it past so with us at present til future Experience cou'd inform us
better.[84]

About 4 a Clock this afternoon Jumble advanc't from the rest of his
Company to tell me, that his Collegues for Carolina wanted to speak with
me. I desired if they had anything to communicate, that they wou'd please
to come forward. It was some time before I heard any more of these worthy
Gentlemen, but at last Shoebrush, as the Mouth of the rest, came to acquaint
me that their Government had order'd them to run the Line but 30 or [90]
40 Miles above Roanoke that they had now carry'd it near 50, & intended
to go no farther. I let them know, it was a little unkind they had not been

so gracious as to acquaint us with their Intentions before. That it had been Neighbourly to have inform'd us with their Intentions before we set out, how far they intended to go that we might also have received the Commands of our Government in that Matter. But since they had fail'd in that Civility we wou'd go on without them, since we were provided with Bread for 6 Weeks longer. That it was a great Misfortune to loose their Company: but that it wou'd be a much greater to loose the Effect of our Expedition, by doing the Business by halves. That tho' we went by our selves, our Surveyors wou'd continue under the same Oath to do impartial Right both to his Majesty, & the Lords Proprietors; & tho' their Government might chuse perhaps whether it wou'd be bound by our Line, yet it wou'd at least be a direction to Virginia how far his Majesty's Land extended to the Southward.

Then they desired that the Surveyors desired that the [Surveyors]^m might make a fair Plat of the distance we had run together, and that of this there might be two Copys signed by the Commissioners of both Governments. I let them know I agreed to that, provided it might be done before Monday Noon, when, by the Grace of God, we wou'd proceed without Loss of time, because the Season was far advanc't, & wou'd not permit us to waste one Moment in Ceremony to Gentlemen who had shew'd none to us. Here the Conversation ended 'til after Supper, when the Subject was handled with more Spirit by Firebrand. On my repeating what I had said before upon this Subject, he desir'd a Sight of our Commission. I gave him to understand, that since the Commissioners were the same that acted before, all which had heard the Commission [91] read, & since those for Carolina had a Copy of it, I had not thought it necessary to cram my Portmanteau with it a second time. And was therefore sorry I cou'd not oblige him with a Sight of it. He immediately said he wou'd take a Minute of this, and after being some time in scrabbling of it, he read to this Effect. That being ask't [by him]^n for a sight of my Commission, I had deny'd it upon Pretense that I had it not with me. That I had also refus'd the Commissioners of Carolina, to tarry on Monday, til the necessary Plats cou'd be prepar'd & exchang'd, but resolv'd to move forward as soon as the Tent shou'd be dry, by which means the Surveyors wou'd be oblig'd to work on the Sunday. To this I answer'd, that this was a very smart Minute, but that I objected to the word Pretence, because it was neither decent, nor true, that I deny'd him a Sight of our Commission upon any pretense, but for the honest Reason that I had it not there to shew; most of the Company thinking my Objection just, he did vouchsafe to soften that

---

^{m}*Phrase copied twice in A:* Then they desired that the Surveyors desired that the Surveyors ^{n}*Phrase copied twice in A:* by him by him

Expression, by saying I refus'd to shew him the Commission, alledgeing I had not brought it.

Soon after when I said that our Governor expected that we shou'd carry the Line to the Mountains, he made answer, that the Governor had exprest himself otherwise to him, & told him that 30 or 40 Miles wou'd be sufficient to go beyond Roanoke River. Honest Meanwell hearing this, & I suppose, not giving entire Credit to it, immediately lugg'd out his Pencil, saying in a Comical Tone, that since he was for Minutes, I Gad he wou'd take a Minute of that. The other took Fire at this, & without any preface or Ceremony seized a Limb [92] of our Table, big enough to knock down an Ox, and lifted it up at Meanwell, while he was scratching out his Minutes. I happening to see him brandish this dangerous Weapon, darted towards him in a Moment, to stop his Hand, by which the Blow was prevented; but while I hinder'd one Mischief, I had like to have done another, for the Swiftness of my Motion overset the Table, & Shoebrush fell under it, to the great hazard of his gouty Limbs. So soon as Meanwell came to know the favour that Firebrand intended him, he saluted him with the Title he had a good right to, namely, of Son of a W<   >e, telling him if they had been alone he durst as well be damn'd as lift that Club at him. To this the other reply'd with much Vigour; that he might remember, if he pleas'd, that he had now lifted a Club at him.

I must not forget that when Firebrand first began this Violence, I desir'd him to forbear, or I should ^be oblig'd to^ take him in Arrest. But he telling me in a great Fury that I had no Authority, I call'd to the Men, & let him know, if he wou'd not be easy, I wou'd soon convince him of my Authority. The Men instantly gather'd about the Tent ready to execute my Orders, but we made a Shift to keep the Peace without coming to Extremities. One of the People, hearing Firebrand very loud, desired his Servant to go to his Assistance. By no means, said he, that's none of my Business, but if the Gentleman will run himself into a Broil, he may get out of it as well as he can.

This Quarrel ended at last as all Publick Quarrels do, without Bloodshed, as Firebrand has experience'd several times, believing that on such Occasions [93] a Man may shew a great deal of Courage with very little Danger. However knowing Meanwell was made of truer Metal, I was resolv'd to watch him narrowly, to prevent further Mischief. As soon as this Fray was compos'd the Carolina Commissioners retir'd very soon with their Champion, to flatter him, I suppose, upon the great Spirit he had shew'd in their Cause against those who were join'd with him in Commission.

6.   This being Sunday we had Prayers, but no Sermon, because our Chaplain was indispos'd. The Gentlemen of Carolina were all the Morning breaking their Brains to form a Protest against our Proceeding on the Line

any further without them. Firebrand stuck close to them, & assisted in this elegant Speech, tho' he took some Pains to persuade us he did not. They were so intent upon it, that we had not their good Company at Prayers. The Surveyors however found time for their Devotions, which help't to excuse their working upon their Plats when the Service was over. Besides [this being]° a work of necessity, was the more pardonable. We dined together for the last time, not discovering much concern that we were soon to part. As soon as dinner was over the Protesters return'd to their Drudgery to lick their Cubb into shape. While I was reading in the Tent in the Afternoon, Firebrand approach't with a gracious smile upon his Face, & desir'd to know if I had any Commands to Williamsburgh, for that he intended to return with the Carolina Commissioners. That it was his Opinion we had no Power to proceed without them, but he hoped this difference of Sentiment might not widen the Breach that was between us, that he was very sorry any thing [94] had happen'd to set us at Variance, & wish't we might part Friends. I was a little surpriz'd at this Condescension but humour'd his Inclinations to Peace, believing it the only way to prevent future Mischief. And as a proof that I was in earnest, I not only accepted of these peaceable Overtures myself, but was so much his Friend as to persuade Meanwell to be reconcil'd to him. And at last I join'd their Hands & made them kiss one another.

Had not this Pacification happen'd thus luckily, it would have been impossible for Meanwell to put up the Indignity of holding up a Clubb at him, because in a Court of honour, the Shaking of a Cudgel at a Gentleman, is adjudged the same Affront as striking him with it. Firebrand was very sensible of this, & had great Reason to believe that in due time he must have been call'd to an Account for it by a man of Meanwell's Spirit. I am sorry if I do him wrong, but I believe this Prudent Consideration was the true Cause of the Pacifick advances he made to us, as also of his returning back with his dear Friends of Carolina. Tho' there might have still been another Reason for his going home before the Genl. Court. He was it seems left out of the Instructions in the List of Councellors, & as that matter was likely to come upon the Carpet at that time, he thought he might have a better Chance to get the matter determin'd in his favour when 2 of his Adversarys were absent. Add to this the Lucre of his Attendance during the Genl. Court, which would be so much clear Gain if he cou'd get so much Interest as to be paid as bountifully for being out 4 Weeks, as we for being 10, out upon the Publick Service. This I [95] know he was so unconscionable as to expect, but without the least Shadow of Reason or Justice.[85] Our Reconciliation with Firebrand

°*Phrase repeated in A:* this being this being

naturally made us Friends with his Allys of Carolina, who invited us to their Camp to help finish their Wine. This we did as they say, tho' I suspect they reserv'd enough to keep up their Spirits in their Return: while we that were to go forward did from henceforth depend altogether upon pure Element.

7. This Morning I wrote some dispatches home, which Firebrand was so gracious as to offer to forward by an Express, so soon as he got to Williamsburgh. I also wrote another to the Governor signifying how friendly we parted with our Brother-Commissioner. This last I shew'd to my Collegues to prevent all Suspicion, which was kindly taken. The Plats were Countersign'd about Noon, and that which belong'd to Virginia we desir'd Firebrand to carry with him to the Governor. Then the Commissioners for Carolina delivered their Protest sign'd by them all, tho' I did not think Plausible wou'd have join'd in so ill-concerted a Piece. I put it up without reading, to shew the Opinion I had of it, & let the Gentlemen know we wou'd endeavour to return an Answer to it in due time. But that so fine a Piece may be preserv'd, I will give both that & the Answer to it a place in my Journal. The Protest is in the following Words: WE THE UNDERWRITTEN COMMISSIONERS[p] for the Government of North-Carolina in Conjunction with the Commissioners on the part of Virginia, having run the Line for the Division of the 2 colonys from Coratuck [96] Inlet to the Southern Branch of Roanoke River, being in the whole about 170 miles, & near 50 Miles without the Inhabitants, being of Opinion we had run the Line as far as would be requisite for a long time, judg'd the carrying of it farther wou'd be a needless charge & trouble; & the Grand Debate which had so long subsisted between the Two Governments about Weyanoak River or Creek being settled at our former meeting in the Spring, when we were ready on our Parts to have gone with the Line to the Outmost Inhabitants, which if it had been done, the Line at any time after might have been continu'd at an easy Expence by a Surveyor on each Side, & if at any time hereafter there shou'd be occasion to carry the Line on farther than we have now run it, which we think will not be in an Age or Two, it may be done in the same easy Manner without the great Expence that now attends it; and on a Conference of all the Commissioners, we having communicated our Sentiments thereon, declared our Opinion that we had gone as far as the Service requir'd, & thought proper to proceed no farther, to which it was answer'd by the Commissioners for Virginia, that they shou'd not regard what we did, but if we desisted, they wou'd proceed without us. But we, conceiving by his Majesty's Order in Council, they were directed to act in Conjunction with the Commissioners appointed for Carolina, & having

[p]*Written in A in double-sized letters.*

accordingly run the Line jointly so far, & exchanged Planns, thought they
cou'd not, carry on the Bounds singly, but that their Proceedings without
us wou'd be irregular & invalid & that it wou'd be no Boundary, [97] and
thought it proper to enter our Dissent thereto; Wherefore for the Reasons
aforesaid, in the Name of His Excellency the Palatine, & the rest of the true &
absolute Lords Proprietors of Carolina, we dissent & disallow of any farther
Proceedings with the bounds without our Concurrence, & pursuant to our
Instructions do give this our dissent in writing.

| October | Plausible | Jumble |
| 7th, 1728 | Puzzlecause | Shoebrush |

To this protest the commissioners for Virginia made the following answer:

WHEREAS on the 7th day of October a Paper was deliver'd to us by the
Commissioners of N. Carolina in the Style of a Protest, against our carrying
any farther without them the Dividing Line between the 2 Governments, we
the underwritten Commissioners on the part of Virginia having maturely
consider'd the Reasons offer'd in the said Protest, why those Gentlemen
retir'd so soon from that Service, beg leave to return the following Answer.

They are pleas'd to alledge in the first Place by way of Reason, that having
run the Line near 50 Miles without the Inhabitants it was sufficient for a long
time, & in their Opinion for an Age or two.q To this we answer, that they by
breaking off so soon, did very imperfectly obey his Majesty's Order, assented
to by the Lords Proprietors. The plain meaning of that Order was, to ascertain
the Bounds betwixt the 2 Governments, as far toward the Mountains as we
cou'd, that neither the King's Grants may hereafter encroach upon the Lords
Proprietors, nor theirs on the Right [98] of his Majesty. And tho' the distance
towards the Mountains be not precisely determin'd by the said Order, yet
surely the West Line shou'd be carried as near to them as may be, that both
the Land of the King, & of the Lords may be taken up the faster, & that his
Majesty's Subjects may as soon as possible extend themselves to that Natural
Barrier. This they will do in a very few Years, when they know distinctly in
which Government they may enter for the Land, as they have already done
in the more Northern Parts of Virginia; So that 'tis strange the Carolina
Commissioners shou'd affirm, that the distance of 50 Miles beyond the
Inhabitants should be sufficient to carry the Line for an Age or two, especially
considering that a few days before the Signing of this Protest Astrolabe had
taken up near 2000 Acres of Land, granted by themselves, within 5 Miles
of the Place where they left us. Besides if we reflect on the goodness of the
Soil in those Parts, & the fondness of all Degrees of People to take up Land,

qA: *The number 2 partly erased, and the word overwritten.*

we may venture to foretell, without the Spirit of Divination, that there will
be many settlements much higher than these Gentlemen went in less than
ten years, & perhaps in half that time. The Commissioners of N. Carolina
protested against proceeding on the Line for another Reason, because it
wou'd be a needless charge & trouble alledging that the rest may be done by
one Surveyor on a Side, in an easy Manner when it shall be thought necessary.
To this we answer, that Frugality of the Publick Money is a great Vertue,
but when the Publick Service must suffer by it, it degenerates into a Vice, &
this will [99] ever be the Case, when Gentlemen execute the Orders of their
Superiors by halves. But had the Carolina Commissioners been sincerely
frugal for their Government, why did they carry out Provisions sufficient to
support themselves & their Men for 8 Weeks, when they intended to tarry out
no longer than half that time. This they must confess to be true, since they
had provided 500 lb. of Bread, & the same Weight of Beef & Bacon, which was
sufficient allowance for their Complement of Men for 2 Months, if it had been
carefully managed. Now after so great an Expence in their Preparations, it
had been but a small Addition to their Charge, if they had endur'd the Fatigue
a Month longer. It wou'd have been at most no more than what they must
be at, whenever they finish their work, even tho' they think proper to entrust
it to the Management of a Surveyor, who must have a necessary Strength
to attend him both for his Attendance & Defence. These are all the Reasons
these Gentlemen think fit to mention in their Protest, tho' in Truth they had
a much stronger Argument for their retiring so abruptly, which because they
forgot, it will be but neighbourly to help them out, and remind them of it.
The Provisions they brought along with them, for want of Providing Horses
to carry it, was partly left behind upon a high Tree to be taken down as
they return'd, and what they did carry, was so carelessly handled, that after
18 Days, which was the whole time we had the honour of their Company,
they had by their own confession no more left [100] than 2 lb. of bread for
each Man to carry them home. However tho' in Truth this was an invincible
Reason why they left the Business unfinish't, it was none at all to us who had
at that time Biscuit sufficient for 6 Weeks longer. Therefore lest their want
of Management shou'd put a Stop to his Majesty's Service, we conceiv'd it
our Duty to proceed without them, & have extended the Dividing Line so far
West, as to leave the Mountains on each Hand to the Eastward of us. This
we have done with the same Fidelity & Exactness, as if those Gentlemen had
continu'd with us. Our Surveyors acted under the same Oath which they had
taken in the Beginning, & were Persons whose Integrity will not be call'd in
Question. However tho' the Government of N. Carolina shou'd not hold itself
bound by the Line we made in the absence of its Commissioners, yet it will

continue to be a direction to the Government of Virginia, how far the King's Lands reach toward Carolina, & how far his Majesty may grant them ^away^ without Injustice to the Lords Proprietors. To this we may also ^add^, that having the Authority of our Commission to act without the Commissioners of N. Carolina in case of their Disagreement or Refusal, we thought it necessary on their deserting, to finish the Dividing Line without them, lest his Majesty's Service might suffer by any Neglect or Mismanagement on their Part. Given under our Hands the 7th of December, 1728.

      Meanwell   Steddy [101]

Tho' the foregoing Answer was not immediately return'd to the Protest, as appears by the Date, yet it can't be placed better in this Journal than next to it, that the Arguments on each Side may be the better compared & understood. Thus after we had compleated our Business with our dear Friends of Carolina, & supply'd 'em with some small Matters that cou'd be spared, they took their Leave, & Firebrand with them, full of Professions of Friendship & good Will. Just like some Men & their Wives, who after living together all their time in perpetual Discord & uneasiness, will yet be very good Friends at the Point of Death, when they are sure they shall part forever.

A General Joy discover'd itself thro' all our Camp, when these Gentlemen turned their Backs upon us, only Orion had a Cloud of Melancholly upon his Face, for the loss of those with whom he had spent all his leizure hours. Before those Gentlemen went he had perswaded Puzzlecause to give him a Certificate concerning the quarrel betwixt Firebrand & Meanwell, not because he was ignorant how it was, because he was sitting by the Fire within hearing all the time of the Fray, but because he shou'd not be able to tell the Truth of the Story, for fear of disobliging his Patron, & to disguise and falsify the Truth, besides making himself a Lyar, wou'd give just Offence to Meanwell. In this Dilemma he thought it safest to perswade Puzzlecause to be the Lyar by, giving him a Certificate which soften'd some things & left out others, & so by his New England way of cooking the Story, made it tell less shocking [102] on the side of Firebrand. This was esteem'd wonderful Politick in Orion, but he was as blameable, to circulate an untruth in another's Name, & under another's hand, as if it had been altogether his own Act & Deed, & was in Truth as much resented by Meanwell, when he came to hear it.

Because Firebrand desired that one of the Men, might return back with him, I listed one of the Carolina Men to go on with us in his room, who was indeed the best Man they had. One of our Horses being missing, we quitted not our Camp 'til 2 a Clock. This & the thick Woods were the reason we carry'd the Line not quite 3 Miles. We crost Hico-atto-moni-Creek once more in this day's work, & encampt near another Creek that runs into it call'd

Buffalo Creek, so call'd from the great Signs we saw of that Shy Animal. Now we drank nothing but the Liquor Adam drank in Paradise, & found it mended our Appetite, not only to our Victuals, of which we had Plenty, but also to Women of which we had none. It also promoted Digestion, else it had been impossible to eat so voraciously, as most of us did, without Inconvenience.[86]

Tom Short kill'd a Deer, & several of the Company kill'd Turkeys. These 2 kinds of Flesh together, with the help of a little Rice, or French Barley, made the best Soup in the World. And what happens very rarely in other good things, it never cloys by being a constant Dish. The Bushes being very thick, began to tear our Bread Bags so intollerably that we were [103] obliged to halt several times a day to have them mended. And the Carolina Men pleas'd themselves with the Joke of one of the Indians, who said we shou'd soon be forced to cut up our House (meaning the Tent) to keep our Baggs in Repair.[87] And what he said in Jest wou'd have happen'd true in Earnest, If I had not order'd the Skins of the deer which we kill'd, to be made use of in covering the Bags. This prov'd a good expedient by which they were guarded, & consequently our Bread preserv'd. I cou'd not forbear making an Observation upon our Men, which I believe holds true in others, that those of them who were the foremost to Stuff their Guts, were ever the most backward to work, & were more impatient to eat their Supper than to earn it. This was the Character of all the Carolina Men, without Exception.

8. We hurry'd the Surveyors out about 9, & follow'd ourselves with the Baggage about 11, yet the Woods were so thick we cou'd advance little better than 4 Miles. I spirited up our Men by telling them that the Carolina Men were so arrogant as to fancy we cou'd make no Earnings of it without them. Having yet not Skins enough to cover all our Bread Bags, those which had none suffer'd much by the Bushes, as in Truth did our Clothes & our Baggage, nor indeed were our Eyes safe in our Heads. Those difficulty's hindered Tom Jones from coming up with some of the loaded Horses to the Camp where we lay. He was forc'd to stop short about a Mile of us, where there was not a drop of Water, But he had the Rum with him, which was some Comfort. I was [104] very uneasy at their Absence, resolving for the future to put all the Baggage before us.

We were so lucky as to encamp near a fine Spring, & our Indian killed a fat Doe, with which Providence supply'd us just time enough to hinder us from going supperless to Bed. We called our Camp by the Name of Tear-Coat Camp, by reason of the rough thickets that surrounded it. I observ'd some of the Men were so free as to take what share of the Deer they pleas'd and to secure it for themselves, while others were at work, but I gave such Orders as put a stop to those Irregularitys, & divided the people into Messes, among which the Meat was fairly to be distributed.

9. The Surveyors went to work about 9, but because the Bushes were so intollerably thick, I order'd some hands to clear the way before them. This made their Business go on the slower; however they carry'd the Line about 6 Miles, by reason the Thicket reach't no farther than a Mile, & the rest of the Way was over clear Woods & even Grounds. We tarry'd with the Rear Guard till 12 for our absent Men, who came to the Camp as hungry as Hawks, for having no Water to drink, they durst not eat for fear of Thirst, which was more uneasy than Hunger. When we had supply'd our Wants, we followed the Track of the Surveyors, passing over 2 Runs of Excellent Water, one at 3, & the other at 4 Miles' Distance from our ^last^ Camp. The Land was for the most part very good, with Plenty of wild Angelica growing upon it. Several deer came into our Sight [105] but none into our Quarters, which made short commons & consequently some discontent. For this reason some of the Men call'd this Bread & Water Camp, but we call'd it Crane-Camp, because many of those Fowls flew over our Heads being very clamorous in their Flight. Our Indian kill'd a Mountain Partridge resembling the smaller Partridge in the Plumage, but as large as a Hen. These are common toward the Mountains tho' we saw very few of them, our Noise scareing them away.[88]

10. We began this day very luckily by killing a Brace of Turkeys & one Deer, so that the Plenty of our Breakfast this Morning, made amends for the Shortness of our Supper last Night. This restor'd good Humour to the Men, who had a mortal Aversion to fasting. As I lay in my Tent, I overheard one of them, call'd James Whitlock, wish that he were at home. For this I reprov'd him publickly, asking him whether it was the Danger, or the Fatigue of the Journey that dishearten'd him, wondring how he cou'd be tired so soon of the Company of so many Brave Fellows. So seasonable a Reprimand put an effectual Stop to all Complaints, and no Body after that day was ever heard so much as to wish himself in Heaven. A small distance from our Camp we crossed a Creek which we call'd Cocquade Creek, because we there began to wear the Beards of Wild-Turkey-Cocks in our Hats by way of Cocquade. A little more than a Mile from thence we came to the [106] true Southern Branch of Roanoke River, which was about 150 Yards over, with a swift Stream of Water as clear as Chrystal. It was fordable near our Line, but we were oblig'd to ride above 100 Yards up the river to the End of a Small Island, & then near as far back again on the other Side of the Island before we cou'd mount the Bank. The West Side of this fine River was fringed with tall Canes, a full furlong in Depth, thro' which our Men clear'd a Path Broad enough for our Baggage

406 } *The Secret History of the Line*

to pass, which took up a long time. The Bottom of the River was pav'd with Gravel, which was every where Spangled with small Fleaks of Mother of Pearl, that almost dazzled our Eyes. The Sand on the Shoar sparkled with the same. So that this seem'd the most beautiful River that I ever saw. The Difficulty of passing it & cutting thro' the Canes hinder'd us so much, that we cou'd carry the Line little more than 3 Miles. We crost a Creek 2½ Miles beyond the River, call'd Cane Creek, from very tall Canes, which lin'd its Banks. On the West Side of it we took up our Quarters. The Horses were very fond of those Canes, but at first they purg'd them exceedingly, & seem'd to be no very heartening Food. Our Indian kill'd a Deer, & the other Men some Turkeys, but the Indian begg'd very hard that our Cook might not boil Venison & Turkey together, because it wou'd certainly spoil his luck in Hunting, & we should repent it with fasting & Prayer. We call'd this South Branch of Roanoke the Dan, as I had call'd the North [107] Branch the Stanton before.[89]

11.   We hurry'd away the Surveyors at 9, & follow'd with the Baggage about 11. In about 4½ Miles we crost the Dan the 2d. time, & found it something narrower than before, being about 110 Yards over. The West Banks of it, were also thick set with Canes, but not for so great a Breadth as where we past it first. But it was here a most charming River, having the Bottom spangled as before, with a limpid Stream gently flowing, & murmuring among the Rocks, which were thinly scatter'd here & there to make up the Variety of the Prospect. The Line was carry'd something more than 2 Miles beyond the River, in which Distance the Thickets were very troublesome. However we made a Shift to run 6½ Miles in the whole, but encampt after Sun-set. I had foretold on the Credit of a Dream which I had last Sunday-Night, that we shou'd see the Mountains, this day, & it prov'd true, for Astrolabe discover'd them very plain to the NW of our Course, though at a great Distance. The Rich Land held about a Mile broad on the West Side the River. Tom Jones kill'd a Buck, & the Indian a Turkey, but he wou'd not bring it us, for fear we shou'd boil it with our Venison against his ridiculous Superstition. I had a moderate Cold which only spoil'd my Voice, but not my Stomach. Our Chaplain having got rid of his little lurking Feavers, began to eat like a Cormorant.[90]

12.   The Surveyors were dispatch't by 9, but the thick Woods made the Horses so hard to be found, that we [108] did not follow with the Baggage, til after Twelve. The Line was extended something more than 5 Miles, all the way thro' a Thicket. We judg'd by the great Number of Chestnut-Trees that we approach't the Mountains, which several of our Men discover'd very plainly. The Bears are great Lovers of Chestnuts, and are so discreet as not to venture their unwieldy Bodys upon the smaller Branches of the Trees, which will not bear their Weight. But after walking upon the Limbs as far

as is safe, they bite off the Limbs which falling down, they finish their Meal upon the Ground. In the same cautious Manner they secure the Acorns that grow on the outer Branches of the Oak. They eat Grapes very greedily which grow plentifully in these Woods, very large Vines wedding almost every Tree in the Rich Soil. This shews how natural the Situation of this Country is to Vines. Our Men kill'd a Bear of 2 Years Old which was very fat. The Flesh of it hath a good relish, very savoury, & inclining nearest to that of Pork. The Fat of this Creature is the least apt to rise in the Stomach of any other. The Men for the most part chose it rather than Venison, the greatest inconvenience was that they eat ^more^ Bread with it. We who were not accustom'd to eat this rich Dyet tasted it at first with some squeamishness, but soon came to like it. Particularly our Chaplain lov'd it so passionately, that he wou'd growl like a Wild-Cat over a Squirrel. Towards the Evening the Clouds gath'red thick, & threaten'd Rain, [109] & made us draw a Trench round the Tent, & take the necessary Precautions to secure the Bread, but no Rain fell. We remember'd our Wives & Mistresses in a Bumper of excellent Cherry-Brandy. This we cou'd afford to drink no oftener than to put on a clean Shirt, which was once a Week.

13.   This being Sunday we rested from our Fatigue, & had a Sermon. Our Weather was very louring with the Wind hard at NW with great likelihood of Rain. Every Sunday I constantly order'd Peter Jones to weigh out the weekly allowance of Bread to each Man, which hitherto was 5 pounds. This with Plenty of Meat was sufficient for any reasonable Man, & those who were unreasonable, I wou'd by no means indulge with Superfluitys. The rising ground where we encampt was so surrounded with Thickets, that we cou'd not walk out with any Comfort; however after Dinner, several of the Men ventur'd to try their Fortune, & brought in no less than 6 Wild Turkeys. They told us they saw the Mountains very distinctly from the Neighbouring Hills.[91]

In the Evening I examin'd our Indian Ned Bearskin concerning his Religion, & he very frankly gave me the following Account of it. That he believ'd there was a Supream Being that made the World & every thing in it. That the same Power that made it still preserves and governs it. That it protects and prospers good People in this World, & punishes the bad with Sickness & Poverty. That after Death all Mankind are conducted into one great Road, in which both the good & bad travel in Company to a certain [110] Distance, where this great Road branches into 2 Paths, the one extremely Levil, & the other Mountainous. Here the good are parted from the bad, by a flash of Lightening, the first fileing to the Right, the other to the Left. The Right-hand Road leads to a fine warm Country, where the Spring is perpetual, & every Month is May. And as the Year is always in ^its^ Youth,

so are the People, and the Women beautifull as Stars, & never scold. That in
this happy Climate there are Deer innumerable perpetually fat, & the Trees
all bear delicious Fruit in every Season. That the Earth brings forth Corn
spontaneously without Labour, which is so very wholesome, that none that
eat of it are ever Sick, grow Old or Die. At the Entrance into this blessed Land
sits a venerable old Man who examines every one before he is admitted, &
if he has behav'd well the Guards are order'd to open the Chrystal Gate
& let him into this Terrestrial Paradise. The Left-hand Path is very rough
& uneven, leading to a barren Country, where 'tis always Winter, the Ground
was cover'd with Snow, & nothing on the Trees but Icicles. All the People are
old, have no teeth, & yet are very hungry. Only those who labour very hard
make the Ground produce a Sort of Potato pleasant to the Tast, but gives
them the dry Gripes, & fills them full of Sores, which stinks and are very
painfull. The Women are Old & ugly arm'd with sharp Claws like a Panther,
& with those they gore the Men that slight their Passion. For it seems these
haggard old Furies [111] are intollerably fond. They talk very much, & very
shrill, giving most exquisite Pain to the Drum of the Ear, which in that horrid
Climate grows so tender, that any sharp Note hurts it. On the Borders sits
a hideous Old Woman whose Head is cover'd with Rattlesnakes instead of
Tresses, with glaring white Eyes, sunk very deep in her Head. Her Tongue
is 20 Cubits long arm'd with sharp Thorns as strong as Iron. This Tongue
besides the dreadfull Sound it makes in pronouncing Sentence, serves the
Purpose of an Elephant's Trunk, with which the Old Gentlewoman takes up
those she has convicted of Wickedness & throws them over a vast high Wall
hewn out of one Solid Rock, that surrounds this Region of Misery, to prevent
Escapes. They are receiv'd on the inside by another Hideous Old Woman who
consigns them over to Punishments proper for their Crimes. When they have
been Chastis'd here a certain Number of Years according to their ^degrees of^
Guilt, they are thrown over the Wall again, & driven once more back into this
World of Trial, where, if they mend their Manners they are conducted into
the abovementioned fine Country after their Death. This was the Substance
of Bearskin's Religion, which he told us with a Freedom uncommon to the
Indians.

14. It began to rain about 3 a Clock this Morning but so gently that
we had Leisure to secure the Bread from damage. It continued raining all
Night, & till near Noon, when it held up; the clouds look't [112] very heavy,
& frighten'd us from all thoughts of decamping. Meanwell & I lay abed all
the Morning, believing that the most agreeable situation in wet Weather.
The Wind blowing hard at NE made the Air very raw & uncomfortable.
However several of the Men went a hunting in the afternoon, & kill'd 3 Deer &

4 Turkeys, so that the Frying Pan was not cool til next Morning. The Chaplain disdaining to be usefull in one Capacity only, condescended to darn my Stockins; he acquired that with his other University Learning at the College of Dublin. At 6 it began to rain again, & held not up til 9, when the Clouds seem'd to break away & give us a Sight of the Stars. I dreamt the 3 Graces appear'd to me in all their Naked Charms, I singled out Charity from the rest, with whom I had an Intrigue.[92]

15.   The Weather promiseing to be fair, we hurry'd away the Surveyors as early as we cou'd, but did not follow with the Baggage til one a Clock, because the thick Woods made it difficult to find the Horses. I interpos'd very seasonably to decide a Wager betwixt two of the Warmest of our Men, which might otherwise have inflamed them into a Quarrel. In about a Mile's march we past over a large Creek whose Banks were fring'd with Canes. We call'd it Sable Creek from the Colour of its Water. Our Surveyors crost the Dan twice this Day. The first time was 240 Poles from our Camp, & the Second in 1 Mile & 7 Poles farther, & from thence [113] proceeded with the Line only 59 Poles, in all no more than one Mile & 300 Poles. The difficulty they had in passing the River twice, made their days work so small. The Baggage did not cross the River at all but went round the Bent of it; & in the Evening we encampt on a charming Piece of Ground that commanded the Prospect of the Reaches of the River, which were about 50 Yards over & the Banks adorn'd with Canes. We pitch't the Tent at the Bottom of a Mount, which we call'd Mount Pleasant, for the Beauty of the Prospect from thence.[93]

This Night Astrolabe's Servant had his Purse cut off, in which he lost his own Money, & some that my Man had put into his keeping. We cou'd suspect no Body but Holmes of the Kingdom of Ireland, who had watched it seems that Night for several of the Men, without which he cou'd not have had an Opportunity. He had also the Insolence to strike Meanwell's Servant, for which he had like to have been toss't in a Blanket. Astrolabe's Horse fell with him in the River, which had no other Consequence but to refresh him, & make the rest of the Company merry. Here the Low-Ground was very narrow, but very dry, & very delightfull.[94]

16.   The Surveyors got to work about 9, & we follow'd with the Baggage at 11. They carry'd the Line about 4½ Miles, & were stop't by the River over which they cou'd not find a Ford. We past a small Creek near our Camp, which had Canes on each [114] Side on which our Horses had feasted. The constant Current in the River may be computed to run about 2 Knots, & we discover'd no Falls over which a Canoe might not pass. Our Journey this day was thro' very Open Woods. At 3 Miles distance we crost another Creek, which we call'd Lowland Creek from a great Breadth of Low Ground made by this Creek & the

River, which ran about ¼ of a Mile to the Northward of us. We were obliged to go 2 Miles higher than where our Line intersected the River, because we cou'd not find a Ford. In our way we went thro' several large Indian Fields where we fancy'd the Sauro Indians had formerly planted Corn.[95] We encampt near one of these Indian Corn Fields, where was excellent Food for our Horses. Our Indian kill'd a Deer & the Men knock't down no less than 4 Bears & 2 Turkeys, so that this was truly a Land of Plenty both for Man & Beast. Dr. Humdrum at this Camp first discover'd his Passion for the delicious Flesh of Bear.

17.   The Surveyors mov'd early, & went back at least 2 Miles on the South Side of the River before they cou'd get over. Nor was it without difficulty, & some Danger, that they & we crost this Ford, being full of Rocks & Holes, & the Currant so swift that it made them giddy. However Heaven be prais'd, we all got safe on the other Side, only one Baggage Horse stumbled, & sopt a little of the Bread. The Puzzle in crossing the River, & the thick Woods [115] hinder'd our Surveyors from carrying the Line farther than 2 Miles & 250 Poles, to the Banks of Caskade Creek, so call'd from several Water-Falls that are in it. We encampt the sooner because it threaten'd Rain, the Wind strong at NE. In our way to this Place, we went over abundance of good Land, made so by the River, & this Creek. Our Dogs catch't a Young Cubb, & the Indian kill'd a Young Buck. Near the Creek we found a very good kind of Stone that flaked into thin Pieces fit for Pavement. About a Mile SW from our Camp was a high Mount that commanded a full Prospect of the Mountains, & a very extensive View of all the flat Country. But being with Respect to the Mountains no more than a Pimple, we call'd it by that name.[96]

18.   The Weather clearing up with a brisk NWester, we dispatch't the Surveyors about 9, who carry'd the Line about 6 Miles & 30 Poles to a Branch of the Dan, which we call'd the Irvin. We did not follow with the Baggage til 12. We crost Cascade Creek over a Ledge of Rocks, & march't thro' a large Plane of good Land but very thick Woods, for at least 4 Miles together. We met with no Water in all that Distance. A little before Sunset we crost the Irvin at a deep-Ford, where the Rocks were so slippery the Horses cou'd hardly keep their Feet. But by the great Care of Tom Jones we all got safe over, without any Damage to our Bread. We encamp't on a Pleasant Hill in [116] Sight of the River, the Sand of which is full of shining Particles. Bearskin kill'd a fat Doe, & came across a Bear, which had been kill'd & half-devoured by a Panther. The last of these Brutes reigns King of the Woods, & often kills the poor Bears, I believe more by surprize than fair Fight. They often take them Napping, Bears being very Sleepy Animals, & tho' they be very strong, yet is their Strength heavy, & the Panthers are much nimbler. The Doctor grutch't

the Panther this Dainty Morsel, being so fond of Bear, that he wou'd rise before day to eat a Griskin of it.[97]

19.　About 9 the Surveyors took their Departure, & advance with the Line 5 Miles & 135 Poles, nor was this a small Day's-work, considering the way was more uneven & full of Thickets than ever. We did not follow them til 12 because some of the Bread-Horses were missing. Astrolabe wou'd have feign sent out 2 of the Men to find out where the Dan & the Irvin fork't, but I wou'd not consent to it, for fear they shou'd fall into some disaster, we being now near the Path which the Northern Indians take when they march against those of the South. Something more than 4 Miles from our Camp we crost Matrimony Creek, which receiv'd its Name from being very Noisy, the Water murmuring Everlastingly amongst the Rocks. Half a Mile beyond this Creek we discoverd 5 Miles to the NW of the Line, a small Mountain which we call'd the Wart. We would willingly have marcht to a good Place for our Horses, which began to grow very weak, but Night coming on, we were oblig'd to [117] encamp on very uneven Ground, so overgrown with Bushes & Saplins, that we cou'd with difficulty see 10 Yards before us. Here our Horses met with short Commons, & so shou'd we too, if we had not brought a Horse Load of Meat along with us. All that our Hunters cou'd kill was only one Turkey, which helpt however to season the Broth.[98]

20.　This being Sunday, I wash't off all my Weeks Dirt, & refresht my self with clean Linnen. We had Prayers & a Sermon. We began here to fall from 5 to 4 Pounds of Bread a Man for the following Week, computeing we had enough at that rate to last us a Month longer. Our Indian had the Luck to kill a monstrous fat Bear, which came very seasonably, for our men having nothing else to do, had eat up all their Meat, & began to look very pensive. But our starv'd Horses had no such good Fortune, meeting with no other Food, but a little Wild Rosemary that grows on the high Ground. This they love very well if they had had enough of it, but it grew only in thin Tuffts here & there. Tom Short brought me a Hat full of very good Wild-Grapes, which were plentifull all over these Woods. Our Men, when the Service was over, thought it no Breach of the Sabbath to wash their Linnen, & put themselves in Repair, being a Matter of indispensible necessity. Meanwell was very handy at his Needle, having learnt the Use of that little Implement at Sea, & flourisht his Thread with as good a Grace as any Merchant-Taylor.[99]

21.　Our Surveyors got to work about 9, & carry'd the [118] Line 4 Miles & 270 Poles, great Part of that Distance being very hilly, & grown up with Thickets. But we cou'd not follow them ^til after 2^. Both Hamilton & his Horse were missing, & tho' I sent out several Men in quest of them, they were able to find neither. At last fearing we shou'd not overtake the Surveyors, I left Tom Jones & another Man to beat all the adjacent Woods for them. We past thro' intolerable Thickets to the great Danger of our Eyes, & Damage of our Cloaths, Insomuch that I had enough to do to keep my Patience & sweet Temper. With all our Diligence, we cou'd fight our way thro' the Bushes no farther than 2½ Miles before Sunset, so that we cou'd not reach the Surveyors. This was a sensible Grief to us, because they had no Bedding with them, & probably no Victuals. And even in the last Article we were not mistaken, for tho' our Indian kill'd a Bear, he had left it on the Line for us to pick up. Thus our Dear Friends run a risque of being doubly starv'd, both with Cold & Hunger. I knew this wou'd ill agree with Orion's delicate Constitution, but Astrolabe I was in less pain for, because he had more Patience & cou'd subsist longer upon licking his Paws. We had the Comfort to encamp where our Horses fared well, and we drank Health to our Absent Friends in pure Element. Just as it was dark Tom Jones brought poor Hamilton to us without his Horse. He had contriv'd to loose himself being no great Woodsman, but pretended that he was only bogued. He looked very melancholly [119] for the Loss of his Horse, til I promis't to employ my Interest to procure him satisfaction. For want of Venison Broth for Supper, we contented ourselves with some Greasy Soupe de Jambon, which tho' it slip't down well enough, sat not very easy on our Stomachs. So soon as we encampt I dispatch't John Evans to look for the Surveyors, but he return'd without Success, being a little too sparing of his Trouble. We saw a small Mountain to the N.W., which we call'd the Wart.[100]

22. This Morning early I sent John Evans with Hamilton back to our last Camp to make a farther Search for the Stray Horse, with Orders to spend a whole day about it. At the same time I dispatch't Richd. Smith to the Surveyors with some Provisions to stop their Mouths as well as their Stomachs. It was 11 a Clock before we cou'd get up all the Horses, when we follow'd our Surveyors, & in a Mile & a half reach't the Camp where they had lain. The Woods were extremely thick in the beginning of this day's March, but afterwards grew pretty open. As we rode along, we found no less than 3 Bears & half a Deer left upon the Line, with which we loaded our light Horses.

We came up with the Surveyors on the Banks of the Western Branch of the Irvin, which we call'd the Mayo. Here they had halted for us, not knowing the Reason why we staid behind so long. And this was the Cause they proceeded no farther with the line than One Mile & 230 Poles. About a mile before [120] we reach't this River, we crost a small Creek, which we call'd Miry Creek because several of the Branches of it were Miry. We past the Mayo just below a Ledge of Rocks, where Meanwell's Horse slipt, & fell upon one of his Legs, &

wou'd have broke it, if his Half-Jacks had not guarded it. As it was, his Ancle was bruis'd very much, & he halted several Days upon it.[101]

After the Tent was pitch't, Astrolabe, Humdrum, & I clamber'd up a high Hill to see what we could discover from thence. On the Brow of the Hill we spy'd a young Cubb on the top of a high Tree at Supper upon some Acorns. We were so indiscreet as to take no Gun with us, & therefore were oblig'd to halloo to the Men to bring one. When it came, Astrolabe undertook to fetch the Bear down, but mist him. However the poor Beast hearing the Shot rattle about his Ears, came down the Tree of his own Accord, & trusted to his Heels. It was a pleasant Race between Bruin & our grave Surveyor, who I must confess, runs much better than he shoots; yet the Cubb out ran him even down Hill, where Bears are said to Sidle, lest their Guts shou'd come out of their Mouths. But our Men had better luck, & kill'd no less than 6 of these unwieldy Animals. We sent our Horses back to Miry Creek, for the benefit of the Canes & Winter Grass which they eat very greedily. There was [121] a Waterfall in the River just by our Camp, the Noise of which gave us Poetical Dreams, & made us say our Prayers in Metre when we awaked.[102]

23. Our Surveyors mov'd forward & proceeded with the Line 4 Miles & 69 poles. At the distance of 62 Poles from our Camp, we past over another Branch of the Irvin with difficulty about half a Mile from where it fork't. It was extremely Mountainous great Part of the Way, & the last Mile we encounter'd a dreadfull Thicket enterlaced with Briars & Grape Vines. We crost a large Creek no less than 5 Times with our Line, which for that Reason we call'd Crooked Creek. The Banks of it were steep in many Places & border'd with Canes. With great luck for our Horses we encampt where these Canes were plentifull. This Refreshment was very seasonable after so tiresome a Journey, in which these poor Beasts had clamber'd up so many Precepices. About Sunset Evans & Hamilton came up with us, but had been so unlucky as not to find the Horse. Our Men eat up a Horse-load of Bear, which was very unthrifty Management, considering we cou'd meet with no Game all this Day. But Woodsmen are good Christians in one Respect: by never taking Care for the Morrow, but letting the Morrow care for itself, for which Reason no Sort of People ought to pray so fervently for their [122] daily Bread as they.[103]

24. The Men feasted so plentifully last Night, that some of them paid for it by fasting this Morning. One who had been less provident than the rest broke his fast very oddly. He sing'd all the Hair off of a Bearskin, & boil'd the Pelt into Broth. To this he invited his particular Friends, who eat very heartily & commended the Cookery, by supping it clean up. Our Surveyors hurry'd away a little after 8, & extended the Line 6 Miles & 300 Poles. We did not follow them till about 11, & crost a Thicket 2 full Miles in Breadth, without any

great Trees near it. The Soil seem'd very rich & Levil, hanging many Locust & Hiccory Saplins. The reason why there are no high Trees, is probably, because the Woods in these remote Parts are burnt but seldom. During those long intervals the Leaves & other Trash, are heapt so thick upon the Ground, that when they come to be set on Fire, they consume all before them, leaving nothing either standing or lying upon the Ground. Afterwards our way was Mountainous & the Woods open for about 2½ Miles. Then Level & overgrown with Bushes all the remaining distance. The Line crost Crooked Creek 10 times in this day's work, & we encampt upon a Branch of it, where our Horses fared but indifferently. The Men came off better for the Indian kill'd 2 Bears on which they feasted till the Grease ran out of their Mouths. Till this Night I had always lain in my Night-Gown, but upon Tryal [123] I found it much warmer to strip to my shirt, & lie in naked Bed with my Gown over me. The Woodsmen put all off, if they have no more than one Blanket to lye in, & agree that 'tis much more comfortable than to lye with their Cloaths on, tho' the Weather be never so cold.

25.   The Surveyors got to work soon after 8, & run the Line 4 Miles & 205 Poles. We did not follow them til near 2, by Reason Holm's Horse cou'd not be found. And at last we were forced to leave Robin Hix & William Pool behind, to search narrowly for him. The Woods were so intollerably thick for near 4 Miles, that they tore the very Skins that cover'd the Bread-Bags. This hinder'd us from overtaking the Surveyors, tho' we used our utmost diligence to do it. We cou'd reach but 4 Miles, & were oblig'd to encamp near a small run, where our Horses came off but indifferently. However they fared very near as well as their Masters, for our Indian met with no Game, so we had nothing to entertain ourselves with, but the Scanty Remnant of Yesterday's Plenty. Nor was there much Luxury at the Surveyors' Camp, either in their Lodging or Diet. However they had the Pleasure as well as we, to see the Mountains very Plain both to the North & South of the Line. Their distance seem'd to be no more than 5 or 6 miles. Those to the North appear'd in 3 or 4 Ledges rising one above another, but those to the South made no more than one [124] Single Ledge, and that not entire, but were rather detach't Mountains lying near one another in a Line. One was prodigiously high, & the west end of it a Perpendicular Precipice. The next to it was lower but had another rising out of the East End of it, in the form of a Stack of Chimneys. We cou'd likewise discern other Mountains in the Course of the Line but at a much greater Distance. Til this day we never had a clear View of any of these Mountains, by reason the Air was very full of Smoak. But this Morning it clear'd up & surpriz'd us with this wild Prospect all at once. At Night the Men brought Holm's Horse.

26. We had Ambassadors from our hungry Surveyors setting forth their
Wants, which we supply'd in the best Manner we cou'd. We mov'd towards
them about 11, & found them at the Camp where they lay, near a Rivulet,
which we judg'd to be the Head of Deep River, otherwise call'd the North
Branch of Cape Fear. We resolv'd to encamp here, because there was great
Plenty of Canes for the poor Horses, which began to grow wondrous thin.
However the Surveyors measured 300 Poles this day, which carry'd the Line
to the Banks of the Rivulet. The last Line Tree they mark't, is a red Oak
with the Trees around it blazed. We determin'd to proceed no farther with
the dividing Line, because the way to the West grew so Mountainous that
our jaded Horses were not in Condition to climb over it. Besides we had
no more Bread than wou'd last us a Fortnight [125] at short allowance. And
the Season of the Year being far advanc'd, we had reason to fear we might
be intercepted by Snow, or the swelling of the Rivers, which lay betwixt us
& home. These Considerations check't our Inclination to fix the Line in the
Ledge of Mountains, & determin'd us to make the best of our way back the
same Track we came. We knew the worst of that, & had a strait Path to carry
us the nearest Distance, while we were ignorant what difficulties might be
encounter'd if we steer'd any other Course.[104]

We had intended to cross at the Foot of the Mountains over to the head
of James River, that we might be able to describe that Natural Boundary.
But prudence got the better of Curiosity, which is always the more necessary
when we have other Men's welfare to consult as well as our own. Just by our
Camp we found a pair of Elks Horns, not very large, & saw the Track of the
Owner of them. They commonly keep more to the Northward, as Buffalos do
more to the Southward. In the Afternoon we walk't up a high Hill North of our
Camp, from whence we discover'd an Amphitheatre of Mountains extending
from the NE round by the West to the SE. 'Twas very unlucky that the
Mountains were more distant just at the head of our Line towards the West
by 30 or 40 Miles. Our Chaplain attempted to climb a Tree, but before he got
6 Feet from the Ground, Fear made him cling closer to the Tree, than Love
wou'd make him [126] cling to a Mistress. Meanwell was more venturesome,
but more unfortunate, for he bruised his Foot in a tender place, by which he
got a gentle Fit of the Gout. This was an improper Situation to have the cruel
Distemper in, & put my Invention upon contriving some way or other to carry
him back. In the mean while he bath'd his Foot frequently in cold Water, to
repell the Humour if Possible, for as the Case was, he cou'd neither put on
Shoe nor Boot. Our Men kill'd 2 Bears, a Buck, & a Turkey, a very seasonable
supply, & made us reflect with gratitude on the goodness of Providence. The
whole Distance from Coratuck Inlet where we began the Line to this Rivulet

where we ended it, was 241½ Miles & 70 Poles. In the Night the Wind blew fresh at SW with moderate Rain.

27.   This being Sunday, we gave God thanks for protecting & sustaining us thus far by his Divine Bounty. We had also a Sermon proper for the Occasion. It rain'd small Rain in the Morning, & look't lowring all day. Meanwell had the Gout in form, his Foot being very much swell'd; which was not more Pain to him, than it was disturbance to the rest. I order'd all the Men to visit their Horses, & to drive them up that, they might be found more easily the next Morning. When the distribution of Bread was made among the Men, I recommended good Husbandry to them, not knowing how long we shou'd be oblig'd to subsist [127] upon it. I sat by the Riverside near a small Cascade, fed by a Stream as clear as liquid Chrystal, & the Murmur it made compos'd my Sences into an agreeable Tranquillity. We had a Fog after Sunset that gave an unpleasant dampness to the Air, which we endeavour'd to correct by a rousing Fire. This with the Wetness of the Ground where we encampt made our Situation a little unwholesome; yet thank God all our Company continu'd in a perfect Health.[105]

28.   We ordered the Horses up very early, but the likelihood of more Rain prevented our decamping. And we judg'd right, for about 10 a Clock it began to Rain in good earnest. Meanwell made an excellent Figure with one Boot of Leather & the other of Flannel. So accoutred, he intended to mount, but the Rain came seasonably to hinder him from exposeing his Foot to be bruis'd & tormented by the Bushes. We kept snug in the Tent all Day spending most of our time in reading, & Dr. Humdrum being disturb'd at Astrolabe's reading Hudibras aloud, gabbled an old Almanack 3 times over, to drown one Noise with another. This Trial of Lungs lasted a full Hour, & tired the Hearers as much as the Readers. Powell's Ague return'd, for which I gave him the Bark & Pool took some Anderson's Pills to force a Passage thro' his Body. This Man had an odd Constitution, [128] he eat like a Horse, but all he eat stay'd with him 'til it was forc'd downwards by some purging Physick. Without this Assistance his Belly & Bowells were so swell'd he cou'd hardly Breath. Yet he was a Strong Fellow & used a world of Exercise. It was therefore wonderfull the Peristaltick Motion was not more vigorously promoted. Page was muffl'd up for the Tooth-ach, for which Distemper I cou'd recommend no Medicine but Patience, which he seem'd to possess a great Share of. It rain'd most part of the Night.[106]

29.   In the Morning we were flatter'd with all the Signs of a fair Day, the Wind being come about to the NW. This made us order the Horses to be got up very early, but the Tent-Horse cou'd not be found. And 'tis well he stop't us,

for about 10, all our hopes of fair Weather blew over, and it rain'd very smartly for some time. This was all in Favour of Meanwell's gouty Foot, which was now grown better, & the Inflammation assuaged. Nor did it need above one Day more to bring it down to its natural Proportion, and make it fit for the Boot. Being confin'd to the Tent til Dinner, I had no Amusement but reading. But in the Afternoon I walk't up to a Neighbouring Hill, from whence I cou'd view the Mountains to the Southward, the highest of which our Traders fancy'd to be the Katawa Mountain, but it seems to be too Northerly for that. Our men went out a driveing and had the [129] Luck to kill 2 Bears, one of which was found by our Indian asleep, & never waked. Unfortunate Hamilton straggling from the rest of the Company, was lost a second time. We fired at least a Dozen Guns, to direct him by their Report to our Camp, but all in vain, we cou'd get no tidings of him. I was much concern'd lest a disaster might befall him being alone all Night in that dolefull Wilderness.

30.   The Clouds were all swept away by a kind NWester, which made it pretty cold. We were all impatient to set our Faces towards the East, which made the Men more alert than Ordinary in catching their Horses. About 7 our Stray Man found the Way to the Camp, being directed by the Horses' Bells. Tho' he had lain on the bare Ground without either Fire or Bed Cloaths, he catch't no Cold. I gave order that 4 Men shou'd set off early, & clear the way, that the Baggage Horses might travel with less difficulty & more Expedition. We follow'd them about 11, and the Air being clear we had a fair Prospect of the Mountains both to the N & S. That very high one to the South, with the Precipice at the West End we called the Lover's cure, because one Leap from thence wou'd put a sudden Period both to his Passion & his Pain. On the highest Ledge, that stretch't away to the N.E., rose a Mount in the Shape of a Maiden's Breast, which for that reason we call'd by that Innocent Name. And the main Ledge itself we call'd Mount Eagle. [130] We march'd 11 Miles from the End of the Line & encampt upon Crooked Creek near a Thicket of Canes. In the Front of our Camp was a very beautifull Hill which bounded our Prospect at a Mile's Distance, & all the intermediate Space was cover'd with Green Canes. Firewood was scanty with us, which was the harder, because twas very cold. Our Indian kill'd a Deer that was extremely fat, & we pick't his Bones as clean as a Score of Turkey Buzzards cou'd have done.

By the favour of a very clear Night, we made another Essay of the Variation & found it much the same as formerly, 2° 30'. This being his Majesty's Birth Day we drank his Health in a Dram of excellent Cherry Brandy, but cou'd not afford one Drop for the Queen & the Roial Issue. We therefore remember'd them in Water as clear as our Wishes. And because all loyal rejoicings shou'd be a little noisy, we fired Canes instead of Guns, which made a Report as loud as a Pistol, the heat expanding the Air shut up within the Joints of this Vegetable, & making an Explosion.

The Woods being clear'd before us by the Pioneers, & the way pretty Levil, we travell'd with Pleasure encreas'd by the hopes of making haste home.

31. We dispatch't away our Pioneers early to clear away the Bushes, but did not follow them till 11 a Clock. We crost Crooked Creek several times, the Banks of which being very steep, jaded our poor Horses very much. Meanwell's Baggage Horse gave out the [131] first, & next to him one of the Bread horses, so that we were oblig'd to drop them both by the way. The second time we crost Crooked Creek, by endeavouring to step off my Horse's Back upon the Shoar, I fell all along in the Water. I wet myself all over & bruis'd the back part of my Head; yet made no Complaint, but was the merriest of the Company at my own disaster. Our Dreamer Orion had a Revelation about it the Night before, & foretold it fairly to some of the Company.

The Ground was so Mountainous, & our Horses so weak, that with all our diligence we cou'd not exceed 4 Miles. Indeed, we spent some time in crossing the Dan & the Mayo, the Fords being something deeper than when we came up. We took up our Camp at Miry Creek, & regal'd ourselves with one Buck & 2 Bears, which our Men kill'd in their march. Here we promoted our Chaplain from the Deanery of Pip, to the Bishopric of Beardom. For as those Countrys where Christians inhabit are call'd Christendome, so those where Bears take up their residence may not improperly go by the Name of Beardom. And I wish other Bishops loved their Flock as intirely as our Doctor loves his.

November 1. The Pioneers were sent away about 9 a Clock, but we were detain'd till near 2 by reason John Evan's his Horse cou'd not be found, & at last we were oblig'd to leave 4 Men behind to look for him. [132] However we made a Shift to go 6 Miles, & by the way had the Fortune to kill a Brace of Does, 2 Bears, and one Turkey. Meanwell's Riding Horse tir'd too by the way, so that we were oblig'd to drop him about a Mile short of the Camp. Many more of our Horses were so weak they stagger'd under their Riders, so that in Compassion to the poor Animals we walkt great part of the way notwithstanding the Path was very rough, & in many Places uneven. For the same good-natur'd Reason we left our bears behind, choosing rather to carry the Venison, for which our Bishop had like to have mutiny'd. We endeavour'd about Noon to observe the Latitude, but our Observation was something imperfect, the Wind blowing too fresh. By such a one as we cou'd make, we found the Latitude no more than 36° 20′. In this Camp our Horses had short Commons, & had they been able to speak like Balaam's Ass, would have bemoan'd themselves very much.[107]

2.   We lost all the Morning in hunting for Powell's Mare, so that it was 2 a Clock before we decampt. Our Zeal to make the best of our way made us set out, when it was very like to rain, & it rain'd in good earnest before we had march't a Mile. We bore it patiently while it was moderate, & repast Matrimony Creek about 1½ Miles from our Camp. But soon after the Rain fell more violently, & oblig'd us to take up our Quarters upon an Iminence, that we might not be drown'd. This was [133] the only time we were catch't in the Rain upon the Road during the whole Journey. It us'd to be so civil as to fall in the Night, as it did while Herod was building the Temple or on a Sunday, or else to give us warning enough to encamp before it fell. But now it took us upon the way, & made our Lodging uncomfortable, because we were oblig'd to pitch the Tent upon wet Ground. The worst Circumstance of all was, that there was hardly any picking for the Horses, which were now grown so lean & so weak, that the Turkey-Buzzards began to follow them. It continu'd raining till 3 a Clock in the Morning, when, to our great Joy it clear'd up with a NWester.[108]

3.   It was my Opinion to rest in our Camp, bad as it was, because it was Sunday: but every body was against me. They urg'd the Danger of starving the Horses, & the short March we made Yesterday, which might justify making a Sabbath Day's Journey to day. I held out against all these Arguments on Account of resting the Horses, which they greatly needed, as well as because of the Duty of the Day; 'til at last the Chaplain came with a Casuistical Face, & told me it was a Case of necessity that oblig'd us to remove from a Place that wou'd famish all our Horses, that Charity to those poor Animals wou'd excuse a small Violation of the 4th Commandment. I answer'd, that the the Horses wou'd lose as much by the Fatigue of travelling, as they wou'd gain by the bettering their Food; that the Water was rais'd in the River Irvin, & we shou'd be [134] forc't to stay 'til it was fallen again, & so shou'd gain no Distance by travelling on the Sunday. However on condition the Dr. wou'd take the Sin upon himself, I agreed to move 3 or 4 Miles, which carry'd us to the Banks of the Irvin. By the way our Indian kill'd 4 Deer & a Bear. When we came to the River, we found the Water 3 or 4 Foot higher than when we came up, so that there was no likelihood of getting over under 2 Days. This made good my Argument, & put our hasty Gentlemen into the Vapours, especially Orion, who was more impatient than any Body. I cou'd find no other Reason for it, but because he had dream't that Colo. Beverley was dead, & imagined his Absence

might hinder him from making Interest for his Place of Surveyor Genl. In the Evening we perceiv'd the Water began to fall in the River, which gave some of the Company the Vain hopes of getting over the next day.[109]

4. In the Morning we measured the Marks we had set up at the River, & found the Water had not fallen above a foot, by this we were convinced, that we should be oblig'd to halt there a day longer. We sent some Men to endeavour to bring up 2 Horses, which tired on Saturday, but the Horses were too well pleas'd with their Liberty, to come along with them. One of these manumitted Horses belong'd to Abraham Jones, and being prick't in the Mouth, he bled him self quite off his Leggs.

There being great Plenty in our Camp the [135] Men kept eating all day to keep them out of Idleness. In the Evening it look't very dark, & menaced us with more Rain to our great Mortification, but after a few Drops, I thank God it blew over. Orion sigh'd heavily while it lasted, apprehending we shou'd take up our Winter Quarters in the Woods. John Ellis who was one of the Men we had sent to bring up the tired Horses told us a Romantick Adventure which he had with a Bear on Saturday last. He had straggled from his Company, & treed a young Cubb. While he was new priming his Gun to shoot at it, the old Gentlewoman appear'd, who seeing her Heir Apparant in Distress, came up to his Relief. The Bear advanced very near to her Enemy, rear'd up on her Posteriours, & put herself in Guard. The Man presented his Piece at her, but unfortunately, it only snapp't, the Powder being moist. Missing his Fire in this Manner, he offer'd to punch her with the Muzzle of his Gun; which Mother Bruin being aware of, seiz'd the Weapon with her Paws, & by main strength wrencht it out of his Hand. Being thus fairly disarm'd, & not knowing in the Fight but the Bear might turn his own Cannon upon him, he thought it prudent to retire as fast as his Legs cou'd carry him. The Brute being grown more bold by the Flight of her Adversary, immediately pursued, and for some time it was doubtfull, whether [136] Fear made one Run faster, or Fury the other. But after a fair Course of 40 Yards, the poor man had the Mishap to stumble over a Stump, and fell down at his full length. He now wou'd have sold his Life a Penny-worth: But the Bear apprehending there might be some Trick in this Fall, instantly halted, & look't very earnestly to observe what the Man cou'd mean. In the mean time he had with much Presence of Mind, resolv'd to make the Bear believe he was dead, by lying breathless on the Ground, upon the hopes that the Bear wou'd be too generous to kill him over again. He acted a Corps in this Manner for some time, til he was rais'd from the Dead by the Barking of a Dog, belonging to one of his Companions. Cur came up seasonably to his Rescue and drove the Bear from her Pursuit of the

Man, to go and take care of her innocent Cubb, which she now apprehended might fall into a second Distress.

5.ʳ We found this Morning that the River had fallen no more than 4 Inches the whole Night, but a North-Wester had swept away all the Clouds. About 10 we resolv'd to pass the River, which we did very safely, thank God, only Tom Short's Horseˢ fell with him, & sopp't him all over. In the Distance of 6 Miles we crost Cascade Creek, & from thence proceeded in near 3 Miles to the Dan, which we [137] forded with some difficulty, because the Water was deeper than when we came over it before. Unfortunate Mr.ᵗ Short was duck't a Second Time by the Fall of his Horse but receiv'd no hurt. My Horse made a false Step, so that his Head was all underwater, but recover'd himselfᵃ with much adoe.ᵇ

Having day enough left, we proceeded as far as Low-land Creek, where we took up our Quarters, and had great Plenty both of Canes & Winter Grass for the Horses, but Whitlock's Horse tired 2 Miles offᶜ, and so did one of Astrolabe's. The Truth of it is, we made a long Journey, not less than 14 Miles in the round about Distance we came, tho' it did not exceed 10 upon the Line. I favour'd my Steed by walking great Part of [the] way on Foot; it being Levelᵈ & well clear'd made the Fatigue more Tolerable. The Indian kill'd a young Buck, the Bones of which we pick't very clean, but want of Bear made Dr. Humdrumᵉ less gay, than he used to be where that delicious Food was Plenty.

6. We set not out til near 12, & past over very uneven Ground, tho' our Comfort was that it was open and clear of Bushes. We avoided crossing the Dan twice, by going round the Bent of it. About 3 we past by Mount Pleasant, and proceeded along the River Side to Sable Creek, which we crost, and encampt a little beyond it near the Banks of the [138] Dan. The Horses fared Sumptuously here upon Canes & Grass. Hamilton wounded a Buck, which made him turn upon the Dogs, & even pursue them 40 Yards with great Fury. But he got away from us, choosing rather to give the Wolves a Supper, than to more cruel Man. However our other Gunners had better Fortune, in killing a Doe & a 2-year-old Cubb. Thus Providence supply'd us every day with Food sufficient for us, making the Barren Wilderness a Theater of Plenty. The Wind

---

ʳ*Here the fragment CWR.s (C) begins.*   ˢC: Tho.   ᵗC: Tho ˆMʳ.ˆ   ᵃC: but he recover'd hims[elf]   ᵇC: *A vertical line here to break paragraph (break present in A, not in C).*
ᶜC: but James Whitlock's Horse tired 2 Miles short of our camp ˆoffˆ   ᵈC: [the] way
ˆitˆ ([the] *is conjecturally assumed where the paper is torn*)   ᵉC: *The paper here is heavily erased. A hole along the horizontal path of erasure obliterates the original writing.*

blew very Cold, & produced a hard Frost. Our Journey this day did not exceed 5 Miles, great part of which in Complement to my Horse, I perform'd on Foot[f], notwithstanding the way was Mountainous, and the Leaves that cover'd the Hills as slippery as Ice.

7.   After dispatching away our Pioneers[g] at 8 a Clock, we follow'd them[h] at 10. The Ground was very hilly, and full of Underwood, but our Pioneers had helpt that Inconvenience. Our Journey was 8 Miles by the Line, but near 10 by our Path, which was not quite so strait. The Hunters were more fortunate than ordinary, killing no less than 4 Deer, & as many Turkeys. This made them impatient to encamp early, that they might enjoy the Fruits of their good Luck. We arriv'd at 2 a Clock on the Banks of the Dan, where we mark't out our Quarters, where[i] the Horses had as great Plenty as ourselves. However they[j] were now grown so weak, that they stagger'd when we dismounted: [139] and those which had been used to the Stable & dry Food throve least upon Grass & Canes, & were much sooner jaded than the rest.

8.   The Pioneers took their Departure about 9, and we set out upon their Track at 10, & found the Ground rising & falling all the way between the 2 Fords of the River. The first of these we past at first setting out, but Robin Hix & the Indian undertook to go round the Bent of the River, without crossing it all. This they perform'd, making the Distance no more than 12 Miles. About a Mile from our Camp[k], they met with a Creek whose Banks were fortify'd with high Cliffs, which gain'd it the name of Cliff-Creek. Near 3 Miles beyond that they forded over another Creek, on whose Margin grew plenty of Canes. And this was call'd Hix's Creek from the Name of the Discoverer. Between these 2 Creeks lies a Levil of exceeding good Land, full of large Trees, and a black Mold.[110]

We that march't upon the Line past over Cane-Creek something more than 4 Miles from the Camp, & 3 Miles beyond that we forded the Dan for the last time, passing thro' a Forest of Canes before we got at it. It was no small Joy ^to us^ to find ourselves safe over all the Waters that might[l] retard our Journey home. Our Distance upon the Line was 7 Miles, & where we encampt afforded good Forrage for the Horses, which we had favour'd by walking the greater Part of the way. The Indian brought us the primeings of a fat Doe, which he had kill'd too far [140] off for him to carry the whole. This & 2 Turkeys that our Men shot, made up our Bill of Fare this Evening.

9.   Dr. Humdrum[m] got up so early, that it made him quite peevish, especially now we were out of the Latitude of Fat Bear, with which he us'd

---

[f]C: afoot   [g]C: dispatching our Pioneers away   [h]C: 'em   [i]C: and the ^where^
[j]C: ^However^ they   [k]C: our ^the^   [l]C: could ^might^   [m]C: Dr Humdrum

to keep[n] up his good Humour. It was necessary to hurry out the Pioneers by 8 a Clock because great part of the Journey was overgrown with Bushes. However about 5 Miles of this Day's work were very open & tolerably Level[o]. The Distance in all was 12 Miles by the Line, tho' we made 15 of it by picking our way[p]. Of this I footed it at least 8 Miles, notwithstanding my Servant had scorcht my Boots by holding them too near the Fire. The Length of our March harass'd the Horses much[q], so that Page was oblig'd to leave his, 2 Miles short of our Journey's End[r], and several others had much adoe to drag one Leg after another. In less than half a Mile from the Dan we crost Cocquade Creek, so call'd from our beginning there to wear the Turkey Beard in our Hats by way of Cocquade. This we made one of the Badges of a new Order, call'd the Order of Ma-osty[s], signifying in the Sapponi-Language, a Turkey's Beard. The other Badge is a Wild Turkey in Gold, with the rings expanded, & a Collar round its neck, with this Motto engraven upon it, *Vice Coturnicum.* As most Orders have been religious in [141] their Original, so this was devis'd in gratefull Remembrance of our having been supported in the Barren Wilderness so many Weeks, with Wild Turkeys instead of Quails. From thence we continu'd our March to Buffalo-Creek, on which we encampt. Here our Horses made better Cheer than we, for the Indian kill'd nothing but one Turkey. However ^with^ what remain'd of our former good Fortune, this was sufficient to keep Famine out of the Camp[t].[111]

10.   This being Sunday we observ'd the 4th Commandment[a], only our Hunters went out to provide a Dinner for the rest which was matter of necessity. They fired the Woods in a Ring[b], which burning Inwards drove the Deer to the Center, where they were easily kill'd. This Sport is call'd Fire-hunting, & is much practised by the Indians, & some English as barbarous as Indians[c]. Three Deer were slaughter'd in[d] this Manner, of which they brought one to the Camp, and were content only[e] to prime the other Two. Besides these Tho. Short brought in a Doe which made us live in Luxury[f]. William Pool complained that tho' his Stomach was good, and he eat a great deal yet he hardly ever went to Stool without the help of Physick. This made him very full and uneasy; giving him Pains both in his Stomach and Bowels.

424 } The Secret History of the Line

First I gave him a Dose of Anderson's Pills, which afforded[g] him very little ease. Then I prescribed a small [142] Dose of Ipecoaccanna to be taken in hot Broth well season'd with Salt, which took off the Emetick Quality & turn'd it downwards[h]. This not only empty'd him, and gave him ease, but brought him to be very regular in his Evacuations, by being now and then repeated. Page went out in quest of his Horse and brought him to the Camp pretty well recruited. The absence of most of the[i] Men diminish't our Congregation so much, that we who remain'd behind were contented with Prayers. I read a great deal, and then wrote a letter[j] with design to send an Express with it so soon as we got amongst the Inhabitants.

11.   By the favour of good Weather, & the impatience of being at home, we decampt early[k]. But there was none of the Company so very hasty as Orion[l]. He cou'd not have been more uneasy even tho' he had a Mistress at Williamsburgh. [But I suspect the true reason for his being so much upon the Spur, was the belief he had in his own Dreams. He had dream't it seems that Colo. Beverly was dead who was Surveyor Genll., the Succession of which Place he had been promised by his Patron the Commissary. But he fancy'd his absence might prejudice that Pretention, and give his Competitors too great an advantage. This made him peevish when any thing happen'd to delay our Motion, nor cou'd I escape being suspected of makeing less hast than I ought to have done. All the ground he had was my fixt Resolution of observing the Sabbath and favouring the Horses.][m] ^He found much Fault with^ my scrupulous observing the Sabbath. I reprov'd him for his uneasiness[n], letting him understand that I had both as much Business and as much Inclination to be at home as he had, but for all that was determin'd to make[o] no more hast than good Speed.[p]

We crossed Hico-ottomoni Creek twice in this[q] March, and travers'd very thick and very uneven[r] Woods as far as Sugar-Tree Creek. This was no more than 7 Miles, but equal [143] in fatigue to double that distance on good Ground. Near this Creek our man kill'd a young Buffalo of 2 Years[s] Old, that was as big as a large Ox. He had short[t] Legs, and a deep Body with Shagged Hair on his Head and Shoulders. His Horns were short, and very strong. The

---

[g]C: gave ^afforded^   [h]C: downwards into a gentle Purge   [i]C: our ^the^   [j]C: a letter to my wife   [k]C: we decampt as soon as we cou'd ^early^   [l]C: Erasure, with the name Orion overwritten.   [m]This passage, canceled in C, does not appear in A. I have restored it here, as have earlier editors. Over the cancellation Byrd inserted ^He found much fault with my^   [n]C: unjust suspicion ^uneasiness^   [o]C: wou'd ^was determin'd to^ make   [p]C: A vertical line here to break paragraph (break present in A, not in C).   [q]C: our ^this^   [r]C: very uneaven and very thick   [s]C: Year   [t]C: very short

Hair on the Shoulders is soft, resembling Wool, and may be spun into Thread. The Flesh is arrant Beef, all the difference is that the Fat of it inclines more to be Yellow. The Species seems to be the same, because a Calf produced betwixt tame Cattle and these will propagate. Our People were so well pleas'd with Buffalo-Beef, that the Gridiron was upon the Fire all Night. In this Day's March[a] I lost one of the[b] Gold Buttons out of my Sleeve, which I bore the more patiently because that, and the burning of my Boots were all the Damage I had suffered[c].

12.   We cou'd not decamp before 11, the People being so much engaged with their Beef; I found it always a Rule that the greater our Plenty, the later we were in fixing out. We avoided[d] 2 Miles of very uneven Ground, by leaving the Line on our Left, and keeping upon the Ridge. Something less than 3 Miles Distance from the Camp we past over Blewing Creek, and 5 Miles beyond this, over that of Tewahominy. Thence we travers'd a very large Level of rich high Land near 2 Miles in [144] breadth and encamped on a branch three and a half miles beyond the last-named creek, so that our whole distance this day was more than eleven miles.

Here was very scanty fare for the horses, who could pick only here and there a sprig of wild rosemary, which they are fond of; the misfortune was there was not enough of it. John Ellis killed a bear in revenge for the fright one of that species had lately put him into. Nor was this revenge sweeter to him than a griskin of it was to the Doctor, who of all worldly food conceives this to be the best. Though, in truth, 'tis too rich for a single man and inclines the eater of it strongly to the flesh, insomuch that whoever makes a supper of it, will certainly dream of a woman or the devil, or both.

13.   This morning I wrote a letter to the Governor, intending to dispatch it away by an express from the outermost inhabitants. We mounted about ten, and after proceeding three miles crossed a large branch and two miles farther reached Ohimpamony Creek. Beyond that three and a quarter miles we came to Yapatsco or Beaver Creek. Here those industrious animals had dammed up the water in such a manner that we could with difficulty ford over it. However, we all got happily over and continued our march three miles farther to Massamony Creek, so that the [145] day's journey was in all eleven and a quarter miles. But to make the horses some amends, we encamped in the midst of good forage. Both Meanwell's horses could hardly carry their saddles, no more being required of them; nor was it much better with many others in the company. On our way we had the fortune to kill a deer and a

[a]C: In our March this day ^this days March^   [b]C: my ^the^   [c]C: I ^had^ suffered
[d]*Here the first section (three pages) of C ends.*

turkey, sufficient for our day's subsistence; nor need anyone despair of his daily bread whose faith is but half so big as his stomach.

14.   About eight in the morning, I dispatched two men to Miles Riley's and by the way to hire John Davis to carry my letters to Major Mumford's with all expedition. I also gave them orders to get a beef killed and likewise some meal ground to refresh the men on their arrival amongst the inhabitants.

We decamped after them at eleven a clock and at the end of seven and a quarter miles crossed Nutbush Creek. From thence we proceeded about four miles farther to a beautiful branch of Great Creek, where we arrived in good order about four a Clock in the afternoon. We encamped on a rising ground that overlooked a large extent of green reeds with a crystal stream serpenting through the middle of them. The Indian killed a fawn and one of the other men a raccoon, the flesh of which is like pork, but truly we were better fed than to eat it. The clouds gathered and [146] threatened rain, but a brisk northwester swept them all away before morning.

15.   We were ready to march about ten o'clock and at the distance of six miles passed Great Creek. Then, after traversing very barren grounds for near five miles, we crossed the trading path used by our traders when they carry goods to the southwest Indians. In less than a mile from thence we had the pleasure to discover a house, though a very poor one, the habitation of our friend Nat on Major Mumford's plantation. As agreeable a sight as a house was, we chose our tent to lie in as much the cleanlier lodging. However, we vouchsafed to eat in the house, where nothing went down so sweetly as potatoes and milk. In order for that, a whole ovenful of potatoes were provided, which the men devoured unmercifully.

Here all the company but myself were told that my little son was dead. This melancholy news they carefully concealed from me for fear of giving me uneasiness. Nothing could be more good-natured and is a proof that more than thirty people may keep a secret. And what makes the wonder the greater is that three women were privy to this my supposed misfortune.

I drew out the men after dinner and harangued them on the subject of our safe return in the following terms:

"Friends and fellow travelers, it is with abundance of pleasure that I now have it [147] in my power to congratulate your happy arrival among the inhabitants. You will give me leave to put you in mind how manifestly Heaven has engaged in our preservation. No distress, no disaster, no sickness of any consequence has befallen anyone of us in so long and so dangerous a journey. We have subsisted plentifully on the bounty of Providence and been day by day supplied in the barren wilderness with food convenient for us. This is surely an instance of divine goodness never to be forgotten, and, that it may still be more complete, I heartily wish that the same protection may have been extended to our families during our absence. But lest amidst so many blessings there may be some here who may esteem themselves a little unfortunate in the loss of their horses, I promise faithfully I will do my endeavor to procure satisfaction for them. And as a proof that I am perfectly satisfied with your service, I will receive your pay and cause a full distribution to be made of it as soon as possible. Lastly, as well to gratify your impatience to see your several families as to ease the expense of the government, I will agree to your discharge so fast as we shall approach the nearest distance to your respective habitations."

16.   It was noon before we could disengage ourselves [148] from the charms of Madam Nat and her entertainments. I tipped her a pistole for her civilities and ordered the horses to the ford, while we and the baggage were paddled over in the canoe. While the horses were marching round, Meanwell and I made a visit to Cornelius Keith, who lived rather in a pen than a house with his wife and six children. I never beheld such a scene of poverty in this happy part of the world. The hovel they lay in had no roof to cover those wretches from the injuries of the weather, but when it rained or was colder than ordinary the whole family took refuge in a fodder stack. The poor man had raised a kind of a house, but for want of nails it remained uncovered. I gave him a note on Major Mumford for nails for that purpose and so made a whole family happy at a very small expense. The man can read and write very well and by way of a trade can make and set up quernstones, and yet is poorer than any Highland Scot or bogtrotting Irishman. When the horses came up, we moved forward to Miles Riley's, another of Major Mumford's quarters. Here was a young steer killed for us and meal ground, and everything also provided that the place afforded. There was a huge consumption of potatoes, milk, and butter, which we found in great plenty.[112]

This day I discharged Robin Hix, Thomas Wilson, and Charles Kimball, allowing them two days [149] to reach their homes. I also dismissed our honest Indian Bearskin, after presenting him with a note of £3 on Major Mumford, a pound of powder with shot in proportion. He had, besides, the skins of all the deer he had killed in the whole journey and had them carried for him into the bargain. Nothing could be happier than this honest fellow was with all these riches, besides the great knowledge[e] he had gained of the country. He killed a fat buck, great part of which he left us by way of[f] legacy;

[e]*Here the fourth page of C begins.*   [f]C: for a ^by way of^ Legacy

the rest he cut into pieces, toasted them before the fire, and then strung them upon his girdle to serve him for his provisions on[g] his way to Christanna Fort, where his nation lived.[113]

We lay in the tent, notwithstanding there was a clean landlady and good beds, which gave the men an opportunity of getting a house over their heads after having for two months had no covering but the firmament[h].

17.   Being Sunday[i], besides performing the duties of the day, we christened Thomas Page[j], one of our men who[k] had been bred a Quaker, and Meanwell[l] and I were his gossips. Several of the neighbors came, partly out of curiosity and partly out of devotion. Amongst the rest came a young woman which lives in comfortable fornication with Cornelius Cargill and has several children by him. Meanwell[m] bought a horse of this man, in which he was jockeyed. Our eyes as well as our taste were blest with [150] a sirloin of roast beef, and we drank pleasure to our wives in a glass of shrub. Not content with this moderate refreshment, my friends carried on the joke with bombo made of execrable brandy, the manufacture of the place. I preached against it, though they minded me as little at night as they had Humdrum[n] in the morning, but most of them paid for it by being extremely sick. This day I discharged John Holmes and Thomas[o] Page with a reasonable allowance of days for their[p] return home.[114]

18.   This day we endeavored to set out early but were hindered by Powell's[q] not finding some of his horses. This man had almost[r] been negligent in that particular but amongst the inhabitants was more careless than ordinary. It was therefore thought high time to discharge him and carry our baggage as well as we could to Cornelius Cargill's, who lived about seven miles off, and there hire his cart to transport it as far as Major Mumford's. We made the best shift we could and, having crossed Mrs. Riley's hand with a pistole[s], we moved toward Cargill's, where we arrived about 2 a clock. Here we put the heavy baggage into the cart, though I ordered mine to continue on my own horses lest some disaster might happen to this frail vehicle. Then, appointing a guard to attend the baggage, we proceeded five miles farther to George Hix's plantation, where preparation was [151] made to entertain us.[t,115]

By the way we met John Davis that brought me letters from home and from Major Mumford, in answer to those I had sent to them by this express.

---

[g]C: in   [h]C: that of Heaven ^the Firmament^   [i]C: ^This^ being Sunday   [j]C: Tho. Page   [k]C: that ^who^   [l]C: Meanwell   [m]C: Meanwell   [n]C: Humdrum   [o]C: Tho.   [p]C: to ^for their^   [q]C: Edw[d] Powels   [r]C: ever ^almost^   [s]C: <haveing presented Mrs. Riley with a Pistole,> haveing ^crosst^ Mrs Rileys ^hand^ with a Pistole   [t]C: *A vertical line here to break paragraph (break present in A, not in C).*

He had indeed been almost as expeditious as a carrier pigeon, for he went from Miles Riley's on Saturday, and he met us this day being Monday early in the afternoon three miles before we got to George Hix's. By the letters he brought I had the pleasure to hear that all my family was well, that my heir apparent had been extremely ill but was recovered; nevertheless, the danger he had been in gave birth to the report that he was dead.[a] All my company expected that now the bad news would be confirmed. This made Meanwell take a convenient station to observe[b] with how much temper I should receive such melancholy tidings. But not finding any change in my countenance, he ventured to ask me how it fared with my family. And I must gratefully own that both he and the whole company discovered a great deal of satisfaction that the report proved false[c]. They then told me with how much care they had concealed from me the fame[d] of his being dead, being unwilling to make me uneasy upon so much incertainty.[e,116]

We got to George Hix's before 4 a clock, and both he and his lively little wife received us courteously[f]. His house stands on[g] an eminence, from [152] whence is a good prospect. Every thing looked clean and wholesome, which made us resolve to quit the tent and betake ourselves to the house.[h]

All the grandees of the Saponi nation waited here to see us, and our fellow traveler, Bearskin[i], was amongst the gravest of them. Four ladies of quality graced their visit[j], who were less besmeared with grease and dirt than any copper-coloured beauties I had ever seen[k]. The men too had an air of decency very uncommon, and, what was a greater curiosity, most of the company[l] came on horseback. The men rode more awkwardly than sailors, and the women, who sat astride, were so bashful they would not mount their ponies till[m] they were quite out of sight.[n]

Christanna Fort, where these Indians live, lies three miles from George Hix's[o] plantation. He has considerable dealings with them and supplies them too plentifully with rum, which kills more of them than the northern Indians

[a]C: my family was well, thank God. That my little Son ^Heir Apparent^ had been extreamly ill but was recover'd, however ^nevertheless^ the danger he had been in had given ^gave^ birth to the Report that he was dead.   [b]C: This made Meanwell stand at a convenient distance ^take a convenient station^ to observe   [c]C: when they understood my Heir apparent was alive ^that the Report prov'd false^   [d]C: Report ^fate^   [e]C: *A vertical line here to break paragraph (break present in A, not in C).*   [f]C: receiv'd us very civilly ^courteously^   [g]C: ^on^   [h]C: *A vertical line here to break paragraph (break present in A, not in C).*   [i]C: Fellow Travellor, Ned Bearskin   [j]C: came with them ^graced their visit^   [k]C: copper-colour'd Beautys I had ever seen *(Though Byrd canceled* ever *in C, the word still appears in A.)*   [l]C: good Company   [m]C: Naggs ^Ponys^ til   [n]C: *A vertical line here to break paragraph (break present in A, not in C).*   [o]C: Geo. Hixes

do and causes much disorder[p] amongst them. Major Mumford was so good as to send me a horse, believing that mine was sufficiently jaded, and Colo. Bolling sent me another. With the last I complimented Orion[q], who had marched on foot good[r] part of the way from the mountains. When we saluted Mrs. Hix, she bobbed up her mouth with more than ordinary Elasticity[s] [153] and gave us a good opinion of her other motions[t]. Capt. Embry, who lives on[a] Nottoway River, met us here and gave us an invitation to make our next stage at his house. Here I discharged John Evans Stephen Evans William[b] Pool George Tilman George[c] Hamilton and James Petillo, allowing them for their distance[d] home. Our course from Miles Rileys inwards held generally about northeast and the road level[e].[117]

19.   We dispatched away the cart under a guard by 9 a clock, and after complimenting our landlord with a pistole for feeding us and our horses, we followed about eleven. About a mile from the house we crossed Meherrin River which being very low, was not more than twenty yards wide. About five miles farther we passed Meherrin Creek almost as wide as the River. From thence eight miles we went over Sturgeon Run[f], and six miles beyond that we came upon Waqua Creek[g], where the stream is swift, and tumbles over the rocks very solemnly[h]. This makes broad low-grounds in many places and abundance of rich land[i].

About two miles more brought us to our worthy friend Capt. Embrys habitation, where we found the housekeeping much better than the house. In that the noble Capt. is not very curious, his Castle containing of one dirty room with a dragging door[j] to it that will neither open nor shut. However [154] my Landlady made us amends by providing a supper sufficient for a battalion[k]. I was a little shocked[l] at our first alighting with a sight I did not expect. Most of the men I discharged yesterday were got here before us and within a few good-downs of being drunk. I showed so much concern at this that they had the[m] modesty to retire. Mr. Walker met us here and kindly invited us to his house being about five miles wide of this place. I should have been glad to accept of his civility but could not with decency put a slur upon our good friend[n] the Captain, who had made abundant provision for

[p]C: all the ^much^   [q]C: Orion   [r]C: great ^good^   [s]C: <bobb'd up her mouth like an Eel> bobbed up her mouth ^with more than ordinary Elasticity^   [t]C: her other ^motions^   [a]C: upon ^on^   [b]C: Wm.   [c]C: Geo.   [d]C: time to go ^for their distance^ [e]C: about N.E. and the road very levil   [f]C: Creek ^Run^   [g]C: met with ^came upon^ Wick-quoi Creek   [h]C: agreeably ^solemnly^   [i]C: good ^rich^ land   [j]C: an ancient door ^a dragging door^   [k]C: compleat Regiment ^Battalion^   [l]C: choqued   [m]C: so much ^the^   [n]C: put such a slur upon our kind friend

us. For this reason we chose to drink water, and stow thick in a dirty room, rather than give our black-eyed landlady the trouble of making a feast to no purpose. She had set all her Spits, Pots, Frying pans, Gridirons, and Ovens to work to pamper us up after fasting so long in the wilderness[o]. The worst point of her civility was that she made us eat part of everything which obliged two of the nine that lay in the[p] room to rise at a very unseasonable time of night.

20.   Mr. Walker came to us again in the morning and was so kind as to bring us some wine and cider along with him. He also lent Meanwell[q] a horse for himself, and me another for one of my men[r]. We had likewise a visit from Colo. Bolling, who had been surveying in the neighborhood. Our landlord, who [155] is a dealer in rum, let me have some for the men and had the humility, though a Captain, to accept of a pistole for our entertainment. I discharged John Ellis and James Whitlock at this place[s]. It was 12 a clock before we could get loose from hence[t], and then we passed Nottoway River just below Capt. Embrys house, where it was about fifteen yards over. This river divides Prince George County from Brunswick. We had the company of Colo. Bolling and Mr. Walker along with us, who could not heartily approve of our Lithuanian custom[a] of walking part of the way.[b,118]

At the distance of eleven miles we crossed Stony Creek, and five miles farther we went over Gravelly Run, which is wide enough to merit the name of a Creek. We passed by Sapony Chapel [8 miles this side Nottoway] and after thirty good miles arrived[c] safe at Colo. Bollings, where we were entertained with much plenty and civility. Among abundance of other good things he regaled us with excellent cider. While Meanwell[d] and I fared deliciously here, our two surveyors and the Reverend Doctor[e] in compliment to their horses stuck close to the baggage. They reached no farther than eighteen miles, and took up their quarters at James Hudsons, where their horses were better provided for than their masters. There was no more than one bed to pig into, with one cotton sheet and the other of brown Osnaburgs[f] made browner by a months perspiration.[g] This mortified Orion[h] to the Soul, so that the other two were happy enough in laughing at him. Though I think they ought all to have

[o]C: Spits, Pots, Frying pans, ^Gridirons,^ and Ovens at work to pamper us up after fasting so long, as she thought, in the wilderness   [p]C: our ^the^   [q]C: ^Meanwell^
[r]C: servants ^men^   [s]C: allowing them a reasonable time to go home ^at this Place^
[t]C: the civilitys of this place ^hence^   [a]C: ^Lithuanian^ Custome   [b]C: *A vertical line here to break paragraph (break present in A, not in C).*   [c]C: ^8 miles this side Nottoway^ and after 30 good miles we arriv'd *(the first phrase inserted and canceled)*
[d]C: ^Meanwell^   [e]C: & the Revd. ^Doctor^   [f]C: one Cotten Sheet and the other of Brown Ozzenbrugs   [g]C: service ^Perspiration^   [h]C: ^Orion^

been perfectly satisfied with the mans hospitality who was content to lie out of his own bed to make room for them.[119]

21. These gentlemen quitted their sweet lodging so early, that they reached Colo. Bollings time enough for Breakfast[i]. Mr. Mumfords pretty Wife[j] was very ill here, which had altered her pretty face[k] beyond all knowledge. I took upon me to prescribe to her and my advice succeeded well[l] as I understood afterwards. About 11 a clock we took leave and proceeded to Majr. Mumfords, where I discharged the Cart, and the few men that remained with me, assuring them that their behavior had engaged me to do them any service that lay in my power. I had no sooner settled these[m] affairs but my Wife and eldest daughter arrived in the chair to meet me. Besides the pleasure of embracing them, they made me happy by letting me understand the[n] rest of the family were extremely well.[o] Our treatment was as civil as possible in this good family. I wrote a letter to send by Orion[p] to the Governor, and the evening we spent giving an account of our Travels[q] and drinking the best cider I ever tasted[r].[120]

22. I sent away Meanwells[s] baggage and my own about ten a clock, he intending to take Westover[t] in his way home. When we had [157] fortify'd our selves[a] with a meat breakfast,[b] we took leave about twelve.[c] My Wife and I rode[d] in the Chair, and my Daughter on an easy Pad she had borrowed.[e] Mrs. Mumford was[f] so kind as to undertake to spin my Buffalo's Hair in order to knit me a pair of stockings[g]. Orion took the nearest way to Williamsburgh, Astrolabe to Goochland, and Humdrum to Mount Misery.[h] We called on Mr. Fitzgerald, to advise him what method to take with his sick child; but Nature had done the business before we came[i]. We arrived at Coggins Point

---

[i]C: to eat a hearty meal ^for^ Breakfast   [j]C: ^pretty^ wife   [k]C: ^pretty face^   [l]C: very well   [m]C: all these   [n]C: that the   [o]C: well, blessed be God.   [p]C: ^Orion^
[q]C: at Cards, and in ^giving an account of our Travels^   [r]C: tasted in my life. The men I discharg'd this day were Peter Jones, Thomas Jones Junr, Richard Smith, Thomas Short and Abraham Jones, who were not far from their several habitations. These were all chosen men & had been very usefull, and very obligeing the whole Journey and wou'd on any occasion attend me without expecting any pay.   [s]C: ^Meanwells^   [t]C: go along with me ^take Westover^   [a]C: fill'd our Bellys ^fortify'd our selves^   [b]C: a meat Breakfast, and finisht our Business,   [c]C: 12, and turn'd our faces toward Westover [d]C: ^rode^   [e]C: Mrs Betty Mumfords Horse ^on an easy Pad she had borrow'd^ [f]C: had been ^was^   [g]C: to knit me some ^a pair of^ Stockins   [h]C: Orion took his ^the^ nearest way to Williamsburgh, Astrolabe to Goochland, and Humdrum to Mount Misery, the place of his Habitation.   [i]C: Nature had done her own ^the^ business, and removed his feaver before we came

about four, where my servants attended with boats[j] in order to transport us to Westover. I had the happiness to find all the family well[k]. This crowned all my other blessings and made the journey truly prosperous, of which I hope I shall ever retain a grateful remembrance[l]. Nor was it all that my people were in good health, but my business was likewise in good order. Everyone seemed to have done their duty, by the joy they expressed at my return. My neighbors had been kind to my wife, when she was threatened with the loss of her son and heir[m]. Their assistance was kind as well as seasonable[n], when her child was threatened with fatal symptoms and her husband upon a long journey exposed to great variety of perils. Thus, surrounded with the most fearful apprehensions, Heaven was pleased to support [158] her spirits and bring back her child from the grave and her husband from the mountains, for which blessings may we be all sincerely thankful.[o,121]

[j]C: where William Wilkins ^my servants^ attended with both my Boats   [k]C: to find all my ^the^ Family well Blessed be God.   [l]C: made the Journey truly prosperous, For ^of^ which I hope I shall ^ever^ retain a gratefull remembrance as long as I live.   [m]C: when she was distrest by the dangerous illness ^threaten'd with the Loss^ of her Son & Heir   [n]C: Their Assistance was then very ^kind as well as^ seasonable   [o]Heaven was pleas'd to support her Spirits, to ^and^ bring back her dear Child from the Gates of Death, and soon after ^from the grave and^ her Husband from howling Desart in Safety & Reputation ^the mountains^, for which Blessings may we be ^all^ sincerely & everlastingly thankfull.

THE NAMES OF THE COMMISSIONERS TO DIRECT THE RUNNING OF
THE LINE BETWEEN VIRGINIA AND NORTH CAROLINA

Steddy
Firebrand } Commissioners for Virginia
Meanwell

Judge Jumble
Shoebrush
Plausible } Commissioners for North Carolina
Puzzlecause

Orion
Astrolabe } Surveyors for Virginia

Plausible
Boötes } Surveyors for North Carolina

The Reverend Doctor   Humdrum Chaplain

NAMES OF THE MEN EMPLOYED ON THE PART OF VIRGINIA TO RUN
THE LINE BETWEEN THAT COLONY AND NORTH CAROLINA

On the first expedition	On the second expedition [159]
I. Peter Jones	Peter Jones
2. Thomas Short	Thomas Short
3. Thomas Jones	Thomas Jones
4. Robert Hix	Robert Hix
5. John Evans	John Evans
6. Stephen Evans	Stephen Evans
7. John Ellis	John Ellis
8. Thomas Wilson	Thomas Wilson
9. George Tilman	George Tilman
10. Charles Kimball	Charles Kimball
11. George Hamilton	George Hamilton
12. Robert Allen	Edward Powell
13. Thomas Jones, Junior	Thomas Jones, Junior
14. John Ellis, Junior	William Pool
15. James Petillo	James Petillo
16. Richard Smith	Richard Smith
17. John Rice	Abraham Jones
18.	William Calvert
19.	James Whitlock
20.	Thomas Page [160]

ACCOUNT OF EXPENSE OF RUNNING THE LINE BETWEEN
VIRGINIA AND NORTH CAROLINA

To the men's wages in current money	£277	10	0
To sundry disbursements for provisions, etc.	174	1	6
To paid the men for seven horses lost	44	0	0
	£495	11	6

The sum of £495 11*s.*6*d.* current money reduced at 15% to sterling amounts to	£430	8	10
To paid Steddy	142	5	7
To paid Meanwell	142	5	7
To paid Firebrand	94	0	0
To paid the Chaplain Humdrum	20	0	0
To paid Orion	75	0	0
To paid Astrolabe	75	0	0
To paid for a tent and marquee	20	0	0
	£1000	0	0

This sum was discharged by a warrant out of His Majesty's quitrents from the lands in Virginia.

THE DISTANCES OF PLACES MENTIONED IN THE FOREGOING HISTORY
OF THE DIVIDING LINE BETWEEN VIRGINIA AND NORTH CAROLINA

	M[iles]	Q[uarters]	P[oles]
From Currituck Inlet to the Dismal	21	2	16
The course through the Dismal	15	0	0
To the east side of Blackwater River	20	1	43
We came down Blackwater to the mouth of Nottoway 176 poles, from whence to Meherrin	13	2	46 [161]
To Meherrin River again	1	67	
To Meherrin River again	2	0	40
To the ferry road	1	2	60
To Meherrin again			22
To Meherrin the fifth and last time	2	3	66
To the middle of Jack's Swamp	11	0	25
To a road	1	2	52
To Beaver Pond Creek the first time	3	3	8
To a road from Bedding Field southward	11	0	37
To Pea Hill Creek	3	1	33
To a road	2	0	30
To Lizard Creek	3	38	
To Pigeon Roost Creek	3	1	72
To Cocke's Creek	2	3	24
To Roanoke River		2	48
To the west side of Do [ditto]			49
To the Indian trading path	8	0	20
To Great Creek	4	3	28
To Nutbush Creek	7	0	6
To Massamony Creek	7	1	4
To Yapatsco Creek	3	0	30
To Ohimpamony Creek	3	1	38
To Tewahominy Creek	8	2	54
To Bluewing Creek	4	3	10
To Sugartree Creek	2	3	10
To Hycootomony Creek	3	1	76
To the same			18
To the same		2	64
To the same		2	66 [162]

	M[iles]	Q[uarters]	P[oles]
To the same again			42[?]
To Buffalo Creek	1	8	40
To Cockade Creek	11	3	6[?]
To the south branch of Roanoke called the Dan		1	26
To the west side including the island		34	
To Cane Creek	2	2	42
To Dan River the second time	4	1	38
To the west side of Do [ditto]			24
To Dan River the third time	8	0	68
To the northwest side aslant		53	
To the Dan River the fourth time	1	0	7
To the west side			21
To Lowland Creek	3	2	50
To Dan River the fifth time	1	0	18
To the northwest side aslant		66	
To Cascade Creek	2	3	10
To Irvin River, a branch of the Dan	6	0	30
To Matrimony Creek	4	0	31
To Miry Creek	7	1	68
To Mayo River, another branch of the Dan	1	36	
To Dan River the sixth and last time	1	2	
To Crooked Creek the first time	2	1	77
To Ne plus ultra Camp	13	0	35
To a red oak, marked on three sides with four notches and the trees blazed about it, on the east bankof a rivulet supposed to be either a branch of Roanoke or Deep River		3	60
The whole distance	241	2	70

NOTES

1. The expectations of the governor and Council (including Byrd) that the largest part of the contested region would prove to be part of Virginia were not borne out by the survey.

2. While revising *The Secret History* Byrd replaced the names of the major participants in the expedition with these nicknames. *Steddy* is Byrd himself; *Merryman,* Virginia councillor Nathaniel Harrison; *Astrolabe,* Virginia surveyor William Mayo; *Capricorn,* Virginia councillor John Allen; *Firebrand,* surveyor general of Customs and Virginia councillor Richard Fitzwilliam; *Meanwell,* Virginia councillor and commissioner William Dandridge; *Burly,* Virginia Church of England commissary the Reverend James Blair; and *Dr. Humdrum,* the Reverend Peter Fontaine.

3. Byrd gave the North Carolina Commissioners satirical names. *Judge Jumble* was Chief Justice Christopher Gale; *Shoebrush,* Secretary John Lovick; *Plausible,* Surveyor General Edward Moseley; *Puzzlecause,* Attorney General William Little.

Mercury and the Moon in conjunction: According to astrological calculations, a conjunction occurs when the angle two planets make is 0°, when heavenly bodies viewed from the earth appear to be in approximately the same direction. However, contemporary almanacs do not register such a conjunction on March 5, 1728. Titan Leeds, in *The American Almanack for the Year of Christian Account, 1728* (Philadelphia, [1727]), recorded a sextile of the sun and Jupiter; Nathaniel Whittemore, in *An Almanack for the Year of Our Lord, 1728* (Boston, [1727?]), a conjunction of Saturn and Mercury; and London almanac writer Francis Moore, in *Vox Stellarum: Being a Loyal Almanack for the Year of Humane Redemption, 1728* (London, 1728), a sextile of the sun and Saturn.

Astrology does not play any significant part anywhere in Byrd's writing, so it is natural to conclude that Byrd's astrological allusion is an ironic comment referring to the supposed influences of the moon and Mercury. Mercury influenced liveliness, volatility of temperament, spirit, inconstancy, and wit. Mercury's astrological qualities are "convertible, in Nature mutable." The constantly shifting phases of the moon traditionally suggest mutability of character and changeable physical and mental health. The negative influence produces "Vagabonds, an idle, lazy, drunken Companion, given to Sottishness, delighting to love careless and beggarly, one of no Spirit or Forecast, a perfect hater of Labour, a mutuable, unsettled and unconstant person" (Richard Ball, *Astrology Improv'd; or, A Compendium of That Most Noble Science* [London, 1723], 3, 58, 60). Those of Byrd's readers familiar with astrology (or its use as a literary device) would have no difficulty recognizing Byrd's allusion as a satirical comment on the difficulty of getting the Carolina Commissioners to agree on a date.

4. *Marquis:* marquee, a large officer's field tent. *Gentiles:* heathens or pagans, that is, nominal but unbaptized Christians.

5. The actual letter, preserved in the records of North Carolina's Executive Council, is nearly identical, save for a few variant readings:

Secret History	Executive Council Letter
by your Governor.	by your Governors Letter
find each other.	find one another.
We shall have full powers to agree	We are fully Impowred to agree
It is very proper	We think it very proper

that so you Gentlemen who are appointed	that so that you being appointed
Honour to your Government	Honor to your Country
Marquis	Marques
We shall be provided with as much Wine and Rum as just enable us	We bring as much Wine and Rum as will enable us
many Gentiles on your Frontiers	many Gentiles on the frontier
And whoever of your Province shall be desirous of Novelty may repair on Sundays to our Camp and hear a Sermon	and whoever in that Neighboorhood is desirous of Novelty may come and here a Sermon
the News that such able Commissioners are appointed for that Government	the News of your being appointed Commissioners for that Government
converse with prodigious Pleasure	converse with a great deal of Pleasure

—Robert J. Cain, ed., *Records of the Executive Council, 1735–1754,* CRNC, VII, (Raleigh, N.C., 1988), 558

6. The letter as it appears in *The Secret History* is very close to the letter on file in the Board of Trade records, saving some variants:

Secret History	Board of Trade Letter
from Williamsburgh, dated the 16th of December	from Williamsburgh the 16 Decr.
there can no difficulty arise	there can be no Difficulties arise
We think so too; but if no dispute shou'd arise in construing	we think so too, if no disputes should arise in construing
yet the Manner of our Proceeding in the Execution	yet the manner of Our Proceeding in the Executing them
by Letters, about any Matters previously to be adjusted	by Letter any matters previously to be adjusted
to desire by this Messenger, you will let us know	to desire you will by this Messenger let us know
to go thro' the Great Swamp	to go thro the Dismall
to run a due West Line to the Swamp, & then to find the said Latitude on the West Side the Swamp, & continue thence a due West Line to Chowan River	to run a due West Line to the West side of the Swamp and to continue a Due west Line to Chowan River
& find the Variation with	and find the Variation of the Compass with
which we hope will not happen again, after we in so remote a place	we hope will not happen againe nor any other Difficulty that may occasion any Disappointment or delay after we have been at the trouble of meeting
the Circumstances of things will admit; And what we want in necessaries	the Circumstances of things will admit us, and what we may want in necessaries

your Chaplain, of whom we shall give Notice as you desire; & doubt not of making a great many Boundary Christians	your Chaplain of whom we shall give Notice as you desire to all Lovers of Novelty and doubt not of a great many Boundary Christians
To conclude, we promise a Singular Pleasure to us, that you Gentlemen are nam'd	To conclude, Gentlemen, we promise a Singular Pleasure to us that you are named
being assur'd your Characters	being assured Gentlemen of your Characters

—Board of Trade records, CO 5, 306, f. 29

Contrary to Byrd's satirical assertion, the Board of Trade's copy is in fact dated January 24.

7. The 1728 surveyors came much better prepared than those of 1710, when the North Carolina Commissioners found fault with a loosely fixed instrument furnished by the Virginians. This instrument for calculating the magnetic variation proved to be not "fast in the ring" and so produced erratic readings. Byrd acknowledged the justice of their complaint, for the 1710 quadrant had allowed "an Error of near 30 Minutes either in the Instrument, or in those, who made use of it."

8. Colonel Robert Mumford (or Munford) was a prominent planter in Prince George County, where he was also justice of the peace, colonel of the militia, and burgess in 1720–1722. In his youth he had worked for Byrd and was instrumental in recruiting the Virginia men for the 1728 expedition.

The rendezvous point has not been identified. Warren's Mill must have been located somewhere south and east of Westover, in the direction of the journey toward Norfolk. Byrd relates that he and Mayo, setting out from Westover, first crossed "the River" (the James). Thus it is unlikely to have been the Warren Mill of today, eight miles northwest of Williamsburg, apparently named for a gristmill established in 1792.

9. For details about the Virginia men, see Appendix 1: Dramatis Personae.

10. *Capricorn's Elegant Seat:* the home of Colonel John Allen (ca. 1674–1742) in Surry County, built in 1665 by his grandfather, Arthur Allen. Because it had been garrisoned by Nathaniel Bacon's forces in 1676, it came to be known as Bacon's Castle. It is located due south of Williamsburg, thus placing it squarely along the projected route. Allen's wife, Elizabeth Bassett Allen, predeceased him.

Young Astrolabe: William Mayo's brother, Joseph Mayo, whose plantation, Powhatan Seat, lay on the south side of the James in Henrico County.

Dr. Arsmart: Dr. George Nicholas of Williamsburg. Byrd's name for Nicholas is witty, for *Arsmart* was a common name for *Polygonum hydropiper,* now known as smartweed. The plant possesses the property of irritating the skin; it was sometimes applied to the hindquarters of a weary horse to impart artificial vigor, hence its name.

Orion: Alexander Irvin, professor of mathematics at William and Mary, 1729–1732. Byrd later counters this exaggerated praise of Irvine's accomplishments with many examples of his incompetence in the field.

Rack Punch: strong punch made with arrack, a liquor distilled from fermented palm sap or rice, sugar, and coconut juice, originally made in southeastern Asia but imported into Virginia from the West Indies.

Pistole: "A Spanish gold double-escudo dating from the 1530s and surviving into the

19th cent.; (also) any various coins derived from or resembling this from the 17th and 18th centuries, *esp.* the louis d'or issued in 1640–3 (during the reign of Louis XIII), an Irish coin issued in 1642–3 (in the reign of Charles II), and the Scottish twelve pound piece issued in 1701 (during the reign of William III)" *(OED)*. If Byrd refers to to the last coinage, this is a way of saying the Virginia Commissioners expected to be paid sixty pounds.

11. *The Widdow Allen:* Katherine Baker Allen, the widow of Arthur Allen II.

12. *Mr. Baker:* Probably the planter William Baker, whose plantation was in the neighborhood of Wickham's Swamp. He was the eldest son of Henry Baker of Isle of Wight (1632–1712), and his brother Henry Baker was sheriff, militia captain, burgess, justice, and surveyor in Nansemond County, Virginia. The Dividing Line placed the Baker plantation in North Carolina. *DNCB,* I, 28.

Colo. Thomas Godding: Thomas Godwin, planter, burgess for Nansemond County, county lieutenant, militia commander, sheriff, and tobacco agent. His eager son, another Thomas Godwin, was later a justice of peace in Nansemond. Hugh Drysdale, "The Present State of Virginia with Respect to the Colony in General," *VMHB,* LXVIII (1940), 143; John Bennett Boddie, *Seventeenth Century Isle of Wight County, Virginia . . .* (Baltimore, 1994), 465; *Council,* IV, 235, 273, 319.

13. *Majr. Crawford:* William Crawford, Norfolk County burgess, sheriff, and judge. His plantation was on the west side of the Elizabeth River. *DNCB,* I, 458; *Council* IV, 86; H. R. McIlwaine, ed., *Journals of the House of Burgesses of Virginia, 1727–1734, 1736–1740* (Richmond, Va., 1910), viii–ix; Thomas C. Parramore, Peter C. Stewart, and Tommy L. Bogger, *Norfolk: The First Four Centuries* (Charlottesville, Va., 1994), 66.

Colo. Newton: George Newton, Norfolk County burgess, sheriff, militia officer, and merchant. His wife was Aphia Wilson Newton. McIlwaine, ed., *Burgesses, 1727–1734, 1736–1740,* vii, xi; Drysdale, "Present State of Virginia," *VMHB,* XLVIII (1940), 148; *Council,* V, 237, 285; Rogers Dey Whichard, *The History of Lower Tidewater Virginia* (New York, 1959), I, 374; Parramore, Stewart, and Bogger, *Norfolk,* 67.

14. *Old Colo. Boush:* Samuel Boush (d. 1736), attorney, ship chandler, merchant, landowner, militia commander, and first mayor of Norfolk. He traded on the Elizabeth River, owned two Norfolk ferries, bought and sold lands, and served as county magistrate, coroner, deputy escheator, tobacco agent *(DVB,* II, 125–126; Parramore, Stewart, and Bogger, *Norfolk,* 63; *Council,* II, 234, III, 176, 196, 215, 217, 229, 335, 380, 419, 543, IV, 12; Drysdale, "Present State of Virginia," *VMHB,* XLVIII [1940], 148). Boush, whose mercantile activities included supplying ships, chandler, was well suited to provide the expedition with provisions.

William Wilkins: a planter in Norfolk and Prince George Counties, in 1729 justice of the peace for Norfolk County. In the 1704 quitrent rolls he was listed for two hundred acres in Norfolk County and nine hundred in Prince George. Louis des Cognets, Jr., ed., *English Duplicates of Lost Virginia Records* (1958; Baltimore, 1990), 44, 125, 227.

Sam Smith: Samuel Smith (d. 1739), Norfolk merchant, shipowner, and land speculator. In 1726 and 1729 he was listed as justice of the peace and served as sheriff in 1730–1731 and Norfolk alderman in 1736. *DNCB,* V, 388; Drysdale, "Present State of Virginia," *VMHB,* XLVIII (1940), 148; Beverley Fleet, *Virginia Colonial Abstracts* (Baltimore, 1988), II, 324; *Council,* IV, 215, 235; des Cognets, ed., *English Duplicates of Lost Virginia Records,* 37.

15. *Codrus and the 2 Decii:* Two ubiquitous classical exemplars of patriotism in the face

of certain death. Codrus, the last king of Athens, went out from his besieged city to fight the Dorian invaders and die. Sir Francis Bacon explained, "There is an Honour likewise which may be ranked amongst the greatest, which happeneth rarely, that is, of such as sacrifice themselves to Death or Danger for the Good of their Country as . . . the Two *Decii*" ("Of Honour and Reputation," in *The Essays, or Councils, Civil and Moral, of Sir Francis Bacon* . . . [London, 1718], 145). Byrd had copies of Bacon's *Essays* and *Opera* (*Hayes* 623, 826). Valerius Maximus, *Memorable Doings and Sayings (Factorum et dictorum memorabilium IX libri)*, trans. D. R. Shackleton Bailey (Cambridge, Mass., 2000), includes these two among his examples of patriotism *(De pietate erga patriam)*, 5.6. Byrd owned copies of works by Valerius Maximus (*Hayes* 1636, 1701, 2474).

Byrd's servant Tom first appeared in the *Secret Diary* in February 1709; thereafter Byrd mentions him briefly in numerous entries, often as "my man Tom." He carried letters for Byrd, conveyed orders to outlying plantations, and brought back news to Westover. Byrd also occasionally mentions treating Tom's illnesses or disciplining him (*SD*, esp. 5). Byrd's language does not specify his status; he might have been enslaved, indentured, or a salaried employee. Most writers on Byrd assume Tom was enslaved, though without introducing evidence.

16. *Mr. Marston:* the Reverend Richard Marsden (ca. 1675–1742); see *History of the Dividing Line,* note 44.

Powder-Point: at the fork of the east and south branches of the Elizabeth River, across from Norfolk, Royal Navy ships were careened (removed from the water and turned on their sides for cleaning, caulking, and repairing). A naval powder magazine was built there; hence the name. Parramore, Stewart, and Bogger, *Norfolk,* 60.

17. *Captain Wilkins:* Probably John Wilkins, who patented land in 1719 near tracts held by Thomas and William Wilkins in Northampton County, and probably the son of William Wilkins, Norfolk County justice and planter, which would fit the identification of his father's plantation, or "Castle," east of the Dismal Swamp (*C&P,* III, 78, 213). Boyd, who mistranscribed this name as "Wilson," identifies him as Captain Willis Wilson, Jr. (*Boyd,* 39). Confusingly, several lines later Boyd identifies "Capt. Wilkins" as William Wilkins (41). Also confused, Wright identified Wilkins as the Captain James Wilson mentioned later in *The Secret History of the Line* (*Prose Works,* 53).

On the classical significance of laurel (bay) and myrtle, see *History of the Dividing Line,* note 46.

Andrew Dukes: In *History of the Dividing Line* Byrd does not name Duke, merely asserting that he "was lately removed Bag and Baggage from Maryland, thro' a strong Antipathy he had to work, and paying his Debts." There were Dukes in Calvert County, Maryland. James Duke of "Mary's Dukedom" wedded Mary Dawkins and had three children, James, Andrew, and Elizabeth. The younger James (ca. 1670–1731) wedded Martha Mackall, and they had six children, including another eldest son, James (ca. 1691–1754), and a second son, Andrew (to whom he left only one shilling in his will). This second-generation Andrew is probably the one who left Maryland. The name Andrew Duke appears in Currituck Precinct, North Carolina, records between 1726 and 1740. He might well have been poor and probably owned little land (quitrent rolls for 1735 record only 89.5 acres in his name), which fact would perhaps conform somewhat to Byrd's description of the accommodations. It is not clear whether the Maryland Dukes were related to the Virginia family of the same name. Mary Byrd, daughter of William Byrd I, married the Virginian James Duke of James City County and later Charles City County. A member of the Virginia Executive Council, James Duke was "a close friend and political associate to both colonels Byrd of Westover." His eldest son, William, was educated at Westover by his uncle William Byrd II. Elise Greenup Jourdan, *Early Families of Southern Maryland* (Westminster, Md., 2007), V, 7–8; John Anderson Brayton, comp., *Transcriptions of Provincial North Carolina Wills, 1663–1729/30* (Memphis, Tenn., Baltimore, 2003–2005), II, 119, 120, 139–140; Gordon C. Jones, *Abstracts of Wills and Other Records, Currituck and Dare Counties, North Carolina (1663–1850)* (Philadelphia, 1958), 4; *DNCB*, II, 118–119.

Chinches: bedbugs.

18. Jumble (Christopher Gale) was *not* in fact the brother of the famous antiquary Thomas Gale, dean of York (1635–1702) (*Boyd,* 43). North Carolina's turbulent political history was distasteful to Byrd, who had so much invested in his own patrician authority. He believed Carolina's government had been weak and in crisis throughout the proprietary era, and he maintained that the rule of law there was uncertain. Thomas Lowndes, provost marshal of Carolina (who remained in England and carried out his business by means of a deputy), famously summed up the colony as "a receptacle for pyrates, thieves and vagabonds of all Sorts." Lowndes to Council of Trade and Plantations, Dec. 8, 1729, *CSP,* XXXVI, 544, no. 1008.

Moseley had been a student until 1697 at Christ's Hospital (known as the "Blue-Coat School") in Newgate, founded in 1552. The charter of 1672 established a mathematical program designed to train young men for careers at sea, as navigators. Byrd characterizes Moseley, both in the nickname he gives him and by asserting he was qualified to be a Jesuit, as an untrustworthy, sophistical, equivocating person.

Bo-otes: North Carolina surveyor Samuel Swann, Jr. He represented Perquimans in the North Carolina Assembly from 1725 to 1734. He is given the name of the constellation Boötes, just as the surveyor Irvin is called Orion; there may be an ironic distinction here, for Boötes was merely a plowman, whereas Orion was a noble hunter, and his is one of the brightest constellations.

19. *Stiff Buckle:* Samuel Johnson defined "buckle" as the "state of the hair crisped and curled by being kept long in the same state" (cited in *OED*). Joseph Addison, in *Spectator* no. 129 (July 28, 1711), describes the "monstrous flaxen periwig" of a country dandy who "lets his wig lye in buckle for a whole half year" between special occasions (*The Works of the Right Honourable Joseph Addison, Esq.* [London, 1721], III, 84 [*Hayes* 1848]). Byrd thus suggests that Irvin was comically and quaintly overdressed for the expedition, yet at the same time neglecting matters of hygiene.

20. In their report of the abortive survey of 1710, Ludwell and Harrison complained that Moseley was intent on making the survey impossible, and the Virginia government was concerned that Moseley might prove difficult again in 1728. After a heated debate about the spot on the shore from which the line should proceed westward, Moseley persuaded his party to accept a compromise—after Byrd showed him papers he had brought along to serve such an occasion. Byrd designates the effective document a letter from Governor Spotswood to Queen Anne, but it was something more than that. Among the documents Byrd appended to *The History of the Dividing Line* was the Board of Trade's report on the 1710–1711 survey sent to the Queen in Council. This report included Spots-

wood's correspondence to the Board, reference to the Ludwell Harrison journal, and the Council's own recommendations. "A Journal of the Proceedings of Philip Ludwell and Nathaniel Harrison Commissioners Appointed for Settling the Boundary between Her Majesty's Colony and Dominion of Virginia and the Province of North Carolina," Board of Trade and Plantations Journal, 1316, ff. 174r–183r.

Copies of these documents were included with the Virginia Commissioners' instructions, together with copies of the Carolina charter and the Eden-Spotswood proposals, over the signature of Edward Southwell, clerk of the Privy Council. The Board of Trade report had laid out the difficulties Virginia had encountered previously with getting the survey of the Virginia–North Carolina boundary underway. From Spotswood's reports they documented all North Carolina's delays, and the Board agreed with his allegation that officials there were benefiting from the uncertain state of the controverted lands, patenting land in the disputed region and collecting quitrents:

> So unfair hath Mr. Moseley and the other Surveyors of that Province been, tho' they pretend no farther than a West line from the mouth of Nottoway River, yet upon making out that line, I find several people, seated even to the Northward of it, who hold their Lands by Carolina Patents.
> —Spotswood to Board of Trade, July 21, 1714, in R. A. Brock, ed., *The Official Letters of Alexander Spotswood, Lieutenant-Governor of the Colony of Virginia, 1710–1722* (Richmond, Va., 1882), II, 70–72

See the Privy Council report, signed by Edward Southwell, included in the documents Byrd appended to *The History of the Dividing Line.* The Privy Council document included the entire panoply of charges Ludwell and Harrison had made against Moseley, corroborated by Spotswood. It stressed Moseley's prevarication and his obstruction of the survey because it tended "so manifestly to his disadvantage." This, then, was the document Byrd showed Moseley, who was sufficiently chastened or alarmed that he refrained from further obstructing the negotiated agreement about the starting point. He continued to be the most civil of the Carolina Commissioners, at least according to Byrd's report.

21. *Japon:* yaupon or yaupon holly, also known as cassena *(Ilex vomitoria).*

22. William Harding held Virginia land patents in Virginia. He died in 1748 in Currituck, and his will was proven in North Carolina; his wife Jane was coexecutor. *NCHGR,* I (1900), 226.

Byrd again mocks the dress and manners of the Carolina Commissioners, ridiculing Lovick for wearing mismatched clothing and stressing his unknown origins. In attributing Puritan origins to Little, Byrd might have been ridiculing his sober dress, more appropriate for the law courts than the frontier.

The relation between Alexander Irvin and Commissary Blair to which Byrd alludes was their professional connection at the College of Willam and Mary: Blair as the head of the college was Irvin's superior. Boyd might well have been right to call Irvine Blair's "protégé" *(Boyd,* xiii).

23. There were Heaths throughout the region. James and John Heath each had land on the west side of the North River, just south of Richard Eisland's plantation, and the families were connected by marriage. The "Surveyors' Journal or Field Book" entry for March 9 lists "John Heaths House S 64° E" and "James Heaths S 70° 30′ E."

Salute: originally denoting speech expressing "good wishes, respect, or homage," and then by extension, "to kiss, or greet with a kiss" *(OED).*

Grandee: originally "a Spanish or Portuguese nobleman of the highest rank," by extension, "a person of high rank or position, or of eminence in any line" *(OED).* Byrd's use of this elevated term may well be ironic.

Capt. White: Solomon White, Princess Anne County militia officer, justice of the peace. In 1714 he was granted 890 acres in Norfolk County, and in 1717 he patented 2,136 acres in Princess Anne County, in Lynhaven Parish, Currituck, and Knott's Island (Lloyd DeWitt Bockstruck, *Virginia's Colonial Soldiers* [Baltimore, 1988], 219; des Cognets, ed., *English Duplicates of Lost Virginia Records,* 9, 27, 51, 100, 111, 254; *C&P,* III, 103).

Mr. Moss: Probably Francis Moss, in 1728 a justice of peace in Currituck; he died in Jamaica in 1742 en route to Cartagena (Robert J. Cain, ed., *Records of the Executive Council, 1735–1754,* CRNC, VIII [Raleigh, N.C., 1988], 183; Bockstruck, *Virginia's Colonial Soldiers,* 157).

24. *Eyland:* Richard Eiland, Jr. (ca. 1681–1733), was a planter on the west side of North River. The Eilands' plantation was just to the north of John Heath's; Richard Eiland, Jr., married Elizabeth Heath, daughter of James Heath. In 1731 he represented Currituck in the North Carolina Assembly. In his will, dated March 7, 1733, he left five hundred acres of land to his children, excluding the home plantation, which went to his wife during her life, and property on the shore that he ordered sold to pay debts. The extent to which the boundary split the plantation may be seen in the language of Eiland's will: "the major part lying in Princess Ann Co. in Virginia, the lesser part in Corotuck, North Carolina." Worth S. Ray, ed., *Ray's Index and Digest to Hathaway's North Carolina Historical and Genealogical Register* (Baltimore, 1997), 75. Thanks to Diane Eiland for help with this investigation.

Mr. Merchant: Probably Christopher Merchant, Jr. (grandson of Willoughby Merchant of Princess Anne County), in 1728 justice of Currituck Precinct Court—or his brother Willoughby, briefly sheriff of Princess Ann County in 1726 (*DNCB,* IV, 255; *Council,* IV, 100).

25. Gen. 32:24–32.

26. *Capt. Willis Wilson:* There were two Willis Wilsons in the Norfolk area. The first was a Norfolk shipowner and trader, justice of the peace for King and Queen County, and captain of the Elizabeth County Militia in 1698. The man Byrd mentions was his nephew, Captain Willis Wilson (ca. 1687–ca. 1750), sometimes called Willis Wilson, Jr., to distinguish him from his uncle. He was a trader, burgess for Norfolk in the 1718 and 1720–1722 Assemblies, sheriff in 1724, and justice of the peace. *Council,* I, 411, IV, 67, 273, V, 92; Bockstruck, *Virginia's Colonial Soldiers,* 23; McIlwaine, ed., *Journals of the House of Burgesses, 1712–1714* . . . , ix, x; Patti Sue McCrary, *Wilson Families in Colonial Virginia and Related Mason, Seawell, Goodrich, Boush Families: Ancestors and Kin of Benjamin Wilson, 1733–1814* (Westminster, Md., 2007), 2, 8.

Yaws: An infectious tropical disease (treponematosis) generically related to syphilis but transmitted by skin contact.

27. *Monsr. Broglie:* François Marie, duc de Broglie (1671–1745), marshal of France, who in 1709 fought at Malplaquet, in the War of the Polish Succession, and the War of the Austrian Succession. He also served as French ambassador to Great Britain from 1724 to 1731. The shocking incident of his narrow escape occurred in September 1734, when the army

of the Austro-Hungarian Empire crossed the Secchia River in Lombardy and surprised Broglie's quarters before nearby troops commanded by the dauphin could prevent it. Dispatches reported he "saved himself only *en chemise.*" John L. Sutton, *The King's Honor and the King's Cardinal: The War of the Polish Succession* (Lexington, Ky., 1980), 173.

28. *A la Dragon:* to do something like a dragon is to act fiercely—perhaps with a pun on swearing like a "dragoon," one of the British horse soldiers famous for strong language.

Mr. Balance: William Balance (d. 1732), a planter who in 1697 patented 950 acres in Norfolk County on the southwest bank of Northwest River. The patent description—"nigh the runn branch, on Little Br., dividing this and the White Oake Ridge, nigh mouth of the Cyprus Swamp"—accords with Byrd's itinerary (*C&P*, III, 13).

The young woman might in fact have suffered from yaws, her scabs resulting from the characteristic inflammatory lesions, and perhaps the pain in her wrist resulted from the disease's attack on bone.

29. John Ellis, Sr., one of the men recruited by Colonel Mumford in Bristol Parish. Charles Kimball was an Indian trader and interpreter to the Saponi. George Hamilton was a planter in Surry County.

30. *Pioneers:* in military usage, infantrymen sent in advance to clear terrain for the main body of troops.

White Cedar: Byrd correctly distinguishes the Atlantic white cedar *(Chamaecyparis thyoides)* from the eastern red cedar *(Juniperus virginiana).* Both trees are native to the region, and both share a wetland habitat.

31. *Capt. Meade:* Andrew Meade (d. 1745) emigrated to Virginia from Ireland in 1685 and settled along the Nansemond River. He served as burgess for Nansemond County, 1727–1734, justice of the peace, captain of the militia, and vestryman in the Upper Parish of Suffolk. P. Hamilton Baskervill, *Andrew Meade of Ireland and Virginia . . .* (Richmond, Va., 1921), 23–25; *C&P*, III, 336.

Mr. Pugh: Daniel Pugh, planter and sheriff of Nansemond County. In 1698 he patented 415 acres in Nansemond "on the east side of of Bennett's Creek, and the north side of the mouth of Spights' Branch," and in the following five years he patented an additional 756 acres; in 1724 he took on another 398 acres. In 1726 and 1729 he was justice of the peace and served as coroner in 1729. In 1732 and 1738 he represented Nansemond in the House of Burgesses. *C&P*, III, 22, 24, 32, 37, 41, 274; des Cognets, ed., *English Duplicates of Lost Virginia Records*, 32, 44, 49, 67.

Timothy Ives: Timothy Ives (ca. 1685–1743), son of Timothy Ives (1640–ca. 1716), who lived in Elizabeth River Parish, Norfolk County. "Honest Timothy Ives" the son apparently lived on or near his father's land. Ives had three daughters, Elizabeth, Mary, and Rachel (*C&P*, III, 116, 173; W. Mac Jones, "The Ivey Family," *WMQ*, 2d Ser., VII [1927], 92–96, 181–192). As for the young woman, "sandy" denotes hair of a yellowish-red color *(OED)*, which might have had some significance as a folkloric sign of a sexual nature, now unclear.

32. *John Ives:* In 1704 John Ives was listed in the Norfolk County quitrent rolls as owning 434 acres. He was probably related to Timothy Ives, perhaps a cousin. Timothy Ives, Sr., had a brother, John Ives (d. 1716), and this John Ives was possibly his son. Des Cognets, ed., *English Duplicates of Lost Virginia Records*, 94; Annie Laurie Wright Smith, *The Quit Rents of Virginia . . . 1704 . . .* (Baltimore, 1975), 48.

Mr. Oshield: David O'Sheall, who owned land in both Nansemond County, Virginia, and North Carolina. He was an active attorney in Virginia and North Carolina. He was admitted in 1726 to plead before the North Carolina General Court by Chief Justice Christopher Gale, and in 1737 he was named recorder of Norfolk County, Virginia. *NCHGR,* II (1901), 448; Cain, ed., *Records of the Executive Council, 1664–1734,* CRNC, VII, 551; William S. Price, Jr., *North Carolina Higher-Court Minutes, 1709–1723,* CRNC, V (Raleigh, N.C., 1977), esp. 185, 335; des Cognets, ed., *Virginia Duplicates of Lost Virginia Records,* 314.

Captain Meade: In 1726, Andrew Meade was listed among Nansemond County's twenty justices of the peace; in 1729 he represented Nansemond in the House of Burgesses. Drysdale, "Present State of Virginia," *VMHB,* XLVIII (1940), 146; des Cognets, ed., *English Duplicates of Lost Virginia Records,* 49.

33. *Hibernian Bull:* A narrative jest involving self-contradiction and ridiculous inconsistency, commonly associated with the Irish, who supposedly speak this way without knowing they do so.

34. *Thomas Speight:* (1670–1737) merchant, planter, and attorney, justice of the peace and member of the North Carolina Assembly for Perquimans Precinct in 1725, assistant justice of the General Court in 1726. Briefly, in 1700, he was identified in deeds as residing in Nansemond, Virginia, but otherwise the records show him in Perquimans, and later in Bertie County. At the time of the expedition Speight had three daughters, Rachel (b. 1708), Ruth (b. 1712), and Zilpah (b. 1716), and two sons, Isaac and Moses. Cain, ed., *Records of the Executive Council, 1664–1734,* CRNC, VII, 141, 164, 202, 231; *NCHGR,* I (1900), 391.

Truss: "Of a thick rounded form, like a bundle or parcel; neatly and compactly framed; tight, compact" *(OED).*

35. *Morocco-Embassadors:* see *History of the Dividing Line,* above, note 96.

36. *Majr. Alston:* John Alston (1653–1753), whose plantation on Bennet's Creek, Chowan County, lay within the controverted region. He was justice of the peace and major of the militia for Chowan County, collector of revenue, assistant justice of the Court of Oyer and Terminer, and assistant justice of the General Court. The Dividing Line ran to the north of his properties.

Capt. Baker: Henry Baker's lands also lay within the controverted region. He had previously served as sheriff, captain of the militia, justice of the peace, surveyor, and burgess for Nansemond County, Virginia. The Dividing Line ran to the north of his property, rendering him a North Carolinian.

Rank Butter & Glyster Sugar: apparently the butter garnishing the grits was rancid, and the sugar was of the crude sort used for glysters (clysters), "medicine injected into the rectum, to empty or cleanse the bowels, to afford nutrition, etc." *(OED).*

Rachel: Thomas Speight's eldest daughter, born in 1708, Rachel was twenty years old at the time of the expedition. She married Thomas Jordan of Virginia sometime in the 1730s.

37. *3 Cormorants:* The cormorant is a bird known for its voracious appetite. Judge Jumble's brother was Edmund Gale, member of the Assembly, treasurer of Pasquotank, associate justice of the General Court, commissioner of Edenton, and member of Governor Everard's Council. Shoebrush's brother was Thomas Lovick, collector of Customs—in which capacity Fitzwilliam was his superior, though I have found no evidence Fitzwilliam appointed him—justice of the peace for Chowan County, and associate justice of the General Court.

Capt. Genneau was probably Joseph Jenoure of Edenton. In 1728, Governor Everard charged him with scandal and defamation; Jenoure was defended by David O'Sheill. At the end of the proprietary government, Jenoure was appointed to Governor Burrington's Council in 1730, and succeeded Moseley as surveyor general in 1731.

38. *Ruth:* Thomas Speight's daughter Ruth (b. 1712) was eighteen at the time of the expedition. In the 1730s she married Joseph Jordan, brother to her sister Rachel's husband.

39. *Baker . . . the Surveyor of Nansimond:* Henry Baker, Jr., sometime sheriff, captain in the Nansemond Militia, burgess (1723–1726), justice of the peace, and surveyor in Nansemond County, Virginia. The Dividing Line placed the Baker family's land in North Carolina. By the will of his father, Henry Baker, Jr., in 1712 inherited twenty-five hundred acres at Bucklands. He married first Angelica Bray, and second Ruth Chancey. His will was probated in Chowan County, North Carolina, in 1739. By his first wife he had two sons, Henry and David, and by his second Ruth, Mary, Zadock, Sarah, Samuel, and John. John Bennett Boddie, *Southside Virginia Families* (Baltimore, 1996), I, 9; *DNCB,* I, 28.

40. All the North Carolina Commissioners, including Moseley and Little, were deeply immersed in controversy with Governor Everard at the the time of the expedition. Indeed, at one point Everard called Little, Gale, and Lovick "the only enemies to the Repose and quiet of the colony" (*DNCB,* IV, 73).

41. *Capt. Foot:* Byrd's reasons for thus renaming Captain Genneau (Jenoure) remain obscure, unless Jenoure's erstwhile command had been a company of foot soldiers, traditionally less glamorous than cavalry. Or perhaps he intended a pun on the name "Genneau," alluding to the French phrase "ce soulier mon pied gêne" ("this shoe pinches my foot").

Peter Brinkley: eldest son of Jacob Brinkley, who emigrated to Virginia in 1684. A planter in Perquimans Precinct, west of the Great Dismal Swamp, Peter Brinkley married Anne Eley and had a large family. Freddie L. Brinkley, *The Brinkley and Allied Families of Nansemond County, Virginia, and Gates County, North Carolina: A Family History* (Pasadena, Md., 1994), 17–18.

Madeira Wine: a fortified wine from the Spanish island of Madeira. *Pottle Bottles of Strong Beer:* half-gallon pots or tankards. *Jamaica Rum:* liquor distilled from sugarcane, one of the chief commodities exchanged between the West Indies and Virginia. It should be noted that all three are strong drinks.

Naples Biscuit: a rosewater-flavored pastry, rather a genteel confection for a rough expedition.

42. The headwaters of all these rivers do in fact lie within the boundaries of the Dismal drainage area, except the Perquimans, which starts up a little to the west. See Robert Q. Oaks, Jr., and Donald R. Whitehead, "Geologic Setting and Origin of the Dismal Swamp, Southeastern Virginia and Northeastern North Carolina," in Paul W. Kirk, ed., *The Great Dismal Swamp* (Charlottesville, Va., 1979), 1–24.

43. In Byrd's era, it was understood that diseases not caused by diet or direct contact with the ill could be transmitted in the moist air of insalubrious locations.

44. *Majr. Alston's Daughter:* John Alston's will names five daughters: Mary, Elizabeth, Sarah, Charity, and Martha. At the time of the expedition, Mary was probably twenty-one, Sarah nineteen, and Elizabeth seventeen. Charity and Martha were ten years old or younger. *NCHGR,* I (1900), 163.

45. *Wife & Heir Apparent:* Mary Hinton Speight (d. 1743); Isaac Speight (ca. 1703–ca. 1752).

46. I have not identified Captain Robins or his ship. Presumably they were involved in exporting North Carolina tobacco, bypassing the export duties imposed by Customs officers at Virginia's ports.

Richard Parker: Richard Parker, Jr. (d. 1751), planter in Surry County, and vestryman of Nansemond Parish. The Journal of the North Carolina Commissioners records that on March 30 the Line was run just to the north of Richard Parker's house, west of the Dismal "and 515 Chain west of the road that leads from Perquimmons to the White Marsh in Virginia." Cain, ed., *Records of the Executive Council, 1664–1734,* CRNC, VII, 567.

47. *William Speight:* William Speight (ca. 1674–ca. 1749) of the Upper Parish, Nansemond County, Virginia. His lands appear to have been in both jurisdictions: in 1711 and 1719 he patented land in Virginia (*C&P,* III, 118, 215); in 1716 he witnessed a lease for a tract of land in Chowan Precinct, North Carolina (Margaret M. Hofmann, *Chowan Precinct, North Carolina, 1696 to 1723* [Three Rivers, Mass., 2000], 147). In 1726 Parker paid quitrents to North Carolina (Cain, ed., *Records of the Executive Council, 1664–1734,* CRNC, VII, 551). In 1728 as a resident of Nansemond County he sold property in Virginia that was registered in a North Carolina document (*NCHGR,* II, [1901], 444). In 1735 he sold lands on Horse Pen Branch, North Carolina (*NCHGR,* I [1900], 109, III [1902], 128).

The Journal of the North Carolina Commissioners reported that on April 1 the Line crossed Sommerton Road 1.5 miles south of the Chapel and Meherrin Ferry Road "near William Speights whose plantation was Split by the Line Posts marked being put up on the main Roads where the Line crost them" (Cain, ed., *Records of the Executive Council, 1664–1734,* CRNC, VII, 567–568). Speight's activities recorded in the documents of both provinces suggest he preferred to remain Virginian, but he was also a vestryman of Saint Paul's Parish in Chowan Precinct, North Carolina.

48. Byrd's distrust of the Meherrin may be traced to skirmishes with Anglo-Virginians in the wake of Bacon's Rebellion, seemingly at odds with their alliance with the colonists during the rebellion itself. Still more troubling was the rumor of Meherrin support for the Tuscarora in the war of 1711, a rumor confirmed by the discovery of clothing in Meherrin possession taken from German Protestants killed in North Carolina. The Meherrin also continued to insist forcefully on their right to their land at Meherrin Neck. *Council,* III, 291, and see Shannon Lee Dawdy, "The Meherrin's Secret History of the Dividing Line," *North Carolina Historical Review,* LXXII (1995), 386–415.

49. That is to say, the surveyed border between counties did not follow natural or geographic features or landmarks.

50. *Chevaux de Frise:* defensive battle devices consisting of rows of large, pointed timbers fastened together in a row, used to stop cavalry charges.

51. *Carolus Anderson:* Carolus Anderson (ca. 1694–1753) had patented land in Virginia on the south side of the Meherrin River, but, after the Dividing Line passed, his lands were in North Carolina. Byrd comments that Anderson's given name is "learned"—it is the Latin form of "Charles"—but this was not an affectation but a family name. Ironically, Anderson himself was probably illiterate, for he signed his will with an *X. NCHGR,* I (1900), 165.

Mr. Kinchen: William Kinchen (d. 1736) owned land in Isle of Wight County, Virginia;

between 1702 and 1726 he took out patents for 510 acres. Kinchen was a vestryman at the church near Smithfield from 1724 to 1736 and served as justice of the peace in 1726 and sheriff in 1729. The line placed his house in North Carolina by a mile. The fact that he continued to participate in the political life of Virginia confirms the success of the Virginia Commissioners' negotiations to make variances when the line split properties. Kinchen also appears in a few North Carolina records, including a petition to relocate the seat of the government of Bertie Precinct, and his 1736 will identifies him as "William Kitching, of Perquimans." He was married to Elizabeth Ruffin, daughter of Robert Ruffin of Surry County. Boddie, *Seventeenth Century Isle of Wight County,* 230; *C&P,* III, 61, 320; Drysdale, "Present State of Virginia," *VMHB,* XLVIII (1940), 145; Cain, ed., *Records of the Executive Council, 1664–1734,* CRNC, VII, 299; *NCHGR,* I (1900), 56; *Boyd,* 111.

52. *Plat:* a surveyor's map or chart.

Prick't, pipp't: A "pricked" line is a dotted line. The chaplain substitutes the "maidenly" term "pip" (a spot such as markings on playing cards) in an awkward attempt to avoid the double entendre.

53. *Corker:* Probably an unidentified descendant of John Corker, who represented James City, Chickahominy, and Pasbehay in the House of Burgesses in 1632, 1633, 1645; he also served as clerk of the House. In 1657 John Corker patented 1,150 acres in Surry County on the south side of the James. William Corker (d. 1677) represented James City in the Assembly of 1657–1658. William G. Stanard and Mary Newton Stanard, *The Colonial Virginia Register: A List of Governors . . .* (1902; Baltimore, 1989), 57–58, 64, 73; *C&P,* III, 81, 374; Fleet, *Virginia Colonial Abstracts,* III, 40–41.

Capt. Gerald: Possibly Thomas Gerald, who was justice of peace in Isle of Wight County in 1729; des Cognets, ed., *English Duplicates of Lost Virginia Records,* 47. No militia officer of that name is listed in Bockstruck, *Virginia's Colonial Soldiers.*

Bolton's Ferry: A 1732 law regulating Virginia ferries stipulated the fares for crossing the Nottoway River "at Bolton's ferry, on the land of John Simmons, gentleman, the price for a man three pence, and for an horse three pence" (*Hening,* IV, 363). John Simmons (or Simons) had incurred the wrath of the Executive Council in 1714 by advising his neighbors, the Nottoway, to petition the House of Burgesses to reverse legislation requiring them to relocate (*Council,* III, 363–364, 367). Simmons also represented the Nottoway before the Council in 1739, when they petitioned to be allowed to sell the remainder of their reserved land (*Council,* IV, 345, 444).

Sally Parker: In the 1751 will of Richard Parker of Albemarle Parish, Surry County, Sarah is listed as his eldest daughter; she was named for her mother. Lyndon H. Hart III, *Surry County, Virginia, Wills, Estate Accounts, and Inventories, 1730–1800* (Easley, S.C., 1983), 48.

54. *Molly Izzard:* I have not been able to identify this woman or her immediate family. The first known member of the Izard family of Virginia, Richard Izard, settled in Isle of Wight County as early as 1655 (Boddie, *Seventeenth Century Isle of Wight County,* 523). In 1704, Francis Izard was listed in the New Kent County quitrent rolls as owning 1,233 acres (des Cognets, ed., *English Duplicates of Lost Virginia Records,* 166).

The Nottoway are an Iroquian nation, probably the people identified by Smith and Strachey as "Mangoags," an Algonquian term meaning "stealthy ones." They did not call themselves Nottoway; this was an Algonquian term meaning "snakes" or "enemies." Rather, they called themselves "Chiroenhaka." James Mooney, *The Siouan Tribes of the*

East, U.S., Bureau of American Ethnology, *Bulletin,* no. 22 (Washington, D.C., 1899), 7; Helen C. Rountree, "The Termination and Dispersal of the Nottoway Indians of Virginia," *VMHB,* XLV (1987), 193–214; Maurice A. Mook, "The Ethnological Significance of Tindall's Map of Virginia, 1608," *WMQ,* 2d Ser., XXIII (1943), 383.

The earliest records of contact are from Edwin Bland's expedition south of the James in 1650. In 1675, the Nottoway and the nearby Meherrin supported the Anglo-Virginians in Bacon's Rebellion. By signing the Treaty of Middle Plantation in 1677, they hoped to benefit from growing trade with the settlers at the same time that the alliance would provide protection from the customary raids of hostile nations. They became peaceful tributary Indian nations, and during the Tuscarora War the Nottoway again supported the Anglo-Virginian government. The war was concluded at a parley called by Spotswood at Nottoway Town, attended by the militia of three counties, a large contingent of tributary Indians, and delegations from eight of the Tuscarora towns. At this same meeting, the Nottoway were among the first to agree to place the children of their chiefs in the Indian school at Christanna. However, they resisted Spotswood's attempt to move them there, and in 1728 they were still living in their town in Isle of Wight County, where they absorbed some allied contiguous people displaced by Anglo-Virginian settlement.

55. *Queen of Weyanoke:* The Weyanoke were an Algonquian people allied with the Powhatan Confederacy and governed by a female chief, or "Queen." They signed the 1677 Treaty of the Middle Plantation to become tributary Indians. With the continued attacks of Iroquoian enemies (including the Nottoway), they sought protection among the English colonists. In 1710, during testimonials about the location of the place where the boundary should begin, some Weyanoke were living among the Nottoway.

56. *Jones:* There were many small planters in Surry County named Jones with whom Byrd might have taken chocolate. In 1704, James Jones was registered in the Surry County quitrent rolls as owner of 100 acres. Robert Jones was granted 120 acres in Surry County on November 13, 1713. On the same day, John Jones received 330 acres, and Henry Jones 250 acres. On June 16, 1714, Jno. Jones was granted 170 acres, and William Jones 280 acres. On March 23, 1715, Thomas Jones was granted 370 acres. Des Cognets, ed., *English Duplicates of Lost Virginia Records,* 95, 96, 100, 104, 212.

Henry Harrison: Henry Harrison, prominent planter in Surry County, was appointed sheriff in 1712, justice of the peace in 1726, burgess in 1715, 1718, 1720–1722, 1723–1726, and member of the Executive Council in 1731. Harrison, his brother Nathaniel, and several others took up twenty thousand acres in Henrico, Surry, and Prince George Counties between 1719 and 1721. McIlwaine, ed., *Journals of the House of Burgesses, 1712–1714 . . . ,* viii–xi, *1727–1734, 1736–1740,* viii–xi; *Council,* III, 394, 515, 526, 548, IV, 234.

57. *Boller Cocke:* Bowler Cocke (1696–1771), Byrd's neighbor at Bremo, was clerk of Henrico County, 1728–1752, vestryman for Henrico Parish, 1730–1743, and militia officer.

58. *Prince George Court:* the seat of Prince George County, about five miles south of the James River and four miles east of Petersburg.

59. Here and in the preceding paragraph Byrd neglected to revise the earlier mode of first person narrative to the third, leaving "I" in the place where usually he would have written "Steddy."

60. *Upon the Irish:* figuratively, in the supposedly hyperbolic and mendacious manner of the Irish, especially in using contradictory statements, as in Irish bulls.

61. *Mr. Banister:* William Byrd I became the guardian of John Banister, Jr., at the death of his father the naturalist in 1692. The younger Banister became collector of Customs for the Upper James and served as Byrd's business manager.

62. Fitzwilliam's claim to rank, Byrd insinuates, amounts to no more than being born a Fitzwilliam of Ireland, not in itself very significant. Nor is his office especially worthy, for he is, not a legislator, but a mere "Publican," that is, a "tax-gatherer" or "collector of toll, tribute, customs, or the like" *(OED)*. Unlike other colonial officers whose appointment was presented for the king's approval by the Privy Council, Fitzwilliam was named to his position by the Customs Office. All in all, Byrd is concerned to emphasize that Fitzwilliam attempted to portray himself in a light considerably above his station.

63. The minutes of the Executive Council meetings on August 15 and 16, 1728, include no roll call (not the usual practice). The full Council met on August 22.

64. *Kings of Brentford:* Byrd alludes to characters in Buckingham's farce, *The Rehearsal,* whose actions are identical and absurd: for instance, all of them come on stage together, smelling the same nosegay. [George Villiers, duke of Buckingham], *The Rehearsal, as It Was Acted at the Theatre Royal* (London, 1672).

65. As noted above, both Edmund Gale and Thomas Lovick held posts as collectors of Customs and as such were technically under Fitzgerald's supervision.

66. *Ravenscroft's Landing:* Thomas Ravenscroft (1688–1736), in 1722 sheriff of James City County, in 1723 purchased the Maycox plantation across the James River from West-over. Though his plantation was closer to Petersburg than the river, he maintained a landing for transportation and commerce. He was burgess for Prince George County from 1727 until his death. In 1736 Byrd recommended Ravencroft's son John to his fellow Templar, Chief Justice Benjamin Lynde of Massachusetts (*Correspondence*, II, 473–474; *Boyd*, 141).

Bristol Parish, in the vicinity of Petersburg, maintained a church at Bermuda Hundred and a chapel at City Point, near the Falls, called the "Ferry Chapel." Additionally, there were chapels at Saponi and Namoisen Creeks, expanded in 1729. In 1723 the parish contracted Thomas Jefferson, Sr., to build a new church near Chesterfield, which is no doubt the rendezvous. William Meade, *Old Churches, Ministers, and Families of Virginia* (Philadelphia, 1900), I, 439–440.

67. *Tiring Room:* a dressing room, and not "Fireing Room," as previous editors have transcribed. Heating is not required in a cold springhouse.

Byrd himself once bathed in cold water regularly, writing in 1706 to recommend the practice to Sir Hans Sloane, but two years later wrote that he had discontinued it after "a violent diarraea" brought on by cold bathing. Byrd to Sloane, Apr. 20, 1706, Sept. 10, 1708, *Correspondence*, I, 260, 269.

68. Byrd and his companions followed the Courthouse Road south and west, crossing the Blackwater River below the town of Isle of Wight, then crossing a branch of the Assamoosick Swamp to the Parker plantation.

Scots Mist: A heavy mist of a thickness proverbially native to Scotland. A Scottish proverb says, "A Scots Mist will weet an Englishman to the Skin." Alan Ramsay, *A Collection of Scots Proverbs* (Edinburgh, 1737), 7.

69. Philip Ludwell, Jr. (d. 1728), son of Philip Ludwell (ca. 1638–ca. 1723), who had served as governor of South Carolina and North Carolina and as member and speaker

of the Virginia House of Burgesses. Ludwell, Jr., was a member of the Virginia Executive Council and a colonel of the militia; he married Hannah Harrison, daughter of Benjamin Harrison. He was Byrd's ally in Williamsburg.

70. *Capt. Hix:* Robert Hix (or Hicks) of Surry County, one of the principal Indian traders licensed by Spotswood in 1712. In 1709 Hix had patented 1,280 acres on the north side of the Meherrin River and set up a trading post halfway between Fort Henry and the Tuscarora towns and near Meherrin Town. He helped survey the site for the fort and school at Christanna in 1716, assisted Spotswood in the 1722 treaty with the northern Indians at Albany, and negotiated with the Catawba in 1730 and the Saponi in 1733.

Capt. Drury Stith: Drury Stith was a justice of Charles City County Court, sheriff of the county from 1718, and surveyor from 1720. In 1728 he was designated alternate surveyor in the Dividing Line expedition should Alexander Irvine decline the position. Stith relocated to Brunswick County, where he became justice of the peace, lieutenant colonel, and then major of horse in the Brunswick County Militia. He also surveyed the boundaries between Brunswick and Prince George, Surry, and Isle of Wight Counties. *Council*, III, 470, 500, IV, 66, 86, 167; McIlwaine, ed., *Journals of the House of Burgesses, 1712–1714 . . .* , 135, *1727–1734, 1736–1740,* 225; Drysdale, "Present State of Virginia," *VMHB,* XLVIII (1940), 149.

71. Almost certainly a conscious echo of Henry Fielding's *Jonathan Wild:* "He in a few Minutes ravished this fair Creature, or at least would have ravished her, if she had not, by a timely Compliance, prevented him." *The Life of Mr. Jonathan Wild the Great,* in *Miscellanies* (London, 1743), III, 230 (*Hayes* 1879, A24). It is interesting to note that Fielding's character is named "Fireblood," though this resonance may be coincidental.

72. On the gendered, aggressive (or defensive) use of the contents of chamberpots, see *Commonplace Book,* §351 and §389, 159, 164–165.

73. *John Hill:* I have not been able to identify which of the many John Hills in Virginia to whom Byrd refers.

74. *Been Piqued:* that is, not *being* piqued.

Sent for the silver bowl: A proverbial reference to hospitable drinking and the tradition of drinking toasts, common in early modern English neoclassical verse, originating with Anacreon's Odes 17 and 18, "On a Silver Bowl." Byrd owned editions of Anacreon in Greek and in French translation (*Hayes* 1683, 1449).

75. *Fresh-colored:* blooming, looking healthy or youthful; brisk, vigorous, active *(OED)*.

76. *At Rack & Manger:* wasteful or improvident use of abundant supplies; lack of proper management; waste and destruction *(OED)*.

77. *Fountain's Creek:* Named for John Fontain or Fountain, a free black Indian trader active in the early eighteenth century, and now known as Fountaine Creek, located in Sussex County, Virginia, between Emporia and the North Carolina border. The date of Fountain's death is unclear; a Jno. Fountain (together with Peter Winn) was granted 175 acres in Prince George County, July 15, 1717. Des Cognets, ed., *English Duplicates of Lost Virginia Records,* 110.

It is not clear whom Byrd meant by "Captain Stiff," but the lass's retort is consistent with Byrd's persistent pattern of sexual innuendo in his ridicule of Irvin.

Byrd insisted that Virginia's "Indian Physick" *(Gillenia stipulata* or *Porteranthus tri-*

foliatus) was "the true Ipocoacanna," identical with the Brazilian shrub ipecacuanha *(Cephaelis ipecacuanha),* used in European medicine after colonists and Jesuits brought it back to France in the seventeenth century. Indian physick came to be called "American Ipecacuanha." In the *Philosophical Transactions,* one Dr. Douglass acknowledged four kinds of "the true *Ipecacuanha,*" all of which originated in South America. He also identified two "false Kinds" brought "from *Maryland* in 1725, by one M. *Seymour* a Surgeon, who informed me that they grow there in great Plenty, being called *Ipecacuanha* by the Inhabitants, and used as a Vomit by those of inferior Rank." Sir Hans Sloane informed Douglass that the "false Brown Kind was the same that was formerly sent to him from *Virginia* for the true *Ipecacuanha,* and which he afterwards discovered to be the Root of a poisonous Apocynum described by him in his *Natural History of Jamaica.*" Significantly, it was Byrd himself who sent these samples of "hippocoacanna" to Sloane. *Philosophical Transactions,* XXXVI (1729–1730), 152, 157; Byrd to Sloane, Sept. 10, 1708, *Correspondence,* I, 266–267.

Many Virginia plants were identified as useful in treating snakebite. In 1687, the Reverend John Clayton wrote skeptically of the great number of plants credited with the virtue of curing snake bites:

> I have had 40 several Sorts, or near that Number, shewed me as great Secrets, for the *Rattle-snake-root,* or that kind of *Snake-root* which is good for curing the Bite of the *Rattle-snake:* But I have no Reason to believe, that any of them are able to effect the Cure.
> —"A Letter from the Revd. Mr. John Clayton . . . to Dr. Grew," *Philosophical Transactions,* XLI (1739–1741), 153

Compare the somewhat briefer list provided by Thomas Amy:

> They have three sorts of the *Rattle-Snake Root* which I have seen; the *Comous* or *Hairy,* the *Smooth,* the *Nodous,* or *Knotted* Root: All which are lactiferous, or yielding a *Milkie Juice;* and if I do not very much in my Observations err, the Leaves of all these Roots of a Heart had the exact Resemblance: They are all Sovereign against the Mortal Bites of that Snake, too frequent in the *West Indies:* In all *Pestilential Distempers,* as *Plague, Small Pox,* and *Malignant Fevers,* it's a Noble *Specifick;* when stung, they eat the Root, applying it to the Venemous Wound; or they boyl the Roots in Water; which drunk, fortifies and corroborates the Heart, exciteing strong and generous Sweats; by which endangered Nature is relieved, and the Poyson carried off, and expelled.
> —*Carolina; or, A Description of the Present State of That Country, and the Natural Excellencies Thereof* (London, 1682), 11–12

78. *Epaphroditus Bainton:* Epaphroditus Benton, of Nansemond County, Virginia (where he patented land as early as 1682), and Chowan Precinct, North Carolina (where he proved headrights for land in 1716). In 1700 he kept a ferry over the Chowan River at Cow Landing. *C&P,* III, 25, 41, 334; *NCHGR,* I (1700), 150; Hofmann, *Chowan Precinct, North Carolina, 1696 to 1723,* 223.

Majr. Mumford: Robert Mumford, planter with extensive land holdings in several counties, militia officer and burgess (1720–1722) for Prince George County, vestryman of Bruton Parish, former associate of Byrd's, and supplier of men and provisions for the expedition.

Miles Riley: The overseer of one of Robert Mumford's plantations, probably a descendant of the Miles Riley who immigrated from Ireland to Virginia in 1663, or possibly of the Miles Riley transported to Virginia in the *Bonaventure* in 1634.

Young Mumford: Robert Mumford, Jr., who in September 1728 patented land on the Roanoke River above Occaneechee Islands in Brunswick County and in 1731 on Buckskin Creek in Prince George County.

Mr. Walker: David Walker, who patented land adjoining that of Robert Mumford, Jr., both on the Roanoke and on Buckskin Creek.

Natt: The difficulty of identifying Natt, another of Mumford's overseers, is exacerbated by the fact that the name is both a first name (often short for Nathaniel, and often found in colonial records as a single name for an enslaved African or for an Indian) and a surname (Natt or Nott). The Natt family was established in Virginia as early as 1625, when a list of titles and landowners in Virginia itemized a patent for two hundred acres near Mulberry Island by Nathaniel Natt. "The Randolph Manuscript: Virginia Seventeenth Century Records," *VMHB,* XVI (1908), 13.

79. *John Young:* possibly John Young of Prince George County. The 1704 quitrent rolls show that he held two hundred acres. Des Cognets, ed., *English Duplicates of Lost Virginia Records,* 222.

Charles Kimball: Byrd neglects to mention that Kimball had in fact served as official interpreter to the Saponi for at least sixteen years.

80. *Poison'd fields:* land where large trees were destroyed by fire or insects, where nothing but saplings will grow. Fires might have been caused by lightning or set by Indians to clear undergrowth for improving hunting range or for driving game. Stephen Conrad Ausband speculates the damage could also have been caused by caterpillars. *Byrd's Line: A Natural History* (Charlottesville, Va., 2008), 80.

81. *Mossamony Creek:* a tributary of the Roanoke, now known as Island Creek.

Yapatsco, or Beaver Creek, was so called because of a large beaver dam. Byrd translates the name *Ohimpamony Creek* in *The History of the Dividing Line,* not as "Fishing Creek," but "Jumping Creek from the frequent Jumping of Fish during the Spring Season." He identifies the word as "Saponi" rather than the generic "Indian." The stream is now known as "Grassy Creek." For the Siouan linguistic background of the Saponi names given here, see Mooney, *The Siouan Tribes of the East,* 46.

The Hebrews of the Old Testament were considered stubborn and discontented, so much so that they grumbled when God nourished them in the desert with manna. The allusively biblical comment implies there was sufficient food to make reasonable travelers content.

82. *Tewahominy or Tuscaruda Creek:* The former appears to be a Saponi word for *Tuscarora,* and the second is an alternate spelling sometimes found in colonial documents (Mooney, *The Siouan Tribes of the East,* 46). The stream is now known as *Aaron's Creek.*

83. *Blewing Creek:* Blue Wing Creek, a tributary of the Hicotomony—then sometimes called a creek (now known as the Hyco River) named after the blue-winged teal.

Sugar-Tree Creek: another tributary of the Hyco. In 1742 Byrd purchased 105,000 acres for £525 on both sides of the Dan River and its branches, including the "Hiconomy" and Sugar Tree Creek. Rebecca Johnston, "William Byrd Title Book," *VMHB,* L, (1942), 177–178.

84. Bearskin was in fact right: the Hyco runs into the Dan River, which in turn runs into the Roanoke River.

85. Fitzwilliam's name had been omitted in the king's instructions to the governor, as noted in Council on October 13, 1728. However, in 1725 Fitzwilliam, then surveyor general of Customs for "South America," produced a letter from the Lords Justices in Council "directing his being sworn and admitted one of his Ma[jesty's] Council in Virginia, South Carolina and Jamaica," and he was sworn in on December 15, 1725 (*Council,* IV, 93–94; the order is recorded in *CSP,* XXXIV, no. 702). Governor Gooch noted this fact in 1728 and declared that he "did not think it proper to remove him from the other untill his Majesty's pleasure be known therein." The Council concurred with his ruling—and Byrd was present at this meeting (*Council,* IV, 90). Thus, Byrd's suggestion that Fitzwilliam left the expedition in order to confirm his status in the Council in their absence is inaccurate, if not disingenuous.

86. *Best Man:* Probably John Holmes, to whom the narrative refers later, but whose name is not present in the lists of the Virginia men on the expedition.

87. The placement of this anecdote in the narrative is confusing, for by this date all the Carolina men (except Holmes, hired to replace the man attending Fitzwilliam) had departed, and Bearskin ("our Indian") was the only Saponi still with the party.

88. *Hungry as hawks:* See John Ray, *A Compleat Collection of English Proverbs,* 3d ed. (London, 1737), 219.

89. *Dan River:* apparently named after the river in the Holy Land, a tributary of the Jordan.

Stanton River: The Staunton River is actually not a separate river, but a section of the Roanoke River renamed, extending from its emergence from the Blue Ridge to the mouth of the Dan River. Though popular legend has it that the river was named after a Captain Henry Stanton (or Staunton) (details of whose identity are unclear), it is more likely that the river was given its name to honor Lady Rebecca Staunton, the wife of Governor Gooch. Members of the Staunton family who settled in this area appear to have arrived some time after the expedition. Byrd's phrasing—"We call'd," "I had call'd"—implies that the names date from the expedition. Although other rivers and streams were named by the Dividing Line party, I have not been able to confirm that 1728 was the earliest date for the names *Dan* and *Stanton.*

90. *Cormorant:* a "large and voracious sea-bird," and figuratively an "insatiably greedy or rapacious person" *(OED).*

91. *Louring:* frowning or scowling; figuratively of weather, "gloomy, dark, threatening" *(OED).*

92. *Chaplain:* Fontaine received his B.A. in 1715 at Trinity College, Dublin; shortly afterward he was licensed as a minister to Virginia. Byrd is apparently making a mild joke at Fontaine's expense, having to do with the penurious life of a student, or perhaps an implicit slur on Trinity College, or even a reference to common experience, since both Fontaine and Byrd had studied law.

Charity is *not* one of the Three Graces, who in classical mythology were the daughters of Zeus and the nymph Eurynome, deities of radiance, joy, and fertility. He has conflated the Graces with the three cardinal virtues (faith, hope, and charity) proclaimed by Paul in 1 Cor. 13:13.

93. Mount Pleasant, a peak (elevation 4,071 feet) east of the main range of the Blue Ridge, is still known for the view from its heights. Note that Byrd refers to the view or prospect even though the expedition did not reach that point. He might have heard of the view or seen it himself at a later date.

94. *Toss't in a Blanket:* a spontaneous mode of punishment in which an offender is thrown up and caught, repeatedly and roughly, by four men holding the corners of a blanket.

95. By the time of the expedition the Sauro had abandoned the region.

96. *Caskade Creek,* a tributary of the Dan, still bears the name Byrd and his company gave it.

A Pimple: probably one of the hills now known as Mountain Hill, near the Dan River; see Ausband, *Byrd's Line,* 101.

97. *Irvin River:* a tributary of the Dan River, named in 1728 after the Virginia surveyor Alexander Irvin, but now known as Smith River.

Griskin: the lean portion of a pork or beef loin (or, in this case, of bear).

98. *Matrimony Creek:* a tributary of the Dan River, still retaining the name given it by Byrd.

The Wart: Ausband has identified this peak as the one now known as Chestnut Knob; see Ausband, *Byrd's Line,* 99.

99. Byrd's allusion to Dandridge's use of the needle at sea suggests a late date for the inclusion of this passage. At the time of the expedition, Dandridge was a merchant, planter, and shipowner. In the late 1730s he was commissioned in the Royal Navy, commanding several vessels and serving in important naval engagements.

100. *Bogued:* bogged, sunk or tangled in a bog or quagmire. *Soupe de Jambon:* ham soup. *The Wart:* Byrd here repeats the entry from the nineteenth.

101. *Mayo River:* Named for Virginia surveyor William Mayo, this tributary of the Dan River is one of several rivers named during the expedition. *Half-Jacks:* Jackboots are strong cavalry boots reaching above the knee; thus, a half-jackboot extends partway to the knee.

102. A curious tenet of early modern folk zoology was that bears do not have a breastbone, thereby imperiling their internal organs. The momentum of a downhill run could force their lights (lungs) to rise in their throats. See *History of the Dividing Line,* note 278.

103. An ironic reference to Matt. 6.14: "Take therefore no thought for the morrow: for the morrow shall take thought for the things of itself. Sufficient unto the day is the evil thereof."

104. *North Branch of Cape Fear:* Boyd identifies the stream as Peter's Creek, on the border of Stokes County, North Carolina (*Boyd,* 234).

105. *The Gout in form:* Dandridge's gout had now developed fully "in form," that is, according to the recognized mode of the affliction.

106. *Hudibras:* Byrd may be exaggerating when he describes the chaplain's reluctance to hear anything of *Hudibras,* Samuel Butler's satire of the English Civil War and Interregnum, unless Fontaine was uncomfortable with satire directed against differences among Protestants as a noxious form of contempt for the clergy.

Anderson's Pills: a proprietary laxative, first sold in England in the 1630s. The pills were available in the colonies, advertised in the *Virginia Gazette* as early as May 27, 1737, continuing right up into the 1780s.

107. *Balaam's Ass:* When the soothsayer Balaam beat his ass unjustly, the beast spoke reproachfully to him (Num. 22:21–41).

108. *Herod:* Byrd here refers to Josephus, *Antiquities of the Jews* 15.11 (*Hayes* 8, 153, 1227, 1610, 1742, 1826).

109. *Colo. Beverley:* As it turned out, William Beverley (ca. 1698–1756) was not dead.

110. *Hix's Creek:* now known as Hicks Creek.

111. *Cocquade Creek:* a tributary of the Dan River.

The Order of Ma-osty: a fanciful order, the emblem of which was a turkey comb, and the motto a reference to the quails provided the Hebrews on their exodus.

112. *Cornelius Keith:* Though professing to be a stranger to Keith, Byrd had in fact been acquainted with him. In 1721, Byrd, together with Keith, James Terry, and Jno. Kembro, had jointly patented a large tract of land in New Kent County. *Council,* IV, 5.

113. Indian traders transported deerskins in packs of fifty, three to a horse. W. Stitt Robinson, *The Southern Colonial Frontier, 1607–1763* (Albuquerque, N.Mex., 1979), 86.

114. *Gossip:* "one who has contracted spiritual affinity with another by acting as a sponsor at a baptism. . . . A godfather or godmother" *(OED).*

Cornelius Cargill: Cornelius Cargill, a colorful "rogue and opportunist," at the time of the expedition owned land adjoining Robert Mumford at Beaverpond Creek, on the north side of the Roanoke. During his life he accumulated more than three thousand acres of land, mostly in Brunswick County. He was married six times, often to widows. Some time after the death of his second wife, Mary, Cargill took up with Elizabeth Daniel, listed in some deeds as his wife. That no record of this marriage has been found has led family historian Patty Barthell Myers to speculate she might have been a common-law wife. Their relationship might have started as early as 1720, and she "was still a femme sole in 1731, although by that time she was the mother of several children by Cornelius Cargill." Patty Barthell Myers, *Cargill/Cargile/Cargal of the South and Southwest . . .* (San Antonio, Tex., 1997), 19–47.

Shrub: a drink made with rum, lemon juice, orange juice, and sugar.

Bombo (also bumbo): a drink made with rum (or other liquor), sugar, water, and nutmeg.

115. *George Hix:* George Hix, son of the Indian trader Captain Robert Hix, owned land at Poplar Creek, on the north side of the Roanoke in Brunswick County.

116. *My heir apparent:* William Byrd III (1728–1777) had just been born on September 6, less than a fortnight before his father left Westover for the second part of the expedition.

117. *Capt. Embry:* officer of the Surry County militia, later sheriff and burgess, who in 1728 conducted a police action against the Saponi. McIlwaine, ed., *Journals of the House of Burgesses, 1727–1734, 1736–1740,* 64; Lyon Gardiner Tyler, ed., *Encyclopedia of Virginia Biography* (New York, 1915), I, 229; Bockstruck, *Virginia's Colonial Soldiers,* 8; *VMHB,* XXIX (1921), 507–508.

118. *Colo. Bolling:* Robert Bolling, who was appointed surveyor of Charles City County in 1726, and not Colonel John Bolling (1700–1757), as Boyd would have it. Drysdale, "Present State of Virginia," *VMHB,* XLVIII (1940), 143; *Boyd,* 311

119. *Sapony Chapel:* built by Bristol Parish ca. 1728.

James Hudson: a planter in Bristol Parish, Prince George County. His land was about twenty miles south of Petersburg, on Hatches Run, which flows into Monk's Neck Creek, which in turn empties into the Nottoway River about fifty miles above where it joins the Blackwater. Churchill Gibson Chamberlayne, ed., *Vestry Book and Register of Bristol Parish, Virginia, 1720–1789* (Richmond, Va., 1898), 312–316; *Council,* IV, 302, 328.

120. *Mr. Mumfords pretty Wife:* Anne Munford. She appears to have been frequently ill; in his diary entry for October 15, 1711, Byrd mentioned hearing from his men from Appomattox that she was very sick again. *SD,* 421.

121. *Coggins Point:* A point across the James from Westover, one of the two spots for the ferry across the James from Westover.

Appendix 1 *Dramatis Personae*

THE VIRGINIA COMMISSIONERS

On November 2, 1727, Governor William Gooch appointed Byrd, Dandridge, and Fitzwilliam commissioners to supervise the expedition. All three were members of the Executive Council and were men of considerable status.[1]

William Byrd (Steddy)

For Byrd's background, see Introduction. Though it is not always easy to distinguish between fact and flattering self-presentation in the Dividing Line histories, Byrd was the senior commissioner, responsible for assembling the personnel and supplies needed for the expedition, supervision along the way, and disbursing payment after the expedition concluded. Whether Byrd in fact delivered motivational speeches to the assembled men, as represented in his narratives, cannot be determined. However, his letters to Governor Gooch and his role in reporting to the Board of Trade and submitting an account of the expedition's costs clearly establish his leadership, though Fitzwilliam disputed Byrd's precedence.

William Dandridge (Meanwell)

William Dandridge (1689–1743) was a wealthy merchant and shipowner with a wharf and trade at Hampton. He moved to King William County upon his marriage in 1719 to Unity West, daughter of prominent planter Colonel Nathaniel West. There he was appointed justice of the peace and invested in land in several counties. Dandridge had been a member of the Council for less than a year when he was named to the Dividing Line Commission. Byrd found him a man of integrity, both reasonable and cooperative; hence the name "Meanwell" by which he is known in *The Secret History*.

Later on he became better known as a naval officer. After serving as lieutenant on a navy ship, he went to London seeking promotion, bearing letters of introduction including a commendation as an "honest gentleman" by Commissary James Blair. This mission was successful, for he soon was given the command of the Royal Navy ship *Wolf* at the Virginia Station, and then in 1741 as captain of the *South Sea* he participated in James Oglethorpe's attack on the Spanish port of Saint Augustine and Admiral Edward Vernon's siege of Cartagena.[2]

Richard Fitzwilliam (Firebrand)

Byrd portrays Fitzwilliam as a monster of bad temper, greed, love of power, obstructionism, sneering, bad language, outright violence, and a deep and insatiable vanity. Byrd no

---

1. *Council*, IV, 155–156.

2. Blair to the bishop of London, Aug. 11, 1734, in Herbert L. Ganter, "Documents Relating to the Early History of the College of William and Mary and to the History of the Church in Virginia," *WMQ*, 2d Ser., XX (1940), 120; Wilson Miles Cary, "The Dandridges of Virginia," *WMQ*, 1st Ser., V (1896), 30–39; *Council*, III, 439, 516, 528, esp. IV, 122, 124.

doubt exaggerated, but Fitzwilliam's public life in the decade of the Dividing Line expedition provides some corroboration. In 1718, Fitzwilliam appeared in court as Customs collector of the Lower District of the James River, disputing the right of the district naval officer to seize a ship for illegal trading with Jamaica. He contended that only Customs had the right to seize ships violating the Trade Act, though the naval officers, who supervised ports and cargos, were empowered by the act of Parliament establishing the service to seize illicit cargos. The issue was the one-third share granted to the arresting officer. The Council ruled against Fitzwilliam and repudiated instructions to the same effect from the Commissioners of Customs.[3]

In 1725, Fitzwilliam was named surveyor general of Customs for South America (the mid-Atlantic and Caribbean). Serving under the authority of the Lords of the Treasury, the surveyor general supervised collectors who took in duties on tobacco and other goods at every colonial port, examined their accounts, and issued instructions. Customs reports bypassed colonial governors and legislatures, going directly to the Treasury, the Customs House, and the Board of Trade. Soon after his appointment Fitzwilliam petitioned for admission to the Executive Councils of Virginia, Carolina, and Jamaica, "the better to enable him to recover some debts due to the Crown and doe the duty of his Office." The petition was approved and referred to the Board of Trade, and on August 5, 1725, it appointed Fitzwilliam to all three councils. On December 15, 1725, he was sworn and admitted a member of the Virginia Council. Fitzwilliam's commitment to Virginia was marginal, and his commission made it clear that his primary loyalty was to the Customs House and not the colonies, all of which could have increased Byrd's resentment. In practice Fitzwilliam's attendance at meetings of the Council was sporadic. Moreover, his duties took him to other colonies, where he likewise claimed a place in the upper legislative body. In 1727, for instance, he was admitted to North Carolina's Council and even served briefly as judge of the Court of Chancery, without question drawing a stipend for the session.[4]

Though Byrd makes Fireblood's venality a special issue in *The Secret History,* the pursuit of remunerative public services was characteristic of the patrician elite at large. Still, Byrd censures Fitzwilliam's attempt "to be paid as bountifully for being out 4 Weeks, as we for being 10, out upon the Publick Service." On April 29, 1730, Governor Gooch read the royal warrant authorizing him to apportion payment for "the charges of running and Settling the Boundaries between this Colony and North Carolina" as he saw fit. He divided the commissioners' salaries "according to the time of their attendance on that Service." Fitzwilliam protested, requesting permission to explain "why he left the other Commissioners before they had finished the line by them run." The Council ruled his re-

---

3. On the roles of district collector and naval officer, see Percy Scott Flippin, *The Financial Administration of the Colony of Virginia,* Johns Hopkins University Studies in Historical and Political Science, XXXIII, no. 2 (Baltimore, 1915), 28–32; May 1, 1718, *Council,* III, 467–468, Nov. 21, 1719, 490–491, 492.

4. Flippin, *Financial Administration of the Colony of Virginia,* 23–27, 34–57; *Council,* IV, 93–94; *CSP,* XXXIV, 405, no. 691; Robert J. Cain, ed., *Records of the Executive Council, 1664–1734,* CRNC, VII (Raleigh, N.C., 1984), 169; Cain, ed., *North Carolina Higher-Court Minutes, 1724–1730,* CRNC, VI (Raleigh, N.C., 1981), 661.

quest out of order, since the king had already approved their proceedings. Fitzwilliam left shortly thereafter, missed the next two meetings on May 6 and 29, returning only twice, on June 11 and 17, 1730. Here he provoked another major controversy, protesting a resolution of the Burgesses that their wages should be paid in money, rather than in tobacco, with funds from taxes on imported liquor. Fitzwilliam commented in Council that having their payroll approved by the Council would make the Burgesses "subservient to the wishes of the Council in other matters than independent legislators should be." He further accused the Burgesses of avarice, arguing it would be unfair to burden West Indies traders "with so heavy a Duty on their Liquors with a view only to have the greatest share of it distributed among the Burgesses." A committee of Burgesses concluded Fitzwilliam's charges were false, scandalous, malicious, and designed to "bring the House into disgrace" with the king. The House adopted this much of the committee's report but fell short of sending a formal complaint to the King in Council by a tie vote of twenty-eight to twenty-eight, broken by the speaker's vote. Governor Gooch reported to the Board of Trade that the Burgesses considered Fitzwilliam "a person of a turbulent Spirit unfit for Society," and he added that for the sake of peace he had interposed to convince them not to petition the king for Fitzwilliam's removal. Though the Burgesses did not send their petition, the Board of Trade naturally learned of the crisis through the governor's letter and the proceedings of the House, which were routinely submitted to them.[5]

Fitzwilliam then left Virginia, a departure so welcome that his name seems to have disappeared from all Virginia and North Carolina records except for transfers of his Virginia property. He was replaced as surveyor general of Customs in December 1731. Some Virginia historians have concluded that he had returned to England, where he either died or retired into obscurity, but this was not the case. He resurfaced in London as an expert in colonial commerce, his proposals to the Board of Trade supported by the Customs House. Perhaps the Customs House considered his attention to increasing revenue more important than rumors of clashes with colonial authorities. Particularly noteworthy was his report of June 30, 1729, on the Bahamas, which offered a very optimistic view of the islands' potential for development of natural resources. Probably this letter was instrumental in securing Fitzwilliam an appointment as governor of the Bahamas in early January 1733. However, it should come as no surprise that his term as governor was marked by discord, power struggles, and litigation.[6]

5. H. R. McIlwaine, ed., *Journals of the House of Burgesses of Virginia, 1727–1734, 1736–1740* (Richmond, Va., 1910), xxi–xxii. Curiously, *The Executive Journals of the Council of Colonial Virginia* do not record Fitzwilliam's inflammatory comments. Gooch's letter is given in full in *CSP,* XXXVII, 201–220, esp. 210, no. 348.

6. On December 10, 1731 the Board of Trade petitioned the king that the new surveyor general, Mr. Phenney, be added to the executive councils of the colonies in his district "in the room of Mr. Fitzwilliam, the late Surveyor Genl. of the Customs in the Southern District of America." *CSP,* XXXVIII, 368, no. 543. On October 3, 1729, the Board of Trade considered Fitzwilliams's report, forwarded by the Customs House: CO 23, 2. ff. 249, 250–251, 252.

The Chaplain (the Reverend Dr. Humdrum)

Though not a commissioner, another important member of the Virginia party was the Reverend Peter Fontaine (1691–ca. 1757), who came along at Byrd's invitation to serve as chaplain to the expedition. One of the sons of a Huguenot minister who emigrated to Ireland, Fontaine had been educated at Trinity College, Dublin, and ordained by the bishop of London in 1715, arriving in Virginia in 1716. He had an especially close relationship with Byrd and served as a minister in Westover Parish for nearly forty years. In the 1720s, the parish stretched over thirty square miles, populated by 233 families. Unlike his brother John Fontaine, who in 1724 became rector of Yorkhampton Parish (a position he left to become professor of oriental languages at the College of William and Mary), Peter Fontaine was not granted a permanent living (as rector), but performed divine service thrice weekly at Westover, Weyanoke, or Wallingford Church for an annual salary in the 1720s of sixteen thousand pounds of tobacco (valued around £80). Later in life, Fontaine retired to Lunenburg County, where he patented twenty-four hundred acres on Wynne's Creek and Polecat Creek.[7]

THE NORTH CAROLINA COMMISSIONERS

Like their Virginia counterparts, the North Carolina Commissioners all held positions of power in the government of their colony and were all members of the Executive Council. In status and authority within their province, they were at the very least on equal terms with the Virginia Commissioners, and, despite Byrd's bias, they came from a patrician elite comparable to that of Virginia. They considered their status proportional to their merit and sought and employed the power that came with rank and all the attendant advantages.

Christopher Gale (Judge Jumble)

The senior member of the North Carolina party was Chief Justice Christopher Gale (ca. 1679–1735). The extent of his legal training is unclear; it seems probable that he studied with a provincial lawyer, clerking for "a country attorney at Lancaster." In 1703 Gale was commissioned as one of the justices of the General Court (the highest court of the colony), and in 1704 he became attorney general. In 1712 he joined the Executive Council, but, lacking any talent or skill for the politic art of deference, for thirty-five years he was caught up in "conflicts and struggles of increasing intensity and bitterness with nearly every governor of North Carolina." He acquired much wealth, first through marrying the daughter of Governor Thomas Harvey shortly after his arrival in 1702, and then through trade, government benefits, and land speculation.[8]

7. George MacLaren Brydon, *Virginia's Mother Church and the Political Conditions under Which It Grew* (Richmond, Va., Philadelphia, 1947–1952), I, 370–372; Sept. 6, 1748, *Council,* V, 341.

8. Charles Knowles Bolton, *The Founders: Portraits of Persons Born Abroad Who Came to the Colonies in North America before the Year 1701* (Boston, 1919–1926), I, 29; *DNCB,* II, 260.

John Lovick (Shoebrush)

Born in England, John Lovick (ca. 1691–1733) came to North Carolina in 1713 with Governor Edward Hyde. There is no evidence to support Byrd's *Secret History* assertion that Lovick had been Hyde's valet (hence the name "Shoebrush"). Lovick might have served Hyde in some capacity, perhaps as a secretary or manager. During his career Lovick was secretary to the colony, member of the Executive Council, delegate to the Assembly, chief justice, and surveyor general. He was mired in controversy when Governor Charles Eden left him his entire estate at the expense of Eden's stepchildren, but not long afterward he married Eden's widow, Penelope, and ensuing appeals by the stepchildren were dismissed. Like Gale, Lovick clashed with North Carolina's governors.

William Little (Puzzlecause)

William Little (1691–1734) first appeared in North Carolina in 1720. He served as attorney general for a brief period under Governor George Burrington but resigned after only eight months, "probably because he assisted Christopher Gale in efforts to remove Burrington from office." He was returned to the position by Governor Richard Everard in 1725 and was named receiver general in 1726, the year that he married Gale's daughter Penelope. Little was continually embroiled in controversy. As receiver general, he oversaw the issuance of blank patents "by which hundreds of thousands of acres of land were illegally engrossed." The North Carolina Assembly accused him "of instituting suits to harass individuals and then accepting bribes to dismiss the actions." Little's reputation for sharp, illegal practices continued to grow after 1728.[9]

Edward Moseley (Plausible)

Born in London, Edward Moseley (ca. 1682–1749) was trained as a navigator and surveyor at the London charity school Christ's Hospital. He served as apprentice in 1697 aboard the *Joseph* in the Spanish trade. After some time at sea, he arrived in Albemarle in 1704, and in 1705 he married Ann Lillington Walker, widow of the late governor, Henderson Walker. Moseley's rise was remarkably quick; he was appointed justice of the peace, vestryman, and member of the Executive Council, all in the year of his marriage. He was elected to the Assembly in 1708 and served frequently thereafter. In 1711 he was named to the commission for paper currency and served as treasurer, judge of the Vice-Admiralty Court between 1724 and 1728, and briefly as chief justice in 1744. He served in the capacity of North Carolina surveyor general from 1706 to 1711, and again from 1724 to 1728. Moseley oversaw land surveys and prepared plats, participated in county boundary surveys, and made at least one important map, printed in London in 1733. The extent of his acquisition of land, facilitated by his position as surveyor general, may be seen in the fact that at his death he owned more than thirty thousand acres in several counties as well as lots in Edenton and Cape Fear.[10]

9. *DNCB,* IV, 73.

10. For the life of Moseley, see *DNCB,* IV, 332–333; William S. Powell, "Moseley, Edward (1682–1749)," *ODNB.*

THE SURVEYORS

Four surveyors, two from each colony, carried out the actual surveying, with the assistance of a crew of pioneers and chain-carriers.

Edward Moseley

According to Byrd, Moseley served primarily as a commissioner and only took on the "Drudgery" of surveying for North Carolina when his associate Samuel Swann was granted permission to return to his new wife from the field.

Samuel Swann (Bo-otes)

Born in Perquimans Precinct, Samuel Swann II (1704–1744) was the son of a prominent Virginian who moved to North Carolina. At the time of the expedition he was a young man in his twenties; he might have learned elements of surveying from his father, but he does not appear to have been a professional surveyor. Byrd, whose testimony is not necessarily reliable, called him "a young Man of much Industry, but no Experience." Later in life he followed his father's example, serving for many years in the North Carolina Assembly.[11]

Alexander Irvin (Orion)

Initially Colonel John Allen (ca. 1674–1742) — named Capricorn in *The Secret History* — had been appointed surveyor for Virginia. Allen was highly qualified; he served as surveyor of Isle of Wight and Surry Counties and attended Ludwell and Harrison on the 1710 survey. He declined because his wife was gravely ill. Allen was replaced by Alexander Irvin (d. 1731), professor of mathematics at the College of William and Mary in 1728–1729, and later professor of natural philosophy. Educated at Edinburgh and without question an accomplished mathematician, Irvin had no practical experience with the applied mathematics of surveying. The appointment was no doubt urged upon the Council by Commissary Blair, the president of the college, who was present at the meeting when Allen's withdrawal was announced. Byrd, who might have suggested a more suitable alternate, was not present at the meeting. The appointment of Irvin seems to have surprised and annoyed Byrd, ostensibly because Irvin was not prepared to perform at Mayo's level but also perhaps because the appointment was a token of the powerful influence of Commissary Blair. The Council's appointment of William Mayo at Byrd's recommendation had confirmed his claim to leadership, whereas the appointment of Irvin became a constantly irritating reminder of rival powers. Throughout the two narratives Byrd displays a fierce antagonism toward Irvin, either sarcastically emphasizing Irvin's supposed qualifications or unrelentingly mocking the misplaced professor's awkwardness.[12]

11. *DNCB*, V, 487–488. Boyd asserts Swann was Moseley's nephew, but I can find no evidence of such a relation, Much confusion attends the name: "The confusion caused by Swann's having more than one son bearing his name is compounded by his having several grandsons and great-grandsons named Samuel, some of whom historians have confused with their fathers or uncles."

12. *DVB*, I, 77; *Council*, III, 340. The Executive Council acknowledged Allen's withdrawal from the expedition on February 27, 1728:

William Mayo (Astrolabe)

Before he arrived in Virginia, William Mayo (1684–1744) worked as a surveyor in Barbados. There the Assembly commissioned him to develop a comprehensive map of the island, which Byrd identifies in *The History of the Dividing Line* as "the accurate Mapp of Barbadoes." The completed map set the "true and real boundaries" of the parishes, and on July 21, 1720, the legislature declared the map "legal evidence in all disputes respecting the bounds of the parishes." In 1721 Mayo was in London, where a presentation copy gained Mayo the approval and thanks of the Royal Society. The king granted him sole royal privilege to publish his map, and he set out to publish a deluxe edition by subscription; it was to be five feet in length, with vignettes, a city plan, and appropriate illustrations and was published in 1782.[13]

In 1722, Caribbean trader William Tryon sent a letter to the Board of Trade recommending Mayo, who was preparing to reside in North America. With his wife, Frances Gould Mayo, whom he had married in Barbados in 1709, and their four daughters, Mayo arrived in Virginia in 1722 or 1723 and took up residence in Henrico County. He set up as a surveyor and began to acquire land in his own name. He was listed as a justice of peace for Henrico County in 1726 and, moving to Goochland County just before the expedition, was appointed justice of peace there. In 1730, he became major in the Goochland militia and, ten years later, colonel. At the end of *The History of the Dividing Line* Byrd singles Mayo out, praising him for his "eminent degree of Skill" and positive attitude alike. In 1733 Mayo accompanied Byrd on his journey to look over the lands they both had acquired along the Dividing Line, described in Byrd's "Journey to the Land of Eden," and several years later Mayo and Byrd participated in the survey establishing the limits of Lord Fairfax's claim to the Northern Neck of Virginia, a large tract of land between the Potomac and Rappahannock Rivers. In 1737, Byrd devised a scheme to create a town he named Richmond on his property near the falls of the James. Mayo surveyed the site and laid out the lots. In his accounts of the 1728 expedition, Byrd keeps Mayo in the forefront

---

This Board having received information that Mr Allen one of the Surveyors appointed for running the dividing line between this Colony and No. Carolina declines going on that service being hindred by the dangerous indisposition of his wife the Governor with the advice of the Council was pleased to nominate and appoint Mr Alexander Irwin Professor of the Mathematicks in the College of William and Mary in the room of the said Mr Allen, and in case he shall refuse to undertake the same, then Mr Drury Stith is appointed for that service.
—*Council*, IV, 167

See also Thad W. Tate, "The Colonial College, 1693–1782," in Susan H. Godson, Ludwell H. Johnson, Richard B. Sherman, Thad W. Tate, and Helen C. Walker, *The College of William and Mary: A History* (Williamsburg, Va., 1993), I, 69–70.

The appointment of Irvin was not without precedent, for the charter of the College of William and Mary empowered the president and faculty "to appoint all surveyors, who gave bond to secure the College one-sixth of all their fees." "Journal of the Meetings of the President and Masters of William and Mary College," *WMQ*, 1st Ser., I (1892–1893), 134.

13. Robert H. Schomburgk, *The History of Barbados* . . . (1848; London, 1971), 7.

of the narration, stressing his professionalism and calm assurance. A talented and enterprising man, Mayo clearly benefited from Byrd's friendship and patronage.[14]

THE OTHER VIRGINIA MEN

The mediating presence of Byrd so dominates the Dividing Line narratives that little attention has been paid to other participants in the expedition. A social divide separated the commissioners from the other members of the party, but the divide might not have been as radical as the narratives suggest. Byrd implies that the rest of the company were men of no status: if not servants, then little more than hired hands, a notion accepted on faith by later historians. No doubt some were "servants or laborers," but in fact many of them were men of property, with considerable experience on the frontier, in the Indian trade, and in official positions. Others were planters in their own right, many of whom lived not far from Westover and were well acquainted with Byrd and his circle. In early-eighteenth-century Virginia, the major landowning elite—2–5 percent of the population—owned half to two-thirds of the land. Jack Greene has noted that in the longer-settled parts of Virginia "householders and landholders together usually constituted no more than half of the free adult male population." Ownership of land, in Byrd's neighborhood and farther

---

14. Feb. 23, 1722, *CSP,* XXXIII, 22, no. 57. Attached to the Board of Trade journal entry are copies of the subscription proposal and the royal privilege:

> Proposals for printing by subscription, a new large and correct map of the Island of Barbadoes in America; with a particular and exact plan of the Bridge-Town *etc.*, by William Mayo. The Royal Society, upon communicating the Map to them, ordered him the thanks of that illustrious body. It is proposed that a prospect of Codrington College *etc.* shall be added by way of embellishment to the engraving which is to be at least five feet long. Price to subscribers, two guineas each map *etc.* London. Nov. 20, 1721.
>
> Copy of H.M. license to William Mayo for the sole privilege of publishing said Map. *Countersigned,* Townshend. St. James's, 11th Nov., 1721.

In 1726 and 1727, Mayo was granted 3,000 acres on Fine Creek (or the Fluvanna, as the upper branch of the James was then known), 3,000 acres north of the western branch of Deep Creek (in partnership with Bowler Cocke), and 6,000 acres between the Appomattox River and Flatt Creek in Prince George County. After the expedition, Mayo's land acquisition accelerated—in 1730, 2,800 acres on Willis's Creek and 9,350 acres in Goochland County; in 1731, 2,850 acres on Willis Creek in Goochland; in 1734, 800 additional acres adjacent to his land in Prince George County; in 1737 (with Tarlton Fleming and Stephen Hughes), 4,300 acres consolidated in one patent; in 1738, 800 more acres near Willis Creek (with Fleming and Hughes); in 1741, 1,600 acres on Angola and Great Guinea Creek in Goochland; in 1742, 1,000 acres on the Fluvanna above Buffalo; and in 1742 (with five others), 20,000 acres on the branches of the James. *Council,* IV, 224, 340, 410, 419, V, 66, 107, 145; *C&P,* III, 393, 403; Hugh Drysdale, "The Present State of Virginia with Respect to the Colony in General," *VMHB,* XLVIII (1940), 145; *Council,* IV, 172; Lloyd DeWitt Bockstruck, *Virginia's Colonial Solders* (Baltimore, 1988), 16; *Virginia Gazette,* Apr. 15–22, 1737.

into the frontier, conferred a degree of status and importance not reflected in Byrd's account of the Virginia men. Though they were not members of the major landowning elite, they were largely enterprising and established men, and not the mere servants and contract woodsmen of Byrd's narratives.[15]

Robert Mumford, Recruiter

A key figure in recruiting the Virginia men was Robert Mumford (or Munford), who recommended "15 able Woodsmen, most of which had been Indian Traders." Mumford's plantation was a staging point for the expedition, and Byrd acknowledges his generous assistance to the endeavor on several occasions. As a young man Robert Mumford had managed Byrd's plantation at Appomattox, and he acted as Byrd's attorney from 1706 to 1711. In 1709 Byrd attempted to get him an appointment as clerk of the Prince George County Court, but competing factions frustrated that plan. Around the same time, Mumford assisted Byrd in various business matters, including trade in deerskins and exchange goods. Mumford also used his influence with Byrd to aid his friends; in 1710, he asked Byrd to support the nomination of Peter Jones (later one of the Virginia men in the expedition) as sheriff of Prince George County. Mumford, who soon came to own considerable land, purchased headrights from Byrd in 1710. Their early relationship seems to have been very cordial, for Byrd's diaries often mention Mumford's dining, drinking claret, playing billiards, and taking walks with him. Mumford rose to a position of consequence, elected burgess for Prince George County in the sessions of 1720 and 1722 and to the vestry of Bristol Parish in 1720.[16]

15. See, for instance of the assumed social divide, Ralph Bauer's account of the composition of the survey party: "seven commissioners, four surveyors, forty laborers, and a chaplain" (Bauer, *The Cultural Geography of Colonial American Literatures: Empires, Travel, Modernity* [Cambridge, 2003], 187). See also Jack P. Greene, *Pursuits of Happiness: The Social Development of Early Modern British Colonies and the Formation of American Culture* (Chapel Hill, N.C., 1988), 90, 92, 195. In North Carolina, Robert E. Gallman reports that in 1720/1 10 male-headed landowning households in Perquimans Precinct held fewer than 100 acres, 134 households between 100 and 900, but only 19 households more than 900. Of that land, 64.5 percent was held by 25 percent of households. "Influences on the Distribution of Landholdings in Early Colonial North Carolina," *Journal of Economic History*, XLII (1982), 552.

16. His legal tasks were various. Mumford represented Byrd at the "outcry" of his uncle's estate (June 10, 1710, *SD*, 194, 198); in 1711, Byrd noted in his diary that Mumford and William Kennon assisted in drawing up "certificates of rights" (Feb. 13, 1711, *SD*, 301). Byrd delegated him to "treat with H——sh about letting me have money for bills at 10 per cent" (July 15, 1711, *SD*, 374). Mumford called on Byrd to inquire if he had "any service before the General Court" (Oct. 12, 1711, *SD*, 420).

On clerk appointment, see *SD*, esp. 8. The court had refused three times to admit Robert Bolling to the position, and Byrd wrote several times on Mumford's behalf to Edmund Jenings, the president of the Council and acting lieutenant governor. Jenings ordered the court not to convene until it assented to Bolling's nomination. Meanwhile, the burgess of

A better man for the task of finding personnel for the surveying expedition could not have been found. The majority of the company came from Bristol Parish: John Davis, John Ellis, John Evans, Abraham Jones, Peter Jones, Thomas Jones, Thomas Jones, Jr., James Petillo, William Pool, Edward Powell, Thomas Short, Richard Smith, and George Tillman.

John Davis was an Indian trader who spent the last years of his life in Bristol Parish. John Ellis was also an Indian trader who appeared in the Bristol Parish records.[17]

A good deal more is known about John Evans, an experienced Indian trader who in 1708 carried messages from the Virginia Council to the Tuscarora. In 1710, Byrd recorded in his diary that "Robin Hix" had asked him to advance him seventy pounds to purchase

---

Prince George County, Edward Goodrich, promised Bolling that he should have the position on the condition he give Goodrich half the profit of the first three years, but President Jenings would not allow such a commission. Jenings sent Byrd a letter granting him the right to name the clerk, and Byrd presented the president's commission to Mumford. Still, the appointment went to Robert Bolling after the Prince George justices, reversing their position, wrote to the president on Bolling's behalf, and Jenings replied favorably. Byrd was angry, complaining that his protégé had a commission and Bolling only a letter.

On business matters: "Robin Hix and Robin Mumford came to discourse about the skin trade" (June 2, 1710, *SD,* 186). Byrd, Mumford, and Mr. Bland consulted on dividing trade goods that had arrived on the sloop (June 10, 1710, *SD,* 198); Byrd's sloop brought "abundance of goods for Mr. Mumford from Mr. Bland" (June 22, 1712, *SD,* 547). Mumford wrote letters to England for Byrd (July 16, 1711, *SD,* 375). Jones: Nov. 10, 1710, *SD,* 260. Headrights: Mar. 17, 1710, *SD,* 315.

A Robert Mumford was burgess for Prince George in 1732; this might have been our Mumford, or his son Robert Mumford, Jr., who was burgess for Prince George 1738 and 1740. William G. Stanard and Mary Newton Stanard, *The Colonial Virginia Register: A List of Governors* . . . (1902; Baltimore, 1989), 103, 109, 112, 170; Churchill Gibson Chamberlayne, ed., *Vestry Book and Register of Bristol Parish, Virginia, 1720–1789* (Richmond, Va., 1898), 1. Mumford served on the vestry continuously to 1742 (Louis des Cognets, Jr., ed., *English Duplicates of Lost Virginia Records* [1958; Baltimore, 1990], 51).

17. In 1704, North Carolina governor Robert Daniel accused three Virginia traders, John Davis, John Fontaine, and "Hubert (a Negro)," of encouraging the Tuscarora "to cutt off the Inhabitants" and fomenting war between the Windaw and Wawee. They appeared before the Virginia Council and were acquitted. In 1708, Council ordered payment of £9.7s.6d each to Davis, Joshua Wynne, and Jno. Evans for going to the Tuscarora for them (*Council,* II, 390, 402, III, 198). It is probable that Davis owned land, but, because his name is common and land transactions are recorded for men of the same name in Nansemond, Surry, and Isle of Wight counties, it is impossible to determine which Davis owned which property. In 1732, the vestry of Bristol Parish acquitted Davis of paying the parish levy (Chamberlayne, ed., *Bristol Parish,* 62). The vestry in 1720 paid for a doctor to treat Ellis's son for a badly broken leg. Vestry records also mention Ellis's debts to the parish, and in 1726 he was acquitted from paying the parish levy (Chamberlayne, ed., *Bristol Parish,* 3, 12, 29).

"two negroes" from John Evans. In 1711 Evans took out a license in Charleston to trade with South Carolina Indians; in December of that year Byrd's agent told him that "Captain Evans and another Indian trader were come from Carolina and had brought abundance of skins." Some years later John Evans assisted Meredith Hughes, factor of the South Carolina outpost at Wineau, with the deerskin trade, before the post was closed because of the restlessness of the Cheraws. Before 1723 Evans owned land in Prince George County, and in 1731 he patented one thousand acres on Saponi Creek in Prince George County (including his earlier holdings).[18]

Peter and Abraham Jones also lived in Bristol Parish. Captain Peter Jones was named to the vestry in 1724; he and his son Abraham were commissioned to count tobacco plants in the upper precinct of the parish, and Abraham continued in the position. Counters tallied the number of plants at every plantation, a task designed to control the market price of tobacco by limiting production. In 1731–1732 Peter served as tobacco inspector at Appomattox, Munford, and Powels Creek. Both men were active in processioning parish land. (*Processioning* was the formal term for circumambulating a body of land to determine its bounds. It was an annual duty of vestrymen.) Peter owned at least twenty-seven hundred acres in Prince George and Henrico Counties, and in 1729–1730 the Council granted Abraham four thousand acres in Prince George County.[19]

Thomas Jones is somewhat more elusive, again because the name is so common. He might be Thomas Jones, son of Richard Jones of Prince George County, who in 1723 was granted one thousand acres on a tributary of the Nottoway River. It is more likely that he was another son of Peter Jones of Bristol Parish, who processioned parish boundaries in 1727 and 1731. It is also likely that he is the woodsman who petitioned the Council that same year "in behalf of the late Virginia Indian Company" for expenses "in repairing the Fortifications of Christanna."[20]

James Petillo (ca. 1692–ca. 1760), of Bristol Parish, Prince George County, first appears in the county records in 1724, when he witnessed the will of one Richard Smith. In that

---

18. *Council,* III, 198; *SD,* 186, 447–448; W. L. McDowell, ed., *Journals of the Commissioners of the Indian Trade, September 20, 1710–August 29, 1718* (Columbia, S.C., 1955), 7.

Evans's land is cited as a landmark for a 1723 patent by Peter Jones, another of the men employed in the expedition (*Council,* IV, 50, 241); in 1733 the Council minutes mention "Capt. Evans' quarter" on the Nottoway River as a landmark for another patent (*Council,* IV, 305).

19. Chamberlayne, ed., *Bristol Parish,* 17–18, 33–35, 54, 77; *Council,* IV, 58, 181, 212, 219, 237, 285, 380.

20. There was an Indian trader of that name who settled in Yamassee territory until the South Carolina Commissioners of Trade expelled him in 1711 (McDowell, ed., *Journals of the Commissioners of the Indian Trade,* 11, 17). A Thomas Jones helped survey the boundary of the Northern Neck in 1705 (*Council,* III, 131). A Thomas Jones was active in Isle of Wight County in 1713–1718; see John Anderson Brayton, *Colonial Families of Surry and Isle of Wight Counties, Virginia,* VIII, *Isle of Wight County, Virginia, Will and Deed Book 2 (1666–1719)* (Memphis, Tenn., 2004), 445, 514. *Council,* IV, 43, 51; Chamberlayne, ed., *Bristol Parish,* 35, 55.

same year, he was granted 200 acres of land adjacent to the property of James Tillman (another participant in the Dividing Line expedition). Virginia records indicate an ambitious and steady course of land acquisition over a long and eventful life. In 1726 he patented 242 acres in Brunswick County, and in 1727 he petitioned the Council for leave to take up 1,000 acres in Prince George County. After the expedition he continued to acquire land, mostly in Prince George—1,200 acres in in 1730, 844 acres in 1734, 250 acres in 1735, 1,000 acres in 1739, 993 acres in 1745, 234 acres in 1753, and 600 acres in 1758. Though he sold some of this land during his lifetime, an accumulation of more than 6,300 acres should serve to indicate that James Petillo was something more than a mere woodsman. Indeed, in 1728 Petillo was appointed tobacco inspector and processioned bounds of land in Bristol Parish, both activities appropriate to a landholding gentleman of some status in his county. It is not known how Byrd came to know Petillo, but he apparently found him useful, for in January 1729 Petillo served as witness to Byrd's purchase of land from George Hicks.[21]

One of Petillo's tracts adjoined George Tillman's property, with whom Petillo was later involved in a land dispute. In 1737, Petillo entered a petition (or "Caveat") against George Tillman and one Robert Abernathy, Jr., laying claim to a tract of land once surveyed for Tillman, who then sold it to Abernathy. However, Tillman's patent had apparently never been properly registered; that oversight provided an opportunity for someone else to assert a claim. It turned out that a negligent deputy surveyor had taken fees from Abernathy without ever filing the patent, but the Council found against Petillo and granted the patent retroactively. But, because Tillman had never paid quitrent, the Council ordered him to compensate Petillo fifty shillings "for his trouble and Expence in prosecuting his Caveat." Petillo continued to acquire land in this manner, by claiming land improperly patented or seated. Between 1740 and 1745 he picked up thirty-four hundred acres in Prince George and Brunswick Counties.[22]

The Bristol Parish vestry book records the births of William Poole's children in 1725, 1726, and 1731, but very little more information has been discovered. Edward Powell, too, lived in Bristol Parish, where his children were born in 1727, 1743, and 1746. In 1730, the Council granted him one thousand acres in Prince George County. It is difficult to establish when Thomas Short arrived in Brunswick Parish, but by 1736 he was appointed tobacco inspector at Maycock's Warehouse, and in 1739 at Mumford's. In 1740 he was named to the vestry.[23]

21. *C&P*, III, 323; *Council*, IV, 163; Melba C. Crosse, *Patillo, Pattillo, Pattullo, and Pittillo Families* (Fort Worth, Tex., 1972), 24–28. According to Crosse, the name is a variation of the Scottish Pittiloch (or Pettiloch); many versions of the name occur in Scotland and Virginia. Crosse also noted (23) that, in 1716, a Jacobite prisoner named James Pittillo was transported to Virginia on the *Elizabeth and Anne*. Those convicts without means to pay their fare were obliged to a term as indentured servants, but Petillo's name does not appear in any indenture records.

Byrd: Rebecca Johnston, "William Byrd Title Book," *VMHB*, L (1942), 178.

22. *Council*, IV, 276, 411, V, 13, 50, 79, 184; *C&P*, 3, 376.

23. Chamberlayne, ed., *Bristol Parish*, 107, 350–352, 355; *Council*, IV, 344, 382. A

Identifying Richard Smith is also problematic, for the name is very common. It is tempting to identify him as the Virginia Indian trader who in 1711 took out a license to operate in South Carolina. Land grants and patents assigned to men named Richard Smith can be found in the records of half a dozen counties; more to our purpose, in 1717 Richard Smith, Sr., was granted tracts of 370 and 83 acres in Prince George County. In 1727 the Bristol Parish vestry book notes that he processioned parish lands in 1727, 1731, and 1735.[24]

The last member of the expedition from Bristol Parish was George Tillman, who was established as early as 1711 in Prince George County. The births of his children were recorded in the vestry book in 1720, 1723, and 1731. Gradually through the 1720s he accumulated 568 more acres in Prince George and Brunswick Counties. He processioned parish lands in 1727, 1731, and 1735.[25]

Charles Kimball

Besides these neighbors of Robert Mumford, several other members of the expedition were also selected for their experience as Indian traders. Charles Kimball had been an Indian trader for many years. In 1715 he and several others came under suspicion of trading with the Tuscarora and encouraging the Seneca to attack Virginia Indians. The charges must have been dropped, since only the preliminary charges appear in the records. Kimball had also served as the Virginia government's official interpreter to the Saponi and allied Indian nations since 1712. He appeared before the Council during the break between the two parts of the expedition to request an augmentation of his salary as interpreter. Kimball's office as interpreter receives no mention in Byrd's account, even when he writes in *The Secret History* that he "sent Charles Kimball to Christanna" to recruit two Saponi huntsmen "to go the Journey to help supply us with Meat."[26]

Robert Hix

Robert (Robin) Hix or Hicks (d. 1739) gets some respect from Byrd for his resistance to Fitzwilliam's rudeness. Robin Hix was the son of the famous Indian trader Captain Robert Hix, whose visit to the camp so delighted Byrd. Robert, Jr., was himself an Indian trader and planter; in his diary Byrd mentions discussing the Indian trade with him at West-

---

William Poole, possibly his son, was cornet of Dragoons in the Brunswick County Militia (Bockstruck, *Virginia's Colonial Soldiers,* 9). Thomas Short may be one of six persons in 1714 imported by Thomas Jones of Prince George County for a patent of 370 acres of new land in Surry County (*C&P,* III, 176–177).

24. McDowell, *Journals of the Commissioners of the Indian Trade,* 6–7; *C&P,* III, 194; Chamberlayne, ed., *Bristol Parish,* 43, 57, 77.

25. Extant records mention his property as a landmark for a 1711 patent, but I have not located his prior patent. *C&P,* III, 124, 312, 313; Chamberlayne, ed., *Bristol Parish,* 48, 56, 82, 371, 372, 375.

26. Apr. 27, 1728, *Council,* IV, 174, and III, 321; McIlwaine, ed., *Journals of the House of Burgesses, 1712–1714 . . . ,* 10, 327, 412, *1727–1734, 1736–1740,* 15. Both Byrd and Dandridge were present at this meeting, indicating Byrd was fully aware of Kimball's status.

over on several occasions, long before the expedition. The Hix family settled along the Roanoke River in Brunswick County. In the 1720s Hix acquired 580 acres near the land owned by his father and brothers. After the expedition in 1730 (now identified as "Robert Hix, Gent."), he patented an additional 2,610 acres on Miry Branch, along the north side of the Meherrin River in Surry County, along the route of the surveying expedition.[27]

George Hamilton

George Hamilton, another member of the expedition, patented 780 acres of land in Surry County in 1715. Further information about Hamilton has not been discovered.[28]

Servants and Slaves

Among the company were several men attending in the capacity of servants. In *The Secret History* Fitzwilliam's man is identified only as "Tipperary." Byrd mentions the misbehavior of "my Man Tom," but further identification has proved elusive; he might have been a slave. Byrd apparently had at least one other servant in attendance, for in *The Secret History* he comments that Fitzwilliam "instructed one of the 3 Men which he listed on the Publick Service to call him Master, thereby endeavouring to pass him on the Carolina Commissioners for his Servant, that he might seem to have as many Servants as Steddy." These three men were probably not servants as such, but persons employed to assist in his business as commissioner.

Other members of the expedition might have brought uncounted and unnamed servants. For example, one accompanied Mayo; in *The Secret History* Byrd mentions in passing that "Astrolabe's Negro" fell ill.

27. July 19, 1709, *SD*, 61. Hix and Robert Mumford dined with Byrd and discussed the "skin trade" on June 2, 1710 (*SD*, 186). Hix came to Byrd in 1712 for "some rights" and talked "very foolishly" (*SD*, 502). *C&P*, III, 322, 387, 392; "Hicks Family," *WMQ*, 1st Ser., XI (1902), 130–131.

28. Des Cognets, *English Duplicates of Lost Virginia Records*, 105.

Appendix 2 Bibliographical Notes

COPY-TEXTS

This edition takes as its copy-text for *The History of the Dividing Line* the version included in the Westover Manuscripts at the Virginia Historical Society (MSS1 B9966), with constant reference to the American Philosophical Society copy (975.5 B99h), the British Library manuscript (Add. MS 28260), and extant fragments. A fresh transcription was done from VHS microfilm and then carefully checked against the manuscript itself. The Westover Manuscripts include a set of miscellaneous texts by William Byrd, gathered in a vellum-bound folio that for many years was treated as a family treasure. The pages devoted to "The History of the Dividing Line betwixt Virginia and North Carolina Run in the year of our Lord 1728" are numbered from 1 to 139. This text, in a middle-eighteenth-century hand, was produced by a secretary or copyist. Additionally, throughout the manuscript there are frequent corrections, emendations, and expansions in Byrd's own hand. Authorial interventions are indicated in the textual notes on each page, where variant readings also appear.[1]

The APS manuscript of *The History of the Dividing Line* is written in a hand very similar to that of the APS manuscript of the *Secret History*. Earlier editors have speculated that the hands may be the same; a close inspection neither confirms nor rules out this presumption. Three sections of the original APS *Secret History* manuscript are missing (pp. 1–28, 122–128c, and 138a–140). The missing passages were supplied in another hand much later, inserted and written on a different paper stock (not laid paper, as in the older, larger portion). The inserted passages are written in a small, regular nineteenth-century steel-pen hand; the ink is very light or faded. The nineteenth-century copyist does not use (or preserve) the capitalization standard in other Byrd manuscripts. Sometime after the APS acquired its *History of the Dividing Line* manuscript, Peter DuPonceau, the head of the APS publications committee, arranged with Benjamin Harrison, executor of the estate of William Byrd III, to have the missing text supplied from the Westover Manuscripts, then in the hands of George Evelyn Harrison, great-grandson of the author. These nineteenth-century sections silently incorporate nearly all of the Byrd corrections and additions in the VHS manuscript, whereas the remainder of the APS manuscript mostly resembles the state of the VHS narrative before Byrd worked on it.[2]

1. The descendants of the Byrd family who long held the Westover Manuscripts occasionally allowed them to be read. In 1816 James Kirke Paulding read "The History of the Dividing Line" with considerable enjoyment and praised the author: "Judging by the work, the author was a deep scholar; a man of great observation, and a sly joker on womankind." The writing drew praise: "The style of this work is, I think, the finest specimen of that grave, stately, and quaint mode of writing fashionable about a century ago, that I have ever met with any where." *Letters from the South, Written during an Excursion in the Summer of 1816* (New York, 1817), I, 28–29. See also Floyd C. Watkins, "James Kirke Paulding and the Manuscripts of William Byrd," *Modern Language Notes,* LXVII (1952), 56–57.

2. Kathleen L. Leonard, "Notes on the Text and Provenance of the Byrd Manuscripts," in *Prose Works,* 418.

It would seem that, when Byrd commissioned the copy now known as the APS manuscript, he was still making revisions; these are discussed below. It seems probable that multiple copies of the two narratives existed at one time, perhaps in various stages of revision and polishing; the extant copies were also subject to authorial attentions.

The copy-text for *The Secret History* is the APS manuscript (975.5 B99h), supplemented with fragments in the Brock Collection at the Huntington Library (BR box 256.28) and at the Rockefeller Library, Colonial Williamsburg Foundation (MS 40.2). The APS text, contained in an oblong notebook much resembling a surveyor's notebook, was donated to the library by Thomas Jefferson in 1816. The manuscript was missing pages 155–156 (the entries for November 20–22), but the Huntington fragments provided the lost text.[3]

VARIATIONS BETWEEN THE VHS AND THE APS *DIVIDING LINE*

The Virginia Historical Society's manuscript of *The History of the Dividing Line,* bound with copies of other Byrd texts in a collection known as the Westover Manuscripts, has long been recognized as the better version. Its pages feature numerous revisions, corrections, and additions in Byrd's hand, and so previous editors have concluded that the APS version was a copy of the VHS manuscript. Many of the changes to V—interlinear and marginal insertions, erasures and overwriting—recur in the body of APS.d. For instance, on page 52 of V Byrd added these lines:

> The same Humour prevails at this day in the Kings of Denmark, who order all the East India ships of that nation to call at the Cape of Good Hope and take in a But of Water from a Spring on the Table Hill and bring it to Coppenhagen for Their Majestys own Drinking.

The fact that the APS.d incorporates this addition indicates the copy was made after Byrd's revisions to V. Notation of variants lists numerous similar instances of changes to V that appear in APS.d; this fact tends to support the conclusion that APS.d was a copy of V.

However, collation of the manuscripts reveals two patterns of variance that call this conclusion into question. First, there are a number of revisions to V that do not appear in APS.d. Some of these variants might have been the result of carelessness on the part of the copyist, which may be seen in the substantial number of typical scribal errors, including transposition, omission, anticipation, and eye-skip. But there are many other instances when V revisions not appearing in APS.d cannot be explained as scribal errors. One of the most common forms of revision to V occurs when Byrd expanded in the space at the end of the last line of a paragraph and the indentation at the beginning of the next. For instance, on page 47 of V, where the copyist's paragraph ended "being desirous to husband the publick Money," Byrd added the words "as much as possible." This addition, like many other end-of-line additions, does not appear in APS.d. Such variations can be explained by the supposition that Byrd had a copy of V made at a stage when he had made some but not all of the extant revisions. This supposition is supported by other small revisions to V, as when on page 28 Byrd inserted the cogent word "fatal" above the line in the passage concerning secular marriage in North Carolina, "a Country Justice can tie the fatal Knot as fast as an Arch-Bishop." The word "fatal" is absent in APS.d. This small but character-

3. Ibid., 419.

istic addition—Byrd peppers his narratives with many wry comments about the state of matrimony—and at least sixty more editorial additions must have been made after APS.d was copied from V. Naturally, the nineteenth-century sections of APS.d. faithfully replicate all the VHS.d revisions. By this logic, APS.d was a copy of V in an intermediate state.

The second class of variants is still more puzzling. On a number of occasions there appears to have been additional material added to APS.d, revisions not found in V. For instance, the passage on page 25 of V—"accompany'd with a strong Wind"—is enriched in APS.d by the addition of the phrase "that made us all tremble." On page 26, V's "any more than Robinson Cruso did" becomes "any more than Robinson Crusoe was able to do." On page 60, V's "Nor are these Birds the only Animals that appoint Scouts to keep the main Body from Being surprizd" is extended with "by the Enemy." In the same passage APS.d records many improvements, as when V's "and scour away to the Mountains as fast as they can" becomes the more lively "scour away to the Mountains as fast as their Legs will carry them." Many more such variations, some revising or improving phrases, some involving only the addition of a suitable word or phrase, are provided in textual footnotes. From this evidence it is reasonable to conclude that Byrd must have had copies made of his work in progress and that on occasion he must have made revisions to one stream of copied manuscripts (represented by APS.d) that do not appear in the other stream (represented by V). Revisions made to the V manuscript after the APS.d copy was taken naturally do not appear in the APS.d stream, nor do revisions to APS.d appear in V.

MANUSCRIPTS AND FRAGMENTS

Again, Byrd circulated copies of his narratives to select friends; it may be that the extant manuscripts were prepared for this purpose, but there is no way of knowing how many copies Byrd commissioned for circulation. What follows is a brief description of what manuscripts remain.

V

The version of the *Dividing Line* in the Westover Manuscripts is written on laid paper in the early- to mid-eighteenth-century hand of an unidentified copyist, with frequent revisions in Byrd's hand. Most of these revisions occur as erasures with overwriting in the resulting opening or as insertions above the text line, usually with a ^ to indicate the precise placement of the insertion. Another common pattern is the addition or revision of phrases crowded into the space at the end of a paragraph and the indentation at the beginning of the next, resulting in a conjoined paragraph. Some longer additions appear vertically in the margins. While V apparently began as a fair copy of an advanced state of the narrative, it was also a working manuscript, an editing project to which Byrd returned from time to time, mostly making small stylistic adjustments of the sort described above. It occupies a stage of development after the major phase of compiling and amplifying. All of the major digressions and illustrative materials are already present.

APS.d

In the American Philosophical Society's manuscript copy of the *Dividing Line* (975.5 B99h) the original APS.d copyist seems to have introduced nonauthorial variations. Standard early-eighteenth-century practice was to capitalize abstract nouns; extant manuscripts in

Byrd's hand indicate his own practice was not so consistent. The two manuscripts reveal no discernible pattern of capitalization, though the APS.d copyist appears to like capitalizing adjective-noun pairs, such as "Cardinal Vertues." Both APS.d and V use contractions *(watch'd* or *watch't* for *watched,* and *cou'd* for *could);* APS.d uses the uncontracted forms slightly more often. Some spelling differences are common, but none appears to be significant. Additionally, it is possible to spot common scribal errors in APS.d. Repetition occurs occasionally—APS.d lists "Philadelphia, Buckingham, Philadelphia, and Chester Counties," corrected by a line drawn through the first "Philadelphia." Transposition is common, as when the APS.d copyist replaces the description of a man thrown from a horse into a stream and "not carry'd down the Stream very far" with "not being carry'd very far down the Stream." The APS.d copyist commits and then corrects an anticipation error: V describes the town of Norfolk as "built on a level Spot of Ground upon Elizabeth River" (p. 11); APS.d has "built upon," but when the copyist reached the "upon" six words later, he apparently recognized his mistake and drew a line through the letters "up" in the first, incorrect instance. Doubtless the most amusing scribal error is the substitution when the APS.d copyist has the portly figure of the buffalo "disgrac'd by a shabby little Tail not above 12 Feet long." The proper effect of disproportion may be seen in V—a somewhat less spectacular 12-*inch* tail (p. 103).

APS.s

The American Philosophical Society owns the only copy of *The Secret History of the Line* (975.5 B99h). It is also written in an early- to mid-eighteenth-century hand, very similar to the hand of the Society's copy of *The History of the Dividing Line.* Two missing pages (containing the entries for November 21–22) are supplied from a manuscript fragment in the Brock Collection at the Huntington Library (H); the whole manuscript is collated with H and with the fragments in the Rockefeller Library (CWR.s).

CWR.s

The Rockefeller Library at Colonial Williamsburg owns a fragment of *The Secret History* (MS 40.2). This fragment consists of 4½" by 7¼" leaves from the last part of *The Secret History,* taken at some point from a bound journal or blank book, consisting of partial signatures. The pages bear copious marks of revision and addition in Byrd's hand, including erasure and overwriting, interlineal and end-of-line additions, and cancellations with interlineal replacements. At several places there are heavily scraped erasures of actual names, with Byrd's farcical names for his companions overwritten. In nearly every case, revisions made here were integrated into the APS version of *The History of the Dividing Line.*

CWR.d

A fragment of *The History of the Dividing Line* in the Rockefeller Library (MS 40.2) consists of fourteen leaves from a working copy in Byrd's hand, with revisions also in Byrd's hand. This manuscript is collated with the copy-text. Most of Byrd's revisions here occur as erasures and overwriting, with occasional insertions above the line, indicating how thoroughly the manuscript was reworked.

H

The Brock Collection of the Huntington Library includes several pages from an early version of *The Secret History* (BR box 256.28). This fragment consists of 4½" by 7¼" leaves from a bound journal or blank book, partial signatures, numbered: [7] (illegible; recto) and 8 (verso; a separate torn sheet); 9r and 10v; 11r and 12v (one set of four pages, that is, a single sheet folded, is missing); 17r and 18v; 19r and 20v. The manuscript bears copious marks of revision and addition, including erasure and overwriting, interlineal and end-of-line additions, and cancellations with interlineal replacements. The manuscript is in Byrd's hand, as are the editing marks. Physical evidence—the erasure of actual names and replacing them with farcical names, and the replacement of first-person pronouns with the name Byrd gives himself (Steddy)—indicate that this is an early state, and it shows the extent of revision needed to translate the relatively staid first-person narration to the raucous third.

MANUSCRIPTS

"Articles of Agreement indented and made between John Custis of York County Gentleman and Frances his Wife on the one part, and William Byrd of Charles City County Esqr on the other." New York Historical Society, Miscel. MS B.

"A Journal of the Divideing line Drawn between the Colonies of Virginia & North Carolina begun March 5: 1728—[per] Colo. Byrd & others." British Library Add. MS 28260.

"History of the Dividing Line." American Philosophical Society Library, MS 975.5 B99h.

"History of the Dividing Line" (fragment). John D. Rockefeller, Jr., Library, Colonial Williamsburg, MS 40.2.

"The History of the Dividing Line betwixt Virginia and North Carolina Run in the year of our Lord 1728." Westover Manuscripts, Virginia Historical Society, MS 62-4347.

Huntington Manuscript BR 744 (notebook including Byrd's case for recovering slave ship seized by France).

"A Journal of the proceedings of the Commissioners for settling the Bounds betwixt Virginia and Carolina." Board of Trade Journals, National Archives, U.K., CO 5, 1321.

"Secret History of the Line" (fragment). The Huntington Library, BR box 256.28.

"Secret History of the Line" (fragment). John D. Rockefeller, Jr., Library, Colonial Williamsburg, MS 40.2.

The Westover Manuscripts, 1692-1739. Virginia Historical Society, Mss1 B9966 a.

> This bound volume includes the following: "The History of the Dividing Line betwixt Virginia and North Carolina Run in the Year of Our Lord 1728" (pp. 1-139); "A Journey to the Land of Eden Anno 1733" (pp. 141-176); "A Progress to the Mines in the Year 1732" (pp. 177-217); "An Essay on Bulk Tobacco" (pp. 289-301); and "The Female Creed" (enclosure).
>
> Miscellaneous essays and recipes include the following: "To the Honble Commissioners of their Majesty's Customs. An Answer . . . for Some Reasons for Suspending the Laws for Paying Debts in Country Commodities of Virginia" (pp. 302-310); "The Method of Curing Red and Pickle Herrings" (p. 311); "Pickle Herrings" (p. 311); "The Method of Planting Vineyards & Making Wine" (pp. 311-314); "Mrs. Otway's Receipts for Clary & Cherry Wines" (pp. 321-322); "Mrs. Shuts Receipt for Making Birch Wine" (p. 322); "Duchesse of Lorreign's Receipt for Making Soupe" (pp. 322-323); "The Method Used in Cornwall in Making Earthen Floors for Malt Houses" (pp. 323-324); "To Cure Misletoe of the Oak" (p. 324); Mr. Catesby's Receipt to Pickle Sturgeon & Make Caviar" (pp. 324-325); "The Method of Making Tar in Muscovy" (pp. 339-340); and "To Make Plaster to Resemble Ashler" (pp. 341-342).

"William Byrd's Secret history of the line between Virginia and North Carolina." American Philosophical Society Library, MS 62-2548.

WORKS PUBLISHED IN BYRD'S LIFETIME

"An Account of a Negro-Boy That Is Dappel'd in Several Places of His Body with White Spots. By Will. Byrd, Esq, F.R.S." *Philosophical Transactions,* XIX (1695–1697), 781–782.

[Attributed to Byrd]. *A Discourse concerning the Plague, with Some Preservatives against It.* By a Lover of Mankind. London: Printed for J. Roberts, 1721.

Tunbrigalia; or, Tunbridge Miscellanies for the Year 1719. London, 1719 (includes poems by "Mr. Burrard").

POSTHUMOUSLY PUBLISHED WORKS

"A Description of the Dismal Swamp, in Virginia, with Proposals for and Observations on the Advantages of Draining It." *Columbian Magazine,* III (1789), 230–234.

"Proposal to Drain the Dismal Swamp." *Farmer's Register,* IV (1837), 521–524 (with editorial comments by Edmund Ruffin).

The Westover Manuscripts: Containing the History of the Dividing Line betwixt Virginia and North Carolina; A Journey to the Land of Eden, A.D. 1733; and A Progress to the Mines: Written from 1728 to 1736, and Now First Published. Petersburg, Va. Printed by Edmund and Julian C. Ruffin, 1841 (as a supplement to the *Farmer's Register*).

History of the Dividing Line and Other Tracts: From the Papers of William Byrd, of Westover, in Virginia, Esquire. Ed. Thomas H. Wynne. Richmond, Va., 1866.

The Writings of "Colonel William Byrd of Westover in Virginia, Esqr." Ed. John Spencer Bassett. New York, 1901.

A Journey to the Land of Eden and Other Papers. Ed. Mark Van Doren. New York, 1928 (includes *History of the Dividing Line, A Journey to the Land of Eden,* and *A Progress to the Mines*).

William Byrd's Histories of the Dividing Line bewixt Virginia and North Carolina. Ed. William Boyd. Raleigh, N.C., 1929.

William Byrd's Natural History of Virginia; or, The Newly Discovered Eden. Ed. and trans. from a German version by Richmond Croom Beatty and William J. Mulloy. Richmond, Va., 1940. (The German section [109 pages] is a reprint of the title page and pages 96–202 of *Neu-gefundenes Eden; oder, Ausführlicher Bericht von Süd- und Nord-Carolina, Pensilphania, Mary-Land & Virginia. . . .* In truck verfertiget durch Befehl der Helvetischen Societät. 1737.)

The Secret Diary of William Byrd of Westover, 1709–1712. Ed. Louis B. Wright and Marion Tinling. Richmond, Va., 1941.

Another Secret Diary of William Byrd of Westover, 1739–1741, with Letters and Literary Exercises 1696–1726. Ed. Maude Woodfin and Marion Tinling. Richmond, Va., 1943.

The London Diary (1717–1721) and Other Writings. Ed. Louis B. Wright and Marion Tinling. New York, 1958.

The Great American Gentleman: William Byrd of Westover in Virginia, His Secret Diary for the Years 1709–1712. Ed. Louis B. Wright and Marion Tinling. New York, 1963. (Selections from *The Secret Diary of William Byrd of Westover, 1709–1712.*)

The Prose Works of William Byrd of Westover: Narratives of a Colonial Virginian. Ed. Louis B. Wright. Cambridge, Mass., 1966.

William Byrd's Histories of the Dividing Line betwixt Virginia and North Carolina. Intro. by Percy G. Adams. New York, 1967. (Reproduces the 1929 Boyd edition, with additional material from Wright.)

Tinling, Marion, ed. *The Correspondence of the Three William Byrds of Westover, Virginia, 1684–1776.* Charlottesville, Va., 1977.

Martin, Wendy, ed. *Colonial American Travel Narratives.* New York, 1994. (Includes the *Secret History* as published in the 1967 Dover edition.)

The Commonplace Book of William Byrd II of Westover. Ed. Kevin Berland, Jan K. Gilliam, and Kenneth A. Lockridge. Chapel Hill, N.C., 2001.

Index